INTERNATIONAL LAW AND THE POLITICS OF HISTORY

As the future of international law has become a growing site of struggle within and between powerful states, debates over the history of international law have become increasingly heated. *International Law and the Politics of History* explores the ideological, political, and material stakes of apparently technical disputes over how the legal past should be studied and understood. Drawing on a deep knowledge of the history, theory, and practice of international law, Anne Orford argues that there can be no impartial accounts of international law's past and its relation to empire and capitalism. Rather than looking to history in a doomed attempt to find a new ground for formalist interpretations of what past legal texts really mean or what international regimes are really for, she urges lawyers and historians to embrace the creative role they play in making rather than finding the meaning of international law.

ANNE ORFORD is Redmond Barry Distinguished Professor and Michael D. Kirby Chair of International Law at the University of Melbourne. She has held visiting professorships at Harvard, Lund, Gothenburg, and Paris 1, and lectured at the Hague Academy of International Law. Her publications include *Reading Humanitarian Intervention* (2003), *International Authority and the Responsibility to Protect* (2011), *Pensée Critique et Pratique du Droit International* (2020), and the co-edited collections *The Oxford Handbook of the Theory of International Law* (2016) and *Revolutions in International Law: The Legacies of 1917* (2021).

International Law and the Politics of History

ANNE ORFORD

The University of Melbourne

CAMBRIDGE
UNIVERSITY PRESS

CAMBRIDGE
UNIVERSITY PRESS

University Printing House, Cambridge CB2 8BS, United Kingdom

One Liberty Plaza, 20th Floor, New York, NY 10006, USA

477 Williamstown Road, Port Melbourne, VIC 3207, Australia

314–321, 3rd Floor, Plot 3, Splendor Forum, Jasola District Centre, New Delhi – 110025, India

103 Penang Road, #05–06/07, Visioncrest Commercial, Singapore 238467

Cambridge University Press is part of the University of Cambridge.

It furthers the University's mission by disseminating knowledge in the pursuit of education, learning, and research at the highest international levels of excellence.

www.cambridge.org
Information on this title: www.cambridge.org/9781108480949
DOI: 10.1017/9781108691765

First published 2021

A catalogue record for this publication is available from the British Library.

ISBN 978-1-108-48094-9 Hardback
ISBN 978-1-108-70362-8 Paperback

Contents

Acknowledgements   *page* ix

1 **Neoformalism and the Turn to History in International Law**   1
   1.1 Turning to History   1
   1.2 The Hermeneutic of Suspicion and the History of
        International Law   5
   1.3 The Politics of Making International Law   9
   1.4 Overview of the Argument   12

2 **Situating the Turn to History in International Law**   18
   2.1 International Law at the End of History   19
        2.1.1 US Hegemony and the Transformation of
               International Law   19
        2.1.2 The Turn to History as a Critical Response to
               US Expansionism   30
   2.2 The Turn to History and the War on Terror   36
        2.2.1 Liberal Internationalism Must Be Defended   36
        2.2.2 The End of the Affair: The Turn to History and the
               American Project   40
   2.3 Historicising the Crises   44
        2.3.1 International Law and the Triple Crisis   44
        2.3.2 The Turn to History in a Time of Crisis   47
   2.4 The Rise of China and the End of the Revolution   56
   2.5 From Law to History   68

3 **History and the Turn to the International**   70
   3.1 Turning to the International   71
   3.2 History as Completion and Correction   75

3.3 The Empiricist Rules of the Historical Game   81
3.4 Challenging Empiricist Historiography   86
3.5 Interpretation and the Cambridge School   93
3.6 The Past as Law or History?   99

4   **History's Lawyers**   105
    4.1 The Figure of the Lawyer in Contextualist History   105
    4.2 Herbert Butterfield and the Lawyer as
        Whig Constitutionalist   112
        4.2.1 Butterfield's England and the Challenge to
              Constitutional History   112
        4.2.2 The Competing Legacies of FW Maitland   115
        4.2.3 Butterfield and the Whig Historian as 'God and Judge' 119
        4.2.4 Christian Realism and the Truth of History   122
    4.3 JGA Pocock and the English Common Lawyer   127
        4.3.1 Pocock and the Cambridge School   127
        4.3.2 Pocock and 'the Common-Law Mind'   131
    4.4 Quentin Skinner and the Scholastic Lawyer   135
        4.4.1 Skinner, Revolution, and the Turn to Method   135
        4.4.2 Skinner's Lawyers: Scholastics, Humanists, and
              the 'Genuinely Historical Spirit'   144
        4.4.3 Skinner, Panofsky, and the Myth of the
              Italian Renaissance   149
        4.4.4 The 'Triumphant Methodology' of the
              Cambridge School   156
    4.5 Ian Hunter and the Lawyer as Metaphysician   157
        4.5.1 Hunter and International Law as Factional Politics   157
        4.5.2 Hunter on Contextualist Historians and Their
              'Scholastic Enemies'   165
        4.5.3 The Politics of Contextualist Method   169
    4.6 Contextualist Method as the End of Legal History?   172

5   **The Past in the Practice of International Law**   178
    5.1 International Law Scholars between the Academy and the
        Legal Profession   185
        5.1.1 The Invisible College as a Form of Life   185
        5.1.2 Legal Education as Training   189
    5.2 The Plural Roles of International Lawyers: Beyond the
        Judge and the Historian   194
        5.2.1 The Judge and the Historian   194

5.2.2 Standpoint, Role, and the Nature of International Legal Argument 197

5.2.3 Judging and the Legacies of Colonialism and Fascism 201

5.3 All Realists Now: International Law after Metaphysics 206

5.3.1 Contextualist History and the International Lawyer as Metaphysician 206

5.3.2 Realism and American Anti-formalism in International Law 208

5.3.3 European Anti-metaphysical Approaches to International Law 212

5.3.4 Decolonisation and the Challenge to European Metaphysics 215

5.4 The Past in the Making of International Law 217

5.4.1 'Finding' the Facts 218

5.4.2 Arguing about Past Precedents 223

5.4.3 Debating the Nature and Interpretation of Treaties 226

5.4.4 Custom and the Interpretation of Past Practice 235

5.4.5 Transmitting Legal Concepts and Fictions 243

5.4.6 Teleology: From Technique to Ideology 245

5.5 The Realist Challenge and the Making of International Legal Argument 249

6 **The History of What?** 253

6.1 How Historians Make Law Too 253

6.2 British Colonial Networks as the Origins of International Law 257

6.3 US Internationalism and the Real History of Human Rights 262

6.4 Ordoliberalism and the Intellectual History of International Economic Law 265

6.5 Historians and the International Legal Field 283

7 **Why Study the Past of International Law? History as Politics** 285

7.1 Legal Argument as Making Not Finding 287

7.2 History of International Law as Neoformalism 294

7.2.1 Neoformalism in a Post-Realist Field 294

7.2.2 Fact Laundering through History: Ordoliberalism as the Truth of the WTO 296

7.2.3 Method Laundering through History: From Carl Schmitt to Reinhart Koselleck 299

7.3 Method as Politics: How We Study the Past Depends
on Why We Study the Past 310
7.3.1 The Hermeneutic of Suspicion and the Global Rule
of Lawyers 310
7.3.2 Politics All the Way Down 315

Bibliography 321
Index 373

Acknowledgements

International Law and the Politics of History has been many years in the making. It began life as the first chapter of a companion book, which is entitled *The Battle for the State: Democracy, International Law, and Economics*. I wrote this book as it was becoming increasingly clear that a consensus was emerging in the field of international law around the question of what count as 'objective' methods for undertaking legal work with a historical consciousness, and that this dogmatic consensus would get in the way of having the kind of debate about the relation of international law to social, political, and economic transformation that I feel is vital and timely. To prevent a focus upon a particular historical method becoming the measure of scholarly rigour, it seemed necessary to intervene before that new consensus began to be taken as gospel and all other ways of writing about the past of international law dismissed or ruled out of bounds by the gatekeepers of the field's journals, conferences, and publishers. Indeed, for many of the early career scholars with whom I was working, that effect on legal research was already becoming apparent.

I have presented much more of this work than I have been able to write down until now, and the conversations that followed those presentations have been central to developing the ideas set out here. In particular, for engagement with the arguments developed in *International Law and the Politics of History*, I would like to thank the organisers of and participants in the following events at which I presented aspects of this work: the Colloquium on *Les Nouvelles approches sur le Tiers Monde: Bilan et perspectives*, Université Paris 1, 2010; the Australia New Zealand Law and History Society Annual Conference, University of Technology Sydney, 2012; the European Society of International Law Public Lecture on *Histories of International Law and Empire*, Université Paris 1, 2013; the Conference on *History and Histories of International Law*, University of Helsinki, 2014; the Australian Historical

Association Annual Conference, University of Sydney, 2015; the Conference on *History, Politics, Law: Thinking through the International*, University of Cambridge, 2016; the 350th Anniversary Symposium of the Faculty of Law, Lund University, 2017; the Conference on *Rethinking and Renewing the Study of International Law in/from/about Latin America*, co-hosted by the Universidad de los Andes, Universidad del Rosario, and Universidad Externado de Colombia, 2017; and the Conference on *What Is International History Now?*, University of Sydney, 2018.

I am particularly grateful to Karen Knop, Kerry Rittich, and Jutta Brunnée for inviting me to present the 2014 Katherine Baker Memorial Lecture on *Food Security, Free Trade, and the Battle for the State* at the University of Toronto and creating the opportunity for the rich interdisciplinary conversation subsequently published in (2015) 11 *Journal of International Law and International Relations* 1–180; to Anne Saab and Fuad Zarbiyev for inviting me to discuss the outline of the book with colleagues in international law and international history as part of the *International Law Literature Forum* series at the Graduate Institute Geneva in 2018; to Chen Yifeng for inviting me to workshop the first chapter with colleagues from law, history, and international relations at Peking University Law School in 2019 as part of their *Empire and International Law* workshop series; and to Juan Pablo Scarfi and Fabia Veçoso for inviting me to discuss this work in its late stages at the roundtable on *Beyond 'Gringo Histories' of International Law* at Universidad Nacional de San Martin as well as in our wanderings around the streets, coffee shops, and bars of Buenos Aires in October 2019.

Many of my interlocutors at workshops and conferences over the past years have been historians, and I have learnt a great deal from those interactions, in particular with David Armitage, Annabel Brett, Shaunnagh Dorsett, Ian Duncanson, Marco Duranti, Lars Edgren, Sheila Fitzpatrick, Ann Genovese, Lena Halldenius, Randall Lesaffer, Mark Mazower, Janne Nijman, Glenda Sluga, Bo Stråth, Christopher Tomlins, Richard Tuck, and Zhang Yongle. I hope that this book does justice to the many ways in which I learn from historians, as well as helping to shape ongoing relations between the two fields of international law and history.

I have previously published fragments of the methodological arguments made here in 'The Past as Law or History? The Relevance of Imperialism for Modern International Law' in Mark Toufayan, Emmanuelle Tourme-Jouannet, and Hélène Ruiz Fabri (eds), *International Law and New Approaches to the Third World: Between Repetition and Renewal* (Société de Législation Comparée, 2013), 97; 'On International Legal Method' (2013) 1 *London Review of International Law* 166; 'Food Security, Free Trade, and the

Battle for the State' (2015) 11 *Journal of International Law and International Relations* 1; 'Theorizing Free Trade' in Anne Orford and Florian Hoffmann (eds), *The Oxford Handbook of the Theory of International Law* (Oxford University Press, 2016), 701; and 'International Law and the Limits of History' in Wouter Werner, Marieke de Hoon, and Alexis Galán (eds), *The Law of International Lawyers: Reading Martti Koskenniemi* (Cambridge University Press, 2017), 297.

I am grateful to the Australian Research Council (ARC) for the support provided for this work under three projects: an Australian Professorial Fellowship (2007–2011), a Future Fellowship (2012–2015), and an Australian Laureate Fellowship (2015–2021). I appreciate the great privilege I have enjoyed as a recipient of these ARC fellowships, as well as the space, time, and funding they have provided to engage with and help build a global collective of scholars and practitioners thinking critically about the role of international law in contemporary social, political, economic, and ecological transformations.

At Cambridge University Press, I thank Tom Randall and as always Finola O'Sullivan for their support and stewardship of this book. I am also grateful to the anonymous readers of the proposal for their thoughtful feedback.

The writing of this book and its companion volume has taken place over a particularly challenging and rewarding period of transformation in my life and work. I have been inspired, supported, and energised during this time by colleagues at academic homes in three countries.

In Australia, I thank the wonderful group of doctoral students, postdoctoral fellows, and visiting early career fellows who worked with me at Melbourne Law School from 2015 to 2021 as part of the program funded by my Laureate Fellowship, and the many colleagues and visiting professors who engaged with the work of the program, including Hilary Charlesworth, Alison Duxbury, Luis Eslava, Ann Genovese, Jan Klabbers, Martti Koskenniemi, Susanne Krasmann, Dino Kritsiotis, Shaun McVeigh, Naz Modirzadeh, Gregor Noll, Rose Parfitt, Glenda Sluga, and Pål Wrange.

In Sweden, I am grateful to the colleagues at Gothenburg University and Lund University who have enriched my work over the past decade. I have made numerous visits to the Law School and the Raoul Wallenberg Institute at Lund University since 2005, and I thank my host and colleague Gregor Noll for his life-changing invitations to visit Sweden for the first time in 2005 and since, and Morten Kjaerum for welcoming me as Raoul Wallenberg Visiting Professor from 2015 to 2017. I made a series of visits to Gothenburg University as the Torgny Segerstedt Visiting Professor for 2011–2012, and I thank Eva-Maria Svensson and the Torgny Segerstedt Foundation for that invitation and for generously hosting those visits. During 2014–2015, I was the Hedda

Andersson Visiting Chair in the History Department at Lund University. My thanks to my host Lena Halldenius, and colleagues at the Human Rights Program, the History Department, and the Law School, for a rich year of interdisciplinary discussions that informed my thinking on the questions explored in this book.

In the United States, I am grateful to Dean John Manning for the invitation to spend the Spring Term of 2019 as Visiting Professor and John Harvey Gregory Lecturer on World Organization at Harvard Law School. This book might never have been finished without the inspiration to keep writing that I received from the energetic, argumentative, and brilliant community of scholars into which I was welcomed. My thanks in particular to William Alford, Elizabeth Bartholet, Gabriella Blum, Dan Danielsen, Naz Modirzadeh, and Lucie White for their collegiality and hospitality, and to David Kennedy, Janet Halley, and Duncan Kennedy for the many forms of generosity they extended to me in Cambridge and for our many stimulating conversations about law and life.

Finally, my love and thanks to my family, Andrew, Isobel, and Felix, for your company on this and our many other journeys over the past decade. Andrew, thank you for reading and reflecting upon every word of this manuscript, and for recognising those mornings when I was 'dogged by debilitating presentism' and particularly needed cheering on. Isobel, thank you for helping me to see the world in new ways and for all your careful work putting together the bibliography, which at times looked like it might end up longer than the manuscript! Felix, our apprentice chef extraordinaire, thank you for thinking about and making wonderful meals and for reminding me to live in the present. In all this time spent thinking about the past, the three of you give me hope for the future.

1

Neoformalism and the Turn to History in International Law

1.1 TURNING TO HISTORY

International lawyers are very familiar with the claim that international law has taken a turn to history. Indeed, for some more dramatically inclined legal scholars, there is a 'struggle for the soul' of international law being played out through debates about the past.[1] This book seeks to grasp the political stakes of that historical turn. It does so by situating debates over the origins of international law and the meaning of past legal material within the broader field of political, social, economic, and institutional transformation that has reshaped the theory and practice of international law since the end of the Cold War.

The tumultuous decade of the 1990s was the initial context in which international lawyers took what has since been characterised as a 'turn to history'.[2] That is not to say that this was the moment at which international lawyers first began talking and writing about history. International law has

---

[1] A Carty, 'Visions of the Past of International Society: Law, History or Politics?' (2006) 69 *Modern Law Review* 644, at 645 (on the 'struggle for the soul' of international law being played out in debates about the past); P Alston, 'Does the Past Matter? On the Origins of Human Rights' (2013) 126 *Harvard Law Review* 2043, at 2077 (arguing that 'there is a struggle for the soul of the human rights movement, and it is being waged in large part through the proxy of genealogy').

[2] GRB Galindo, 'Martti Koskenniemi and the Historiographical Turn in International Law' (2005) 16 *European Journal of International Law* 539; M Craven, 'Introduction: International Law and Its Histories' in M Craven, M Fitzmaurice, and M Vogiatzi (eds), *Time, History, and International Law* (Leiden: Martinus Nijhoff, 2007), 1, at 3; T Skouteris, 'The Turn to History in International Law' in A Carty (ed), *Oxford Bibliographies Online* (Oxford: Oxford University Press, 2016); M Craven, 'Theorizing the Turn to History in International Law' in A Orford and F Hoffmann (eds), *The Oxford Handbook of the Theory of International Law* (Oxford: Oxford University Press, 2016), 21. For an early account challenging the utility of the 'move to history' in international law theory, see AL Paulus, 'International Law after Postmodernism: Towards Renewal or Decline of International Law?' (2001) 14 *Leiden Journal of International Law* 727.

1

been an intensely historical field of practice for as long as there have been international lawyers. Past texts, concepts, and practices are regularly retrieved and taken up as a resource in international legal argumentation, and past events or figures are invoked to situate current developments within a longer narrative and provide a meaningful teleology for the discipline. The tendency to equate the history of international law with the progress of humanity accompanied the organisation of international lawyers into a profession in the late nineteenth century.[3] In the aftermath of formal decolonisation scholars also turned to history to place newly independent states within a longer internationalist tradition,[4] or to insist that international law needed to be renovated if it were to treat new states on equal terms and move beyond the Christian and imperial bases of the European variant of international law.[5]

Nonetheless, the end of the Cold War marked a moment at which history began to play a more central role in international legal argumentation.

[3] M Koskenniemi, 'A History of International Law Histories' in B Fassbender and A Peters (eds), *The Oxford Handbook of the History of International Law* (Oxford: Oxford University Press, 2012), 943, at 943–944.

[4] See, for example, KA Nilakanta Sastri, 'International Law and Relations in Ancient India' (1952) 1 *Indian Yearbook of International Affairs* 97; M Khadduri, 'Islam and the Modern Law of Nations' (1956) 50 *American Journal of International Law* 358; MK Nawaz, 'The Law of Nations in Ancient India' (1957) 6 *Indian Yearbook of International Affairs* 172; CJ Chacko, 'India's Contribution to the Field of International Law Concepts' (1958) 93 *Recueil de Cours* 117; H Chatterjee, *International Law and Inter-State Relations in Ancient India* (Calcutta: KL Mukhopadhyay, 1958); CH Alexandrowicz, 'Treaty and Diplomatic Relations between European and South Asian Powers in the Seventeenth and Eighteenth Centuries' (1960) 100 *Recueil des Cours* 203; CH Alexandrowicz, 'Kautilyan Principles and the Law of Nations' (1965–1966) 41 *British Yearbook of International Law* 301; M Khadduri, *The Islamic Law of Nations: Shaybānī's Siyar* (Baltimore: John Hopkins Press, 1966); CH Alexandrowicz, *An Introduction to the History of the Law of Nations in the East Indies (16th, 17th and 18th Centuries)* (Oxford: Clarendon, 1967); I Keishiro, 'The Principles of International Law in the Light of Confucian Doctrine' (1967) 120 *Recueil des Cours* 1; CH Alexandrowicz, 'The Afro-Asian World and the Law of Nations (Historical Aspects)' (1968) 123 *Recueil des Cours* 117; MT Al Ghunaimi, *The Muslim Conception of International Law and the Western Approach* (The Hague: Martinus Nijhoff, 1968); N Singh, *India and International Law* (Delhi: S. Chand and Co, 1969); TO Elias, *Africa and the Development of International Law* (Leiden: AW Sijthoff, 1972); RP Anand, *Origin and Development of Law of the Sea: History of International Law Revisited* (Leiden: Martinus Nijhoff, 1983); CG Weeramantry, *Islamic Jurisprudence* (New York: St Martin Press, 1988).

[5] See, for example, FC Okoye, *International Law and the New African States* (London: Sweet and Maxwell, 1972); RP Anand, *New States and International Law* (Delhi: Vikas, 1972); UO Umozurike, *International Law and Colonialism in Africa* (Enugu: Nwamife, 1979); M Bedjaoui, *Towards a New International Economic Order* (Paris and New York: UNESCO/ Holmes and Meier, 1979); RP Anand, 'Sovereign Equality of States in International Law' (1986) 197 *Recueil des Cours* 9; FE Snyder and S Sathirathai (eds), *Third World Attitudes toward International Law* (Dordrecht: Nijhoff, 1987).

The sense that more recent historically minded work in international law represented a radical turning point lay not in the mere fact of scholarship engaging with the past, nor even of engaging with the past as 'history'. Rather, the sense that twenty-first-century scholarly trends signalled renewal and innovation was related to two developments – first, the turn to history as a way of understanding or critiquing the role of international law in a shifting global situation and second, the turn to history as a means of professionally engaging with the past. Both the turn to history as a means of intervening in current legal debates and the turn to history as a professional method for studying the past presented themselves as correctives to problems with earlier scholarship and both captured a sense of energy, innovation, and movement.

The first phenomenon that could be characterised as marking a 'turn to history' – the turn to history as a means of critically engaging with a rapidly changing legal and political situation – gained ground during the 1990s. Given the context of a unipolar world in which international law was being remade in the image of the sole remaining hegemonic power, it is perhaps unsurprising that the history of international law became a field of increasing interest and attention. With the break-up of the Soviet Union, international law became the vehicle for an ambitious US-led project of remaking relations between and within states. While for most of the twentieth century, international adjudication had played a relatively minor role in the broader international law field, that began to change. The twin processes of judicialisation and constitutionalisation began to intensify, particularly in areas that were central to the global economy. Appeals to the history of international law played a significant role in debates over the legitimacy of that expansionist project and the far-reaching regimes of investment, trade, and human rights adjudication that were consolidated as a result.

That focus on international law's history only intensified as the project of realising a new international law for a world of liberal states began to falter in the first decades of the twenty-first century.[6] In the wake of the war on terror, the subsequent financial, energy, climate, food, and humanitarian crises, and the disruptions to the US-led international order posed by the rise of China and the populist backlash against liberal multilateralism, history again became a site of struggles over the nature, meaning, and proper role of international law. The sense that history may not have ended and that a world of liberal states was not necessarily our destination re-entered the

---

[6]   For the description of the US-led vision for international law in those terms, see A-M Slaughter, 'International Law in a World of Liberal States' (1995) 6 *European Journal of International Law* 503.

mainstream of international legal debate. The consequences of those wars, crises, disruptions, and uprisings re-enlivened debates about how the world had come to take this form and what alternatives to the current global order were possible. Some scholars looked to the past to understand the role international law had played in contributing to the global financial crisis, climate change, mass displacement of people, and the growing vulnerability, insecurity, and inequality that were increasingly apparent within and between states. Others sought to muster a defence of existing international institutional arrangements and treaty regimes by linking their development to progress narratives.

Much of that initial scholarly work engaging with the history of international law was motivated by what historians call 'presentist' concerns. Lawyers assembled past texts, concepts, practices, and institutions to make arguments directed at rationalising, shaping, or resisting the transformation of international law over the turbulent decades following the end of the Cold War. Legal scholars engaged with the past in the process of participating in the everyday routines of international legal work. They attempted to understand what role international law had played in shaping the rapidly changing global situation, relied on inherited legal concepts, rethought received interpretations of treaties or state practice in relation to new contexts, suggested analogies for current situations requiring legal responses, and participated in exercises of regulatory redesign in the aftermath of financial, security, climate, energy, refugee, and food crises. While some of those international lawyers saw themselves as undertaking historical projects, most did not. In general, the work being undertaken by international lawyers did not conform to professional historical protocols in either style or method.

The idea that international law turned to history in the late twentieth century has also been used to describe a second scholarly trend that emerged during that period. That version of the 'turn to history' followed in the wake of more politically charged interventions. The scholars involved in the turn to history in this second sense urged international lawyers to take a more professional, less instrumentalist, and less partisan approach to history. As the history of international law and international institutions became more visible as public sites of contestation and struggle over the legitimacy of liberal internationalism, historians of international law began to challenge the accounts of the past offered by international lawyers on methodological grounds. Surprisingly quickly, international lawyers and historians became caught up in debates over the appropriate methods, styles, and protocols for engaging with texts, concepts, ideas, institutions, practices, or events considered to belong in and to the 'past' of international law, most notably in the fraught discussion over the past and present relation of international law and empire. A growing body of literature began to argue that those engaged in a substantive turn to history in legal scholarship should become more professional and less amateurish. That literature called on legal scholars to adopt proper historical methods, represented as a unified set of basic rules and standards.

The argument for taking a more professional approach to studying the history of international law was initiated by legal historians advocating the adoption of specific empiricist or contextualist historical techniques. They were joined by a group of professional historians who had begun to take an interest in international law as part of a broader turn to the international and the global amongst historians. Both the global turn in history and the international turn in intellectual history fuelled a new interest in histories of international law and fed into ongoing discussions about the way in which the past was drawn upon to inform current legal debates. Over time, the encounter between historians of international law and international lawyers has been increasingly characterised by the insistence that empiricist historical methods can produce professional, impartial, and verifiable interpretations of past texts, events, concepts, and practices, and that such methods are needed to correct or complete the misuses of history in international legal argument.

The end result has been that historical claims have begun to take on a new status within international legal debates. Despite over a century of anti-formalist scholarship in both law and history insisting that law is made not found, the turn to history has seen numerous historians and like-minded international lawyers treat historical research as if it offered an objective ground for determining what a past legal text really means, what an international institution was really designed to achieve, or what the field of international law is really for. In addition, numerous lawyers and historians have tended to treat at least some international lawyers (often those on the other side of a debate) as naïve scholastics who have yet to learn the lessons taught by centuries of historicising humanism.

1.2 THE HERMENEUTIC OF SUSPICION AND THE HISTORY OF INTERNATIONAL LAW

This book is concerned with the structure of argument that has resulted from that meeting of empiricist historical methods and international law. In short, I argue that the encounter is structured around a cross-disciplinary hermeneutic of suspicion. The claim that contemporary legal thought is structured around a hermeneutic of suspicion has been made by Duncan Kennedy in an article focused on the situation in US legal circles.[7] Kennedy argues that the widespread adoption of a hermeneutic of suspicion amongst US lawyers both in practice and in the academy is a way of dealing with the challenges posed to formalism and to metaphysics, first by the American legal realists of the early twentieth century and subsequently by the self-styled Critical Legal Scholars (or CLS) movement of the 1980s and beyond. The adoption of a hermeneutic of suspicion provides a way to deal with the challenge posed by anti-metaphysical and anti-formalist thinkers to any vestigial traces of the idea that law can be formalist, positivist, and possess a meaning that can be determined free of partisanship or ideology. The technique works by claiming that the lawyers on the other side in any dispute are exhibiting partisanship and engaging in ideological ways with legal rules, texts, or processes. Our side is in contrast simply offering a verifiable account of any legal rule or text and acting in good faith in accordance with processes or canons of interpretation to determine what the law is.

In the debate with which I am engaged in this book, a hermeneutic of suspicion is deployed across and between the disciplines of law and history. It is structured around claims about the ideological character of interpretations of the past by international lawyers and the scientific virtues of empiricist historiography. That cross-disciplinary hermeneutic presents legal scholars as partisan actors who interpret legal rules, texts, or processes politically, while empiricist historical research can offer verifiable and evidence-based interpretations of past legal material.

An argument structured in those terms plays a significant role in the post-realist field of contemporary international law. I characterise the field as post-realist because what counts as a persuasive legal argument in international law has been deeply affected by the realist challenge to the idea that law is a system of rules, the meaning of which is determinate and the consequences of which in any individual case can be mechanically derived from those rules. Yet that challenge to the tenets of formalism and positivism led the early American realists in two different directions, both of which have also shaped international law. On the one hand, the realist challenge fuelled a more sceptical version of legal thinking, which rejected the idea that there was a rational solution to every legal problem that could be uncovered by the use of the

---

[7]   D Kennedy, 'The Hermeneutic of Suspicion in Contemporary American Legal Thought' (2014) 25 *Law and Critique* 91. The idea that there exists a recognisable hermeneutic of suspicion was developed by Paul Ricoeur to describe the mode of interpretation inspired by Freud, Marx, and Nietzsche, the three 'masters of suspicion'. See P Ricœur, *Freud and Philosophy: An Essay on Interpretation* (New Haven: Yale University Press, 1970), 32–36.

correct method, model, or process. On the other hand, the realist challenge also inspired a search for more scientific foundations for the law. For those whose response to the realist challenge led in this direction, law might be politics all the way down, but perhaps other fields of human knowledge could still offer neutral, verifiable, or objective grounds for legal reasoning.

Over the intervening decades, there have been numerous attempts 'to recreate, to some extent, the idea of an objective standpoint' that lawyers can use to make decisions about 'complex legal issues without taking sides in desperate social struggles'.[8] Some have sought to find those new foundations in allegedly neutral processes or non-controversial decision-making procedures (such as the democratic process, the veil of ignorance, or game theory). Others have posited abstract values or criteria for judgment that are said to trump or transcend political divisions (appealing to categories such as rights, dignity, welfare, equality, or efficiency). Others have sought to turn normative disputes into debates about social scientific data or facts. In each case, the ambition has been 'to create a new foundation' for adjudication or legal reasoning 'to replace the discredited foundations of formalism'.[9]

The core argument of this book is that appeals to history do the same work in international law today. Empiricist historians make the neo-formalist claim that reconstructing historical contexts can offer us a verifiable means of interpreting past legal texts, practices, or institutions. Where social science methods are appealed to for objective accounts of the social world in which law operates,[10] historical methods are appealed to for objective accounts of past contexts. International lawyers are repeatedly told that contextualist historical methods can offer us a new foundation for grounding our arguments about the real history of a regime, the origins of international law, or the meaning of a past text. Accepting such claims allows lawyers to avoid the sceptical conclusions to which the realist critique ultimately leads. Rather than fully accepting uncertainty and our responsibility for the politics of our legal arguments, we can use the work of historians to establish truths about international law. In much contemporary international law scholarship, historical claims provide an exit from the uncertainty, self-doubt, or existential dread produced by arguments about the indeterminacy of legal rules or the lack of transcendent values upon which to base a shared law.

---

[8] JW Singer, 'Legal Realism Now' (1988) 76 *California Law Review* 465, at 516.
[9] Singer, 'Legal Realism Now', 516. See also G Peller, 'The Metaphysics of American Law' (1985) 73 *California Law Review* 1151 (comparing realism as critique and realism as science).
[10] D Trubek, 'Where the Action Is: Critical Legal Studies and Empiricism' (1984) 36 *Stanford Law Review* 575.

As debates over the interpretation of past texts, events, and practices have heated up in the context of a rapidly changing field of international law, history offers a silver bullet. While international lawyers may all be realists now, we tend to be realists about the opponent's argument while appealing to objective foundations to ground our own. In the case of the interdisciplinary version of the hermeneutic of suspicion that I study in this book, we find in history a new foundation for arguments about the meaning of law to ground our interpretations or indict our opponents. International lawyers may be biased, partisan, and political, but historical accounts and methods can still offer us knowledge that is objective, impartial, and factual. Numerous historians and like-minded international lawyers have argued that the adoption of professional historical methods can lift debates about legal meaning out of the realm of partisan politics and into the calmer domain of empiricist science. The overall effect is that history is presented as offering a new foundation for formalism in international law.

It is possible to see the resulting debates over the turn to history as simply a form of departmental rivalry – a petty clash between two groups of scholars, concerned with an arcane set of issues focused on style and method. The claim that one discipline is trying to exercise a form of 'scientific imperialism' over another certainly has something of that inside baseball quality to it.[11] Indeed, those of you who are reading this because you are interested in producing better histories of international law might look at my description of this debate and wonder what the fuss is about. Don't lawyers have something to gain from accepting the counsel of professional historians, if their methods can offer us an evidence-based account of the true origins of international law or allow us to understand the real meaning of the historical texts with which we routinely go to work? After all, what could be wrong with a commitment to rigorous engagement with evidence, careful work in documentary archives, articulating with precision the intentions informing particular utterances, and correcting partisan or instrumentalist misuse of the past? Don't we secretly hope for an interpretative method that would allow us to understand what a legal text really means once and for all, and escape from the relentless nihilism of anti-formalist legal theory and its insistence that the meaning of legal texts is indeterminate?

And those of you who are reading this because you are interested in thinking critically about international law might also wonder why I would baulk at an argument structured along those lines. Isn't it valuable to discover

---

[11] See generally U Mäki, A Walsh, and MF Pinto (eds), *Scientific Imperialism: Exploring the Boundaries of Interdisciplinarity* (London and New York: Routledge, 2018).

the true origin of the legal regimes with which we are working and thus be able to prove beyond doubt that everything else we have been told about them is simply an effect of mythologising or the invention of tradition? Shouldn't we adopt a relentlessly suspicious attitude towards the arguments made by lawyers and embrace any methods we can find in other disciplines to help us demonstrate the instrumentalising and misuse of the historical record by our opponents? Shouldn't we welcome a method that can empirically establish the misleading nature of international law's claims to embody universal values or represent all of humanity? And don't we believe – or perhaps fear – in our secret hearts that lawyers' amateurish approaches to interpreting texts, society, agency, and human behaviour need to be corrected by professional historians or social scientists, who can provide us with the empirical data that will expose the dangerous rhetoric with which lawyers pull the wool over everyone's eyes, including, on our worst days, our own?

I want to try and persuade you that this clash is not simply a passing and superficial squabble. Rather, it raises a set of issues that have a longer provenance and that go to the heart of questions around the role of lawyers in contemporary international politics. While many of us may want to believe that the truth is out there and that this time it is historians who will help us to find it, I want to suggest that the structure of that argument will lead us down the wrong path. It matters that the debate with which I am engaging is structured around a cross-disciplinary hermeneutic of suspicion, in which the interpretations of lawyers are presented as partisan or ideological, while those of empiricist historians are presented as objective and scientific. The first proposition – that is, that lawyers instrumentalise and politicise the past – is a useful insight, but the second – that is, that historians can save us – is a misguided attempt to avoid the responsibility that comes with moving beyond formalism. I am interested in exploring instead how international lawyers might think about our roles if we accepted the first of the twinned propositions at play in this debate – that lawyers instrumentalise and politicise history – without succumbing to the second – that empiricist historical method might save us from having to take responsibility for actively constructing accounts of the law's past when we argue about law in the present.

1.3 THE POLITICS OF MAKING INTERNATIONAL LAW

This book is an argument for a different way of thinking about the work of making legal arguments about the past. Rather than using history as a way of establishing the truth of our own account or accusing our opponents of ideological error, I ask what might be possible if we took responsibility for our own creativity and generativity in the project of making the law and making its history. What if we acknowledged the work we do, individually and collectively, in assembling and conferring power on the objects of our scholarly practice?[12]

At present, the combined moves made by historians and lawyers in producing and deploying empiricist histories of international law mean that both can avoid admitting their active and creative role in making international law in the past and in the present. Both sides of the disciplinary divide rely on the truth effects of the other discipline to bolster their own arguments and both deploy a hermeneutic of suspicion to project the agency involved in that process somewhere else. Historians rely on accounts produced by international lawyers for a sense of what international law is today, as if those accounts were objective, and international lawyers rely on accounts by historians for a sense of what international law was in the past, as if those accounts were objective. The result is that lawyers can escape interpretative uncertainty and our own responsibility for legal argument by suggesting that we are uncovering something about the law, discovering the truth of a regime by pointing to its real 'origins', or revealing the history of a field rather than constructing it. That approach continues to constrain and limit our understanding of the active work that is involved in any attempt to construct an account of international law through narrating its past.

This book challenges the suggestion that the empiricist historian offers a technically correct or professional method for interpreting all past texts, while the lawyer offers a politically motivated or instrumental reading. The current attempt to impose a particular empiricist style of historical research in international law is a political intervention in a field that is already organised around interpretative controversies. However, my elaboration of the limitations of the particular turn to empiricist history explored in this book is not meant as a call to the barricades, or for the building of a new wall to separate law and history, present and past. Quite the opposite – this is a call to think in new ways about that relation. This book seeks to show that law is already shot through with history, that history is already shot through with law, that the two are intimately related, and that the advocacy of a particular kind of historical method is inevitably bound up with a particular struggle for the meaning of law.

---

[12] For such an approach, see E Sedgwick, 'Paranoid Reading and Reparative Reading: Or, You're So Paranoid: You Probably Think This Essay Is about You' in E Sedgwick, MA Barale, J Goldberg, and M Moon (eds), *Touching Feeling: Affect, Pedagogy, Performativity* (Durham: Duke University Press, 2002), 123, at 149–150.

The arguments made in this book about the limits of empiricist historical method should not upset those historians whose professional commitment is to produce an accurate or verifiable account of the past rather than having any specific form of engagement with the present. If your professional commitment and goal is to produce scholarship that complies with historical protocols rather than to intervene in the present work of international law, then the claim that this turn to history does not always have critical purchase in the present should be uninteresting and without relevance to your scholarship. In addition, the work of people who understand themselves as engaged in a professional historical project often *does* have relevance for contemporary work in international law without historians themselves having to sign up to that project. Those historians can leave now with my blessing. This book is not for or about you.

However, a body of detailed work on the history of 'international law' is now accumulating at an increasing rate, much of it conforming to historical protocols but lacking an overt reflection on how such work might help us to think about the potential of international law. Indeed, the opposite is at times true – historical protocols are called upon to police innovative work in the field and to ensure that 'presentism' does not inform the way the past is engaged. Making use of the past as a means of engaging with contemporary legal practice requires a form of reflexivity that is not only discouraged but often discredited in the meeting of international law and history.

So if your ambition is that somehow your study of the past can, and perhaps even should, inform an engagement with and potential transformation of the work that an object called 'international law' or people called 'international lawyers' are doing in the present, this book is written for you. Its writing was animated by my commitment to studying the history and transformation of international law as a basis for enabling international lawyers to intervene in the current situation in politically productive ways. In so doing, I hope to establish the theoretical and conceptual foundations for a more nuanced conversation between international lawyers and scholars in related fields about the philosophical foundations and political stakes of the apparently technical debate over the proper 'methods' for engaging with the past of and as international law.

This book aims to enhance the awareness by international lawyers and other scholars of the methodological choices we make when we think and write about legal materials from the 'past', and to increase sensitivity to the political stakes of those choices in particular situations. I also want to encourage scholars of international law to evaluate, choose among, or create

methods based not on whether they are 'correct' but on what they help to
make visible or possible.[13]

1.4 OVERVIEW OF THE ARGUMENT

This is a book about the politics of the turn to history in international law at a
time of disruption, change, and challenge. Chapter 2 explores the political,
social, and economic conditions in which this turn to history and the
accompanying interdisciplinary hermeneutic of suspicion has taken shape
since the early 1990s. I focus in particular on the break-up of the Soviet
Union and the 'end of history' narrative that accompanied a period of
ambitious liberal expansionism, the crisis of liberal internationalism triggered by the war on terror, the subsequent financial, energy, food, asylum,
and climate crises of the early twenty-first century, and the shift in geopolitics
caused by the rise and influence of the BRICS and particularly of China as
an economic power. I consider the effects of those conditions on the ways in
which international lawyers have made use of the past as part of professional
and academic arguments.

Chapter 3 relates the turn to history in international law to the corresponding 'international turn' taken in the discipline of history, and points to the
effects of translating the stakes of those turns into a technical debate involving
the more abstract question of the proper scientific methods for understanding
the past of international law. That chapter explores a wide-ranging set of
claims about empiricist history and criticisms of international law that have
accompanied the turn to history. The claims made on behalf of empiricist
history were organised around the vocabulary of science. Historical
approaches were presented as a means of upholding 'standards of veracity
and verifiability',[14] 'distinguishing the abuses from the uses of history',[15] and
resisting 'the political manipulation of the past for present political purposes'
and the growing 'indifference to the verifiability of political discourse' in
contemporary culture.[16] The criticisms made of international lawyers took
many forms, but the basic idea was that international lawyers impose some
kind of organising scheme on past material, often with a view to addressing

---

[13] For a related approach, see WW Fisher III, 'Texts and Contexts: The Application to American
Legal History of the Methodologies of Intellectual History' (1997) 49 *Stanford Law Review* 1065.

[14] L Benton, 'Beyond Anachronism: Histories of International Law and Global Legal Politics'
(2019) 21 *Journal of the History of International Law* 1, at 3.

[15] S Moyn, *Human Rights and the Uses of History* (2nd edition) (London: Verso, 2017), xii.

[16] A Fitzmaurice, 'Context in the History of International Law' (2018) 20 *Journal of the History of
International Law* 5, at 13, 15, 30.

presentist legal issues. International lawyers have been rebuked for writing history 'from present to past',[17] making 'fanciful connections' between texts from different periods,[18] '[m]ining the past for analogues',[19] taking 'daring jumps' that destroy the 'complexity and pluralism of the discourses from various (and often very divergent) centuries',[20] engaging in 'a cherry-picking of historical events',[21] imposing a 'hermeneutic template' on the past,[22] or generally drawing incidents, events, or figures from the past into morality plays or progress narratives. As Chapter 3 shows, central to these arguments was a set of claims about what 'the basic rules of historical methodology' required,[23] including the prohibition on anachronism, presentism, or abridged versions of history. International lawyers proved very receptive to the idea that empiricist historical methods offered a set of technical rules to which legal scholars should conform when writing about the past and quickly began to call out their colleagues for violating those 'rules'.

Chapter 4 traces the traditions for thinking about meaning and history on which those methodological arguments are built. I argue that claims about what history can offer international law are part of a longer tradition, in which humanist disenchantment and secularisation promised to lift Europe out of the divided world of religious wars and into a new era of civil peace. A particular vision of law and a particular figure of the lawyer has been central to the work of empiricist historians of political thought for at least a century. The chapter explores the work of Herbert Butterfield, JGA Pocock, Quentin Skinner, and Ian Hunter – four influential scholars whose work has influenced the method debates in international law. I draw out the particular figure of the lawyer as apologist for power who reappears in their texts and against which their historicising methods are staged. That figure of the lawyer appears in different guises – as Whig constitutionalist for

---

[17] R Lesaffer, 'International Law and Its History: The Story of an Unrequited Love' in M Craven, M Fitzmaurice, and M Vogiatzi (eds), *Time, History, and International Law* (Leiden: Martinus Nijhoff, 2007), 27, at 34–35.

[18] G Cavallar, 'Vitoria, Grotius, Pufendorf, Wolff and Vattel: Accomplices of European Colonialism and Exploitation or True Cosmopolitans?' (2008) 10 *Journal of the History of International Law* 181, at 207.

[19] K Purcell, 'On the Uses and Advantages of Genealogy for International Law' (2020) 33 *Leiden Journal of International Law* 13, at 27.

[20] Cavallar, 'Accomplices of European Colonialism and Exploitation or True Cosmopolitans?', 207–208.

[21] CR Rossi, *Whiggish International Law: Elihu Root, the Monroe Doctrine, and International Law in the Americas* (Leiden: Brill, 2019), 36.

[22] I Hunter, 'About the Dialectical Historiography of International Law' (2016) 1 *Global Intellectual History* 1, at 6.

[23] Lesaffer, 'International Law and Its History', 37.

Butterfield, as English common lawyer for Pocock, as Italian scholastic lawyer for Skinner, and as nineteenth-century Prussian natural lawyer for Hunter. In each case, however, the function of this figure in the narrative about the arrival of a new method is the same. The lawyer as scholastic textualist, university metaphysician, or Whig apologist functions as the foil against which a new figure is opposed, a figure who will challenge the oppressive authority of received tradition with the liberating methods of historicising contextualism. In each account, while the villain of the story is the scholastic, common, natural, or international lawyer who offers indefensible claims about authority based on appeals to transcendence, metaphysics, or timeless origins, the hero of the story is the humanist (deploying methods that bear a striking resemblance to those of the context-ualist historian), who arrives on the scene to offer an anti-metaphysical challenge to authority. I argue that the debate over the turn to method in international law is part of that longer narrative, in which historians are able to take up their preordained place as radical disrupters of orthodoxy. It is this narrative that helps make sense of the certainty with which historians understand their role as at once objective, scientific, and revolutionary.

Chapter 5 challenges the representations of international law that dom-inate the turn to history. The vision of international law as metaphysically grounded and of lawyers as scholastics or moralising judges is resonant because it shores up a familiar fantasy. Yet that vision bears little relation to the ways in which contemporary international lawyers use the past in the practice of making legal arguments. This chapter challenges that fantasised vision of law, by giving a sense of the broader field of the past out of which lawyers assemble legal arguments and the varied standpoints we take up in doing so. Despite the contextualist assumption that the past centuries of humanist scholarship have not yet registered in international legal argu-mentation, international lawyers are already immersed in a centuries-long debate over the grounds of law's authority, into which historicising tech-niques and anti-metaphysical approaches have long been incorporated. Many influential forms of international legal thought, including legal realism, positivism, critical legal studies, and game theory, have been informed by an anti-metaphysical orientation. Anti-formalist arguments and the historicisation of legal texts are firmly established aspects of legal argumentation in both theory and practice.[24] In that sense it can be said of

---

[24] S Seppänen, 'Anti-formalism and the Preordained Birth of Chinese Jurisprudence' (2018) 14 *China Perspectives* 31, at 37.

international lawyers, as it was said of American lawyers decades ago: 'Realism is dead: we are all realists now.'[25]

Chapter 5 explores two issues that flow from that constant reiteration of a default position for law in debates over its history. The first issue is analytical and concerns whether these methods help in understanding the way that lawyers use the past in making legal meaning or the roles that lawyers play in doing so. I argue that if we want to understand meaning as it is made in law, and to intervene in that process, it is necessary to pay attention to the language games within which lawyers work as scholars, teachers, and practitioners. It is only by exploring the many roles of the international law scholar and the many uses we make of the past that scholars can understand the work that the argument for empiricist methods does when it is translated into the contemporary field of international legal argumentation. Rather than treat law as a subfield of history and try to 'professionalise' the amateuristic approach that lawyers take to the past, that chapter asks what it might mean to 'take legal amateurism as seriously as any other knowledge practice one might want to study'.[26] The second issue is political and relates to the claim that empiricist historicising is both impartial and liberatory when applied to law. The debate explored in this book makes a set of claims about what historicising can do that are premised upon 'assumptions about the historical position and normative commitments' of both the historian and their audience.[27] Ideas about historicising law are designed to challenge particular forms of orthodoxy that depend upon or are committed to metaphysical ideals like truth or mythical origin stories.[28] In order for the work of historicising international law to have the kind of critical purchase that is claimed for it, the authority of international law would need to be based on a claim to be timeless, natural, or self-evident, or organised around preserving tradition for its own sake. For this form of work to have that effect, there need to be people who hold those beliefs. As Chapter 5 argues, however, there are very few lawyers for whom the idea that international law is historically situated or political is novel or even controversial. Such arguments are already an entrenched part of the argumentative field of international law. To put this differently,

---

[25] W Twining, *Karl Llewellyn and the Realist Movement* (London: Weidenfeld and Nicholson, 1973), 382.

[26] A Riles, 'Legal Amateurism' in J Desautels-Stein and C Tomlins (eds), *Searching for Contemporary Legal Thought* (Cambridge: Cambridge University Press, 2017), 499.

[27] L Carlson, 'Critical for Whom? Genealogy and the Limits of History' (2019) 31 *Method and Theory in the Study of Religion* 185, at 187.

[28] Carlson, 'Critical for Whom?', 199.

the reader for whom contextualist history or even genealogy is written is not stable through time.[29]

Chapter 6 takes up the claim that historians are able to offer value-free, impartial, and verifiable observations about the history of something called 'international law'. While numerous historians have criticised international legal scholars for misusing the past to tell stories, draw analogies, or link material from diverse periods, historical work is presented as a process of finding evidence rather than making arguments, committed to reality rather than myths. This chapter argues that histories of international law are necessarily as partisan and political as those produced by the most pragmatic of lawyers. Any study that is described as offering a history of something called 'international law', or of a subfield of international law like international economic law or human rights law, necessarily makes choices about what international law is, where its precursors are to be found, who or what counts as a subject of international law, what past practice is relevant to the field of international law, which figures, texts, or events are central to understanding how the field developed, how the technical details of legal practice relate to ideological claims about what the law is for, and why any of this might matter. In so doing, they become part of presentist debates about what international law is and where it is to be found. To show how that works in practice, I explore three empiricist historical accounts that are overtly presented as offering correctives to the distorted, presentist, or incomplete histories of international law produced to date – Lauren Benton and Lisa Ford's *Rage for Order*, Samuel Moyn's *The Last Utopia*, and Quinn Slobodian's *Globalists*.[30] I focus in each case on the normative and political choices involved in deciding what the history of international law, international human rights law, or international economic law is properly a history of.

Chapter 7 returns to take up the argument that the interplay between international law and empiricist history offers a new grounding for formalism in an extremely fraught political context. Historical work is increasingly relied upon as a source of substantive claims about what law really means and of scientific methods for studying the past. Lawyers rely on the scientific tone and resulting truth effects of accounts presented by professional historians to intervene in contemporary debates by using the claims made in those

---

[29] See L Carlson, *Contingency and the Limits of History* (New York: Columbia University Press, 2019).

[30] L Benton and L Ford, *Rage for Order: The British Empire and the Origins of International Law, 1800–1850* (Cambridge: Harvard University Press, 2016); S Moyn, *The Last Utopia: Human Rights in History* (Cambridge: Belknap Press, 2010); Q Slobodian, *Globalists: The End of Empire and the Birth of Neoliberalism* (Cambridge: Harvard University Press, 2018).

narratives about international law's 'true' origins or 'real' history. Appeals to contextualist histories allow lawyers to present their arguments as being grounded on evidence and to characterise the other side in a legal debate as ideologically motivated, presentist, or engaged in myth-making rather than proper scholarship. Yet if international lawyers cannot look to historians (or anyone else for that matter) to save the day with impartial and verifiable evidence-based interpretations of what international law really is, means, or stands for, what then is to be done? I conclude by exploring why and how we might nonetheless study the international legal past even knowing that writing histories of international law is inevitably a partisan act. There *is* a struggle for the soul of international law currently being played out, as there is a struggle being played out for many of the inherited institutions and laws of the past centuries. The kind of historical methods being proposed for legal scholars offer one set of weapons that international lawyers might take up to be part of this struggle, but they do not have to be accepted wholesale. Rather, legal scholars need to think hard about the historical baggage, the time-bound assumptions, the working premises, the institutional conditions, the visions of politics, the possibilities, and the inevitable limitations that are part of any method we borrow or take up.

Situating the Turn to History in International Law

This chapter explores the political stakes involved in the turn to history in international law by situating that turn within a broader political, social, economic, and institutional context. My starting point is that in order to understand what international legal scholars were doing when they turned to history, it is necessary to pay attention to the contemporaneous arguments being made in international legal practice. As Annelise Riles has argued, the legal academy is 'integrated first into the profession and only secondarily into the social science division of the modern university'.[1] Legal scholars work as part of an interpretative community that encompasses legal practice and the academy. Legal scholarship, including legal scholarship that refers to the past, needs to be understood as an attempt both to make sense of and to intervene in a rapidly shifting field of argumentative practice and to do so while conforming to the conventions of the modern university.

With that relation to practice in mind, I focus in this chapter on four broad conditions that have propelled the turn to history in the field of international law since the early 1990s. The first condition was the break-up of the Soviet Union and the 'end of history' narrative that accompanied the expansionist liberal internationalism of the 1990s. The second was the attack on the United States of 11 September 2001 and the war on terror initiated by the United States in response. The third involved the financial,

---

[1]   A Riles, 'Legal Amateurism' in J Desautels-Stein and C Tomlins (eds), *Searching for Contemporary Legal Thought* (Cambridge: Cambridge University Press, 2017), 499, at 501, 514. For a sociological exploration of that relationship, see Y Dezalay and BG Garth, *Dealing in Virtue: International Commercial Arbitration and the Construction of a Transnational Legal Order* (Chicago: University of Chicago Press, 1996). I explore the relation of international lawyers in practice and the university in more detail in Chapter 5.

energy, food, asylum, and climate crises of the early twenty-first century and the backlash against multilateralism that they triggered. The fourth was the shift in geopolitics caused by the rise and influence of the BRICS, and particularly China, as economic powers, and the corresponding sense of a decline in US hegemony.

International lawyers in practice and the academy have drawn on past events, practices, cases, negotiating histories, and institutional experiments as argumentative resources in adjudicatory settings, as well as in debates over how to shape, understand, justify, enable, challenge, narrate, or resist the legal transformations that have taken place in that changing international situation. Appeals to the history of international law initially played a significant role in debates over the legitimacy of expansionist liberal internationalism during the 1990s and the far-reaching regimes of investment, trade, and human rights adjudication that were consolidated during that decade. As that project came under pressure, appeals to history played a significant role in the subsequent debates over how to make sense of the perceived crisis of liberal internationalism. Those who have sought to muster a defence of existing international institutional arrangements and treaty regimes have linked their development to progressive narratives, while those who have sought to challenge aspects of existing international regimes have linked them to historical processes including imperialism, neoliberalism, and fascism.

As part of that broad field of legal ferment and contest, international law scholars also began to undertake more conventionally historical work. Over time, the turn to history began to be understood as a project that should be distanced from the argumentative practice of international law and instead measured against the empiricist protocols of academic historians. In this chapter, I return it to the context of international legal argumentation from which it arose, in order to gain a better understanding of what work the turn to history was initially doing as an intervention in struggles over the meaning and role of international law in the present.

2.1 INTERNATIONAL LAW AT THE END OF HISTORY

2.1.1 *US Hegemony and the Transformation of International Law*

The first set of conditions shaping the turn to history in international law resulted from the break-up of the Soviet Union in 1989 and the accompanying claim that something momentous had occurred in 'mankind's ideological evolution', leaving no alternative to liberal democracy as the ideal form of government that resolved all the serious contradictions that had undermined other forms of political life.[2] The subsequent and contested attempts to remake international law in the image of liberal internationalism saw fierce struggles play out over the meaning of international law's past in both practice and theory. The sense that an interventionist liberal international law represented the end of history was conditioned by the break-up of the Soviet Union and the emergence of the United States as the sole superpower at the end of the Cold War. Over the decade of the 1990s, the United States was increasingly able to shape a new world order in its own image. The transformation of international law was central to that process. 'The end of history' became a useful shorthand for the claim that human society had been progressing in a determinate direction over the previous century, and that liberal democracy represented the destination of that history.

While some – but far from all – international lawyers embraced that vision of the destiny of international law, determining what a liberal international legal order would mean in practice proved controversial. In particular, liberal internationalists imagined the post-Cold War project of transforming international law in two quite different ways. On the one hand, the claim that the conduct of relations between states should take place according to liberal ideals had already shaped many of the principles that are often seen as foundational to the international order, among them the principles of sovereign equality, self-determination, collective security, non-intervention in the internal affairs of other states, and the commitment to peaceful settlement of disputes. For some international lawyers, the end of the Cold War meant the opportunity to see these liberal ideals realised through the UN system. Other more muscular liberal internationalists looked to law as a vehicle for transforming all states into liberal democracies, protecting the rights of individuals, entrenching market logic at the heart of government, and promoting freedom. In this vision, the true destiny of international law was 'a world of liberal states'.[3] The moral certainty underpinning that project sat uneasily with the pluralistic foundations of the thinner liberal conception of international law expressed in documents such as the UN Charter. Those two visions of what it might mean to entrench liberal internationalism have often been in tension, but never more so than when crusading liberal states have emerged as hegemonic.

---

[2]   See famously F Fukuyama, *The End of History and the Last Man* (New York: Free Press, 2006), xiii, xxi.

[3]   A-M Slaughter, 'International Law in a World of Liberal States' (1995) 6 *European Journal of International Law* 503.

From the beginning of the early 1990s, liberal democracies took advantage of the new geopolitical situation by attempting a systematic process of remaking international law across a wide range of fields. The 1990s was the period during which international law began to be seen as a vehicle for entrenching a particular approach to economic policy-making through international and regional economic integration.[4] This was largely realised through negotiating ambitious new multilateral or regional agreements. To take one example, the creation of the World Trade Organization (WTO) at the completion of the Uruguay Round in 1995 led to a significant expansion in the range of activities brought within the scope of the international trade regime. The WTO dispute settlement system was referred to as the 'jewel in the crown' of the organisation.[5] Scholars argued that 'the importance of the mere existence of the Appellate Body to a shift in organizational legal culture' could not be overestimated.[6] It was lauded as an approach to mandatory dispute settlement that 'surpasses' in 'effectiveness and sophistication' anything 'achieved by other international tribunals, such as the International Court of Justice'.[7] For those who saw international law as contributing to the creation of a liberal international order, 'WTO admission and participation would set up a kind of tutorial in rule-of-law values' and might provide the means to push a state 'not only to change its trade and trade-related practices, but also to reform its domestic government, liberalize its political system, expand the rights and opportunities of women and other disadvantaged groups, and so on'.[8]

A related set of developments initiated during the 1990s was the process of creating a raft of new international courts and tribunals and increasing the resort to existing processes of international arbitration. For most of the twentieth century, international adjudication had played a relatively minor role in the broader international law field. To the extent that there were international

---

4   See further A Orford, 'Theorizing Free Trade' in A Orford and F Hoffmann (eds), *The Oxford Handbook of the Theory of International Law* (Oxford: Oxford University Press, 2016), 701; A Orford, 'International Law and the Populist Moment' (2020) 35 *American University International Law Review* 427.

5   CD Creamer, 'From the WTO's Crown Jewel to Its Crown of Thorns' (2019) 113 *AJIL Unbound* 51.

6   JHH Weiler, 'The Rule of Lawyers and the Ethos of Diplomats: Reflections on the Internal and External Legitimacy of WTO Dispute Settlement' (2001) 35 *Journal of World Trade* 191, at 199.

7   See R Howse, 'Adjudicative Legitimacy and Treaty Interpretation in International Trade Law: The Early Years of WTO Jurisprudence' in JHH Weiler (ed) *The EU, the WTO, and the NAFTA: Towards a Common Law of International Trade?* (Oxford: Oxford University Press, 2000), 35.

8   Remarks of LF Damrosch, 'Human Rights, Terrorism and Trade' (2002) 96 *Proceedings of the ASIL Annual Meeting* 128, at 130.

courts and tribunals, their jurisdiction was not mandatory, and states did not generally allow issues that were perceived as central to their national interest to be subjected to binding adjudication. With the ending of the Cold War that began to change. The twin processes of judicialisation and constitutionalisation began to intensify, with the creation of international courts and tribunals as part of specialised regimes, including international criminal courts, regional economic courts, and regional human rights courts.[9] The result has been a form of uneven judicialisation, with 'a new paradigm of routinised litigation and judicial governance' developing alongside 'the traditional paradigm of episodic international (inter-state) dispute settlement by tribunals'.[10]

The 1990s was the most fertile period for this process of judicialisation. The emergence of international criminal tribunals was heralded as signalling the emergence of 'a new world order based on the rule of international law',[11] with the highpoint being the adoption in 1998 of the Rome Statute establishing the International Criminal Court. The UN Convention on the Law of the Sea (UNCLOS) entered into force in 1994, and the International Tribunal for the Law of the Sea (ITLOS) began to operate in 1997, with commentators hailing the creation of a mandatory dispute settlement mechanism under UNCLOS as 'one of the most significant developments in dispute settlement in international law, even as important as the entry into force of the United Nations Charter'.[12] Regional human rights courts in Europe and Latin America became far more active and influential.

The most significant developments in terms of international adjudication, however, were in the areas that were central to entrenching a global capitalist economy, through the expanded operation of adjudicatory regimes in the fields of investment and trade. As I noted earlier, the creation of the WTO with its mandatory dispute settlement system replacing the old world of GATT panels staffed by trade diplomats was heralded by many as a key moment in the development of a global rule of law.[13] In addition, perhaps the most

---

[9]   See A Orford, 'A Global Rule of Law' in M Loughlin and J Meierhenrich (eds), *The Cambridge Companion to the Rule of Law* (Cambridge: Cambridge University Press, 2021), 538.

[10] B Kingsbury, 'International Courts: Uneven Judicialisation in Global Order' in J Crawford and M Koskenniemi (eds), *The Cambridge Companion to International Law* (Cambridge: Cambridge University Press, 2012), 203, at 210.

[11] A Cassese, 'On the Current Trends towards Criminal Prosecution and Punishment of Breaches of International Humanitarian Law' (1998) 9 *European Journal of International Law* 2, at 8.

[12] N Klein, *Dispute Settlement in the UN Convention on the Law of the Sea* (Cambridge: Cambridge University Press, 2009), 2.

[13] Weiler, 'The Rule of Lawyers and the Ethos of Diplomats'; Howse, 'Adjudicative Legitimacy and Treaty Interpretation', 35.

effective mechanism through which the international facilitation of economic liberalisation took place was through the consolidation of a transnational regime of investment protection.

Home states had sought to internationalise the protection of foreign investment and justify the lawfulness of actions to protect private rights since the nineteenth century.[14] The creation of mixed commissions or tribunals to settle disputes concerning the property rights of aliens was not a new phenomenon,[15] and precedents also existed for granting standing to private investors to make claims before such tribunals. However, historically those international claims institutions had been the 'stepchildren of war and rebellion', and were typically constituted by victorious states or aggrieved neutrals seeking compensation for their nationals.[16] States only consented to private actors bringing such claims in relation to 'past, strictly circumscribed events in the aftermath of war or revolution',[17] such as the capture, confiscation, or destruction of property, or the inability to collect debts during conflict. International claims practice was thus a 'retributive instrument of international power politics',[18] while also championed by the peace movement as a means of preventing further conflict.[19]

That situation had begun to change during the era of formal decolonisation, when foreign investors and their home states perceived a threat to the security and profitability of investments in newly independent states and sought to introduce greater protections for investments and private property. A key procedural step was the development by the World Bank of a form of international machinery to address disputes between states and investors. The resulting International Convention on the Settlement of Investment Disputes between States and Nationals of Other States (ICSID Convention) 1966 established a centre for facilitating the settlement of disputes. Its proponents

---

[14] See generally K Miles, *The Origins of International Investment Law: Empire, Environment and the Safeguarding of Capital* (Cambridge: Cambridge University Press, 2013).

[15] K Greenman, 'Aliens in Latin America: Intervention, Arbitration and State Responsibility for Rebels' (2018) 31 *Leiden Journal of International Law* 617.

[16] DJ Bederman, 'The United Nations Compensation Commission and the Tradition of International Claims Settlement' (1994) 27 *New York University Journal of International Law and Politics* 1, at 3.

[17] J Pauwelyn, 'Rational Design or Accidental Evolution? The Emergence of International Investment Law' in Z Douglas, J Pauwelyn, and JE Viñuales (eds), *The Foundations of International Investment Law: Bringing Theory into Practice* (Oxford: Oxford University Press, 2014), 11, at 36.

[18] Bederman, 'The United Nations Compensation Commission', 6.

[19] HL Bray, 'Understanding Change: Evolution from International Claims Commissions to Investment Treaty Arbitration' in SW Schill, CJ Tams, and R Hofmann (eds), *International Investment Law and History* (Cheltenham: Edward Elgar, 2018), 102, at 119.

stressed that its operation would be founded upon state consent, that ICSID tribunals would only have jurisdiction over disputes that parties specifically agreed to submit for arbitration, and that states could carve out disputes they did not want to submit to ICSID.[20] However, what had seemed like a purely procedural commitment was later interpreted in combination with dispute settlement provisions in bilateral investment treaties to provide grounds for jurisdiction.[21]

The resulting transnational regime for investment protection was consolidated and expanded during the 1990s with the negotiation of many new BITs and other broad-reaching agreements such as the Energy Charter Treaty and the North American Free Trade Agreement (NAFTA). The result was a significant increase in resort to international adjudication. Broad interpretations of substantive provisions addressing direct or indirect 'expropriation' served to protect investors against the effects on profits of routine government regulation aimed at protecting public health and safety or the environment. Whereas in earlier eras international claims processes had been directed towards loss suffered during conflict, in the era of BITs the focus of arbitral scrutiny became the everyday conduct of government regulation and its impacts on the profits of foreign investors.[22] An expansive sense of the relation between treaty terms and emerging principles of customary international law (largely dependent upon interpreting the past practice of major Western states) shaped the decisions of arbitral tribunals in that field of investment law.[23] The overall effect was increasingly to disembed the economic relations of host states and foreign investors from the political situation in which

---

[20] AR Parra, *The History of ICSID* (Oxford: Oxford University Press, 2012), 25.

[21] In the 'revolutionary' award of *AAPL v Sri Lanka*, the tribunal found that the article of the UK–Sri Lanka BIT consenting to submit investment disputes to ICSID gave rights to investors to bring direct claims of treaty breach against Sri Lanka even in the absence of a contract between the investor and the government: *AAPL v. Sri Lanka*, ICSID/ARB/87/3 (1990). For the characterisation of that award as revolutionary, see Pauwelyn, 'Rational Design or Accidental Evolution?', 31.

[22] Bray, 'Understanding Change', 104, 118.

[23] For a sense of debates over the role that custom plays as a means for justifying new interpretations of legal obligations in the field of international investment law, see S Schwebel, 'The Influence of Bilateral Investment Treaties on Customary International Law' (2004) 98 *Proceedings of the ASIL Annual Meeting* 27; JE Alvarez, 'A BIT on Custom' (2009) 42 *New York University Journal of International Law and Policy* 17; CL Lim, 'The Worm's View of History and the Twailing Machine' in CL Lim (ed), *Alternative Visions of the International Law on Foreign Investment: Essays in Honour of Muthucumaraswamy Sornarajah* (Cambridge: Cambridge University Press, 2016), 3; CL Lim, 'The Strange Vitality of Custom in the International Protection of Property, Contracts, and Commerce' in CA Bradley (ed), *Custom's Future: International Law in a Changing World* (Cambridge: Cambridge University Press, 2016), 205.

investments were made and to establish international arbitration as the principal mode of resolving investment disputes.

The high political, strategic, and financial stakes of the new forms of international adjudication placed stress on the need to present international law as neutral, impartial, and free of politics.[24] The privileging of international adjudication over both interstate negotiation and domestic political processes as a means of resolving conflicts between competing interests, values, and ideologies inevitably embroiled judges and arbitrators in controversies and political struggles. The claim that humanity was making progress towards realising a global rule of law played an important role in arguments justifying the desirability of these new regimes and processes.[25] The new forms of international adjudication relied upon the symbolic capital of international lawyers, with arbitral tribunals located in internationalist cities such as The Hague and Geneva, and senior international law professors and judges taking up roles as investment arbitrators or WTO Appellate Body members.[26]

In addition, the United States and its allies began to argue for new understandings of international law on the use of force. During periods when the US President was a Republican those novel arguments tended to focus on the flexibilities purportedly available to states using force in individual or collective self-defence, and during periods when the US President was a Democrat those novel arguments tended to focus on the flexibilities enabled by expansive readings of collective security authorised by the Security Council or appeals to an alleged customary rule of humanitarian intervention. What remained stable was the ongoing attempt to reshape international law on the use of force in order to enable US interventionism.

To take one contested example, it was during the 1990s that international lawyers began to argue in favour of the evolution of customary international law rules that were said to permit unilateral or regional humanitarian intervention.[27] The claim that states might unilaterally resort to force for

---

[24] See further Chapter 6. For a discussion of the political stakes and increased controversy surrounding international investment arbitration, see A Orford, *International Law and the Social Question* (The Hague: Asser Press, 2020).

[25] Orford, 'A Global Rule of Law'.

[26] Dezalay and Garth, *Dealing in Virtue*.

[27] From a very broad literature arguing initially for the need to expand the role of the Security Council to include humanitarian intervention, and then more ambitiously for the emergence of a customary norm permitting humanitarian intervention without Security Council authorisation, see for example TG Weiss, 'On the Brink of a New Era? Humanitarian Interventions, 1991–94' in DCF Daniel and BC Hayes (eds), *Beyond Traditional Peacekeeping* (Hampshire and New York: Palgrave Macmillan, 1995); FR Tesón, 'Collective Humanitarian Intervention' (1996) 17 *Michigan Journal of International Law* 232; TJ Farer, 'Intervention in

humanitarian motives of course predates the 1990s. However, the changed geopolitical and institutional conditions of the 1990s saw a shift in support for the notion of humanitarian intervention, at least amongst liberal states. For many in the West, humanitarian intervention was presented as a means to allow the international community, or at least an alliance of liberal states, to bring human rights and democracy to those suffering at the hands of punitive, authoritarian, or 'failed' states. A simple roll call of names – Somalia, Haiti, Rwanda, Bosnia, Kosovo, Timor-Leste – serves as a reminder of the sense of humanitarian crisis which pervaded the 1990s. Looking back on that period, from an era when security, preventive self-defence, and the war on terror largely dominate the foreign policy agenda of militaristic states, it can be difficult to remember the anguished intensity with which this concern for saving strangers manifested itself in the 1990s.[28]

A turning point in debates over humanitarian intervention came with the eleven-week NATO bombing of Kosovo during 1999. NATO's Operation Allied Force, launched on 24 March 1999, and undertaken without Security Council authorisation, was the first major military campaign undertaken by the alliance in its history. NATO intervened in the context of an ongoing civil war between the Kosovo Liberation Army and the Yugoslav army, concerns that Belgrade was planning the systematic ethnic cleansing of Kosovar Albanians, and a potential regional crisis caused by the growing numbers of internally displaced persons and refugees from the conflict.

To the extent that NATO governments offered a legal defence for their action, it was premised on the principle of humanitarian intervention. According to a UK Foreign and Commonwealth Office note, military intervention by NATO was 'lawful on grounds of overwhelming humanitarian necessity'.[29] In general, even international lawyers sympathetic to NATO's

---

Unnatural Humanitarian Emergencies: Lessons of the First Phase' (1996) 18 *Human Rights Quarterly* 1; WM Reisman, 'Kosovo's Antinomies' (1999) 93 *American Journal of International Law* 860. For a revival of that debate in the context of Libya and Syria, see D Bethlehem, 'Stepping Back a Moment – The Legal Basis in Favour of a Principle of Humanitarian Intervention', *EJIL: Talk!*, 12 September 2013, available at www.ejiltalk.org/?s=bethlehem; HH Koh, 'Syria and the Law of Humanitarian Intervention (Part II: International Law and the Way Forward)', *Just Security*, 2 October 2013, available at http://justsecurity.org/1506/koh-syria-part2/; A-M Slaughter, 'A Regional Responsibility to Protect' in D Held and K McNally (eds), *Lessons from Intervention in the 21st Century: Legality, Feasibility and Legitimacy* (London: Global Policy, 2014), 60.

[28] For a critical account written during that period, see A Orford, *Reading Humanitarian Intervention: Human Rights and the Use of Force in International Law* (Cambridge: Cambridge University Press, 2003).

[29] The note is reproduced in A Roberts, 'NATO's "Humanitarian War" over Kosovo' (1999) 41 *Survival* 102, at 106.

position did not accept that argument for the legality of the intervention. Many US and European international lawyers nonetheless supported the NATO intervention in Kosovo, arguing that the NATO action was 'illegal but legitimate', that international law could sometimes tolerate a delict if it was for the collective good, that the failure of the Security Council to condemn the NATO intervention or its subsequent resolution 1244 (1999) amounted to an implicit authorisation of the action, or that a customary principle of humanitarian intervention had continued to exist alongside the UN Charter.[30] Interpretations of the legitimacy or legality of the NATO intervention supported the position put by political leaders such as British Prime Minister Tony Blair, who portrayed the NATO intervention in Kosovo as a 'just war, based not on territorial ambitions, but on values'.[31]

Even Samuel Moyn, an intellectual historian who two decades later would produce a series of scathing critiques indicting international lawyers and human rights activists for their complicity with US expansionism and neoliberalism during the 1990s,[32] was in 1999 working at the White House to develop legal arguments in favour of the NATO intervention. Moyn, who at that time was

[30] For a range of arguments made by European and US lawyers, many expressing some reservations about the legality of the resort to force but nonetheless ending in support of the intervention, see B Simma, 'NATO, the UN and the Use of Force' (1999) 10 *European Journal of International Law* 1; A Cassese, '*Ex iniuria ius oritur*: Are We Moving towards Forcible Humanitarian Countermeasures in the World Community?' (1999) 10 *European Journal of International Law* 23; MJ Glennon, 'The New Interventionism: The Search for a Just International Law' (1999) 78 *Foreign Affairs* 2; L Henkin, 'Kosovo and the Law of "Humanitarian Intervention"' (1999) 93 *American Journal of International Law* 826; R Wedgwood, 'NATO's Campaign in Yugoslavia' (1999) 93 *American Journal of International Law* 828; C Greenwood, 'Humanitarian Intervention: The Case of Kosovo' (1999) 10 *Finnish Yearbook of International Law* 168; M Matheson, 'Justification for the NATO Air Campaign in Kosovo' (2000) 94 *Proceedings of the ASIL Annual Meeting* 301; S Murphy, 'The Intervention in Kosovo: A Law-Shaping Incident' (2000) 94 *Proceedings of the ASIL Annual Meeting* 303; S Sur, 'Le recours à la force dans l'affaire du Kosovo et le droit international', *Les notes de l'Ifri – no 22* (Paris: Institut français des relations internationales, 2000); A Sofaer, 'International Law and Kosovo' (2000) 36 *Stanford Journal of International Law* 13; A Pellet, 'Brief Remarks on the Unilateral Use of Force' (2000) 11 *European Journal of International Law* 385; M Koskenniemi, '"The Lady Doth Protest Too Much" Kosovo, and the Turn to Ethics in International Law' (2002) 65 *Modern Law Review* 159.

[31] T Blair, 'Doctrine of the International Community', Speech given to the Economic Club of Chicago, Chicago, 22 April 1999.

[32] See S Moyn, 'Martti Koskenniemi and the Historiography of International Law in the Age of the War on Terror' in W Werner, M de Hoon, and A Galán (eds), *The Law of International Lawyers: Reading Martti Koskenniemi* (Cambridge: Cambridge University Press, 2016), 340; S Moyn, *Human Rights and the Uses of History* (2nd edition) (London: Verso, 2017), 51–67; S Moyn, *Not Enough: Human Rights in an Unequal World* (Cambridge and London: Belknap Press, 2018).

'motivated by his "romance" with the idea of a human-rights-driven foreign policy', was working with National Security Advisor Sandy Berger.[33] In that role, Moyn helped to draft op-eds such as 'A Just and Necessary War', which was published under US President Bill Clinton's byline in the *New York Times* towards the end of the bombing campaign in May 1999.[34] That op-ed appealed to history in order to argue that the United States and its allies 'must do for southeastern Europe what we did for Western Europe after World War II and for Central Europe after the cold war'.[35] It drew on a historical narrative in which '[f]reedom, respect for minority rights, and prosperity are powerful forces for progress'.[36] 'The Balkans', Moyn's co-written op-ed concluded, 'are not fated to be the heart of European darkness'.[37]

Yet the legitimacy of the intervention undertaken by NATO, as well as the legality of humanitarian intervention, remained extremely questionable for many states outside the NATO alliance, as was made clear in collective statements issued by the Non-Aligned Movement, the Rio Group, and the Commonwealth of Independent States,[38] and in addresses before the Security Council and General Assembly over the following year.[39] India's representative summed up the nature of the opposition to NATO's intervention during a Security Council debate concerning NATO's actions:

> Those who continue to attack the Federal Republic of Yugoslavia profess to do so on behalf of the international community and on pressing humanitarian grounds. They say that they are acting in the name of humanity. Very few

---

[33] J Baskin, 'The Disillusionment of Samuel Moyn', *The Chronicle of Higher Education*, 27 October 2017. In that interview, Moyn now says of that period: 'I was confused in that time in the White House about who I was serving ... I thought I was serving humanity. But I was serving what in retrospect has to be seen as an assertion of American hegemony.'

[34] Baskin, 'The Disillusionment of Samuel Moyn'.

[35] WJ Clinton, 'A Just and Necessary War', *New York Times*, 23 May 1999, available at www .nytimes.com/1999/05/23/opinion/a-just-and-necessary-war.html.

[36] Clinton, 'A Just and Necessary War'.

[37] Clinton, 'A Just and Necessary War'.

[38] Movement of Non-Aligned Countries, Statement, Geneva, 9 April 1999; Declaration Adopted by the Inter-Parliamentary Assembly of States Members of the Commonwealth of Independent States, 3 April 1999, UN Doc A/53/920-S/1999/461, Annex II, 22 April 1999, reprinted in H Krieger, *The Kosovo Conflict and International Law: An Analytical Documentation 1974–1999* (Cambridge: Cambridge University Press, 2001), 487, 496–497.

[39] See, for example, UN Security Council, 3989th Meeting, 26 March 1999, S/PV.3989 (statements made by Russia, India, Ukraine, Belarus, and Cuba); UN General Assembly, 54th session, 4th plenary meeting, 20 September 1999, A/54/PV.4 (statement made by Algeria); UN General Assembly, 55th session, 24th plenary meeting, 20 September 2000, A/55/PV.24 (statements made by Namibia, Cyprus, Ecuador, China, Malaysia, and Russia); UN General Assembly 55th session, 30th plenary meeting, 27 September 2000, A/55/PV.30 (statements made by the Democratic People's Republic of Korea, India, Cuba, Iraq, and Namibia).

members of the international community have spoken in this debate, but even among those who have, NATO would have noted that China, Russia and India have all opposed the violence which it has unleashed. The international community can hardly be said to have endorsed their actions when already representatives of half of humanity have said that they do not agree with what they have done.[40]

In addition, critics argued that the conduct of NATO's bombing campaign had put civilians at risk rather than protecting them. The air campaign appeared to have caused minimal damage to the Yugoslav military, but rather to have succeeded through putting pressure on the Serbian government as a result of the destruction caused to roads, bridges, energy infrastructure, and industry, all of which also harmed the civilian population. The use of depleted uranium projectiles and cluster bombs by NATO created a hazardous environment for the population. It became clear that the killing and displacement of Kosovar Albanians had increased dramatically after the bombing commenced, creating doubts as to 'whether, in the absence of the NATO bombing, ethnic cleansing would have proceeded with such speed and viciousness'.[41]

Despite such concerns and reactions, across multiple regimes US and allied international lawyers continued to experiment with the flexibilities of international law, testing it to see how far it could accommodate novel legal theories and interpretations. A great deal of legal energy went into developing innovative legal frameworks, concepts, and categories through which to understand the global situation, enable new legal relations, justify intensified processes of control, liberalisation, harmonisation, and competition, and consolidate US power. International lawyers made historical arguments not only to ground new interpretations of legal treaties, customs, principles, and concepts, but also to make links between specific doctrinal or technical innovations and broader ideological commitments to freedom, security, justice, or efficiency.

Appeals to the past played multiple roles in these interrelated processes of rationalising or challenging new directions in international law. The past was appealed to in arguments about the content of the law, the form of the law, the *telos* of the law, and the foundations of the law. International lawyers looked to past practice in order to justify the emergence of new customary law, or to explain the difference between current contexts and the conditions in which earlier interpretations of treaties took place. While some of the scholars engaged in such work saw themselves as undertaking historical projects, most

---

[40] UNSC, 3989th Meeting, 26 March 1999, S/PV.3989, 16.
[41] Roberts, 'NATO's "Humanitarian War"', 113–114.

saw themselves as writing international law rather than history, doing the everyday work of lawyers by weaving together elements of past practice, legal interpretations of that practice, and the history of meanings attached to legal concepts in order to make legal arguments.[42]

2.1.2 *The Turn to History as a Critical Response to US Expansionism*

That then was the context in which the turn to history began to take shape as a critical response to liberal, and particularly US, interventionism. Much of the initial historically conscience work undertaken by international lawyers during those early years of US-led legal transformation did not conform to empiricist historical protocols in either style or method. While legal scholars did respond to the ways in which the past was being used to justify increased intervention and offer progress narratives underpinning particular forms of integration, the aim of that work was unashamedly and overtly presentist. Critical international law scholars were focused on grasping and in many cases critiquing or resisting the attempt to remake international law in the image of the sole remaining superpower. Those interventions were a response to the work of establishment lawyers who were arguing in favour of more permissive interpretations of the norms relating to the use of force or more expansive interpretations of the obligations upon states to protect the property of foreign investors.

For example, critical international lawyers pointed to the ways in which overarching teleological narratives of progress towards freedom, human rights, development, or a global rule of law were being used to shore up a particular form of US hegemony. Lawyers who sought to oppose crusading forms of liberal internationalism pushed back against attempts to use international law as a vehicle for transforming all states into liberal capitalist democracies,[43] and challenged the attempt to entrench a particular form of market logic at the

---

[42] See further the discussion in Chapter 5.

[43] OC Okafor, 'The Global Process of Legitimation and the Legitimacy of Global Governance' (1997) 14 *Arizona Journal of International and Comparative Law* 117; R Gordon, 'Saving Failed States: Sometimes a Neocolonialist Notion' (1997) 12 *American University Journal of International Law and Policy* 903; A Orford and J Beard, 'Making the State Safe for the Market: The World Bank's *World Development Report 1997* ' (1998) 22 *Melbourne University Law Review* 196; A Anghie, 'Universality and the Concept of Governance in International Law' in EK Quashigah and OC Okafor (eds), *Legitimate Governance in Africa: International and Domestic Legal Perspectives* (The Hague: Kluwer, 1999), 21; JT Gatthi, 'Good Governance as a Counter Insurgency Agenda to Oppositional and Transformative Social Projects in International Law' (1999) 5 *Buffalo Human Rights Law Review* 107; JT Gatthi, 'Neoliberalism, Colonialism and International Governance: Decentring the International Law of Governmental Illegitimacy' (2000) 98 *Michigan Law Review* 1996.

heart of government in the name of promoting economic development and economic integration through law.[44]

International lawyers also turned to history as part of a broader attempt to resist the entrenching of a narrow vision of human rights at the centre of the international law discipline and profession. Legal scholars argued that the highly individualist visions of rights that were beginning to be promoted by some US and European lawyers too readily functioned as the handmaiden of neoliberalism and economic fundamentalism.[45] Critical work on human rights stressed the need to focus on the ways in which inequality, dispossession, exploitation, and insecurity were being produced through international economic law and institutions,[46] challenged the US privileging of a narrow

---

[44] See for examples of literature from that period M Sornarajah, 'Power and Justice in Foreign Investment Arbitration' (1997) 14 *Journal of International Arbitration* 103; C Thomas, 'Causes of Inequality in the International Economic Order: Critical Race Theory and Postcolonial Development' (1999) 9 *Transnational Law and Contemporary Problems* 1; AA Shalakany, 'Arbitration and the Third World: A Plea for Reassessing Bias under the Specter of Neoliberalism' (2000) 41 *Harvard International Law Journal* 419; A Orford, 'Globalization and the Right to Development' in P Alston (ed), *Peoples' Rights* (Oxford: Oxford University Press, 2001), 127; K Rittich, 'Who's Afraid of the *Critique of Adjudication?*: Tracing the Discourse of Law in Development' (2001) 22 *Cardozo Law Review* 929; K Rittich, *Recharacterizing Restructuring: Law, Distribution, and Gender in Market Reform* (The Hague: Kluwer, 2002); H Mann, 'International Investment Agreements: Building the New Colonialism?' (2003) 97 *Proceedings of the ASIL Annual Meeting* 247; BS Chimni, 'Third World Approaches to International Law: A Manifesto' in A Anghie, B Chimni, K Mickelson, and O Okafor (eds), *The Third World and International Order: Law, Politics, and Globalization* (Leiden/Boston: Martinus Nijhoff, 2003), 47.

[45] P Alston, 'The Myopia of the Handmaidens: International Lawyers and Globalization' (1997) 8 *European Journal of International Law* 435; KJ Guest, 'Exploitation under Erasure: Economic, Social and Cultural Rights Engage Economic Globalisation' (1997) 19 *Adelaide Law Review* 74; A Orford, 'Contesting Globalization: A Feminist Perspective on the Future of Human Rights' (1998) 8 *Transnational Law and Contemporary Problems* 171; A Orford, 'The Subject of Globalization: Economics, Identity, and Human Rights' (2000) 94 *American Society of International Law* Proceedings 146; P Alston, 'Resisting the Merger and Acquisition of Human Rights by Trade Law: A Reply to Petersmann' (2002) 13 *European Journal of International Law* 815; A Orford, 'Beyond Harmonization: Trade, Human Rights and the Economy of Sacrifice' (2005) 18 *Leiden Journal of International Law* 179; U Baxi, 'Market Fundamentalisms: Business Ethics at the Altar of Human Rights' (2005) 5 *Human Rights Law Review* 1.

[46] A Orford, 'Locating the International: Military and Monetary Interventions after the Cold War' (1997) 38 *Harvard International Law Journal* 443; K Rittich, 'Transformed Pursuits: The Quest for Equality in Globalized Markets' (2000) 13 *Harvard Human Rights Journal* 231; OC Okafor, 'Poverty, Agency and Resistance in the Future of International Law: An African Perspective' (2006) 27 *Third World Quarterly* 799; J Oloka-Onyango and D Udagama, *The Realization of Economic, Social and Cultural Rights: Globalization and Its Impact on the Full Enjoyment of Human Rights, Preliminary Report to the UN Sub-Commission on the Promotion and Protection of Human Rights* (E/CN.4/Sub.2/2000/13); J Oloka-Onyango and Deepika Udagama, *Globalization and Its Impact on the Full Enjoyment of Human Rights, Progress Report to the*

range of civil and political rights over economic, social, cultural, and group rights,[47] and argued that the most important task facing human rights lawyers in industrialised states was to resist the triumphalist liberalism that was taking over the field and instead work 'in solidarity with activists in other parts of the world to challenge exploitation and inequality'.[48]

Many legal scholars were also sceptical about the legality of humanitarian intervention, and some turned to history as a challenge to that position.[49] They looked to history in order to resist the claim that humanitarian intervention had played a role in official justifications for the use of force in earlier eras. Critics argued that humanitarian intervention had throughout the Cold War been perceived as a doctrine that was closely tied to nineteenth-century imperialism.[50] General Assembly resolutions passed during the 1970s reasserted the principle of non-intervention and made no exception for

UN Sub-Commission on the Promotion and Protection of Human Rights (E/CN.4/Sub.2/2001/ 10); G Hernández-Uriz, 'To Lend or Not to Lend: Oil, Human Rights and the World Bank's Internal Contradictions' (2001) 14 *Harvard Human Rights Journal* 197; J Olaka-Onyango and D Udagama, *Economic, Social and Cultural Rights: Globalization and Its Impact on the Full Enjoyment of Human Rights, Final Report* (E/CN.4/Sub.2/2003/14); Chimni, 'Third World Approaches to International Law'.

[47] From a broad literature during that period, see P Alston, 'U.S. Ratification of the Covenant on Economic, Social and Cultural Rights: The Need for an Entirely New Strategy' (1990) 84 *American Journal of International Law* 365; B Stark, 'Postmodern Rhetoric, Economic Rights and an International Text: "A Miracle for Breakfast"' (1993) 33 *Virginia Journal of International Law* 433; J Olaka-Onyango, 'Beyond the Rhetoric: Reinvigorating the Struggle for Economic and Social Rights in Africa' (1995) 26 *California Western International Law Journal* 1; I Merali and V Oosterveld (eds), *Giving Meaning to Economic, Social and Cultural Rights* (Philadelphia: University of Pennsylvania Press, 2001); C Odinkalu, 'Analysis of Paralysis or Paralysis of Analysis: Implementing Economic, Social and Cultural Rights under the African Charter on Human and Peoples' Rights' (2001) 23 *Human Rights Quarterly* 328; SC Agbakwa, 'Reclaiming Humanity and Economic, Social and Cultural Rights as the Cornerstone of African Human Rights' (2002) 5 *Yale Human Rights and Development Law Journal* 177; J Olaka-Onyango, 'Reinforcing Marginalised Rights in an Age of Globalization' (2003) 18 *American University International Law Review* 851; Chimni, 'Third World Approaches to International Law'.

[48] Orford, 'Globalization and the Right to Development', 183.

[49] For a sample of legal responses from the 1990s and early 2000s challenging legal arguments in favour of humanitarian intervention, see Orford, 'Locating the International'; M Sornarajah, 'Power and Justice in International Law' (1997) 1 *Singapore Journal of International and Comparative Law* 28; A Orford, 'Muscular Humanitarianism: Reading the Narratives of the New Interventionism' (1999) 10 *European Journal of International Law* 679; C Gray, *International Law and the Use of Force* (Oxford: Oxford University Press, 2000); S Chesterman, *Just War or Just Peace?: Humanitarian Intervention and International Law* (Oxford: Oxford University Press, 2001); H Charlesworth, 'International Law: A Discipline of Crisis' (2002) 65 *Modern Law Review* 377; Orford, *Reading Humanitarian Intervention*.

[50] Sornarajah, 'Power and Justice in International Law', 48.

intervention on humanitarian grounds.[51] While India's intervention in East Pakistan, Vietnam's intervention in Cambodia, and Tanzania's intervention in Uganda were cited by commentators as Cold War examples of humanitarian intervention, legal scholars argued that none of the intervening states had justified their actions on humanitarian grounds at the time.[52]

In addition, critical international lawyers drew attention to the continuities that existed between patterns of argument used to justify humanitarian intervention and the ways in which certain peoples and territories continued to be internationalised and their political struggles defined as matters of global concern long after decolonisation. Legal scholars drew attention to the techniques of distinguishing between politics and economics, status and control, sovereignty and property, or freedom and coercion, that had long enabled informal empire.[53] Legal scholars argued that techniques of imperial ordering that were perceived as abandoned remained embedded in and transmitted through legal concepts, practices, doctrines, hierarchies, techniques, institutions, and professional sensibilities.[54]

---

[51] Friendly Relations Declaration, GA Resolution 2625 (1970); Declaration on the Definition of Aggression, GA Resolution 3314 (1974).

[52] For India's justification of its use of force against Pakistan in the Security Council debate on this question, see S/PV.1606 (1971), at 14–18. See also the materials related to this incident collected as 'Documents: Civil War in Pakistan' (1971) 4 *New York University Journal of International Law and Policy* 524. For Vietnam's justification of its use of force against Kampuchea as self-defence in a border war, see the Security Council debate: S/PV.2108 (1979), at 12. As the Security Council 'passed over in silence the several efforts to have it convened' in relation to the Tanzanian intervention that ousted Idi Amin, there is no Security Council debate on this question, but Tanzania claimed to be responding to Ugandan border incursions: see TM Franck, *Recourse to Force: State Action against Threats and Armed Attack* (Oxford: Oxford University Press, 2002), at 143–145.

[53] D Kennedy, 'The International Style in Postwar Law and Policy: John Jackson and the Field of International Economic Law' (1995) 10 *American University Law Review* 671; Orford, 'Locating the International'; Shalakany, 'Arbitration and the Third World'; Chimni, 'Third World Approaches to International Law'; A Anghie, 'Time Present and Time Past: Globalization, International Financial Institutions, and the Third World' (2000) 32 *New York University Journal of International Law and Policy* 243.

[54] A Riles, 'The View from the International Plane: Perspective and Scale in the Architecture of Colonial International Law' (1995) 6 *Law and Critique* 39; N Berman, 'Beyond Colonialism and Nationalism? Ethiopia, Czechoslovakia, and "Peaceful Change"' (1996) 65 *Nordic Journal of International Law* 421; N Berman, 'In the Wake of Empire' (1999) 14 *American University International Law Review* 1521; DP Fidler, 'A Kinder, Gentler System of Capitulations? International Law, Structural Adjustment, and the Standards of Liberal, Globalized Civilization' (2000) 35 *Texas International Law Journal* 387; AWB Simpson, *Human Rights and the End of Empire: Britain and the Genesis of the European Convention* (Oxford: Oxford University Press, 2001); A Anghie, 'Colonialism and the Birth of International Institutions: Sovereignty, Economy, and the Mandate System of the League of Nations' (2002) 34 *New York University Journal of International Law and Politics* 513; Orford, *Reading Humanitarian Intervention*.

Scholars associated with the Third World Approaches to International Law (TWAIL) movement were important players in the ongoing debate about the relevance of the history of imperialism to modern international law.[55] The question of whether – and how – the imperial past is relevant to international law was and remains hotly disputed. For many international lawyers writing in the aftermath of the Cold War, decolonisation had successfully taken place, international law and the international community were essentially anti-colonial, and the real political question should now become how that truly universal international law could best realise peace and equality.[56] In contrast, critical and TWAIL scholars argued against the willed forgetting of inter-national law's imperial past, and insisted that imperialism is 'ingrained in international law as we know it today'.[57] The aim was not (or not only) to argue about responsibility for past unjust relations but rather to resist the perpetuation of such relations through present law.

The stakes of the debate about the legacies of the imperial past in the multinational present remained high, because the authority of international law in the post-Cold War era rested on its claim to have transcended its European heritage and to operate as a universal law capable of representing humanity. The suggestion that international law still operated in a differenti-ated fashion undermined that claim to universality. In addition, the idea that imperialism was of no relevance to the contemporary global order played a significant part in justifying the status quo. Much international legal debate assumed that extremes of uneven development, inequality, mass movement of peoples, civil war, food insecurity, and poverty were the consequence of the inherent characteristics or failed leadership of post-colonial states, rather than the effects of a historically constructed global political and economic system that could yet be challenged.[58] Questioning the legacies of empire in international law was thus an intervention in contemporary global politics.

---

[55] The classic text is A Anghie, *Imperialism, Sovereignty and the Making of International Law* (Cambridge: Cambridge University Press, 2008), arguing that if 'the colonial encounter, with all its exclusions and subordinations, shaped the very foundations of international law, then grave questions must arise as to whether and how it is possible for the post-colonial world to construct a new international law that is liberated from these colonial origins' (8).

[56] For responses to that tendency to draw a line between yesterday's imperialism and today's international law, see Berman, 'In the Wake of Empire'; Orford, *Reading Humanitarian Intervention*, 40–51.

[57] Gathii, 'Neoliberalism, Colonialism and International Governance', at 2020.

[58] Orford, 'Locating the International'; A Orford, 'The Past as Law or History? The Relevance of Imperialism for Modern International Law' in M Toufayan, E Tourme-Jouannet, and H Ruiz Fabri (eds) *Droit international et nouvelles approches sur le tiers-monde: entre repetition et renouveau* (Paris: Société de Législation Comparée, 2013), 97.

The focus on the links between imperialism and contemporary liberal internationalism sought to address the blind spot created by 'the fact that, while the United States [had] stepped into the shoes of the European imperial powers', US lawyers and officials understood US authority to come 'from an anti-imperialism long dressed in benevolent ideals'.[59]

A related body of critical scholarship initiated during the 1990s sought to counter celebratory accounts of the new liberal international law as the latest stage in the development of a profession self-evidently working collectively in the interests of a common humanity and universal values, by providing a more complex and nuanced history of the discipline. These historically oriented projects were part of a broader body of international law scholarship that sought to explore the self-understanding and liberal sensibilities of international lawyers.[60] They related the emergence of the profession to a range of political, social, and cultural developments in the late nineteenth and early twentieth centuries that in turn reflected great power machinations, imperial ambitions, and economic relations.[61] The expansion of historically minded scholarship by international lawyers also sought to make visible the processes involved in constructing international institutions, and the political choices involved in those processes.[62] The focus was on grasping the projects that

---

[59] Y Dezalay and BG Garth, *The Internationalization of Palace Wars: Lawyers, Economists, and the Contest to Transform Latin American States* (Chicago and London: University of Chicago Press, 2002), 4.

[60] For other work along those lines, see D Kennedy, 'Autumn Weekends: An Essay on Law and Everyday Life' in A Sarat and TR Kearns (eds), *Law in Everyday Life* (Ann Arbor: University of Michigan Press, 1993), 191; A Orford, 'Embodying Internationalism: The Making of International Lawyers' (1998) 19 *Australian Year Book of International Law* 1; D Kennedy, 'When Renewal Repeats: Thinking against the Box' (2000) 32 *New York University Journal of International Law and Politics* 335.

[61] See, for example, N Berman, '"But the Alternative is Despair": European Nationalism and the Modernist Renewal of International Law' (1993) 106 *Harvard Law Review* 1792; A Riles, 'Aspiration and Control: International Legal Rhetoric and the Essentialization of Culture' (1993) 106 *Harvard Law Review* 723; N Berman, 'Between "Alliance" and "Localization": Nationalism and the New Oscillationism' (1994) 26 *New York University Journal of International Law and Politics* 449; D Kennedy, 'International Law and the Nineteenth Century: History of an Illusion' (1997) 17 *Quinnipiac Law Review* 99; O Korhonen, *International Law Situated: An Analysis of the Lawyer's Stance towards Culture, History and Community* (The Hague: Kluwer, 2000); M Koskenniemi, *The Gentle Civilizer of Nations: The Rise and Fall of International Law 1870–1960* (Cambridge: Cambridge University Press, 2001). The *European Journal of International Law* published a series on the work of European international lawyers (including Georges Scelle, Dionisio Anzilotti, Alfred Verdross, Hersch Lauterpacht, Hans Kelsen, Alf Ross, Max Huber, Walther Schücking, FF Martens, James Lorimer), and the *Leiden Journal of International Law* published a series on lawyers from the 'periphery' (including Alejandro Álvarez and Taslim Olawale Elias).

[62] See, for example, D Kennedy, 'The Move to Institutions' (1986–1987) 8 *Cardozo Law Review* 841.

international lawyers tried to advance through their professional practice, their struggles for power within the discipline, their attempts to delineate the profession from other disciplines, and their engagement in the reproduction of cultural, social, economic, and political hierarchies.[63] In addition, critical counter-histories sought to challenge the vision of international law as the property of European or US internationalists.[64]

Collectively, these studies interrogated the claim that a continuous tradition of liberal international law could be traced back to a period before the late nineteenth century in Europe, while also offering an implicit challenge to the idealised notion that international law exists as a coherent system of objective rules and principles that determine state behaviour and treat all states as equals. Rather, what international lawyers championed as either scientifically deduced rules (in the European formalist version) or progressive developments in the realisation of liberal democracy as the end of history (in the US hegemonic version) were after all just human constructions – the product of struggles between people with political projects, seeking to establish the domination of their vision for the world, trying to assert power over others, and effecting the distribution of material and spiritual resources towards one group rather than another.

2.2 THE TURN TO HISTORY AND THE WAR ON TERROR

2.2.1 *Liberal Internationalism Must Be Defended*

A second condition and turning point for historical engagement with international law was the September 11 attack on the United States and the resulting initiation of a decades-long war on terror conducted by the United States and its allies. It gradually became clear that if existing international law did not prove sufficiently malleable or other states refused to agree to new

---

[63] See, for example, Kennedy, 'International Law and the Nineteenth Century'; Koskenniemi, *The Gentle Civilizer of Nations*; L Obregón, *Completing Civilization: Nineteenth Century Criollo Interventions in International Law*, PhD thesis, Harvard Law School, 2002; L Obregón, 'Completing Civilization: Creole Consciousness and International Law in Nineteenth-Century Latin America' in A Orford (ed), *International Law and Its Others* (Cambridge: Cambridge University Press, 2006), 247.

[64] Y Onuma, 'When Was the Law of International Society Born? – An Inquiry of the History of International Law from an Intercivilizational Perspective' (2000) 2 *Journal of the History of International Law* 1; A Anghie, 'Civilization and Commerce: The Concept of Governance in Historical Perspective' (2000) 45 *Villanova Law Review* 887; Obregón, *Completing Civilization*; Obregón, 'Completing Civilization: Creole Consciousness and International Law", 247.

rules, the United States would even be willing to walk away from its Western allies or the multilateral treaties upon which they had relied to create the international order after the Second World War. In that sense, the Iraq invasion of 2003 without Security Council authorisation was a turning point. While for those outside Europe, concern with resort to force absent Security Council authorisation had already emerged in the aftermath of Kosovo, it was only after the split between Europe and the United States over the Iraq invasion that liberal internationalists began to express widespread concern about US unilateralism.

The invasion of Iraq and the broader war on terror gave rise to a new set of historically focused debates about the evolution of international legal rules and doctrines. US international lawyers looked to history in support of the 'Bush Doctrine' of pre-emptive self-defence as set out in the National Security Strategy of the United States published in 2002. They argued that the 'new phenomenon' of terrorism as practiced in the September 11 attacks required 'adjustments' to the law,[65] focused on the changes in context between the drafting of the UN Charter and the war on terror,[66] and insisted that the law on the use of force needed to be altered to meet new threats posed by non-state actors. Anne-Marie Slaughter and William Burke-White famously suggested that the September 11 attacks on the United States gave rise to a 'constitutional moment' for international law, in which a fundamental change in the threats facing the international community paved the way for the rapid development of customary international law.[67]

Lawyers for the United States, the United Kingdom, and allied states self-consciously developed new interpretations of international law as 'a means of imposing discontinuity between what went before and what is intended for the future',[68] and US lawyers also looked to history in support of practice

---

[65] TM Franck, 'Criminals, Combatants, or What? An Examination of the Role of Law in Responding to the Threat of Terror' (2004) 98 *American Journal of International Law* 686, at 688.

[66] A Sofaer, 'On the Necessity of Pre-Emption' (2003) 14 *European Journal of International Law* 209; MN Schmitt, 'Preemptive Strategies in International Law' (2002–2003) 24 *Michigan Journal of International Law* 534; RJ Delahunty and J Yoo, 'The "Bush Doctrine": Can Preventive War Be Justified?' (2009) 32 *Harvard Journal of Law and Public Policy* 851.

[67] A-M Slaughter and W Burke-White, 'An International Constitutional Moment' (2002) 43 *Harvard International Law Journal* 1. See also MP Scharf, *Customary International Law in Times of Fundamental Change: Recognizing Grotian Moments* (Cambridge: Cambridge University Press, 2013).

[68] This is the language of the then Legal Advisor to the UK Foreign and Commonwealth Office, Daniel Bethlehem: D Bethlehem, 'A Transatlantic View of International Law and Lawyers: Cooperation and Conflict in Hard Times' (2009) 103 *Proceedings of the ASIL Annual Meeting* 455, at 456.

supporting their expansive interpretation of the law relating to self-defence. In a speech delivered at the London School of Economics in 2006, US State Department Legal Adviser John Bellinger III argued that 'over a century of state practice' supported the US position that the inherent right to individual and collective self-defence under the UN Charter permits states to respond with military force to attacks from non-state actors on the territory of another state 'at least where the harbouring state is unwilling or unable to take action to quell the attacks'.[69] According to that US position, depriving the international community of a 'reasoned basis for using force' through treating the UN Charter as a 'value-free document' that 'lends itself to a mechanical reading' would threaten 'Charter interests and values', rather than supporting and advancing them.[70] These lawyers appealed to the past to explain why the United States should be understood as leading the development of international law in ways that conformed to the logics of history.

More broadly, American political commentators invoked history to charge Europeans with failing to recognise that the survival of the liberal international order depended upon an understanding of the historical role of the United States. That position was famously expressed by Robert Kagan,[71] whose essay on the theme was widely circulated and influential amongst Bush administration officials in the build-up to the invasion of Iraq.[72] According to Kagan, while Europe had entered a 'post-historical paradise of peace and

---

[69] JB Bellinger III, 'Legal Issues in the War on Terrorism' (2006) 8 *German Law Journal* 735, at 739. That language was subsequently taken up in the academic work of Bellinger's former colleague Ashley Deeks. See AS Deeks, '"Unwilling or Unable": Toward a Normative Framework for Extraterritorial Self-Defense' (2012) 52 *Virginia Journal of International Law* 483. For other arguments by UK and US legal scholars offering expansive readings of the right to self-defence in support of US interventions post-September 11, see T Franck, 'Editorial Comments: Terrorism and the Right of Self-Defense' (2001) 95 *American Journal of International Law* 839; S Murphy, 'Terrorism and the Concept of "Armed Attack" in Article 51 of the UN Charter' (2002) 43 *Harvard International Law Journal* 41; Franck, *Recourse to Force*; J Yoo, 'International Law and the War in Iraq' (2003) 97 *American Journal of International Law* 574; WM Reisman, 'Assessing Claims to Revise the Laws of War' (2003) 97 *American Journal of International Law* 82; C Greenwood, 'International Law and the Pre-emptive Use of Force: Afghanistan, Al-Qaida, and Iraq' (2003) 4 *San Diego International Law Review* 7; SD Murphy, 'The Doctrine of Preemptive Self-Defense' (2005) 50 *Villanova Law Review* 699; WM Reisman and A Armstrong, 'The Past and the Future of the Claim of Preemptive Self-Defense' (2006) 100 *American Journal of International Law* 525.

[70] Sofaer, 'On the Necessity of Pre-Emption', at 212–213, 225.

[71] See R Kagan, *Paradise and Power: America and Europe in the New World Order* (London: Atlantic, 2003), which is an extended version of an article that first appeared in *Policy Review* in 2002.

[72] JL Goldsmith, *The Terror Presidency: Law and Judgment Inside the Bush Administration* (New York and London: WW Norton, 2007), 126–127.

relative prosperity', the United States remained 'mired in history', destined to operate in a Hobbesian world 'where international laws and rules are unreliable, and where true security and the defense and promotion of a liberal order still depend on the possession and use of military might'.[73] It was the effective exercise of American power 'according to the rules of the old Hobbesian order' that had 'made it possible for the Europeans to believe that power was no longer important'.[74] The liberal order depended upon the existence of a powerful state or states willing to assume the responsibility for its defence.

The US government position, developed in tandem with the United Kingdom and other close allies, was subsequently promoted by academic lawyers, many of whom had previously been government legal advisors. To take one influential example, in 2012 former Legal Advisor to the UK Foreign and Commonwealth Office, Daniel Bethlehem, published his influential 'principles relevant to the scope of a state's right of self-defence against an imminent or armed attack by nonstate actors' in the *American Journal of International Law*.[75] Bethlehem described himself as having the very scholarly 'intention of stimulating debate on the issues' rather than purporting 'to reflect a settled view of the law or the practice of any state'.[76] He made clear, however, that unlike other scholarship on the question that showed too little 'intersection between the academic debate and the operational realities', his principles had 'been informed by detailed discussions over recent years with foreign ministry, defense ministry, and military legal advisers from a number of states who have operational experience in these matters'.[77] The 'Bethlehem principles' were subsequently endorsed by the Legal Adviser at the US Department of State, the UK Attorney General, and the Australian Attorney General.[78]

---

[73] Kagan, *Paradise and Power*, 3.

[74] Kagan, *Paradise and Power*, 73.

[75] D Bethlehem, 'Self-Defense against an Imminent or Actual Armed Attack by Nonstate Actors' (2012) 106 *American Journal of International Law* 770.

[76] Bethlehem, 'Self-Defense', 775.

[77] Bethlehem, 'Self-Defense', 773. For an analysis based on documents revealed by *WikiLeaks* suggesting that the principles were the product of a joint endeavour between the United States, the United Kingdom, Australia, Canada, and New Zealand, see V Kattan, 'Furthering the "War on Terrorism" through International Law: How the United States and the United Kingdom Resurrected the Bush Doctrine on Using Preventing Military Force to Combat Terrorism' (2018) 5 *Journal on the Use of Force and International Law* 97.

[78] B Egan, 'International Law, Legal Diplomacy, and the Counter-ISIL Campaign: Some Observations' (2016) 92 *International Studies* 235; J Wright, 'The Modern Law of Self-Defence', speech presented at the International Institute for Strategic Studies, London (11 January 2017), *EJIL:Talk!*, available at www.ejiltalk.org/the-modern-law-of-self-defence/; G Brandis, 'The Right of Self-Defence against Imminent Armed Attack in International

2.2.2 *The End of the Affair: The Turn to History and the American Project*

As the United States intensified its argument for using force pre-emptively in the aftermath of the September 11 attacks, the languages of security and crime became the new lingua franca for international law. As a result, many international law scholars turned their attention away from critiquing the uses or misuses of human rights or development rhetoric,[79] and began to focus more intently on understanding the' ways in which sweeping narratives about defence of the liberal order were being used to justify the reshaping of international norms relating to security and counterterrorism.[80]

European critics of US actions looked to the past in support of the argument that the United States and its allies were undermining the cosmopolitan or universal order that had been painstakingly constructed over the twentieth century. In the aftermath of the Iraq invasion, the United States began to be

---

Law', speech presented at the TC Beirne School of Law, University of Queensland (11 April 2017), *EJIL:Talk!*, available at www.ejiltalk.org/the-right-of-self-defence-against-imminent-armed-attack-in-international-law/.

[79] For arguments exploring the need to shift away from human rights as the core focus of critical legal scholarship, see D Kennedy, 'The International Human Rights Movement: Part of the Problem?' (2002) 15 *Harvard Human Rights Journal* 101; A Orford, 'Biopolitics and the Tragic Subject of Human Rights' in E Dauphinee and C Masters (eds), *The Logics of Biopower and the War on Terror: Living, Dying, Surviving* (Hampshire and New York: Palgrave Macmillan, 2007), 205.

[80] For examples from an extensive legal literature placing the transformations of international law on the use of force to enable the war on terror into a broader historical context, see A Anghie, 'The Bush Preemption Doctrine and the United Nations' (2004) 98 *Proceedings of the ASIL Annual Meeting* 326; A Carty, 'The Iraq Invasion as a Recent United Kingdom "Contribution to International Law"' (2005) 16 *European Journal of International Law* 143; SC Neff, *War and the Law of Nations: A General History* (Cambridge: Cambridge University Press, 2005); JN Maogoto, *Battling Terrorism: Legal Perspectives on the Use of Force and the War on Terror* (London and New York: Routledge, 2005); D Kennedy, *Of War and Law* (Princeton: Princeton University Press, 2006); T Ruys, '*Armed Attack*' and Article 51 of the UN Charter: Evolutions in Customary Law and Practice (Cambridge: Cambridge University Press, 2010); A Alexander, 'A Short History of International Humanitarian Law' (2015) 26 *European Journal of International Law* 109; J Goldsmith, 'The Contribution of the Obama Administration to the Practice and Theory of International Law' (2016) 57 *Harvard International Law Journal* 455; O Corten, 'The "Unwilling or Unable" Test: Has It Been, and Could It Be, Accepted?' (2016) 29 *Leiden Journal of International Law* 777; D Kritsiotis, 'Theorizing International Law on Force and Intervention' in A Orford and F Hoffmann (eds), *The Oxford Handbook of the Theory of International Law* (Oxford: Oxford University Press, 2016), 655; M Gunneflo, *Targeted Killing: A Legal and Political History* (Cambridge: Cambridge University Press, 2016); N Tzouvala, 'TWAIL and the "Unwilling or Unable" Doctrine: Continuities and Ruptures' (2016) 109 *AJIL Unbound* 266; G Blum, 'Prizeless Wars, Invisible Victories: The Modern Goals of Armed Conflict' (2017) 49 *Arizona State Law Journal* 633; Kattan, 'Furthering the "War on Terrorism"'.

portrayed by European and internal US critics as a rogue hegemon whose actions threatened to undermine the rule of law in international affairs. 'Formalist' scholars argued that the UN Charter had established a 'law against war',[81] and that the US attempt to justify recourse to force as a form of preventive police action signalled a movement 'toward a fundamentally different kind of legal order'.[82] By the early 2000s, international law and international relations journals were awash with articles and symposia about the future of international law in the age of a single superpower.[83]

Scholarly attention to the relation of international law and imperialism also began to expand during that period. That scholarship built on work undertaken by an earlier generation of international lawyers from newly independent states.[84] It looked to the past in order to explore whether imperialism might be a productive concept or historical referent through which to understand and anticipate the emerging global legal order being promoted by the

---

[81] M Bothe, 'Terrorism and the Legality of Pre-emptive Force' (2003) 14 *European Journal of International Law* 227; O Corten, 'The Controversies over the Customary Prohibition on the Use of Force: A Methodological Debate' (2006) 16 *European Journal of International Law* 803; O Corten, *Le droit contre la guerre: l'interdiction du recours à la force en droit international contemporain* (Paris: Pedone, 2008); J Kammerhofer, 'The Future of Restrictive Scholarship on the Use of Force' (2016) 29 *Leiden Journal of International Law* 13; G Nolte, 'Preventive Use of Force and Preventive Killings: Moves into a Different Legal Order' (2004) 5 *Theoretical Inquiries in Law* 111.

[82] Nolte, 'Preventive Use of Force', 113.

[83] See, for example, JR Bolton, 'Is There Really "Law" in International Affairs?' (2000) 10 *Transnational Law and Contemporary Problems* 1 (arguing that Americans should see themselves as 'unashamed, unapologetic, uncompromising American constitutional hegemonists' at 48); HJ Richardson III, 'US Hegemony, Race, and Oil in Deciding United Nations Security Council Resolution 1441 on Iraq' (2003) 17 *Temple International and Comparative Law Journal* 27; JE Alvarez, 'Hegemonic International Law Revisited' (2003) 97 *American Journal of International Law* 873. See also the series of symposia held on these questions published as 'Unilateralism in International Law: A United States–European Symposium' (2000) 11 *European Journal of International Law* 1; 'The Single Superpower and the Future of International Law' (2000) *ASIL Proceedings* 64; 'Symposium: American Hegemony and International Law' (2000) 1 *Chicago Journal of International Law* 1.

[84] For examples of work by the first generation of thinkers from newly independent states arguing that a decolonised international law needed to move beyond the Christian, imperial, exploitative, and predatory bases of the European variant, see FC Okoye, *International Law and the New African States* (London: Sweet and Maxwell, 1972); RP Anand, *New States and International Law* (Delhi: Vikas, 1972); UO Umozurike, *International Law and Colonialism in Africa* (Enugu: Nwamife, 1979); M Bedjaoui, *Towards a New International Economic Order* (Paris and New York: UNESCO/Holmes and Meier, 1979); RP Anand, 'Sovereign Equality of States in International Law' (1986) 197 *Recueil des Cours* 9; FE Snyder and S Sathirathai (eds), *Third World Attitudes toward International Law* (Dordrecht: Nijhoff, 1987).

United States and its allies.[85] Legal scholars challenged the idea that the current situation was a novel one that represented unprecedented challenges to liberal industrialised states and that justified new forceful means to secure the Western way of life. They argued both that the same logics had justified earlier forms of imperial action and that the very claim of 'newness' made by those seeking to abandon legal restraints on resort to force was itself a familiar 'technology of imperialism'.[86] A related body of scholarship asked similar questions in relation to notions of hegemony or great power politics as useful heuristics.[87] More generally, international lawyers looked to the past to explore analogies, patterns, or precedents for making sense of the ways that powerful states developed legal justifications for their resort to force and control over foreign territory, people, and resources.[88]

---

[85] See, for example, S Marks, 'Empire's Law' (2003) 10 *Indiana Journal of Global Legal Studies* 449; S Laghmani, *Histoire du droit des gens: du jus gentium impérial au jus publicum europaeum* (Paris: Pedone, 2004); BS Chimni, 'International Institutions Today: An Imperial Global State in the Making' (2004) 15 *European Journal of International Law* 1; A Anghie, *Imperialism, Sovereignty and the Making of International Law* (Cambridge: Cambridge University Press, 2005); E Jouannet and H Ruiz Fabri (eds), *Le droit international et l'impérialisme en Europe et aux Amériques* (Paris: Société de droit et de legislation comparée, 2007); S Laghmani, 'L'ambivalence du renouveau du *jus gentium*' in H Ruiz Fabri, E Jouannet, and V Tomkiewicz (eds), *Select Proceedings of the European Society of International Law, Volume 1 2006* (Oxford and Portland: Hart, 2008). For overviews of the work that the concept of 'imperialism' has done in international law, see A Anghie, 'Imperialism and International Legal Theory' in A Orford and F Hoffmann (eds), *The Oxford Handbook of the Theory of International Law* (Oxford: Oxford University Press, 2016), 156; R Knox and N Tzouvala, 'Looking Eastwards: The Bolshevik Theory of Imperialism and International Law' in K Greenman, A Orford, A Saunders, and N Tzouvala (eds), *Revolutions in International Law: The Legacies of 1917* (Cambridge: Cambridge University Press, 2021), 27. For a focus on imperialism as an economic enterprise focused on exploitation rather than a political enterprise focused on domination, see Orford, *Reading Humanitarian Intervention*, 47, 68, 77, 142.

[86] OC Okafor, 'Newness, Imperialism, and International Legal Reform in Our Time: A TWAIL Perspective' (2005) 43 *Osgoode Hall Law Journal* 171, at 180.

[87] See particularly DF Vagts, 'Hegemonic International Law' (2001) 95 *American Journal of International Law* 843; S Sur, 'Peut-on parler d'une hégémonie américaine?' in *Travaux et Recherches de l'IFRI, Observation et théorie des relations internationales* (Paris: IFRI, 2001), 83; U Mattei, 'A Theory of Imperial Law: A Study on US Hegemony and the Latin Resistance' (2003) 10 *Indiana Journal of Global Legal Studies* 383; Alvarez, 'Hegemonic International Law Revisited', 873; G Simpson, *Great Powers and Outlaw States: Unequal Sovereigns in the International Legal Order* (Cambridge: Cambridge University Press, 2004); N Krisch, 'International Law in Times of Hegemony: Unequal Power and the Shaping of the International Legal Order' (2005) 16 *European Journal of International Law* 369.

[88] A Anghie, 'The War on Terror and Iraq in Historical Perspective' (2005) 43 *Osgoode Hall Law Journal* 45; K Mickelson, 'Leading towards a Level Playing Field, Repaying Ecological Debt, or Making Environmental Space: Three Stories about International Environmental Cooperation' (2005) 43 *Osgoode Hall Law Journal* 135; F Mégret, 'From "Savages" to

For many US international lawyers and legal historians, this is seen as the moment at which the field took a turn to history. While, as the previous section shows, international law scholars had been engaging in struggles over the interpretation of legal history for decades, the crisis to US leadership and moral legitimacy set in train by the invasion of Iraq brought these questions to the forefront of the American political imaginary. This, for example, is the narrative recounted by Samuel Moyn. Moyn's self-described '"romance" with the idea of a human-rights-driven foreign policy' was clearly over by the time he began the new stage of his career as a prolific writer of histories of human rights and international law in the mid-2000s.

According to Moyn, the US war on terror is the political context within which the turn to history in international law 'should be understood'.[89] In Moyn's US-focused interpretation of context, the accompanying internal US debates about liberal internationalism provided 'the true conditions of possibility of the new historiography of international law'.[90] For Moyn, the 'extraordinary spike of scholarly attention to the history of international law that shows no sign of abating' is really a 'proxy for burning political debate' over 'the promise and perils of international law in the novel circumstances of the nation's "war on terror"'.[91] Debates over how we think about the history of international law are for Moyn properly understood as minor skirmishes in the struggle that really matters; that is, the struggle between factions competing for power within the US establishment.

Certainly, there is something to be said for this view. As we will see in later chapters, many of the historians who have since developed an interest in international law are based in the United States. Very few of the hundreds of legal scholars cited in this book ever appear in the work of those revisionist historians of international law. Instead, the scholarship of a small group of international lawyers whose work speaks to US historians is taken out of the context of the legal field and presented as part of a collective historical rather than legal project, one that should be conducted according to empiricist historical protocols. However, if September 11 and the resulting war on terror are the defining traumas for a generation of American liberal internationalists, they are just one part of a much broader history for many other participants in the field of international law.

"Unlawful combatants": A Postcolonial Look at International Humanitarian Law's "Other"' in Orford (ed), *International Law and Its Others*, 265; JL Beard, *The Political Economy of Desire: International Law, Development, and the Nation State* (New York: Routledge, 2006).

[89] Moyn, 'Martti Koskenniemi and the Historiography of International Law', 341.

[90] Moyn, 'Martti Koskenniemi and the Historiography of International Law', 349.

[91] Moyn, 'Martti Koskenniemi and the Historiography of International Law', 340.

2.3 HISTORICISING THE CRISES

2.3.1 *International Law and the Triple Crisis*

During the heyday of liberal internationalism in the 1990s and after the outbreak of the war on terror in the early 2000s, international lawyers had struggled to grasp the new world order that was taking shape and to craft forms of law that were adequate to the new situation. Nonetheless, the dominant sense that liberal internationalism represented the end of history shaped the field of international law for most of the 1990s and to a degree survived even into the first decade of the twenty-first century. While some critical international lawyers sought to unsettle the self-evidence of that account, much of the discipline and the field was shaped by newly dominant liberal states and remained organised around ideas about progress (or temporary barriers to progress) towards a liberal international order. International law may have been a discipline organised around other people's crises, but international law in its liberal guise was on the right side of history.

However, beginning in 2006 with what was often referred to as the 'triple crisis' of finance, food, and climate change, a sense that history may not have ended re-entered the mainstream of international legal debate. The external challenge to the self-evidence of liberal internationalism as the end of history resulted in part from the interrelated financial, food, energy, climate, security, and refugee crises of the early twenty-first century. Those crises gave a new urgency to questions about the adequacy of the existing institutions of the liberal international order as a response to global challenges. The consequences of those crises re-enlivened debates about how the world had come to take this form and what alternatives to the current global order were possible. In addition, the growing awareness that climate change was beginning to have tangible effects created a sense of being reinserted into history, as people began to face the possibility that the world as we know it was coming to an end.[92] In the face of the disruptions of a warming world, politics appeared far less likely to be simply a field of endless return and repetition.[93]

In response to the growing conditions of insecurity experienced by many people globally, a particular set of tendencies that had already been present in the first decades of the post-Cold War period began to accelerate. For once dominant liberal states, those tendencies included a move towards

---

[92] D Chakrabarty, 'The Climate of History: Four Theses' (2009) 35 *Critical Inquiry* 197.
[93] S Hamilton, 'Foucault's End of History: The Temporality of Governmentality and Its End in the Anthropocene' (2018) 46 *Millennium* 371.

intensification of resort to military force justified in the language of self-defence and 'protection', the normalisation of the practice of detaining displaced people, and a greater use of naval policing to maintain the security of the oceans as liberal spaces through which only certain goods and people could move. At the same time, expansive readings of the jurisdiction of international tribunals and dispute settlement bodies saw an acceleration of the process of removing decisions relating to investment, financial regulation, and national budgets from democratic processes.

Given the wide geopolitical, material, and ideological divisions within and between states, few major international legal or institutional initiatives could be agreed upon in the areas of refugee resettlement, climate change mitigation or adaptation, international financial regulation, or energy policy. Instead, international lawyers consolidated new forms of legal regulation through transnational guilds and networks, particularly involving monetary, surveillance, and intelligence experts. Legal scholars from Europe and the United States began to discuss new forms of international law-making that could bypass the need for consent by states or democratic publics.[94] International lawyers proposed new mechanisms for law creation, including through the development of standards by transnational networks of experts working to realise public goods.[95]

The financial, refugee, and climate crises also began to fuel a backlash against the existing order within states that had been committed to liberal internationalism. With the Brexit vote in the United Kingdom and the election of Donald Trump as US President on an overtly anti-globalist platform, that sense of rupture became palpable. The idea that there was a backlash against liberal internationalism was driven by the rise of populist movements explicitly attacking the politics of multilateralism, the shifting priorities of US foreign policy under the Trump administration, and multiple high-profile instances of states leaving, denouncing, withdrawing, and unsigning international agreements.[96]

International investment law was the first field in which commentators began to express concerns about a backlash against liberal internationalism,

---

[94] LR Helfer, 'Nonconsensual International Lawmaking' (2008) *University of Illinois Law Review* 71; AT Guzman, 'Against Consent' (2012) 52 *Virginia Journal of International Law* 747; N Krisch, 'The Decay of Consent: International Law in an Age of Global Public Goods' (2014) 108 *American Journal of International Law* 1.

[95] AM Slaughter, *A New World Order* (Princeton: Princeton University Press, 2005); HH Koh, 'Is There a "New" New Haven School of International Law?' (2007) 32 *Yale Journal of International Law* 559.

[96] See further the discussion in Orford, 'International Law and the Populist Moment'.

in the context of mounting criticism of the perceived excesses of investor–state dispute settlement (or ISDS) awards.[97] This began with the withdrawal from the procedural ICSID Convention by a group of Latin American states (Bolivia, Ecuador, and Venezuela) beginning in 2007, part of a broader process through which the newly elected left-wing governments in the region responded to the popular backlash against neoliberal policies and attempted to reverse the privatisation of essential services and resources that had taken place under IMF and World Bank supervision during the 1990s.[98] Since then numerous states in Latin America, Asia, and Africa have announced their intention to terminate some or all of their bilateral investment treaties or BITS, including Bolivia, Ecuador, India, Indonesia, South Africa, and Venezuela. Perhaps more strikingly, as Western states increasingly became respondents in investor–state proceedings, a growing political resistance to ISDS emerged within Canada, Europe, and more recently the United States, as evidenced by the popular challenge to inclusion of ISDS provisions in the Transatlantic Trade and Investment Partnership between the EU and the United States and the EU–Canada Comprehensive Economic and Trade Agreement. In addition, Italy and Russia have withdrawn from or unsigned the Energy Charter Treaty, one of the major multilateral agreements under which ISDS proceedings have been brought.

Similar trends began to emerge in the fields of international trade law, international criminal law, international environmental law, and international human rights law. For example, in the field of trade agreements, the United States initiated a renegotiation of the NAFTA, the United Kingdom signalled its withdrawal from the European Union, the United States 'unsigned' the Trans-Pacific Partnership, and both the Obama and Trump administrations blocked appointments to the Appellate Body of the WTO. In the field of international criminal law, Burundi and the Philippines withdrew from the ICC, Russia and the United States withdrew their signatures from the Rome Statute, and the African Union adopted a coordinated 'Withdrawal Strategy' arguing that the court has become a political instrument targeting Africans. The United States announced its intention to withdraw from the Paris Agreement on Climate Change, while populist and counter-populist attempts

---

[97] See M Waibel, A Kaushal, K Chung, and C Balchin (eds), *The Backlash against Investment Arbitration: Perceptions and Reality* (The Netherlands: Wolters Kluwer, 2010).

[98] For a discussion of the context informing legal disputes over energy resources in Bolivia during that period, see FC Morosini and MS Badin, 'Petrobras in Bolivia: Is There a Rule of Law in the "Primitive" World?' in H Muir Watt, L Bíziková, A Brandão de Oliveira, and DPF Arroyo (eds), *Global Private International Law: Adjudication without Frontiers* (Cheltenham: Edward Elgar, 2019), 381.

to shape climate politics emerged from the right and the left, as illustrated by the *Gilets Jaunes* protests in France, the Extinction Rebellion actions in London, and student climate strikes globally.[99] States in Europe and Latin America argued that regional human rights courts had engaged in jurisdictional overreach, African states withdrew from regional human rights agreements, and the United States withdrew from the UN Human Rights Council.

2.3.2 *The Turn to History in a Time of Crisis*

In response to those financial, material, and social crises, a new wave of historically oriented scholarship began to emerge. Legal scholars still continued to publish work exploring the relationship of international law to European imperialism and the question of whether and to what extent international law had been decolonised, maintaining the momentum generated by the critical work that had been initiated during the triumphant phase of liberal internationalism.[100] However, another body of international law

---

[99] For a range of analyses of the Gilets Jaunes movement that address its relation to and significance for broader political struggles of working people, see C Askan and J Bailes (eds), *One Question Gilets Jaunes* (2019), available at https://stateofnatureblog.com/one-question-gilets-jaunes/. For the interpretation of the Gilets Jaunes as inventing a form of 'counter-populism', see É Balibar, '"Gilets Jaunes": The Meaning of the Confrontation', *Open Democracy*, 20 December 2018, available at www.opendemocracy.net/en/can-europe-make-it/gilets-jaunes-meaning-of-confrontation/.

[100] See, for example, M Craven, *The Decolonization of International Law* (Oxford: Oxford University Press, 2007); R Wilde, *International Territorial Administration: How Trusteeship and the Civilizing Mission Never Went Away* (Oxford: Oxford University Press, 2008); C Stahn, *The Law and Practice of International Territorial Administration: Versailles to Iraq and Beyond* (Cambridge: Cambridge University Press, 2008); JT Gathii, 'A Critical Appraisal of the International Legal Tradition of Taslim Olawale Elias' (2008) 21 *Leiden Journal of International Law* 317; BS Chimni, 'International Law Scholarship in Post-colonial India: Coping with Dualism' (2010) 23 *Leiden Journal of International Law* 23; A Orford, 'International Territorial Administration and the Management of Decolonization' (2010) 59 *International and Comparative Law Quarterly* 227; U Natarajan, 'Creating and Recreating Iraq: Legacies of the Mandate System in Contemporary Understandings of Third World Sovereignty' (2011) 24 *Leiden Journal of International Law* 799; F Johns, T Skouteris, and W Werner, 'The League of Nations and the Construction of the Periphery Introduction' (2011) 24 *Leiden Journal of International Law* 797; S Pahuja, *Decolonizing International Law* (Cambridge: Cambridge University Press, 2011); L Nuzzo and M Vec (eds), *Constructing International Law: The Birth of a Discipline* (Frankfurt am Main: Vittorio Klostermann, 2012); B Bassbender and A Peters, *The Oxford Handbook of the History of International Law* (Oxford: Oxford University Press, 2012); Toufayan, Tourme-Jouannet, and Ruiz Fabri (eds), *Droit international et nouvelles approches sur le tiers-monde*; M Fakhri, *Sugar and the Making of International Trade Law* (Cambridge: Cambridge University Press, 2014); A Becker Lorca, *Mestizo International Law: A Global Intellectual History 1842–1933* (Cambridge: Cambridge University Press, 2014); I de la Rasilla del Moral, *In the Shadow of Vitoria: A History of*

scholarship began to emerge during that period, which was more directly responsive to the disruptions caused by the financial, food, and climate crises and their consequences. That scholarship looked to the past in the attempt to understand the role international law had played in contributing to the global financial crisis, the rapidly heating planet, the mass dislocation and dispossession of people in North Africa and the Middle East, and the growing vulnerability, insecurity, and inequality that were increasingly apparent within and between states. Lawyers looked to the past both to diagnose how international law had contributed to these problems and to argue over what regulatory changes or new legal techniques, forms, and institutions should be developed in response.

To take one example, in the aftermath of the financial crisis international lawyers began to consider the failings of the pre-2008 regulatory system and whether it needed to be redesigned. Here the 'turn to history' by lawyers was part of a broader approach to questioning the foundations of the regulatory regime that had contributed to the financial crisis. Rethinking the (recent) 'past' here included rethinking fundamental assumptions about whether we know what a financial system is and how to regulate it, which sources or forms of law (treaties, private contracts, soft law, domestic court judgements, local regulations) had shaped the global regulatory field, the implications of international financial systems for how we understand sovereignty, and whether the analytical focus should be on the forms of law that create capital or the forms of law that purport to regulate capital once it is created.[101] Legal scholars looked to earlier centuries in order to understand the continuities and

---

International Law in Spain (1770–1953) (Leiden and Boston: Brill, 2017); M Koskenniemi, W Rech, and M Jiménez Fonseca (eds), *International Law and Empire: Historical Explorations* (Oxford: Oxford University Press, 2017); A Alexander, 'International Humanitarian Law, Postcolonialism and the 1977 Geneva Protocol I' (2016) 17 *Melbourne Journal of International Law* 15; L Eslava, M Fakhri, and V Nesiah (eds), *Bandung, Global History, and International Law: Critical Pasts and Pending Futures* (Cambridge: Cambridge University Press, 2017); J von Bernstorff and P Dann (eds), *The Battle for International Law: South-North Perspectives on the Decolonization Era* (Oxford: Oxford University Press, 2019); R Parfitt, *The Process of International Legal Reproduction: Inequality, Historiography, Resistance* (Cambridge: Cambridge University Press, 2019).

[101] F Johns, 'Financing as Governance' (2011) 31 *Oxford Journal of Legal Studies* 391; B Maurer, 'Regulation as Retrospective Ethnography: Mobile Money and the Arts of Cash' (2011) 21 *Banking and Finance Law Review* 299; K Pistor, 'A Legal Theory of Finance' (2013) 41 *Journal of Comparative Economics* 315; G Mallard and J Sgard (eds), *Contractual Knowledge: One Hundred Years of Legal Experimentation in Global Markets* (Cambridge: Cambridge University Press, 2016); K Pistor, 'From Territorial to Monetary Sovereignty' (2017) 18 *Theoretical Inquiries in Law* 491.

discontinuities in the treatment of money and finance over time.[102] They also looked to recent history in order to work out the role of regulatory arbitrage and other games that lawyers play in contributing to the global financial crisis, the feedback loops between regulators and market actors that complicate the effect of new laws, whether the evidentiary record supported the claim that complexity was the best solution to complexity or suggested the limits of that approach, and how much of the regulatory system had depended on a dominant US economy allowing US regulators to set the rules of the game for everyone else.[103] In addition, that legal scholarship tried to determine which if any of those conditions would still exist when the next crisis began to develop.

While much of that legal scholarship addressing financial regulation included some study of the past, the goal was not the historical one of producing a complete account of the crisis, discovering its true origins, or dispelling disciplinary myths. Rather the goal was the presentist and legal one of understanding the involvement of law and regulation in contributing to the conditions in which the crisis unfolded. Lawyers sought to become 'aware of the tensions between our inherited concepts and our methodological tools',[104] in order to inform highly contested debates about what regulatory and governance changes were needed to avert another global financial crisis and its destructive effects.

Similarly, in the context of the backlash that had begun to emerge against international investment arbitration, numerous studies began to engage with the history of that field. Some of that work turned to history to find more objective grounds for formalist doctrinal interpretations of treaty terms or customary international law.[105] Other scholars drew on the past to offer

---

[102] R Kreitner, 'The Jurisprudence of Global Money' (2010) 11 *Theoretical Inquiries in Law* 177.

[103] See, for example, C Bradley, 'Rhetoric and the Regulation of the Global Financial Market in a Time of Crisis: The Regulation of Credit Ratings' (2009) 3 *Transnational Law and Contemporary Problems* 24; C Brummer, 'Territoriality as a Regulatory Technique: Notes from the Financial Crisis' (2010) 79 *University of Cincinnati Law Review* 499; JW Head, 'The Global Financial Crisis of 2008–2009 in Context – Reflections on International Legal and Institutional Failings, "Fixes", and Fundamentals' (2010) 23 *Global Business and Development Law Journal* 43; A Riles, 'Managing Regulatory Arbitrage: A Conflict of Laws Approach' (2014) 47 *Cornell International Law Journal* 63; DR Holmes, 'Communicative Imperatives in Central Banks' (2014) 47 *Cornell International Law Journal* 15; A Riles, 'New Approaches to International Financial Regulation', *Cornell Law School Research Paper No 15-03*, Cornell Law School, 2014; M Ortino, 'The Governance of Global Banking in the Face of Complexity' (2019) 22 *Journal of International Economic Law* 177.

[104] C Joerges, 'Europe's Economic Constitution in Crisis and the Emergence of a New Constitutional Constellation' (2014) 15 *German Law Journal* 998.

[105] T Weiler, *The Interpretation of International Investment Law: Equality, Discrimination and Minimum Standards of Treatment in Historical Context* (Leiden and Boston: Martinus Nijhoff, 2013); J Kammerhofer, 'The Challenges of History in International Investment Law: A View

normative accounts of the field's legitimacy (or at least its preferability to alternatives such as gunboat diplomacy),[106] to offer revisionist interpretations of landmark decisions,[107] or to reflect upon the development of core concepts, principles, and institutions.[108] In addition, critics of the international investment regime turned to history to show the field's origins in supporting imperialism and the interests of capitalist states.[109] Legal scholars developed historically informed accounts of the processes through which trade, investment, and regional economic agreements had been used as vehicles to embed a set of costs and constraints on states seeking to implement environmental, labour, or health and safety measures, pointed to the lack of political institutions to provide checks and balances to international arbitrators, and traced the structural asymmetry provided to corporate actors who were empowered to challenge government decision-making in their role as foreign investors.[110]

For a number of us who had been working to understand the relation of international law to the rapidly accelerating project of global economic liberalisation unfolding during the 1990s,[111] the publication (in 2004 in French and in 2008 in English) of Michel Foucault's groundbreaking

from Legal Theory' in Schill, Tams, and Hofmann (eds), *International Investment Law and History*, 164.

[106] SW Schill, 'Private Enforcement of International Investment Law: Why We Need Investor Standing in BIT Dispute Settlement' in Waibel, Kaushal, Chung, and Balchin (eds), *The Backlash against Investment Arbitration*, 29; SM Schwebel, 'In Defense of Bilateral Investment Treaties' (2015) 31 *Arbitration International* 181.

[107] See, for example, J Cantegreil, 'The Audacity of the Texaco/Calasiatic Award: René-Jean Dupuy and the Internationalization of Foreign Investment Law' (2011) 22 *European Journal of International Law* 441; JW Yackee, 'The First Investor-State Arbitration: The Suez Canal Company v Egypt (1864)' (2016) 17 *The Journal of World Investment and Trade* 401.

[108] Parra, *The History of ICSID*; J Pauwelyn, 'At the Edge of Chaos? Foreign Investment Law as a Complex Adaptive System, How It Emerged and How It Can Be Reformed' (2014) 29 *ICSID Review* 372; M Kinnear, GR Fischer, JM Almedia, LF Torres, and MU Bidegain (eds), *Building International Investment Law: The First 50 Years of ICSID* (The Netherlands: Wolters Kluwer, 2016).

[109] Miles, *The Origins of International Investment Law*; M Sornarajah, *Resistance and Change in the International Law on Foreign Investment* (Cambridge: Cambridge University Press, 2015).

[110] See, from a large literature, M Renner, 'The Dialectics of Transnational Economic Constitutionalism' in C Joerges and J Falke (eds), *Karl Polanyi, Globalisation and the Potential of Law in Transnational Markets* (Oxford: Hart, 2011), 419; D Schneiderman, *Resisting Economic Globalization: Critical Theory and International Investment Law* (Hampshire and New York: Palgrave Macmillan, 2013); NM Perrone, 'The Governance of Foreign Investment at a Crossroad: Is an Overlapping Consensus the Way Forward?' (2015) 15 *Global Jurist* 1; Lim (ed), *Alternative Visions of the International Law on Foreign Investment*; Greenman, 'Aliens in Latin America'; Orford, 'A Global Rule of Law'.

[111] In Chapter 6 I explore this legal scholarship in more detail and discuss its relation to subsequent scholarship in intellectual history covering the same ground.

1978–1979 lectures at the Collège de France was influential.[112] While a handful of legal scholars and economic historians in France, Germany, Italy, and Sweden had been studying the Ordoliberal approach to economic ordering and its relation to the project of European integration since the 1960s,[113] it was the publication of Foucault's legendary series of lectures as an edited volume that made Ordoliberal thinking appear relevant again for legal and political thinkers outside Germany.[114] The timing of the English-language version of Foucault's lectures, arriving as they did in the same year as the financial and Eurozone crisis, contributed to a renaissance of interest in Ordoliberalism amongst historical, legal, and political scholars. Over the next decade, legal scholars and economic historians developed a significant body of scholarship linking the mid-century Central European ordoliberals to contemporary transnational and international economic ordering through law.

---

[112] M Foucault, *Naissance de la Biopolitique: Cours au Collège de France, 1978–1979* (Paris: Éditions de Seuil/Gallimard, 2004); M Foucault, *The Birth of Biopolitics: Lectures at the Collège de France, 1978–79* (trans Graham Burchell) (Hampshire and New York: Palgrave Macmillan, 2008).

[113] See, for example, F Bilger, *La pensée economique libérale dans l'Allemagne contemporaine* (Paris: Librairie Générale de Droit et de Jurisprudence, 1964); H Willgerodt and A Peacock, 'German Liberalism and Economic Revival' in A Peacock and H Willgerodt (eds), *Germany's Social Market Economy: Origins and Evolution* (London: Palgrave Macmillan, 1989); C Joerges, 'The Market without the State? The "Economic Constitution" of the European Community and the Rebirth of Regulatory Politics' (1997) *European Integration online Papers (EIoP)* Vol. 1 No. 19 (http://eiop.or.at/eiop/texte/1997-019a.htmJoerges); C Joerges, 'State without a Market? Comments on the German Constitutional Court's Maastricht-Judgement and a Plea for Interdisciplinary Discourses', *European Integration Online Papers (EIoP)* Vol. 1, No. 20 (http://eiop.or.at/eiop/texte/1997-020a.htm); C Joerges, 'The Science of Private Law and the Nation-State' in F Snyder (ed), *The Europeanisation of Law: The Legal Effects of European Integration* (Oxford: Hart, 2000), 47; M Wegmann, *Früher Neoliberalismus und Europäische Integration* (Baden-Baden: Nomos, 2002); P Commun (ed), *L'ordolibéralisme allemande: Aux sources de l'Économie sociale de marché* (Cergy-Pontoise: CIRAC, 2003); C Joerges, 'Europe a Großraum? Shifting Legal Conceptualisations of the Integration Project' in C Joerges and NS Ghaleigh (eds), *Darker Legacies of Law in Europe: The Shadow of National Socialism and Fascism over Europe and Its Legal Traditions* (Oxford: Hart, 2003), 167; C Joerges and F Rödl, '"Social Market Economy" as Europe's Social Model?', *EUI Working Paper Law No. 2004/8*; VJ Vanberg, 'The Freiburg School: Walter Eucken and Ordoliberalism', *Freiburg Discussion Papers on Constitutional Economics*, No. 04/11 (2004); C Joerges, 'What Is Left of the European Economic Constitution? A Melancholic Eulogy' (2005) 30 *European Law Review* 461.

[114] An early example of such work was Keith Tribe's *Strategies of Economic Order*, published as part of the Cambridge school-inspired *Ideas in Context* series, which engaged in subtle and complicated conversation with Foucault's as then unpublished 1979 lectures: K Tribe, *Strategies of Economic Order: German Economic Discourse 1750–1950* (Cambridge: Cambridge University Press, 1995). Tribe's final two chapters exploring European integration show what informed economic history can add to Foucault's brilliant but somewhat eclectic genealogy.

Perhaps the most extensive study of the relation of Ordoliberalism to transnational economic integration was in relation to the economic constitution of the European Union. The question of how to make sense of the growing disenchantment with European integration also contributed to an intensification of the scholarly conversation around the legacies of Ordoliberalism in Europe. The Eurozone crisis provided the context for much of that scholarly conversation about Ordoliberalism and its relation to transnational projects of economic ordering. In France, the rediscovery of Foucault's lectures led to a new wave of historical, economic, and philosophical scholarship studying the theories of neoliberals and their relation to modern political developments.[115] Controversies about German Ordoliberalism and its role in shaping responses to the Eurozone crisis became 'part of the public debate in France'.[116] In Germany, the financial crisis led to a new interest in Ordoliberalism in both scholarly and public debates.[117] Around Europe, collectives of scholars at many universities began to revisit the political and legal history of European integration and the role of the Ordoliberal vision of an 'economic constitution' in that history.[118]

---

[115] P Dardot and C Laval, *La nouvelle raison du monde. Essai sur la société néolibérale* (Paris: La Découverte, 2010); S Audier, *Néo-libéralisme(s). Une archéologie intellectuelle* (Paris: Grasset, 2012); S Audier, *Le colloque Lippmann: Aux origines du 'néo-libéralisme'* (Paris: BDL editions, 2012); P Commun, *Les Ordolibéraux: Histoire d'un libéralisme à l'allemande* (Paris: Les Belles Lettres, 2016).

[116] A Lechevalier, 'Why and How Has German Ordoliberalism Become a French Issue? Some Aspects about Ordoliberal Thoughts We Can Learn from the French Reception' in J Hien and C Joerges (eds), *Ordoliberalism, Law and the Rule of Economics* (Oxford and Portland: Hart, 2017), 23.

[117] See further A Wigger, 'Debunking the Ordoliberal Myth in Post-War Europe' in Hien and Joerges (eds), *Ordoliberalism, Law and the Rule of Economics*, 161; T Biebricher and F Vogelmann (eds), *The Birth of Austerity. German Ordoliberalism and Contemporary Neoliberalism* (London and New York: Rowman & Littlefield, 2017).

[118] See, for example, H Schulz-Forberg and B Stråth, *The Political History of European Integration: The Hypocrisy of Democracy-Through-Market* (Abingdon: Routledge, 2010); K Tuori and S Sankari (eds), *The Many Constitutions of Europe* (Surrey: Ashgate, 2010); C Joerges and E-U Petersmann (eds), *Constitutionalism, Multilevel Trade Governance and International Economic Law* (Oxford: Hart, 2011); M Maduro, K Tuori, and S Sankari (eds), *Transnational Law: Rethinking European Law and Legal Thinking* (Cambridge: Cambridge University Press, 2014); C Joerges and C Glinski (eds), *The European Crisis and the Transformation of Transnational Governance: Authoritarian Managerialism versus Democratic Governance* (Oxford: Hart, 2014); Joerges, 'Europe's Economic Constitution in Crisis', 986; JE Fossum and AJ Menéndez (eds), *The European Union in Crises or the European Union as Crises?* (Oslo: Arena Report Series, 2014); J Solchany, 'Wilhelm Röpke as a Key Actor of Transnational Neoliberalism after 1945' in H Schulze-Forberg and N Olsen (eds), *Re-Inventing Western Civilisation: Transnational Reconstructions of Liberalism in Europe in the Twentieth Century* (Cambridge: Cambridge Scholars, 2014), 95; J Solchany, *Wilhelm Röpke, l'autre Hayek. Aux origines du néolibéralisme* (Paris: Publications de la Sorbonne, 2015); D Chalmers,

The work focused on understanding the practical impact of Ordoliberalism on the process of European integration and subsequently on exploring the relevance of that history to the decisions being taken during the financial crisis. The collective nature of that work was vital to enabling new insights about the relation of law and political economy.

In the context of law and development, Kerry Rittich was one of the first critical legal scholars to stress the significance of Friedrich von Hayek and Wilhelm Röpke for understanding the 'theoretical antecedents of neoliberalism' and show their significance for grasping the role of law in economic globalisation.[119] I brought Ordoliberal thinking into relation with projects of remaking the state through the UN in the early era of decolonisation under the leadership of the economist Dag Hammarskjöld, and traced the Ordoliberal influence on the project of European integration, the GATT, and the WTO.[120] In the field of international investment law, David Schneiderman and Ntina Tzouvala both linked the constitutionalism of international investment law to German Ordoliberalism and Freiburg school theorising.[121]

M Jachtenfuchs, and C Joerges (eds), *The End of the Eurocrats' Dream: Adjusting to European Diversity* (Cambridge: Cambridge University Press, 2016); Hien and Joerges (eds), *Ordoliberalism, Law and the Rule of Economics*; J Hien and C Joerges, 'Dead Man Walking? Current European Interest in the Ordoliberal Tradition' (2018) 24 *European Law Journal* 14; C Joerges, '"Where the Law Runs Out": The Overburdening of Law and Constitutional Adjudication by the Financial Crisis and Europe's New Modes of Economic Governance' in S Garben, I Govaere, and P Nemitz (eds), *Critical Reflections on Constitutional Democracy in the European Union* (Oxford: Hart, 2019), 168; C Joerges and M Everson, 'The Legal Proprium of the Economic Constitution' in PF Kjaer (ed), *The Law of Political Economy: Transformations of the Function of Law* (Cambridge: Cambridge University Press, 2020), 33.

[119] Rittich, *Recharacterizing Restructuring*.

[120] A Orford, 'Europe Reconstructed' (2012) 75 *Modern Law Review* 275; A Orford, 'On International Legal Method' (2014) 1 *London Review of International Law* 166; A Orford, 'Hammarskjöld, Economic Thinking, and the United Nations' in H Melber and C Stahn (eds), *Peace, Diplomacy, Global Justice, and International Agency: Rethinking Human Security and Ethics in the Spirit of Dag Hammarskjöld* (Cambridge: Cambridge University Press, 2014), 156; A Orford, 'Food Security, Free Trade, and the Battle for the State' (2015) 11 *Journal of International Law and International Relations* 1; A Orford, 'Law, Economics, and the History of Free Trade: A Response' (2015) 11 *Journal of International Law and International Relations* 155; Orford, 'Theorizing Free Trade'.

[121] D Schneiderman, *Constitutionalizing Economic Globalization: Investment Rules and Democracy's Promise* (Cambridge: Cambridge University Press, 2008), 6; D Schneiderman, 'Constitutional Property Rights and the Elision of the Transnational: Foucauldian Misgivings' (2015) 24 *Social and Legal Studies* 65; N Tzouvala, 'The Ordo-Liberal Origins of Modern International Investment Law: Constructing Competition on a Global Scale' in JD Haskell and A Rasulov (eds), *New Voices and New Perspectives in International Economic Law* (Cham: Springer, 2020), 37 (posted on Academia in 2015).

Across international law, critical scholars also turned to history in an attempt to shape or engage with legal responses to the environmental, asylum, security, and food security crises. International lawyers explored the framing assumptions about law and the forms of legal thinking that underpinned and constrained the efficacy of international environmental law,[122] or that shaped international laws liberalising the movement of some people and products while policing and controlling the movement of others.[123] Legal scholarship focused on the changing nature of international law relating to the use of force, tracing the processes through which particular states and legal networks had sought to expand the legal meaning of terms like self-defence, engaged in forms of carceral internationalism focused on promoting criminal law responses to issues of social control, and reintroduced the language of

---

[122] J Purdy, 'The Politics of Nature: Climate Change, Environmental Law, and Democracy' (2010) 119 *Yale Law Journal* 1122; U Natarajan, 'TWAIL and the Environment: The State of Nature, the Nature of the State, and the Arab Spring' (2012) 14 *Oregon Review of International Law* 177; U Natarajan and K Khoday, 'Fairness and International Environmental Law from Below: Social Movements and Legal Transformation in India' (2012) 25 *Leiden Journal of International Law* 415; I Porras, 'Appropriating Nature: Commerce, Property, and the Commodification of Nature in the Law of Nations' (2014) 27 *Leiden Journal of International Law* 641; U Natarajan and K Khoday, 'Locating Nature: Making and Unmaking International Law' (2014) 27 *Leiden Journal of International Law* 573; I Porras, 'Binge Development in the Age of Fear: Scarcity, Consumption, Inequality, and the Environmental Crisis' in B Stark (ed), *International Law and Its Discontents: Confronting Crises* (Cambridge: Cambridge University Press, 2015), 25; K Mickelson, 'International Law as a War against Nature? Reflections on the Ambivalence of International Environmental Law' in Stark (ed), *International Law and Its Discontents*, 84; S Humphreys and Y Otomo, 'Theorizing International Environmental Law' in Orford and Hoffmann (eds), *The Oxford Handbook of the Theory of International Law*, 797; J Dehm, 'International Law, Temporalities and Narratives of the Climate Crisis' (2016) 4 *London Review of International Law* 167; T Stephens, 'Reimagining International Environmental Law in the Anthropocene' in L Kotzé (ed), *Environmental Law and Governance for the Anthropocene* (Oxford: Hart, 2017), 31; J Dehm, 'One Tonne of Carbon Dioxide Equivalent ($1tCO_2e$)' in J Hohmann and D Joyce (eds), *International Law's Objects* (Oxford: Oxford University Press, 2018), 305.

[123] BS Chimni, 'The Birth of a "Discipline": From Refugee to Forced Migration Studies' (2009) 22 *Journal of Refugee Studies* 11; J McAdam, 'An Intellectual History of Freedom of Movement in International Law: The Right to Leave as a Personal Liberty' (2011) 12 *Melbourne Journal of International Law* 27; S Dehm, 'Framing International Migration' (2015) 3 *London Review of International Law* 133; Orford, 'Theorizing Free Trade' (arguing that the policing of 'surplus' population is one of the conditions of the free trade project and of its material limits); C Thomas, 'Transnational Migration, Globalization, and Governance: Theorizing a Crisis' in Orford and Hoffmann (eds), *The Oxford Handbook of the Theory of International Law*, 882; SB Woldemarian, A Maguire, and J von Meding, 'Forced Human Displacement, the Third World and International Law: A TWAIL Perspective' (2019) 20 *Melbourne Journal of International Law* 1.

protection into North–South relations.[124] International law scholars questioned the idea that liberal internationalism was still, if it ever had been, the alpha and omega of international law.[125] Critical legal scholars pointed to the possibility that other authoritarian forms of transnational law were being given expression through new international legal arguments.[126] That work, for example, explored the legacies of *Großraum* thinking that were being promoted by expansive interpretations of collective self-defence or regional projections of force,[127] and noted the echoes of the alliance between Carl Schmitt's vision of a strong state and the Ordoliberal vision of economic ordering in the relation of doctrines justifying increased Western military intervention read with the project of international economic constitutionalism.[128]

Appeals to the history of international law also played a major role in debates about how to make sense of the perceived crisis of liberal internationalism and in debates over the legitimacy of the 'liberal international order'. Those who sought to muster a defence of existing international institutional arrangements and treaty regimes linked their development to progress narratives,[129] while those who sought to challenge aspects of existing international

[124] A Orford, *International Authority and the Responsibility to Protect* (Cambridge: Cambridge University Press, 2011); A Orford, 'Moral Internationalism and the Responsibility to Protect' (2013) 24 *European Journal of International Law* 83; A Orford, 'NATO, Regionalism, and the Responsibility to Protect' in I Shapiro and A Tooze (eds), *Charter of the North Atlantic Treaty Organisation together with Scholarly Commentaries and Essential Historical Documents* (New Haven: Yale University Press, 2018), 302; T Ruys and O Corten with A Hofer (eds), *The Use of Force in International Law* (Oxford: Oxford University Press, 2018); J Halley, P Kotiswaran, R Rebouché, and H Shamir (eds), *Governance Feminism: Notes from the Field* (Minneapolis and London: University of Minnesota Press, 2019).

[125] For the contrasting claim that 'the international legal system has since 1999 moved … in the direction of an individual-centred, humanized system' and that 'this humanistic principle is also the *telos* of the international legal system', see A Peters, 'Humanity as the A and Ω of Sovereignty' (2009) 20 *European Journal of International Law* 513.

[126] The groundbreaking 2003 collection edited by Christian Joerges and Navraj Singh Ghaleigh was ahead of its time in that respect: Joerges and Ghaleigh, *Darker Legacies of Law in Europe*. See now the work being done by Rose Parfitt, including R Parfitt, 'Fascism, Imperialism and International Law: An Arch Met a Motorway and the Rest Is History …' (2018) 31 *Leiden Journal of International Law* 509; R Parfitt, 'Series Introduction – Fascism and the International: The Global South, the Far-Right and the International Legal Order', *TWAILR: Reflections #5/2019*; R Parfitt, 'Is This (Brazilian) Fascism? The Far-Right, the Third World and the Wrong Question', *TWAILR: Reflections #6/2019*.

[127] Orford, 'NATO, Regionalism, and the Responsibility to Protect'; R M Mitchell, 'Chinese Receptions of Carl Schmitt Since 1929' (2020) 8 *Penn State Journal of Law and International Affairs* 181.

[128] Orford, 'On International Legal Method', 189–194; Orford, 'Hammarskjöld, Economic Thinking, and the United Nations', 172–174; Orford, 'Theorizing Free Trade'.

[129] P Alston, 'The Populist Challenge to Human Rights' (2017) 9 *Journal of Human Rights Practice* 1; I Hull, 'Anything Can Be Rescinded' (2018) 40(8) *London Review of Books* 25; J Crawford,

regimes variously linked them to histories involving culture wars, democratic deficits, exploitation, growing inequality, or the rise of cosmopolitan elite rule.[130] Overall, across the field and around the globe, international lawyers sought to develop interpretations of legal transformations in practice while making clear their presentist commitments to intervening in post-crisis debates about the legal regimes then being imagined for the future.

2.4 THE RISE OF CHINA AND THE END OF THE REVOLUTION

International law is a field informed (at least in theory) by the practice of 195 states. Its legitimacy depends in part upon a claim to universality. As a result, while the continued influence of scholarship and practice from the United States and its Western allies is undeniable, international lawyers are also engaged with the legal arguments being made by scholars and practitioners from beyond the North Atlantic.[131] As a result, understanding the forces shaping the turn to history in international law requires attending to the political, economic, and social moment in which it took place beyond the United States and Europe.

'The Current Political Discourse Concerning International Law' (2018) 81 *Modern Law Review* 1; F Fukuyama and R Muggah, 'Populism Is Poisoning the Global Liberal Order', *The Globe and Mail*, 29 January 2018; G Shaffer, 'A Tragedy in the Making? The Decline of Law and the Return of Power in International Trade Relations' (2019) 44 *Yale Journal of International Law* 1.

[130] E Posner, 'Liberal Internationalism and the Populist Backlash', *University of Chicago, Public Working Paper No. 606*, 11 January 2017; M Koskenniemi, *International Law and the Far Right: Reflections on Law and Cynicism* (The Hague: Asser Press, 2019); Orford, 'International Law and the Populist Moment'; JHH Weiler, 'The European Circumstance and the Politics of Meaning: Not on Bread Alone Doth Man Liveth (Deut. 8:3; Mat 4:4)' (2020) 21 *German Law Journal* 96; Orford, *International Law and the Social Question*.

[131] For the ongoing influence of powerful states in the production of knowledge about international law, see D Kennedy, 'What Is New Thinking in International Law?' (2000) 94 *Proceedings of the ASIL Annual Meeting*, 104, at 121 ('the ideas about international law popular at a given moment in some countries are more influential than those popular in others simply because some countries are more powerful; money, access to institutional resources, relationships to underlying patterns of hegemony, and influence – is central to the chance that a given idea will become influential or dominant within the international law profession'); Chimni, 'Third World Approaches to International Law', 47 ('Unfortunately, TWAIL (third world approaches to international law) has neither been able to effectively critique neo-liberal international law or project an alternative vision of international law. The ideological domination of Northern academic institutions, the handful of critical third world international law scholars, the problems of doing research in the poor world, and the fragmentation of international legal studies has, among other things, prevented it from either advancing a holistic critique of the regressive role of globalising international law or sketching maps of alternative futures').

The turn to history in international law after 1989 did not of course only play out in the West. The break-up of the Soviet Union and the twenty-first century crises of liberal internationalism were events that reverberated outside the North Atlantic centres of power. In addition, the rise of China, alongside the other 'BRICS' (Brazil, Russia, India, and South Africa) during this period had significant implications for international law and global order. Given that the moment of American hegemony that had initially prompted the end of history debate began to appear relatively short-lived, it is unsurprising that new histories of international law with different actors as historical agents began to emerge. As a result, a growing body of work in international law and international relations began to explore the implications of these geopolitical shifts for the future international order,[132] in part through rethinking international history from the perspectives opened up by a focus on historical agents outside Europe and North America. I focus here in particular on new histories of international law that centre on the role of China.

The 'reform and opening-up policy' initiated in the late 1970s within the Chinese Communist Party under the leadership of Deng Xiaoping began a process of transformation that had significant implications for how the past, present, and future of international law were understood both by Chinese scholars and more broadly. The break-up of the Soviet Union in 1989 was a historically meaningful event for China, not only because it ended the Cold War stand-off between the United States and the USSR, but also because it marked the 'global domination of neoliberalism in economic and political

---

[132] See, for example, C Cai, 'New Great Powers and International Law in the 21st Century' (2013) 24 *European Journal of International Law* 755; VI Lo and M Hiscock (eds), *The Rise of the BRICS in the Global Political Economy* (Cheltenham: Edward Elgar, 2014); A Hurrell, 'Hegemony, Liberalism and Global Order: What Space for Would-Be Great Powers?' (2016) 82 *International Affairs* 1; RJ Neuwithr, A Svetlicinii, and DDC Halis (eds), *The BRICS-Lawyers' Guide to Global Cooperation* (Cambridge: Cambridge University Press, 2017). For examples of varied US foreign policy responses to the challenges posed to the vision of a US-led world order by the rise of China, see SP Huntington, *The Clash of Civilizations and the Remaking of World Order* (New York: Touchstone, 1996); RD Kaplan, 'How We Would Fight China' (June 2005) *The Atlantic* 49; GJ Ikenberry, 'The Rise of China and the Future of the West: Can the Liberal System Survive?' (2008) 87 *Foreign Affairs* 23; H Kissinger, *On China* (New York: Penguin, 2011); P Navarro, *Death by China: Confronting the Dragon – A Global Call to Action* (New Jersey: Pearson FT Press, 2011). For broader reflections on the role of the Third World international lawyer, see G Abi-Saab, 'The Third World Intellectual in Praxis: Confrontation, Participation or Operation behind Enemy Lines?' (2016) 37 *Third World Quarterly* 1957; M Sornarajah, 'On Fighting for Global Justice: The Role of a Third World International Lawyer' (2016) 37 *Third World Quarterly* 1972.

structures'.[133] In the words of Wang Hui, 1989 in China represented the 'end of the revolution' rather than the end of history.[134]

Revolutionary politics in China had been one twentieth-century response to resolving the contradiction between modernisation and democracy, which had been presented in China 'by the arrival in the late nineteenth century of the most undemocratic form of global modernizationism: the form known as capitalist-imperialism'.[135] The apparent demise of revolutionary politics in 1989 cemented the triumph of neoliberalism with Chinese characteristics, created through an embrace of 'radical marketization' alongside the continuity of China's political system.[136] International law has been one field through which scholars have sought to interpret the meaning of those changes for China and for the world. The engagement with international law by scholars within China can be understood as part of a broader 'attempt to rethink the contours of modern Chinese history and the basic historical narrative shaping views of China's past and future'.[137]

In the political version of that story, Chinese legal scholars focus on the emergence of China from a century of humiliation,[138] the founding of the People's Republic of China (PRC) in 1949, and the historical role subsequently played by the new China as a force for resisting imperialist war and promoting new principles of international law.[139] Those accounts stress the peaceful rise of China and contrast that with a history in which Western states gained power through imperialism, coercion, and unequal treaties.[140] The history of oppression stretching from the first Opium War through the century of unequal treaties, foreign concessions, extraterritoriality, and other related privileges of colonial powers 'was not merely a piece of history' but explained

---

[133] H Wang, *The End of the Revolution: China and the Limits of Modernity* (London and New York: Verso, 2009), 19.

[134] Wang, *The End of the Revolution*.

[135] R Karl, 'Foreword to the English Edition' in Wang, *The End of the Revolution*, vii, at viii.

[136] Wang, *The End of the Revolution*, 19.

[137] D Ownby and T Cheek, 'An Introduction to Jiang Shigong on "Philosophy and History: Interpreting the 'Xi Jinping Era' through Xi's Report to the Nineteenth National Congress of the CCP"', *The China Story*, 11 May 2018, www.thechinastory.org/cot/jiang-shigong-on-philosophy-and-history-interpreting-the-xi-jinping-era-through-xis-report-to-the-nineteenth-national-congress-of-the-ccp/.

[138] On the relation of international law to that century of oppression by colonial powers, see T Wang, 'International Law in China: Historical and Contemporary Perspectives' (1990) 221 *Recueil des Cours* 195, at 237–262.

[139] See Wang, 'International Law in China'; H Xue, *Chinese Contemporary Perspectives on International Law: History, Culture, and International Law* (Pocketbooks of The Hague Academy of International Law) (Leiden/Boston: Brill/Nijhoff, 2012).

[140] Wang, 'International Law in China'.

'why China always attaches such importance to the principle of sovereign equality in international affairs'.[141]

China's 'past colonial history and bitter experience under imperialist oppression' meant that it found 'common grounds and sentiments with the newly independent and non-aligned countries on the world stage', while as a socialist country it was also aligned with the Soviet Union and its allies.[142] The founding of the PRC was thus 'part of the historical process that fundamentally transformed the political landscape of the world in the wake of WWII', as 'a large number of Asian and African countries gained independence'.[143] The new China was 'very critical of traditional international law that primarily protected the interests of the colonial and imperialist powers to the detriment of the most undeveloped nations and peoples'.[144] It did not, however, opt to be an 'outlaw'.[145] Rather than accepting or rejecting international law in its entirety, China voluntarily accepted those rules and norms that reflected a commitment to 'peace, equality, and mutual respect in international relations'.[146] As a result, its 'attitude and practice towards international law' manifested 'both realism and idealism'.[147]

The Korean War represents a turning point in those histories of the PRC's role in resisting imperialism. In Chinese international law scholarship, the Korean War figures as part of a longer history of resisting aggression and imperialist invasion, which has shaped China's commitment to mutual non-aggression as a foundational principle of international law.[148] In the aftermath of the Korean War, China and India formally committed to the Five Principles of Peaceful Coexistence as the foundation for a new international law.[149] The subsequent incorporation of those principles in the closing declaration of the Bandung Conference reflected China's re-establishment of its links with Asia and Africa,[150] and the moment at which it emerged as a leader

---

[141] Xue, *Chinese Contemporary Perspectives on International Law*, 28.
[142] Xue, *Chinese Contemporary Perspectives on International Law*, 24.
[143] Xue, *Chinese Contemporary Perspectives on International Law*, 34.
[144] Xue, *Chinese Contemporary Perspectives on International Law*, 23.
[145] Xue, *Chinese Contemporary Perspectives on International Law*, 23.
[146] Xue, *Chinese Contemporary Perspectives on International Law*, 34.
[147] Xue, *Chinese Contemporary Perspectives on International Law*, 2.
[148] M Li, *Five Principles of Peaceful Coexistence: Continuity and Challenges* (A Series of Lectures at the Xiamen Academy of International Law) (2017), 61–63.
[149] For arguments stressing the significance of the Five Principles of Peaceful Co-existence for China's role in shaping international law, see Wang, 'International Law in China', 263–287; H Xue, 'Meaningful Dialogue through a Common Discourse: Law and Values in a Multi-Polar World' (2011) 1 *Asian Journal of International Law* 13; Li, *Five Principles of Peaceful Coexistence*.
[150] Wang, 'International Law in China', 267–268.

of the Third World.[151] The histories narrated by international lawyers link China's opposition to US acts of aggression during the Korean War with China's definition of the Vietnam War as a US war of aggression, China's opposition to armed interventions by the United States in Latin America, China's condemnation of the Soviet Union invasion of Afghanistan, and Chinese outrage at the US bombing of the Chinese embassy in Belgrade during the NATO intervention of 1999.[152]

Those legal accounts reinforce the work of other Chinese scholars who stress the significance of the Korean War for understanding China's role in the twentieth century. To take one example, Wang Hui places the War to Resist US Aggression and Aid Korea into an international context that includes the preceding revolution and people's wars of twentieth-century China and the subsequent structures of 'division, separation and confrontation' that persist in Northeast Asia.[153] Wang insists on the creative work done by any choice of context for a historical event, both when that choice is made by empiricist historians operating according to the 'supposedly non-ideological' methods of 'contemporary social sciences and historical studies' and when, as in Wang's case, it is made by a scholar who presents himself as occupying a position within a field of 'principles, values and confrontational politics that shaped the actions of people in that period'.[154] Wang resists the tendency to present the significance of the war 'from the standpoint of relations between nations and national interests', and instead insists on the need to interpret it through 'such antagonistic categories as capitalism and socialism, imperialism and inter-nationalism'.[155] In that telling, the UN was exposed as a 'tool of the imperialists' during the Korean War, which 'paved the way for a subsequent political struggle within the UN' and 'promoted the formation of a worldwide united front of oppressed nations'. That situation 'could only have been enabled by the appearance of a new political subject' in the form of the New China.[156]

A key turning point in those legal narratives was the shift in China's international status that resulted from the recognition of the PRC as the lawful

---

[151] For that narrative, see M Sornarajah and J Wang, 'China, India, and International Law: A Justice Based Vision between the Romantic and Realist Perceptions' (2019) 9 *Asian Journal of International Law* 217. For a discussion of China's role at the Bandung conference, see Y Chen, 'Bandung, China, and the Making of World Order in East Asia' in Eslava, Fakhri, and Nesiah (eds), *Bandung, Global History, and International Law*, 177.

[152] Li, *Five Principles of Peaceful Coexistence*, 64–65.

[153] H Wang, *China's Twentieth Century: China's Twentieth Century: Revolution, Retreat and the Road to Equality* (London and New York: Verso, 2016), 112.

[154] Wang, *China's Twentieth Century*, 111–112.

[155] Wang, *China's Twentieth Century*, 111.

[156] Wang, *China's Twentieth Century*, 134–135.

representative of China at the UN in 1971.[157] With the end of the Cultural Revolution and the reinstatement of legal education after 1979, the period of reform and opening up saw a new embrace of international law in practice and in the universities. China's approach to international law was linked to a history of China's good neighbourliness based on respect for principles of sovereign equality, non-intervention, and peaceful settlement of disputes,[158] and its peaceful approach to international relations traced to the traditional notion of *tianxia* (all under Heaven).[159] The notion of China's commitment to a 'harmonious world', a sister concept to that of the 'harmonious society', was declared by President Hu Jintao at the United Nations in 2005,[160] and subsequently taken up in international law scholarship.[161] Chinese international lawyers have stressed that China's approach to international law differs from that of other major powers, particularly the United States, in its resistance to interfering in the systems of other states and its preference for peaceful resolution of international disputes over either the resort to force or international adjudication.[162] Historically informed normative visions of China's place in the international order have thus focused on the role of China in shaping alternatives to international liberal legalism.

A second way of telling the story of China's role since the end of the Cold War foregrounds economics. The 1980s saw the rise in power and influence of China's reformist economists, who sought to remake the relation between state and market with the help of foreign economic advisors and international organisations such as the World Bank. By 1993, the Chinese Communist Party officially renamed China a 'socialist market economy', in recognition of the range of reforms that had been introduced over the previous decades aimed at achieving greater deregulation, marketisation, and competition within the

---

[157] UN General Assembly Resolution 2758, 'Restoration of the Lawful Rights of the People's Republic of China in the United Nations', A/RES/2758 (XXVI), 25 October 1971. See further Xue, *Chinese Contemporary Perspectives on International Law*, 41; Li, *Five Principles of Peaceful Coexistence*, 45–48.

[158] Xue, *Chinese Contemporary Perspectives on International Law*.

[159] T Zhao, 'A Political World Philosophy in Terms of All-Under Heaven (*Tian-xia*)' (2009) 56 *Diogenes* 1. See further the discussion in MA Carrai, *Sovereignty in China: A Genealogy of a Concept since 1840* (Cambridge: Cambridge University Press, 2019), 223–224.

[160] Hu J, 'Build towards a Harmonious World of Lasting Peace and Common Prosperity', New York, 15 September 2005, https://www.un.org/webcast/summit2005/statements15/china050915eng.pdf.

[161] See, for example, S Yee, 'Towards a Harmonious World: The Roles of the International Law of Co-progressiveness and Leader States' (2008) 7 *Chinese Journal of International Law* 99.

[162] Li, *Five Principles of Peaceful Coexistence*, 130–138.

Chinese economy.[163] China's accession to the WTO in November 2001, after fifteen years of negotiations, was seen as a significant achievement of the Chinese economic reformists who supported neoliberal transformation.[164]

China's transformation intensified in the second decade of the twenty-first century. In the wake of the global financial crisis and prolonged US engagement in an open-ended war on terror, China became the world's second largest economy and largest exporter. The economic rise of China began to shift the global balance of power. Under Xi Jinping's leadership, China began a more ambitious phase of engagement with international law, effectively forming negotiating blocs at the WTO, undertaking institutional entrepreneurialism through the creation of the Asian Infrastructure Investment Bank, providing infrastructure for development as part of the Belt and Road Initiative, and challenging US military power and credibility in the South China Sea and East China Sea.

A wide range of historically oriented work has since sought to interpret the success of China's economic model in the period since 1989, particularly as 'experts in economic development policy have lost confidence in the neoliberal package of policy ideas once promoted with enthusiasm across the globe'.[165] With the apparent demise of revolutionary politics, scholars attempted to make sense of the 'special character' of Chinese neoliberalism produced by China's embrace of 'radical marketization' premised upon the 'continuity of its political system'.[166] For Chinese scholars and those engaged

---

[163] The story of that period is told, with strikingly different ideological valences, in H Wang, *China's New Order: Society, Politics and Economy in Transition* (Cambridge, MA: Harvard University Press, 2003); G Arrighi, *Adam Smith in Beijing: Lineages of the Twenty-First Century* (London and New York: Verso, 2007); Wang, *The End of the Revolution*; JY Lin, M Liu, and R Tao, 'Deregulation, Decentralization, and China's Growth in Transition' in D Kennedy and J Stiglitz (eds), *Law and Economics with Chinese Characteristics* (Oxford: Oxford University Press, 2013), 467; J Gewirtz, *Unlikely Partners: Chinese Reformers, Western Economists, and the Making of Global China* (Cambridge, MA: Harvard University Press, 2017).

[164] For analyses of the implications of China's accession for both China and the WTO, see K Zeng and W Liang, *China and Global Trade Governance: China's First Decade in the World Trade Organization* (London and New York: Routledge, 2013); M Wu, 'The WTO and China's Unique Economic Structure' in BL Liebman and CJ Milhaupt (eds), *Regulating the Visible Hand? The Institutional Implications of Chinese State Capitalism* (Oxford: Oxford University Press, 2015), 313; M Wu, 'The "China, Inc" Challenge to Global Trade Governance' (2016) 57 *Harvard International Law Journal* 261; PC Mavroidis and A Sapir, 'China and the World Trade Organisation: Towards a Better Fit', *Working Paper, Issue 06*, 11 June 2019, Bruegel, available at www.bruegel.org/2019/06/china-and-the-world-trade-organisation-towards-a-better-fit/.

[165] D Kennedy, 'Law and Development Economics: Toward a New Alliance' in Kennedy and Stiglitz (eds), *Law and Economics with Chinese Characteristics*, 19.

[166] Wang, *The End of the Revolution*, 19.

with their work, the economic rise of China offers a different model to that offered by Western states – a 'Beijing Consensus' to compete with the widely derided neoliberal 'Washington Consensus' of the 1990s.[167] In that account, Chinese socialism has offered an alternative to the forms of international order developed by powerful Western states that depended upon dispossession as the foundation of capital accumulation, the interdependence of military force and financial power, and extravagant energy consumption. For scholars associated with China's New Left, for example, the history of China's rise is related to the 'social origins of the Chinese ascent', the development of an alternative model of rural/urban relations under market conditions, the avoidance of entrenched rigid bureaucratic systems (in part through the Cultural Revolution), investment in village and workers' education, and a continued focus on anti-corruption as conditions of China's success and attractiveness to investors.[168] In those accounts, China successfully competed with the United States, at least in part, by providing an educated and disciplined workforce rather than simply a cheap workforce.[169] International law scholars have echoed that story, arguing that despite the high price that China had to pay to join the WTO, a significant factor in its subsequent economic success has been the strength of the Chinese system in implementing economic policy combined with 'the Chinese people's hard-working spirit', 'the high qualities of the Chinese people', and 'the countless ordinary Chinese people working diligently to improve their living environment'.[170]

The Belt and Road Initiative introduced by China in 2013 is also presented as part of a historical narrative foregrounding China's unique historical role. Unlike the US attempt during the 1990s to achieve regulatory alignment through multilateral treaties and institutions, China's Belt and Road Initiative resembles something more like the Marshall Plan, where relations

---

[167] See Arrighi, *Adam Smith in Beijing*, 379–389; W Chen (ed), *The Beijing Consensus: How China Has Changed Western Ideas of Law and Economic Development* (Cambridge: Cambridge University Press, 2017).

[168] Arrighi, *Adam Smith in Beijing*, 351–378; Wang, *The End of the Revolution*.

[169] The accounts offered by Chinese scholars differ markedly from the focus of much US scholarship, which tends to concentrate on China as a threat to the United States, and sees China's economic success either as a result of access to cheap labour or as an effect of the differences between Chinese and Western approaches to issues such as intellectual property protection or the treatment of state-owned enterprises. Those differences are represented largely as an effect of unfair practices on the part of China or as China acting in breach of universal norms, rather than as the expression of two divergent forms of economic organisation. More broadly, US historians describing China's economic transformation have stressed the role of Western economists in facilitating a transition from communism to China's version of capitalism.

[170] Li, *Five Principles of Peaceful Coexistence*, 117–118.

are established through the financing of infrastructure and the embedding of Chinese companies into domestic economies. The Belt and Road Initiative has been normatively framed by international lawyers as a contribution to creating a 'regional community of common destiny'.[171] Just as 'the Silk Road represented friendship, peace, and commerce', the Belt and Road Initiative is said to embody 'the idea of cooperative international law'.[172] As a result of its economic power, 'China can advocate and carry out infrastructure connectivity with the countries along the land and sea Silk Roads'.[173] Legal scholars have suggested that the new concept and structure offered by the Belt and Road Initiative could lead to a 'style of lawyering' directed not just to addressing the short-term interests of a particular client but also the long-term interests of the Belt and Road 'situation'.[174] At the same time, China is ensuring control over the forms of investor–state dispute settlement that will be developed to protect Chinese investments in those infrastructure projects.

Chinese international lawyers have also stressed the capacity of China to join with other states in resisting Western hegemonic reinterpretations of international law. For example, the approach to international order that Russia and China have collectively sought to consolidate has been expressed in legal terms, evidencing their intention to contest US control over the meaning of international law. In 2016 Russia and China jointly issued a declaration on the promotion of international law,[175] positioning the two states as champions of the approach to international law set out in the UN Charter and the Friendly Relations Declaration. The Russian-Chinese Declaration made clear their disagreement with Western powers over 'foundational constitutional principles of international law',[176] and more generally over the vision of the rule of law that should underpin the future of international order. In addition, scholars have argued that in collaboration China and India acting together could 'make changes in international law

[171] L Zeng, 'Conceptual Analysis of China's Belt and Road Initiative: A Road towards a Regional Community of Common Destiny' (2016) 15 *Chinese Journal of International Law* 517.

[172] Li, *Five Principles of Peaceful Coexistence*, 119–120.

[173] Li, *Five Principles of Peaceful Coexistence*, 120.

[174] S Yee, 'Dispute Settlement on the Belt and Road: Ideas on System, Spirit and Style' (2018) 17 *Chinese Journal of International Law* 907, at 911.

[175] The Declaration of the Russian Federation and the People's Republic of China on the Promotion of International Law, Ministry of Foreign Affairs of the Russian Federation, 25 June 2016, available at www.mid.ru/en/foreign_policy/news/-/asset_publisher/cKNonkJEo2Bw/content/id/2331698.

[176] L Mälksoo, 'Russia and China Challenge the Western Hegemony in the Interpretation of International Law', *EJIL: Talk!*, 15 July 2016, available at www.ejiltalk.org/russia-and-china-challenge-the-western-hegemony-in-the-interpretation-of-international-law/

and shift it from its present Euro-American moorings', jointly marshalling their power 'to displace rules of international law that emanate from imperial roots or are perceived as unjust'.[177]

Despite those appeals to a history of resisting imperialism and aggression, China's legal scholars are also beginning to articulate a new and more ambitious role for China in the region and the world. Just as the US developed interpretations of international law that appealed to history as a source of rights to self-defence and humanitarian intervention that exist alongside the UN Charter, so have Chinese legal arguments asserted the concept of historic rights of continental states possessing outlying archipelagos existing alongside UNCLOS. In both cases, the work of legal advisers and legal scholars has supported new interpretations of the law based on innovative readings of history.[178] In both cases, the appeal to the past is better analysed in terms of its performative effects rather than as a descriptive statement.[179] History is used to help shape a normative understanding of hegemonic state power and the purposes for its use. Here the critical and TWAIL scholarship that had begun in response to the 'end of history' thesis in the 1990s has now begun to reappear in a new guise. TWAIL scholarship is now invoked to justify the authority of states such as China and India taking the lead in the project of rethinking existing international law.[180]

In that context, a number of influential Chinese legal and philosophical scholars including Jiang Shigong, Wang Hui, and Liu Xiaofeng have begun to draw on the work of Halford Mackinder and on Carl Schmitt's *Großraum* thinking to shape possible interpretations of China's role in resisting US

---

[177] Sornarajah and Wang, 'China, India, and International Law', 217.

[178] Just as former UK legal adviser Daniel Bethlehem's note on the 'principles relevant to the scope of a state's right of self-defence against an imminent or armed attack by nonstate actors' was first published in 2012 in the *American Journal of International Law* as an academic study that closely resembled UK and US government positions, so too the Chinese Society of International Law's critical response to the South China Sea arbitration was published in the *Chinese Journal of International Law* as an academic study that closely resembled Chinese government positions. See further Bethlehem, 'Self-Defense'; Chinese Society of International Law, 'The South China Sea Arbitration Awards: A Critical Study' (2018) 17 *Chinese Journal of International Law* 207.

[179] S Seppänen, 'Performative Uses of Sovereignty in the Belt and Road Initiative' in Y Zhao (ed), *International Governance and the Rule of Law in China under the Belt and Road Initiative* (Cambridge: Cambridge University Press, 2018), 32.

[180] See, for example, the references to TWAIL scholarship in The Hague lectures of Judge Xue: see Xue, *Chinese Contemporary Perspectives on International Law*, 35–36, 257. See also Sornarajah and Wang, 'China, India, and International Law'.

imperialism through constituting new forms of spatial order.[181] Their use of Schmitt to critique US interventionism mirrors that of European international lawyers a decade earlier.[182] More broadly, Jiang portrays China's new developmental path as part of a 'glorious epic' acted out by generations of Chinese people on a 'great historical stage', founded upon the 'mutual absorption of Marxism and Chinese culture'.[183] Such narrating of history in contemporary Chinese international law argumentation positions China within world and communist history, drawing on its past contributions to 'the development of civilisation in East Asia' and its modern struggles against Western domination to produce a narrative of China's role in shaping 'the future of the civilisation of humanity at large'.[184] In these accounts, we get a sense of what a *Großraum* with Chinese characteristics might look like – one in which China will deliver a new regional order that ends American hegemony in Asia, draws inspiration from Confucian culture, Hegelian philosophy, and international communism, and represents those people who live in Third World states.

Studying the history of international law from the perspective of China requires more than simply expanding the scope of standard global histories.[185] As attending to the work that has been done in this field over the past decades makes clear, the inclusion of China in the histories of the twentieth century, including the history of international law, raises foundational questions about

---

[181] S Jiang, 'The Internal Logic of Super-Sized Political Entities: "Empire" and World Order' (trans D Ownby), available at www.readingthechinadream.com/jiang-shigong-empire-and-world-order.html; X Liu, 'New China and the End of American "International Law"' (2019) III (3) *American Affairs* 155. See further the discussion in Mitchell, 'Chinese Receptions of Carl Schmitt'. For the argument that US legal scholars have advocated a similar *Großraum*-based vision of international order through their formulation of legal norms underpinning new forms of regional policing, see Orford, 'NATO, Regionalism, and the Responsibility to Protect'.

[182] For a critical reflection on that use of Schmitt by European scholars, see M Koskenniemi, 'International Law as Political Theology: How to Read *Nomos der Erde?*' (2004) 11 *Constellations* 492.

[183] S Jiang, 'Philosophy and History: Interpreting the "Xi Jinping Era" through Xi's Report to the Nineteenth National Congress of the CCP', *The China Story*, 11 May 2018, available at www.thechinastory.org/cot/jiang-shigong-on-philosophy-and-history-interpreting-the-xi-jinping-era-through-xis-report-to-the-nineteenth-national-congress-of-the-ccp/.

[184] Jiang, 'Philosophy and History'.

[185] See, for example, the methodological questions raised in WP Alford, 'Law, Law, What Law? Why Western Scholars of Chinese History and Society Have Not Had More to Say About Its Law' (1997) 23 *Modern China* 398; M Dutton, *Policing Chinese Politics: A History* (Durham and London: Duke University Press, 2005); T Ruskola, 'China in the Age of the World Picture' in Orford and Hoffmann (eds), *The Oxford Handbook of the Theory of International Law*, 138 (noting that China 'is rarely, if ever, approached as a *theoretical* question' but that its inclusion should unsettle the historiography of international law); S Seppänen, *Ideological Conflict and the Rule of Law in Contemporary China: Useful Paradoxes* (Cambridge: Cambridge University Press, 2016); Jiang, 'Philosophy and History'.

philosophy and methodology. As Michael Dutton has argued, writing histories of China involves questions not only of substance but also of historiography – how should the story of political transformation in China be told?

Professional historians from the West who turn to China see it as part of their role 'to revisit and debunk' the 'model of historical causality' internal to the Chinese Community Party, which saw the 'idea of a "two-line struggle"' as the key to history.[186] That two-line struggle refers to Mao's thesis that the party was a unity of opposites and that without the two-line struggle against errone-ous ideas and the recognition that class struggle and contradictions between classes had their reflection within the party, the life of the party would come to an end. Dutton notes that leading historians from the West treat that as 'a simplistic and historically inaccurate method through which to analyse polit-ical history'.[187] As a result there is 'no recent contemporary political history of China', other than those histories written by members of the Communist Party, 'that does not reject the idea of the two-line struggle as a method for approaching the history of China'.[188]

Most professional historians agree that the best method for demonstrating the falsity of the two-line struggle as a heuristic for interpreting Chinese political history is simply 'to look at the historical facts' with 'the eye of an erudite scholar'.[189] Such work 'marshals the archival material to produce a dense and detailed portrait of elite politics that belies a simple binary inter-pretation'.[190] The resulting depoliticised histories produced by Western histor-ians 'replace politics with personality'.[191] The evidence then proves that history cannot be reduced to the two-line struggle. This is 'of course, historically speaking, absolutely correct'.[192] But is it correct to speak 'historically' about politics, particularly revolutionary politics? As Dutton argues, 'while history is more complex than this, politics is not'.[193] That mechanical rendering of the political in the form of individualist elite politics misses the intensity of the commitment politics organised around the two-line struggle or the friend/ enemy dyad that propelled revolutionary Chinese history.

The references to Schmitt in elite Chinese legal and philosophical argu-ment should serve to remind us that commitment politics 'produces the

---

[186] Dutton, *Policing Chinese Politics*, 311.
[187] Dutton, *Policing Chinese Politics*, 311.
[188] Dutton, *Policing Chinese Politics*, 311.
[189] Dutton, *Policing Chinese Politics*, 311.
[190] Dutton, *Policing Chinese Politics*, 312.
[191] Dutton, *Policing Chinese Politics*, 9.
[192] Dutton, *Policing Chinese Politics*, 213.
[193] Dutton, *Policing Chinese Politics*, 312.

intensity that propels history forward' precisely by removing complexity and reducing everything to the friend/enemy distinction.[194] It is worth being curious about rather than dismissive of that commitment politics when we study the history of international law from a Chinese perspective. When historians of China apply the allegedly apolitical methods of empiricist history to their studies, they bring with those methods a philosophy and indeed a politics that inevitably shapes the historical accounts they produce.

Empiricist historians take as given that history is made by innovating individuals and that 'the personalized machinations of the leadership group' rather than any form of commitment politics were the real engines of change throughout China's revolutionary decades.[195] At stake in the writing of those revisionist histories is a shift in the very concept of the political, from a revolutionary or collectivist conception of politics to one organised around the form of liberal individualism. The standard conventions of professional historiography that dominate the field assume the latter and thus impose an alien understanding onto a form of politics that was not narrated or experienced as the product of self-interested individuals. That revolutionary political binary may have been replaced by economic distinctions internally, yet it continues to inform narratives about China's historical role on the world stage. Understanding what that means for the present and future of international law requires taking the practice and self-understanding of Chinese lawyers and officials more seriously than the sceptical reason of dominant historiography allows.

2.5 FROM LAW TO HISTORY

In characterising the conditions that have shaped the turn to history in international law that began in the early 1990s, I have so far focused on those that involve 'the intertwined relationship between the identities of the legal scholar and the legal practitioner'.[196] Yet while the legal academy is integrated into the profession, it is also integrated into the modern university. International legal scholars are also in conversation with debates in the humanities and social sciences, and our work is enriched, influenced, and shaped by engaging with work from many other disciplines, among them sociology, philosophy, international relations, economics, anthropology, geography, literature, and history. This aspect of the situation of international

---

[194] Dutton, *Policing Chinese Politics*, 312.
[195] Dutton, *Policing Chinese Politics*, 314.
[196] Riles, 'Legal Amateurism', 500.

lawyers informs the second version of the turn to history in international law, which was shaped in part by the corresponding 'international turn' taken in the academic discipline of history. The growing awareness that the archives of international law represented an untapped resource for historians was part of that broader global turn in historical scholarship. Beginning in the second decade of the twentieth century, a group of historians began to produce work that explicitly presented itself as offering histories of an object called 'international law'. It is that quite different version of the turn to history in international law that I will examine in the next chapter.

3

History and the Turn to the International

This chapter explores a second set of scholarly trends that have been characterised as part of the turn to history in international law in the late twentieth
century. The claim that we witnessed a turn to history in international law
during that period can refer to two quite distinct projects of innovation and
renewal. On the one hand, international legal scholars and practitioners have
turned to the past as a resource for engaging in presentist arguments over the
promise or limitations of international law in the new geopolitical situation
taking shape following the end of the Cold War. That was the aspect of the
turn to history that I explored in Chapter 2.

The second tendency characterised as a turn to history in international law
has been heralded as offering a more professional orientation to engaging with
the past. Those involved in this version of the turn to history followed in the
wake of more politically charged debates, urging international lawyers to take
a less functional, less partisan, and less presentist interest in the history of their
field and to do so by adopting empiricist historical methods. The turn to
history as method treated the origin of international law and meaning of past
texts and practices as objective matters that could be established through
employing the proper scientific techniques.

The combined effect of the turn to history amongst international lawyers
and the turn to the global or the international amongst historians has been to
produce two streams of debate about the past of international law that have sat
alongside each other and at times intersected or overlapped. One stream saw
the turn to history as a means of intervening in a field of legal practice in the
present. The other saw the turn to history as a way of producing verifiable and
objective accounts of the past to correct and complete the flawed scholarship
of international lawyers. The two versions of the turn to writing histories of
international law were driven by different motivations, professional styles, and
scholarly ambitions.

My interest in this chapter is in the encounter between the two. As this chapter will show, that encounter has been increasingly dominated by a growing insistence that empiricist historical methods can produce professional and impartial interpretations of past texts, events, or concepts that can correct or complete the misuses of history in international legal argument. It is that meeting of empiricist historical methods with international legal argumentation that has come to offer a new foundation for formalism in international law.

3.1 TURNING TO THE INTERNATIONAL

The early twenty-first century saw historians take a growing interest in global, transnational, world, international, and imperial history,[1] while historians of political thought began to engage in and describe an 'international turn in intellectual history', 'a renaissance in the history of international thought', and the emergence of 'global intellectual history'.[2] Historians also began to undertake innovative research exploring the history of internationalism and international institutions.[3] Both the global turn in history and the international

---

[1] For reflections on the conditions, promises, and limits of that trend, see M van Ittersum and J Jacobs, 'Are We All Global Historians Now? An Interview with David Armitage' (2012) 36 *Itinerario* 7; L Hunt, *Writing History in the Global Era* (New York and London: WW Norton and Company, 2014); DA Bell, 'Questioning the Global Turn: The Case of the French Revolution' (2014) 37 *French Historical Studies* 1; J Adelman, 'What Is Global History Now?' *Aeon*, 2 March 2017: https://aeon.co/essays/is-global-history-still-possible-or-has-it-had-its-moment; R Drayton and D Motadel, 'Discussion: The Futures of Global History' (2018) 13 *Journal of Global History* 1; S Beckert and D Sachsenmaier (eds), *Global History, Globally* (London: Bloomsbury, 2018).

[2] D Armitage, 'The Fifty Years' Rift: Intellectual History and International Relations' (2004) 1 *Modern Intellectual History* 97, 108–109; S Moyn and A Sartori (eds), *Global Intellectual History* (New York: Columbia University Press, 2013); D Armitage, 'The International Turn in Intellectual History' in DM McMahon and S Moyn (eds), *Rethinking Modern European Intellectual History* (Oxford: Oxford University Press, 2014), 232; G Sluga, 'Turning International: *Foundations of Modern International Thought* and New Paradigms for Intellectual History' (2015) 41 *History of European Ideas* 103.

[3] See, for example, ALS Staples, *The Birth of Development: How the World Bank, Food and Agriculture Organization, and World Health Organization Changed the World, 1945–1965* (Kent: The Kent State University Press, 2006); S Amrith and G Sluga, 'New Histories of the United Nations' (2008) 19 *Journal of World History* 251; E Rothschild, 'The Archives of Universal History' (2008) 19 *Journal of World History* 375; M Mazower, *No Enchanted Palace: The End of Empire and the Ideological Origins of the United Nations* (Princeton: Princeton University Press, 2013); H Melber and C Stahn (eds), *Peace, Diplomacy, Global Justice, and International Agency: Rethinking Human Security and Ethics in the Spirit of Dag Hammarskjöld* (Cambridge: Cambridge University Press, 2014); S Pedersen, *The Guardians: The League of Nations and the Crisis of Empire* (Oxford: Oxford University Press, 2015);

turn in intellectual history fuelled a new interest in histories of international law and international relations and fed into ongoing discussions in those fields about the way in which the past was drawn upon to inform current debates.

The turn to the international and the global by historians had a strong effect on the scholarly landscape in the fields of international law and international relations. For international relations scholars, the theoretical and methodological influences upon historically oriented scholarship were and have remained diverse. Contextualist intellectual historians had a major influence on scholarship in international relations through reinterpretations of canonical texts and thinkers in the history of international thought,[4] and through a number of influential revisionist disciplinary histories.[5] Yet so too did scholars informed by, inter alia, historical materialism, Foucauldian genealogy, social

G Sluga and P Clavin (eds), *Internationalism: A Twentieth-Century History* (Cambridge: Cambridge University Press, 2017); G Scott-Smith and JS Rofe, *Global Perspectives on the Bretton Woods Conference and the Post-War World Order* (London: Palgrave Macmillan, 2017).

4　See, for example, J Tully, *An Approach to Political Philosophy: Locke in Contexts* (Cambridge: Cambridge University Press, 1993); K Tribe, *Strategies of Economic Order: German Economic Discourse 1750–1950* (Cambridge: Cambridge University Press, 1995); R Tuck, *The Rights of War and Peace: Political Thought and the International Order from Grotius to Kant* (Oxford: Oxford University Press, 1999); I Hont, *Jealousy of Trade: International Competition and the Nation-State in Historical Perspective* (Cambridge, MA: Harvard University Press, 2005); J Pitts, *A Turn to Empire: The Rise of Imperial Liberalism in Britain and France* (Princeton: Princeton University Press, 2005); D Bell (ed), *Victorian Visions of Global Order: Empire and International Relations in Nineteenth-Century Political Thought* (Cambridge: Cambridge University Press, 2007); P Borschberg, *Hugo Grotius, the Portuguese, and Free Trade in the East Indies* (Singapore: National University of Singapore Press, 2011); D Armitage, *Foundations of Modern International Thought* (Cambridge: Cambridge University Press, 2013).

5　For disciplinary histories of IR that drew on contextualist approaches, see P Wilson, 'The Myth of the "First Great Debate"' (1998) 24 *Review of International Studies* 1; G Holden, 'Who Contextualizes the Contextualizers? Disciplinary History and the Discourse about IR Discourse' (2002) 28 *Review of International Studies* 253; D Long and BC Schmidt (eds), *Imperialism and Internationalism in the Discipline of International Relations* (Albany: State University New York Press, 2005); J Quirk and D Vigneswaran, 'The Construction of an Edifice: The Story of a First Great Debate' (2005) 31 *Review of International Studies* 89; D Vigneswaran and J Quirk, 'Past Masters and Modern Inventions: Intellectual History as Critical Theory' (2010) 24 *International Relations* 107; O Wæver, 'The Speech Act of Realism: The Move That Made IR' in N Guilhot (ed), *The Invention of International Relations Theory* (New York: Columbia University Press, 2011), 97; R Devetak, *Critical International Theory: An Intellectual History* (Oxford: Oxford University Press, 2018). For other revisionist disciplinary histories of IR, see T Dunne, *Inventing International Society: A History of the English School* (Hampshire and New York: Palgrave, 1998); BC Schmidt, *The Political Discourse of Anarchy* (New York: State University New York Press, 1998); R Vitalis, *White World Order, Black Power Politics: The Birth of American International Relations* (Ithaca: Cornell University Press, 2015); N Guilhot, *After the Enlightenment: Political Realism and International Relations in the Mid-Twentieth Century* (Cambridge: Cambridge University Press, 2017).

history, constructivism, conceptual history, and reception theory.[6] Methodological debates in international relations scholarship subjected the claims of empiricist historians to critical scrutiny. The political nature of the struggle between the varied projects that can be pursued through engaging with history was overt, and the scholars involved were clear about the relation between theory, politics, and method.

For example, international relations scholars informed by historical materialism argued that the historical turn in international relations was largely based upon statist realist assumptions and ideological accounts of who are the agents of history and what are the social conditions of change.[7] The Weberian vision of politics informing much history of political thought was challenged for its too-ready acceptance of the liberal ideas about what counts as historically meaningful action underpinning Weber's sense of politics as a vocation.[8] Others noted that contextualist historians 'need to have something to contextualise in order to get the enquiry started', and that this 'something' was often the architecture already offered by the existing canon or material of

---

[6] For examples that illustrate the diversity of historically conscious work in international relations, see J Der Derian, *On Diplomacy: A Genealogy of Western Estrangement* (Oxford: Basil Blackwell, 1987); S Gill (ed), *Gramsci, Historical Materialism and International Relations* (Cambridge: Cambridge University Press, 1993); RBJ Walker, *Inside/Outside: International Relations as Political Theory* (Cambridge: Cambridge University Press, 1993); J Bartelson, *A Genealogy of Sovereignty* (Cambridge: Cambridge University Press, 1995); RL Doty, *The Politics of Representation in North–South Relations* (Minneapolis: University of Minnesota Press, 1996); A Linklater, *The Transformation of Political Community: Ethical Foundations of the Post-Westphalian Era* (Cambridge: Polity Press, 1998); E Keene, *Beyond the Anarchical Society: Grotius, Colonialism and Order in World Politics* (Cambridge: Cambridge University Press, 2002); J Haslam, *No Virtue Like Necessity: Realist Thought in International Relations since Machiavelli* (New Haven: Yale University Press, 2002); SM Amadae, *Rationalizing Capitalist Democracy* (Chicago: University of Chicago Press, 2003); B Buzan and G Lawson, *The Global Transformation: History, Modernity and the Making of Modern International Relations* (Cambridge: Cambridge University Press, 2015); P Owens, *Economy of Force: Counterinsurgency and the Historical Rise of the Social* (Cambridge: Cambridge University Press, 2015); P Owens, 'International Historical What?' (2016) 8 *International Theory* 448; T Dunne and C Reus-Smit (eds), *The Globalization of International Society* (Oxford: Oxford University Press, 2017); C Vergerio, 'Context, Reception, and the Study of Great Thinkers in International Relations' (2019) 11 *International Theory* 110.

[7] J Rosenberg, *The Empire of Civil Society: A Critique of the Realist Theory of International Relations* (London and New York: Verso, 1994); M Rupert and H Smith, *Historical Materialism and Globalization* (London and New York: Routledge, 2002); B Teschke, *The Myth of 1648: Class, Geopolitics and the Making of Modern International Relations* (London: Verso, 2003); R Shilliam, *German Thought and International Relations: The Rise and Fall of a Liberal Project* (Hampshire and New York: Palgrave Macmillan, 2009).

[8] S Eich and A Tooze, 'The Allure of Dark Times: Max Weber, Politics, and the Crisis of Historicism' (2017) 56 *History and Theory* 197.

the international relations tradition.[9] In addition, theorists noted that the tendency of revisionist disciplinary historians of international relations to mobilize anti-Whig arguments in order to produce a normative rehabilitation of realism fed into a broader presentist account of the statist nature of international relations – an account that both informed and was reproduced in those histories.[10]

In the field of international law, the situation has been somewhat different. The turn to history was accompanied by an intensifying insistence that any work engaging with the past of international law, where the past was understood very broadly to include 'past' texts, ideas, practices, cases, or concepts, should adopt specific empirical historical methods. Historians began to produce work that explicitly presented itself as correcting or completing the work of international lawyers or as contributing to debates about the historiography of an object called 'international law'.[11] That group was largely made up of historians from the East Coast of the United States, with a smattering of other historians based in Australia and the United Kingdom, whose previous work had focused on the history of political thought, histories of US or European foreign policy, or histories of empire and colonialism. The turn to the international was seen to 'open up a vast domain of international law' for

---

[9] E Keene, 'International Intellectual History and International Relations: Contexts, Canons and Mediocrities' (2017) 31 *International Relations* 341.

[10] N Guilhot, 'Portrait of the Realist as a Historian: On Anti-whiggism in the History of International Relations' (2015) 21 *European Journal of International Relations* 3.

[11] For examples of historical work that is explicitly presented as offering revisionist histories of international law or the historiography of international law, see S Moyn, *The Last Utopia: Human Rights in History* (Cambridge and London: Belknap Press, 2010), 176–211; J Pitts, 'Empire and Legal Universalisms in the Eighteenth Century' (2012) 117 *American Historical Review* 92; A Fitzmaurice, 'Liberalism and Empire in Nineteenth-Century International Law' (2012) 117 *American Historical Review* 92; IV Hull, *A Scrap of Paper: Breaking and Making International Law during the Great War* (Ithaca and London: Cornell University Press, 2014); J Pitts, 'The Critical History of International Law' (2015) 43 *Political Theory* 541; L Benton and L Ford, *Rage for Order: The British Empire and the Origins of International Law, 1800–1850* (Cambridge: Harvard University Press, 2016); I Hunter, 'About the Dialectical Historiography of International Law' (2016) 1 *Global Intellectual History* 1; S Moyn, 'Martti Koskenniemi and the Historiography of International Law in the Age of the War on Terror' in W Werner, M de Hoon, and A Galán (eds), *The Law of International Lawyers: Reading Martti Koskenniemi* (Cambridge: Cambridge University Press, 2016), 340; J Pitts, 'International Relations and the Critical History of International Law' (2017) 31 *International Relations* 282; J Pitts, *Boundaries of the International: Law and Empire* (Cambridge: Harvard University Press, 2018); Q Slobodian, *Globalists: The End of Empire and the Birth of Neoliberalism* (Cambridge: Harvard University Press, 2018); A Fitzmaurice, 'Context in the History of International Law' (2018) 20 *Journal of the History of International Law* 5; L Benton, 'Beyond Anachronism: Histories of International Law and Global Legal Politics' (2019) 21 *Journal of the History of International Law* 1.

historians to study,[12] while international institutions offered a new set of archives, practices, and techniques that could 'keep an army of graduate students and scholars busy for a long time'.[13]

3.2 HISTORY AS COMPLETION AND CORRECTION

Initially, it seemed serendipitous that international lawyers, legal historians, and historians more broadly were developing a collective interest in the past of international law. Not only did this offer areas of substantive overlap, but lawyers and historians seemed to have a common project – complicating overly simplistic accounts of the inevitability of a newly triumphant liberal international law. And indeed, as I outlined in Chapter 2, one of the reasons that many international legal scholars sought to engage with history was precisely as a means of complicating universalist or transcendental claims for the various transformations that international law began to undergo after the end of the Cold War.

Initially, critical scholarship engaging with past texts, events, practices, and concepts in ways that were innovative, self-reflexive, and methodologically heterogeneous was welcomed as part of a broader set of historically minded attempts to rethink the nature of international law as a profession, field, and discipline.[14] Yet as debates over history of international law and international institutions became more visible and contested, a growing number of historians of international law began to challenge the accounts of the past offered by international lawyers on methodological grounds. The earlier pluralism of the 1990s during which international law scholars had exuberantly embarked upon historically oriented projects was met with a swelling tide of responses from empiricist historians, who insisted that there were a set of canons with which legal scholars must comply in order to do proper historical work. Historians began to insist that the 'vast domain' offered by international law was one that not only could but must be studied using a given set of empiricist

---

[12] Fitzmaurice, 'Context in the History of International Law', 29.

[13] S Pedersen, 'Review Essay: Back to the League of Nations' (2007) 112 *The American Historical Review* 1091, at 1116.

[14] See, for example, the scholars included with the 'small international circle of international law historians' described in IJ Hueck, 'The Discipline of the History of International Law – New Trends and Methods on the History of International Law' (2001) 3 *Journal of the History of International Law* 194, at 208. The scholars listed there included Anthony Carty, Martti Koskenniemi, David Kennedy, Nathaniel Berman, Yasuaki Onuma, David Caron, Emmanuelle Tourmé-Jouannet, Randall Lesaffer, and Kinji Akashi. Only some of that group would be treated as engaged in methodologically correct historical research in the current climate.

historical techniques.[15] That turn to method would have significant effects for the conduct and reception of historically oriented work in the field of international law.

The argument for taking a more professional approach to the history of international law was initiated by legal historians, who equated professionalism with the adoption of a specific set of empiricist or contextualist historical techniques. International lawyers were accused of 'misusing' history, either to produce an instrumentalist form of 'foreign office international legal history' or in the service of manufacturing celebratory myths of origin. For example, David Bederman cautioned against the professional tendency to engage in what had been dismissively described elsewhere as 'law office history',[16] or in the case of international law, 'foreign office international legal history'.[17] Bederman expressed concern that 'international law advocacy and scholarship could be tainted' by 'improper historiographic methods'.[18] The problem as he saw it was that lawyers take up the past instrumentally in order to win an argument as advocates, and that as a result law office or foreign office history was distorted by the adversarial culture in which it was put to use. This criticism of the 'misuses' of the past by lawyers was in effect a 'criticism of forensic advocacy'.[19] Bederman instead called on legal scholars to adopt proper historical methods or 'best practices'.[20] At the same time, he noted that it was necessary to recognize the complicated situation of the lawyer. While '[a]s international lawyers we are called upon to "do" international legal history', it is also necessary to recognize that 'legal history and legal truth are not always the same thing, and they certainly cannot be ascertained by the same means and modalities'.[21]

Randall Lesaffer similarly cautioned 'the scholar studying the history of international law' to 'approach the past with proper respect', which 'means that he should make use of the basic rules of historical methodology'.[22] Lesaffer dismissed the 'deplorable' results of 'genealogic history from present to past' that 'leads to anachronistic interpretations of historical phenomena,

---

[15] Fitzmaurice, 'Context in the History of International Law', 29.

[16] AH Kelly, 'Clio and the Court: An Illicit Love Affair' (1965) 119 *Supreme Court Review* 121.

[17] DJ Bederman, 'Foreign Office International Legal History' in M Craven, M Fitzmaurice, and M Vogiatzi (eds), *Time, History, and International Law* (Leiden: Martinus Nijhoff, 2007), 43.

[18] Bederman, 'Foreign Office International Legal History', 46.

[19] JP Reid, 'Law and History' (1993) 27 *Loyola of Los Angeles Law Review* 193, at 203.

[20] Bederman, 'Foreign Office International Legal History', 43.

[21] Bederman, 'Foreign Office International Legal History', 62–63.

[22] R Lesaffer, 'International Law and Its History: The Story of an Unrequited Love' in M Craven, M Fitzmaurice, and M Vogiatzi (eds), *Time, History, and International Law* (Leiden: Martinus Nijhoff, 2007), 27, at 37.

clouds historical realities that bear no fruit in our own times and gives no information about the historical context of the phenomenon one claims to recognise'.[23] He noted the 'amateurism' of international lawyers when it came to history, which had been possible because '"professional" legal historians' had 'disdained to plough the field'.[24] Lesaffer called for a more professional engagement with the past of international law, where professionalisation was equated with adopting very specific historical methods, and for a clearer delimitation of the history of international law 'as a field and as a discipline'.[25] In arguing that 'the rudiments of classical historical methodology should be respected' by international lawyers, Lesaffer argued that this approach was 'what historians have been doing since the days of humanist scholarship: the textual and contextual analysis of their written sources'.[26]

The argument that international legal scholars were failing to comply with empiricist historical methods began to intensify in response to the emergence of postcolonial legal scholarship, particularly that of TWAIL scholars or lawyers exploring the legacies of imperialism in international law. TWAIL scholars were charged with having 'abandoned' the 'standards of historiographical analysis',[27] engaging in a 'whole new trend of *historical revisionism*' that produced 'simple but rather stunning' interpretations,[28] and constructing 'fanciful connections' between the modern discipline of international law and texts from earlier periods.[29] For the critics of postcolonial scholarship, the claim that there existed any tradition connecting earlier figures like Vitoria to modern international law involved 'assuming a false continuity and connectedness that is in fact the work of the interpreter's mind' and taking 'daring jumps' that destroy the 'complexity and pluralism of the discourses from various (and often very divergent) centuries'.[30]

In addition, the 'postcolonial complaints' of TWAIL scholars were cited as examples of 'whiggish international law' – that is, legal scholarship that failed to heed '[Herbert] Butterfield's admonishment about the retrospective

---

[23] Lesaffer, 'International Law and Its History', 34–35.

[24] Lesaffer, 'International Law and Its History', 35.

[25] Lesaffer, 'International Law and Its History', 41.

[26] Lesaffer, 'International Law and Its History', 38.

[27] P Zapatero, 'Legal Imagination in Vitoria: The Power of Ideas' (2009) 11 *Journal of the History of International Law* 221, at 268, 271.

[28] Zapatero, 'Legal Imagination in Vitoria', 268 (emphasis in original).

[29] G Cavallar, 'Vitoria, Grotius, Pufendorf, Wolff and Vattel: Accomplices of European Colonialism and Exploitation or True Cosmopolitans?' (2008) 10 *Journal of the History of International Law* 181, at 207.

[30] Cavallar, 'Accomplices of European Colonialism and Exploitation or True Cosmopolitans?', 207–208.

tendency toward pre-judgment' and engaged in 'selective and moralizing ratification' of presentist concerns.[31] While it may have 'become common-place to blame colonialism for the horrors of the present', such 'stories of good and evil are rarely satisfying'.[32] 'Fortunately', empiricist historians could offer 'other, better ways to take the measure of influence of . . . imperial formations in world history'.[33]

The most sustained critique of critical and postcolonial legal scholarship along these lines was made by an Australian intellectual historian, Ian Hunter. Hunter declared that the work of critical or postcolonial international law scholars was 'dogged by debilitating anachronism and "presentism"',[34] pre-sumed 'a single normative telos for the historiography of *jus naturae et gentium*',[35] and mistakenly assumed that 'there is a global principle of justice capable of including European and non-European peoples'.[36] According to Hunter, the 'tacitly universalist presumption sustaining this account' is that 'relations between European and New World peoples should and could have been rendered fair and just on the basis of a common global normative order'.[37] In addition, histories that traced the emergence of the international law profession to the late nineteenth century represented 'a tendentious mangling of the historical record' and 'in fact a factional cultural politics rather than scholarship'.[38]

The idea that mainstream lawyers had somehow misused or distorted history in ways that could be corrected by historians informed a new wave of revisionist international law histories. As disciplinary histories of international law and human rights began to develop into a more recognizable

---

[31] CR Rossi, *Whiggish International Law: Elihu Root, the Monroe Doctrine, and International Law in the Americas* (Leiden: Brill, 2019), 31. In Chapter 4 we will come back to the questions of who the Whigs were and why their way of writing history is considered so timelessly and acontextually bad that we still talk about it centuries after there have been any Whigs to write history.

[32] Benton and Ford, *Rage for Order*, 180.

[33] Benton and Ford, *Rage for Order*, 180.

[34] I Hunter, 'The Figure of Man and the Territorialisation of Justice in "Enlightenment" Natural Law: Pufendorf and Vattel' (2013) 23 *Intellectual History Review* 289.

[35] I Hunter, 'Vattel's Law of Nations: Diplomatic Casuistry for the Protestant Nation' (2010) 31 *Grotiana* 108, at 111–112.

[36] I Hunter, 'Global Justice and Regional Metaphysics: On the Critical History of the Law of Nature and Nations' in S Dorsett and I Hunter (eds), *Law and Politics in British Colonial Thought: Transpositions of Empire* (New York: Palgrave Macmillan, 2010), 11.

[37] Hunter, 'Global Justice and Regional Metaphysics', 13–14.

[38] Hunter, 'About the Dialectical Historiography of International Law', 19. That essay can be compared to Hunter's earlier treatment of Koskenniemi, in which he characterized *Gentle Civilizer* as 'an illuminating contextualization of international-law thought': I Hunter, 'Postmodernist Histories' (2009) 19 *Intellectual History Review* 265, at 266.

subdiscipline of historical work, the writing of such histories became increasingly conventional in terms of historical method. The truth claims of disciplinary histories were premised on being able to provide a more 'professional' form of history-writing than was offered by the self-mythologizing histories produced by those seeking to establish disciplinary myths of origin. International lawyers were characterised as having been engaged in 'myth-making rather than historical argument' and chided for 'smuggling in a kind of normative judgment in the form of historical narrative'.[39] Even as such histories revealed the constructed nature of the disciplines they were critiquing, they reinforced the claims to impartiality and verifiability of historical methods.[40]

To take one influential example, in his ground-breaking *The Last Utopia: Human Rights in History*, Samuel Moyn critiqued what he called the 'church history' of human rights offered by the American mainstream of liberal internationalists.[41] He argued that contemporary accounts of human rights had 'adopted a celebratory attitude toward the emergence and progress of human rights', 'recast world history as raw material for the progressive ascent of international human rights', and provided 'uplifting backstories' for 'recent enthusiasms'.[42] For Moyn, such narratives looked to history to 'provide the myths that the new movement wants or needs'.[43] He sought to correct 'the glaring confusions' that marred those attempts to find 'the "precursors" of human rights',[44] and to argue against the idea that human rights could be 'discovered rather than made in history'.[45]

When Moyn suggested that rights were 'made in history', he did not mean that they were made by historians or that we all construct the past as partisan actors in the present. Rather, he meant that human rights were made in the past by specific historical protagonists, 'people thinking and acting on their convictions' whose thought and actions could be studied. Moyn presented his work as a corrective – an 'alternative history' that revealed the 'true origins' of

---

[39] Pitts, 'The Critical History of International Law', 541, at 547.
[40] For the claim that disciplinary histories have had that effect more generally, see W Breckman, 'Intellectual History and the Interdisciplinary Ideal' in DM McMahon and S Moyn (eds), *Rethinking Modern European Intellectual History* (Oxford: Oxford University Press, 2014), 275, at 281.
[41] Moyn, *The Last Utopia*, 8.
[42] Moyn, *The Last Utopia*, 5.
[43] Moyn, *The Last Utopia*, 6.
[44] Moyn, *The Last Utopia*, 12
[45] Moyn, *The Last Utopia*, 6.

the human rights programme and its place in 'real history'.[46] His narrative sought to counter the 'misuse of history' by the church historians of rights, whose *longue durée* narrative 'distorts the past to suit the present'.[47] Moyn stressed the need for 'distinguishing the abuses from the uses of history' and differentiating between 'ideologues' who 'through selective evidence or misleading interpretation, betray the dead', and those who are 'anxious about the threat of anachronism' and respect the alterity of the past.[48]

The language used by those historians seeking to engage with international lawyers through the imposition of method was the empirical vocabulary of science. Historians pointed out elements of the history of international law or international relations that were not yet 'fully corrected' and presented historical work as capable of responding to 'unsystematic' assessments and offering studies that were 'balanced' in order to rectify the 'imbalance' of legal scholarship.[49] The 'distortions' produced by international lawyers' reliance on the wrong 'methods' could be corrected, and the 'problems' caused by such distortions resolved, through the adoption of 'better ways' to study the past.[50] Historical approaches to interpretation were presented as offering the means to 'uphold standards of veracity and verifiability'.[51] In such accounts, lawyers and historians were opposed, and that opposition was not founded upon the language of politics, struggle, or ideology, but rather – at least initially – upon the language of science. These accounts insisted that empiricist historical methods offered the benchmark or standard against which to measure the utility and propriety of legal scholarship.

In addition, historians suggested that there was something not only empirically wrong and intellectually unsophisticated but also morally questionable about what international lawyers did with the past. Along with references to the errors, flaws, and distortions produced by legal methods of interpretation, lawyers were challenged in language that suggested bad faith, partisanship, or indifference to the truth. International lawyers were accused of suspending 'empirical history altogether' in order to 'adopt a speculative or prophetic

---

[46] Moyn, *The Last Utopia*, 5, 7. For an alternative reading that resists the idea of Moyn as an 'orthodox historian' and interprets his reference to the 'true history' of human rights as a rhetorical strategy, see B Golder, 'Contemporary Legal Genealogies' in J Desautels-Stein and C Tomlins (eds), *Searching for Contemporary Legal Thought* (Cambridge: Cambridge University Press, 2017), 80, at 87.

[47] S Moyn, *Human Rights and the Uses of History* (2nd edition) (London: Verso, 2017), 1.

[48] Moyn, *Human Rights and the Uses of History*, xii.

[49] Benton and Ford, *Rage for Order*, 19, 209, 268, 270.

[50] Benton and Ford, *Rage for Order*, 202.

[51] Benton, 'Beyond Anachronism', 3.

stance' in the pursuit of a morally suspect 'academic anti-positivism'.[52] Legal scholarship exploring the relation of European imperialism and international law was mocked for adopting a 'self-congratulatory posture, allowing its exponents to bask in the glow of being on the right historical side'.[53] And international lawyers who questioned the capacity of historical method to guarantee the true meaning of past texts were seen to present 'new dangers'.[54]

While international lawyers were portrayed as misusing and distorting the past, historical work could employ professional methods to produce scrupulously accurate and impartial historical narratives. So Moyn promised to reveal the 'true origins' of human rights and their 'real history'.[55] Isabel Hull introduced her history of 'international law during the Great War' as a corrective to accounts that 'mislead us about what international law is and how it works, and about its relation to power and high politics'.[56] In so doing, she presented her scholarship as a challenge to 'self-styled "realists", international-legal skeptics, cynics, and pacifists'[57] that was nonetheless 'careful to avoid the anachronistic practice of reading backward'.[58] According to Lauren Benton and Lisa Ford, while other scholars of international law had imposed 'organizing rubrics' that offered 'oversimplified, but ever fashionable, proofs of imperial indifference' or 'the more uplifting but misleading fictions of the origins of human rights law', their work was an 'effort to capture the complexity of imperial legal change' and its relation to the history of international law.[59] Historical approaches to interpretation were presented as offering the means to resist 'the political manipulation of the past for present political purposes' and the growing 'indifference to the verifiability of political discourse' in contemporary culture.[60]

3.3 THE EMPIRICIST RULES OF THE HISTORICAL GAME

Central to these arguments was a set of claims about what 'the basic rules of historical methodology' in fact were. The claims that were invoked to critique contemporary international law scholarship turned around a core set of what

[52] Hunter, 'About the Dialectical Historiography of International Law', 7, 23.
[53] Hunter, 'The Figure of Man', 291.
[54] Fitzmaurice, 'Context in the History of International Law', 30.
[55] Moyn, *The Last Utopia*, 5, 7.
[56] Hull, *A Scrap of Paper*, 3.
[57] Hull, *A Scrap of Paper*, 322.
[58] Hull, *A Scrap of Paper*, x.
[59] Benton and Ford, *Rage for Order*, 25.
[60] Fitzmaurice, 'Context in the History of International Law', 13, 15, 30.

we might think of as empiricist dogmas that were treated as uncontroversial. At their heart were fundamental ideas about the nature of time, evidence, objectivity, and meaning.

The first, as we have seen, was the prohibition against the kind of 'debilitating anachronism' with which international legal scholarship was repeatedly diagnosed.[61] According to contextual historians, 'critiques of anachronism' were driven by the desire to avoid 'distorted understandings of the past'.[62] According to historians of international law, the prohibition of anachronism amounted only to 'the relatively innocuous methodological recommendation to use evidence-based findings of the past to inform legal analyses of the present'.[63] The claim that international legal argument must avoid anachronism would 'incite controversy only if one holds that historical evidence does not matter and that historical studies need not take account of it'.[64]

The second and related rule of methodology invoked in the debate over the turn to history was the call to contextualise legal texts. According to empiricist historians of international law, context determines meaning. All past texts are essentially historical, and their meaning can only be understood by locating them within the temporal context in which they were authored. To a degree, the idea that past texts, events, people, or artefacts should be placed in historical context in order to be understood is a commonplace of historical method. However, the stronger version of the claim – and the one brought into play in the debate over the history of international law – is that there is a single, defined context for every text. That context is the historical period in which the text was authored. It is that context, and not any broader tradition, that gives the text its meaning once and for all. According to Andrew Fitzmaurice, historians 'oppose themselves to anachronism' not because of any 'political commitment' but because of a philosophical perspective on how meaning is made: 'we can only reliably understand the meaning of a . . . text, through reconstructing the context' of its creation.[65]

That way of thinking about meaning assumes that the proper historical context for each text is given and self-evident. The study of that context should not be contaminated by other contexts, and particularly by the present context.

[61] Hunter, 'The Figure of Man', 289.
[62] Fitzmaurice, 'Context in the History of International Law', 15.
[63] Benton, 'Beyond Anachronism', 10.
[64] Benton, 'Beyond Anachronism', 10.
[65] Fitzmaurice, 'Context in the History of International Law', 13.

Historical time is an index of difference.[66] An object placed in its proper historical context will be different from the object placed in another context. In addition that approach assumes that the object and its context will resemble each other. Only particular thoughts are thinkable in any give historical context. As Lesaffer put this:

> We cannot correctly interpret a rule or dogma without knowing who made it ... Over the past decades, the 'Cambridge School of Political Thought' has made headway in the contextual study of historical political thought. Authors are studied from the perspective of their own life, their time and their context rather than from their impact on the future ... A similar approach should be made towards past law, and particularly historical jurisprudence and dogmatic history. It is only through the reconstruction of the historical context of the law that it can take on meaning outside the world of its own logic, or rather our present-day logic.[67]

The third methodological rule invoked in the turn to history debate was the prohibition against presentism. Presentism for historians refers to the tendency to interpret the past in terms of present interests, values, or concepts.[68] Its prohibition is driven by a concern 'with the use of the present as the lens through which we understand the past'.[69] While the past can inform the present, the present (which is dynamic, living, or in process) must not inform or contaminate the study of the past (which is static, dead, or finished). In the words of Lesaffer: 'The past does not change; if it does, it wasn't the past to begin with'.[70] Lawyers are routinely seen to have violated this rule, given that 'the interest displayed by international lawyers in their history is functional and dictated by current needs',[71] and almost all international lawyers 'look at history because they need it to better understand current issues and trends'.[72] Historians have criticised international lawyers for being dogged by presentism.[73]

---

[66] For a critical reflection on that assumption, see KM Parker, 'Repetition in History: Anglo-American Legal Debates and the Writings of Walter Bagehot' (2014) 4 *UC Irvine Law Review* 121, at 123.

[67] R Lesaffer, 'Law and History. Law between Past and Present' in B van Klink and S Taekema (eds), *Law and Method: Interdisciplinary Research into Law* (Tübingen: Mohr Siebeck, 2011), 133, at 151.

[68] Lynn Hunt, 'Against Presentism', *Perspectives on History* (May 2002).

[69] Fitzmaurice, 'Context in the History of International Law', 9.

[70] Lesaffer, 'Law and History', 152.

[71] Lesaffer, 'International Law and Its History', 29.

[72] Lesaffer, 'International Law and Its History', 33.

[73] Hunter, 'The Figure of Man', 289.

The fourth concern expressed by historians about international legal scholarship involved what the Cambridge historian Herbert Butterfield had referred to as 'abridgement' – the writing of narratives about the past that moved between periods or treated history 'on the broad scale'.[74] According to Butterfield, the attempt to do so produced 'what is really a gigantic optical illusion'.[75] Historians criticised the style of relating different temporal contexts that was adopted by international lawyers, referring disparagingly to lawyers making a 'mad dash' between periods,[76] or offering 'daring jumps' between 'divergent' centuries.[77] It was taken as given that there was something wrong with the 'mad dash' or 'daring jumps' involved in assembling material from different periods into arguments that were not structured around linear histories.

International lawyers appeared receptive to the idea that empiricist historical methods offered a set of technical rules to which legal scholars should conform when writing about the past. International legal scholars began to call out their colleagues for violating those rules. For example, international lawyers were criticised for displaying 'a tendency to anachronism' and urged to recognise 'the political importance of the critique of anachronism' and make 'efforts to avoid its most dangerous forms'.[78] International lawyers warned each other against committing 'the sin of anachronism' or creating the false sense that it might be 'possible to carry a timeless conversation on perennial problems between the living and the dead'.[79] International lawyers announced that 'the anachronistic tendencies of international law's use of history' should 'be both historicized and challenged'.[80] The critique of anachronism in international law was presented as a 'response to the ideological use of history, particularly that [which] Herbert Butterfield famously

---

[74] Butterfield, *The Whig Interpretation of History*, 15.

[75] Butterfield, *The Whig Interpretation of History*, 29. See further the discussion of Butterfield in Chapter 4.

[76] Benton and Ford, *Rage for Order*, 18.

[77] Cavallar, 'Accomplices of European Colonialism and Exploitation or True Cosmopolitans?', 208.

[78] K Purcell, 'On the Uses and Advantages of Genealogy for International Law' (2020) 33 *Leiden Journal of International Law* 13, at 14, 31, 35.

[79] M Koskenniemi, 'Histories of International Law: Dealing with Eurocentricity' (2011) 19 *Rechtsgeschichte* 152, at 166. See also M Koskenniemi, 'A History of International Law Histories' in B Fassbender and A Peters (eds), *The Oxford Handbook of the History of International Law* (Oxford: Oxford University Press, 2012), 943, at 969 (offering a 'word of caution' to international lawyers who seek to write 'a history of legal concepts or institutions that travel, as it were, unchanged through time' as that would be 'anachronistic').

[80] Purcell, 'On the Uses and Advantages of Genealogy', 31.

identified as "whiggish"'.[81] Postcolonial legal scholars were particularly singled out for embedding 'elements of anachronistic thinking or whiggish hanging judge narration' in their work,[82] or for producing historical narratives that 'neglect the complexity of the moment'.[83]

International lawyers also took up the prohibition against presentism, rebuking colleagues for their 'almost desultory present-centeredness'.[84] The resulting 'staged, pro-establishment or anti-imperial narratives' produced by lawyers worked 'to retrofit new circumstances' or 'moral values' into 'the old story'.[85] And international lawyers policed the work of legal colleagues that offered abridged accounts of history. International lawyers were accused of producing 'a sense of Whiggish preordination' by engaging in 'a cherry-picking of historical events', rather than tracing incremental shifts in meaning or focusing on the kind of compressed time scales that had become *de rigueur* in history faculties.[86] The effect was a 'loss of specificity and temporal sequence' in legal scholarship.[87] Such 'straight-line whiggish abridgments' may appeal due to their 'simplicity' and 'the promotion of ideology' but lead to 'a moral deterioration in the historical understanding of international law'.[88] 'Legal scholars, foreign policy analysts, court decisions and the judges who construct them, diplomats and academics who apply and interpret them' were all indicted for contributing to 'the articulation of a whiggish straight-line analysis and the attending abridgements of factual or contextual circumstance'.[89] The proper context within which to write about past texts was to consider their meaning for their 'contemporaries'.[90] International lawyers engaging with the past were advised to treat 'legal vocabularies and institutions as open-ended platforms on which contrasting meanings are projected at different periods, each complete in themselves'.[91]

---

[81] Purcell, 'On the Uses and Advantages of Genealogy', 29.

[82] Rossi, *Whiggish International Law*, 30–31.

[83] M Koskenniemi, 'Empire and International Law: The Real Spanish Contribution' (2011) 61 *University of Toronto Law Journal* 1, at 10–11.

[84] Rossi, *Whiggish International Law*, 34.

[85] Rossi, *Whiggish International Law*, 51.

[86] Rossi, *Whiggish International Law*, 34, 36.

[87] Rossi, *Whiggish International Law*, 31.

[88] Rossi, *Whiggish International Law*, 38, 51.

[89] Rossi, *Whiggish International Law*, 195.

[90] Koskenniemi, 'A History of International Law Histories', 969.

[91] Koskenniemi, 'A History of International Law Histories', 969.

More broadly, international legal scholars chastised each other for lacking 'awareness of historiographical methods',[92] or for being 'rarely and often superficially engaged' with historiography.[93] International lawyers were told they should map and 'clarify the range of available options' made available by historians, from which they could then choose the appropriate method for the next job.[94] As 'there can be no central body for the imposition' of the 'professional standards of international legal history', it was up to international legal scholars to stop producing research that was 'tainted' by 'improper historiographic methods' and 'to pass judgment on what are, and what are not, legitimate and proper techniques of historiography' for international law.[95] '[S]cholars and practitioners of international law' were urged to adopt the 'attitude of suspicion' made possible by 'far-ranging historical investigation'.[96]

Overall, as the turn to history in international law intensified, the legitimacy of empiricist historical rules was increasingly treated as given and the application of those rules to international law treated as unquestionable. Any debate over the utility or propriety of applying these methods to law was a trivial diversion: 'contextualism in history stands for nothing more than a commitment to empirically careful study that treats political thought as an activity open to investigation and interpretation alongside other historical phenomena'.[97] The 'deeply flawed debates' over empiricist historical methods merely served as 'distractions from weightier discussions'.[98] It was widely agreed that historians had something to teach international lawyers, usually by explaining more slowly and carefully that anachronism and presentism were bad, contextualising was good, time flowed from past to present in a linear, unidirectional fashion, and texts had definable contexts and specific authors whose historically available intentions reflected in historical evidence offered a guide to the true meaning of law.

3.4 CHALLENGING EMPIRICIST HISTORIOGRAPHY

If one attended only to the debate playing out in relation to international law, it would seem that international lawyers were the first scholars ever to question

---

[92] V Vadi, 'International Law and Its Histories: Methodological Risks and Opportunities' (2017) 58 *Harvard International Law Journal* 311, at 320.

[93] M Clark, 'Ambivalence, Anxieties/Adaptation, Advances: Conceptual History and International Law' (2018) 31 *Leiden Journal of International Law* 747, at 757.

[94] Vadi, 'International Law and Its Histories', 334.

[95] Bederman, 'Foreign Office International Legal History', 63.

[96] Purcell, 'On the Uses and Advantages of Genealogy', 35.

[97] Benton, 'Beyond Anachronism', 28.

[98] Benton, 'Beyond Anachronism', 1–2.

the self-evident nature of concepts such as 'context' or 'anachronism'. Yet there has been a lively debate playing out for some time amongst historians, philosophers, literary scholars, art historians, postcolonial theorists, and anthropologists challenging the concepts of 'context', 'anachronism', and 'presentism' that have been so self-confidently wielded in the debate over method in international law.

For example, work questioning the self-evidence of anachronism as an 'error' has become a widespread contribution to debates about the utility of current historical orthodoxies.[99] As the 'chronism' in anachronism indicates, the criticism of anachronism is premised upon a theory of time as 'chronos' – something akin to a naturally existing medium that flows in a uniform fashion from past to present and within which history unfolds. In the words of Lesaffer, 'the clock [should] always run forward', to avoid the risk of legal history 'deforming' and becoming 'some kind of genealogy of modern practices'.[100] To commit the sin of anachronism is to place an object in the wrong time. Critical scholars, however, have noted that the representation of chronological time as moving steadily in one direction 'from before to after' or 'as a series of points strung along a line' is itself historically situated and 'an effect of its figurations'.[101] That scholarship explores the historically specific notions of time or chrono-logics that underpin the idea of anachronism.

Others have resisted the imposition of 'heterotemporality' on the past,[102] attempted to loosen the hold of a linear conception of time in the form of 'chronology' on our thinking,[103] and more broadly argued that 'the truth of anachronism' is 'worth defending'.[104] Postcolonial theorists, literary theorists,

---

[99] For examples of work questioning the self-evidence of anachronism as an error, see N Loraux, 'Éloge d'anachronisme en histoire' (1993) 27 *Le Genre Humain* 23; J Rancière, 'Le concept d'anachronisme et la vérité de l'historien' (1996) 6 *L'Inactuel: Psychoanalyse & Culture* 53 (republished as J Rancière, 'The Concept of Anachronism and the Historian's Truth' (2015) 3 *In/Print* 21); G Didi-Huberman, *Devant le temps: histoire de l'art et anachronism des images* (Paris: Les Éditions de Minuit, 2000); M de Grazia, 'Anachronism' in B Cummings and J Simpson (eds), *Cultural Reformations: Medieval and Renaissance in Literary History* (Oxford: Oxford University Press, 2010), 13; A Nagel and CS Wood, *Anachronic Renaissance* (New York: Zone Books, 2012); S Palfrey, 'The Truth of Anachronism' in S Palfrey, *Shakespeare's Possible Worlds* (Cambridge: Cambridge University Press, 2014), 147; M Rubin, 'Presentism's Useful Anachronisms' (2017) 234 *Past and Present* 236.

[100] Lesaffer, 'Law and History', 147–148.

[101] Nagel and Wood, *Anachronic Renaissance*, 9. See further Chapter 4 for a detailed exploration of the critical work done by art historians to unsettle the myth of Italian Renaissance humanism and its triumph over anachronism.

[102] D Chakrabarty, *Provincializing Europe: Postcolonial Thought and Historical Difference* (Princeton: Princeton University Press, 2000), 8.

[103] de Grazia, 'Anachronism', 32.

[104] Palfrey, 'The Truth of Anachronism', 147–159.

queer theorists, and heterodox historians have gone so far as to 'celebrate anachronism as a visible site of dislocation of what counts as timely and what constitutes history',[105] while anthropologists and philosophers of history continue to put into question the 'regimes of historicity' underpinning mainstream historical methods and to argue that the charge of anachronism operates as a political dismissal of expressions of time that do not conform to the order of a linear chronology.[106]

In addition, historians have argued for the need to revisit the contained scale that has dominated Anglo-American history-writing and urged a return to *longue durée* approaches in order to make sense of global transformations such as growing inequality or climate change.[107] The challenge to assumptions that the temporal context for a text or artwork is narrow, contained, or self-evident has become a key feature of attempts to develop more diverse historical methods.[108] And numerous historians and lawyers have produced

---

[105] ML Mullen, 'Anachronism' (2018) 46 *Victorian Literature and Culture* 567.

[106] E Hirsch and C Stewart, 'Introduction: Ethnographies of Historicity' (2005) 16 *History and Anthropology* 261; H Harootunian, *Marx after Marx: History and Time in the Expansion of Capitalism* (New York: Columbia University Press, 2015), 22–24; C Stewart, 'History and Anthropology' (2016) 45 *Annual Review of Anthropology* 79; M Hodges, 'History's Impasse: Radical Historiography, Leftist Elites, and the Anthropology of Historicism in Southern France' (2019) 60 *Current Anthropology* 391. The concept of 'regimes of historicity' is taken from François Hartog, although he takes a more historically orthodox approach to the question of presentism than I do: F Hartog, *Regimes of Historicity: Presentism and Experiences of Time* (New York: Columbia University Press, 2015).

[107] J Guldi and D Armitage, *The History Manifesto* (Cambridge: Cambridge University Press, 2014); D Chakrabarty, 'Planetary Crises and the Difficulty of Being Modern' (2018) 46 *Millennium* 259.

[108] For examples of scholarship complicating the role played by 'context' in historiographic debates, see D LaCapra, *Rethinking Intellectual History: Texts, Contexts, Language* (Ithaca and London: Cornell University Press, 1983); P Burke, 'Context in Context' (2002) 8 *Common Knowledge* 152; B Young, 'The Tyranny of the Definite Article: Some Thoughts on the Art of Intellectual History' (2002) 28 *History of European Ideas* 101; M Bevir, 'The Role of Contexts in Understanding and Explanation' (2000) 23 *Human Studies* 395; R Felski, '"Context Stinks!"' (2011) 42 *New Literary History* 573; M Jay, 'Historical Explanation and the Event: Reflections on the Limits of Contextualization' (2011) 42 *New Literary History* 557; P Kelly, 'Rescuing Political Theory from the Tyranny of History' in J Floyd and M Stears (eds), *Political Philosophy versus History? Contextualism and Real Politics in Contemporary Political Thought* (Cambridge: Cambridge University Press, 2011); C Tomlins, 'After Critical Legal History: Scope, Scale, Structure' (2012) 8 *Annual Review of Law and Social Science* 31; D Armitage, 'What's the Big Idea? Intellectual History and the *Longue Durée*' (2012) 38 *History of European Ideas* 493; PE Gordon, 'Contextualism and Criticism in the History of Ideas' in DM McMahon and S Moyn (eds), *Rethinking Modern European Intellectual History* (Oxford: Oxford University Press, 2014), 32; S Moyn, 'Imaginary Intellectual History' in DM McMahon and S Moyn (eds), *Rethinking Modern European Intellectual History* (Oxford: Oxford University Press, 2014), 112; Guldi and Armitage, *The History Manifesto*; Keene, 'International Intellectual History and International Relations', 341; E Kleinberg, J Wallach Scott, and

sophisticated reflections about the ways that interdisciplinary work across law and history unsettles the methodological certainties of both fields.[109]

More broadly, historians have begun to express concern about the ways in which a demand for conformity with specific empiricist conventions is deployed within the field of academic history.[110] In *The History Manifesto*, for example, Jo Guldi and David Armitage questioned the particular 'training in thinking about time' that has dominated Anglophone history departments since the 1970s. They pointed particularly to the insistence on 'micro-histories', a genre borrowed from the Italian academy where it had been linked to the study of larger political and social questions, but which in the Anglophone academy 'produced a habit of writing that depended upon shorter and shorter

---

G Wilder, *Theses on Theory and History* (Wild on Collective, May 2018); R Parfitt, *The Process of International Legal Reproduction: Inequality, Historiography, Resistance* (Cambridge: Cambridge University Press, 2019).

[109] For examples from a broad literature, see Reid, 'Law and History', 193; WW Pue, 'In Pursuit of Better Myth: Lawyers' Histories and Histories of Lawyers' (1995) 33 *Alberta Law Review* 732; WW Fisher III, 'Texts and Contexts: The Application to American Legal History of the Methodologies of Intellectual History' (1997) 49 *Stanford Law Review* 1065; RW Gordon, 'Foreword: The Arrival of Critical Historicism' (1997) 49 *Stanford Law Review* 10; N Berman, 'In the Wake of Empire' (1998–1999) 14 *American University International Law Review* 1521; D Sugarman and WW Pue, 'Introduction: Towards a Cultural History of Lawyers' in WW Pue and D Sugarman (eds), *Lawyers and Vampires: Cultural Histories of Legal Professions* (Oxford: Hart, 2003), 1; A Carty and R Smith, *Sir Gerald Fitzmaurice and the World Crisis: A Legal Advisor in the Foreign Office 1932–1945* (The Hague: Kluwer, 2000), 1–36; D Ibbetson, 'What Is Legal History a History Of?' in A Lewis and M Lobban (eds), *Law and History* (Oxford: Oxford University Press, 2004), 33; C Fasolt, *The Limits of History* (Chicago: University of Chicago Press, 2004); A Carty, 'Visions of the Past of International Society: Law, History or Politics?' (2006) 69 *Modern Law Review* 644; A Curthoys, A Genovese, and A Reilly, *Rights and Redemption: History, Law and Indigenous People* (Sydney: University of New South Wales Press, 2008); KM Parker, 'Law "In" and "As" History: The Common Law in the American Polity, 1790–1900' (2011) 1 *UC Irvine Law Review* 587; A Carty, 'Doctrine versus State Practice' in B Fassbender and A Peters (eds), *The Oxford Handbook of the History of International Law* (Oxford: Oxford University Press, 2012), 973; Tomlins, 'After Critical Legal History', 31; R Parfitt, 'The Spectre of Sources' (2014) 25 *European Journal of International Law* 297; Parker, 'Repetition in History'; RH Fallon Jr 'The Meaning of Legal "Meaning" and Its Implications for Theories of Legal Interpretation' (2015) 82 *The University of Chicago Law Review* 1235; S McVeigh, 'Afterword: Office and the Conduct of the Minor Jurisprudent' (2015) 5 *UC Irvine Law Review* 499; H Irving, 'Outsourcing the Law: History and the Disciplinary Limits of Constitutional Reasoning' (2015) 84 *Fordham Law Review* 957; RW Gordon, *Taming the Past: Essays on Law in History and History in Law* (Stanford: Stanford University Press, 2017); E Cavanagh, 'Legal Thought and Empires: Analogies, Principles, and Authorities from the Ancients to the Moderns' (2019) 10 *Jurisprudence* 463; Parfitt, *The Process of International Legal Reproduction*.

[110] J Guldi and D Armitage, *The History Manifesto* (Cambridge: Cambridge University Press, 2015), 49.

time-scales and more and more intensive use of archives'.[111] Increasing specialisation had resulted in a shift in the university training of historians, with
doctoral students urged to narrow their research questions temporally and
spatially 'in favour of ever tighter rhetorical and temporal contextualisation'.[112]
They pointed to a similar reaction against 'various long-range tendencies in
the field' that had emerged in intellectual history.[113] Guldi and Armitage
commented that students were being taught 'to emulate the specialisation of
a society run by experts, each of whom competes in terms of narrowness with
others in their field'.[114] Doctoral students were urged 'to narrow, not to
broaden, their focus on place and time', and 'time-scales of between five
and fifty years became the model' for work perceived as ground-breaking.[115]
The resulting historical game 'rewarded intensive subdivision of knowledge'
and led to what Guldi and Armitage termed 'the triumph of the short *durée*'.[116]
Their summary of both the conditions seen as evidencing technical mastery of
the discipline and the resulting effects on historical scholarship resonated with
the situation taking shape as historians began to impose those dogmas in
international law.

> The combination of archival mastery, micro-history, and an emphasis on
> contingency and context, powered by a suspicion of grand narratives, a
> hostility to whiggish teleologies, and an ever-advancing anti-essentialism,
> determined an increasing focus on the synchronic and the short-term across
> wide swathes of the historical profession.[117]

In their *Theses on Theory and History*, the historians Ethan Kleinberg, Joan
Wallach Scott, and Gary Wilder expressed a related concern about the way in
which an 'obsession' with empiricist methodology as the measure of historical
competence on the part of the field's 'gatekeepers' was working to normalise and
reinforce an 'anti-theoretical and unreflexive orientation' amongst historians.[118]
They argued that academic history was committed to an eighteenth-century
vision of itself as an 'empiricist enterprise' committed to a 'scientistic method
intrinsically linked to positivism', or what Horkheimer called 'modern empiricism'.[119] The dominant commitment in academic history was to that 'method of

---

[111] Guldi and Armitage, *The History Manifesto*, 46.
[112] Guldi, and Armitage, *The History Manifesto*, 48.
[113] Guldi and Armitage, *The History Manifesto*, 47.
[114] Guldi and Armitage, *The History Manifesto*, 51.
[115] Guldi and Armitage, *The History Manifesto*, 45.
[116] Guldi and Armitage, *The History Manifesto*, 52.
[117] Guldi and Armitage, *The History Manifesto*, 54.
[118] Kleinberg, Scott, and Wilder, *Theses on Theory and History*, 1, 4.
[119] Kleinberg, Scott, and Wilder, *Theses on Theory and History*, 1.

gathering facts in order to produce interpretations by referring them to sup-posedly given contexts and organizing them into chronological narratives'.[120]

The result was a form of 'methodological fetishism' that treated 'reified appearances (i.e. immediately observable, preferably archival, evidence) as embodying the real and containing the truth of social relations'.[121] Kleinberg, Scott, and Wilder argued that the field 'evaluates scholarship based on whether this empiricist method has been capably employed', with the effect of reinforcing 'the scholarly and political status quo'.[122] The fact that historians 'typically write for other professional historians, paying special attention to the disciplinary norms and gatekeepers upon which career advancement depends' meant that empiricist methods were able to exercise a tight hold on the academic history field, with the 'disciplined' being 'rewarded by the guild' and 'the innovators' being 'punished'.[123] Kleinberg, Scott, and Wilder noted that debates over method were treated as trivial, precisely because the empiricists failed to acknowledge that the 'preoccupa-tion with empirical facts and realist argument' was founded upon 'a set of uninterrogated theoretical assumptions about time and place, intention and agency, proximity and causality, context and chronology'.[124] While their argument was primarily directed to historians, Kleinberg, Scott, and Wilder explained that one of their intentions in writing the *Theses* was 'reminding scholars in other fields that professional history does not possess a monopoly on modes of historical thinking or means of historical insight'.[125]

Yet little if any of that scholarship registered in debates about historiography in international law, where empiricist historians and the international lawyers who adopted their approaches continued to insist on the propriety of a narrow set of methodological dogmas for scholarship that engages with the past in international law. The literature questioning the assumptions underpinning concepts such as 'context' or 'anachronism' has not been taken up in the field of international law with anything approaching the level of enthusiasm, cer-tainty, or interest that has greeted claims that ideas need to be placed in their context or the denunciations of presentism and anachronism. As is often the case with the field of law, it is not the methods of critical or heterodox scholars

---

[120] Kleinberg, Scott, and Wilder, *Theses on Theory and History*, 1.
[121] Kleinberg, Scott, and Wilder, *Theses on Theory and History*, 1.
[122] Kleinberg, Scott, and Wilder, *Theses on Theory and History*, 1, 5.
[123] Kleinberg, Scott, and Wilder, *Theses on Theory and History*, 1–2.
[124] Kleinberg, Scott, and Wilder, *Theses on Theory and History*, 5.
[125] E Kleinberg, JW Scott, and G Wilder, 'From the Authors of the "Theses on Theory and History"', *In the Moment Blog*, 10 July 2018, available at https://critinq.wordpress.com/2018/07/10/from-the-authors-of-the-theses-on-theory-and-history/.

that have been introduced as standards, best practices, or rules of engagement. Very specific understandings of temporality, change, evidence, and meaning were being transposed from empiricist historiography to international law by those seeking to stamp out anachronism or presentism, with no recognition of the criticisms of and challenges to those understandings within and beyond the discipline of history. Those challenges seem not to have shaken the confidence with which international lawyers were presented with a set of rules to be followed in order to comply with proper historical methods.

Instead, the turn to international law was seen to offer new archives, practices, institutions, or figures, which could be studied by historians using a given set of techniques that were already in place. There was almost no sense that the attempt to understand and study the practices of international legal argumentation might *unsettle* the methods already developed by historians. Rather, the turn to international law seemed to shore up the certainty with which many historians and international lawyers went to work with a set of established empiricist methods. While, as we have seen, intense debates about historiography continue unabated amongst historians, engagement with law seemed to provide a reassuring ground on which to reassert conventional empiricist methods and, perhaps more surprisingly, to propose those methods as if to do so were somehow revolutionary. Historical work was presented as offering verified techniques for correcting or completing the amateurish approach that lawyers took to the past.

In contrast, the lack of sustained challenges to the axioms of empiricist historiography in international law shored up the status of history as a master interpretative discipline that was capable of producing verifiable and impartial accounts of international law. The 'tone of certainty' in which these historians described both the virtue of their own methods and the constructed nature of everyone else's truth claims seemed to leave historical method as the last remaining procedure of verification.[126] They claimed that international lawyers who questioned the universal applicability of empiricist historical rules across time, space, and situation revealed only ignorance or a 'misunderstanding' of historical methods rather than raising any deeper philosophical, analytical, or political concerns.[127]

---

[126] For a related argument describing the 'tone of certainty' adopted in the field of art history, see G Didi-Huberman, *Confronting Images: Questioning the Ends of a Certain History of Art* (trans John Goodman) (University Park: The Pennsylvania State University Press, 2005 [1990]), 2.

[127] Fitzmaurice, 'Context in the History of International Law', 15 ('critiques of the contextual methodology of the Cambridge School approach to the history of international law from within the discipline itself are based upon a misunderstanding of the contextual methodology'); Benton, 'Beyond Anachronism', 2 ('debate about the merits of historical methods in the study

3.5 INTERPRETATION AND THE CAMBRIDGE SCHOOL

The methodological tenets being proposed for international law as part of the turn to history debate have been strongly championed by proponents of the Cambridge School or 'contextualist' approach to the history of political thought. I borrow the idea of a 'Cambridge School' from historians, who began to identify the existence of such a school in the 1970s.[128] The reference to a Cambridge School in the history of political thought is usually taken to include at least the work of JGA Pocock, Quentin Skinner, and John Dunn.

of international law' is based on a 'fundamental misunderstanding'); Purcell, 'On the Uses and Advantages of Genealogy', 23 (questions about the 'critique of anachronism' are based on a 'misunderstanding').

[128] S James, 'JGA Pocock and the Idea of the "Cambridge School" in the History of Political Thought' (2019) 45 *History of European Ideas* 83 (dating the first use of the term 'Cambridge School' to 1973). For discussions of the common methodological enterprise in which scholars associated with the Cambridge School have understood themselves to be engaged, see J Tully (ed), *Meaning and Context: Quentin Skinner and His Critics* (Princeton: Princeton University Press, 1988); N Phillipson and Q Skinner, 'Preface' in *Political Discourse in Early Modern Britain* (Cambridge: Cambridge University Press, 1993), xii (referring to the 1960s as 'the beginning of a revolution in our ways of thinking about the history of political theory'); J Dunn, *The History of Political Theory and Other Essays* (Cambridge: Cambridge University Press, 1996), 11; DSA Bell, 'The Cambridge School and World Politics: Critical Theory, History and Conceptual Change', *The Global Site*, 2001, 5 ('During the 1960's a number of young historians, either based in or trained at Cambridge University, helped to re-orient the study of the history of political thought. Three scholars in particular stand out in this endeavor, namely J.G.A Pocock, John Dunn and Quentin Skinner. For the sake of convenience, and following convention, I will term these authors representatives of the "Cambridge School" methodology'); D Runciman, 'History of Political Thought: The State of the Discipline' (2001) 3 *British Journal of Politics and International Relations* 84 (arguing that the history of political thought exists 'in the shadow of the great methodological argument that began in the 1960s' and the 'triumphant methodology' developed by the 'group of historians who have become known as the Cambridge School'); JGA Pocock, 'Foundations and Moments' in A Brett and J Tully with H Hamilton-Bleakley (eds), *Rethinking the Foundations of Modern Political Thought* (Cambridge: Cambridge University Press, 2006), 37 (describing himself as being 'present at the creation . . . of the enterprise of which Skinner has become the leader'); JGA Pocock, *Political Thought and History: Essays on Theory and Method* (Cambridge: Cambridge University Press, 2008), vii ('A certain method, or procedure, for defining political thought and studying its history – alternatively, for studying it in history – has been formed and practised . . . at Cambridge and other universities, and is so far associated with the first of these that it is often known by its name'); R Bourke, 'The Cambridge School', 2016, https://projects.history.qmul.ac .uk/hpt/2016/06/27/interview-with-richard-bourke-on-the-cambridge-school-for-the-iranian-journal-farhangemrooz-todays-culture/ ('The existence of a "Cambridge School" was first identified by JGA Pocock in the early 1970s . . . The practitioners whom Pocock had in mind as exemplary members of this School included himself, Quentin Skinner and John Dunn . . . [O]ne thing that distinguishes Pocock, Skinner and Dunn from their predecessors was a determination, at least in the 1960s and 1970s, to justify their procedures in terms of self-conscious methodology. It was above all Skinner who made this terrain his own').

Predecessors are variously taken to include Herbert Butterfield, Peter Laslett, John Burrow, and Duncan Forbes, and later scholars whose work is often characterised as related to the Cambridge School include Richard Tuck, Istvan Hont, James Tully, Annabel Brett, Duncan Bell, Andrew Fitzmaurice, and Jennifer Pitts. In addition, David Armitage, who has sought to rethink contextualist methods in ways that have great purchase for international law, works within and against the Cambridge School tradition. As in many such attempts to characterize an intellectual movement, whether there is such a School, and if so what its adherents agree upon, is debated.[129] Nonetheless, it is useful to focus on the account of method articulated by scholars associated with the Cambridge School for a number of reasons.

First, the approach developed by the Cambridge School has informed many of the methodological arguments being made in the fields of international law and international relations with which this book is concerned. The methodological correctives proposed by scholars such as Bell, Hunter, Lesaffer, Pitts, Fitzmaurice, and Richard Devetak explicitly draw upon the arguments of Skinner or contextualist historians more broadly.[130] Those scholars have referred to Cambridge School methodology both in the process of explaining the limitations of existing approaches to engaging with the past in international relations and international law, and in elaborating the methods needed to replace those approaches.

In addition, many of the new historical studies in international law and international relations have drawn upon a Cambridge School or contextualist approach to shape their practice. For example, contextualist intellectual

---

[129] For example, Richard Bourke describes Istvan Hont being flown in to introduce a Japanese audience to 'the finer points of the distinctively "Cambridge" approach to intellectual history' and then 'insisting that no such school existed': R Bourke, 'Revising the Cambridge School: Republicanism Revisited' (2018) 46 *Political Theory* 467.

[130] See, for example, Bell, 'The Cambridge School and World Politics'; DSA Bell, 'International Relations: The Dawn of a Historiographical Turn?' (2001) 3 *British Journal of Politics and International Relations* 115; Lesaffer, 'Law and History'; Pitts, 'The Critical History of International Law', 541; R Devetak and R Walter, 'The Critical Theorist's Labour: Empirical or Philosophical Historiography for International Relations?' (2016) 13 *Globalizations* 520; R Devetak, '"The Battle Is All There Is": Philosophy and History in International Relations Theory' (2017) 31 *International Relations* 261; Pitts, 'International Relations and the Critical History of International Law', 282; Fitzmaurice, 'Context in the History of International Law'; Devetak, *Critical International Theory*. For Hunter's articles relating his approach to that of Pocock, Skinner, and contextualist historians, see I Hunter, 'The History of Philosophy and the Persona of the Philosopher' (2007) 4 *Modern Intellectual History* 571; I Hunter, 'Natural Law, Historiography, and Aboriginal Sovereignty' (2007) 11 *Legal History* 137; I Hunter, 'Talking about My Generation' (2008) 34 *Critical Inquiry* 583; Hunter, 'Postmodernist Histories'; I Hunter, 'The Contest over Context in Intellectual History' (2019) 58 *History and Theory* 185.

historians have had a major influence on scholarship in the discipline of international relations through the development of revisionist disciplinary histories of that field.[131] Scholars informed by the contextualist history of political thought have also offered influential reinterpretations of key texts, concepts, or figures in the international law and international relations canons.[132] Influential international law scholars such as Martti Koskenniemi have suggested that studies by scholars such as Skinner and Tuck associated with the 'Cambridge School' offer a model for the kind of work that is needed 'to contextualise the legal ideologies or concepts within the intellectual, social, and political environment in which they have operated' and develop an 'intellectual history' of international law,[133] and pointed to the significance of contextualist histories of early modern political thought by Tuck, Hunter, and Brett for thinking about international law.[134]

Perhaps most importantly, the methodological manifestos associated with the proponents of the Cambridge School approach have provided the clearest, most compelling, most influential, and at times most polemical accounts of why the extension of particular kinds of empiricist historical methods from the interpretation of past events or figures to the interpretation of 'past' ideas, texts, or thought is not only desirable but necessary.[135] The commitment to

---

[131] For disciplinary histories of IR that drew on contextualist approaches, see the references cited in footnote 5.

[132] See, for example, Tully, *An Approach to Political Philosophy*; Tribe, *Strategies of Economic Order*; Tuck, *The Rights of War and Peace*; JE Nijman, *The Concept of International Legal Personality: An Inquiry into the History and Theory of International Law* (Asser: The Hague, 2004); Hont, *Jealousy of Trade*; Bell (ed), *Victorian Visions of Global Order*; Borschberg, *Hugo Grotius, the Portuguese, and Free Trade in the East Indies*; Armitage, *Foundations of Modern International Thought*; Pitts, *Boundaries of the International*. For reflections upon both the usefulness and the limitations of Cambridge School methods for such work, see MJ van Ittersum, *Profit and Principle: Hugo Grotius, Natural Rights Theories and the Rise of Dutch Power in the East Indies (1595–1615)* (Leiden: Brill, 2006), xxxviii–xliv; Keene, 'International Intellectual History and International Relations', 341.

[133] M Koskenniemi, 'Why History of International Law Today?' (2004) 4 *Rechtsgeschichte* 61, at 64.

[134] Koskenniemi, 'A History of International Law Histories', 943, at 966.

[135] For examples of the early methodologically oriented statements of scholars later referred to as the Cambridge School, see JGA Pocock, 'The History of Political Thought: A Methodological Inquiry' in P Laslett and WG Runciman (eds), *Philosophy, Politics, and Society*, Second Series (Oxford: Oxford University Press, 1962), 183; J Dunn, 'The Identity of the History of Ideas' (1968) XLIII *Philosophy* 85; Q Skinner, 'Meaning and Understanding in the History of Ideas' (1969) 8 *History and Theory* 3; JGA Pocock, 'Languages and Their Implications: The Transformation of the Study of Political Thought' in JGA Pocock, *Politics, Language, and Time* (Chicago: University of Chicago Press, 1971), 3, at 11 ('what we can claim to be living through is nothing more or less than the emergence of a truly autonomous method, one which offers means of treating the phenomena of political thought strictly as historical phenomena . . .

empiricist methods is shared by much mainstream historical work, and in particular there is nothing very remarkable about the claim that an event or a specific historical figure should be placed in historical context. International law, however, is not an event or a person that can be located straightforwardly in a specific historical context, and nor is it self-evident that a legal text or concept has a single historical context from which its meaning can be determined. It was scholars associated with the Cambridge School, however, who argued strongly for the extension of empiricist methods to the interpretation of ideas, texts, or concepts and to the study of fields such as law, philosophy, or theology.

Early Cambridge School texts argued that empiricist historical methods offered a verifiable means of interpreting legal, philosophical, literary, artistic, or theological material, all of which in turn could only be understood by locating it in a specific historical context. The manifestos produced by scholars such as Skinner offered a strong case for the extension to law of the methodological axioms that are a commonplace of empiricist historical work and that are now being mandated as standards in the debate over international law scholarship. The ambition of Skinner, as well as of fellow travellers such as Laslett, Pocock, and Dunn, was to demonstrate the necessity of treating the 'historical character' of texts in fields such as political philosophy, theology, or law as 'fundamental'.[136] Their assertion was that Cambridge School methods were not only applicable, but mandatory, for correctly understanding the meaning of all texts in any field. As spelt out by Skinner, his approach was designed to offer more than simply 'a method for doing the history of ideas', and rather to set out a set of 'methodological implications' for the 'process of interpretation itself'.[137] His ambition was 'to establish and prove the case for this methodology – to establish it not as a suggestion, an aesthetic preference, or a piece of academic imperialism, but as a matter of conceptual propriety, a matter of seeing what the necessary conditions are for the understanding of utterances'.[138]

A similar structure of argument was introduced to US constitutional interpretation in the 1980s, where the 'originalist' approach to legal interpretation of the US constitution had gained ground in the US Supreme Court under

we are beginning to see historical daylight'); Q Skinner, 'Motives, Intentions and the Interpretation of Texts' (1972) 3 *New Literary History* 393.

[136] Dunn, *History of Political Theory*, 19.

[137] Q Skinner, 'A Reply to My Critics' in J Tully (ed), *Meaning and Context: Quentin Skinner and His Critics* (Princeton: Princeton University Press, 1988), 231, at 234.

[138] Skinner, 'Meaning and Understanding in the History of Ideas', 3, at 49.

the influence of Justice Scalia.[139] As the US debate makes clear, applying ideas about context and authorship to a field like law is complicated.[140] Much turns on the question of how to determine which legal texts or concepts are properly thought of as 'past' and thus not to be contaminated by the present – which texts, in other words, should be thought of as 'dead' rather than 'living'.[141] The problem for law is that the past and the present cannot be separated clearly, particularly when the past is expanded to mean past texts, past concepts, or past ideas.[142] In addition, there seemed little room in contextualist accounts for thinking about forms of identity and repetition across time,[143] or for the idea that a text might have multiple temporal contexts.[144] Due to the institutional situation in which they arise, questions about the 'meaning and

[139] Originalists attempt to resolve a perceived tension between constitutionalism and democracy by arguing that judges interpreting the constitution are not an unelected elite imposing their will on the majority, but are merely enforcing an agreement that represents the popular will, the meaning of which was determinate at a particular moment in the past and can be understood by reference to the intentions of its authors. See, for example, E Meese III, 'Toward a Jurisprudence of Original Intent' (1988) 11 *Harvard Journal of Law and Public Policy* 5; A Scalia, 'Originalism – The Lesser Evil' (1989) 57 *University of Cincinnati Law Review* 849; RH Bork, *The Tempting of America: The Political Seduction of the Law* (New York: Macmillan, 1990).

[140] There is a large literature debating the merits and politics of originalism. Engaging with that literature in any detail is beyond the scope of this book. Of particular relevance, however, are those contributors to the debate who explore the relation of originalism to contextualist intellectual history, ask whether the production of legal texts differs from the production of texts in other situations, and complicate the assumptions of empiricist historical methodology when applied to law. See, for example, S Cornell, 'Meaning and Understanding in the History of Constitutional Ideas: The Intellectual History Alternative to Originalism' (2013) 82 *Fordham Law Review* 721; B Meyler, 'Accepting Contested Meanings' (2013) 82 *Fordham Law Review* 803; RH Fallon Jr, 'The Meaning of Legal "Meaning" and Its Implications for Theories of Legal Interpretation' (2015) 82 *The University of Chicago Law Review* 1235; LB Solum, 'Intellectual History as Constitutional Theory' (2015) 101 *Virginia Law Review* 1111; J Gienapp, 'Historicism and Holism: Failures of Originalist Translation' (2015) 84 *Fordham Law Review* 935; H Irving, 'Outsourcing the Law: History and the Disciplinary Limits of Constitutional Originalism' (2015) 84 *Fordham Law Review* 957; Gordon, *Taming the Past*, 361–381; W Baude and SE Sachs, 'Originalism and the Law of the Past' (2019) 37 *Law and History Review* 809.

[141] On the dead past, see M Oakeshott, *Experience and Its Modes* (1933), 106 ('What the historian is interested in is a dead past'), discussed in Gordon, 'Foreword', 1023, at 1025.

[142] For the argument that drawing the line between law and history involves debating 'where the past ends and where the present begins', see Fasolt, *The Limits of History*, 227.

[143] Parker, 'Repetition in History', 123.

[144] A Orford, 'The Past as Law or History? The Relevance of Imperialism for Modern International Law' in M Toufayan, E Tourme-Jouannet, and H Ruiz Fabri (eds), *Droit international et nouvelles approches sur le tiers-monde: entre repetition et renouveau* (Paris: Société de Législation Comparée, 2013), 97; A Orford, 'International Law and the Limits of History' in W Werner, M de Hoon, and A Galán (eds), *The Law of International Lawyers: Reading Martti Koskenniemi* (Cambridge: Cambridge University Press, 2016), 297.

understanding' of international law, to borrow Skinner's foundational formulation,[145] are not questions that can be answered once and for all in some determinate, objective manner through reaching for the correct tools. More importantly, any mode of interpretation applied to legal materials will inevitably be political and instrumental.

Even a brief consideration of the kinds of interpretative issues that arise in international law illustrates why a contextualist concern with reading the past through the present becomes complicated when it is applied to legal material. Disputes often turn on questions about whether there is a single historical context for grasping the meaning of terms in legal texts, such as the term 'sacred trust of civilization' in the League Covenant, 'self-defence' in the UN Charter, or 'fair and equitable treatment' in investment agreements, or on whether a particular treaty term should be informed by attention to context rather than merely the text of the treaty itself, and if so what counts as the relevant context (the treaty negotiations, the broader field of legal obligations existing at the time the treaty was negotiated, the overall purpose of a legal regime, the history of meaning attached to a term, or all of the above).

As Chapter 5 will argue, there are no politically innocent answers to such 'method' questions in situations when disputes over these interpretative issues are themselves part of a political struggle. The question of which actors should be treated as the authors of collectively drafted texts or of customary international law principles and of whose intentions are relevant in determining the meaning of the law cannot be answered as a matter of historical fact. Such questions necessarily involve normative considerations around issues of who counts as a legal subject at any given time, whether treaties or customs are understood to be living law that changes over time, why new actors should be taken to have consented to specific texts or principles, and the relationship between the nature of international law-making and the basis of legal authority.

From a practical, philosophical, or political perspective, the claim that international lawyers should adopt empiricist historical methods when engaging with any 'past' text or concept should have given international law scholars pause. From a practical perspective, the claim that looking at discrete historical contexts was the best way to make sense of the 'meaning' of legal texts seemed to ignore how those texts function – to go against the grain of international law as it is practised. From a philosophical perspective, something in these methodological prescriptions seemed to skip over the key

---

[145] Skinner, 'Meaning and Understanding'.

normative decisions that were involved in choosing which texts, concepts, or practices should be treated as relevant to a history of present-day 'international law'. And from a political perspective, given the nature of the legal field, any argument about how legal texts or concepts should be interpreted always operates within a field of contestation (even better if the interpretation can be portrayed as offering a historical truth about the text) and thus will inevitably become part of that partisan struggle.

3.6 THE PAST AS LAW OR HISTORY?

The overall effect of the turn to history as method in international law and the turn to international law by empirical historians has been to recast the nature of international legal scholarship. Rather than understanding legal scholarship as part of a field that includes contemporary legal practice, historians approached international legal scholarship as a field that existed only in a relationship to the academic world of the humanities and social sciences. That had a number of effects on the way that legal scholarship engaging with the past of international law was represented and understood.

First, in the work of historians, the scope and scale of international legal argumentation engaged with the past was radically narrowed. Historians of international law treated as interlocutors only a handful of lawyers based in the United States and Europe whose published monographs specifically engaged with historical themes. Despite representing historians and lawyers as being part of a shared enterprise, or at least claiming sufficient knowledge of the legal field to be able to correct the historical understanding of international lawyers, those historians of international law largely did not acknowledge, let alone engage with, the work of most scholars and practitioners who are part of the contemporary field. Yet, as we saw in Chapter 2, the narrow segment of international legal scholarship that has been noticed by historians exists as part of a far broader field of legal argumentation.

To the extent that the broader field of contemporary legal scholarship and practice was mentioned by historians of international law, it was to dismiss the working premises of international lawyers as methodologically irrelevant and intellectually impoverished. For example, Samuel Moyn argued that historians do not and should not understand international lawyers as having any involvement in an intellectual project of engaging with the past of international law. Moyn compares the 'typically doctrinal focus of work done by trained lawyers – "law office history" even when written in the academy' – with that of 'trained historians' who have been willing 'to take the subject

seriously for the first time'.[146] For Moyn, 'card-carrying historians' have more
commonly adopted the assumption that '[l]egal ideas were relevant, but less as
doctrines working themselves pure than as ideology' or 'even as apologetics for
state interest and power'.[147] In that account, lawyers had to be taught by
historians that international law can function as an apology for power and
have otherwise retained a naïve and scholastic faith in doctrine. The initial
and 'undoubtedly crucial' task for historians of international law was thus 'to
reclaim law from the lawyers in order to think about its role in the history of
international affairs', and not to collude with lawyers, 'with whose foreshortened version of intellectualism' historians 'rightly saw the need to break'.[148]

According to Lauren Benton, 'historians and lawyers can find a settled
foundation' for a 'shared enterprise' that does not 'require particular methodological commitments'.[149] All that international lawyers need to do if they want
to be intellectually respectable participants in that shared enterprise is to
undertake the 'pursuit of evidence-based history' and the development of
'sharper analytical tools' to gain 'analytical coherence'.[150] International lawyers
must comply with empiricist historical methods '[r]egardless of their training
and the questions they prefer'.[151] Benton not only assumes that historians and
lawyers are engaged in a 'shared enterprise', but makes clear that this enterprise is one that should be defined by professional historians. There is no
recognition or acknowledgement that international legal scholarship is also
produced in dialogue with legal argumentation in practice.

Second, the repeated claim made in the work of historians of international
law is that their histories challenge conventional narratives of international
law by correcting those narratives or completing them, whether by recovering
something that has been forgotten, by historicizing something that has been
treated as ahistorical, by finding the proper context for something that has
been treated as having no context, the wrong context, or too many contexts, by
revealing the true origins of something for which false origins have been
offered, or by offering the real history of international law in place of an
unreal history or a myth. For this 'ta dah' move to work, historians must first
establish that there is a 'conventional narrative' that is parlayed by international lawyers, whether through ignorance, sloth, villainy, naivety, or all
of the above. That conventional narrative is then presented as a foil against

---

[146] Moyn, 'Martti Koskenniemi and the Historiography of International Law', 348.
[147] Moyn, 'Martti Koskenniemi and the Historiography of International Law', 348.
[148] Moyn, 'Martti Koskenniemi and the Historiography of International Law', 353.
[149] Benton, 'Beyond Anachronism', 27.
[150] Benton, 'Beyond Anachronism', 27.
[151] Benton, 'Beyond Anachronism', 27.

which the radical work of historicizing can take place. Yet the resulting picture of the conventional narrative in the international law field is often unrecognisable because of the failure to engage with the work of contemporary international lawyers.

For example, in 2018 Quinn Slobodian published an intellectual history linking Ordoliberalism to the GATT, WTO, and EU, which he presented as a 'neglected' history of thought that has been 'lost' in other accounts of international economic law.[152] According to Slobodian, his history 'corrects' the existing storyline,[153] scholars working on issues of European integration or international economic law have completely overlooked the thinking of Ordoliberals such as Röpke, Mises, Robbins, and Haberler, and passed over the relevant work of Hayek,[154] that the fact that 'questions of empire, decolonization, and the world economy were at the heart of the neoliberal project' has been '[a]ll but ignored' and 'chronically overlooked',[155] and that other scholars 'fail to notice that the real focus of neoliberal proposals is not on the market per se but on redesigning states, laws, and other institutions to protect the market'.[156] Slobodian presented his history as '[c]orrecting this elision', which 'is critical because it was the European neoliberals who were most attentive to questions of international order'.[157] His intellectual history would put 'the neoliberal project into a broader framework than other scholars have provided to date'.[158] Yet, as we saw in Chapter 2, the study of Ordoliberalism and its relation to international economic ordering had been undertaken by international and European lawyers for over a decade, as had work on the relation of Ordoliberal economic ordering to decolonisation.[159] It is only by erasing the legal scholarship on this question that Slobodian could present his intellectual history as a corrective to and completion of existing accounts.[160]

---

[152] Slobodian, *Globalists*, 257.

[153] Slobodian, *Globalists*, 2.

[154] Slobodian, *Globalists*, 105.

[155] Slobodian, *Globalists*, 14, 24.

[156] Slobodian, *Globalists*, 6.

[157] Slobodian, *Globalists*, 8.

[158] Slobodian, *Globalists*, 24.

[159] For the decades of work that Slobodian's narrative closely mirrors but fails to acknowledge, see the references cited in Chapters 2 and 6.

[160] In Chapter 6, I explore in detail the analytical and political effects that flow from Slobodian's decision to produce a historical narrative of recent decades that erases the substantial body of work undertaken by legal scholars and historians making the arguments he claimed to introduce. In brief, I argue there that his translation of the story we told into the form of an intellectual history organised around a small group of men and their mentees stripped the institutional and legal context out of our work. The overall effect was that the complex account offered in our legal scholarship about the ways in which international law imperfectly

To take a second example, Samuel Moyn has argued that human rights lawyers have only very recently begun to concern themselves with inequality or argued for 'social constraint on markets',[161] that 'global inequality simply went missing from human rights politics in a neoliberal age',[162] and that 'the field has failed to respond to – or even recognise – neoliberalism's obliteration of any constraints on inequality'.[163] Having produced an account of the 1990s and 2000s in which no human rights lawyers discussed or were aware of exploitation or inequality, Moyn could conclude that 'the critical reason that human rights have been a powerless companion of market fundamentalism is that they simply have nothing to say about material inequality'.[164] It took an American historian arriving in the twenty-first century to bring those issues to the attention of international lawyers.

According to Moyn, 'for those activists and lawyers who have inherited the world's stock of idealism in our day, there ought to be some shame in succeeding only amid the ruins of materially egalitarian aspiration on every scale'.[165] Yet as Chapter 2 showed, international lawyers and human rights lawyers have been engaged in heated debates over the material inequality produced by neoliberalism in concert with US military interventionism for decades.[166] While Moyn has described himself as involved in a 'romance' with US human-rights-driven foreign policy during the 1990s,[167] many international lawyers from other parts of the world have never been enamoured with that approach. Indeed, writing the work of critical international lawyers back into the recent history of the field would raise a different and more difficult question. How can it be that, after decades of legal arguments that have made the same points that Moyn now claims to be introducing to the field for the first time, we nevertheless *still* find ourselves 'amid the ruins of materially egalitarian aspiration'?

---

routinised Ordoliberal ideological commitments was translated into a far more overdetermined and simplistic story of the relations between a small number of European men who had determined the future of the world through programming the EU, the GATT, and the WTO.

[161] S Moyn, *Not Enough: Human Rights in an Unequal World* (Cambridge and London: Belknap Press, 2018), 210.

[162] Moyn, *Not Enough*, 209.

[163] Moyn, *Not Enough*, 217.

[164] Moyn, *Not Enough*, 216.

[165] Moyn, *Not Enough*.

[166] For some of the scholarly literature that Moyn's claims erase, see the references discussed in Chapter 2.

[167] J Baskin, 'The Disillusionment of Samuel Moyn', *The Chronicle of Higher Education*, 27 October 2017. See further the discussion in Chapter 2.

Whether or not they acknowledge the contemporary field of legal practice, historians too are 'ideological performers',[168] taking up a position as part of an interpretative community that is responsible for shaping the public reaction to particular interpretations of what international law has been, what it is, and what it might yet become. Indeed, in his argument about the shame that human rights lawyers should feel when they reflect on their history, Moyn, who holds degrees and chairs in both law and history, suggests the depth of that complicated identification with the law. As Carlo Ginzburg has argued, 'the country one belongs to is not, as the usual rhetoric goes, the one you love but the one you are ashamed of'.[169] The same may be true of disciplinary affiliations. 'Shame', says Ginzburg, 'can be a stronger bond than love'.[170]

As these examples illustrate, historians of international law rarely refer to or engage with the work of most contemporary international legal scholars, and when they do, it is to treat lawyers as, at best, second-rate historians. The debates over method that have accompanied the turn to history assume that legal thought is primarily an academic practice that to date has failed to conform to a modernist ideal. Despite their lack of engagement with most contemporary international legal scholarship, historians seem to have little doubt that empiricist historical methods provide a timeless standard against which legal scholarship can be measured and, often, found wanting. For lawyers to question the universal applicability of empiricist historical rules across time, space, and situation signals only a lack of intellectual sophistication or 'misunderstanding' of historical methods rather than posing more significant challenges to the uniform applicability of contextualism.[171]

The debate over the proper methods for engaging with the past of international law has focused on the work that engaging with history can do for the practice of international lawyers. Indeed, the use of the language of 'the turn to history' in international law to describe this scholarly encounter makes very clear who is doing the turning and who is standing still. In the next chapter, I explore a question that has been given less attention – what role has turning

---

[168] On the judge as an 'ideological performer' in that sense, see DM Davis, 'Adjudication and Transformation: Out of the Heart of Darkness' (2001) 22 *Cardozo Law Review* 817, at 820. For that role of the judge, see more broadly D Kennedy, *A Critique of Adjudication: Fin de Siècle* (Cambridge: Harvard University Press, 1997).

[169] C Ginzburg, 'The Bond of Shame' (2019) 120 *New Left Review* 35.

[170] Ginzburg, 'The Bond of Shame'.

[171] Fitzmaurice, 'Context in the History of International Law', 15 Benton, 'Beyond Anachronism', 2; Purcell, 'On the Uses and Advantages of Genealogy', 23.

to law played as an intervention in the practice of history? My answer, in short, is that the work of contextualist historians has depended upon a longer tradition in which the reproduction of a particular image of law and lawyers has played a central role. That longer tradition helps make sense of the certainty with which Anglophone historians have claimed to be authoritative interpreters of international law's true meaning, using methods that are presented as at once objective, scientific, and radical.

4

History's Lawyers

4.1 THE FIGURE OF THE LAWYER IN CONTEXTUALIST HISTORY

As Chapter 3 showed, the turn to history in international law has been marked by an intense debate about the proper methods that international lawyers should adopt when drawing on the past in legal arguments. Historians have criticised international lawyers for exhibiting anachronistic tendencies,[1] being dogged by presentism,[2] producing abridged narratives that cherry-pick events from different periods rather than offering linear chronologies,[3] making moral

---

[1] R Lesaffer, 'International Law and Its History: The Story of an Unrequited Love' in M Craven, M Fitzmaurice, and M Vogiatzi (eds), *Time, History, and International Law* (Leiden: Martinus Nijhoff, 2007), 27, at 34–35 (criticising international lawyers for producing 'anachronistic interpretations of historical phenomena'); I Hunter, 'The Figure of Man and the Territorialisation of Justice in "Enlightenment" Natural Law: Pufendorf and Vattel' (2013) 23 *Intellectual History Review* 289 (describing international lawyers as 'dogged by debilitating anachronism'); CR Rossi, *Whiggish International Law: Elihu Root, the Monroe Doctrine, and International Law in the Americas* (Leiden: Brill, 2019), 34 (criticising 'elements of anachronistic thinking' in international legal scholarship); K Purcell, 'On the Uses and Advantages of Genealogy for International Law' (2020) 33 *Leiden Journal of International Law* 13, at 14, 31, 35 (criticising international lawyers for 'a tendency to anachronism', calling for 'the anachronistic tendencies of international law's use of history to be historicized and challenged', and arguing that international lawyers should take the 'dangers of anachronism 'seriously').

[2] Hunter, 'The Figure of Man and the Territorialisation of Justice', 289 (describing international lawyers as 'dogged by debilitating ... "presentism"'); Rossi, *Whiggish International Law*, 34 (criticising the 'almost desultory present-centeredness' of international legal scholarship).

[3] G Cavallar, 'Vitoria, Grotius, Pufendorf, Wolff and Vattel: Accomplices of European Colonialism and Exploitation or True Cosmopolitans?' (2008) 10 *Journal of the History of International Law* 181, at 207–208 (criticising international lawyers for taking 'daring jumps' that destroy the 'complexity and pluralism of the discourses from various (and often very divergent) centuries'); L Benton and L Ford, *Rage for Order: The British Empire and the Origins of International Law, 1800–1850* (Cambridge: Harvard University Press, 2016), 18 (criticising work that makes a 'mad dash' between periods); Rossi, *Whiggish International Law*, 38, 51 (criticising international lawyers for making 'straight-line whiggish abridgments' that

or normative arguments,[4] and generally producing scholarship that is 'tainted' by 'improper historiographic methods'.[5] The sense that the legitimacy of those rules is unquestionable, that the method of applying them is determinate, and that it is self-evident that those rules can and should be applied to legal scholarship emerges strongly from the tone in which this debate is conducted. In the turn to history debates in international law, it is treated as self-evident that a text, a concept, or a political thought has its own temporal context, and that there is something dangerous about placing a text, concept, or political thought in the wrong context. Interpreting the past from the perspective of the present is bad, as are progress narratives and myths. Making moral judgements about material from the past should be avoided. Most of the scholarly work admonishing lawyers for ignoring or questioning these axioms simply asserts the normative desirability of those rules without further explanation. Historians of international law insist that historians and lawyers are part of a 'shared enterprise' that should be conducted according to empiricist historical rules.[6] International lawyers should have no problem with the 'relatively innocuous methodological recommendation to use evidence-based findings of the past' to correct our partisan or instrumentalist misuses of history.[7]

To the extent that any broader justification for the application of those rules to international law is given, it is in the claim that empiricist historical methods offer an evidence-based challenge to the distortions, myths, or dangerously misleading stories about the past presented in legal arguments. Empiricist historians present their methods as a means to avoid 'distorted understandings of the past',[8] 'uphold standards of veracity and verifiability',[9] resist 'the political manipulation of the past for present political purposes',[10] and challenge the growing 'indifference to the verifiability of political

---

appeal due to their 'simplicity' but lead to 'a moral deterioration in the historical understanding of international law').

4   Rossi, *Whiggish International Law*, 30–31 (criticising legal scholars for failing to heed 'Butterfield's admonishment about the retrospective tendency toward pre-judgment and the selective and moralizing ratification of what is right in the present' and for producing 'whiggish hanging judge narration').

5   DJ Bederman, 'Foreign Office International Legal History' in M Craven, M Fitzmaurice, and M Vogiatzi (eds), *Time, History, and International Law* (Leiden: Martinus Nijhoff, 2007), 43, at 46.

6   L Benton, 'Beyond Anachronism: Histories of International Law and Global Legal Politics' (2019) 21 *Journal of the History of International Law* 1, at 27.

7   Benton, 'Beyond Anachronism', 10.

8   A Fitzmaurice, 'Context in the History of International Law' (2018) 20 *Journal of the History of International Law* 5, at 15.

9   Benton, 'Beyond Anachronism', 3.

10 Fitzmaurice, 'Context in the History of International Law', 13.

discourse' in contemporary culture.[11] International lawyers, in contrast, are said to be engaged in 'factional cultural politics rather than scholarship',[12] 'the promotion of ideology',[13] and the pursuit of a morally suspect 'academic anti-positivism'.[14] International lawyers who question the contextualist historical approach to 'the creation of meaning' present 'new dangers'.[15] International lawyers are urged to adopt 'the attitude of suspicion' towards juridical methods that depart from those advocated by historians.[16] Empiricist historical methods can and should be used to unveil, challenge, and correct the misleading, ideological, distorted, and partisan accounts produced by international lawyers. The application of contextualist historical methods to international law simply represents 'what historians have been doing since the days of humanist scholarship: the textual and contextual analysis of their written sources'.[17]

This chapter explores what lies behind this sense of the dangers posed by styles of legal argument that do not comply with empiricist historical methods. In order to do so, it focuses on the work of a group of historians of political thought whose approach has been a touchstone for many participants in the debate over the correct methods for studying the past in international law. As I argued in Chapter 3, many of the historians who have engaged with the turn to history in international law have been associated with or influenced by what is often referred to as the Cambridge School of contextualist history. This chapter explores in more detail the methodological arguments made by four historians associated with or influenced by the Cambridge School: Herbert Butterfield, JGA Pocock, Quentin Skinner, and Ian Hunter.

A style of historical argument that advocated the mastery of narrowly defined temporal contexts and denounced anachronism and presentism developed in the Anglophone university world, and particularly in English universities, in the late nineteenth century.[18] *The Whig Interpretation of History*, a short pamphlet by Hebert Butterfield published in 1931, was to become the most famous articulation of that position[19] and has remained in print ever since its

---

[11] Fitzmaurice, 'Context in the History of International Law', 30.
[12] I Hunter, 'About the Dialectical Historiography of International Law' (2016) 1 *Global Intellectual History* 1, at 19.
[13] Rossi, *Whiggish International Law*, 38, 51.
[14] Hunter, 'About the Dialectical Historiography of International Law', 7, 23.
[15] Fitzmaurice, 'Context in the History of International Law', 30.
[16] Purcell, 'On the Uses and Advantages of Genealogy', 35.
[17] Lesaffer, 'International Law and Its History', 27, at 38.
[18] M Bentley, *Modernizing England's Past: English Historiography in the Age of Modernism 1870–1970* (Cambridge: Cambridge University Press, 2005).
[19] H Butterfield, *The Whig Interpretation of History* (New York: WW Norton, 1965 [1931]).

publication, with far-reaching effects.[20] The idea that 'Whig history' is something to be avoided has continued to inform contemporary historical debates long after and far beyond the world in which there were any Whig historians to cause such trouble. Butterfield's challenge to Whig history has been explicitly invoked in debates over international law,[21] and many of his methodological arguments against anachronism, presentism, progress narratives, and abridgment have become the common sense of the historical field.

During the 1960s, a group of historians associated with the University of Cambridge began to argue for and develop an approach to studying the history of political thought that built in part on the work of an earlier generation of Cambridge historians, including Butterfield. As I noted in Chapter 3, the idea that those scholars formed a 'Cambridge School' began to emerge as early as the 1970s.[22] The reference to a Cambridge School is usually taken to include at least the work of JGA Pocock, Quentin Skinner, and John Dunn. For many commentators, the major contribution made by the Cambridge School was the development of new methods for studying intellectual history.[23]

[20] M Bentley, *The Life and Thought of Herbert Butterfield: History, Science and God* (Cambridge: Cambridge University Press, 2011), 99.

[21] Rossi, *Whiggish International Law*; Purcell, 'On the Uses and Advantages of Genealogy', 29.

[22] S James, 'JGA Pocock and the Idea of the "Cambridge School" in the History of Political Thought' (2019) 45 *History of European Ideas* 83 (dating the first use of the term 'Cambridge School' to 1973).

[23] See J Tully (ed), *Meaning and Context: Quentin Skinner and His Critics* (Princeton: Princeton University Press, 1988); N Phillipson and Q Skinner, 'Preface' in N Phillipson and Q Skinner (eds), *Political Discourse in Early Modern Britain* (Cambridge: Cambridge University Press, 1993), xii (referring to the 1960s as 'the beginning of a revolution in our ways of thinking about the history of political theory'); J Dunn, *The History of Political Theory and Other Essays* (Cambridge: Cambridge University Press, 1996), 11; DSA Bell, 'The Cambridge School and World Politics: Critical Theory, History and Conceptual Change', *The Global Site*, 2001, 5 ('During the 1960's a number of young historians, either based in or trained at Cambridge University, helped to re-orient the study of the history of political thought ... namely JGA Pocock, John Dunn and Quentin Skinner. For the sake of convenience, and following convention, I will term these authors representatives of the "Cambridge School" methodology'); D Runciman, 'History of Political Thought: The State of the Discipline' (2001) 3 *British Journal of Politics and International Relations* 84 (the history of political thought exists 'in the shadow of the great methodological argument that began in the 1960s' and the 'triumphant methodology' developed by the 'group of historians who have become known as the Cambridge School'); JGA Pocock, 'Foundations and Moments' in A Brett and J Tully with H Hamilton-Bleakley (eds), *Rethinking the Foundations of Modern Political Thought* (Cambridge: Cambridge University Press, 2006), 37 (describing himself as being 'present at the creation ... of the enterprise of which Skinner has become the leader'); JGA Pocock, *Political Thought and History: Essays on Theory and Method* (Cambridge: Cambridge University Press, 2008), vii ('A certain method, or procedure, for defining political thought and studying its history – alternatively, for studying it in history – has been formed and practised ... at Cambridge and other universities, and is so far associated with the first of these that it is often

Those scholars sought 'to extend into the domain of intellectual history the methods and procedures that, during the post-war years, had come to be characteristic of professional history in general', and in particular the 'sensitivity to anachronism' that Butterfield had powerfully expressed in *The Whig Interpretation of History*.[24] For the Cambridge School, the 'historical character' of all texts including philosophical, theological, and (most importantly for this book) legal texts was 'fundamental'.[25] The contextualist approaches to the history of political thought developed by Pocock and Skinner have been regularly invoked or defended as guides to the conduct of international law and international relations scholarship.[26]

The most sustained critique of contemporary international lawyers for their failure to conform with contextualist historical methods has been developed by Ian Hunter, an intellectual historian strongly influenced by the Cambridge School.[27] As we saw in Chapter 3, Hunter has been highly critical of international legal scholarship for breaching the methodological protocols of contextualist historians, accusing lawyers of being 'dogged by debilitating anachronism and "presentism"',[28] imagining 'a single normative telos' for international law,[29] wrongly suggesting that 'there is a global principle of justice capable of including European and non-European peoples',[30] and producing 'a tendentious mangling of the historical

known by its name'); R Bourke, 'The Cambridge School', 2016, https://projects.history.qmul.ac .uk/hpt/2016/06/27/interview-with-richard-bourke-on-the-cambridge-school-for-the-iranian-journal-farhangemrooz-todays-culture/ ('The existence of a "Cambridge School" was first identified by JGA Pocock in the early 1970s … The practitioners whom Pocock had in mind as exemplary members of this School included himself, Quentin Skinner and John Dunn … [O]ne thing that distinguishes Pocock, Skinner and Dunn from their predecessors was a determination, at least in the 1960s and 1970s, to justify their procedures in terms of self-conscious methodology').

[24] F Oakley, *Politics and Eternity: Studies in the History of Medieval and Early-Modern Political Thought* (Leiden: Brill, 1999), 9.

[25] Dunn, *The History of Political Theory and Other Essays*, 19.

[26] See the lengthy list of examples discussed in Chapter 3.

[27] On the relation of his approach to that of Pocock, Skinner, and contextualist historians, see I Hunter, 'The History of Philosophy and the Persona of the Philosopher' (2007) 4 *Modern Intellectual History* 571; I Hunter, 'Natural Law, Historiography, and Aboriginal Sovereignty' (2007) 11 *Legal History* 137; I Hunter, 'Talking about My Generation' (2008) 34 *Critical Inquiry* 583; I Hunter, 'Postmodernist Histories' (2009) 19 *Intellectual History Review* 265; I Hunter, 'The Contest over Context in Intellectual History' (2019) 58 *History and Theory* 185.

[28] Hunter, 'The Figure of Man and the Territorialisation of Justice', 289.

[29] I Hunter, 'Vattel's Law of Nations: Diplomatic Casuistry for the Protestant Nation' (2010) 31 *Grotiana* 108, at 111–112.

[30] I Hunter, 'Global Justice and Regional Metaphysics: On the Critical History of the Law of Nature and Nations' in S Dorsett and I Hunter (eds), *Law and Politics in British Colonial Thought: Transpositions of Empire* (New York: Palgrave Macmillan, 2010), 11.

record'.[31] Hunter's writings offer a clear sense of the hermeneutic of suspicion that structures the debate over method, presenting international lawyers as the scholastic enemies of contextualist historians, and as engaged in 'factional cultural politics rather than scholarship'.[32]

Butterfield, Pocock, Skinner, and Hunter have each advocated the need for new methods to modernise interpretation in their fields and beyond, emphasised empiricist canons of evidence and verifiability, and stressed the centrality of those methods to the production of accounts of the past free from ideology and presentism. We can see in their work a clear articulation of each of the methodological axioms that are currently being proposed for engaging with the history of international law. In addition, Butterfield, Pocock, Skinner, and Hunter have each presented their methods as offering a fundamental challenge to forms of authority based upon invented traditions, progress narratives, and metaphysical foundations. And perhaps most significantly for my argument in this book, each has related those illegitimate forms of authority to law and lawyers.

Rather than treat the methodological arguments of these contextualist historians as establishing an instruction manual for understanding the true meaning of past legal texts, events, cases, or practices, my aim in this chapter is to explore the normative claims that underpin those arguments. The methodological debate which the turn to history in international law has generated is shaped by a European story about the liberating power of historical consciousness. The insistence that challenging legalist misuses of the past is a sign of methodological and indeed political progress plays a major role in that European story. Narratives about conflicts between law and history turn out to be central to contextualist historiography. In those narratives, historians are seen as radical disrupters of legal, theological, and thus political orthodoxy.

My particular interest in this chapter is the central role that law and lawyers play in the work of the empiricist historians whose interpretative techniques are being brought to bear on legal scholarship. In particular, I explore the figure of the lawyer as scholastic apologist for power or as moralising judge that reappears in the texts of contextualist historians of political thought and against which their historicising methods are staged. That figure of the lawyer appears as Whig constitutionalist in the writings of Butterfield, as English common lawyer in the writings of Pocock, as Renaissance Italian scholastic lawyer for Skinner, and as Prussian natural lawyer for Hunter.

---

[31] Hunter, 'About the Dialectical Historiography of International Law', 19.
[32] Hunter, 'About the Dialectical Historiography of International Law', 19.

In addition, Butterfield, Pocock, Skinner, and Hunter each offer historical narratives in which the figure of the lawyer functions as the foil against which a second figure is opposed – a figure who arrives on the scene to challenge the oppressive authority of received tradition with the liberating methods of historicising contextualism. The hero of those stories is the historicising humanist, who deploys methods that bear a striking resemblance to those of the contextualist historian. Like many revolutionary histories, the story of the emergence of contextualist method is organised around a narrative of struggle taught through example. It is also framed by a binary choice between friend and enemy, or between heroes of methodological progress and their opponents. Surprisingly often, those binary choices and the examples which illustrate them involve lawyers. Lawyers, it turns out, are everywhere in the work of contextualist historians, both in their manifestos about method and in the narratives they produce using those methods.

The figure of the lawyer as judge or scholastic metaphysician reappears throughout the methodological writings and the narrative histories studied in this chapter. That figure is presented either as holding anachronistic beliefs about the possibility of representing values that transcend the specific political situation or as a naïve formalist who advocates 'outmoded ideals of "applying law mechanically" through a process of logical deduction'.[33] In the texts of contextualist historians, lawyers believe – or at least cynically claim – that the ideals they represent are universal and timeless. Lawyers are dangerous because the more successfully they can perform as apolitical representatives of timeless metaphysical ideals, the more easily they can smuggle in their own politics and ideology under the guise of formal law.

In such accounts, 'history serves a negative function and it serves that function against a well-defined enemy' – that is, 'law's pretended atemporal foundations, its pretended claim to autonomy, its insistence on its impervious to its outside'.[34] By situating the turn to method in international law as part of a longer narrative, this chapter helps to make sense of the certainty with which historians understand their role as at once objective, scientific, and revolutionary. That certainty depends upon their insistent invocation of a metaphysical mode of legal thought and a formalist mode of legal argument as foil and antagonist. As we will see, the methodological struggle in which modernising

---

[33] For a discussion of the ways in which ideological opponents deploy notions of formalism in those terms in contemporary China, see S Seppänen, *Ideological Conflict and the Rule of Law in Contemporary China: Useful Paradoxes* (Cambridge: Cambridge University Press, 2016), 39–40.

[34] See KM Parker, 'Law "In" and "As" History: The Common Law in the American Polity, 1790–1900' (2011) 1 *UC Irvine Law Review* 587, at 590.

historians understand themselves to be involved seems to have depended in some significant way upon a static image of lawyers as the enemies of history and the enemies of humanism.

4.2 HERBERT BUTTERFIELD AND THE LAWYER AS WHIG CONSTITUTIONALIST

4.2.1 *Butterfield's England and the Challenge to Constitutional History*

Butterfield was a major influence upon the early proponents of the Cambridge School method, particularly through his role as supervisor and early mentor of JGA Pocock.[35] While Butterfield did not employ precisely the same vocabulary as the generation of historians referred to as the Cambridge School, his work foreshadowed the methods they brought to bear on the history of political thought.[36] Butterfield was also an important point of contact between modernising historians and the new field of international relations.[37] He was the founder of the Rockefeller-sponsored British Committee on the Theory of International Politics and one of the leading figures in the resulting English School of international relations.[38]

---

[35] For varying assessments of Butterfield's influence upon the Cambridge School in general and Pocock in particular, see further JGA Pocock, *The Ancient Constitution and the Feudal Law: A Reissue with a Retrospect* (Cambridge: Cambridge University Press, 1987 [1957]), vii, viii, xiv; Bentley, *Modernizing England's Past*, 150–151; Richard Bourke, 'Pocock and the Presuppositions of the New British History' (2010) 53 *The Historical Journal* 747; KB McIntyre, *Herbert Butterfield: History, Providence, and Skeptical Politics* (Wilmington: ISI Books, 2011), 46; James, 'JGA Pocock and the Idea of the "Cambridge School"'; JGA Pocock, 'A Response to Samuel James's "JGA Pocock and the Idea of the 'Cambridge School' in the History of Political Thought"' (2019) 45 *History of European Ideas* 99.

[36] See further Oakley, *Politics and Eternity*, 9; Bentley, *Modernizing England's Past*, 150–151; McIntyre, *Herbert Butterfield*, 46.

[37] E Keene, 'The English School and British Historians' (2008) 37 *Millennium* 381; R Soffer, *History, Historians, and Conservatism in Britain and America: From the Great War to Thatcher and Reagan* (Oxford: Oxford University Press, 2008), 179–220; N Guilhot, 'Portrait of the Realist as a Historian: On Anti-Whiggism in the History of International Relations' (2015) 21 *European Journal of International Relations* 3.

[38] T Dunne, *Inventing International Society: A History of the English School* (Hampshire: Palgrave, 1998), 71–88. The ground-breaking work of Reba Soffer explored the role played by the Rockefeller Foundation in the creation of the British Committee on the Theory of International Politics and the broader milieu of Christian Realism informing collaborations between scholars, journalists, and policy-makers in the United Kingdom and the United States: Soffer, *History, Historians, and Conservatism*, 179–220. See also Bentley, *Life and Thought of Herbert Butterfield*, 270–271; N Guilhot, 'Introduction: One Discipline, Many Histories' in N Guilhot (ed), *The Invention of International Relations Theory* (New York: Columbia University Press, 2011), 1, at 4; O Wæver, 'The Speech Act of Realism' in N Guilhot (ed), *The*

In writing *The Whig Interpretation of History*, Butterfield summarised, systematised, and publicised a set of challenges to Whig historiography, in a context in which Victorian liberals had begun to seem like yesterday's heroes.[39] In the decades prior to the publication of *The Whig Interpretation of History*, a growing body of scholarship had emerged that criticised English liberal historiography of the nineteenth century. That liberal historiography had been organised around the progressive development of constitutionalism, parliamentary monarchy, and Anglican Protestantism.[40] Central to the critical project that emerged to challenge that dominant historiography was the call to abandon the supposedly amateurish scholarship of an earlier generation and replace it with a new, systematic, and professional mode of enquiry.

Constitutional history was a core focus of those opposed to progressive or Whig historiography, in part because of the central place that claims about constitutionalism had played in narratives about the English past.[41] During the early nineteenth century, moderate Whigs had developed an account of the gradual emergence of an idealised parliamentary constitutional monarchy as a challenge to radical alternatives, whether in the form of revolutionary or reformist movements. Key events such as the signing of the Magna Carta, the Glorious Revolution, opposition to the authoritarianism of George III, and the Parliamentary Reform Bills of the nineteenth century had been presented by Whig historians as part of a master narrative of progress, enlightenment, and freedom. In that story, institutional stability, incremental change, and the ancient constitution had served as a check against both centralised monarchy and revolutionary politics. The plausibility of such accounts depended upon a shared sense of continuity with the past. The continuity of the unwritten constitution could be presented as a force in English history because England had neither experienced a lasting revolution that irrevocably altered pre-existing laws nor been occupied by a foreign power bringing with it a new legal code. Unlike the continental European legal systems, England had retained an unwritten constitution and a customary legal system allegedly extending back to time immemorial.

The political faith in gradualism and the experience of institutional continuity was put under pressure throughout the mid-nineteenth century.

Invention of International Relations Theory (New York: Columbia University Press, 2011), 97, at 116–117; Guilhot, 'Portrait of the Realist as a Historian', 9–10.

[39] JP Young, *Yesterday's Hero*, 1975, www.youtube.com/watch?v=KVSEiveFY7g.

[40] PBM Blaas, *Continuity and Anachronism: Parliamentary and Constitutional Development in Whig Historiography and in the Anti-Whig Reaction between 1890 and 1930* (The Hague: Springer, 1978), 2.

[41] Blaas, *Continuity and Anachronism*, 34.

The American and French revolutions of the late eighteenth century had already begun to influence British thinking about internal government, empire, and foreign policy.[42] The issue of how to respond to the threat of revolution both in Europe and in European colonies began to confront landed elites in England and Ireland, while manufacturing and working-class campaigners agitated for repeal of the Corn Laws, reform of restrictive land laws, new factory legislation, the abolition of the East India Company monopolies in China and India, and the expansion of the franchise.[43] Ongoing deadlocks and crises in the House of Commons and opposition in the House of Lords to liberal and democratic Bills from the Commons undermined the 'cult of Parliament' that had been central to Whig historiography.[44] Both the Crimean War and the Franco-Prussian War gave rise to rumblings against the 'old-fashioned amateurism' and anti-militarism of the Whig tradition, with critics challenging the utility of a parliamentary system in a time of war. The opposition to liberal parliamentarianism intensified with the British defeat in the first Boer War and calls for more 'scientific management' of the military.[45] A new political vocabulary of 'efficiency' emerged to challenge the value of tradition,[46] with calls for greater military efficiency matched by calls for greater political efficiency in the face of disruptions caused by industrialisation and bureaucratisation.

The academic reaction to Whig historical writing was informed by those broader challenges to the political and social tradition of nineteenth-century liberalism.[47] In the face of such transformations, there was an increased sense of discontinuity between past and present and the devaluation of tradition as a guide – 'the past came to be thought of as ballast, as something of no use, as an anachronism'.[48] In the legal field, the forms of property law that had been inherited from the feudal era and the voting rights that flowed from them became more clearly dysfunctional in a rapidly industrialising England, and calls for law reform began to produce a sense of distance between present needs and past rules. In that context, academic critics of Whig historiography

---

[42] B Hilton, *A Mad, Bad, and Dangerous People? England 1783–1846* (Oxford: Clarendon Press, 2006).

[43] A Orford, 'Food Security, Free Trade, and the Battle for the State' (2015) 11 *Journal of International Law and International Relations* 1, at 39–42.

[44] Blaas, *Continuity and Anachronism*, 205.

[45] Blaas, *Continuity and Anachronism*, 223.

[46] Blaas, *Continuity and Anachronism*, xiv.

[47] Blaas, *Continuity and Anachronism*, xii, 33; N Guilhot, *After the Enlightenment: Political Realism and International Relations in the Mid-Twentieth Century* (Cambridge: Cambridge University Press, 2017).

[48] Blaas, *Continuity and Anachronism*, xiv, 28.

began to argue that liberal constitutional histories had downplayed context, chance, conflict, and discontinuity in their narratives of constitutional persistence and political evolution.[49]

4.2.2 *The Competing Legacies of FW Maitland*

One of the key figures who initiated a new approach to studying the history of English law and its relation to political history was FW Maitland. Maitland had studied at Cambridge where he was awarded a Whewell International Law Scholarship, was called to the Bar at Lincoln's Inn in 1876, returned to Cambridge in 1884 to take up a readership in English Law, and was elected to the Downing Professorship of the Laws of England at the University of Cambridge in 1892, a position which he held until his death in 1906.[50] Maitland was influential in opening up a new set of questions about the adequacy of existing English constitutional and legal history.[51]

Amongst lawyers, Maitland is remembered as the instigator of the study of legal history in England and of a more scholarly relationship to the common law.[52] Maitland discovered and published volumes of original legal sources, wrote a comprehensive interpretative overview of the history of English law as well as detailed histories of particular periods, and engaged in careful studies of technical legal documents, the evolution of legal doctrines, and systems of pleading, proof, and procedure. While Maitland's training in philosophy and

---

[49] Blaas, *Continuity and Anachronism*, 35.

[50] F Pollock, 'Frederic William Maitland, 1850–1906' (1905–1906) 2 *Proceedings of the British Academy* 1.

[51] See, for example, FW Maitland, 'Why the History of English Law Is Not Written' in HAL Fisher (ed), *The Collected Papers of Frederic William Maitland* (Cambridge: Cambridge University Press, 1911 [1888]), 480; FW Maitland, *Domesday Book and Beyond: Three Essays in the Early History of England* (Cambridge: Cambridge University Press, 1897); FW Maitland, 'A Prologue to a History of English Law' (1898) 14 *Law Quarterly Review* 13; F Pollock and FW Maitland, *The History of English Law* (2nd edition) (Cambridge: Cambridge University Press, 1968 [1898]); F Maitland, *English Law and the Renaissance* (Cambridge: Cambridge University Press, 1901); FW Maitland, *Constitutional History of England – A Course of Lectures Delivered* (Cambridge: Cambridge University Press, 1908); FW Maitland, *The Forms of Action at Common Law* (Cambridge: Cambridge University Press, 1965 [1909]); FW Maitland and FC Montague, *A Sketch of English Legal History* (New York and London: GP Putman's Sons, 1915); FW Maitland, *State, Trust and Corporation*, eds D Runciman and M Ryan (Cambridge: Cambridge University Press, 2003).

[52] See JH Baker, 'Why the History of English Law Has Not Been Finished' (2000) 59 *Cambridge Law Journal* 62; SFC Milsom, 'Maitland' (2001) 60 *Cambridge Law Journal* 265; J Getzler, 'Law, History, and the Social Sciences: Intellectual Traditions of Late Nineteenth- and Early Twentieth-Century Europe' in A Lewis and M Lobban (eds), *Law and History* (Oxford: Oxford University Press, 2004), 215, at 242–248.

engagement with German historians influenced his approach to legal history,[53] so too did the practical experience he gained during the seven years he spent as an equity lawyer and conveyancer at Lincoln's Inn.[54] Maitland's ability to enliven the law through attention to its history was a result of the legal training that 'enabled him to grapple with legal technicalities and to perceive their full significance'.[55]

Maitland criticised specific concepts and doctrines of the common law in language that would later be taken up by Pocock and others as the foundation for a historical critique of the inadequacies of the 'common-law mind'.[56] Maitland referred to English law as 'obscure and antiquated', dogged by 'misplaced antiquarianism', and leading to cases in which the merits 'disappear beneath the accumulated rubbish of ages'.[57] Yet his opposition to the 'archaisms' embedded in the 'historical institution' of real property law was not a result of an abstract commitment to contextualist method, but rather was based upon his concern that such archaisms rendered property law practically inconvenient and so obscure as to be unworkable.[58] His criticisms were directed to the presentist goal of advocating reform of the law of real property (and, as a result, the law relating to the Parliamentary franchise which flowed from it).

For Maitland, legal reform required an adequate understanding of the changing social function of legal concepts, practices, and institutions related to land law and property in new economic circumstances, and legal history offered the means of achieving such an understanding. He argued that it was profitable 'to trace the origin of legal rules in the social and economic conditions of a by-gone age', and that anyone who had 'the historic sense' must 'dislike to see a rule or an idea unfitly surviving in a changed

---

[53] Getzler, 'Law, History, and the Social Sciences', 245–248; J Kirby, 'History, Law and Freedom: FW Maitland in Context' (2019) 16 *Modern Intellectual History* 127.

[54] See Maitland, 'Why the History of English Law Is Not Written', 495; Blaas, *Continuity and Anachronism*, 241; Milsom, 'Maitland', 265–268.

[55] Pollock, 'Frederic William Maitland', 2.

[56] See Pocock, *The Ancient Constitution and the Feudal Law*, 58, 66.

[57] See FW Maitland, 'The Law of Real Property' in HAL Fisher (ed), *The Collected Papers of Frederic William Maitland Volume 1* (Cambridge: Cambridge University Press, 1911 [1879]), 162, at 163, 191. For a study of the history of English land law, which conveys some flavour of both the training which young common lawyers all over the world still undergo when we are taught the law of real property and of the strange, feudal world into which we are still inducted in the process, see AWB Simpson, *A History of the Land Law* (2nd edition) (Oxford: Clarendon Press, 1986).

[58] Maitland, 'The Law of Real Property', 194, 200; Maitland, 'Why the History of English Law Is Not Written', 493 (on the 'many good reasons for wishing that some parts of our law, notably our land-law, were thoroughly purged of their archaisms').

environment'. Such an 'anachronism' should offend both reason and taste.[59] While the lawyer had a different relation to the past from the historian, both relations were valid. In a famous passage in his inaugural lecture, Maitland wrote:

> A lawyer finds on his table a case about rights of common which sends him to the Statute of Merton. But is it really the law of 1236 that he wants to know? No, it is the ultimate result of the interpretations set on the statute by the judges of twenty generations. The more modern the decision the more valuable for his purpose ... Thus we are tempted to mix up two different logics, the logic of authority, and the logic of evidence. What the lawyer wants is authority and the newer the better; what the historian wants is evidence and the older the better.[60]

More pointedly, Maitland argued that to understand the history of English law required first engaging with the details of modern law. Maitland insisted that it was necessary to study property law in order to understand constitutional history, as 'our whole constitutional law seems at times to be but an appendix to the law of real property'.[61] For Maitland, 'it is utterly impossible to speak of our medieval constitution except in terms of our medieval land law'.[62] In addition, Maitland argued that it was 'quite impossible' to speak of England's medieval constitution without also studying medieval criminal law and criminal procedure.[63] Maitland considered that 'only a trained lawyer could deal with the technical material necessary to write good legal history'.[64] For that reason, Maitland counselled that 'any one who aspires to study legal history should begin by studying modern law' and advised students 'that a thorough training in modern law is almost indispensable for any one who wishes to do good work on legal history'.[65] As a result, '[i]t would be disastrous ... as well as stupid advice, were I to tell you that you could read constitutional history without studying land law – you cannot do this, no one can do it'.[66] Historians

[59] FW Maitland, 'The Making of the German Civil Code' in HAL Fisher (ed), *The Collected Papers of Frederic William Maitland Volume 3* (Cambridge: Cambridge University Press, 1911 [1879]), 474, at 486.

[60] Maitland, 'Why the History of English Law Is Not Written', 490–491.

[61] Maitland, *Constitutional History of England*, 538.

[62] Maitland, *Constitutional History of England*, 24.

[63] Maitland *Constitutional History of England*, 538.

[64] DM Rabban, *Law's History: American Legal Thought and the Transatlantic Turn to History* (Cambridge: Cambridge University Press, 2013), 391.

[65] Maitland, *Constitutional History of England*, 494.

[66] Maitland, *Constitutional History of England*, 538.

of law 'will often have to work from the modern to the ancient, from the clear to the vague, from the known to the unknown'.[67]

Maitland's rethinking of English legal history led in a number of directions. On the one hand, Maitland was part of a broader transatlantic turn to studying the history of the common law, which included American scholars such as James Bradley Thayer, James Barr Ames, and Oliver Wendell Holmes with whom Maitland was in conversation.[68] Scholars like Thayer and Ames explored legal history as a guide to reforming the common law and removing elements that had become dysfunctional. Indeed, it was often 'precisely those people who took the most pragmatic view of present law', including Maitland, who urged 'the study of the past' at least 'partly for the sake of ridding the present of the deadwood of irrelevant survivals'.[69] Here the work of the German private law codifiers was also influential.[70] For Holmes, appeals to the past served a more strongly iconoclastic function and were employed in a polemical spirit to attack legal formalism and undo 'the pretended ahistorical foundations of law'.[71]

In the hands of the legal realists, whose scholarship built on the ground-clearing historical work of Holmes and his generation, the goal of continuing that anti-foundational critique remained the functionalist one of engaging with present law in a pragmatic spirit. In the work of figures like Karl Renner, Hugo Sinzheimer, and Otto Kahn-Freund in Europe or of Roscoe Pound and J Willard Hurst in the United States, historical jurisprudence fed into an emerging sociological jurisprudence.[72] The shared approach underlying those streams of historical and sociological jurisprudence treated the social context of the law as knowable, whether in the past through the work of history or in the present through the work of social science. In all of that legal scholarship, critical historical analysis was motivated by presentist concerns.

---

[67] Maitland, *Constitutional History of England*, 493.

[68] Rabban, *Law's History*, 383–422.

[69] RW Gordon, 'J Willard Hurst and the Common Law Tradition in American Legal Historiography' (1975) 10 *Law and Society Review* 9, at 28.

[70] MW Reimann, 'Holmes's *Common Law* and German Legal Science' in RW Gordon (ed), *The Legacy of Oliver Wendell Holmes, Jr* (Stanford: Stanford University Press, 1992), 72; Rabban, *Law's History*, 92–114; Kirby, 'History, Law and Freedom', 127.

[71] KM Parker, 'Writing Legal History Then and Now: A Brief Reflection' (2016) 56 *American Journal of Legal History* 168, at 170. See also T Grey, 'Holmes and Legal Pragmatism' (1989) 42 *Stanford Law Review* 787; Reimann, 'Holmes's *Common Law* and German Legal Science'.

[72] See generally K Renner, *The Institutions of Private Law and Their Social Functions* (trans A Schwarzschild) (London: Routledge and Kegan Paul, 1949); Gordon, 'J Willard Hurst', 9; O Kahn-Freund, 'Hugo Sinzheimer 1875–1945' in O Kahn-Freund, *Labour Law and Politics in the Weimar Republic* (Oxford: Basil Blackwell, 1981), 73; C Joerges, 'German Perspectives and Fantasies' (2011) 12 *German Law Journal* 10; Rabban, *Law's History*, 423–471, 499.

In contrast, historians have tended to portray Maitland as initiating a more profound challenge to lawyers and legal historiography.[73] Maitland's critique of the anachronisms that persisted in the English legal system has been embraced as representing 'the historical spirit incarnate' and as a counter to the 'untruthful history' produced by other lawyers.[74] For example, in his early Cambridge school history of the common law, Pocock wove some of the insights offered by Maitland into a broader repudiation of the insularity and 'defect' of the 'common-law mind'.[75] Critics of Whig constitutional history drew on Maitland's arguments to attack the anachronism and presentism of English constitutionalism more broadly, while ignoring his claims about the need for historians of law to study the details of contemporary legal practice in the present. Over time, the challenge to Whig historiography and common law thinking began to be framed in the more abstract language of methodological flaws, with critics dismissing the 'severely anachronistic manner of interpretation' adopted by nineteenth-century constitutional historians and the 'linear historical evolutionism of the Whigs'.[76]

4.2.3 Butterfield and the Whig Historian as 'God and Judge'

The new sensitivity to the anachronism and presentism of Whig progress narratives evidenced by Butterfield and his generation was in part shaped by the new constitutional historiography inspired by scholars like Maitland and in part by factors external to the university. The emergence during the interwar period of an experience of distance from the past, and the related sense that tradition was no longer a reliable guide to present law or politics, allowed historians to carve out a broader sphere of academic influence in early twentieth-century Britain.

For Butterfield and his generation, methodological and substantive challenges to liberal historiography began to appear desirable and possible because of broader political and economic transformations that challenged the dominance of liberal politics within Britain and beyond. In *The Whig Interpretation of History*, Butterfield offered a concise and compelling articulation of that view. In that methodological manifesto, we can find many of the arguments that are now treated as axiomatic in debates about the need to

---

[73] RL Schuyler, 'The Historical Spirit Incarnate: Frederic William Maitland' (1952) LVII
American Historical Review 303; Blaas, *Continuity and Anachronism*, 240; Kirby, 'History, Law and Freedom', 127, 146.

[74] Schuyler, 'The Historical Spirit Incarnate', at 303, 305.

[75] See Pocock, *The Ancient Constitution and the Feudal Law*, 58, 66.

[76] Blaas, *Continuity and Anachronism*, xi, xv.

adopt empiricist historical methods in international law. Yet rather than present methodological issues as technical rules, Butterfield's rejection of presentism, anachronism, Whig narratives, and abridged or *longue durée* histories was explicitly normative. It was grounded in a theological account of the historian's role and a conservative vision of politics.

Butterfield argued that the Whig interpretation of history had tended 'to emphasize certain principles of progress in the past and to produce a story which is the ratification if not the glorification of the present'.[77] The Whig approach imposed an order on the past that was structured according to the principle that the winners (which in the English context of the 1930s meant Whigs and Protestants) represented progress and the future, and the losers (in that context Tories and Catholics) represented regression and the past. For Butterfield, that problematic Whig narrative of history was also 'associated with certain methods of historical organisation and inference'.[78] *The Whig Interpretation of History* was aimed at diagnosing the problems of method produced by or associated with the liberal desire to judge the past.

The first mistake which Butterfield attributed to the Whig historian involved 'studying the past for the sake of the present'.[79] The tendency to study the past 'with one eye to the present' was, for Butterfield, 'the source of all sins and sophistries in history, starting with the simplest of them, the anachronism'.[80] 'Real historical understanding' could not be achieved by subordinating the past to the present.[81] Rather, the historian must try 'to understand the past for the sake of the past', by 'making the past our present and attempting to see life with the eyes of another century than our own'.[82]

Butterfield's second methodological concern related to what he termed 'abridgment' – the writing of historical surveys that covered long periods or studied great transitions. Butterfield stated unequivocally that 'all history must tend to become more whig in proportion as it becomes more abridged'.[83] The problem of distortion arose when the historian attempted the move from special to general, and tried to 'treat of history on the broad scale'.[84] The attempt to do so produced 'what is really a gigantic optical illusion'.[85]

[77] Butterfield, *The Whig Interpretation of History*, v.
[78] Butterfield, *The Whig Interpretation of History*, v.
[79] Butterfield, *The Whig Interpretation of History*, 16.
[80] Butterfield, *The Whig Interpretation of History*, 31–32.
[81] Butterfield, *The Whig Interpretation of History*, 16.
[82] Butterfield, *The Whig Interpretation of History*, 16.
[83] Butterfield, *The Whig Interpretation of History*, 7.
[84] Butterfield, *The Whig Interpretation of History*, 15.
[85] Butterfield, *The Whig Interpretation of History*, 29.

The problematic attitude of the abridger was one into which even careful specialists could slide if they attempted to relate a 'special piece of work to the larger historical story'.[86] Butterfield argued that a new attitude 'intervenes between the work of the historical specialist and that work, partly of organisation and partly of abridgement, which the general historian carries out'.[87] Despite the best intentions of the historian, that attitude 'inserts itself at the change of focus that we make when we pass from the microscopic view of a particular period to a bird's-eye view of the whole; and when it comes it brings with it that whig interpretation of history which is so different from the story that the research student has to tell'.[88]

As a result, the scale of historical work had to be limited to tracing events 'from one generation to another'.[89] 'It is only by this method', he argued, 'that the great 'lessons of history' can 'be learned in detail' – that is, that human change is complex and the consequences of any act or decision are unpredictable.[90] Those lessons are not only 'bound to be lost in abridgment',[91] but 'abridgments of history are sometimes calculated to propagate the very reverse of the truth of history'.[92] The truth of history, which for Butterfield was also 'a truth of philosophy', is that it is 'the whole of the past, with its complexity of movement, its entanglement of issues, and its intricate interactions, which produced the whole of the complex present'.[93] Butterfield therefore championed 'the more concentrated labours of historical specialists', focused on 'seeing things in their context'.[94]

The concern with abridgment was linked to the third aspect of Whig interpretation critiqued by Butterfield, which involved organising the narrative of history around the division of the world into 'the friends and enemies of progress'.[95] For Butterfield, writing progress narratives was an example of the dangers into which a form of abridged history could fall. The Whig interpretation of history had organised 'the whole course of centuries upon what is really a directing principle of progress'.[96] The result of that method was 'to impose a certain form upon the whole of the historical story' that purported to

---

[86] Butterfield, *The Whig Interpretation of History*, 15.
[87] Butterfield, *The Whig Interpretation of History*, 15–16.
[88] Butterfield, *The Whig Interpretation of History*, 15–16.
[89] Butterfield, *The Whig Interpretation of History*, 20.
[90] Butterfield, *The Whig Interpretation of History*, 21.
[91] Butterfield, *The Whig Interpretation of History*, 21.
[92] Butterfield, *The Whig Interpretation of History*, 22.
[93] Butterfield, *The Whig Interpretation of History*, 19.
[94] Butterfield, *The Whig Interpretation of History*, 5, 117.
[95] Butterfield, *The Whig Interpretation of History*, 5.
[96] Butterfield, *The Whig Interpretation of History*, 101.

show 'throughout the ages the workings of an obvious principle of progress, of which the Protestants and whigs have been the perennial allies while Catholics and tories have perpetually formed obstruction'.[97] That problem was not simply reducible to bias and nor was that approach to history only the property of Whigs. Rather, it arose from an 'error' that was more widely shared – that is, the practice of 'judging' things 'apart from their context'.[98]

Butterfield insisted that behind all the mistakes of the Whig historian lay 'the passionate desire to come to a judgment of values, to make history answer questions and decide issues and to give the historian the last word in a controversy', to 'show which party was in the right'.[99] Butterfield argued that to take up the position of judge was to misunderstand the role of the historian. The historian is not 'the avenger', who judges the parties and rivalries of past generations and 'can punish unrighteousness, avenge the injured or reward the innocent'.[100] Rather, the proper role of the historian 'is to describe' and in doing so 'he stands impartial'.[101] History can 'show us that all our judgments are merely relative to time and circumstance'.[102] The historian should not be 'moved to indignation by something in the past', which may seem 'wicked to our own day', and instead should 'bring this thing into the context where it is natural'.[103] Butterfield argued that the Whig historian confused 'the importance which courts of legal justice must hold, and the finality they must have for practical reasons in society, with the most useless and unproductive of all forms of reflection – the dispensing of moral judgments upon people or upon actions in retrospect'.[104] The idea of history as 'the arbiter of controversy' was 'history raised into something like the mind of God'.[105]

4.2.4 *Christian Realism and the Truth of History*

In order to understand why Butterfield understood the role of the historian in those terms, it is useful to consider the place of Christianity in his world view. Butterfield was part of a conservative theological milieu that rejected liberal narratives of progress and 'rationalistic *hubris*' and sought to return theology 'to

[97] Butterfield, *The Whig Interpretation of History*, 12.
[98] Butterfield, *The Whig Interpretation of History*, 31.
[99] Butterfield, *The Whig Interpretation of History*, 65.
[100] Butterfield, *The Whig Interpretation of History*, 1.
[101] Butterfield, *The Whig Interpretation of History*, 73–74.
[102] Butterfield, *The Whig Interpretation of History*, 75.
[103] Butterfield, *The Whig Interpretation of History*, 17.
[104] Butterfield, *The Whig Interpretation of History*, 108.
[105] Butterfield, *The Whig Interpretation of History*, 113.

the frontlines of intellectual life'.[106] Butterfield's approach brought him into anti-liberal circles that extended beyond Britain. While there are debates over the extent of his sympathy for Nazism,[107] Butterfield nonetheless accepted an invitation in 1938 to visit Hitler's Germany and present a sponsored series of lectures about the Whig interpretation of history at Berlin, Bonn, Cologne, and Münster, strongly supported the Vichy regime during the war, despised de Gaulle and his exiled government in London ('a poor unhappy unrepresentative handful of people'), and reportedly enjoyed shocking liberal Cambridge friends and colleagues during the war with remarks such as 'Hitlerism will be alright . . . when it has won'.[108]

After the war Butterfield's mind 'turned most urgently to the fate of a devastated and humiliated Germany'.[109] He was particularly opposed to what he saw as the injustices of the denazification program when applied to those in the academy 'who had joined the Nazi party simply in order to keep their jobs and support their families',[110] and wrote numerous testimonials in support of Nazi academics. Butterfield's 'sensitivity to Germany's plight', along with the lectures he gave during the early 1950s on Christianity and international relations, widened his influence and were part of the reason that he was approached by the Rockefeller Foundation to establish the British Committee on the Theory of International Politics.[111] Through that collaboration, Butterfield found common ground with other international relations theorists in Britain and the United States who rejected liberal historiography and indeed 'any version of politics availing itself of the meaning of history'.[112] The repudiation of the liberal narrative of history as progress would become a central theme in the emergence of realist thought in international relations.[113]

---

[106] Guilhot, 'Portrait of the Realist as a Historian', 9; Guilhot, *After the Enlightenment*, 70.

[107] See, for example, the charitable view expressed in Bentley, *Life and Thought of Herbert Butterfield*, 137–157.

[108] Bentley, *Life and Thought of Herbert Butterfield*, 137–141 (on Butterfield's 1938 lecture series); 154 (on his comments about Hitlerism); 156–157 (on Vichy and de Gaulle).

[109] Bentley, *Life and Thought of Herbert Butterfield*, 267.

[110] Bentley, *Life and Thought of Herbert Butterfield*, 267.

[111] Bentley, *Life and Thought of Herbert Butterfield*, 270.

[112] Guilhot, 'Portrait of the Realist as a Historian', 12.

[113] See more broadly C Craig, *Glimmer of a New Leviathan: Total War in the Realism of Niebuhr, Morgenthau, and Waltz* (New York: Columbia University Press, 2003); Guilhot, *After the Enlightenment*, 69–99. For the relation of that Christian realist world view to contemporary forms of moral internationalism, see A Orford, 'Moral Internationalism and the Responsibility to Protect' (2013) 24 *European Journal of International Law* 83, at 93–108.

Christian Realism informed Butterfield's ideas about the 'truth of history', as well as his view of international relations and diplomacy.[114] For Butterfield, there was a broader meaning to be found in history, but the secular liberals were mistaken in thinking that the academic historian could offer that meaning. Instead, for Butterfield, it was Christianity that offered 'the key' to the interpretation of 'the whole human drama' – 'it is the combination of the history with a religion, or with something equivalent to a religion, which generates power and fills the story with significance'.[115] Butterfield believed that there was order in history, but he understood the existence of that order in theological terms.[116] The process of history was not the result of human design, as human beings were not 'sovereign makers of history' but rather 'are born to co-operate with Providence'.[117] Throughout history, the greatest danger had been posed by people who did not accept that their understanding of the world was incomplete and partial and who sought to impose their view of order on the world. To the extent that there was order in history, it was a sign that 'in the workings of history there must be felt the movement of a living God'.[118]

Butterfield thus had no time for the struggles that resulted from competing political interpretations of past events – 'the liberal, the Jesuit, the Fascist, the Communist, and all the rest may sail away with their militant versions of history, howling at one another across the interstellar spaces'.[119] The historian must recognise 'the history-making that was going on over men's heads, at cross purposes with them'.[120] History was a story of contingency and unpredictability because of 'that historical process which so cheats men of their purposes – that providence which deflects their labours to such unpredictable results'.[121] The role of the historian was therefore not to judge the conduct of others but rather to increase 'human understanding, extending it to all the ages, and binding the world into one'.[122] Rather than 'being moved to

---

[114] I Hall, 'History, Christianity, and Diplomacy: Sir Herbert Butterfield and International Relations' (2002) 28 *Review of International Studies* 719; P Sharp, 'Herbert Butterfield, the English School and the Civilizing Virtues of Diplomacy' (2003) 79 *International Affairs* 855.

[115] H Butterfield, *Christianity and History* (London: G Bell and Sons, 1950), 22–23.

[116] See, for example, Butterfield, *Christianity and History*; H Butterfield, 'The Scientific versus the Moralistic Approach in International Affairs' (1951) 27 *International Affairs* 411; H Butterfield, *Christianity, Diplomacy and War* (London: Epworth Press, 1953).

[117] Butterfield, *Christianity and History*, 99.

[118] Butterfield, *Christianity and History*, 111.

[119] Butterfield, *Christianity and History*, 23.

[120] Butterfield, *The Whig Interpretation of History*, 49.

[121] Butterfield, *The Whig Interpretation of History*, 49.

[122] Butterfield, *The Whig Interpretation of History*, 130–131.

indignation by something in the past which at first seems alien and perhaps even wicked to our own day', the historian should make 'the effort to bring this thing into the context where it is natural'.[123]

Butterfield believed that anachronism, presentism, Whig histories, and progress narratives were wrong and dangerous. Paying attention to his conservative Christian world view helps to remind us of *why* he believed they were wrong and dangerous. For Butterfield, progress narratives gave too much agency to human beings and propped up their grandiose fantasies that they could shape history or effect change. Indeed, '[j]udgment in history falls heaviest on those who come to think themselves gods, who fly in the face of Providence and history, who put their trust in man-made systems and worship the work of their own hands'.[124] Liberal progress narratives gave historians the false sense that they could judge the arc of history. Butterfield, in contrast, believed that human understanding was limited. The workings of Providence were mysterious and did not equate with the plans of any individuals or collectives. History plays out above the heads of human actors.

The political stakes of that position were made clear in Butterfield's reflections upon Germany's role in the Second World War. For Butterfield, 'the judgment which lies in the structure of history gives none of us the right to act as judges over others'.[125] While outsiders may 'say that Germany has come under judgment', they have 'no *right* to say any such thing'.[126] Certainly it was not 'within the competence of the technical historian' to make such a judgment'.[127] The question of a nation's guilt was 'a matter between itself and God – we as outsiders, or third parties, are not entitled to presume upon it'.[128]

Indeed, Butterfield considered that overly moralistic Europeans were in part responsible for creating the conditions in which Hitler's Germany became the aggressor. According to Butterfield, the problem for Europe after 1914 was that the conception of war within the European order had become 'more like the eighteenth-century conception of a war between the European

---

[123] Butterfield, *The Whig Interpretation of History*, 17.
[124] Butterfield, *Christianity and History*, 60.
[125] Butterfield, *Christianity and History*, 62.
[126] Butterfield, *Christianity and History*, 62.
[127] Butterfield, *Christianity and History*, 62.
[128] Butterfield, *Christianity and History*, 63. For examples of critical reactions to Butterfield's argument at the time from colleagues who saw it as too apologetic, see Soffer, *History, Historians, and Conservatism*, 203 (referring, for example, to Martin Wight's response that 'in seeking to avoid self-righteousness about the tyrant and the aggressor' Butterfield had lost sight of the implications for victims and the international community, and Stuart Hampshire's comment that 'Humility, and an appeal to historical complexities, can also be an evasion').

order as a whole and barbarism outside it'.[129] Such an approach should not
have been adopted within the European states system, which Butterfield
considered a model for international order. In his view, during earlier centuries European thinkers had responded to the wars of religion and the transfer of
the scientific method to the field of politics by developing a 'science of policy',
in which containing conflict and preventing revolution were the primary
ends.[130] That approach had been premised upon the Christian understanding
that political action was not 'sovereign action' but rather 'a co-operation with
time and providence'.[131] The result had been a 'science for the preservation of
a civilized order'.[132] According to Butterfield, the foundational premise of the
resulting 'European States-System' had been 'to accept the fact of human
conflict' but seek to prevent that conflict from overthrowing 'the whole
civilized order of things'.[133] The European system of balance of power 'stood
as a special civilized area and a providential order', within which it was
recognised that political actions are performed 'on the margin of deeper
historical processes'.[134] European states had failed by 'making diplomacy an
ideological affair' and rushing into 'blind moralistic angers and indignations'
about the behaviour of other states, rather than finding ways of working with
them to create a stable European order.[135] Thus Butterfield concluded that 'if
before Heaven it matters that Hitler was a wicked man, before men it is far
more relevant to consider how we ourselves helped to decide the form that his
wickedness would take'.[136]

Butterfield's challenge to Whig history was not then simply an expression of
the kind of impartial and objective scientific spirit for which his work is
regularly invoked, nor was he 'standing up for "History" in general'.[137]
Rather, Butterfield condemned the progress narratives of liberal Whig historians because his view of history, international relations, and diplomacy was
premised on an opposing and decidedly anti-liberal Christian Realist world
view.[138] His methods were not value-free, but derived from a very specific
vision of politics and of history. In time, Butterfield's methodological premises

[129] Butterfield, 'The Scientific versus the Moralistic', 418.
[130] Butterfield, 'The Scientific versus the Moralistic', 415–416.
[131] Butterfield, 'The Scientific versus the Moralistic', 416.
[132] Butterfield, 'The Scientific versus the Moralistic', 416.
[133] Butterfield, 'The Scientific versus the Moralistic', 417.
[134] Butterfield, 'The Scientific versus the Moralistic', 418.
[135] Butterfield, 'The Scientific versus the Moralistic', 421.
[136] Butterfield, 'The Scientific versus the Moralistic', 420.
[137] Keene, 'The English School and British Historians', 382.
[138] Hall, 'History, Christianity, and Diplomacy'; Sharp, 'Herbert Butterfield, the English School
and the Civilizing Virtues of Diplomacy', 866.

would become dogmas and his attack on 'Whig' history would become short-hand for those dogmas, but in his writing we can see his methods being articulated and justified on normative grounds, as an attack on the hubris of utopian politics and an articulation of conservative Christian Realism. In other words, here we see spelt out an account of what this method was for and not just what it was against.

There was, however, one form of progress narrative that Butterfield continued to countenance. That narrative concerned the methodological progress manifested in the embrace of contextualist methods. For Butterfield, '[t]he whole process of historical study is a movement towards historical research – it is to carry us from the general to the particular, from the abstract to the concrete'.[139] The approach advocated by Butterfield and his modernising generation treated contextualist methods as the telos of the professionalised field of history. Their approach had a powerful influence on the field of history in the United Kingdom and beyond for the remainder of the twentieth century, informing the growing focus on the 'micro-examination of detail' and the study of short periods with a view to accumulating evidence about the past.[140] That approach, and those who championed it, increasingly dominated the field and helped 'impose a view of correct method in the historical discipline'.[141] The language of method was used to undermine the claims of other approaches to 'represent serious historical work'.[142] That was the intellectual world in which the Cambridge School emerged.

4.3 JGA POCOCK AND THE ENGLISH COMMON LAWYER

4.3.1 *Pocock and the Cambridge School*

During the interwar period, Butterfield and other English modernisers had argued against 'Whig history' and its sweeping narratives of progress. They

---

[139] Butterfield, *The Whig Interpretation of History*, 69–70.

[140] Bentley, *Modernizing England's Past*, 195, 207.

[141] Bentley, *Modernizing England's Past*, 207.

[142] Bentley, *Modernizing England's Past*, 209. For critical responses from historians to the ways in which the demand for conformity with specific empiricist conventions has been deployed, see C Fasolt, *The Limits of History* (Chicago: University of Chicago Press, 2004); C Tomlins, 'After Critical Legal History: Scope, Scale, Structure' (2012) 8 *Annual Review of Law and Social Science* 31; PE Gordon, 'Contextualism and Criticism in the History of Ideas' in DM McMahon and S Moyn (eds), *Rethinking Modern European Intellectual History* (Oxford: Oxford University Press, 2014), 32; J Guldi and D Armitage, *The History Manifesto* (Cambridge: Cambridge University Press, 2015); E Kleinberg, JW Scott, and G Wilder, *Theses on Theory and History* (Wild on Collective, May 2018).

claimed that events and characters should only be considered in discrete contexts, and historians should not attempt to consider those contexts together or impose a broader form on the historical story. Two decades later, the idea that people or events must be understood in their 'context' was extended in a new and more radical argument made by a group of scholars who would come to be referred to as the Cambridge School. Their argument was that concepts, ideas, and even 'thought' could also only be meaningfully understood in their own discrete and temporally confined contexts.

In addition to focusing on the development of contextualist methods for the study of the history of political thought, a number of the original proponents of the Cambridge School method were also preoccupied with the 'intimate relationship' between 'the study of history and the study of law'.[143] That theme was the focus of one of the earliest texts to be associated with the Cambridge School – JGA Pocock's doctoral thesis, subsequently published as *The Ancient Constitution and the Feudal Law*.[144] While Pocock's methodological writings have had less direct influence on debates in international law,[145] it is worth pausing to reflect upon the significant role that *The Ancient Constitution* played as a bridge between the more concrete legal histories written by Maitland and the more abstract claims about legal method that would become central to narratives about the radical character of contextualist history as a challenge to the dangers, distortions, and myths of legal argument.

Pocock has dated the emergence of the 'Cambridge method' to around 1949.[146] At that point Pocock, who was a doctoral student supervised by Butterfield, became aware of the work of Peter Laslett. Laslett's studies of Robert Filmer and John Locke offered what were seen as ground-breaking contextualist readings that revised how both figures were received and, more broadly, challenged the idea that classical philosophical texts addressed time-less philosophical questions.[147] Pocock has described Laslett's pioneering

---

[143] James, 'JGA Pocock and the Idea of the "Cambridge School"', 88.

[144] Pocock, *The Ancient Constitution and the Feudal Law*.

[145] For examples of Pocock's methodological writings, see the essays collected in JGA Pocock, *Politics, Language and Time: Essays on Political Thought and History* (Chicago: University of Chicago Press, 1971); JGA Pocock, *Virtue, Commerce, and History: Essays on Political Thought and History, Chiefly in the Eighteenth Century* (Cambridge: Cambridge University Press, 1985); JGA Pocock, *Political Thought and History: Essays on Theory and Method* (Cambridge: Cambridge University Press, 2009).

[146] Pocock, 'Foundations and Moments', 37, at 37–38.

[147] For examples of Laslett's scholarship, see P Laslett, 'Sir Robert Filmer: The Man versus the Whig Myth' (1948) 5 *The William and Mary Quarterly* 523; R Filmer, *Patriarcha and Other Political Works*, ed P Laslett (Oxford: Basil Blackwell, 1949); P Laslett, 'The English Revolution and Locke's "Two Treatises of Government"' (1956) 12 *Cambridge Historical Journal* 40;

contextualisations of the work of Filmer and Locke as the foundation of the Cambridge School method.[148]

Just as influential for the Cambridge School style was Laslett's understanding of the challenges facing political philosophy in the academic and political world of the 1950s. In one of his most widely cited pronouncements, Laslett famously declared in 1956 that 'political philosophy is dead'.[149] By this he meant that both academic and political developments had 'put an end to philosophy as a pursuit' and 'radically revised the identity of the philosopher as a person'.[150] For Laslett, both 'the world of politics and the methods of studying it' had been radically transformed by the events of the previous half-century.[151] 'Faced with Hiroshima and with Belsen', it made little sense for theorists to devote themselves to offering up neat accounts of political concepts, establishing the existence of timeless principles, or drawing on classics as a source of answers to perennial problems.[152] Politics, Laslett argued, had 'become too serious to be left to philosophers'.[153] In making that claim, Laslett had in mind a very specific image of the philosopher as a figure who participated in formulating timeless and unquestionable principles – such as liberty, utility, or justice – that could guide politicians, political parties, or public opinion. To the extent that remnants of the 'broken' and no longer credible tradition of political philosophy persisted, it was in that 'movement growing every day more powerful for the restoration of a philosophy of all humanity', evidenced by 'international organisation' and 'in such documents – notably once more legal documents – as the Universal Declaration of Human Rights'.[154]

The old methods for studying politics were also being radically transformed. In England, the 'traditional Whig-liberal study of politics as an eclectic mix of

---

J Locke, *Two Treatises of Government*, ed P Laslett (Cambridge: Cambridge University Press, 1988 [1960]).

[148] Pocock, 'Foundations and Moments', 37–38; Pocock, 'A Response to Samuel James', 99–101. The significance of Laslett for the methods of the Cambridge School is more broadly discussed in M Bevir, 'Contextualism: From Modernist Method to Post-analytic Historicism' (2009) 3 *Journal of the Philosophy of History* 211; P Koikkalainen, 'Peter Laslett and the Contested Concept of Political Philosophy' (2009) 30 *History of Political Thought* 336; P Koikkalainen, 'The Politics of Contextualism: Normativity and the New Historians of Political Thought' (2015) 9 *Journal of the Philosophy of History* 347.

[149] P Laslett, 'Introduction' in P Laslett (ed), *Philosophy, Politics and Society* (Oxford: Basil Blackwell, 1956), vii.

[150] Laslett, 'Introduction', xiii.

[151] Laslett, 'Introduction', ix.

[152] Laslett, 'Introduction', vii.

[153] Laslett, 'Introduction', vii.

[154] Laslett, 'Introduction', xii.

history, philosophy, classics and law' that was typical of universities like
Cambridge was being challenged by the rise of a more empiricist
'Americanized' style of political science promising more rigorous methods
and increased accuracy.[155] The influence of analytical philosophy within
English philosophy departments had also revised the sense of what philosophy
was for. Analytical philosophers argued that philosophic inquiry should be
directed towards sharpening the analysis of how language was used and
exposing linguistic confusion, rather than offering a systematic view of all
knowledge or timeless answers to perennial questions. Faced with the rise of
social science in the United States, philosophical positivism in Britain, and
the demise of faith in political philosophy as a guide to action in the aftermath
of two world wars, Laslett concluded that 'winter has set in for the political
philosopher' imagined as a purveyor of the wisdom of the ages.[156]

What then was the future for political philosophy in such a context? For
Laslett the answer was twofold.[157] The first role for political studies he envisaged led in the direction of the Cambridge School. Scholars of political
thought should contribute to hastening the demise of the old vision of political
philosophy, by showing that there was no coherent tradition of philosophical
thought or even of particular schools of thought such as liberalism. Rather,
political theorists could play a role in developing a history of political thought
directed to showing that canonical texts did not in fact reveal political principles or normative statements that existed outside politics. Instead, such texts
should be understood as interventions in past political battles. Second, those
who sought to answer questions about politics should do so without calling
themselves political philosophers or claiming a 'prestige in the world at large
to which we should do better not to pretend'.[158] Rather, the political theorist
should develop an objective and scientific approach to the study of mass
society guided by 'the psychologist, the social anthropologist, and the sociolo-
gist'.[159] Laslett argued that it was vital not to 'believe that we have to wait until
our own problems are solved at the philosophical level' before deciding what
evidence is necessary to develop a 'workable analysis of society'.[160]

---

[155] Koikkalainen, 'Peter Laslett and the Contested Concept of Political Philosophy', 338.

[156] Laslett, 'Introduction', ix.

[157] See further Koikkalainen, 'Peter Laslett and the Contested Concept of Political Philosophy',
348–356.

[158] Laslett, 'Introduction', xiv.

[159] P Laslett, 'The Face to Face Society' in P Laslett (ed), *Philosophy, Politics and Society* (Oxford:
Basil Blackwell, 1956), 157, at 184.

[160] Laslett, 'The Face to Face Society', 184.

4.3.2 *Pocock and 'the Common-Law Mind'*

Pocock's early work can be understood as a historical narrative about the emergence of the form of historiography being advocated and attempted by Laslett. Pocock has described himself as writing the history of 'a form of historiography employed in political argument, and equally a form of political argument that took the form of historiography'.[161] Pocock's narrative was organised around the challenge posed to certain forms of law by history. According to Pocock, the emergence of contextualist historiography as a form of political argument had been profoundly shaped by humanist challenges to legal thought during the sixteenth and seventeenth centuries. Lawyers in Western Europe had been confronted with urgent and 'philosophically profound' problems concerning 'the relation of the past to the present'.[162] The way a sixteenth-century legal scholar thought about those problems 'might permanently affect the historical understanding of his civilization'.[163] For Pocock, 'each nation's thought about its past – it might be said, each nation's relationship with its past – was deeply affected by the character of its law and the ideas underlying it'.[164]

Pocock's narrative was organised around a binary account of the emergence of historical consciousness that was related to the form of law that dominated in any given nation. For Pocock, the distinction between written and unwritten forms of law was central to the way that each European nation had come to think about its past. Nations, like France, that had been strongly influenced by Roman law were able to develop a more modern historical sensibility, because scholars were able to place the original written texts in their correct context. According to Pocock, 'because Roman law was written … it could be reduced to the context of a past society', which allowed a 'critical spirit' to emerge.[165] As a result, the challenge to legal claims about the authority of Roman law had shaped the emergence of historical thought in states that had been strongly influenced by Roman law. In contrast, Pocock believed that nations like England that had maintained or created a form of unwritten or customary law were not able to develop the same historical sense.

---

[161] Pocock, 'A Response to Samuel James', 100.
[162] Pocock, *The Ancient Constitution and the Feudal Law*, 8.
[163] Pocock, *The Ancient Constitution and the Feudal Law*, 8.
[164] Pocock, *The Ancient Constitution and the Feudal Law*, 29.
[165] Pocock, *The Ancient Constitution and the Feudal Law*, 19.

Pocock traced 'the rise of modern historiography' to French universities during the sixteenth century and the change in the techniques of classical scholarship associated with 'the name of humanism'.[166] He argued that French legal humanists developed an approach that challenged the received methods of studying codified Roman law. Donald Kelley later built on Pocock's work to develop a rich account of that *mos gallicus*.[167] The French legal humanists argued that a return should be made to the 'purity' of the original Justinian text rather than relying upon the glosses and commentaries that overlaid it, and that there should also be a return to 'the meaning which these laws had possessed in the minds of the Romans who penned them'.[168] According to Pocock, in so doing, they effectively destroyed the authority of Roman law, by opening up the question of how and why a law should be obeyed when it 'had been framed for utterly different conditions and no longer bore its original meaning'.[169] The effect was to deny 'European civilization the use of one of the principal canons by which she was accustomed to guide herself'.[170] 'The moment', according to Pocock, 'was revolutionary'.[171] Yet the 'heroic' approach of the humanists was undertaken 'in the name of pure scholarship'.[172] The effect 'was to institute a historical outlook and the rudiments of a historical technique in many branches of European scholarship'.[173] According to Pocock, the 'kernel of historical method' developed during that period focused on 'reconstructing the institutions of society in the past and using them as a context in which, and by means of which, to interpret the actions, words and thoughts of men who lived at that time'.[174] For Pocock, that method has ever since 'distinguished' the 'historian's art'.[175]

In contrast, Pocock suggested that nations with a stronger tradition of customary or unwritten law did not develop the same historical consciousness. Customary law depended upon 'the essential medieval idea of law as a thing

---

[166] Pocock, *The Ancient Constitution and the Feudal Law*, 1, 3.
[167] For examples of the early work of Donald Kelley on legal humanism and historical consciousness, see DR Kelley, 'Legal Humanism and the Sense of History' (1966) 13 *Studies in the Renaissance* 184; DR Kelley, *Foundations of Modern Historical Scholarship: Language, Law, and History in the French Renaissance* (New York: Columbia University Press, 1970); DR Kelley, 'History, English Law, and the Renaissance' (1974) 65 *Past and Present* 24.
[168] Pocock, *The Ancient Constitution and the Feudal Law*, 9.
[169] Pocock, *The Ancient Constitution and the Feudal Law*, 10.
[170] Pocock, *The Ancient Constitution and the Feudal Law*, 11.
[171] Pocock, *The Ancient Constitution and the Feudal Law*, 11.
[172] Pocock, *The Ancient Constitution and the Feudal Law*, 11.
[173] Pocock, *The Ancient Constitution and the Feudal Law*, 5.
[174] Pocock, *The Ancient Constitution and the Feudal Law*, 1.
[175] Pocock, *The Ancient Constitution and the Feudal Law*, 1.

ancient, imminent, and unmade'.[176] Pocock argued that in many parts of Europe, the emergence of legal arguments that appealed to national customary and feudal laws was an attempt to respond to the humanist challenge to codified Roman law. He suggested that 'one of the attractions of custom was precisely that it offered a means of escape from the divorce of past and present threatened by the criticisms of the historical school'.[177] Roman law was written and therefore, in Pocock's view, 'unchangeable' because 'it could be subjected to grammatical analysis and proved to belong to a past state of society'. The legal reliance on a 'concept of custom undoubtedly did much to impede the growth of a critical approach to medieval and barbarian history'.[178] Because custom was 'by its nature unwritten' and 'interpreted through the mouths of judges', lawyers could argue that the authority of customary law was derived from its links to practices stretching back to time immemorial and yet it 'never became obsolete'.[179]

Much of Pocock's book was a study of 'the sort of historical thought' that developed in England – 'a country where only one system of law, and that essentially customary, seemed ever to have penetrated'.[180] According to Pocock, something he called the 'common-law mind' represented the survival in England of a medieval way of thinking about law that lacked historical consciousness, was highly insular, and foreshadowed the Whiggish approach to English history diagnosed by Butterfield. In making that diagnosis of the nature of the 'common-law mind', Pocock followed to a degree in the footsteps of Maitland, upon whose work Pocock drew. Like Maitland, Pocock argued that Sir Edward Coke had offered a classical formulation of the seventeenth-century conception of the common law, which was in turn 'the predecessor and to a large extent the parent of the more famous "Whig interpretation"' of English history.[181]

However, unlike Maitland, whose historical arguments were based on fine-grained studies of English legal institutions, doctrines, cases, and procedures across centuries, Pocock's analysis focused primarily on the political writings of Coke. Pocock's account of 'the common-law mind' was explicitly premised on 'assuming that Coke . . . may be taken as a safe guide to the thought of his profession'.[182] For Pocock, the common-law mind was 'monolithic' and could

---

[176] Pocock, *The Ancient Constitution and the Feudal Law*, 16.
[177] Pocock, *The Ancient Constitution and the Feudal Law*, 14.
[178] Pocock, *The Ancient Constitution and the Feudal Law*, 19.
[179] Pocock, *The Ancient Constitution and the Feudal Law*, 15.
[180] Pocock, *The Ancient Constitution and the Feudal Law*, 29.
[181] Pocock, *The Ancient Constitution and the Feudal Law*, 46.
[182] Pocock, *The Ancient Constitution and the Feudal Law*, 45–46.

safely be studied by focusing on one representative.[183] In addition, Pocock focused primarily on Coke's contributions to Parliamentary debates and pamphlet controversies concerning the common law or the constitution.[184] Pocock understood Maitland to have shown that the 'defect of the common lawyers' historical and legal thought' was 'their ignorance of any law other than their own' along with their inability to 'think historically'.[185] Pocock considered that his own work offered further evidence in support of the ignorance and defects of the common lawyer.[186]

By studying 'the acts and arguments performed by Coke and others in parliament',[187] Pocock confidently concluded that English legal thought was based on 'the belief in the antiquity of the common law' and 'belief in the existence of the ancient constitution'.[188] The common-law mind 'was as nearly insular as a human being's could be'.[189] In making such a claim, Pocock did not consider the legal materials that were available to Coke, the accuracy of those materials, the scale of Coke's engagement with medieval sources, his handling of the medieval materials with which he worked, the legal work of his contemporaries, his use of judicial and government records, or the legal theory that informed the treatises of the time.[190] Pocock nonetheless felt able to conclude that Coke's thought – and thus common-law thought in general – was insular, ahistorical, and represented 'a most vigorous survival of the medieval concept of custom in English political thinking'.[191] As a result, the 'common-law interpretation of history' provided 'a powerful stream of medieval thought flowing into the seventeenth and eighteenth centuries'.[192]

Pocock's arguments about the historical sophistication of French legal humanism and the Whiggish quality of claims made by English lawyers were

---

[183] Pocock, *The Ancient Constitution and the Feudal Law*, 265.

[184] Pocock, *The Ancient Constitution and the Feudal Law*, 46, 279.

[185] Pocock, *The Ancient Constitution and the Feudal Law*, 58, 66.

[186] In contrast, where Pocock expressed only contempt for the common-law mind, Maitland 'respected his lawyer colleagues, thought little of the individual Cambridge historians of his time, collectively thought them a quarrelsome lot, and when offered the Regius chair of history near the end of his life he unhesitatingly declined': Milsom, 'Maitland', 267 (references deleted).

[187] Pocock, *The Ancient Constitution and the Feudal Law*, 279.

[188] Pocock, *The Ancient Constitution and the Feudal Law*, 46.

[189] Pocock, *The Ancient Constitution and the Feudal Law*, 56.

[190] For an example of historical work that explores Coke's contribution in that light, see A Musson, 'Myth, Mistake, Invention? Excavating the Foundations of the English Legal Tradition' in A Lewis and M Lobban (eds), *Law and History* (Oxford: Oxford University Press, 2003), 63.

[191] Pocock, *The Ancient Constitution and the Feudal Law*, 51.

[192] Pocock, *The Ancient Constitution and the Feudal Law*, 51.

influential. So too was his premise that written law is 'unchangeable'. When read alongside the subsequent work of Donald Kelley and Quentin Skinner, we see emerging a narrative about the revolutionary humanist challenge to medieval legalism and the relation of that encounter to the emergence of a European historical consciousness. Yet while Pocock's work undoubtedly contributed to the emergence of a Cambridge school method, he himself noted that '90% of the discussion' of the Cambridge School 'is related to Quentin Skinner's "Meaning and Understanding" essay and appeared after its publication in 1969'.[193] It is to Skinner's work, and specifically its engagement with law around questions of methods, that I now turn.

4.4 QUENTIN SKINNER AND THE SCHOLASTIC LAWYER

4.4.1 *Skinner, Revolution, and the Turn to Method*

The work of Quentin Skinner offers the clearest articulation and justification of the development of the method that has come to be associated with a 'Cambridge School'. Skinner was taught at the University of Cambridge by John Burrow, Duncan Forbes, and Laslett, and his conceptualisation of historical method was strongly influenced by the scholarship of Laslett, Pocock, and Dunn.[194] For Skinner, the approach to the history of ideas outside Cambridge in the 1960s was largely 'an unfriendly landscape' in which 'the history of ideas was so little valued . . . due to the power of Marxism . . . as a historical methodology'.[195] He described spending 'the opening years of my academic career in a state of frustrated rage against this particular world-order',

---

[193] Pocock, 'A Response to Samuel James', 101.

[194] Q Skinner, 'A Reply to My Critics' in J Tully (ed), *Meaning and Context: Quentin Skinner and His Critics* (Princeton: Princeton University Press, 1988), 231, 233–234 (discussing his debt to the scholarship of Pocock, Dunn, and Laslett, and suggesting that '[o]ne way of describing my original essays would be to say that I merely tried to identify and restate in more abstract terms the assumptions on which Pocock's and especially Laslett's scholarship seemed to me to be based'; Q Skinner, 'On Encountering the Past: Interview by Petri Koikkalainen and Sami Syrämäki' (2002) 6 *Finnish Yearbook of Political Thought* 34, at 39–42 (pointing to Pocock's *The Ancient Constitution and the Feudal Law*, Dunn's *The Political Thought of John Locke*, and Laslett's introduction to John Locke's *Two Treatises of Government* as path-breaking contextual works that provided models for his scholarship, and recalling his aim to do for Hobbes what Laslett did for Locke). For discussion of the influence of Laslett on Skinner's intellectual formation, see also E Perreau-Saussine, 'Quentin Skinner in Context' (2007) 69 *The Review of Politics* 106; Bevir, 'Contextualism: From Modernist Method to Post-analytic Historicism'; Koikkalainen, 'Peter Laslett'; Koikkalainen, 'The Politics of Contextualism'.

[195] Skinner, 'On Encountering the Past', 37.

and of launching 'a terrorist attack' on that view of the world in the form of his 1969 essay, 'Meaning and Understanding in the History of Ideas'.[196]

When thinking about the nature of Skinner's opposition to the work being undertaken in his field during the 1960s, it is worth recalling the radical situation in which historians of Skinner's generation found themselves. That was the decade of student rebellions at Berkeley, the LSE, the Sorbonne, and Columbia, the French general strike, the Black Panthers, the assassinations of Che Guevara and Martin Luther King, the Prague Spring, the Red Guard, and resistance to the Vietnam war. By 1968, political protest and student mobilisation had produced crises of authority in many societies around the world.[197] Skinner's methodological manifestos were written at the same time as work being done by radical historians in England and beyond, including the Communist Party Historians' Group, the Warwick School, and the History Workshop in the United Kingdom, Lucien Febvre, Fernand Braudel, and the *Annales* school in France, Jean-Claude Perrot and Michel Foucault in France, and Hayden White, Joan Wallach Scott, Linda Gordon, and Natalie Zemon Davis in North America.[198] Skinner's early studies appeared alongside other work offering radical new interpretations of English history, including EP Thompson's *The Making of the English Working Class*, *Whigs and Hunters*, and his co-authored *Albion's Fatal Tree*,[199] Christopher Hill's *Puritanism and Revolution*, *Intellectual Origins of*

[196] Skinner, 'On Encountering the Past', 39.

[197] See generally J Suri, *Power and Protest: The Global Revolution and the Rise of Détente* (Cambridge: Harvard University Press, 2005); R Vinen, *The Long '68: Radical Protest and Its Enemies* (Milton Keynes: Allen Lane, 2018).

[198] For a series of reflections on the radical historical milieu of the era, see MARHO: The Radical Historians Organization, *Visions of History: Interviews with EP Thompson, Eric Hobsbawm, Sheila Rowbotham, Linda Gordon, Natalie Zemon Davis, William Appleman Williams, Staughton Lynd, David Montgomery, Herbert Gutman, Vincent Harding, John Womack, CLR James, and Moshe Lewin* (New York: Pantheon, 1983); D Fassin, *Michel Foucault* (trans B Wing) (London: Faber and Faber, 1992); H Kaye, *The Education of Desire: Marxists and the Writing of History* (New York and London: Routledge, 1992); E Hobsbawm, *Interesting Times: A Twentieth-Century Life* (London: Allen Lane, 2002); C Winslow, D Hay, and P Linebaugh, 'Introduction to the Second Edition' in D Hay, P Linebaugh, JG Rule, EP Thompson, and C Winslow (eds), *Albion's Fatal Tree: Crime and Society in Eighteenth-Century England* (London and New York: Verso, 2011), xix; C Winslow (ed), *EP Thompson and the Making of the New Left* (New York: Monthly Review Press, 2014).

[199] EP Thompson, *The Making of the English Working Class* (London: Victor Gollancz, 1963); EP Thompson, *Whigs and Hunters: The Origins of the Black Act* (New York: Pantheon, 1975); D Hay, P Linebaugh, JG Rule, EP Thompson, and C Winslow, *Albion's Fatal Tree: Crime and Society in Eighteenth-Century England* (London and New York: Verso, 2011 [1975]).

the English Revolution, and *The World Turned Upside Down*,[200] Eric Hobsbawm's *The Age of Revolution, Industry and Empire*, and *Captain Swing* (the latter written with George Rudé),[201] Raymond Williams' genre-challenging works of literary, cultural, and social history, including *Culture and Society, The Long Revolution, The Country and the City*, and *Keywords*,[202] Juliet Mitchell's 'Women: The Longest Revolution',[203] and Sheila Rowbotham's *Women, Resistance and Revolution* and *Hidden from History*.[204] Journals such as the *New Left Review, New Reasoner*, and *Universities and Left Review* were publishing the work of radical historians and initiating programmes of conferences and adult education in which historians took part.[205] For many, the study of the past was directly linked to the project of transforming the present – a position well illustrated by EP Thompson, Raymond Williams, and Stuart Hall's *May Day Manifesto 1968*, which appeared with the names of over seventy signatories associated with the New Left,[206] and by the organisation of the National Women's Liberation Conference in 1970, initially conceived of by historians Sally Alexander and Sheila Rowbotham. It was, in short, 'a time of rebellion, revolution, struggle,

[200] C Hill, *Puritanism and Revolution* (London: Sicker & Warburg, 1958); C Hill, *The Intellectual Origins of the English Revolution* (New York: Oxford University Press, 1965); C Hill, *The World Turned Upside Down* (New York: Viking, 1972).

[201] E Hobsbawm, *The Age of Revolution: Europe 1789–1848* (New York: Vintage, 1962); E Hobsbawm, *Industry and Empire* (New York: Pantheon, 1968); E Hobsbawm and G Rudé, *Captain Swing* (London: Phoenix Press, 1969).

[202] R Williams, *Culture and Society 1780–1950* (London: Chatto & Windus, 1958); R Williams, *The Long Revolution* (London: Chatto & Windus, 1961); R Williams, *The Country and the City* (New York: Oxford University Press, 1973); R Williams, *Keywords: A Vocabulary of Culture and Society* (Oxford: Oxford University Press, 2015 [1976]). In introducing a new edition of *Keywords* in 1983, Williams commented that '[i]t was not easy then, and it is not much easier now, to describe this work in terms of a particular academic subject', and noted that the book had been classified 'under headings as various as cultural history, historical semantics, history of ideas, social criticism, literary history and sociology': R Williams, 'Introduction' in *Keywords*, ix, at xxv. For the argument that Williams 'worked the edges of inherited and inhabited forms', see EC Walker, 'The Long Revolution of Raymond Williams' (2006) 37 *The Wordsworth Circle* 60, at 63.

[203] J Mitchell, 'Women: The Longest Revolution' (1966) I/40 *New Left Review* 11.

[204] S Rowbotham, *Women, Resistance and Revolution* (New York: Pantheon, 1972); S Rowbotham, *Hidden from History* (London: Pluto, 1973).

[205] See S Hall, 'Introducing NLR' (1960) I/1 *New Left Review* 1; S Hall, 'Life and Times of the First New Left' (2010) 61 *New Left Review* 177; EP Thompson, 'The New Left' in C Winslow (ed), *EP Thompson and the Making of the New Left* (New York: Monthly Review Press, 2014), 119; F Foks, 'The Sociological Imagination of the British New Left: "Culture" and the "Managerial Society", C. 1956–1962' (2018) 15 *Modern Intellectual History* 801.

[206] R Williams (ed), *May Day Manifesto 1968* (London: Verso, 2018).

occupations, strikes – and of living, breathing hope that the old order was in collapse, and that a new society was possible'.[207]

For Skinner, too, the 1960s witnessed 'the beginning of a revolution in our ways of thinking about the history of political theory'.[208] Skinner's revolution, however, was methodological. His was not the sensibility of 'a revolutionary writing history'.[209] Indeed, Skinner was opposed to the work being done by politically radical historians in England and beyond. Skinner was dismissive of the 'economic determinism' of the Annales School and its 'baleful effect on the status as well as the methodology of intellectual history',[210] criticised CB Macpherson's *The Political Theory of Possessive Individualism* as manifesting a 'straightforward ideological reflex',[211] described Raymond Williams' *Keywords* as 'confusingly vague', 'question-begging', and illustrative of 'a prevalent but impoverishing form of reductionism',[212] and characterised the work of 'Christopher Hill and other Marxist historians' as 'highly reductionist'.[213] In subsequent reflections, he has argued that 'the intellectual milieu into which I originally launched my bromides' was one in which 'a number of historians were practising their craft in violation of what I proposed as canons of good historical method'.[214]

Skinner's early programme of research was centred on establishing his proposed 'canons of good historical method'. His aim was 'to defend a series of philosophical arguments about interpretation' and couch them 'in the form of precepts about method'.[215] The centrality of method to Skinner's sense of history was evident from his earliest work. The essays he published in the mid-1960s foregrounded 'methodological adequacy',[216] argued against a 'tendency to treat the study of intellectual history as ersatz philosophy' and the

---

[207] O Jones, 'Introduction' in Williams (ed), *May Day Manifesto 1968*, 1.

[208] Phillipson and Skinner, 'Preface', xii.

[209] For the characterisation of CLR James in those terms, see MARHO, *Visions of History*, 263.

[210] Skinner, 'On Encountering the Past', 37–38.

[211] Skinner, 'On Encountering the Past', 38.

[212] Q Skinner, 'The Idea of a Cultural Lexicon' in Q Skinner, *Visions of Politics: Volume I, Regarding Method* (Cambridge: Cambridge University Press, 2002), 158, at 160, 174.

[213] Skinner, 'On Encountering the Past', 39.

[214] Skinner, 'A Reply to My Critics', 234.

[215] Skinner, 'A Reply to My Critics', 233. Commentators on Skinner's early work have also treated the focus on method as a distinguishing feature: see M Goldie, 'The Context of *The Foundations*' in A Brett and J Tully with H Hamilton-Bleakley (eds), *Rethinking the Foundations of Modern Political Thought* (Cambridge: Cambridge University Press, 2006), 3 ('Skinner's early work was devoted as much to questions of method as to substantive historical exposition').

[216] Q Skinner, 'Hobbes's "Leviathan"' (1964) VII *The Historical Journal* 321, at 330.

'confusion' produced by that tendency,[217] endorsed Butterfield's critique of 'whig historiography',[218] and offered scientific accounts of historical method, complete with logical arguments expressed as mathematical formulations.[219]

In 'Meaning and Understanding in the History of Ideas', the most influential of his essays, Skinner set out to establish 'the appropriate methodology for the history of ideas'.[220] For Skinner, the appropriate way to study political thought was through specialised histories of each agent who used an idea or a concept, the specific situation in which they used it, and the intention with which they did so. That focus on understanding 'long-dead thinkers' in their historical context was the key to interpreting all past texts, whether they were political, theological, literary, or legal.[221] Indeed, Skinner rejected as too limited the claim made by a critic that his work simply offered 'a method for doing the history of ideas'.[222] Rather, he explained that his goal was more ambitious: 'to articulate some general arguments about the process of interpretation itself, and to draw from them a series of what I take to be methodological implications'.[223] He claimed that his work 'may be said to establish and prove the case for this methodology – to establish it not as a suggestion, an aesthetic preference, or a piece of academic imperialism, but as a matter of conceptual propriety, a matter of seeing what the necessary conditions are for the understanding of utterances'.[224]

Throughout his career, Skinner continued to insist on the centrality of his method to any attempt to engage with past texts. He dismissed those who were 'against method' as being condemned 'to making unselfconscious use of whatever intellectual tools may happen to be lying around in our environment'.[225] His sense of the centrality of method to his program was indicated by the title subsequently given to the first volume of his collected essays – *Regarding Method*.[226] Skinner described the republication of his essays in *Regarding Method* as a contribution to the 'articulation and defence' of his

---

[217] Skinner, 'Hobbes's "Leviathan"', 333.

[218] Q Skinner, 'History and Ideology in the English Revolution' (1965) VIII *The Historical Journal* 178.

[219] Q Skinner, 'The Limits of Historical Explanations' (1966) 41 *Philosophy* 199.

[220] Q Skinner, 'Meaning and Understanding in the History of Ideas' (1969) 8 *History and Theory* 3, at 49.

[221] Q Skinner, 'General Preface' in Q Skinner, *Visions of Politics: Volume I, Regarding Method* (Cambridge: Cambridge University Press, 2002), vi, at vii.

[222] Skinner, 'A Reply to My Critics', 234.

[223] Skinner, 'A Reply to My Critics', 234.

[224] Skinner, 'Meaning and Understanding, 49.

[225] Skinner, 'A Reply to My Critics', 233.

[226] Q Skinner, *Visions of Politics: Volume I, Regarding Method* (Cambridge: Cambridge University Press, 2002).

method and continued to claim that if the history of ideas is to be written 'in a properly historical style', such a method is needed.[227] The method espoused by Skinner subsequently became 'a kind of orthodoxy across the interpretative social sciences', where it has often been referred to as 'contextualism'.[228] 'Meaning and Understanding' is taught in many first-year history programmes worldwide, and it is regularly cited as setting out the tenets of a contextualist approach to intellectual history. And as we have seen, Skinner's methodological axioms have also been brought into play in debates over the meaning of international law.

For the purposes of the debates with which this book is concerned, three key aspects of the methodological approach proposed by Skinner are worth emphasising. First, in arguing that a contextualist method could be extended to the history of political thought, Skinner was arguing that 'thought' has a determinate temporal context, just as individuals, events, or objects do. Only thoughts that are proper to their time are thinkable in a given context. In order to understand a particular utterance or text, the contextualist historian must therefore reconstruct the possible meanings the author could have intended in the temporal context of 'the given occasion' when an utterance was 'performed' or a text was written.[229]

It is worth pausing to think about the very specific 'problems of verification' to which that claim gives rise.[230] Determining what can be thought in a particular context raises different challenges to those an empiricist historian might face in verifying when an event really took place, when a particular person lived, or what kinds of clothes people wore in a particular period. The contextualist historian of political thought claims to be able to establish what was thinkable in a given temporal context and what was not. In addition, contextualist historians claim to be able to show as a matter of evidence that the particular individual whose texts are being studied resembled their time and thought only the things that their time made thinkable. Applying a contextualist method to intellectual history is thus based on the assertion that thoughts can be fixed in their proper place through logics of resemblance and differentiation. An anachronic thought or idea is one that does not belong in the time in which it has been allegedly located. The rules that determine whether something resembles or belongs to one time or another are treated as general and timeless. Contextualist historians claim to be able to establish

---

[227] Skinner, 'General Preface', vi, at vii.
[228] Gordon, 'Contextualism and Criticism in the History of Ideas', 32.
[229] Skinner, 'Meaning and Understanding', 48.
[230] J Rancière, 'The Concept of Anachronism and the Historian's Truth' (2015) 3 *In/Print* 21, at 28.

whether a thought resembles its time through processes of empirical reconstruction.

Second, Skinner challenged any scholarly or professional arguments that attempted to trace a history of ideas or a tradition of thought across time.[231] Skinner asserted in 'Meaning and Understanding' that it is a mistake even to try to write histories 'tracing the morphology of a given concept over time'.[232] He put this unambiguously: 'there *is* no history of the idea to be written'.[233] Indeed, it would be misguided and 'seem little more than a very misleading fetishism of words' for a historian to try 'to make any sort of historical study out of focusing on the "idea"' of, for example, 'equality', 'sovereignty', or 'natural law', or 'even to retain the form of the history of an idea'.[234] Skinner was similarly scathing about the 'mythology of doctrines', which he saw as illustrated by the 'wholly meaningless' and 'crude' arguments made by lawyers, leading to various 'kinds of historical absurdity' and 'anachronism'.[235]

Skinner claimed that the only history that should be attempted was a history of every statement made with an expression. While, as he recognised, this 'would of course be an almost absurdly ambitious enterprise', it would 'at least be conceptually proper'.[236] If we apply Skinner's argument to legal concepts (as he explicitly did), there is no understanding to be gained about any legal concept (sovereignty, property, investment, expropriation, self-determination, threats to the peace, non-intervention, collective security, crimes against humanity, genocide, aggression, freedom of navigation, occupation, or even international law itself) by considering its development, evolution, transformation, application, or interpretation over time. It is 'foolishly and needlessly naïve' to do anything other than treat each text as 'the embodiment of a particular intention, on a particular occasion' and thus 'specific to its situation'.[237] To 'try to transcend' that temporal context amounts to 'not merely a methodological fallacy, but something like a moral error'.[238] Skinner argued that past texts, including past legal texts, 'are concerned with

---

[231] Skinner, 'Meaning and Understanding', at 3, discussing A Lovejoy, *The Great Chain of Being* (New York: Torchbook, 1960). For a very different reading of the intellectual style and interdisciplinary commitments of Lovejoy, see W Breckman, 'Intellectual History and the Interdisciplinary Ideal' in DM McMahon and S Moyn (eds), *Rethinking Modern European Intellectual History* (Oxford: Oxford University Press, 2014), 275, at 276–278.

[232] Skinner, 'Meaning and Understanding', 48.

[233] Skinner, 'Meaning and Understanding', 38.

[234] Skinner, 'Meaning and Understanding', 38–39.

[235] Skinner, 'Meaning and Understanding', 10.

[236] Skinner, 'Meaning and Understanding', 39.

[237] Skinner, 'Meaning and Understanding', 50.

[238] Skinner, 'Meaning and Understanding', 50, 53.

their own quite alien problems' and not 'somehow concerned with our own problems as well'.[239] As a result, 'we must learn to do our own thinking for ourselves'.[240]

In the lightly revised version of 'Meaning and Understanding' published in 2002 in *Regarding Method*, Skinner insisted that he continued to 'remain sceptical about the value of writing histories of concepts'.[241] However, in a concluding retrospective included in the same volume, Skinner revisited that question in a discussion of the conceptual history project led by Reinhart Koselleck.[242] While Skinner suggested that '[h]ow far one can hope to capture the historicity of concepts by adopting Koselleck's approach remains a question', there nonetheless 'ought not in my view to be doubts about the very idea of writing conceptual histories – or not, at least, if these are histories of how concepts can be put to use over time'.[243]

However, while Skinner gradually came to accept that writing histories of concepts (as opposed to a history of ideas or a mythology of doctrines) might be a respectable academic project, he continued to envisage that project as involving 'the pointillist study of sudden conceptual shifts'.[244] For Skinner, the history of political thought should properly be envisaged as 'a sequence of episodes'.[245] Each of the episodes that make up the ordered succession of human time takes place in a distinct context. Skinner conveyed a pointillist vision of history as an opposition between time as chronos flowing from past to present, and the specific points or contexts that stand out as distinct and self-identical moments within chronological time.

Third, to the extent that Skinner's vision of politics included any account of the movement between one episode or context and the next, it was through his focus on 'the figure of the innovating ideologist'.[246] For Skinner, an 'innovating ideologist' redeploys existing evaluative terms in the attempt to legitimise novel or questionable forms of conduct or action. Skinner focused on 'the position of a political actor', who is 'anxious to engage in a particular

---

[239] Skinner, 'Meaning and Understanding', 52.
[240] Skinner, 'Meaning and Understanding', 52.
[241] Skinner, 'Meaning and Understanding in the History of Ideas' in Skinner, *Regarding Method*, 57, at 86.
[242] For a discussion of Koselleck's conceptual history project and its relevance to international law, see Chapter 7.
[243] Q Skinner, 'Retrospect: Studying Rhetoric and Conceptual Change' in Skinner, *Regarding Method*, 175, at 178.
[244] Skinner, 'Retrospect', 180. For a discussion of Skinner's style in relation to pointillism, see also K Palonen, *Quentin Skinner: History, Politics, Rhetoric* (Cambridge: Polity Press, 2003), 179.
[245] Skinner, 'A Reply to My Critics', 234.
[246] Skinner, 'Moral Principles and Social Change' in Skinner, *Regarding Method*, 145, at 149.

course of action' but also to appear legitimate.[247] The 'problem facing an agent who wishes to legitimate what he is doing at the same time as gaining what he wants' is twofold – he is faced with the 'instrumental problem of tailoring his normative language in order to fit his projects' and with the 'problem of tailoring his projects in order to fit the available normative language'.[248] Innovating ideologists rhetorically manipulate concepts available to them in order to evince, express, or solicit approval or disapproval of particular actions. It is through this way of framing politics that we can 'return to the classic texts themselves with a clearer prospect of understanding them'.[249]

More broadly, Skinner claimed that adopting his method could 'illuminate some of the connections between political theory and practice'.[250] Having placed the figure of the innovating ideologist at the centre of his account of social change, Skinner argued that it is through the effective 'rhetorical manipulation' of evaluative terms by individuals 'that any society succeeds in establishing, upholding, questioning or altering its moral identity'.[251] Innovating ideologists attempt to bring about conceptual change in order to change the linguistic and thus normative constraints on their actions or to produce constraints on the actions of others. Whether or not they succeed will be 'essentially a linguistic matter'.[252] For Skinner, understanding political history involved contesting the 'somewhat marginal role' that historians had assigned 'to political ideas and principles in seeking to explain political behaviour'.[253]

Skinner's focus on individual agency, his privileging of language as the medium of social change, and the idea of the individual as an innovator each carry with them a particular idea of the political.[254] The effect is to substitute a vision of politics as a realm of innovating ideologists for other accounts of political and social change. For Skinner, the agents of history are individual innovating ideologists rather than, say, revolutionary forces, warring classes, workers, capitalists, political parties, or social movements. Societies change

---

[247] Skinner, 'General Preface', xii.
[248] Skinner, 'General Preface', xii–xiii.
[249] Skinner, 'General Preface', xiii.
[250] Skinner, 'General Preface', xi.
[251] Skinner, 'Moral Principles and Social Change', 149.
[252] Skinner, 'Moral Principles and Social Change', 149.
[253] Skinner, 'General Preface', xi.
[254] See also Koikkalainen, 'The Politics of Contextualism'; J Isaac, 'Progress, Innovation and the Problem of Conceptual Change', Paper presented at the *History, Politics, Law: Thinking through the International Conference*, May 2016 (discussing the idea of change inherent in the use of 'innovation').

because of the skill with which individual innovators manipulate language. According to Skinner, his approach offers 'a clearer understanding of the links between political theory and practice'.[255] We cannot 'expect to attain this level of understanding', Skinner claimed, by adopting other methods.[256]

4.4.2 *Skinner's Lawyers: Scholastics, Humanists, and the 'Genuinely Historical Spirit'*

Like Pocock, Skinner traced that version of historical consciousness and that way of thinking about contexts back to the Renaissance and to a debate about the humanist challenges to scholastic interpretations of law. In *The Foundations of Modern Political Thought*,[257] which has been described by Pocock as 'the recognised masterwork of the "Cambridge School"',[258] the opposition between the scholastic lawyer and the historicising humanist emerges in the form of a historical narrative. In the preface, Skinner explained his intention to use his study of medieval and early modern political theory to 'exemplify a particular way of approaching the study and interpretation of historical texts'.[259] He had discussed his 'method' in a series of articles published over the previous twelve years, and suggested that 'if my method has any merits, these will emerge as I try to practise my own precepts'.[260] Reflecting on his reasons for writing *Foundations* decades later, Skinner confirmed that he was 'not primarily interested in making a contribution to the history or the historiography of the subject', but 'was much more concerned in those far-off days with questions about interpretation, explanation and historical method more generally'.[261]

Foundations is a key text in the consolidation of Skinner's methodological project not only because it exemplified his method, but more importantly

---

[255] Skinner, 'General Preface', xiii.

[256] Skinner, 'General Preface', xiii.

[257] Q Skinner, *The Foundations of Modern Political Thought*, 2 volumes (Cambridge: Cambridge University Press, 1978).

[258] For his reference to *Foundations* as the masterwork of the Cambridge School, see Pocock, 'A Response to Samuel James', 103.

[259] Skinner, *Foundations I*, x. See also A Brett and J Tully, 'Preface' in A Brett and J Tully with H Hamilton-Bleakley (eds), *Rethinking the Foundations of Modern Political Thought* (Cambridge: Cambridge University Press, 2006), viii, at ix (commenting that *Foundations* 'was not a book about method in itself, but it was one that self-consciously aimed to exemplify a method').

[260] Skinner, *Foundations I*, x.

[261] Q Skinner, 'Surveying the *Foundations*: A Retrospect and Reassessment' in A Brett and J Tully with H Hamilton-Bleakley (eds), *Rethinking the Foundations of Modern Political Thought* (Cambridge: Cambridge University Press, 2006), 236, at 238–239.

because it offered a progress narrative about the emergence of that contextualist method in Europe during the Renaissance. Law and lawyers play a central role in that story about 'the emergence of humanism'.[262] Skinner's narrative is organised around the encounter between scholasticism and humanism through their shifting relations to Roman lawyers and canon lawyers. Like Pocock, Skinner's story about law was not concerned with the practice of lawyers or their role within legal institutions or the medieval university, but rather focused on arguments about law made in broader political tracts and treatises.[263] As we will see, the method that Skinner traced to the Italian Renaissance bears a strong resemblance to the method that he himself had developed. Although *Foundations* was not overtly about method, Skinner there immersed his readers in a story about good historicising humanists and bad scholastic lawyers.

Skinner introduced *Foundations* as a story about 'the ideal of liberty'.[264] Decades later, Skinner would reflect that the book had helped 'to open a window on to a world that liberalism had closed off', and to articulate a more exacting 'humanist vision of liberty' that he associated with 'the humanism of the Renaissance' and that had been lost with the triumph of a more democratic understanding of political liberty.[265] His narrative opened with the rise of the Northern Italian city-republics in the twelfth century and their centuries-long struggle to resist the rule of the Holy Roman Empire. This was a story of military struggle, in which for two centuries the German Emperors tried and failed to resume control over the *Regnum Italicum*. But it was also a story of ideological struggle, in which the city propagandists developed the concepts of *libertas* and *libertà*, denoting both political independence and republican self-government, as weapons to challenge the claims by the German Emperors to be the legal rulers over the cities of the *Regnum*.

Only a few pages into Skinner's masterwork, a formalist approach to law entered the story on the side of the Empire and as the enemy of liberty. For

---

[262] Skinner, *Foundations I*, 35.
[263] A Brett, 'Scholastic Political Thought and the Modern Concept of the State' in A Brett and J Tully with H Hamilton-Bleakley (eds), *Rethinking the Foundations of Modern Political Thought* (Cambridge: Cambridge University Press, 2006), 130. For an account that does relate Skinner's narrative to the shifting locations of scholasticism and humanism within the medieval university, see HM Höpfl, 'Scholasticism in Quentin Skinner's *Foundations*' in A Brett and J Tully with H Hamilton-Bleakley (eds), *Rethinking the Foundations of Modern Political Thought* (Cambridge: Cambridge University Press, 2006), 113.
[264] This is the title of the first chapter of *Foundations*.
[265] Skinner, 'Surveying the *Foundations*', 256–257.

Skinner, the political problem for those seeking to affirm *libertas* against the Empire was due to the role that Roman law and lawyers played in justifying imperial authority.[266] Ever since the study of Roman law had been revived at the universities of Ravenna and Bologna in the late eleventh century, the Roman civil code had been treated as the basis of law throughout the Holy Roman Empire. The jurists, and particularly the school of Glossators, had adopted the interpretative method of 'following with absolute fidelity the words of Justinian's Code' and arguing that the Emperor was equated with the *princeps* of Justinian's Code and therefore endowed with rights as *dominus mundi*.[267] The result was that 'as long as the literal methods of the Glossators' were accepted as the basis for interpreting Roman law, the cities had no possibility of gaining legal support for their independence from the Empire.[268]

For the cities to succeed in establishing a legal basis for their challenge to the Empire, there needed to be a change in the attitude of their jurists 'towards the authority of the ancient law books'.[269] For Skinner, that 'necessary alteration of perspective' was achieved by the 'great figure', Bartolus of Saxoferrato, who was 'perhaps the most original jurist of the Middle Ages'.[270] Bartolus, who had been a student at Bologna and became a teacher of Roman Law at universities in Tuscany and Lombardy, reinterpreted the Code in a way that gave the cities a legal defence against the claims of the Emperor. According to Skinner, 'Bartolus's primary contribution was thus a methodological one', in that he 'abandoned the cardinal assumption of the Glossators to the effect that, when the law appears to be out of line with the legal facts, the facts must be adjusted to meet a literal interpretation of the law'.[271] For Skinner, that 'methodological' defence of the Italian cities by Bartolus was 'clearly a revolutionary political claim'.[272]

In suggesting that Bartolus offered a 'methodological' contribution based on recognising political 'facts' as the ground of legal authority, Skinner was doing more than simply describing a development in empirical approaches to legal interpretation. Skinner was instead taking the side of Bartolus in a normative debate. Bartolus treated the 'facts' of physical control over territory as offering a definitive answer to a fundamental normative question: Is the exercise of jurisdiction by a worldly authority a matter of right or an effect of the empirical

---

[266] Skinner, *Foundations I*, 7–8.
[267] Skinner, *Foundations I*, 8.
[268] Skinner, *Foundations I*, 8.
[269] Skinner, *Foundations I*, 8.
[270] Skinner, *Foundations I*, 8–9.
[271] Skinner, *Foundations I*, 8–9.
[272] Skinner, *Foundations I*, 11.

'fact' of physical control over people and territory? A similar debate over the grounds of authority plays out in international law today, for example in issues related to the recognition of one party to a civil war as the legitimate government of a state or in doctrines such as the responsibility to protect.[273] As those contemporary debates help to illustrate, to take one or other side in arguments over whether the claim to authority over territory should be understood as a matter of right (for example, by reference to ideas such as popular sovereignty or self-determination) or of fact (by reference to control over territory or the capacity to protect the population) is a necessarily partisan move.

A second key moment in Skinner's narrative occurred when Florentine civic humanists of the early fifteenth century began to adopt a new 'attitude' towards the study of classical antiquity.[274] Until that point, scholars had felt no 'radical discontinuity' between their own culture and that of Greece and Rome. That sense of belonging to 'essentially the same civilization' was felt 'nowhere more strongly than in Italy', where the legal code of Justinian was still in large part the law of the land, Latin was still used on formal occasions, and many people lived on the site of Roman settlements.[275] As a result, Skinner argued that there was no effort made 'to approach the culture of the ancient world on its own terms'.[276] With the birth of the 'genuinely historical spirit characteristic of the Renaissance', however, a 'new sense of historical distance was achieved',[277] or, to adopt a more historical spirit ourselves, we could say that a new sense was constructed. Ancient Rome 'began to appear as a wholly separate culture', that 'deserved – and indeed required – to be reconstructed and appreciated as far as possible on its own distinctive terms'.[278]

According to Skinner, the humanists 'crystallised their identity as a self-conscious intellectual movement' in part through their attack on the scholastic approach to the interpretation of Roman Law.[279] That attack was based on the 'key belief that all the texts of the ancient world should be studied and appraised as far as possible on their own terms', and led to fierce criticisms of scholastics for their 'wilfully anachronistic approach' to interpretation.[280] The 'rejection of scholastic methodology played a key role in helping to establish a

---

[273] A Orford, 'Jurisdiction without Territory: From the Holy Roman Empire to the Responsibility to Protect' (2009) 30 *Michigan Journal of International Law* 981.

[274] Skinner, *Foundations I*, 85.

[275] Skinner, *Foundations I*, 85.

[276] Skinner, *Foundations I*, 85.

[277] Skinner, *Foundations I*, 86–87.

[278] Skinner, *Foundations I*, 86.

[279] Skinner, *Foundations I*, 105.

[280] Skinner, *Foundations I*, 105.

genuinely historical jurisprudence'.[281] This approach was taken up in Italy by
humanists such as Lorenzo Valla, and in France where Guillaume Budé,
Andrea Alciato, François Le Douaren, François Connan, François Baudouin,
and Jacques Cujas sought to humanise the study of law and established the
mos gallicus or French method.[282]

For Skinner, that 'recognition of the ancient law-books as the product of a
wholly different society' was central to the humanist 'campaign against scholasticism'.[283] Humanists challenged the 'orthodox scholastic approach to the
interpretation of the Civil Code' as 'deliberately unhistorical', 'barbarous and
ignorant',[284] and argued that 'a true appreciation of the Code required that its
text should be considered in the light of their own historical and philological
techniques'.[285] Lorenza Valla, for example, staged one of the humanists'
'earliest and most devastating *coups*' with his 'proof that the so-called
Donation of Constantine was a forgery'.[286] Similarly, Skinner suggested that
Justinian's Code 'began to appear under the sustained philological gaze of the
humanists as little more than a "battered relic"'.[287] From there it was just a
matter of time before 'it occurred to a number of jurists that the methods
employed by the humanists in their studies of Roman and feudal law might
equally be applicable to every other known system of law, so that a scientific
theory of politics might eventually be established'.[288]

Humanism spread throughout Northern Europe and initiated 'an intellectual revolution which eventually led to the overthrow of scholasticism'.[289] For
Skinner that revolution was methodological. Humanists were increasingly
'willing to invade scholastic fields of study' and 'to denounce their rivals for
continuing to follow benighted methods'.[290] They insisted 'with increasing
imperialism on the need for the special techniques of humanism to be put to

[281] Skinner, *Foundations I*, 106.

[282] See further Kelley, 'Legal Humanism and the Sense of History', 184.

[283] Skinner, *Foundations I*, 106, 201–202.

[284] Skinner, *Foundations I*, 202.

[285] Skinner, *Foundations I*, 202.

[286] Skinner, *Foundations I*, 202. For related accounts, see JM Levine, *Humanism and History:
Origins of Modern Historiography* (Ithaca: Cornell University Press, 1987); C Ginzburg,
History, Rhetoric, and Proof (Hanover and London: University Press of New England, 1999),
54–70. For a critical response to the use of the scientific language of 'proof' to describe the
rhetorical argument made by Valla, see M de Grazia, 'Anachronism' in B Cummings and
J Simpson (eds), *Cultural Reformations: Medieval and Renaissance in Literary History* (Oxford:
Oxford University Press, 2010), 13, at 21.

[287] Skinner, *Foundations I*, 207.

[288] Skinner, *Foundations I*, 207.

[289] Skinner, *Foundations I*, 197.

[290] Skinner, *Foundations I*, 105.

use throughout the entire spectrum of the intellectual disciplines'. The 'technical core of humanism' was 'the attempt to apply detailed techniques of philological and historical criticism to texts of the ancient world'.[291] According to Skinner, that scientific imperialism 'played a positive role' and left a legacy in the form of 'experimental sciences', 'practical arts', and 'a new vision of history'.[292] Skinner's history of historiography was a progress narrative, in which contextualist methods were squarely on the right side of history in the battle of humanism and liberty against scholasticism and imperial power.

4.4.3 *Skinner, Panofsky, and the Myth of the Italian Renaissance*

As we have seen, the Italian Renaissance represented a turning point in Skinner's narrative. In his telling, it was during the Renaissance and through the influence of humanism that first Italian and then European culture grasped the true meaning of images, objects, and texts. In this story of secularisation and disenchantment, the humanist approach to understanding the meaning of images or texts was an advance on other ways of thinking. As Skinner's description of the Donation of Constantine as a 'forgery' and Justinian's code as a 'relic' illustrates, his narrative supported the view of those who believed that proving legal documents to be forgeries or equating them to religious relics represented progress in disenchanting the world. Just as humanists believed they could prove that faith in religious relics or icons was nothing more than magical thinking, so too they believed that historicising legal texts could prove that their authority was the result of nothing more than magical thinking. For Skinner, humanism had been able to disprove the claim that Justinian's Code was a 'valid source of law' by revealing its history.[293] Humanists disenchanted the Code by treating it 'simply as a text from the ancient world, and hence as an alien document standing in need of interpretation according to the new style of humanist hermeneutics'.[294]

Skinner's account of the methodological progress represented by the emergence of humanism during the Italian Renaissance was based explicitly on a set of lectures that had been given by the art historian Erwin Panofsky in Uppsala and published in 1960.[295] Panofsky was a German émigré scholar whose lectures on the Renaissance in Western art were a major influence on

---

[291] Skinner, *Foundations I*, 201.
[292] Skinner, *Foundations I*, 107, 109.
[293] Skinner, *Foundations I*, 205.
[294] Skinner, *Foundations I*, 205.
[295] Skinner, *Foundations I*, 85–86, 91, referring to E Panofsky, *Renaissance and Renascences in Western Art* (Stockholm: Almqvist & Wiksells, 1960).

historians of early modern Europe during the 1960s.[296] Panofsky's argument founded what art historians have described as the 'myth of the Renaissance' – the idea that the Italian Renaissance was the moment in which European culture developed a historicist understanding of the past.[297] Some art historians, however, have begun to question the resulting narrative of the Renaissance as a moment of progress and disenchantment. Their work helps make visible the analytical and political stakes of treating contextualism as the destination of historiography.

The key point made by Panofsky in his lectures and subsequently taken up by Skinner was that until the Renaissance, there had never been any effort made 'to approach the culture of the ancient world on its own terms'.[298] According to Panofsky, throughout the Middle Ages, classical themes and forms were 'anachronistically modernized', because the artists of the Middle Ages did not experience themselves as existing in a separate time to ancient Romans. It was only with the Renaissance that classical antiquity 'was looked upon, for the first time, as a totality cut off from the present'.[299] It was that acquisition – or alternatively construction – of historical consciousness that for Panofsky and Skinner marked the decisive break between the Middle Ages and the Renaissance. Once that sense of historical distance and a separation between past and present was in place, Florentine Renaissance humanists could reintegrate classical form and classical content, breaking with the medieval practice of nonchalantly combining classical elements of decoration with Christian themes and stories. The most important result of that new approach, according to Skinner, was 'the development of a non-anachronistic' style.[300]

The narrative of the Italian Renaissance that was introduced by Panofsky and subsequently taken up by Skinner assumes that the historicist model of

---

[296] de Grazia, 'Anachronism', 28–30 (discussing Panofksy's influence on how historians have thought about anachronism); A Nagel and CS Wood, *Anachronic Renaissance* (New York: Zone Books, 2012), 45–50 (discussing the influence of Panofsky's 'myth of a prosaically historicist Renaissance' on art historians). For why debates over the meaning of the Italian Renaissance mattered so much in the United States during the period that Panofsky was writing, and why they mattered more specifically to Panosfky as a German émigré, see C Landauer, 'Erwin Panofsky and the Renascence of the Renaissance' (1994) 47 *Renaissance Quarterly* 255.

[297] Nagel and Wood, *Anachronic Renaissance*, 46 (arguing that Panofsky's 'celebrated definition of the Italian Renaissance as the period first capable of seeing historical art in perspective' is the basis for what has since become the myth of a historicist Renaissance in art history).

[298] Skinner, *Foundations I*, 85.

[299] Panofsky, *Renaissance and Renascences*, 106, 113.

[300] Skinner, *Foundations I*, 86.

interpreting texts and images was an advance on, or an emancipation from, superstitious or irrational ways of thinking. For many Christian men and women in late medieval and Renaissance Europe, 'belief in power-laden natural objects' had been general, and 'stretched from the host, through the image, to the relic'.[301] Religious images, icons, or relics were believed to refer back to divine origins through references to founding stories or sacred figures.[302] Such objects and images were associated with a sacred person and worshipped or revered because of their figurative references.[303] Being able to recognise the resemblance between objects and the chain of association to which they referred had been part of what it meant to be educated in a tradition.

The veneration of relics or the belief in the miraculous properties of certain icons reflected a way of thinking about artefacts and images that involved a degree of abstraction from the material world. Relics or icons took their meaning from membership within a chain stretching back in time. Whether objects were part of such a chain depended upon resemblance, which was 'not an intrinsic property of things, but a perspectival effect'.[304] The stability of that system of identity or resemblance depended upon a shared set of references, practices of naming, and ritual usages. In that substitution model of creation, the identity of an object is established through the repetition and recognition of a form across time rather than through the history of its production.

That referential linkage was not interrupted or invalidated by knowledge of 'the particular or local circumstances of an artifact's fabrication'.[305] For example, in relation to texts, any knowledge the reader had about a particular transcription – for example the particular scribe who made the transcription – 'was simply factored out as accidental'.[306] There was no point in trying to 'fix the historical moment' of a text's genesis by dating a parchment or a script.[307] Few scholars tried to date artefacts or texts. Instead, the aim was 'to *identify* them on the basis of an inferred reference either to a prestigious source of

---

[301] RC Trexler, 'Florentine Religious Experience: The Sacred Image' (1972) 19 *Studies in the Renaissance* 7, at 9.

[302] Nagel and Wood, *Anachronic Renaissance*, 9.

[303] Trexler, 'Florentine Religious Experience', 9, 18.

[304] CS Wood, *Forgery Replica Fiction: Temporalities of German Renaissance Art* (Chicago and London: University of Chicago, 2008), 51.

[305] Wood, *Forgery Replica Fiction*, 15.

[306] Wood, *Forgery Replica Fiction*, 35.

[307] Wood, *Forgery Replica Fiction*, 35.

power and meaning – a divine personage, a founder – or to other artifacts, perhaps a notional original artifact'.[308]

While that model of substitution might seem to have been replaced by modern ideas of authorship and creation, it persists in certain taken-for-granted practices. For example, we might think of the restoration of an old building as an expression of the principle of substitution. We accept that the newly renovated or restored building is identical to the building that existed before the restoration, even if most of the materials in the building are no longer the same. What persists is the identity and form of the building. Even today, for those Christians who believe in transubstantiation, it would make no sense to claim to have proved that the bread taken in communion is not the body of Christ by providing evidence that the communion wafers were made in a factory down the road.

However, as ecclesiastical foundations with complex ties to secular power began to proliferate, the resulting conflicts and multiplication of voices began to place stress on the authenticity of images, icons, and relics. In that context, 'written tradition took on ever greater authority'.[309] Lettered patrician elites 'carefully detached themselves from the cycles of hope and reconciliation that revolved around' sacred images, and distanced themselves from the credulous beholder who was considered incapable of distinguishing truth from fiction and thus vulnerable to manipulation by religious images.[310] Debates about time also intensified with the emergence of new reproduction technologies, in particular moveable type and the woodcut.[311] The emergence of mechanical reproduction of images or texts gave rise to a new set of issues around originality and authorship.[312] Over the fifteenth and sixteenth centuries, as prints sent images and texts circulating across Europe, questions about authority began to accelerate.[313]

Those conditions elevated a rival, authorial method of interpreting the meaning of images and texts. The authorial model of temporality and creation purported to drain an object of historical meaning if it could be proved to be of recent or human manufacture rather than a literal relic of divine origin. According to that authorial model, a relic or icon was evidence of nothing other than the skill of its manufacturers and represented nothing more ancient than its date of production. To link such an object back to a divine or mythical

---

[308] Wood, *Forgery Replica Fiction*, 36.
[309] Wood, *Forgery Replica Fiction*, 116.
[310] Wood, *Forgery Replica Fiction*, 256.
[311] Wood, *Forgery Replica Fiction*, 12–13.
[312] Wood, *Forgery Replica Fiction*, 13.
[313] Nagel and Wood, *Anachronic Renaissance*, 50.

origin through a chain of figurative associations was simply a way of misleading the credulous. A similar argument was made by humanists about religious
or cult images, and about texts such as the Justinian Code. According to the
historicist approach, a reproduction of an artwork or a document created long
after the mythical point of origin can only be a copy, a fiction, or a forgery,
rather than an object connected to an ancient past through substitution.[314]

This latter model emerges triumphant from Skinner's narrative of the
Italian Renaissance. The adoption of an authorial model of production is
presented as a form of enlightenment.[315] Yet to present the story as a progress
narrative is to assume that the humanist approach to images and texts was an
advance on other ways of thinking about the temporality of images and texts.
As the art historian Christopher Wood has argued, '[w]henever the history of
Renaissance art is told *as* a story, with a momentum and trajectory', the plot
usually involves the disenchantment of religious or cult images or texts.[316] The
story is presented as part of a larger narrative about the disenchantment of the
pre-modern world. In such narratives, sacred art failed to deliver on its divine
promise, any sense of divine presence was revealed to be a mere psychological
effect, and social power involved manipulating that effect. The sacred or cult
image was doomed to failure because the transcendental or divine signified
could never in fact be reached. All modernist narratives consider the sacred
image 'to be either a psychological effect (an illusion) or a failed reference to a
transcendental object (a theological fable)'.[317]

A similar narrative about the politically revolutionary and scientifically
progressive effects of translating or reducing metaphysical references to physical references remains at the heart of contextualist arguments for historicising
law. The medieval or scholastic mode of interpretation is dismissed because of
its reliance on substitutional or anachronistic chains of identity, while the
Renaissance or humanist mode is portrayed as enlightened and disenchanted
because of its ordered and rational concepts of authorship. That story of
secularisation and disenchantment became central to 'a post-Christian idea
of Europe',[318] and continues to play a significant role in debates over the
meaning of the European tradition of international law.

Yet this methodological progress narrative oversimplifies the outcome of
those struggles over meaning and interpretation. As European cultures were

---

[314] Nagel and Wood, *Anachronic Renaissance*, 49.
[315] Nagel and Wood, *Anachronic Renaissance*, 49.
[316] Wood, *Forgery Replica Fiction*, 75.
[317] Wood, *Forgery Replica Fiction*, 84.
[318] Wood, *Forgery Replica Fiction*, 78.

rationalised and gave up the framework of meaning provided by myths of origin or prophecies, magical or figurative ways of relating objects, images, texts, or ideas across time were permitted to continue, but only in carefully labelled and circumscribed fields.[319] Art and literature emerged as institutions 'responsible for absorbing but at the same time strictly monitoring anachronistic thinking'.[320] Those fictional replacements became the recourse 'of those who are unconvinced that linear sequences of documents or artifacts can tell the whole story'.[321]

Art, for example, was born as a result of the limiting of the imagination in the Renaissance.[322] As Wood argues, '[t]he institution of art was left responsible for a certain kind of truth that used to be dispersed throughout culture'.[323] Art was the name given during the Renaissance to something that could hold together and suspend without deciding between the substitutional and the authorial models of origins, creation, and time.[324] What had until then been the more widely accepted 'time-bending referential rhetoric of the image' became 'quarantined inside a new institution, the work of art'.[325] On the one hand, the work of art was represented and understood as a material object – an object with a history that had been created by identifiable human agents. On the other hand, the work of art could function like a relic, a 'magical conduit to other times and places'.[326] It was in the latter sense that Renaissance art was 'anachronic' – other to the notion of chronological time 'flowing steadily from before to after' that was then gaining the upper hand.[327] Already in the sixteenth century, 'artistic authorship' could almost be defined as 'the capacity to manipulate the two modes within the confines of an aesthetic field'.[328]

It is perhaps not surprising, then, that art history is one field in which we find a challenge to the myth of the Italian Renaissance and to the claim that the historicist approach is an advance on or emancipation from magical, superstitious, or irrational ways of linking present and past. Instead, art historians have argued that we can understand the authorial and the substitutional

---

[319] Wood, *Forgery Replica Fiction*, 19, 22.
[320] Wood, *Forgery Replica Fiction*, 373.
[321] Wood, *Forgery Replica Fiction*, 22.
[322] Wood, *Forgery Replica Fiction*, 373.
[323] Wood, *Forgery Replica Fiction*, 373.
[324] Nagel and Wood, *Anachronic Renaissance*, 18.
[325] Wood, *Forgery Replica Fiction*, 13.
[326] Nagel and Wood, *Anachronic Renaissance*, 17.
[327] Nagel and Wood, *Anachronic Renaissance*, 9.
[328] Nagel and Wood, *Anachronic Renaissance*, 50.

models as two coexisting styles of relating, valuing, and understanding the meaning of objects, texts, images, or ideas. The authorial model that has now been championed by contextualist historians works by persuading its audience that the true meaning of a text or an object can be derived from studying its resemblance to its historical context. The substitutional model that is disparaged by contextualist historians works by persuading its audience that the true meaning of a text or an object can be derived from studying its resemblance to a tradition or a chain of references stretching across time. However, both 'context' and 'tradition' are constructed. An audience learns to find an argument persuasive because they have been educated to recognise one or the other form of resemblance. Context is just as constructed, fabricated, or artificial as tradition.

Law, like art, holds together those different ideas about time.[329] Lawyers make use of both models or styles of making meaning depending on the argument we are trying to make. For example, international lawyers for one party to a dispute might insist that a term has a historical meaning that is known to all and that its inclusion in a treaty clearly signals the parties were referring to that history of meaning, while lawyers on the other side might insist just as vehemently that the meaning of the term was specific to the context in which the two parties were negotiating. More broadly, modern law, like art, severs the referential mechanism from a divine or mystical origin. Modern law, like art, works in part by 'transforming the "as it must have been" of the substitutional chain into the "as if" of fictionality'.[330] On the one hand, we know that the authority of modern law derives from its relation to human acts of creation. We look for human sources of law and are no longer impressed by the pre-democratic idea that law is something that can be assembled from religious morals, natural law, or custom by a group of erudite men.[331] In that sense, we are all contextualists now.

Yet lawyers also engage in elaborate rituals, take up inherited roles such as judge or prosecutor, and stage trials in majestic courthouses involving gowned and bewigged legal actors. The success of such roles and performances depends upon their ability to invoke a tradition that transcends the specific context. We moderns no longer really believe that law has a divine or mystical origin, but we nonetheless act 'as if' lawyers speak in the name of an absent founding reference. Even Hans Kelsen, one of the sternest proponents of

---

[329] A Orford, 'On International Legal Method' (2013) 1 *London Review of International Law* 166, at 175–176.

[330] Wood, *Forgery Replica Fiction*, 374.

[331] A Carty, *Philosophy of International Law* (Edinburgh: Edinburgh University Press, 2007), 2.

twentieth-century positivism, recognised that the norm that is the origin or foundation of any legal order is 'not a positive norm' but 'a genuine or "proper" fiction' and that most of the time we act as if it simply existed in fact.[332] Lawyers have long understood that references to such legal fictions are key elements of our craft.[333]

In order to understand the work of law, it is necessary to grasp both aspects of its operation – the way it relates to a particular, identifiable social context, and the way in which it gestures beyond that context to chains of references that are constructed – sometimes in a neat linear progression, sometimes in wild leaps and bounds – across centuries. To do so requires noticing that lawyers operate in part by making irrational, poetic, mythical, or figurative connections between words and things, or by working as much in the realm of the fictional as the factual, without then immediately dismissing that aspect of legal argument.[334] We need to be willing to study, rather than merely rage against, this 'as if' or artificial quality of legal work if we are to grasp how lawyers make and transmit meaning.

4.4.4 *The 'Triumphant Methodology' of the Cambridge School*

By 2001, David Runciman could argue that the history of political thought existed 'in the shadow of the great methodological argument that began in the 1960s'.[335] To be clear, it was not that Runciman considered that the 'great methodological argument' cast a shadow because it was still raging. As a

---

[332] H Kelsen, *General Theory of Norms* (trans M Hartney) (Oxford: Clarendon Press, 1991 [1979]), 256 ('the Basic Norm of a positive moral or legal system is not a positive norm, but a merely thought norm (ie a fictitious norm), the meaning of a merely fictious, and not a real, act of will. As such, it is a genuine or "proper" fiction (in the sense of Vaihinger's philosophy of "As-If") whose characteristic is that it is not only contrary to reality, but self-contradictory'. For Kelsen, the Basic Norm contradicts reality because there is no such norm in fact, and it is self-contradictory because it is meant to ground the validity of the legal order but 'emanates from an authority – admittedly a fictious authority – even higher than this one. According to Vaihinger, a fiction is a cognitive device used when one is unable to attain one's cognitive goal with the material at hand ... A fiction differs from a hypothesis in that it is accompanied – or ought to be accompanied – by the awareness that reality does not agree with it').

[333] See further H Vaihinger, *The Philosophy of 'As-If'. A System of the Theoretical, Practical and Religious Fictions of Mankind* (trans CK Ogden) (London: Routledge and Kegan Paul, 1924); L Fuller, *Legal Fictions* (Stanford: Stanford University Press, 1967); M Del Mar and W Twining (eds), *Legal Fictions in Theory and Practice* (Heidelberg: Springer, 2015); A Riles, 'Is the Law Hopeful?' in H Miyazaki and R Swedberg (eds), *The Economy of Hope* (Philadelphia: University of Pennsylvania Press, 2017), 126.

[334] For a related argument in relation to art, see Wood, *Forgery Replica Fiction*, 84.

[335] D Runciman, 'History of Political Thought: The State of the Discipline' (2001) 3 *British Journal of Politics and International Relations* 84.

Cambridge man, it was clear to Runciman that the argument had long since been won by the contextualist historians. It was 'practically impossible' to make 'the case against contextual readings' or to argue that texts could be interpreted without reference to 'what their authors may have meant in writing them when and as they did'.[336] Rather, the history of political thought broadly conceived operated in the 'shadow' of that methodological debate because those engaged with material from the past were still working through the debate's repercussions. More specifically, they were figuring out what it meant to comply with 'the precepts of a triumphant methodology'.[337]

For Runciman, the 'group of historians who have become known as the Cambridge School' addressed more than 'the question of method'. At its 'most sophisticated', their argument offered something closer to 'a political philosophical position of its own'.[338] As this chapter has suggested so far, the question of method and the 'political philosophical position' of the Cambridge School bore a striking resemblance to the approach that their narratives attributed to their heroes of Renaissance humanism. And the constant foil for the progressive character of humanist historicism was the oppressive character of scholastic legalism.

4.5 IAN HUNTER AND THE LAWYER AS METAPHYSICIAN

4.5.1 *Hunter and International Law as Factional Politics*

The link between histories of humanism and contemporary contextualist history has been made explicit in the work of the intellectual historian Ian Hunter. Hunter is also the intellectual historian who has most overtly brought the methodological claims of contextualist historians to bear on modern international law scholarship. Hunter has argued that methodological debates over the interpretation of international law involve normative questions, and that at stake in discussions of method is a battle over the philosophy of history that should inform engagement with the past of international law. Here I am again interested in drawing out the central role that lawyers play in the historical narratives Hunter develops about the emergence of contextualist methods, and in the implications Hunter draws from this for the current study of international law.

---

[336] Runciman, 'History of Political Thought', 84.
[337] Runciman, 'History of Political Thought', 84.
[338] Runciman, 'History of Political Thought', 88.

Hunter has written a series of articles that strongly criticise international lawyers for using what he sees as improper methods to study the past and for the normative consequences of that misuse of history. Hunter's first set of articles about international lawyers focused on the work of Third World Approaches to International Law (TWAIL) scholars, indigenous lawyers, and other international lawyers whose work explored the relation between imperialism and international law.[339] Hunter's argument was that those scholars adopted the wrong methods for studying the law. Their methods were wrong because they were 'dogged by debilitating anachronism and "presentism"',[340] and more specifically because they misinterpreted international law as something that could be extended beyond Europe. Hunter insisted instead that the correct approach 'is to acknowledge – indeed to insist on – the particularist or regional European character' of *jus gentium*.[341] International lawyers have wrongly adopted the 'tacitly universalist presumption' that 'relations between European and New World peoples should and could have been rendered fair and just on the basis of a common normative order'.[342] Those lawyers are wrong to presume 'the existence of a universal norm of justice', because in doing so they 'ignore the possibility that the immensely destructive imposition of this European moral anthropology on indigenous cultures was the uncontrollable consequence of a clash of disparate civilizational cultures'.[343] For Hunter, then, indigenous lawyers, TWAIL scholars, and other critical international lawyers have made an empirical mistake in failing to consider that the immense destruction caused by Europeans was the 'uncontrollable consequence' of a clash of civilizations.

In addition, Hunter argues that this methodological mistake in interpreting the past has implications for the present. According to Hunter, we should 'call into question' whether relations between 'European and non-European peoples' could have been brought within a 'single compass of intelligibility and moral or legal judgment, and hence whether they can be today'.[344] According to Hunter, a methodologically correct reading of history demonstrates that 'European colonial war and conquest need not be treated as symptomatic of hypocrisy or the corruption of a potentially just legal order'.[345]

---

[339] Hunter, 'Global Justice and Regional Metaphysics'; Hunter, 'Vattel's Law of Nations'; Hunter, 'The Figure of Man and the Territorialisation of Justice'.
[340] Hunter, 'The Figure of Man and the Territorialisation of Justice', 289.
[341] Hunter, 'Global Justice and Regional Metaphysics', 15.
[342] Hunter, 'Global Justice and Regional Metaphysics', 13–14.
[343] Hunter, 'Global Justice and Regional Metaphysics', 18.
[344] Hunter, 'Global Justice and Regional Metaphysics', 16.
[345] Hunter, 'The Figure of Man and the Territorialisation of Justice', 307.

Hunter thus dismisses contemporary legal arguments premised upon 'a norm of global justice' or the commitment to 'a potentially just legal order' encompassing 'European and non-European peoples' by arguing that such attempts are founded upon an empirical mistake. For Hunter, encounters between 'civilizational cultures' such as played out during European imperial expansion and colonialism inevitably lead to violent conflict, and there was no reason then and is no reason now to expect anything different. Those lawyers, including indigenous lawyers and lawyers from former colonies, who seek to critique international law for its facilitation of European expansion are simply adopting a 'self-congratulatory posture', which allows them 'to bask in the glow of being on the right historical side, as if their exposés could somehow free them from the all-encompassing historical irrationality and cruelty of European imperialism and colonialism'.[346]

Hunter dismisses such legal scholarship because in his view it is 'critical in the philosophico-historical sense of positing norms that project a history of what *jus naturae et gentium* should have been or could have become, as opposed to a history of what it contingently happened to be'.[347] Hunter here opposes lawyers' partisan accounts of what the law 'could have become' with historians' empirical accounts of what the law 'contingently happened to be'. The idea that historians are able to record what the law 'happened to be' in the past assumes that what the law 'happened to be' is a fact that is lying around waiting to be established through the application of the correct historical methods and the accumulation of sufficient evidence. For Hunter, lawyers wrongly understand the task of interpreting past material in order to determine what international law is, what it has become, what it could yet become, and what it 'happened to be' last year or last century as being an aspect of present-day legal struggles. It is historians who can take an objective, impartial, or normatively innocent position in such debates. For Hunter, impartial historians can determine what the law happened to be in the past based on their objective interpretation of legal sources. Yet lawyers – and the historians who engage with them – are not arguing only about whether relations between 'Europeans and New World peoples' should or could have been rendered fair and just in the past, but are also arguing about whether they should and can be rendered fair and just in the present.

In addition, Hunter has been scathing about international legal scholars who have argued that international law emerged as a profession and an

---

[346] Hunter, 'The Figure of Man and the Territorialisation of Justice', 291.
[347] Hunter, 'Global Justice and Regional Metaphysics', 11.

academic discipline in the second half of the nineteenth century.[348] The particular target of that critique by Hunter was the work of Martti Koskenniemi, but he also took aim more broadly at a range of other international lawyers who adopted that 'viewpoint'.[349] However it was Koskenniemi's landmark history of the international law profession, *The Gentle Civilizer of Nations*, that was the main focus of Hunter's polemic.[350]

The subtitle of *The Gentle Civilizer* – 'The Rise and Fall of International Law 1870–1960' – dramatised the book's presentist argument that the history of the field can be mapped onto the invention of the profession of international law as a consciously liberal political project in the 1870s and the decline and fall of that profession after 1960. *The Gentle Civilizer* focused on the 'political and in some cases biographical context' for the work of the early generations of professionals who thought of themselves as international lawyers. The focus was on grasping the self-understanding of those lawyers, the projects they tried to advance through their professional practice, their struggles for power within the discipline, their attempts to delineate the profession from other disciplines and fields of knowledge, and their engagement in the reproduction of cultural and political hierarchies. Koskenniemi presented *The Gentle Civilizer* as a set of essays that 'form a kind of experimentation in the writing about the disciplinary past' aimed at creating 'intuitively plausible and politically engaged narratives about the emergence and gradual transformation of a profession'.[351] Koskenniemi was very clear that this was a narrative with political implications for the present:

> The essays do not seek a neutral description of the past 'as it actually was' – that sort of knowledge is not open to us – but a description that hopes to make our present situation clearer to us and to sharpen our ability to act in the professional contexts that are open to us as we engage in our practices and projects.[352]

Koskenniemi's stress on the emergence of international law as a profession shifted the focus of history-writing away from an ideological focus on the ideational foundation of international law or its fundamental character, and towards a study of how the discipline and profession of international lawyers

---

[348] Hunter, 'About the Dialectical Historiography of International Law'.

[349] Hunter, 'About the Dialectical Historiography of International Law', 1–2. Hunter included there the work of Ingo Hueck, Bardo Fassbender, Anne Peters, Luigi Nuzzo, and Miloš Vec.

[350] M Koskenniemi, *The Gentle Civilizer of Nations: The Rise and Fall of International Law 1870–1950* (Cambridge: Cambridge University Press, 2001).

[351] Koskenniemi, *The Gentle Civilizer of Nations*, 10.

[352] Koskenniemi, *The Gentle Civilizer of Nations*, 10.

was organised.[353] *The Gentle Civilizer* thus challenged standard histories of the discipline that presented an international law tradition as a history of ideas unfolding in an unbroken line from the great European publicists of the sixteenth century through to the modern era. Koskenniemi rejected the claim that a continuous tradition of international law could be traced back to a period before the late nineteenth century.

Hunter described Koskenniemi's claim that international law did not emerge until the nineteenth century as a 'tendentious mangling of the historical record' and 'in fact a factional cultural politics rather than scholarship'.[354] As that passage makes clear, Hunter's critique of the argument made by Koskenniemi was twofold – first, that this account of the history of international law was wrong (representing a 'mangling of the historical record'), and second, that it was improperly partisan ('factional cultural politics rather than scholarship'). For Hunter, the argument that international law in the form we know it today took shape in the 1870s 'is not a falsifiable historical hypothesis' but rather 'a hermeneutic template'.[355] Hunter argued that 'the claim that the historiography of international law did not exist in early modernity because there was no university discipline with that name is the kind of thing that gives anachronism a bad name'.[356]

According to Hunter, the claim that international law emerged in its modern form only in the nineteenth century was an attack on 'the treaty-based historiography of international law'.[357] Hunter argued that as a result of such attacks, the 'historical reality of formidable doctrines and historiographies of international law during the seventeenth and eighteenth centuries' was 'retrospectively erased' by twenty-first-century revisionists.[358] For Hunter, it was simply an empirical error to exclude from a history of the international law profession early modern writers such as Alberico Gentili, Hugo Grotius, and Samuel Pufendorf, eighteenth-century figures such as Vattel, Johann Jakob Moser, and Johann Stephan Pütter, or their early nineteenth-century inheritors such as Georg Friedrich von Martens or Johan Ludvig Klüber,

---

[353] For the argument that this is what a focus on the history of the professionalisation of international law can offer, see A Carty, 'Did International Law Really Become a Science at the End of the 19th Century' in L Nuzzo and M Vec (eds), *Constructing International Law: The Birth of a Discipline* (Frankfurt am Main: Vittorio Klostermann, 2012), 229, at 232.

[354] Hunter, 'About the Dialectical Historiography of International Law', 19.

[355] Hunter, 'About the Dialectical Historiography of International Law', 6.

[356] Hunter, 'About the Dialectical Historiography of International Law', 3.

[357] Hunter, 'About the Dialectical Historiography of International Law', 4.

[358] Hunter, 'About the Dialectical Historiography of International Law', 5.

because it was a 'fact' that they had 'produced an extraordinary body of technical, engaged, and historiographical work in public international law'.[359] Hunter was particularly outraged by Koskenniemi's exclusion of Moser and Martens. Hunter saw that exclusion as a metaphysical attack on the pluralism of German public lawyers who had sought to ground public law on 'agreements and instruments embedded in a chain of public-law peace treaties, whose collection, redaction, and interpretation formed the substance of constitutional law'.[360] Hunter argued that figures like Moser were the proper subjects of a history of international law,[361] as their work focused on a 'fundamentally documentary' form of 'constitutional historiography' that involved interpreting treaties as 'the record of diplomatic and political acts' aimed at achieving peace.[362] Those who argued otherwise turned history into 'a discursive weapon that could be used against positive public international law'.[363]

In other words, Hunter argued that Koskenniemi made a factual mistake and did not correctly understand what the history of international law was a history *of*. By treating the history of international law as a history of the modern profession and taking the self-image of that profession as the guide to what counted as international law, Koskenniemi had adopted a template that distorted what Hunter referred to as the 'historical reality'.[364] The histories produced by international lawyers were 'useless' for investigating the 'concrete' reception of rival philosophies of history within the discipline of international law because international lawyers 'are themselves creatures of that reception'.[365]

Hunter, as a historian, saw himself as able to correct the mistaken accounts of the past produced by international lawyers. As a result, Hunter also believed that he could correct international lawyers' misdiagnoses of 'the present condition of international law'.[366] Hunter argued that by wrongly rejecting positive international law, contemporary international legal scholars could find no 'ready exit' from the oscillation in legal argument between international law as the will of states (apology) and international law as the interest of the international community (utopia) as the foundation of international law

---

[359] Hunter, 'About the Dialectical Historiography of International Law', 5.
[360] Hunter, 'The Contest over Context', 201.
[361] Hunter, 'About the Dialectical Historiography of International Law', 5–6.
[362] Hunter, 'The Contest over Context', 201.
[363] Hunter, 'About the Dialectical Historiography of International Law', 18.
[364] Hunter, 'About the Dialectical Historiography of International Law', 5.
[365] Hunter, 'About the Dialectical Historiography of International Law', 14.
[366] Hunter, 'About the Dialectical Historiography of International Law', 7.

and the structure of legal argument. As a result, the only way out for international lawyers was through speculative exercises such as 'the relegation of intellectual coherence in favour of postcolonial emancipatory action'.[367] For Hunter, in contrast, it was obvious that international law simply involved the embrace of 'positive treaty-law'.[368] Hunter considered that international lawyers simply needed to remain faithful to the legacy of the 'Protestant *Reichspublizisten* and *Völkerrechtler*', who throughout the eighteenth century 'had assiduously collected and interpreted the major constitutional peace treaties, their enabling enactments, the conflicts to which they had given rise, and the ensuing adjudications of the imperial high courts'.[369]

Hunter's critique of both the history and contemporary situation of international lawyers ignores the problems that arise for any attempt to realise an international law grounded on the will of states as expressed through 'positive treaty-law'. International law operates in a situation in which states encounter other territorially organised political groups claiming the monopoly on the legitimate use of force within their territories on a shared planet. How law might be developed to enable the resulting encounters, transactions, signalling, coexistence, or cooperation between those states, and on what grounds the authority of that law might be based, became increasingly pressing questions between Hunter's period of focus in the 1840s and the twenty-first century.

That legal situation has given rise to the standard problems of international law that found the traditions to which Koskenniemi drew attention in his history of the self-consciousness of the legal profession. The oscillating pattern of legal argumentation that Koskenniemi, and before him David Kennedy, made visible is a means of rhetorically mediating the tensions of a liberal form of law that takes territorially organised political communities as its atomistic subjects.[370] The uneasy balance between the need for state consent and the interests of the international community (or of the hegemonic states that speak in its name) underpins the legitimacy of the whole system. Tilt too far one way (towards the interests of a hegemon or the international community) and it is hard to maintain the necessary support of governments for the law supposedly being developed, but tilt too far the other way (towards a strong commitment

---

[367] Hunter, 'About the Dialectical Historiography of International Law', 7.

[368] Hunter, 'About the Dialectical Historiography of International Law', 22.

[369] Hunter, 'About the Dialectical Historiography of International Law', 20.

[370] D Kennedy, *International Legal Structures* (Baden-Baden: Nomos Verlagsgesellschaft, 1987); M Koskenniemi, *From Apology to Utopia: The Structure of International Legal Argument* (Helsinki: Finnish Lawyers' Publishing Company, 1989).

to state consent and non-intervention in the domestic affairs of small states)
and it is hard to maintain the commitment of superpowers or the 'alliances'
they form in the name of collective security or collective self-defence.

International lawyers attempt to square that circle through a form of
argumentation that oscillates somewhat implausibly between attending to
the practices of states and to broader ideological concepts such as peace,
justice, rights, efficiency, or the common good. When Hunter considers that
the choice faced by lawyers is between interpreting positive law on the one
hand and a misleading appeal to metaphysical values on the other, he misses
the ways in which metaphysical appeals lie on both sides of that oscillation.
On the one hand, international lawyers refer to transcendental values such
as the self-preservation or security of the state, the self-determination of a
people, sovereign equality, or *pacta sunt servanda* to ground the authority of
international law on the material practice of states. On the other hand,
international lawyers appeal to transcendental values such as our common
humanity, global justice, conservation, equality, or efficiency to ground the
authority of international law on the interests of an international community. The tension and oscillation between the two sets of metaphysical claims
is a constant feature of international legal argument. Hunter sees only one
set of metaphysical claims – those that gesture beyond the state –
as illegitimate.

In his challenge to international legal scholarship, Hunter nonetheless put
his finger on a problem that faces any claim to produce a 'falsifiable historical
hypothesis' about the past of an object, such as international law, that does
political and normative work in the present. Any history of international law
can offer nothing more than a 'hermeneutic template' for interpreting a mass
of past material that is taken up in contemporary struggles over the meaning of
international law. Hunter, however, does not make that critical point in order
to argue that we should abandon the doomed attempt to produce 'falsifiable'
empirical accounts of the history of international law. Rather, in good hermeneutic of suspicion fashion, he makes that point to discredit the interpretations of international lawyers, while reserving for himself and other
contextualist historians the ability to present an impartial and empirical history
of international law. In criticising the fact that Koskenniemi and other international lawyers openly position ourselves as part of the history we describe,
Hunter seems to imagine that his work can provide something other than a
'hermeneutic template'. For Hunter, it is through contextualist histories that
we can recover an objective account of the emergence of public international
law in Europe and an alternative to the 'mangling of the historical record' by
international lawyers.

4.5.2 *Hunter on Contextualist Historians and Their 'Scholastic Enemies'*

Hunter presented the opposition between contextualist historians and international lawyers as part of a longer struggle organised around a binary structure. On one side are the contextual historians who take a 'properly impartial or historical view' of the past, and on the other are their 'scholastic enemies', who believe in '[m]etaphysical meanings and transcendent norms'.[371] For Hunter, the two modes of intellectual operation 'should be understood as radically and permanently opposed intellectual cultures or comportments'.[372] They were each 'initially shaped by circumstances of religious and political conflict deeply rooted in German history, and neither is capable of recognizing the other except as an intellectual enemy'.[373]

Hunter places international lawyers in the latter category, as part of 'the kingdom of darkness – that is, scholastic philosophy' and its many modern heirs.[374] Hunter includes in that category any scholar who does not conform to contextualist historical methods or who questions the legitimacy of the European state. All such scholars can be regarded as engaged in a single philosophical project, which Hunter variously characterises as 'European university metaphysics',[375] 'philosophical history',[376] 'metaphysical hermeneutics',[377] 'metaphysical hermeneutics of history',[378] 'post-Kantian philosophical history',[379] 'Aristotelian university metaphysics',[380] scholasticism',[381] or 'dialectical historiography'.[382] Over a number of decades, he has listed a range of scholarly groupings in addition to international lawyers as opponents, including the 'post-sixties humanities',[383] 'Cultural Studies',[384] 'poststructuralism',[385]

---

[371] Hunter, 'The Contest over Context', 192.
[372] Hunter, 'The Contest over Context', 188.
[373] Hunter, 'The Contest over Context', 188.
[374] Hunter, 'History of Philosophy and the Persona of the Philosopher', 571.
[375] I Hunter, 'The History of Theory' (2006) 33 *Critical Inquiry* 98.
[376] Hunter, 'The History of Theory', 98.
[377] Hunter, 'The History of Theory', 98.
[378] Hunter, 'The History of Theory', 109.
[379] Hunter, 'The Contest over Context', 207.
[380] Hunter, 'History of Philosophy and the Persona of the Philosopher', 582.
[381] Hunter, 'History of Philosophy and the Persona of the Philosopher', 582.
[382] Hunter, 'About the Dialectical Historiography of International Law'.
[383] I Hunter, 'The Mythos, Ethos, and Pathos of the Humanities' (2014) 40 *History of European Ideas* 11, at 23–30.
[384] Hunter, 'Mythos, Ethos, and Pathos', 23–30.
[385] Hunter, 'The History of Philosophy and the Persona of the Philosopher', 572; Hunter, 'Mythos, Ethos, and Pathos', 30 ('poststructuralist theory is a devolved "existential" form of the mainline of European university metaphysics').

'Theory',[386] 'anticontextual philosophical history' (meaning 'Marxist and left-Hegelian social philosophy' and Frankfurt School critique),[387] 'Marxist theory',[388] 'anti-state social history',[389] and 'postcolonial histories'.[390] In each case, his intellectual programme has been to seek out and denounce any trace of metaphysics, and specifically Christian metaphysics, in social, political, cultural, or legal thought. Hunter has called out an eclectic assortment of figures from the seventeenth through to the twenty-first century for being overt or covert 'university metaphysicians',[391] amongst them Valentin Alberti, Gottfried Wilhelm Leibniz, Christian Wolff, Immanuel Kant, Georg Wilhelm Friedrich Hegel, Heinrich Leo, Ferdinand de Saussure, Ernst Cassirer, Roland Barthes, Louis Althusser, Noam Chomsky, Jürgen Habermas, Jacques Derrida, Stuart Hall, Frederic Jameson, Alain Badiou, Henry Reynolds, Julia Kristeva, Terry Eagleton, Martin Jay, and Martha Nussbaum, as well as international lawyers including Antony Anghie, Emmanuelle Jouannet, and Martti Koskenniemi and indigenous lawyers including Robert A Williams Jr and S James Anaya.[392]

For Hunter, anyone who queries the impartiality or application of contextualism is either overtly or covertly committed to that project of European university metaphysics. In his view, 'what runs through these different iterations of the critique of context is not some common theoretical doctrine but something quite different and far more fundamental: namely, a particular kind of ethical work'.[393] To criticise contextualist history for whatever reason is

---

[386] Hunter, 'The History of Theory', 78.

[387] Hunter, 'The Contest over Context, 207.

[388] Hunter, 'Talking about My Generation', 600 (discussing what 'Marxist theory shares with other confessional metaphysics that makes it available for use as a repressive state ideology', that being the idea that politics 'must aim at something higher' than ensuring 'civil peace' (or in contemporary parlance, national or homeland security)).

[389] Hunter, 'Natural Law, Historiography, and Aboriginal Sovereignty', 142.

[390] Hunter, 'The Figure of Man and the Territorialisation of Justice', 18.

[391] Hunter, 'The History of Theory', 87.

[392] See I Hunter, *Rival Enlightenments: Civil and Metaphysical Philosophy in Early Modern Germany* (Cambridge: Cambridge University Press, 2001) (on Alberti, Leibniz, Wolff, Kant, and Hegel); I Hunter, 'Metaphysics as a Way of Life' (1994) 23 *Economy and Society* 93 (on Habermas); Hunter, 'The History of Theory' (on Saussure, Cassirer, Barthes, Althusser, Chomsky, Habermas, Derrida, Badiou, Kristeva, and Eagleton); Hunter, 'Talking about My Generation' (on Jameson and Eagleton); Hunter, 'Natural Law, Historiography, and Aboriginal Sovereignty' (on Reynolds); Hunter, 'Global Justice' (on Anghie, Williams, and Anaya); Hunter, 'Vattel's Law of Nations' (on Jouannet); Hunter, 'The Figure of Man' (on Anghie and Anaya); Hunter, 'Mythos, Ethos, and Pathos' (on Nussbaum, Derrida, and Hall); Hunter, 'About the Dialectical Historiography of International Law' (on Koskenniemi); Hunter, 'The Contest over Context' (on Hegel, Leo, and Jay).

[393] Hunter, 'The Contest over Context', 208.

to be a defender of scholasticism, an apologist for the 'empire of metaphysics', and engaged in 'the continuation of the post-Kantian war against the historicization of metaphysics in an updated, more covert form'.[394] Any scholar who offers a critical view of the 'sciences of facts', amongst which Hunter includes contextualist history, is 'an improvisation on the figure of the Christian university metaphysician; for that was always the role of this personage'.[395] Any challenge to empirical historians can only be understood as resulting from a commitment to 'transcendental thought', and from that perspective the 'modern anti-contextual critique of the Cambridge School' is 'spiritual or ethical rather than empirical or scholarly'.[396]

Hunter argues that those who are on the 'kingdom of darkness' side of the battle are primarily concerned with 'acts of inner self-transformation' that aim at 'the cultivation of a particular philosophical persona'.[397] Hunter claims that this critical persona is 'characterized by the desire to interrupt ordinary life and knowledge in order to rise above it, to look down on it, to be someone for whom and to whom the world declares itself in all its purity'.[398] Hunter has characterised the scholarly writing of international lawyers as directed towards producing the international lawyer as an 'exalted kind of intellectual persona' and towards the 're-theologization of law'.[399] This persona involves a 'posture of intellectual contempt for the sciences of fact'.[400] At heart is the critical intellectual's 'relationship to himself'.[401] Hunter does not pay any attention to the work with which theorists are engaging, the relation of that work to the theory or teaching in their field, or the political, normative, or strategic intentions that inform their interventions. His claim is simple – any 'enemy' philosopher, theorist, historian, cultural studies scholar, or lawyer who criticises what Hunter sees as the world of 'facts' is engaged in a solipsistic and 'highly specialised spiritual exercise . . . that allows its practitioners to withdraw from formal-positive knowledges and quotidian values'.[402] As a result, their work 'is not suited to the transmission of teachable knowledge'.[403]

---

[394] Hunter, 'History of Philosophy and the Persona of the Philosopher', 594; I Hunter, 'The State of History and the Empire of Metaphysics' (2005) 44 *History and Theory* 289.

[395] Hunter, 'The History of Theory', 87.

[396] Hunter, 'The Contest over Context', 199.

[397] Hunter, 'History of Philosophy and the Persona of the Philosopher', 574, 587, 598.

[398] Hunter, 'The History of Theory', 87.

[399] Hunter, 'About the Dialectical Historiography of International Law', 7.

[400] Hunter, 'The History of Theory', 87.

[401] Hunter, 'Metaphysics as a Way of Life', 98.

[402] Hunter, 'Talking about My Generation', 585.

[403] Hunter, 'Mythos, Ethos, and Pathos', 29.

Hunter characterises broad swathes of scholarship across centuries, disciplines, politics, and styles as reducible to the same project.[404] He argues that critical thinking has the same form, function, and effect wherever it is found. It exists independently of its object.[405] More specifically, all 'weaponized' criticisms of the contextualist historical approach are 'extrapolations from a single core teaching: namely, that ideas or texts cannot be wholly explicated in terms of their historical context because access to context itself has ideational or transcendental conditions'.[406] Hunter characterises the world view and scholarly activities of his many 'enemies' in a way that few of them would recognise and attributes commitments to them that few would willingly adopt.[407] According to Hunter, all are 'unwitting heirs to a thoroughly religious and metaphysical worldview that it is the secular historian's task to uncover'.[408]

On the other side of the battle are the contextualist historians and their allies, who are recognisable by their 'erudite humanist methods' and 'antimetaphysical' stance.[409] Figures lined up on this side of the equation include Samuel Pufendorf, Christian Thomasius, Johann Jakob Moser, Leopold von Ranke, Carl Schmitt, and the Cambridge School. Contextualist interpretation understands that '[e]cclesiastical and juridical documents' are not 'historical expressions of transcendental thoughts and ideas', but 'records of purely historical human acts'.[410] Its proponents stepped outside the world of 'warring religions and philosophies', and in doing so laid the groundwork for a form of politics organised around pluralism.[411] Hunter associates that pluralism with the European – and more specifically the Prussian – state. The 'antimetaphysical stance' of those on that side of the battle allowed them to view theological and juridical doctrines 'in terms of their historical existence rather than their normative validity'.[412] They thus 'removed God from history', and introduced a 'radically historicized outlook' that 'was also "scientific" or scholarly'.[413]

Hunter linked that tradition to 'the Cambridge School historians of political thought, represented most notably by the work of Quentin Skinner and JGA

[404] K Peden, 'The Burden of Intelligibility' (2014) 40 *History of European Ideas* 70, at 77.
[405] Hunter, 'The History of Theory', 80.
[406] Hunter, 'The Contest over Context', 186.
[407] Peden, 'The Burden of Intelligibility', 77.
[408] Peden, 'The Burden of Intelligibility', 77.
[409] Hunter, 'The Contest over Context', 196.
[410] Hunter, 'The Contest over Context', 194.
[411] Hunter, 'The Contest over Context', 209.
[412] Hunter, 'The Contest over Context', 195.
[413] Hunter, 'The Contest over Context', 195.

Pocock'.[414] He argued that 'the Cambridge School inherits a method and an attitude that first appeared in early modern western Europe', in the 'multi-fronted campaign to historicize doctrinal theology and metaphysical philosophy'.[415] These thinkers sought to suspend 'the truth-claims of theology and metaphysics, whose absolute and irreconcilable form was tied to religious civil war'.[416]

4.5.3 *The Politics of Contextualist Method*

As this brief overview makes clear, Hunter explicitly placed contextualist histories within a *longue durée* narrative. He argued that it is 'fundamentally misconceived' to identify contextual historiography 'with a 1960s academic intellectual grouping'.[417] While he suggested that the language of 'contextualism' does date from the mid-twentieth century, contextualist historiography traces its lineage to the seventeenth century.[418] 'Long before the Cambridge School, and as a deep condition of its emergence', argued Hunter, seventeenth-century ecclesiastical historians who were deeply 'rooted in the "learned empiricism" of Renaissance humanism', had already 'developed a full-blown contextual historiography' designed to challenge their 'scholastic enemies'.[419]

More specifically, Hunter argued that the Cambridge School was the 'inheritor' of 'two highly contextual historiographies both rooted in Renaissance humanist erudition' – seventeenth-century humanist ecclesiastical history and eighteenth-century German constitutional history.[420] Both of those traditions sought to interpret documents (theological in the first case, and constitutional in the second) by placing them in the context of the practices, institutions, and conflicts in which they arose.[421] This 'learned empiricism' used these techniques of 'humanist erudition to historicize theological and philosophical texts as a means of combating the treatment of them as expressions of timelessly transcendent truths and meanings'.[422]

---

[414] Hunter, 'History of Philosophy and the Persona of the Philosopher', 575.
[415] Hunter, 'History of Philosophy and the Persona of the Philosopher', 576.
[416] Hunter, 'History of Philosophy and the Persona of the Philosopher', 576.
[417] Hunter, 'The Contest over Context', 189.
[418] Hunter, 'The Contest over Context', 189.
[419] Hunter, 'The Contest over Context', 190, 192.
[420] Hunter, 'The Contest over Context', 187. Hunter makes the same argument in Hunter, 'History of Philosophy and the Persona of the Philosopher', 576; Hunter, 'Talking about My Generation', 594–595; Hunter, 'Postmodernist Histories', 279.
[421] Hunter, 'The Contest over Context', 187.
[422] Hunter, 'The Contest over Context', 188.

Debates over the interpretation of law played a central role in the methodological progress narrative developed by Hunter. According to Hunter,
'German constitutional historiography arrived at a similar document-based,
antimetaphysical contextual method' to that developed by the Cambridge
school.[423] Constitutional historians and jurists rejected the claim that legal
documents were 'expressions of transcendental norms of justice', and instead
grounded their understanding of public law on 'a myriad of documents ...
interpreted contextually'.[424] In the case of constitutional law, that involved
focusing on the negotiation of treaties as the basis for the meaning of the law,
in order to combat the view that German public law 'was grounded in natural
law or a transcendental principle of justice'.[425]

Hunter did explicitly what I have argued Skinner did implicitly – that is,
place contextualist method within a narrative history focused on the humanist
challengers to scholastic lawyers. In Hunter's words, that history should be
understood as part of an ongoing battle. Hunter seeks to show that the
Cambridge school with its 'philological, source-critical, and contextualizing
techniques' has inherited the learned empiricism of earlier ages.[426] All along,
contextualist historians have aimed to challenge 'doctrinal truths' presented as
'emphatically normative' and 'transcendent', and shift them into a register 'of
the worldly conduct of those who held them'.[427]

Having established that lineage, Hunter then treats anyone who questions
contextualism for whatever reason as simply one more participant in the
centuries-long 'factional attempt to annul contextual historiography and its
underlying cultural politics on behalf of a hostile metaphysical confession and
academic clerisy'.[428] Contextualist historians and their allies are engaged in
the ongoing 'campaign' against scholasticism and 'the various "idols" associated with text-based and metaphysically-determined' forms of philosophy and
in 'an unfinished battle with metaphysics'.[429] In any debate, once you have
figured out who is appealing to a metaphysical truth and who is appealing to
an empirically grounded interpretation, you can work out who is your friend
and who is your enemy depending on the side you would have taken in
nineteenth-century Prussia.

---

[423] Hunter, 'The Contest over Context', 192.
[424] Hunter, 'The Contest over Context', 193.
[425] Hunter, 'The Contest over Context', 188.
[426] Hunter, 'The Contest over Context', 208.
[427] Hunter, 'The Contest over Context', 190–191.
[428] Hunter, 'The Contest over Context', 207.
[429] Hunter, 'Postmodernist Histories', 279.

There is obviously something outlandish about the way that Hunter explicitly divides all scholars from the eighteenth century through to today into the friends or enemies of contextualist history, where those he diagnoses as contextualism's enemies offer partisan and misleading accounts of the past that fuel civil war, while those he claims as friends offer impartial or objective accounts of the past that contribute to civil peace. This can make it easy to dismiss his argument. Yet Hunter's account is worth attending to because it makes visible a dichotomy that was present in the three other historical narratives that this chapter has explored – Butterfield's critique of Whig constitutional history, Pocock's disparaging treatment of the 'common-law mind', and Skinner's championing of the humanist challenge to scholasticism in the Italian Renaissance.

It is also important to take Hunter seriously because his argument has been taken up by historians of international law and theorists of international relations as a methodological basis for undermining the work of critical scholars in both fields. Historians have referred to Hunter's work as a methodological corrective to the scholarship of critical international lawyers, suggesting that he has 'pointed to the consequences of anachronism in the history of international law for our understanding of the past' and 'pointed out that much of the history of international law was "critical" in that it proceeded with a normative principle of what the law of nations should have been or could have become'.[430] Lauren Benton and Lisa Ford cite Hunter approvingly as authority for the proposition that the 'problems' of international law scholarship have been 'compounded by a reliance on methods of dialectical philosophical history' and repeat his warning about the 'distortions' that such methods produce.[431] 'Fortunately,' they conclude, the 'distortions' produced by international lawyers with their reliance on the wrong 'methods' can be corrected, and the 'problems' caused by such distortions resolved, through the adoption of 'other, better ways' to study the past offered by historians.[432]

Taking his lead from Hunter, Richard Devetak has argued that contextualist approaches point the way to a new form of critical international scholarship, that 'eschew[s] the dialectical-philosophical approach' adopted by critical theorists of international law and international relations 'for a more empirical one'.[433] Contextualist approaches make it possible 'to enquire into the point or purpose of a text' and to treat that as a question 'to which empirically based

---

[430] Fitzmaurice, 'Context in the History of International Law', 8.
[431] Benton and Ford, *Rage for Order*, 202.
[432] Benton and Ford, *Rage for Order*, 180, 202.
[433] Devetak, *Critical International Theory*, 8.

evidence can be mobilised for answers'.[434] The contextualist historian can trace a 'line of intellectual descent' that 'originates in Renaissance humanism, passes through Absolutist historiographies and feeds into Enlightenment civil histories'.[435] For Devetak, the 'intellectual comportment of the humanist historiographer' lives on 'in the contextualist intellectual historian'.[436] Devetak calls for the defence of this 'alternative humanist intellectual persona', whose commitment to civil peace as the end of politics requires the abandonment of concerns with 'metaphysical' imperatives such as 'emancipation' and a renewed appreciation for 'civil' imperatives such as 'good government, peace, the rule of law, and other mundane achievements of statecraft'.[437]

4.6 CONTEXTUALIST METHOD AS THE END OF LEGAL HISTORY?

This chapter has returned to the work of a series of thinkers who have been touchstones for the methodological debate in international law. It has shown that these scholars have self-consciously understood themselves to be developing and deploying contextualist methods as an intervention in the field of political and legal thought. Their exponents understand contextualist methods to be both a form of historiography *about* political argument and a form of historiography *as* political argument. In the field of international law, and indeed more broadly, that Cambridge School method has been represented as offering a scientific, empirical, impartial, and professional approach to understanding the meaning of past texts (historiography about political argument) and as a revolutionary challenge to theological and imperial forms of authority in the name of individualism and liberty (historiography as political argument).

In current debates about the history of international law, the methodological claims developed by Butterfield, Pocock, Skinner, and Hunter are treated as axioms that can and should be applied without further discussion. Many participants in the debate over method in international law treat it as given that anachronism or presentism are bad and historicism or contextualism are good. The advocacy of those methods in international law goes far beyond recommending their use in situations where they make a specific

---

[434] Devetak, *Critical International Theory*, 8, 9.
[435] Devetak, *Critical International Theory*, 16.
[436] R Devetak, '"The Battle Is All There Is": Philosophy and History in International Relations Theory' (2017) 31 *International Relations* 261, at 269.
[437] Devetak, *Critical International Theory*, 17, 201.

political intervention. Instead, international lawyers are advised that those methods offer timeless means of providing a historically verifiable account of legal meaning.

Rather than accept that those theorists had access to timeless truths, this chapter has returned to the work of Butterfield, Pocock, Skinner, and Hunter to explore the interventions that their arguments were designed to make. In so doing, two features emerge from their writings. The first is that in addition to the more methodologically oriented texts, each of those scholars also offered narratives about moments in European history that witnessed the emergence of contextualist method. Collectively, their work offers a progress narrative, in which a contextualist or humanist 'method' is where we arrive at the end of history. The embrace of a particular historical method is presented by contextualist historians of international law as a corrective to a world of fake news,[438] and as one sign of progress in which we can still have faith.

While historians, like other twenty-first century scholars, no longer believe in progress narratives more broadly, there is an assumption underpinning these self-confident works of empiricist method that the development of a particular way of historicising law represents progress, an advance from the bad old days of naïve or triumphalist Whig histories, of the presentation of two-dimensional historical characters, of misguided attempts to produce morphologies of concepts across time, of the arrogant passing of judgement on past actors according to present values, of misguided valorisation of texts deemed canonical, of misleading narratives of revolutionary change, or of the misuse of history for instrumental and political reasons. They offer a narrative in which we see emerging over time an approach to thinking about history that is presented as progressive, modernising, and revolutionary. That approach is treated as both technically superior in terms of its scientific methods and politically superior because it resists the false claims of those in authority. Contextualist historical method is presented as offering a challenge, both in the past and in the present, to forms of authority based on illusions of transcendence, appeals to universal values, or concerns about the good life.

---

[438] Fitzmaurice, 'Context in the History of International Law', 30 ('a history of international law that questions the centrality of context to the creation of meaning, is one that presents new dangers. We live in an epoch in which politicians are increasingly indifferent to the verifiability of political claims and in which, with the vast proliferation of new media, verity becomes increasingly difficult to establish. Politicians and even some sections of the media are not sufficiently held to account for the truth or falsity of their statements, including their use of history or their understanding of the terms of political discourse ... An historical methodology that resists such indifference to the verifiability of political discourse would seem a better antidote to its perils than one that explicitly embraces anachronism').

In that narrative, historians take up a preordained place as radical disrupters of orthodoxy.

Second, the methodological arguments developed by Butterfield, Pocock, Skinner, and Hunter were structured around a battle between two sides and indeed two kinds of lawyers – the bad, metaphysical, or scholastic lawyers who are apologists for power, and the good, anti-metaphysical, or humanist lawyers, who unmask the strategies of metaphysicians. In the work of those historians, the dual and opposed images of the scholastic or metaphysical lawyer and the humanist or anti-metaphysical lawyer were traced to earlier moments in European history. The story of the emergence of scientific method is related through placing both the lawyer and the contextualist historian into a lineage, in which contemporary international lawyers take up the mantle of scholasticism and contextualist historians inherit the legacy of humanism. International legal scholars are presented as symbols and champions of ahistorical or traditional thinking, who defend the status quo through appealing to continuity and tradition, have a naïve belief that legal concepts or doctrines exist outside or beyond the specific time of their creation, and imagine that legal forms somehow exist independently of the social, economic, or political context in which they operate.

These narratives depend upon that image of the lawyer as scholastic metaphysician so that contextualist historians can be seen as the radical or romantic challengers of the law.[439] The narratives offered by contextualist historians reproduce that image of the law as the condition of contextualism's revolutionary potential. Each of the four historians I have discussed tells a story about the need for methodological innovation, each stages that innovation as radical, each offers an exemplary history in which the historical approach they advocate had a politically revolutionary effect, and each presents that revolutionary effect as a challenge to an oppressive political authority buttressed by an ahistorical form of legality. Those contextualist historians depend upon the image of a formalist, scholastic, metaphysically grounded law (or a related tradition such as philosophy or theology) as the kind of system against which or on behalf of which the agents of the narrative militate. If history ever succeeded in doing away with that image of the law, the power of the narrative in which contextualism is a triumphant modernising force for progress would be sapped.

As we saw in Chapter 3, the axioms as well as the opposition between law and history developed in such accounts have been taken up as the

---

[439] For a related argument about President Trump's relation to the law, see J Butler, 'Genius or Suicide' (2019) 41(2) *London Review of Books* 10.

foundational assumptions informing a new generation of revisionist intellectual historians of international law, who see their work as correcting or completing the scholarship undertaken by or about international lawyers. For those historians, the legal field is either *terra nullius* when it comes to philosophies and self-reflective practices of history, or alternatively it is a field already peopled by the kinds of scholastic lawyers or moralistic judges imagined in the work of Butterfield, Pocock, Skinner, and Hunter, and more broadly in Western historiography.[440] In the new revisionist histories, international law reappears as the kind of universalising, generalising, or moralising authority that has functioned as a foil throughout the work of empiricist historians, and contextualist methods are again presented as offering the kind of radical anti-foundationalist critique of transcendent legal claims that contextualist historians present as a humanist legacy of the European enlightenment.

This is a problem for two sets of reasons, the first to do with how we understand the law, and the second to do with how we use the law. In other words, this matters both for analytical reasons and for political reasons. First, it is a problem because it stops us understanding how law works and the role of lawyers in contemporary politics. The current debate traps all of us, lawyers and non-lawyers alike, in a fantasised ideological battle from earlier centuries, in which lawyers are all imagined as scholastics who work for the Holy Roman Emperor or the Pope, and are yet to understand the truth that lies at the end of (methodological) history – that is, that law is not a transcendental abstraction and that any legal argument, institution, technique, rule, or doctrine can only be understood in relation to the political interests it serves and the projects it furthers. In that fantasised situation, international lawyers are all scholastics, who imagine that there is some position outside of politics from which they can declare a law for humanity.

To be fair, I can think of some international lawyers who comport themselves as if that were possible, but I can also think of generations of international lawyers who have developed sophisticated anti-metaphysical and anti-foundationalist responses to such arguments. To act as if lawyers are all still mindlessly committed to scholasticism not only gives rise to a straw-person image of international law and of international lawyers but also means that

---

[440] For the broad claim that there is an 'intimate relationship' between 'law, historicality, and narrativity', see H White, *The Content of the Form: Narrative Discourse and Historical Representation* (Baltimore and London: The John Hopkins University Press, 1987), 13. For a reflection on White's argument in relation to contemporary American legal thought, see NW Spaulding, 'The Historical Consciousness of the Resistant Subject' (2011) 1 *UC Irvine Law Review* 677.

anything a contemporary international lawyer says is understood as if it had been said by someone committed to pursuing the world view and project of scholasticism in the modern world. Revisiting the early works of the Cambridge School and their image of lawyers as scholastics and metaphysicians helps to explain the impassioned description of the dangers posed by contemporary international lawyers when we question contextualist methods. When international lawyers challenge the claim that contextualist methods can offer verifiable truths about the meaning of law, we are taken to be doing so in order to defend the position that law is based on timeless principles or metaphysical origins.

Yet what if the international lawyer is not, or at least not only, a figure who fits neatly into the lineage of the Italian Renaissance scholastic lawyer, the seventeenth-century English common lawyer, the English Whig constitutionalist, or the Prussian natural lawyer? The debate over method in international law assumes that the methods mandated by empiricist historians and narrated as offering a radical challenge to traditional authority in Renaissance Italy, seventeenth-century England, nineteenth-century Prussia, and twentieth-century Europe necessarily have a similar effect when they are staged as interventions in the practice of twenty-first-century international law. Contextualist historians are presented as arriving on a white charger to liberate us from the heirs of the Holy Roman Empire or liberal Whig constitutionalism. Yet the international legal arguments that dominate today are no longer grounded upon the kinds of metaphysical or transcendent claims to which the historical narratives of the European enlightenment developed by Butterfield, Pocock, Skinner, or Hunter draw our attention.

In other words, the analytical problem with the claim being made by those seeking to historicise law is not that their method is revolutionary or will force lawyers to give up our illusions about the apolitical and transcendental character of international law. The analytical problem with this claim is the opposite – it is *not* a new or radical insight for lawyers. As I will argue in Chapter 5, learning to attack metaphysical claims and argue from concrete legal sources is a commonplace piece of legal training and has been for at least the past century, during which it became possible to claim that 'we are all realists now'.[441] In other words, that methodological position has already been

[441] W Twining, *Karl Llewellyn and the Realist Movement* (London: Weidenfeld and Nicholson, 1973), 382 ('Realism is dead: we are all realists now'). For responses to that claim, acknowledging the unavoidable impact of realism on legal thought while working through the ways in which remnants of metaphysics and formalism continue to inform the legal process school, rights theory, and law and economics, see D Fraser, 'What a Long, Strange Trip It's Been: Deconstructing Law from Legal Realism to Critical Legal Studies' (1988–1989) 5

incorporated within the practices of modern law, such that to make arguments from that position is already to be caught up in the middle of a political battle. To imagine that when international lawyers make arguments from the 'utopian' pole of the apology/utopia divide we do so because we do not know that there is any alternative is to misunderstand the nature of the game that is being played. And to imagine that the political stakes of taking the utopian or indeed the apologetic position in any argument were predetermined in fifteenth-century Italy or nineteenth-century Prussia is to hamper our analytical capacities to make sense of what international lawyers are doing in the present.

Second, the way that this debate continues to perform an unending oscillation between those two positions of science and metaphysics is a problem for politics, which in this case means for the practice of international law. For those of us who are involved in training students to be lawyers, accepting and thinking in the terms offered up by this debate is disabling. For contextualist methods to be reliably corrective and impartial interventions in contemporary debates about international law, the authority of modern international law would need to be based on a naïve faith in metaphysical claims, formalist arguments, and timeless principles. It is not. Empiricist historical interventions have a more complex effect in a field dominated by powerful players and states that have long since incorporated the argument that metaphysical or formalist thinking about law is naïve. Powerful actors routinely argue that international law must be contingent, realist, flexible, responsive to rapidly changing circumstances, and unhampered by the baggage of the past. As 'scholarship relentlessly historizing law pours out',[442] the effects that historians imagine themselves producing in international law by demonstrating law's contingency, revealing its politics, and showing its relation to power have long since been normalised. Understanding how contextualist historical arguments actually intervene in international law today requires having some sense of and curiosity about the institutional, ideological, material, and geopolitical situation in which they go to work. In Chapter 5, I will turn to explore that situation.

Australian Journal of Legal Sociology 35; JW Singer, 'Legal Realism Now' (1988) 76 *California Law Review* 465.

[442] Parker, 'Law "In" and "As" History', 593, making this argument in relation to US legal scholarship.

5

The Past in the Practice of International Law

A core claim made in the debates accompanying the turn to history is that professional historical methods can lift disputes about the meaning of past texts or the origin of current doctrines or institutions out of the realm of partisan politics and into the objective world of science. As we saw in Chapter 4, that narrative about the relation of law and history is part of a longer tradition, in which humanist modes of interpretation are portrayed as challenging oppressive forms of authority grounded on metaphysical meanings and transcendental values. In this chapter, I bring those claims about the promise of contextualist history for law into relation with the ways in which contemporary international lawyers actually use the past in the practice of making legal arguments. I argue that contextualist historical methods cannot offer a new empirical ground for formalist interpretations of international law. The ambiguous or indeterminate nature of past legal texts, practices, cases, or decisions is not a historical problem that can be solved with more evidence and a better understanding of the context in which texts were authored, institutions created, or adjudicative bodies constituted. Rather, the ambiguity over what past texts, practices, cases, or decisions mean is intrinsic to the structure and practice of international law. The key argument of this chapter is that anything historians say about international law will become part of this creative and contested field.

This chapter explores the openness, ambiguity, and capaciousness of the past materials out of which international legal arguments are assembled. In addition, it sketches the broad range of roles and standpoints that international lawyers take up when drawing on the past. The chapter is designed as a challenge to the ideas about law and lawyers to which I drew attention in Chapter 4. As I argued there, when historians of international law argue that contextualist or empirical methods offer better ways of understanding past texts, practices, or concepts than those adopted by legal scholars, they have a particular image of lawyers in mind. As I showed, the received account of law and lawyers that features in the current turn to history debates is part of a longer tradition in the work of empiricist historians. This chapter offers an alternative vision of the role of international lawyers, organised around three key assumptions that recur in the work of contextualist historians. This chapter takes up each of those assumptions in turn.

The first assumption that this chapter seeks to complicate is that international law is primarily an academic discipline, and that the arguments made by legal scholars drawing on the past are in conversation with and should be measured against standards of truth-seeking, fact-finding, or interpretation established by academic historians. As we saw in Chapter 3, historians writing about international law make strong claims about the intellectual and methodological inadequacy of lawyers. Yet the work of historians of international law demonstrates a marked lack of interest in the relation of their claims to contemporary international law as a field of practice. For all the insistence on 'context' in the work of contextualist historians, the discussion of law and lawyers seems strangely disconnected from one of the principal contexts in which legal scholarship intervenes – that is, the context of international legal practice. Today's historians of international law largely steer clear of engaging with arguments about the past developed in the work of legal practitioners.

Of course, the lack of overt engagement by historians with international legal arguments made in the pleadings of international lawyers appearing before courts or tribunals, in recent judgements or arbitral awards, in the published legal opinions of government legal advisors, or in annual digests of state practice makes sense according to the role that contextualist historians envisage for themselves. Historical scholarship is not supposed to be distorted by presentism or anachronistically informed by current thinking, and thus attending to contemporary legal practice outside the academy would only have a negative effect on historical scholarship.

This posture, however, makes it difficult for historians to understand the kinds of interventions that are being performed, or at least attempted, by international legal scholars, whose work engages with legal practice in numerous ways. It also means that historians do not test their assumptions about the contemporary roles played by international lawyers or the situation of international lawyers against the world in which their legal colleagues operate. International legal scholars are all still imagined to be performing our parts in a play that was written in fifteenth-century Italy or nineteenth-century Prussia.

Section 5.1 contests that assumption. I argue that international legal scholars exist in a complex relation to the world of legal practice. That relation to practice involves both the material with which legal scholars work and the role that legal scholars play in training the next generation of lawyers. To understand legal scholarship or legal knowledge production requires recognising the significance of 'relations between the legal academy and the profession'.[1] Legal scholars are part of an interpretative community that encompasses practice and the academy, and we are expected to incorporate developments in professional legal arguments into the research we produce and the courses we teach. In addition, the law school is, at least in part, a place of training in 'what it means to be a lawyer and think like a lawyer',[2] and thus of training in skills of argument, rhetoric, negotiation, and performance. The study of international law in elite law schools is also a site of training in practices of global rule and ways of justifying (or contesting) the exercise of power.[3] Yet while international legal scholars are engaged in reflecting upon, and training students for, a world of practice, historians purport to measure and evaluate international legal scholarship without considering its (and thus their own) relation to the development of legal arguments outside the academy. International legal knowledge cannot be understood without attending to the shifting and complicated relations between the legal academy and the profession.

Second, this chapter seeks to complicate the assumption that if international legal scholars reject empiricist historical methods, we do so in order to adopt the standpoint of the moralising judge or the scholastic formalist. As I showed in Chapter 4, historians have repeatedly imagined a particular role for the lawyer, either as a scholastic apologist for forms of authority grounded on tradition or as a moralising judge bringing present norms to bear on the past. Both roles are assumed to pose problems for making sense of the past. The international lawyer imagined as moralising judge is unaware that the past is a different country governed by different laws and morals. In that story, lawyers need to be taught that we cannot judge the past according to present norms. Alternatively, the international lawyer imagined as scholastic apologist for power naively believes or cynically pretends that the authority of contemporary rule can be traced back to a transcendent origin or is lost in time

---

[1] A Riles, 'Legal Amateurism' in J Desautels-Stein and C Tomlins (eds), *Searching for Contemporary Legal Thought* (Cambridge: Cambridge University Press, 2017), 499, at 501. For a sociological exploration of that relationship, see Y Dezalay and BG Garth, *Dealing in Virtue: International Commercial Arbitration and the Construction of a Transnational Legal Order* (Chicago: University of Chicago Press, 1996).

[2] Riles, 'Legal Amateurism', 500.

[3] D Kennedy, 'Law and the Political Economy of the World' (2013) 26 *Leiden Journal of International Law* 7; D Kennedy, *A World of Struggle: How Power, Law, and Expertise Shape Global Political Economy* (Princeton and Oxford: Princeton University Press, 2016).

immemorial. In that story, lawyers need to be taught that every text is authored by specific individuals with worldly political intentions in determinable historical contexts.

In Section 5.2, I argue that international lawyers in practice and the academy occupy many more roles than those imagined or assumed by historians. Perhaps because the figure of the lawyer as judge or scholastic has such a hold on the historical imagination, it seems difficult for historians to imagine contemporary lawyers adopting any other role or having any intention other than engaging in scholastic legalism or moralising judgement. The judge and the apologist for the system are certainly two of the roles that lawyers might take up in their relation to the past. Yet international lawyers engage with the past in numerous other roles, and grasping those roles is necessary for understanding the more varied ways that lawyers make use of past material. Indeed, one of the things that students learn in the process of legal education is the significance of role to legal practice. If we think about the law only from the position of the judge or as a practice of judgement, we miss many aspects of its operation. As William Twining puts it: 'In studying law the commonest form of stupidity consists in forgetting who one is pretending to be'.[4] As a result, the '[s]elf-conscious clarification of standpoint' is a 'first step in any intellectual procedure concerned with law'.[5] Contextualist historians evince an attention to standpoint when they are engaging with the past, yet that attention seems to disappear when historians engage with contemporary lawyers. Section 5.2 addresses that need for situational awareness. It offers a necessarily brief sketch of the many roles that are played by the broad community of people who practice and identify as international lawyers and points to the significance of the different ways in which that work is organised institutionally.

Third, historians imagine a particular orientation for the international lawyer. Just as scholastic lawyers in the fifteenth century had supported the forms of Papal and imperial authority founded upon metaphysical claims and the sanctification of texts presented as speaking in the name of an absent source, so too contemporary international lawyers are assumed to gain authority by claiming to speak in the name of a law founded upon metaphysical claims and sanctified texts. And just as humanists arrived on the European scene to reveal that spiritual and imperial forms of authority were an illusion, so too impartial historical scholars need to expose the illusory metaphysical

---

[4] W Twining, 'RG Collingwood's Autobiography: One Reader's Response' (1998) 25 *Journal of Law and Society* 603, at 614.

[5] Twining, 'RG Collingwood's Autobiography', 615.

foundations of international law if the world is to be liberated from the oppressive authority that is shored up by partisan international lawyers.

In Section 5.3, I challenge the assumption that international lawyers adopt a scholastic or formalist orientation to the law. While there are of course legal scholars who make legal arguments that continue to rely upon metaphysical claims or adopt formalist methods, they exist alongside a far broader range of orientations and arguments about past material. Indeed, for at least the past century international lawyers, particularly US lawyers and those lawyers influenced by US legal thought, have been trained in antifoundationalist and anti-metaphysical understandings of law. European international law has long been unmoored from the conditions that grounded the authority of scholastics and their legal formalist heirs. International law is no longer tethered to European institutional origins and traditions and has expanded far beyond the territories from which its customs, founders, rituals, and precedents were derived. The most powerful legal actors no longer primarily rely on tradition to ground their authority. Far from being a revolutionary insight, the claim that placing a text in its proper context can determine the intentions of its authors and thus settle the text's determinative meaning is just one of many claims about interpretation that are already part of the broader argumentative world of international lawyers and no more likely than any other method to resolve interpretative controversies or offer the truth of legal history.

Having argued that the understanding of practice is necessary to grasping the work of international legal scholars, I turn in Section 5.4 to sketch some of the ways that the past is used by different players in international legal argumentation. I focus on international law as an argumentative practice, which takes place in institutions organised around managing, channelling, or resolving disputes between heavily armed states on a shared planet, the outcome of which can have significant distributional consequences. That institutional situation means that the kinds of questions to which the turn to history gives rise, such as which method is the correct one for interpreting a legal text, what is the proper context for understanding an event, or what is the true origin and telos of a legal regime, will operate within this argumentative field and necessarily have a partisan effect. Paying attention to the many ways in which international lawyers make use of the past in practice helps to illustrate why the adoption of empirical historical methods cannot deliver an impartial and verifiable means of accessing the true 'meaning' of past legal material.

This chapter invites the reader to approach the use of the past in the practice of international lawyers in a spirit of curiosity. Two essays, one by a contextualist historian and one by an international lawyer, convey the spirit with which this chapter approaches its task. The first is by the Cambridge School historian JGA Pocock. As we saw in Chapter 4, Pocock can be as dismissive of lawyers as the next contextualist historian. But on a more abstract level, Pocock recognised that it might be possible to understand oneself as part of a 'tradition' while having a 'more sophisticated level of consciousness' about what being part of a tradition means.[6] Pocock characterised a 'tradition' as 'an indefinite series of repetitions of an action, which on each occasion is performed on the assumption that it has been performed before', and where each performance is 'authorized' by 'the knowledge, or the assumption, of previous performance'.[7] However, once a tradition is institutionalised, the 'self-awareness' or self-perception of those participating in a form of life organised around the repetitions of actions across time might not 'take a strictly traditional form'.[8]

As a result, those studying a tradition should not proceed on 'the assumption' that participants are limited to transmission as their 'only form of action' and inheritance as their 'only form of knowledge'. It might turn out that participants in a tradition also adopted other modes of action and knowledge, or that there might be conflict and contradiction between traditionalist and non-traditionalist processes or voices.[9] Participants, for example, might recombine or reinterpret past texts into new patterns or new forms of ideology, myth, or history. In such situations, 'every reader' would then be 'a potential radical'.[10] According to Pocock, where a tradition had taken on that more dynamic or pluralist orientation to past material, disinterested historiography would be an impossibility.

> Disinterested historiography is possible only in stable societies, where the past is fortified by means other than the writing of histories ... [I]f the past can be considered dead, this can only mean that society's relation with its past ... has been stabilized by means other than those of the historian.[11]

---

[6]   JGA Pocock, 'Time, Institutions and Action: An Essay on Traditions and their Understanding' in JGA Pocock, *Political Thought and History: Essays on Theory and Method* (Cambridge: Cambridge University Press, 2009), 187, at 191.

[7]   Pocock, 'Time, Institutions and Action', 190.

[8]   Pocock, 'Time, Institutions and Action', 191.

[9]   Pocock, 'Time, Institutions and Action', 192–193, 195.

[10] Pocock, 'Time, Institutions and Action', 203.

[11] Pocock, 'Time, Institutions and Action', 216.

In that essay, Pocock acknowledged that it can take work to understand a tradition. He abandoned his earlier posture of simply dismissing those who understood themselves as operating within a field governed by a broader conception of 'social time'. Instead, he suggested that it might make sense to approach such ways of thinking and acting 'somewhat in the manner of Victorian anthropologists'.[12]

Annelise Riles, a professor in law and in anthropology, has made a similar argument. Riles notes that a recurring complaint about the legal academy is that it is amateuristic. We have seen this complaint already in the suggestion that lawyers who engage with the past should do so in a more professional way. Riles notes that her early response to that aspect of legal scholarship as a young anthropologist was 'the quite naïve ambition to professionalize this amateuristic discipline'.[13] Only later did she realise 'that an anthropologist of law should take legal amateurism as seriously as any other knowledge practice one might want to study'.[14] In that sense, she argues that 'legal amateurism is the very heart of legal professionalism' and is a 'dimension of legal expertise'.[15] Taking this approach to legal amateurism would suggest that 'we abandon the impulse to critique legal scholars from the viewpoint of social scientific standards and instead consider what might be learned from legal amateurism in our hyper-professionalized social scientific disciplines'.[16]

In that spirit of curiosity, this chapter turns to study the uses of the past in international law, not in order to declare which uses are correct and which are incorrect, which history is 'real' and which is a myth, but rather in order to grasp what work appeals to the past are doing in practice. Through taking this approach, we might gain a better feel for the interested historical amateurism of international lawyers rather than immediately moving to measure legal methods against the allegedly disinterested historiography of our professional historical interlocutors. And by studying the situation, roles, orientations, and practices of contemporary international lawyers, we can begin to grasp why the ambitious claims made about the capacity of historicist methods to complete and correct international legal scholarship are misleading.

---

[12] Pocock, 'Time, Institutions and Action', 192, 195.
[13] Riles, 'Legal Amateurism', 499.
[14] Riles, 'Legal Amateurism', 499.
[15] Riles, 'Legal Amateurism', 514.
[16] Riles, 'Legal Amateurism', 515.

5.1 INTERNATIONAL LAW SCHOLARS BETWEEN THE ACADEMY AND THE LEGAL PROFESSION

5.1.1 *The Invisible College as a Form of Life*

International lawyers work in a field and a language that is shared, albeit uneasily, between the world of professional practice and the world of the university. As Riles has argued of law schools more generally, we need to 'understand the legal academy as integrated first into the profession and only secondarily into the social science division of the modern university'.[17] It is not possible to understand what international legal scholars are doing when we write about the past if the contemporaneous arguments being made in international legal practice are ignored. To put this in contextualist terms, even if international lawyers do not make any reference to practice in a piece of writing, the institutional context of international legal scholarship includes the world of international legal practice. Controversies of and about international law are automatically controversies that relate to the practice upon which international law is based.[18] Recognising this aspect of the international lawyers' situation 'sets limits and opens possibilities',[19] including in how we think about the relation of international legal histories to legal practice.

The idea of a relation between theory and practice is everywhere you look in the scholarship of international lawyers. That relation between international legal practice and the academy is a contested one, and practitioners and scholars often disagree over what the proper form of that relation should be. Reflections upon that complicated relationship have featured in the work of lawyers who identify as practitioners, those who identify as scholars, and those who identify as both.[20] Yet there is a widely shared sense that the discursive practice of international law 'inevitably involves both practitioners and scholars'.[21]

---

[17] Riles, 'Legal Amateurism', 514.

[18] O Korhonen, 'New International Law: Silence, Defence or Deliverance?' (1996) 7 *European Journal of International Law* 1.

[19] Korhonen, 'New International Law', 7.

[20] See, as an introductory overview, the essays collected in J d'Aspremont, T Gazzini, A Nollkaemper, and W Werner (eds), *International Law as a Profession* (Cambridge: Cambridge University Press, 2017).

[21] J von Bernstorff, 'The Relationship between Theory and Practice in International Law' in d'Aspremont, Gazzini, Nollkaemper, and Werner (eds), *International Law as a Profession*, 222, at 224.

Oscar Schachter's influential reference to an 'invisible college of international lawyers' is often invoked by international lawyers to describe that relation.[22] Schachter, who had been an advisor at the US Department of State and subsequently a legal advisor at the United Nations before being appointed a professor at Columbia Law School, argued that the professional community of international lawyers dispersed throughout the world 'constitutes a kind of invisible college dedicated to a common intellectual enterprise'.[23] Though international lawyers may be engaged in diverse roles in the governmental, intergovernmental, non-governmental, and academic worlds, the members of that 'college' were part of a unified discipline and a shared endeavour. Increased communication and collaboration between members of the invisible college was desirable not only because the process of reaching solutions to problems could be improved by including plural perspectives, but because issues in international law required answers that 'reflect global positions and actions'.[24]

Of course, not all legal scholars have or desire such a close role with the world of legal practice, and academic lawyers think about their relationship to practice in many ways. For some, the role of the academic scholar is to participate in creating the sense of international law as a coherent and autonomous system. For those scholars who think in these terms, their work is central to upholding the value and autonomy of international legal practice.[25] Other international legal scholars understand their role as presenting an account of the normativity underpinning international law in general or specific fields such as international trade law, often in concert with academics from other fields.[26] For others, academic lawyers have an obligation to maintain a reflexive distance from the profession.[27] The strongest critics of the relation between the world of the law school and that of practice suggest that academic international lawyers are simply engaged in training agents of political power without allowing any room for questioning or doubt.[28]

---

[22] O Schachter, 'The Invisible College of International Lawyers' (1977–1978) 22 *Northwestern University Law Review* 217.

[23] Schachter, 'The Invisible College', 217.

[24] Schachter, 'The Invisible College', 223.

[25] R Collins and A Bohm, 'International Law as Professional Practice' in d'Aspremont, Gazzini, Nollkaemper, and Werner (eds), *International Law as a Profession*, 67.

[26] S Besson, 'International Legal Theory *qua* Practice of International Law' in d'Aspremont, Gazzini, Nollkaemper, and Werner (eds), *International Law as a Profession*, 268.

[27] von Bernstorff, 'The Relationship between Theory and Practice in International Law', 222.

[28] A Rasulov, 'What Is Critique?' in d'Aspremont, Gazzini, Nollkaemper, and Werner (eds), *International Law as a Profession*, 189, at 204–206.

In turn, many current and former legal advisers have expressed a degree of frustration about the way that academic lawyers project an idealised vision of what practice should be onto the actually existing world of advisers. In reflecting upon his time as a 'lawyer-diplomat' employed by the Finnish Ministry of Foreign Affairs, for example, Martti Koskenniemi noted that academic writing about the work of the legal adviser failed to recognise that 'the legal adviser's role is constructed, on the one hand, by critical projection from activist and academic lawyers and, on the other hand, from the "political" colleagues in the operative departments of the home government'.[29] For Koskenniemi, the perception of government legal advisers by academic and activist lawyers was 'coloured by an ambivalent mixture of distancing and envy' that was the result of their cosmopolitan idealism.[30] Koskenniemi imagined that for the idealistic academic scholar, the practitioner's commitment to 'producing justifications for what one's government does may appear as an unappealing and unprincipled opportunism'.[31] From the perspective of the legal advisor, 'the academic's easy moralism ... looks like a facile and irresponsible indulgence in self-aggrandizement and ignorance of the lessons of diplomatic history'.[32] For the practicing lawyer, the academic is 'really an *amateur*, delighting in speaking the language of public governance without responsibility to anyone about his or her statements'.[33]

The sense that there is a relation between international law as a professional practice and international law as an academic discipline is also born out in the organisation of the field. Academics and practitioners regularly take part in conferences and other events that involve exchange between the two worlds. There are multiple arenas in which ideas for codification or development of the law are discussed and debated between practitioners and scholars, including the UN's International Law Commission, the *Institut de Droit international*, and the International Law Association. Many countries and regions have societies of international law that meet annually or other informal arrangements to create bridges between academics and practitioners in international law.

---

[29] M Koskenniemi, 'Between Commitment and Cynicism: Outline for a Theory of International Law as Practice' in *Collection of Essays by Legal Advisors of States, Legal Advisers of International Organizations and Practitioners in the Field of International Law* (New York: United Nations, 1999), 495, at 516.

[30] Koskenniemi, 'Between Commitment and Cynicism', 516.

[31] Koskenniemi, 'Between Commitment and Cynicism', 516.

[32] Koskenniemi, 'Between Commitment and Cynicism', 518.

[33] Koskenniemi, 'Between Commitment and Cynicism', 523.

In addition, international lawyers often move back and forth between the academy and practice. In the United Kingdom and Europe, many international lawyers practice at the international bar while also holding academic posts.[34] In Latin America, most academic international lawyers have been practitioners with extensive professional experience and little scholarly engagement.[35] In the United States, a large number of current international law professors began their careers working with the US government, often in the State Department Legal Advisor's Office (known informally as 'L'). Former State Department Legal Advisor Harold Koh has been candid about the resulting intimacy between the US government and the US international law academy, referring to the 'many alumni' of the State Department 'who have gone on to become professors and scholars of international law' as 'Scholarly L'.[36] Legal academics who were formerly state department lawyers often use their scholarly work to shift the law in directions that bear a close relationship to positions being put by the US government. The Chinese international law academy also regularly supports Chinese government positions.[37]

Academic international lawyers may also be appointed as judges on international courts and tribunals. Indeed some governments make a point of nominating university professors rather than legal advisors to such positions in order to signal the independence of the nominee from the positions of their government.[38] In addition, academic prestige can often be parlayed into lucrative positions as international investment arbitrators, and much of the scholarship in that field is written by people who have an arbitration practice.[39] Indeed, the tendency of international investment lawyers to switch hats regularly between acting as counsel, framing the issues or promoting the

---

[34] See, for example, P Sands and A Sarvarian, 'The Contributions of the UK Bar to International Law' in R McCorquodale and J-P Gauci, *British Influences on International Law, 1915–2015* (Leiden and Boston: Brill Nijhoff, 2016), 497 (describing the movement of individuals between the UK bar, the international law academy, the Foreign and Commonwealth office, and the international judiciary).

[35] L Obregón, 'The Colluding Worlds of the Lawyer, the Scholar and the Policymaker: A View of International Law from Latin America' (2005) 23 *Wisconsin International Law Journal* 145, at 166–167.

[36] HH Koh, 'The State Department Legal Adviser's Office: Eight Decades in Peace and War' (2012) 100 *Georgetown Law Journal* 1747, at 1749.

[37] For a much-discussed example, see Chinese Society of International Law, 'The South China Sea Arbitration Awards: A Critical Study' (2018) 17 *Chinese Journal of International Law* 207.

[38] See the discussion of the UK practice in this respect in *Chagos Marine Protected Area Arbitration (Mauritius v. United Kingdom), Reasoned Decision on Challenge*, PCA Case No. 2011-03, 1 December 2011.

[39] Dezalay and Garth, *Dealing in Virtue*.

system as an academic, and serving as arbitrator or expert witness has become increasingly controversial.[40] In addition, as international lawyers remind each other from time to time, 'the writings of the most eminent publicists' are officially treated as secondary sources of international adjudication in the Statute of the International Court of Justice (ICJ).

5.1.2 *Legal Education as Training*

Legal scholars also relate to the world of practitioners through our role in training future lawyers. The law school is one site of the reproduction and also the legitimation of particular claims about what the law *is*. It is also a site of training in professional cultures, sensibilities, biases, aesthetics, and performative styles. In our role as teachers of international law, academic lawyers cannot ignore the world of legal practice, both because at least some of our students will participate in that world and because we purport to teach our students about that world. It would be a problem, for example, not to update our teaching materials from one year to the next to ensure that we were teaching the most recent case law, treaties, interpretations of customary international law, and so on. As teachers of law students, legal scholars are in part training people to work in the legal profession and become competent members of that professional community. International legal scholars are therefore engaged in the routines of socialising students into a shared set of practices, communicating the processes for assembling legal arguments, and transmitting the law to the next generation. In so doing, the international legal scholar is engaged with the world of practice and a set of shared methods for making that practice legally intelligible.

---

[40] See, for example, G Van Harten, 'Perceived Bias in Investment Treaty Arbitration' in M Waibel, A Kaushal, K-HL Chung and C Balchin (eds), *The Backlash against Investment Arbitration: Perceptions and Reality* (Alphen aan den Rijn: Wolters Kluwer, 2010), 43; SW Schill, 'W(h)ither Fragmentation? On the Literature and Sociology of International Investment Law' (2011) 22 *European Journal of International Law* 875; P Eberhardt and C Olivet, *Profiting from Injustice* (Brussels and Amsterdam: Corporate Europe Observatory and the Transnational Institute, 2012); P Sands, 'Conflict and Conflicts in Investment Treaty Arbitration: Ethical Standards for Counsel,' in A Rovine (ed), *Contemporary Issues in International Arbitration and Mediation: The Fordham Papers* (New York: Brill, 2012), 28. For a frank account of how to be the kind of academic who will be chosen for international judicial and arbitral appointments, see G Sacerdoti, 'From Law Professor to International Adjudicator: The WTO Appellate Body and ISCID Arbitration Compared, a Personal Account' in DD Caron, SW Schill, AC Smutny, and EE Triantafilou (eds), *Practising Virtue: Inside International Arbitration* (Oxford: Oxford University Press, 2015), 204.

One way of thinking about legal academic work, then, lies in understanding the role of the scholar in relation to this process of legal training and transmission. At first glance, it might seem quite conservative to consider the role of the legal academic as someone involved in 'training', if we imagine the terms of such training to be dictated by practitioners whose power and authority are dependent upon their relations with whichever elites are currently dominant in business or politics. Yet many of the intellectual movements or texts that are treated as central to the development of modern, realist, or critical approaches to thinking about the law have been tied up with reflections upon pedagogy and the relation of the legal academy to the profession.[41] The ethos behind that approach to legal education is well captured in the opening words to Oliver Wendell Holmes's classic 'The Path of the Law':

> When we study law we are not studying a mystery but a well known profession. We are studying what we shall want in order to appear before judges, or to advise people in such a way as to keep them out of court. The reason why it is a profession, why people will pay lawyers to argue for them or to advise them, is that in societies like ours the command of the public force is intrusted to the judges in certain cases, and the whole power of the state will be put forth, if necessary, to carry out their judgments and decrees. People want to know under what circumstances and how far they will run the risk of coming against what is so much stronger than themselves, and hence it becomes a business to find out when this danger is to be feared.[42]

Much writing on law takes the relation to practice and the training role of legal scholars seriously as sources of methodological and conceptual

---

[41] See, for example, OW Holmes, 'The Path of the Law' (1897) 10 *Harvard Law Review* 457; K Llewellyn, 'On What Is Wrong with So-Called Legal Education' (1935) 35 *Columbia Law Review* 651; K Llewellyn, 'On the Problem of Teaching "Private" Law' (1941) 54 *Harvard Law Review* 775; D Kennedy, 'Legal Education as Training for Hierarchy' in D Kairys (ed), *The Politics of Law* (New York: Pantheon Books, 1982), 54; P Goodrich, 'The Critic's Love of the Law: Intimate Observations on an Insular Jurisdiction' (1999) 10 *Law and Critique* 343. For studies focusing on the concerns of the realist and critical legal studies movements with legal education, see Comment, 'Legal Theory and Legal Education' (1970) 79 *Yale Law Journal* 1153; W Twining, 'The Bad Man Revisited' (1973) 58 *Cornell Law Review* 275; RW Gordon, 'Critical Legal Studies as a Teaching Method, against the Background of the Intellectual Politics of Modern Legal Education in the United States' (1989) 1 *Legal Education Review* 6; W Twining, 'Other People's Power: The Bad Man and English Positivism 1897–1997' (1997) 63 *Brooklyn Law Review* 189; N Duxbury, *Patterns of American Jurisprudence* (Oxford: Clarendon Press, 1995); J Suk Gersen, 'The Socratic Method in the Age of Trauma' (2017) 130 *Harvard Law Review* 2320.

[42] Holmes, 'The Path of the Law', 457.

innovation.[43] Scholars who work in law schools are 'institutionally committed to teaching and so reproducing law'.[44] Legal scholarship that does not study or engage with the law can hold on to an idealised image of a perfect form of law that transcends the corrupt stuff of worldly practice, but will have only limited effects upon '[t]he law that is taught, the doctrine that is repeated and through repetition reproduced'.[45] Indeed those scholars who refuse to engage with the 'mundane' material of legal practice may end up preserving and reproducing an image of 'substantive law' as something that cannot be questioned,[46] an effect of what Peter Goodrich has diagnosed as the 'critic's love of the law'.[47]

The focus on legal education as 'training' thus captures an important aspect of the broader situation and the distinctiveness of the legal academic. Training someone to engage in the many different roles and tasks involved in contemporary legal practice requires preparing them to engage in the argumentative practices, conduct, and operations of international law. Rather than fetishise the law, the role of legal academics in the law school classroom requires us to engage with law as an institutional practice and make its doctrines, processes, and modes of transmission intelligible. This training in the conduct and performance of that essentially argumentative professional practice is key to the work that goes on in law schools, whether the goal is to transmit, reflect upon, participate in, reinforce, or contest the dominant forms of and trends in practice.

Riles links the 'amateurism' of the legal academy to that focus on professional performance. She argues that the work of the professor in the law school classroom is essentially performative. Legal thought and argument is 'an aesthetic propensity' rather than primarily a theoretical position conforming to a 'modernist ideal' – more particularly, legal practice is 'a genre of self-presentation, a set of skills of thought and performance, a style of life and work'.[48] The law school is a place of training in 'what it means to be a lawyer and think like a lawyer',[49] and in associated forms of self-presentation, modes of argument, and styles of performance.

---

[43] B Meyler, 'Law, Literature, and History: The Love Triangle' (2015) 5 *UC Irvine Law Review* 365; S McVeigh, 'Afterword: Office and the Conduct of the Minor Jurisprudent' (2015) 5 *UC Irvine Law Review* 499; Riles, 'Legal Amateurism'.

[44] Goodrich, 'The Critic's Love of the Law', 349.

[45] Goodrich, 'The Critic's Love of the Law', 360.

[46] Goodrich, 'The Critic's Love of the Law', 348.

[47] Goodrich, 'The Critic's Love of the Law', 343.

[48] Riles, 'Legal Amateurism', 500.

[49] Riles, 'Legal Amateurism', 500.

That training operates in large part through the use of examples, by studying how lawyers or judges in particular cases have produced 'complex arguments that we recognize as exemplary in their power, their ability to create or contest some suggested meaning'.[50] Law school teaching, particularly in common law jurisdictions, is fashioned out of a set of 'cases and materials' that present as a 'collection and display of disparate fragments' rather than a coherent finished essay or textbook.[51] Cases and materials books give a good sense of how legal argument works. The US international law variant is particularly capacious, and can run to well over 1,000 pages in small font packed with material extracted from sources as diverse as the Bible, speeches of US government officials, UN Security Council resolutions, treaties, arbitral awards, ICJ advisory opinions, depository notifications, US Supreme Court judgements, US restatements, and academic writings covering everything from European formalism to game theory to Third World approaches to international law.[52] The casebook may feel 'messy', 'under-theorized', or 'naïve' next to a fully realised work of legal scholarship, but precisely because of that unfinished or amateurish character, casebooks are a gift to the user – 'they leave gaps or opportunities for future work' and allow law professors and law students to pick them up and make them our own.[53]

Teaching with such materials is part of preparing law students for the expectation that they will be able to move between the general and the particular or the present and the past, creating plausible patterns or analogies by assembling material from disparate sources. This is key to understanding what historians criticise as the tendency for legal scholars to make daring leaps or mad dashes between material from different contexts. Legal arguments move between broad strokes and close detail, or the big ideological claim and the small technical question, and link concrete situations with existing rules, principles, precedents, or exceptions expressed at various levels of abstraction. Success in legal performance depends on a lawyer's ability to frame 'a question or set of materials in a sufficiently focused and yet general way, such that debate can be generated in a matter of minutes among the members of the audience'.[54] The ability to do that in a convincing way is one mark of a virtuoso legal argument, and depends upon being able to persuade

---

[50] M Koskenniemi, *From Apology to Utopia: The Structure of International Legal Argument, Reissue with New Epilogue* (Cambridge: Cambridge University Press, 2005), 567.

[51] Riles, 'Legal Amateurism', 504.

[52] See, for example, BE Carter, AS Weiner, and DB Hollis, *International Law* (7th edition) (New York: Wolters Kluwer, 2018).

[53] Riles, 'Legal Amateurism', 512.

[54] Riles, 'Legal Amateurism', 505.

an audience of the plausibility of the big picture 'while understanding that one could always dig deeper into the details on any particular point'.[55] Lawyers are expected to develop the practical skill of being able to 'move quickly from one legal problem and one kind of client to the next with very little knowledge of particulars'.[56]

In order to train law students – even, or perhaps particularly, those who are seeking to contest the status quo – some sense of the shifting nature of what counts as persuasive amongst the profession must be kept in mind. This will mean that lawyers in law schools will have part of their attention focused on trends in the academy, but another part on shifting patterns of professional argument, and the situation in which those arguments are developing. As Riles notes, 'the entire classroom event echoes the experience of the wider professional world' and yet 'it is not actually professional legal work, but a kind of play at professional work'.[57]

Working in a field such as international law, which engages closely with legal material generated in the practice of law and is directed in part to training those who will go on to practice as lawyers, influences the way we approach legal material as scholars. Legal academics, including those who think of themselves as 'critical' or 'theoretical', will need to have a sense of what is happening in practice, because the field of practice is dynamic and constantly shifting. The aim of working with material generated in practice is to remind students and ourselves that any text or apparent consensus is only one point in an ongoing process of struggle over meaning, and that 'the law will always possess reserves for re-opening the debate, undoing the settlement, attacking the ... hegemony of the mainstream'.[58]

As this brief sketch suggests, international legal scholars engage in numerous ways with the practice of international law, through training lawyers, systematising or contesting the legal arguments made by international legal practitioners, or interpreting legal materials for public audiences. The complicated relationship between the international law academy and the international law profession registers both in what international lawyers write and how we teach. To understand international law, it is not enough simply 'to look to the relationship between international law writings and general political events and general cultural or more specifically philosophical

---

[55] Riles, 'Legal Amateurism', 505.
[56] Riles, 'Legal Amateurism', 505.
[57] Riles, 'Legal Amateurism', 506.
[58] Koskenniemi, *From Apology to Utopia*, 597.

currents' – it is necessary to consider in addition 'the way that the profession of international lawyers is itself organized'.[59]

Yet attention to that relation between the academy and the world of practice disappears when we turn to the debate over the history of international law. Historians treat legal knowledge as something located firmly within the university and largely ignore the relation of legal scholarship to the arguments being made by practitioners. In the next three sections I turn to explore how paying attention to the world of practice unsettles the assumptions that historians make about the roles and standpoints that lawyers adopt, the orientations to past material that lawyers take up, and the different ways that the past is used in international legal argument.

5.2 THE PLURAL ROLES OF INTERNATIONAL LAWYERS: BEYOND THE JUDGE AND THE HISTORIAN

5.2.1 The Judge and the Historian

In Chapter 3, I drew out the images of the lawyer that reappeared throughout the historiographical narratives of contextualist historians. In particular, the practice of judgement and the image of the lawyer as moralising judge played a central part in the methodological manifestos published by contextualist historians. For Herbert Butterfield, the particular danger posed by the Whig interpretation of history involved the division of the world into 'the friends and enemies of progress',[60] and arose from an 'error' that was more widely shared – that is, the practice of 'judging' things 'apart from their context'.[61] Butterfield believed that behind all the mistakes of the Whig historian lay 'the passionate desire to come to a judgment of values' and to 'show which party was in the right'.[62] In contrast, he argued that the proper approach to take in studying the past was 'to describe' and in doing so stand 'impartial'.[63] History can 'show us that all our judgments are merely relative to time and circumstance'.[64]

---

[59] A Carty, 'Did International Law Really Become a Science at the End of the 19th Century?' in L Nuzzo and M Vec (eds), *Constructing International Law: The Birth of a Discipline* (Frankfurt am Main: Vittorio Klostermann, 2012), 229, at 232.

[60] H Butterfield, *The Whig Interpretation of History* (New York: WW Norton, 1965 [1931]), 5.

[61] Butterfield, *The Whig Interpretation of History*, 31.

[62] Butterfield, *The Whig Interpretation of History*, 65.

[63] Butterfield, *The Whig Interpretation of History*, 73–74.

[64] Butterfield, *The Whig Interpretation of History*, 75.

For Butterfield, 'the judgment which lies in the structure of history gives none of us the right to act as judges over others'.[65]

Historians and some international lawyers involved in debates over method in international law have also interpreted the work of contemporary legal scholars as attempts to judge the past and the people who inhabited it. Ian Hunter, for example, has characterised the work of international lawyers such as Antony Anghie as an attempt 'to condemn European colonialism as unjust' and to judge whether *jus gentium* was 'condemned or vindicated by this history'.[66] Hunter questioned whether relations between 'European and non-European peoples' could have been brought within a 'single compass of intelligibility and moral or legal judgment' in the past, and therefore 'whether they can be today'.[67] Christopher Rossi has argued that international law scholars have failed to heed 'Butterfield's admonishment about the retrospective tendency toward pre-judgment' and have produced 'whiggish hanging judge narration'.[68] Andrew Fitzmaurice has echoed the argument that 'historians', and in particular those engaged in 'post-colonial studies, or Third World Approaches to International Law (TWAIL) scholarship' have produced work that 'judged the past' through a presentist 'normative framework'.[69] The 'consequence' is that 'past authors were judged to have failed to conform to principles of equality and universality that were themselves products of a post-Kantian European intellectual world whose resources were not available to most of the early modern subjects who had failed to conform to them'.[70] As that language of condemnation, vindication, and judgment makes clear, the dominant assumption is that international lawyers are engaged in a process of judging when we look to the past.

The idea that there is a tension between the roles of the judge and of the historian has deep roots in the writing of historians. The opposition of the judge and the historian is memorably staged by Carlo Ginzburg in his brilliant critical polemic about the trials resulting from the 'accidental death of an

---

[65] H Butterfield, *Christianity and History* (London: G Bell and Sons, 1950), 62.

[66] I Hunter, 'Global Justice and Regional Metaphysics: On the Critical History of the Law of Nature and Nations' in S Dorsett and I Hunter (eds), *Law and Politics in British Colonial Thought: Transpositions of Empire* (New York: Palgrave Macmillan, 2010), 11, at 11–12.

[67] Hunter, 'Global Justice and Regional Metaphysics', 16.

[68] CR Rossi, *Whiggish International Law: Elihu Root, the Monroe Doctrine, and International Law in the Americas* (Leiden: Brill, 2019), 30–31.

[69] A Fitzmaurice, 'Context in the History of International Law' (2018) 20 *Journal of the History of International Law* 5, at 8.

[70] Fitzmaurice, 'Context in the History of International Law', 8.

anarchist' and what they suggest about the Italian legal system.[71] Ginzburg's important study is directed to understanding what he termed in the book's subtitle 'a late-twentieth-century miscarriage of justice', involving one of the many cases that resulted from the aggressive inquisitorial techniques that had been taken up by the Italian criminal justice system as a means of prosecuting anarchists and later the Mafia. For that reason, his focus is on the role of the judge, and indeed on the role of a judge in a criminal trial in a continental legal system.

As Ginzburg comments, '[t]he ties between history and law have always been close'.[72] Ginzburg notes that these ties are traceable back to a quality expected of narrative that the Romans termed *evidentia in narration*. That quality was the ability to use vivid examples of character or situation to make an effective argument that could persuade an audience. In Ginzburg's telling, the production of evidence or evaluation of testimony was properly left to another figure, the antiquarian or savant, and it was not until the eighteenth century that the two roles of historian and antiquarian were combined. That was the point at which comparisons between the judge and the historian began to gain popularity.[73] Ginzburg sketches a tradition of European historiographical scholarship in which the comparison between the judge and the historian became essential.

François Hartog has also focused on the relation between the judge and the historian, presenting it as one of rivalry.[74] The judge and the historian find themselves occupying the same terrain, both 'with full rights to be there'.[75] Hartog argues that judges 'see themselves as charged with the task of pronouncing a decision about almost everything, of "curing" public and private maladies, both past and present, and perhaps even those to come'.[76] This has led historians 'to question the obvious mutual intrusions of the historical and the judicial in each other's traditional domains'.[77]

Hayden White has suggested that there is an 'intimate relationship' between 'law, historicality, and narrativity'.[78] White suggests that the situation that is

---

[71] C Ginzburg, *The Judge and the Historian: Marginal Notes on a Late-Twentieth-Century Miscarriage of Justice* (London and New York: Verso, 1999).

[72] Ginzburg, *The Judge and the Historian*, 12.

[73] Ginzburg, *The Judge and the Historian*, 13.

[74] F Hartog, 'The Present of the Historian' (2014) 4 *History of the Present: A Journal of Critical History* 203.

[75] Hartog, 'The Present of the Historian', 211.

[76] Hartog, 'The Present of the Historian', 211.

[77] Hartog, 'The Present of the Historian', 211.

[78] H White, *The Content of the Form: Narrative Discourse and Historical Representation* (Baltimore and London: The John Hopkins University Press, 1987), 13. For a reflection on

best suited to narrative representation 'is the conflict between desire and the law'.[79] Both history and narrative require some notion of a subject that can serve as the agent of the historical narrative, as well as presupposing 'the existence of a legal system against which or on behalf of which the typical agents of a narrative account militate'.[80] It is the investment in a system of human relations governed by law that creates the narrative possibility of 'the kinds of tensions, conflicts, struggles, and their various kinds of resolutions that we are accustomed to find in any representation of reality presenting itself to us as history'.[81] For White, this raises the suspicion that 'narrative in general ... has to do with the topics of law, legality, legitimacy, or, more generally, authority'.[82]

The narratives of contextualist historians are conditioned upon just such a relationship to law. As I showed in Chapter 4, lawyers and judges play a significant role in the stories that historians tell about their own role and agency. Contextualist historians stage the revolutionary effects of their methods as a challenge to an oppressive political authority buttressed by an ahistorical form of legality. The narratives offered by contextualist historians depend on that image of the lawyer as judge and reproduce a particular scholastic and formalist image of the law as the condition of contextualism's revolutionary potential. If history ever succeeded in doing away with that image of the law, the power of the narrative in which contextualism is a triumphant modernising force for progress would be sapped.

5.2.2 *Standpoint, Role, and the Nature of International Legal Argument*

In order to communicate why this is a problem, we might consider the shared interest of historians and lawyers in standpoint. Contextualist historians draw our attention to the point of view of the author, stressing that the author of a past text or an utterance had an intention and a standpoint when writing the text or making the utterance. Lawyers have also argued that a crucial place in the routines of international law 'is occupied by *roles*'.[83] Different roles are 'reinforced by the different legal practices of international lawyering'.[84]

White's argument in relation to contemporary American legal thought, see NW Spaulding, 'The Historical Consciousness of the Resistant Subject' (2011) 1 *UC Irvine Law Review* 677.

[79] White, *The Content of the Form*, 12–13.
[80] White, *The Content of the Form*, 13.
[81] White, *The Content of the Form*, 14.
[82] White, *The Content of the Form*, 13.
[83] Koskenniemi, *From Apology to Utopia*, 550.
[84] Koskenniemi, *From Apology to Utopia*, 550.

This shared emphasis on role or standpoint offers an initial point of connection between the underlying concerns of historians and international lawyers. It can offer a way of understanding why the assumption that judgement is the emblematic standpoint from which lawyers approach the past is too limiting.

To illustrate, I'll return to Hunter's characterisation of Antony Anghie and postcolonial scholars more generally as being engaged in the moral or legal judgement of colonialism. Hunter sees TWAIL scholars as historians who are wrongly engaged in judging the past, rather than as lawyers intervening in contemporary legal debates. In assuming that such work is written from the standpoint of the judge, Hunter misrecognises what Anghie and other lawyers are doing when they draw on the past in making legal arguments. We can gain a better sense of the interventions made by Anghie and others if we take seriously that question of role or standpoint

The standpoint of the judge is of course one of the positions we can take up when we think and write about the law. An idealised or stylised vision of judging lies at the heart of many theories about law, based upon the idea that judges are impartial, apolitical, and objective.[85] For some international legal scholars, the judge is thought to personify something that 'is more than "how nations behave", that can never be reduced to a partisan position'.[86] The idea that judges would be fundamental to 'the function of law in the international community' has been a core tenet of much international legal thinking.[87] From a formalist perspective, 'even a non-judge (as adviser, academic, activist) must momentarily construct himself or herself as a judge' when 'called upon to perform a legal service'.[88] Yet many legal scholars have noted that the focus on the judge as emblematic of the law, and particularly of international law, can be misleading. This is in part because the place and role of adjudication and thus of the judge within a legal system is culturally specific.[89] Some international legal scholars have argued that the focus on adjudication by European international lawyers is premised on a conflictual style that is alien to other legal systems and creates a distorted vision of international law.[90]

---

[85] Koskenniemi, *From Apology to Utopia*, 550.

[86] Koskenniemi, 'Between Commitment and Cynicism', 512.

[87] H Lauterpacht, *The Function of Law in the International Community* (Oxford: Oxford University Press, 2011 [1933]), 440.

[88] Koskenniemi, 'Between Commitment and Cynicism', 512.

[89] Twining, 'Other People's Power', 197.

[90] See, for example, Y Onuma, A *Transcivilizational Perspective on International Law* (Leiden and Boston: Martinus Nijhoff, 2010), 205 (arguing that there is an 'excessive judicial-centrism in international legal studies ... supported by what I call a (West-centric) domestic model approach').

In addition, the place of adjudication in legal practice is more limited in international law than in many domestic systems. While in some areas, such as international trade and investment, litigation is almost routine, in other areas such as most military and intelligence activities, counterterrorism, migration, or taxation, disputes rarely reach an international court or tribunal.[91] Private lawyers advising clients, government officials deciding when and how to make use of international law in foreign policy, and legal advisors providing advice to the executive on the boundaries of lawful action play at least as important a role in shaping the law as international adjudication.[92] Many of the most controversial matters that arise in relation to international law concern the context of legal advising rather than adjudication, as the conduct of the war on terror illustrates.[93]

The standpoint of the judge is thus only one of many positions from which to think and write as an international lawyer. There are many other roles that lawyers play in relation to law and many other standpoints from which to write about law and legal practice. The community of lawyers involved in practising international law is extremely broad both geographically and functionally, as more and more human activities and interests have become subject to some area of international law.[94]

For example, professionals who make use of international law in their practice include government legal advisors, investment arbitrators, diplomats, domestic judges, international lawyers working for law firms, military lawyers, in-house corporate counsel, scholars and experts involved in negotiating specialised treaties (on issues such as biological weapons or whaling), civil servants and experts responsible for implementing international treaties, and lawyers working with non-governmental organisations and in other activist roles. The practitioners of international law arguably also include the many lawyers involved in the transnational networks that shape global regulation in

---

[91] B Kingsbury, 'International Courts: Uneven Judicialisation in Global Order' in J Crawford and M Koskenniemi (eds), *The Cambridge Companion to International Law* (Cambridge: Cambridge University Press, 2012), 203, at 210.

[92] NW Spaulding, 'Independence and Experimentalism in the Department of Justice' (2011) 63 *Stanford Law Review* 409, at 410.

[93] Spaulding, 'Independence and Experimentalism', 410 ('If there was any doubt about the significance of the counseling function of lawyers, particularly government lawyers, the actions of attorneys working in the Department of Justice during the Bush Administration should dispel it. Torture, indefinite detention, extraordinary rendition, targeted killing, profiling of Arab and Muslim men, and warrantless surveillance all occurred with the *ex ante* approval of government lawyers').

[94] J d'Aspremont, T Gazzini, A Nollkaemper, and W Werner, 'Introduction' in d'Aspremont, Gazzini, Nollkaemper, and Werner (eds), *International Law as a Profession*, 2.

sectors such as banking, finance, transnational policing, surveillance, and intelligence.[95]

Those roles give rise to standpoints from which to think and write about international law that differ from that of the judge.[96] The standpoint of the judge involves sharing in, controlling, or exercising legal power. Such a standpoint might also be adopted by an international lawyer advising a government delegation engaged in treaty negotiations, drafting articles on specific topics as part of the process of codifying international law, or acting as part of the Secretariat to international organs or tribunals. Just as adopting the perspective of the judge gives access to a particular relation to the law, adopting the perspective of other actors can work as a 'cognitive device' for looking at the law in new ways.[97]

The potential insights about law that can be gained from switching standpoints was famously illustrated by Oliver Wendell Holmes when he advised a

---

[95] See A-M Slaughter, *A New World Order* (Princeton: Princeton University Press, 2005); HH Koh, 'Is There a "New" New Haven School of International Law?' (2007) 32 *Yale Journal of International Law* 559, at 572; A Orford, 'The Crisis of Liberal Internationalism and the Future of International Law' (2021) 28 *Australian Year Book of International Law* 3.

[96] For reflections on their work by international lawyers describing their varied roles and functions, see RB Bilder, 'The Office of the Legal Adviser: The State Department Lawyer and Foreign Affairs' (1962) 56 *American Journal of International Law* 633; SM Schwebel, 'Remarks on the Role of the Legal Advisor of the US State Department' (1991) 2 *European Journal of International Law* 131; G Guillaume, 'Droit international et action diplomatique: Le cas de la France' (1991) 2 *European Journal of International Law* 136; Office of Legal Affairs (ed), *Collection of Essays by Legal Advisers of State, Legal Advisers of International Organizations and Practitioners in the Field of International Law* (New York: United Nations, 1999); P Allott, 'The International Lawyer in Government Service: Ontology and Deontology' (2005) 23 *Wisconsin Journal of International Law* 13; M Koskenniemi, 'International Legislation Today: Limits and Possibilities' (2005) 23 *Wisconsin Journal of International Law* 61; I Brownlie, 'Friedmann Award Address: The Work of an International Lawyer' (2006) 45 *Columbia Journal of Transnational Law* 1; MP Scharf and PR Williams, *Shaping Foreign Policy in Times of Crisis: The Role of International Law and the State Department Legal Adviser* (Cambridge: Cambridge University Press, 2010); D Bethlehem, 'The Secret Life of International Law' (2012) 1 *Cambridge Journal of International and Comparative Law* 23; Koh, 'The State Department Legal Adviser's Office'; P Allott, 'Britain and Europe: Managing Revolution' in R McCorquodale and J-P Gauci (eds), *British Influences on International Law, 1915–2015* (Leiden and Boston: Brill Nijhoff, 2016), 56; R Higgins, 'Introduction to the Symposium' (2018) 87 *British Yearbook of International Law* 101; M Wood, 'The Iraq Inquiry: Some Personal Reflections' (2018) 87 *British Yearbook of International Law* 149. The archive of the UK's Chilcot inquiry offers rare insights into the roles played by international lawyers in the lead-up to the war in Iraq and more generally. See, for example, Statement by Sir M Wood, 15 January 2010; Transcript of evidence given by Sir M Wood, 26 January 2010; Transcript of evidence given by Ms E Wilmshurst, 26 January 2010; Statement by Sir D Bethlehem, 24 June 2011, available at https://webarchive.nationalarchives.gov.uk/20171123123237/http://www.iraqinquiry .org.uk/.

[97] Twining, 'Other People's Power', 202.

group of law students to study the law from the viewpoint of the 'bad man' rather than the appellate judge.[98] The standpoint of Holmes' 'bad man' is shared by any other actor who experiences the law as the product of 'other people's power' and engages with it in the mode of calculation, risk management, and prediction.[99] For example, we might imagine that standpoint being adopted by an international lawyer who is acting as counsel in a case before an international court or arbitral body, advising a private corporation on the protection of foreign investments, or advising a government on how to respond to the threat or use of force by a foreign state.

Yet another standpoint is adopted by those actors who take a 'worm's eye view' of the law.[100] Such actors are less alienated than the 'bad man' but have not had any say 'in the design, development, or administration of the system' and are arguing for empowerment, fair treatment, or participation.[101] Such a standpoint might be adopted by international lawyers providing legal advice to a party or an organised minority group within a state, acting on behalf of newly independent states, or assisting or advising non-governmental organisations. Third World international lawyers have seen themselves as offering just such a 'worm's view of history' as a prequel to creating a sense of 'cohesion among the powerless states' and strengthening Third World resistance to neo-conservative forms of international law.[102]

5.2.3 *Judging and the Legacies of Colonialism and Fascism*

Even if we were to assume that a legal scholar like Anghie is taking up the standpoint of a judge when he discusses the legal legacies of imperialism or colonialism, the situation that faces a judge in the postcolonial situation with which TWAIL scholars are concerned is more complex than historians like Hunter and Fitzmaurice suggest. If we want to equate the work of someone like Anghie to that of a judge, it should be a judge who is called upon to interpret laws designed to express colonial, fascist, apartheid, or other such state policies that were developed under previous regimes. In such situations,

---

[98] Holmes, 'The Path of the Law', 459–461.

[99] Twining, 'Other People's Power', 202.

[100] Twining, 'Other People's Power', 212.

[101] Twining, 'Other People's Power', 212.

[102] M Sornarajah, 'Power and Justice: Third World Resistance in International Law' (2006) 10 *Singapore Yearbook of International Law* 19, at 26–30, 57. For a careful articulation of Sornarajah's approach, see CL Lim, 'The Worm's View of History and the Twailing Machine' in CL Lim (ed), *Alternative Visions of the International Law on Foreign Investment: Essays in Honour of Muthucumaraswamy Sornarajah* (Cambridge: Cambridge University Press, 2016), 3.

lawyers do not have the ability to consign all such legal experiments to history but instead have to decide how to make sense of the inheritance of past laws in interpreting present law.

The much-discussed situation of lawyers who were faced with interpreting German law after the Second World War offers a helpful illustration of the challenges this poses.[103] For German lawyers, the years of National Socialism could not simply 'be isolated like some sort of industrial accident'.[104] Legislators, judges, and legal scholars had routinely 'transformed such violent acts as annulment of citizenship, arrest, murder and pogroms into "lawful acts"'.[105] In the words of Christian Joerges, German lawyers faced with the legacies of National Socialism had 'to distinguish between undamaged relics and untenable remnants of tradition', while being motivated by 'the desire to arrive at a positive attitude towards the constitution of the democratic state and social rule of law'.[106] The inheritance of the changes that took place in criminal law, private law, labour law, or corporate law under National Socialism were not something that could be approached 'with the distance of a historian' but were rather a 'problem of the present'.[107]

The same is true of the legal systems developed under French absolutism, Spanish fascism, Australian colonialism, South African apartheid, or any other legal system that is (in theory) relegated to the past. For international lawyers, similar questions arise in relation to European imperialism. Law does not (usually) start again wholesale at Year Zero after a regime, government, or form of rule (such as monarchy, fascism, colonialism, or imperialism) supposedly ends. All of those who are asked to take responsibility for the subsequent law are faced with the question of inherited rights and obligations. Lawyers in such situations have to decide how the legacy of earlier governments or regimes will be addressed as part of the process of transmitting legal material through judicial decisions, academic teaching, or research. This is a presentist obligation that cannot be avoided.

---

[103] See the essays in C Joerges and NS Ghaleigh (eds), *Darker Legacies of Law in Europe* (Oxford and Portland: Hart, 2003).

[104] O Lepsius, 'The Problem of Perceptions of National Socialist Law Or: Was There a Constitutional Theory of National Socialism?' in Joerges and Ghaleigh (eds), *Darker Legacies of Law in Europe*, 19.

[105] M Stolleis, 'Prologue: Reluctance to Glance in the Mirror. The Changing Face of German Jurisprudence after 1933 and Post-1945' in Joerges and Ghaleigh (eds), *Darker Legacies of Law in Europe*, 1, at 10.

[106] C Joerges, 'Continuities and Discontinuities in German Legal Thought' (2003) 14 *Law and Critique* 297, at 304.

[107] Joerges, 'Continuities and Discontinuities in German Legal Thought', 305.

The example of the so-called grudge informer case – a jurisprudential staple in the Anglophone world as a result of the famous Hart–Fuller debate – illustrates the dilemma that arises for the judge in such a situation. The debate was a legacy of the visit by HLA Hart, then Professor of Jurisprudence at Oxford, to Harvard Law School, where he gave the Law School's annual Holmes Lecture in April 1957. While Hart presented the lecture, his host Lon Fuller, then Carter Professor of Jurisprudence at Harvard, reportedly 'paced up and down at the back of the room "like a hungry lion", and later demanded a right to reply'.[108] Hart's lecture and Fuller's response were subsequently published in the *Harvard Law Review*,[109] and the debate is often treated as a set piece in the ongoing struggle between positivist and natural law theories of jurisprudence. Both Hart and Fuller defended their jurisprudential approaches in part by exploring one in a series of cases involving Nazi-era laws that were then being considered in the German courts.[110]

The 'grudge informer' case was a decision of a provincial court of appeal involving an alleged crime committed during the Nazi era. In 1944, a German soldier home on leave for a day had privately made derogatory remarks to his wife expressing disapproval of Hitler and other Nazi leaders. The wife reported his remarks to the local leader of the Nazi party. The husband was tried by court martial and sentenced to death pursuant to a series of statutes that made it illegal to assert statements that were inimical to the welfare of the Third Reich or that impaired the military defence of the German people. In 1949, the wife was indicted for the offense of unlawful deprivation of liberty, which

---

[108] N Lacey, 'Reinterpreting the Context and Reassessing the Significance of the Hart-Fuller Debate' in P Cane (ed), *The Hart-Fuller Debate in the Twenty-First Century* (London: Hart, 2010), 1, at 102.

[109] See HLA Hart, 'Positivism and the Separation of Law and Morals' (1958) 71 *Harvard Law Review* 593; L Fuller, 'Positivism and Fidelity to Law – A Reply to Professor Hart' (1958) 71 *Harvard Law Review* 630.

[110] Hart's attention had been drawn to the 'grudge informer case' by a short note published in the *Harvard Law Review* in 1950: 'Criminal Law. In General. German Citizen Who Pursuant to Nazi Statute Informed on Husband for Expressing Anti-Nazi Sentiments Convicted under Another German Statute in Effect at Time of Act' (1951) 64 *Harvard Law Review* 1005, noting the report in Oberlandesgericht Bamberg July 27, 1949, 5 *Süddeutsche Juristen-Zeitung* 207 (Germany 1950). Hart's treatment of the case was in turn influenced by the German legal philosopher Gustav Radbruch, who had published an influential essay discussing the situation facing German judges in cases involving Nazi laws: G Radbruch, 'Gesetzliches Unrecht und übergesetzliches Recht' (1946) 1 *Süddeutsche Juristenzeitung* 105. Radbruch's essay has since been published in English as G Radbruch, 'Statutory Lawlessness and Supra-Statutory Law (1946)' (2006) 26 *Oxford Journal of Legal Studies* 1 (trans B Litschewski Paulson and SL Paulson). An English translation of the grudge informer case by David Dyzenhaus has been published as an appendix to D Dyzenhaus, 'The Grudge Informer Case Revisited' (2008) 83 *New York University Law Review* 1000, at 1032–1034.

was punishable under the German Criminal Code of 1871. She argued that her husband's imprisonment was pursuant to valid statutes, that his statements were a crime under the law then in force, and that as a result she had committed no offence in reporting him. She was found guilty, on the basis that she had relied on two Nazi statutes that were contrary to the sense of justice of all human beings, that she had no legal obligation to inform on her husband, and that the remarks were made in private.

Hart characterised the case as raising a clash between law and morality. For Hart, any dilemma posed by the case could be resolved by arguing that citizens should disobey unjust laws. Hart's famous resolution did not, however, address the 'complexity of the situation of a judge'.[111] Fuller, in contrast, focused squarely on that situation. He noted that after the collapse of the Nazi regime the German courts were faced with a significant challenge. They could not 'treat as void every decision and legal enactment that had emanated from Hitler's government' without causing massive disruption, but on the other hand 'it was equally impossible to carry forward into the new government the effects of every Nazi perversity that had been committed in the name of law', as 'any such course would have tainted an indefinite future with poisons of Nazism'.[112] Fuller brought into focus that the case 'required the court to take a view not only of doctrine but also of the nature of the judicial role'.[113] In other words, the judges in the grudge informer case 'did not have to decide whether to obey the law', as Hart would have it, but rather 'they had to decide how best to interpret it'.[114]

For the purpose of this book, the central point to note is that the issue for German judges asked to decide on the legality of actions taken during the Nazi era was one of present law not past history.[115] The judges in the grudge informer case were faced with the task of deciding what Nazi-era statutes

---

[111] Dyzenhaus, 'The Grudge Informer Case Revisited', 1018. For discussions of the grudge informer case that illuminate the complicated situation of German judges in the post-Nazi era, see HO Pappe, 'On the Validity of Judicial Decisions in the Nazi Era' (1960) 23 *Modern Law Review* 260; T Mertens, 'Radbruch and Hart on the Grudge Informer: A Reconsideration' (2002) 15 *Ratio Juris* 186; T Mertens, 'Nazism, Legal Positivism, and Radbruch's Thesis on Statutory Injustice' (2003) 14 *Law and Critique* 277.

[112] Fuller, 'Positivism and Fidelity to Law', 648.

[113] Dyzenhaus, 'The Grudge Informer Case Revisited', 1010.

[114] Dyzenhaus, 'The Grudge Informer Case Revisited', 1015.

[115] For related reflections on the ways in which such questions arose both during and after the war for the courts of other countries confronted with the problem of whether to give effect to Nazi law, see D Fraser, '"This Is Not Like Any Other Legal Question": A Brief History of Nazi Law before UK and US Courts' (2003) 19 *Connecticut Journal of International Law* 59; K Knop, 'The Hart-Fuller Debate's Silence on Human Rights' in P Cane (ed), *The Hart-Fuller Debate in the Twenty-First Century* (London: Hart, 2010), 61, at 70–78.

meant in the present. For example, should judges treat as valid law Nazi statutes that granted uncontrolled administrative discretion to Nazi officials, or should they treat such statutes as having no legal relevance for contemporary German law? Given that much Nazi law was enacted in secret, or subject to 'unpublished instructions to those administering the law', should judges in post-Nazi Germany have rummaged through the archives to make sure they were giving proper effect to secret Nazi directives or 'searched for unpublished laws among the files left by Hitler's government so that citizens' rights could be determined by reference to these laws'?[116] Or should those judges have refused to treat secret instructions as legally relevant? If Nazi judges had made a practice of disregarding the clear words of statutes, for example treating the word 'public' as inclusive of statements made between husbands and wives in private, should post-war judges have studied those canons of interpretation and earnestly applied them to Nazi-era statutes?[117]

Such questions are directed to making decisions about present law, although they may, as historians complain, also involve or imply moral judgements about the conduct of people in the past. Yet legal officials cannot simply refuse to address the vestiges of fascism, apartheid, colonialism, or imperialism that are handed on in present law.[118] Lawyers are forced to decide

---

[116] Fuller, 'Positivism and Fidelity to Law', 651–652.

[117] Fuller, 'Positivism and Fidelity to Law', 655.

[118] A similar set of issues arise in the context of cases concerning native title in Australian and other settler colonial courts. A number of the historians engaged in the method debates about international law cut their legal teeth criticising the revolutionary series of decisions made by the High Court of Australia that recognised a form of native title as part of Australian law, in particular the cases of *Mabo* v. *State of Queensland (No 2)* (1992) 175 CLR 1 and *The Wik Peoples* v. *State of Queensland* (1996) 187 CLR 1. That debate is beyond the scope of this book, but for the arguments made by contextualist historians criticising the High Court judges for getting their history wrong in recognising native title, see I Hunter, 'Natural Law, Historiography, and Aboriginal Sovereignty' (2007) 11 *Legal History* 137, at 139 (criticising the 'wave of activity' in common law settler societies focused on indigenous rights that was 'driven by the post-war decolonising agendas of international law, national land rights movements, revisionist academic work on colonialism, and constitutional and juridical reconsideration' for, amongst many other things, 'binding historiography to a common law presentism and a "juridical" relation to the colonial past'); A Fitzmaurice, 'The Genealogy of *Terra Nullius*' (2007) 129 *Australian Historical Studies* 1, at 15 (concluding that 'Mabo is not good history and it may not be very good common law'). For responses to the reactions of such historians that draw out the complex interactions of law and history in that jurisprudence, see L Godden, 'Wik: Legal Memory and History' (1997) 6 *Griffith Law Review* 122; A Curthoys, A Genovese, and A Reilly, *Rights and Redemption: History, Law, and Indigenous People* (Sydney: University of New South Wales Press, 2008); S Motha, 'As If – Law, History, Ontology' (2015) 5 *UC Irvine Law Review* 327.

whether or not fascist, colonialist, or imperialist laws will be transmitted after a change of regime or a change of ideology.

When a legal scholar or practitioner writes about the past, it is useful to try to grasp what standpoint they are occupying and what audience they are imagining in doing so. It could be that a piece of legal scholarship is written from the position of the judge, in which case it might purport to determine relevant facts in relation to a specific dispute or incident, declare the applicable law, perhaps in the form of rules and principles, and apply the law to the facts. That is not, however, a very fashionable style of legal writing, and it does not bear much relation to the TWAIL scholarship that historians have found so objectionable. As Twining has commented, it is 'surprising how often one standpoint is equated with a whole view' in scholarship about law.[119] Imagining the moralising judge or apologist for power as the only roles that a legal scholar might adopt loses touch with the rhetorical and dialectical nature of law and lawyering, and of the many different kinds of roles that lawyers and legal arguments play in a system with diverse ideological, cultural, and institutional foundations.

5.3 ALL REALISTS NOW: INTERNATIONAL LAW AFTER METAPHYSICS

5.3.1 *Contextualist History and the International Lawyer as Metaphysician*

In addition to imagining international lawyers as occupying a limited number of roles when we engage with past material, historians also appear to imagine that lawyers are only capable of taking a limited number of approaches to that material. Contemporary international lawyers are repeatedly presented as committed to a scholastic or doctrinal approach to the interpretation of past texts and having a naïve faith in metaphysical meanings, universal values, and progress narratives. When we make arguments about history, we are characterised as doing so either in search of transcendent foundations or redemptive futures.

According to Andrew Fitzmaurice, for example, 'many scholars in law faculties remain concerned with history as a means of understanding the foundations of the legal system' and ignore the real world of practice for an idealised 'history of doctrine'.[120] Ian Hunter argues that any scholars, including international lawyers, who do not conform to contextualist historical

---

[119] Twining, 'Other People's Power', 217.
[120] Fitzmaurice, 'Context in the History of International Law', 6–7.

methods or who question the legitimacy of the European state can be regarded as engaged in a single philosophical project, which Hunter variously characterises as 'European university metaphysics',[121] 'philosophical history',[122] 'metaphysical hermeneutics',[123] 'metaphysical hermeneutics of history',[124] 'modern anticontextualism', 'post-Kantian philosophical history',[125] 'Aristotelian university metaphysics',[126] scholasticism',[127] and 'dialectical historiography'.[128] For Kate Purcell, international legal scholars assume 'that international law has always been and remains oriented towards justice' and look to the past only to expose '"what went wrong" *en route* towards justice'.[129]

Similarly, Samuel Moyn characterises 'trained lawyers' as engaged in 'doctrinal' work, which he contrasts unfavourably with the sophisticated approach 'more common to card-carrying historians' who understand that '[l]egal ideas were relevant, but less as doctrines working themselves pure than as ideology'.[130] For Moyn, the initial and 'undoubtedly crucial' task for historians of international law is 'to reclaim law from the lawyers' and our 'foreshortened version of intellectualism'.[131] At its starkest, the claim made in the debates over method is that historians have progressed while international lawyers have been left behind in the nineteenth century: 'the distance between the juridical and the historical may in fact be the distance between nineteenth-century approaches to history and more reflexive and critical historical methods'.[132]

As we saw in Chapter 4, there is a long tradition of characterising contextualist historicisation as a radical response to legal traditions that are based on some kind of ancient or timeless point of origin. Butterfield, Pocock, Skinner, and Hunter each described history as presenting a radical challenge to legal

---

[121] I Hunter, 'The History of Theory' (2006) 33 *Critical Inquiry* 78, at 98.

[122] Hunter, 'The History of Theory', 98.

[123] Hunter, 'The History of Theory', 98.

[124] Hunter, 'The History of Theory', 109.

[125] I Hunter, 'The Contest over Context in Intellectual History' (2019) 58 *History and Theory* 185, at 207.

[126] I Hunter, 'The History of Philosophy and the Persona of the Philosopher' (2007) 4 *Modern Intellectual History* 571, at 582.

[127] Hunter, 'History of Philosophy and the Persona of the Philosopher', 582.

[128] I Hunter, 'About the Dialectical Historiography of International Law' (2016) 1 *Global Intellectual History* 1.

[129] K Purcell, 'On the Uses and Advantages of Genealogy for International Law' (2020) 33 *Leiden Journal of International Law* 13, at 18.

[130] S Moyn, 'Martti Koskenniemi and the Historiography of International Law in the Age of the War on Terror' in W Werner, M de Hoon, and A Galán, (eds), *The Law of International Lawyers: Reading Martti Koskenniemi* (Cambridge: Cambridge University Press, 2016), 340, at 348.

[131] Moyn, 'Martti Koskenniemi and the Historiography of International Law', 353.

[132] Purcell, 'On the Uses and Advantages of Genealogy', 34–35.

traditions grounded in Roman law or ancient custom. Empiricist historians have strongly argued that the application of their methods to international law will have the same effect today. In such accounts, the audience for contextualist histories 'always seems curiously the same: untouched by history'.[133] In the case of international law, the imagined reader is invested just enough in the idea of law's metaphysical grounds and the timeless nature of legal concepts to be shocked by the idea that law has a history, but not so invested that they reject the revelations of contextualist historians altogether.

Yet humanist historicising and anti-metaphysical claims have been a central part of international legal jurisprudence and practical legal argumentation for at least the past century. Challenges to scholastic metaphysics and formalist reasoning are already embedded within the existing argumentative field of the international legal academy and legal practice. Far from introducing international lawyers to ideas about empiricist historicisation as the way to understand law, historians are simply intensifying one side of an argumentative debate stretching back centuries. In order to understand the effect of contemporary academic debates in which anti-metaphysical or historicising arguments are portrayed as challenging the metaphysical grounds of law, or in which arguments about the evolution of meaning challenge textualist arguments about meaning, it is helpful to gain a sense of the history of such debates in international legal thought.

5.3.2 *Realism and American Anti-formalism in International Law*

Numerous currents of anti-metaphysical or anti-formalist thinking have informed the modern field of international law over the past centuries. Already by the time that Anglo-American and European international lawyers had begun to imagine themselves as a profession working to generate principles and rules of international law out of a mass of state practice, it was felt necessary to distinguish international law as a science from the vague resort to metaphysics and natural law. The urge to find some scientifically defensible account of international law that amounted to more than an 'unorganized mélange of natural law abstractions, juristic common-sense and a bourgeois conviction about the rightness of one's most banal political beliefs' has driven international lawyers ever since.[134] This is not the place to produce a history of

---

[133] L Carlson, *Contingency and the Limits of History* (New York: Columbia University Press, 2019), 9.

[134] M Koskenniemi, 'Introduction: Alf Ross and Life Beyond Realism' (2003) 14 *European Journal of International Law* 653.

the complex and seemingly never-ending oscillation in the relations between a transcendent natural law and a scientific international law.[135] Suffice to say that for at least some international legal scholars, it can be argued that 'in international law, there is really only one problem, what to do about natural law'.[136]

One particularly influential stream of anti-metaphysical thinking in international law derives from the role played by US lawyers in the development of the contemporary field. The conditions in which American lawyers found themselves in their new republic shaped the emergence of what Peter Goodrich has termed a *mos americanus*.[137] US casebooks in the nineteenth century 'sought early an almost excessive proximity to European law, civilian and common' so as to establish American law's 'legitimacy and legality'.[138] Goodrich gives as an example James Kent's four-volume *Commentaries on American Law*, first published in 1826 and then in revised editions throughout the nineteenth century. It was only after his lengthy first volume addressed 'the law of nations and the place of the United States in the European order of law, the *mos italicus* and its various progeny' that Kent moved on to the US Constitution.[139] While in casebooks through to the mid-twentieth-century US law 'sought to embed itself to the hilt in foreign sources', that invention of a continuous tradition 'across time and geography' was always tenuous and subsequently became 'unmoored, as recent attacks on foreign sources and citations amply prove'.[140] Although the United States retained the form of the common law and the system of precedent from its English forebears, US common law lacked any plausible claim to antiquity, 'being in essence a transplant mingled with local practices'.[141]

The experience of the Civil War in turn led to the emergence of an ethos of realism throughout American culture. Social scientists were aware that 'American culture and traditions had changed' and that 'the cultural traditions of the past were not inevitably or directly related to the here and

---

[135] See further G Gordon, 'Natural Law in International Legal Theory: Linear and Dialectical Presentations' in A Orford and F Hoffmann (eds), *The Oxford Handbook of the Theory of International Law* (Oxford: Oxford University Press, 2016), 279.

[136] P Allott, 'Language, Method, and the Nature of International Law' (1970) 45 *British Yearbook of International Law* 79, at 100.

[137] P Goodrich, '"Who Are We?": Persona, Office, Suspicion, and Critique' in J Desautels-Stein and C Tomlins (eds), *Searching for Contemporary Legal Thought* (Cambridge: Cambridge University Press, 2017), 43, at 44.

[138] Goodrich, 'Who Are We?', 50.

[139] Goodrich, 'Who Are We?', 49.

[140] Goodrich, 'Who Are We?', 50.

[141] Goodrich, 'Who Are We?', 51.

now'.[142] Rather than attempt to solve the problems of law or society through 'looking to history', social scientists believed that 'the traditions and usages of past ages are broken' and that they must look to 'data' to make sense of contemporary reality. The realist ethos and the search for facts soon made their way into law schools.[143] The result was an academic legal culture with a very different relation to the past than the European scholasticism which the humanistic heroes of Pocock and Skinner had sought to challenge.

For at least the past century, US lawyers have been trained in a form of *mos americanus* that is committed to relentlessly anti-metaphysical and anti-formalist understandings of law. Since as far back as Oliver Wendell Holmes, US lawyers have taken an anti-foundationalist stance to the law.[144] Holmes famously rejected as ahistorical the traditional appeal to 'black-letter' rules in favour of experiential approaches that study the social life of the law. Holmes, like many of his American generation and since, rejected tradition as a sufficient ground for law. He saw the search for facts and the study of the real world as central to the work of the legal scholar: 'the black-letter man may be the man of the present, but the man of the future is the man of statistics'.[145]

We might think too of the anti-formalism of early American legal realists like Felix Cohen, who challenged what he saw as the 'transcendental nonsense' of much contemporary legal thought and its attachment to empty forms and metaphysical ideals. Cohen argued that it was necessary to move away from 'legal fictions' that present as 'concepts' and instead look to the '*motions or operations*' that they describe.[146] While it may have once been useful to invent legal terms such as the state or the corporation 'to describe the corporate activities of human beings', it was necessary to avoid falling into the trap of believing that those legal terms describe real things.[147] Cohen aimed 'to substitute a realistic, rational, scientific account of legal happenings for the classical theological jurisprudence of concepts'.[148] This was realism as 'an assault upon all dogmas and devices that cannot be translated into terms of

---

[142] Duxbury, *Patterns of American Jurisprudence*, 94.

[143] Duxbury, *Patterns of American Jurisprudence*, 95.

[144] KM Parker, 'Law "In" and "As" History": The Common Law in the American Polity, 1790–1900' (2011) 1 *UC Irvine Law Review* 587.

[145] Holmes, 'The Path of the Law', 469.

[146] F Cohen, 'Transcendental Nonsense and the Functional Approach' (1935) 35 *Columbia Law Review* 809, at 825.

[147] Cohen, 'Transcendental Nonsense and the Functional Approach', 825.

[148] Cohen, 'Transcendental Nonsense and the Functional Approach', 821.

actual experience' – a 'negative' functionalism that was 'naturally of special prominence in a protestant movement'.[149] Or we might remember Jerome Frank's arguments that scholasticism, the lawyerly faith in word magic, and the formalistic ideal of legal certainty were merely symptoms of the desire to find in the law a substitute Father.[150] For US legal scholars, there was 'no juristic father worth killing, no determinate, historically identified establishment and jurisprudence to overturn' but only the 'freedom' of 'an orphan law' – 'politics all the way down, trench warfare for the foreseeable future'.[151]

In international law, the influence of the realist and pragmatist traditions in American legal thought can be felt in the policy science of the New Haven school and its focus on law as a process of communication and authoritative decision-making,[152] the 'international legal process' scholarship of Abram Chayes, Thomas Ehrlich, Andreas Lowenfeld, and Antonia Chayes,[153] the Weberian-inspired analyses of international law in a world of struggle by David Kennedy,[154] the transnational legal process approach of Harold Koh,[155] Anne-Marie Slaughter's vision of a 'new world order' of networked bureaucratic guilds,[156] the rational choice thinking of Jack Goldsmith and Eric Posner,[157] or the empirical turn championed by Gregory Shaffer and

---

[149] Cohen, 'Transcendental Nonsense and the Functional Approach', 822.

[150] JN Frank, *Law and the Modern Mind* (New York: Coward-McCann, 1930).

[151] Goodrich, 'Who Are We?', 54.

[152] For useful overviews and evaluations, see MS McDougal, 'The Law School of the Future: From Legal Realism to Policy Science in the World Community' (1946–1947) 56 *Yale Law Journal* 1345; MS McDougal and HD Lasswell, 'The Identification and Appraisal of Diverse Systems of Public Order' (1959) 53 *American Journal of International Law* 1; R Higgins, 'Diverging Anglo-American Attitudes to International Law' (1972) 2 *Georgia Journal of International and Comparative Law* 1; R Falk, 'Casting the Spell: The New Haven School of International Law' (1995) 104 *Yale Law Journal* 1991; W Michael Reisman, 'Theory about Law: Jurisprudence for a Free Society' (1999) 108 *Yale Law Journal* 935; WM Reisman, S Wiessner, and AR Willard, 'The New Haven School: A Brief Introduction' (2007) 32 *Yale Journal of International Law* 575; O Jütersonke, 'Realist Approaches to International Law' in Orford and Hoffmann (eds), *The Oxford Handbook of the Theory of International Law*, 327; H Saberi, 'Yale's Policy Science and International Law: Between Legal Formalism and Policy Conceptualism' in Orford and Hoffmann (eds), *The Oxford Handbook of the Theory of International Law*, 427.

[153] A Chayes, T Ehrlich, and A Lowenfeld, *International Legal Process* (Boston: Little Brown & Co, 1968); A Chayes and AH Chayes, *The New Sovereignty: Compliance with International Regulatory Agreements* (Cambridge: Harvard University Press, 1995).

[154] D Kennedy, *The Dark Sides of Virtue: Reassessing International Humanitarianism* (Princeton: Princeton University Press, 2005); Kennedy, *A World of Struggle*.

[155] HH Koh, 'Transnational Legal Process' (1996) 75 *Nebraska Law Review* 181.

[156] Slaughter, *A New World Order*.

[157] JL Goldsmith and EA Posner, *The Limits of International Law* (Oxford: Oxford University Press, 2005).

Tom Ginsburg.[158] US international law scholars over the past century have consistently produced scholarship that is committed to studying law in the social world rather than articulating transcendent rules or historical doctrines and have promoted their methodological approaches with appeals to novelty rather than tradition. Indeed, to the extent that there is any tradition linking each promised American methodological innovation, it is the use of the word 'new' in its branding.[159] Any lawyer who attempts to engage with the American mainstream of international law must orient themselves to that pragmatic and anti-formalist tradition.

5.3.3 European Anti-metaphysical Approaches to International Law

Of course, the development of a realist and anti-metaphysical tradition in international law was not limited to the United States. For example, in the early twentieth century many of the most influential forms of European legal thought were also informed by an anti-metaphysical, modernist turn, which would profoundly unsettle existing relations between law, metaphysics, religion, and history.[160] One example is the work of Hans Kelsen, whose attempt to establish a 'pure theory of law' was informed by a group of scientists, musicians, artists, architects, philosophers, and jurists in interwar Vienna who saw themselves as confronting common problems relating to representation and the limits of language in a society that seemed incapable of adapting to its rapidly changing historical situation.[161]

The concern with the limits of language as an 'instrument of thought' was shared by the intellectuals of Kelsen's Vienna.[162] In this, they were profoundly

---

[158] G Shaffer and T Ginsburg, 'The Empirical Turn in International Law Scholarship' (2012) 106 *American Journal of International Law* 1.

[159] Examples from recent decades include 'New Approaches to International Law', 'New International Legal Process', the 'New World Order' theory, the '"New" New Haven School', 'New International Law Scholarship', and 'New Legal Realism'. See further D Kennedy and C Tennant, 'New Approaches to International Law: A Bibliography' (1994) 35 *Harvard International Law Journal* 417; ME O'Connell, 'New International Legal Process' (1999) 93 *American Journal of International Law* 334; Slaughter, *A New World Order*; JL Goldsmith and EA Posner, 'The New International Law Scholarship' (2006) 34 *Georgia Journal of International and Comparative Law* 463; Koh, 'Is There a "New" New Haven School of International Law?'; G Shaffer, 'The New Legal Realist Approach to International Law' (2015) 28 *Leiden Journal of International Law* 189.

[160] KM Parker, 'Writing Legal History Then and Now: A Brief Reflection' (2016) 56 *American Journal of Legal History* 168, at 169–170.

[161] See the discussion in A Orford, 'Scientific Reason and the Discipline of International Law' (2014) 25 *European Journal of International Law* 369.

[162] A Janik and S Toulmin, *Wittgenstein's Vienna* (Chicago: Ivan R Dee, 1996), 30.

influenced by late nineteenth-century debates about the status of scientific knowledge, and particularly by the methodology and philosophy of science developed by the Austrian physicist Ernst Mach.[163] For Mach, the goal of science was the most economical abstract expression of sense data. He was violently opposed to metaphysical speculation, which he considered to be merely obfuscation.[164] Mach developed a critical and historical approach to the study of physics that was designed to show the points at which factors that were not strict descriptions of sense data had crept into physical theory, thus leading to scientific observations that 'transcended the limits of the observable'.[165] Mach sought to purify science of its theological traces, exploring the history of mechanics in order to point to the moments 'where metaphysics entered in to confuse the physicist'.[166]

Kelsen's call for a pure theory of law echoed the philosophy of Mach – in particular the ideas that representation is a problem of language, that legal science must be stripped of metaphysical or meaningless decoration, and that it is politically necessary for science to avoid imprecise concepts that can lead to misunderstanding and abuse. Kelsen portrayed his project as a science of law – a science that required the study of law to be based upon a scientific method for acquiring knowledge and comprehension of the law.[167] The role of the scientist was to establish a system of concepts, through which the 'immense wealth of positive legal material' could be 'mastered'.[168]

In particular, Kelsen sought to challenge the theory of law as the will of a personified state, seeing in that representation of the relation between law and the state an ideological justification for centralised, imperial, and monarchical politics. Instead, the validity of any legal system was dependent upon the legal fiction that there was a *Grundnorm* or basic norm that is 'presupposed to be valid'.[169] That basic norm 'exists in the juristic consciousness' rather than in some metaphysical appeal to something external to the law. Kelsen argued

---

[163] F Field, *The Last Days of Mankind: Karl Kraus and His Vienna* (London: Macmillan, 1967), 28, 245; J Blackmore, R Itagaki, and S Tanaka (eds), *Ernst Mach's Vienna 1895–1930* (Dordrecht: Kluwer, 2001).

[164] E Mach, *Contributions to the Analysis of the Sensations* (trans CM Williams) (Chicago: Open Court, 1897).

[165] Janik and Toulmin, *Wittgenstein's Vienna*, 137.

[166] Janik and Toulmin, *Wittgenstein's Vienna*, 137, 141.

[167] H Kelsen, *Pure Theory of Law* (trans M Knight) (Berkeley: University of California Press, 1967).

[168] H Kelsen, 'Juristischer Formalismus' [Legal Formalism], 6, cited in J von Bernstorff, *The Public International Law Theory of Hans Kelsen: Believing in Universal Law* (Cambridge: Cambridge University Press, 2011), 238.

[169] H Kelsen, *General Theory of Law and State* (Cambridge: Harvard University Press, 1945), 117.

that international law too was valid not because of some mythical origin in natural law, the common will, or tacit consent, but purely 'because international lawyers assumed it to be valid'.[170] Kelsen thus sought to free international law from the perceived need 'for an ultimate extra-legal foundation'.[171]

Another significant attempt to rethink the role of metaphysics in the social sciences can be found in the work of the post-war generation of jurists, social scientists, and economists in Uppsala and beyond who were influenced by Axel Hägerström's critique of value metaphysics and magical thinking. Hägerström became an icon for those in Swedish intellectual, political, and avant-garde artistic circles who wanted to bring about radical change, including the young economists of the Stockholm School.[172] Since hailed as a founder of Scandinavian Legal Realism, Hägerström sought to uncover the metaphysical elements of legal thinking and provide the foundations for the scientific study of law as a social phenomenon.

Hägerström's approach can perhaps be best illustrated by the motto he chose to open an essay summarising his philosophy: '*Praeterea censeo meta-physicam esse delendam*' ('Moreover I propose that metaphysics must be destroyed').[173] Hägerström argued that modern lawyers had inherited from Roman law and natural law the mystical idea that the law grants rights and imposes obligations that in turn give citizens power over things and persons, and had translated that into the claim that the state by its will could grant rights and duties to legal subjects.[174] For Hägerström, any theory that was organised around the notion of the 'will' of the state or of the law was based on a metaphysical illusion animated by an old belief in animism.[175] No system of

---

[170] J von Bernstorff, 'Hans Kelsen and the Return of Universalism' in Orford and Hoffmann (eds), *The Oxford Handbook of the Theory of International Law*, 192, at 203.

[171] von Bernstorff, 'Hans Kelsen and the Return of Universalism', 203.

[172] For a discussion of the influence of Hägerström on the Stockholm School economists, see G Myrdal, 'Postscript' in P Streeten (ed), *Value in Social Theory* (Oxon: Routledge, 1958), 237, at 250–251. Hägerström's anti-metaphysical thinking about the state and critical thinking about value judgements had an influence on international law through the work of two Stockholm School of economists – Dag Hammarskjöld and Gunnar Myrdal. Both played significant roles in introducing economic thinking about the state to the early practice of the UN. See further A Orford, 'Hammarskjöld, Economic Thinking, and the United Nations' in H Melber and C Stahn (eds), *Peace, Diplomacy, Global Justice, and International Agency: Rethinking Human Security and Ethics in the Spirit of Dag Hammarskjöld* (Cambridge: Cambridge University Press, 2014), 156.

[173] A Hägerström, *Philosophy and Religion* (Oxon: Routledge, 1964), 33, 74.

[174] Hägerström, *Philosophy and Religion*, 72–74.

[175] A Hägerström, *Inquiries into the Nature of Law and Morals* (Uppsala: Almquist & Wiksell, 1953).

law could be organised around the unitary 'will' of the 'state', and any pretence that it could be was simply a cover for those who exercised power in the name of a higher law.[176]

Alf Ross, who had earlier been a student of Hans Kelsen,[177] brought Hägerström's attack on metaphysical thinking to bear on international law and in so doing influenced the next generation of Nordic international lawyers.[178] For Ross, somewhat like Cohen in the United States, the point was not to rid the law of concepts such as 'rights' or 'sovereignty', but rather to be clear about the work that such concepts were doing.[179] A concept like 'rights' was dangerous if superstitious thinkers took it to indicate that something new had been created in the world between a legal fact and a legal consequence.[180] But if lawyers understood a concept like 'rights' as simply a 'tool for the technique of presentation', it could play a useful function in simplifying legal communication.[181]

5.3.4 *Decolonisation and the Challenge to European Metaphysics*

The claims of European international law to a universal status became more controversial in the era of formal decolonisation. As a result, the need to point to sources of international law that offered more legitimacy than European metaphysics intensified. As Onuma Yasuaki has argued, the question of when and where international law was born could not be dissociated from the more foundational question of what international law is. Those who sought to present as a simple factual claim that Europe was the origin of modern international law were doing significant ideological work through an apparently empirical argument.[182] The 'Eurocentric law of nations' was just one regional normative system which applied 'in only a limited area of the earth

---

[176] See further A Carty, 'Scandinavian Realism and Phenomenological Approaches to Statehood and General Custom in International Law' (2003) 14 *European Journal of International Law* 817, at 825–828.

[177] C Landauer, 'Antinomies of the United Nations: Hans Kelsen and Alf Ross on the Charter' (2003) 14 *European Journal of International Law* 767; J Strang, 'Two Generations of Scandinavian Legal Realists' (2009) 32 *Retfærd Årgang* 62.

[178] Koskenniemi, 'Alf Ross and Life Beyond Realism'.

[179] For speculation as to why American and Scandinavian legal realism took similar forms, see H Pihlajamäki, 'Against Metaphysics in Law: The Historical Background of American and Scandinavian Legal Realism Compared' (2004) 52 *American Journal of Comparative Law* 469.

[180] A Ross, 'Tû-Tû' (1957) 70 *Harvard Law Review* 812.

[181] Ross, Tû-Tû', 825.

[182] Y Onuma, 'When Was the Law of International Society Born? – An Inquiry of the History of International Law from an Intercivilizational Perspective' (2000) 2 *Journal of the History of International Law* 1, at 5.

and lasted for a limited period of time'.[183] It was only once European international law was imposed on the rest of the world at the end of the nineteenth century that a claim could be made that it had become a potential 'universal law of the world'.[184] From the late nineteenth century until the mid-twentieth, 'the study of international law focused its attention primarily on Europe, and secondarily on North America'.[185]

That approach became steadily less defensible as the push for decolonisation intensified. Neither positivist approaches that were based on articulating principles of law formulated in another time nor idealist approaches based on 'morality and conscience' could address a situation in which 'different value systems of somewhat equal moral validity are in collision'.[186] In the era of formal independence, as an increasing number of new states joined the United Nations, the overt appeal to civilisational, religious, moral, or cultural origins of international law was abandoned and the formal approach to the sources of international law gained ground.[187] Yet while European metaphysics in the form of arguments grounding legal rules and principles in European customs or ancient texts may have disappeared, Third World and other critical scholars of international law have continued to challenge the cognitive certainties of the European tradition that reappear in the secularised languages of development, humanitarianism, and economics.

International legal scholarship in the twenty-first century expresses in a concentrated form the anti-metaphysical and historicised approaches that have been associated with the kind of 'orphaned' law described by Goodrich. Modern international law has been strongly influenced by US international lawyers who wear their distance from any sense of history, tradition, or institution as a badge of honour, by European appeals to science and systematisation, and by the need for a postcolonial international law to find a new grounding beyond its Christian and European origins. It might be going too far to say that the anti-formalist and anti-metaphysical critiques of international law have won close to universal acceptance,[188] but such

---

[183] Onuma, 'When Was the Law of International Society Born?', 7.

[184] Onuma, 'When Was the Law of International Society Born?', 7.

[185] Onuma, 'When Was the Law of International Society Born?', 54.

[186] M Sornarajah, *The International Law on Foreign Investment* (4th edition) (Cambridge: Cambridge University Press, 2017), 10.

[187] BS Chimni, 'Customary International Law: A Third World Perspective' (2018) 112 *American Journal of International Law* 1.

[188] For the argument that anti-formalist critiques of 'logically formal rationality' have won close to universal acceptance, see D Kennedy, 'The Disenchantment of Logically Formal Legal Rationality, or Max Weber's Sociology in the Genealogy of the Contemporary Mode of Western Legal Thought' (2004) 55 *Hastings Law Journal* 1031, at 1055.

arguments are certainly extremely familiar in international legal scholarship and practice.

In this sense for international lawyers, as for many twenty-first-century lawyers, '[r]ealism is dead: we are all realists now'.[189] Critiques of metaphysical or ahistorical thinking that seek to place international law into a historical context and attack the idea of a transcendental foundation for the law are commonplace. The use of historicising arguments to challenge traditionalist legal claims has been fully incorporated into our patterns of legal argumentation. To take a historicising position or a position that is deeply sceptical about international law as tradition is simply to take one possible side in a shifting legal debate. Of course, this does not mean that metaphysical thinking has disappeared from international law, but rather it means that the claim to have uncovered the remnants of metaphysical or enchanted thinking in the work of fellow scholars is just one more argumentative tool in the international lawyer's toolbox.[190]

All of this goes to say that it would be a mistake to think that attacking formalist or metaphysical forms of legal argumentation is a novel or radical step for international law. In the contemporary international law field, there is a different orientation to metaphysics from that which dominated the Europe of Pocock, Skinner, or even Hunter. As we will see, the project of historicising the law has far more complicated effects in such a situation. To begin to understand how historicist methods operate as interventions in today's international legal situation, we need some sense of the institutional structures, the language games, the patterns of argument, and the styles of performance that make up the contemporary practices of international law.

5.4 THE PAST IN THE MAKING OF INTERNATIONAL LAW

So far, I have suggested that historians of international law have largely failed to engage with the situation of contemporary legal practice and that as a result they misrecognise two aspects of legal scholarship. First, they assume that legal arguments about the past engage with or take up the standpoint of the judge,

---

[189] W Twining, *Karl Llewellyn and the Realist Movement* (London: Weidenfeld and Nicholson, 1973), 382.

[190] For responses that note the unavoidable impact of realism on legal thought while suggesting that remnants of metaphysics and formalism can be found in the legal process school, rights theories, and law and economics, see D Fraser, 'What a Long, Strange Trip It's Been: Deconstructing Law from Legal Realism to Critical Legal Studies' (1988–1989) 5 *Australian Journal of Legal Sociology* 35; JW Singer, 'Legal Realism Now' (1988) 76 *California Law Review* 465.

and second they assume that lawyers adopt a scholastic, formalist, or metaphysical orientation to past texts. I have suggested that the work of international legal scholars cannot be understood without situating it in relation to the world of legal practice, to the different roles and standpoints that lawyers might adopt in practice, and to the varied orientations to the idea of law as tradition or metaphysics that lawyers have already incorporated into patterns of international legal argument.

In this section, I offer some examples of the different ways that the past is drawn upon in the course of contemporary legal arguments. Paying attention to these uses of the past and the varied contexts in which they occur challenges the major claim made by historians and taken up by some international lawyers; that is, the claim that historians can offer us impartial, evidence-based, and verifiable accounts of past legal texts, concepts, ideas, or practices. Some of the ways in which international lawyers make use of the past are likely to be uncontroversial for contextualist historians. For example, international lawyers and contextualist historians would likely find common ground in relation to general principles for engaging with the past, such as that the rights of parties to a dispute must be judged on the basis of the applicable law as it stood at the time or that treaties do not have retroactive effect.[191] However, such points of methodological commonality mask significant differences in the meaning and uses of the past in international law and history. The following sections explore some of the ways in which international lawyers engage with the past as fact and the past as law. The aim is to think through the law, in order to grasp the ambitious nature of the claims that contextualist historians make about what their methods can achieve, and to suggest why those claims are flawed.

5.4.1 'Finding' the Facts

Perhaps the most straightforward way in which historians claim to be able to correct or complete the scholarship of international lawyers is by offering facts about the past rather than contested interpretations. As we saw in Chapter 4, Ian Hunter has insisted that histories of international law should offer 'a falsifiable historical hypothesis' rather than imposing 'a hermeneutic template'

---

[191] There are of course many complications that arise in the application of those general principles in practice. See further R Higgins, 'Time and the Law: International Perspectives on an Old Problem' (1997) 46 *International and Comparative Law Quarterly* 502; FO Vicuña, 'Time in International Law and Arbitration' in Caron, Schill, Smutny, and Triantafilou (eds), *Practising Virtue: Inside International Arbitration*, 584.

on the past.[192] Historians have favourably compared their own ability to offer an 'evidence-based' approach to studying the past based on upholding 'standards of veracity and verifiability',[193] to the approach of international lawyers, who are engaged in 'factional cultural politics rather than scholarship'.[194] They draw a clear line between evidence and interpretation, empirical scholarship and factional politics.

For lawyers, the relation of the world of evidence and the work of interpretation is more complicated.[195] Debates over the relationship between fact and narrative in the work of legal argument can be traced back to at least eighteenth-century controversies amongst lawyers and beyond 'to the convoluted history of rhetoric'.[196] Evidence, fact-finding, and inference play a central role in the interpretation and practice of law more broadly, and determining which facts are relevant to a legal analysis is not simply an empirical process. The presentation of facts has a normative effect. As trial lawyers have pointed out, 'the statement of the facts is not merely a part of the argument, it is more often than not the argument itself.'[197] Once the facts of a legal case are assembled, much of the normative work has been done.

The distinction between questions of fact and questions of law is both central to legal thinking and at the same time slippery and often unsustainable.[198] The 'glue' that holds together reasoning about facts or evidence and the legal conclusions drawn from those facts is made up of background generalisations, processes of story-telling and narrative, and other forms of inferential reasoning and interpretation.[199] The stock of generalisations and inferences that fills in the gaps between facts and law may be made up of

---

[192] Hunter, 'About the Dialectical Historiography of International Law', 6.

[193] L Benton, 'Beyond Anachronism: Histories of International Law and Global Legal Politics' (2019) 21 *Journal of the History of International Law* 1, at 3, 10.

[194] Hunter, 'About the Dialectical Historiography of International Law', 19.

[195] See generally W Twining, *Rethinking Evidence: Exploratory Essays* (2nd edition) (Cambridge: Cambridge University Press, 2006).

[196] W Twining, 'Narrative and Generalizations in Argumentation about Questions of Fact' in Twining, *Rethinking Evidence*, 332.

[197] JW Davis, 'The Argument of an Appeal' (1940) 26 *American Bar Association Journal* 895, at 896. See further KN Llewellyn, *Jurisprudence: Realism in Theory and Practice* (Chicago: The University of Chicago Press, 1962), 342 (suggesting that '[i]t is trite among good advocates, that the statement of the facts can, and should, in the very process of statement, frame the legal issue, and can, and should, simultaneously produce the conviction that there is only one sound result'); JB White, *Heracles' Bow: Essays on the Rhetoric and Poetics of the Law* (Madison: University of Wisconsin Press, 1985), 160; W Twining, 'Lawyers' Stories' in Twining, *Rethinking Evidence*, 286; Twining, 'Narrative and Generalizations', 337.

[198] Twining, 'Narrative and Generalizations', 332.

[199] Twining, 'Narrative and Generalizations', 332.

elements that are 'more or less indeterminate, unarticulated, vague, or precise', and may be supported by 'scientific evidence, "general knowledge", sheer speculation, or prejudice'.[200] 'In short', as William Twining puts it, 'the "glue" for arguments on questions of fact is often historically contingent, culturally relative and value laden'.[201] Such generalisations are all the more powerful (or dangerous, depending on your point of view) when they are left unarticulated or implicit, because they present 'value judgments as if they were empirical facts'.[202] Which version of the facts we believe is not just a matter of probability and logic but also a matter of which narrative we find persuasive.

In addition, lawyers think about facts and evidence in the register of proof rather than truth. We have seen that some historians insist that they can offer a bulwark against those who seek to manipulate the past, that their methods produce something 'verifiable', and that this can be contrasted to the work of lawyers. In a sense, historians are right about lawyers and truth. The lawyer's relationship to truth is indirect. This is not to say that lawyers do not take facts seriously or that we are nonchalant about lying. Rather, the point is that as lawyers we operate in the register of proof and probability rather than truth and falsity. Law students learn that 'propositions which are material to legal controversy can never be proved to be true or false but only to be probable to some degree'.[203]

Lawyers are trained to analyse and communicate a mass of evidence in order to establish its probative value, and to think about how to demonstrate the relevance and materiality of evidence as part of mapping an overall argument. Whether or not a fact is legally relevant is determined by the legal context in which it is invoked.[204] The relevance of evidence relates to the facts that need to be proved to make a case. One of the things that lawyers are doing in making a case is developing 'complex arguments based on mixed masses of evidence'.[205] This involves selecting which evidence is relevant, constructing relations between the propositions of fact which that evidence is said to establish, and then having a theory of the significance of each piece of evidence for the case as a whole.[206]

---

[200] Twining, 'Narrative and Generalizations', 335.
[201] Twining, 'Narrative and Generalizations', 335.
[202] Twining, 'Narrative and Generalizations', 335.
[203] J Michael, *Elements of Legal Controversy* (Brooklyn: The Foundation Press, 1948); W Twining, 'Taking Facts Seriously' in Twining, *Rethinking Evidence*, 14, at 16–17.
[204] R Weis and W Twining, 'Reconstructing the Truth about Edith Thompson: The Shakespearean and the Jurist' in Twining, *Rethinking Evidence*, 344, at 350.
[205] Weis and Twining, 'Reconstructing the Truth about Edith Thompson', 358.
[206] Twining, 'Taking Facts Seriously', 20.

An awareness of the differing nature of the legal and historical engagement with past facts is further intensified if we reflect upon the role that 'legal facts' may play in a case.[207] For instance, in territorial disputes or disputes over maritime delimitations, a court may be asked to determine the legal or 'juridical' facts upon which parties to the case rely in support of their claims to title over territory.[208] In such cases, the clear-cut distinction between empirical fact and interpretation is slippery.

For example, in one of the earliest cases decided by the ICJ, the court was asked to determine whether France or the United Kingdom had produced more convincing proof of title to the Minquiers and Ecrehos islets situated between Jersey and France.[209] In deciding which party had proved its title, the court considered 'the facts' upon which each relied in support of their claim. Those 'facts' included the Norman conquest of England in 1066, a series of medieval treaties concluded between the English and French Kings, and the legal consequences of the 'dismemberment of the Duchy of Normandy' in 1204.

In other cases, evidence of past colonial law is pleaded as fact. States invoking the principle of *uti possidetis juris* ('as you possess under law') often have counsel from a former colonial power on their legal team, because the *jus* according to which boundaries are determined in that formulation is the public law of the former colony.[210] In the case of *Nicaragua* v. *Honduras*,[211] for

---

[207] See R Higgins, 'The Judicial Determination of Relevant Facts, Speech to the Sixth Committee of the General Assembly, 2 November 2007' in R Higgins, *Themes and Theories* (Oxford: Oxford University Press, 2009), 1369, at 1370.

[208] The language of 'juridical fact' invokes the long-running debate amongst international lawyers over the statement made by Max Huber in the *Island of Palmas* arbitration that 'a juridical fact must be appreciated in the light of the law contemporary with it' but that a distinction in relation to 'intertemporal law' must 'be made between the creation of rights and the existence of rights': *Island of Palmas Case (The Netherlands* v. *The United States of America)*, Award (4 April 1928) II RIAA 829. For varied interpretations of the scope and meaning of that passage, see G Fitzmaurice, 'The Law and Procedure of the International Court of Justice 1951–54: Treaty Interpretation and Certain Other Treaty Points' (1951) 28 *British Yearbook of International Law* 1; TO Elias, 'The Doctrine of Intertemporal Law' (1980) 74 *American Journal of International Law* 285; Higgins, 'Time and the Law, 515–519; EE Triantafilou, 'Contemporaneity and Its Limits in Treaty Interpretation' in Caron, Schill, Smutny, and Triantafilou (eds), *Practising Virtue: Inside International Arbitration*, 449, at 454–459.

[209] *France* v. *United Kingdom (Minquiers and Ecrehos case)* [1953] ICJ Reports 47.

[210] *Land, Island and Maritime Frontier Dispute (El Salvador/Honduras: Nicaragua intervening)*, Judgment [1992] ICJ Reports 350, at 558–559 ('It should be recalled that when the principle of the *uti possidetis juris* is involved, the *jus* referred to is not international law but the constitutional or administrative law of the pre-independence sovereign, in this case Spanish colonial law').

[211] *Territorial and Maritime Dispute between Nicaragua and Honduras in the Caribbean Sea (Nicaragua* v. *Honduras)*, Judgment [2007] ICJ Reports 659.

example, the legal teams for both parties included Spanish counsel who presented evidence about the 'complex legal and institutional order of the American territories of the Spanish monarchy during the eighteenth and early nineteenth centuries' and debated the extent and means by which the Spanish Crown had allocated title to cays and islands between colonial provinces.[212]

The ICJ has also been called upon to determine questions of legal fact in the context of advisory opinions. For example, in its Advisory Opinion on the Chagos islands, the ICJ evaluated a broad range of legal matters under the heading of 'the factual context of the separation of the Chagos Archipelago from Mauritius'.[213] These included the implications of discussions between the United Kingdom and the United States concerning the potential strategic use of the Chagos Archipelago by the United States after Mauritian independence, the circumstances leading up to the adoption of the Lancaster House agreement, whether Mauritius could be said to have consented to the terms of that agreement, and the 'factual circumstances', including agreements, law suits, and settlements, related to the removal of the Chagossians from the islands. As such cases illustrate, determining questions of 'fact' can involve interpreting legal material and weighing its probative value for the disputed issues in a case.

All of this can be contrasted with the work of historians. Historians of international law present their work as providing detailed evidence that aims to correct or complete the historical record. This can be compared to the legal context, in which 'completeness and comprehensiveness are only relative matters'.[214] Historians of international law insist on their ability to determine the facts from a standpoint that is general rather than particular, outside of time rather than located within a very specific process. In contrast, the first step in any legal analysis of evidence or historical material involves clarifying 'Who am I? At what stage in what process am I? What am I trying to do?'[215] In situations of a dispute over facts, a key question for law is always 'who determines the facts?' and 'who determines which facts are relevant?' Facts cannot simply be found and disagreements over the facts are often central to legal disputes.[216] The removal of ambiguity through the writing of facts and

---

[212] See further the oral argument presented by Antonio Remiro Brotóns for Nicaragua (CR 2007/3, 8–29), and the discussion in Higgins, 'The Judicial Determination of Relevant Facts', 1371.

[213] *Legal Consequences of the Separation of the Chagos Archipelago from Mauritius in 1965*, Advisory Opinion [2019] ICJ Reports 95, at 119–128.

[214] Weis and Twining, 'Reconstructing the Truth about Edith Thompson', 359.

[215] Weis and Twining, 'Reconstructing the Truth about Edith Thompson', 368.

[216] H Charlesworth, 'International Law: A Discipline of Crisis' (2002) 65 *Modern Law Review* 377, at 382–384.

the determination of whether evidence is relevant is central to the practice of judgement.[217] In international law, where states are reluctant to submit disputes to international adjudication, there is often an ongoing struggle to establish facts and a repeated refusal by powerful states to give up the sovereign authority to determine which facts are relevant.[218] The historical assumption that facts about the past are inert does not fit well with highly contested international situations in which the authority of an international tribunal is at best weak, and at worst non-existent.[219] Without an authoritative decision-maker, 'the facts become as if they were alive as a series of uncoordinated concentrations of state powers'.[220]

Legal scholarship is embedded within those institutional struggles over the historical record. Historians of international law claim to offer accounts of the past that are not shaped by any notion of relevance or by any presentist objectives. They present their accounts of facts in the register of 'verifiability' and truth. In theory, they are not constrained by any sense of which evidence is material to a case and 'are free to frame their questions as they wish without formal constraints'.[221] Yet as we will see in Chapter 6, the evidence historians choose to examine and the questions they choose to answer are often implicitly (and sometimes explicitly) framed by presentist legal arguments and by the choices that have already been made by international lawyers.

5.4.2 *Arguing about Past Precedents*

A second way in which the past is used in international legal practice is in the appeal to precedents. An argument from precedent is an exemplary instance of a number of the problems that historians find in juridical method, such as studying the historical record for presentist purposes or assembling a 'doctrinal' argument about the principles or rules that can be derived from past material. Some of those advocating for the adoption of empiricist historical methods in international law have explicitly criticised lawyers for seeking to

---

[217] N Philadelphoff-Puren and P Rush, 'Fatal (F)laws: Law, Literature and Writing' (2003) 14 *Law and Critique* 191, at 201–202 (arguing that 'the practice of judgement is not reducible to the task of finding the facts, as if the statement of the case is a correct reflection and reproduction of the state of affairs in the world – as if it were possible to find facts and not write them').

[218] A Orford, 'The Destiny of International Law' (2004) 17 *Leiden Journal of International Law* 441 at 456–457.

[219] A Carty and FZ Lone, 'Some New Haven International Law Reflections on China, India and Their Various Territorial Disputes' (2011) 19 *Asia Pacific Law Review* 95, at 107.

[220] Carty and Lone, 'Some New Haven International Law Reflections', 107.

[221] Weis and Twining, 'Reconstructing the Truth about Edith Thompson', 350.

'[mine] the past for analogues' on the basis that searching for 'analogical relevance' obscures the details of history.[222] More broadly, as we have seen, contextualist historians reject the idea that past texts can address present concerns. In the words of Quentin Skinner, past texts 'are concerned with their own quite alien problems' and not 'somehow concerned with our own problems as well'.[223] As a result, 'we must learn to do our own thinking for ourselves'.[224]

Even though legal realists long ago debunked the idea that lawyers could derive abstract legal principles and rules from previous cases and apply them mechanically to the next fact situation, studying and referring to past cases continues to be at the heart of much legal argument. The ways in which lawyers do so has been shaped by the century of realist-inflected legal education that focuses on the malleability of legal terms, on techniques of reading cases broadly to establish a general rule or narrowly to apply to a very specific fact situation, on how to invoke competing rules or move from rule to exception to generate a desired outcome, and on the availability of arguments that appeal to broader social, economic, or policy goals as a way of modifying or shifting attention away from past precedents. Arguments from precedent, to be successful, must amongst other things appear plausible to arbitrators, judges, and other lawyers who are familiar with the same precedents and can be persuaded that the relevant precedents generate the pattern being claimed for them.

Technically, international law does not have a doctrine of *stare decisis*, and the decisions of courts are only relevant to the parties in a particular case. In practice, however, international courts and tribunals routinely appeal to the decisions and reasoning of earlier courts and tribunals. International lawyers study and use past cases both as a source of exemplary patterns of argument and in order to persuade an audience that a particular situation should (or definitely should not) be treated in the same way as an earlier precedent. Martti Koskenniemi has commented that when working as a legal advisor, he often felt his task was akin to being a 'historian of the office'.[225] While for the relevant minister or political decision-maker the situation was always new, the

---

[222] Purcell, 'On the Uses and Advantages of Genealogy', 26–27 (critiquing 'juridical method' that treats history as having 'an analogical relevance', looks to 'analogous situations' to make arguments about present law, or '[mines] the past for analogues').

[223] Q Skinner, 'Meaning and Understanding in the History of Ideas' (1969) 8 *History and Theory* 3, at 52. See further the detailed discussion in Chapter 4 of the place of that claim within Skinner's broader work.

[224] Skinner, 'Meaning and Understanding', 52.

[225] Koskenniemi, 'Epilogue: To Enable and Enchant', 407.

legal advisor's task was 'to show what was done five, fifteen, fifty years ago in an analogous situation' and to persuade the decision-maker to deal with the current situation in the same way as that earlier one.[226]

As that brief description suggests, however, for an argument from precedent to work, the lawyer must be able to convince an interlocutor, whether a political decision-maker, a judge, or an academic audience, that one situation is analogous to another. That requires making a persuasive argument that the incident or case should be understood as part of a pattern or as sharing certain characteristics with the earlier incident or case – that the particular case should be understood as an instance of a general type. And for a lawyer on the opposite side of such an argument, the task is to show why that precedent is not relevant, and to distinguish the current case from the earlier one.

An argument from precedent is better understood as an art than a science. The move between the particular facts of a case that is being invoked as a precedent and the general category for which that case is said to stand necessarily involves interpretation. The basic structure of an argument about whether or not a case stands as precedent for the current situation involves the work of generalisation. The lawyer will argue that in the precedent case X happened, with the legal consequence of Y. As a result, whenever X happens, the legal consequence is Y. As the current situation is a clear case of X, the legal consequence should be Y. In such an argument, X remains constant in the move between the particular and the general, yet how exactly X should be categorised depends upon the interpretation of each situation, the elements of the situation that are considered to be material, and the language used to describe the relevant categories or patterns into which both cases are said to fit. The attraction of case-by-case arguments is that 'one is not forced to define the boundaries of X in advance' – it is possible to argue that the current situation 'is a clear case of X' without defining X.[227] The argument from precedent is valuable as 'a form of argument by analogy which does not commit the arguer to a position beyond what is needed for the case at hand'.[228]

How then does this relate to the arguments made by empiricist historians? For historians, the situation is straightforward: lawyers should just say no to arguing by analogy or making instrumental use of the past in arguments about present law. Yet moving between the particular (the precedent, the treaty provision, the illustrative example, the morality tale, the behavioural science experiment, the incident) and the general (the principle, the rule, the

---

[226] Koskenniemi, 'Epilogue: To Enable and Enchant', 407.
[227] Twining, 'Narrative and Generalizations', 340.
[228] Twining, 'Narrative and Generalizations', 340.

concept, the situation type, the policy, the pattern) is a core part of legal argument. Realising that this involves the work of choice and interpretation rather than empirical science does not mean that such procedures should be prohibited. As I will argue in Chapter 6, the question is not how to rid international law of arguments that move from particular to general, or that assemble elements of the past to make arguments for the present, but rather how to do so in ways that make the linking assumptions underpinning those moves explicit.

5.4.3 *Debating the Nature and Interpretation of Treaties*

In presenting their work as offering a completion to or corrective of existing accounts of international law, historians have regularly waded into debates over the role and meaning of treaties. For Hunter, one of the reasons that international lawyers have misrecognised the history of our own field is that we do not understand the centrality of treaties to the emergence of positive law. It is simply an empirical error to look to anything other than treaties as the basis of international law. The 'historical reality' is that international law is 'positive treaty-law'.[229] In Hunter's account, by the early nineteenth century German public lawyers had properly replaced the natural law reliance on custom or principles with attention to the 'fundamentally documentary' form of the treaty. In so doing, those lawyers recognised that the interpretation of treaties was a matter of 'historiography', premised on understanding that treaties were 'the record of diplomatic and political acts'.[230] According to Hunter, that 'treaty-based historiography of international law' has been 'retrospectively erased' by twenty-first century revisionist international lawyers.[231] Other historians of international law such as Isabel Hull and Quinn Slobodian have presented their work as offering evidence-based accounts that lift the meaning of specific treaties or the purpose of particular treaty regimes out of the stuff of partisan debate and into the realm of fact.[232]

The processes of identifying and interpreting treaties offer some of the most commonplace examples of engaging with the past in international law. Debates over what treaties are, why they bind states, and what they mean, as

---

[229] Hunter, 'About the Dialectical Historiography of International Law', 5, 22.

[230] Hunter, 'The Contest over Context', 201.

[231] Hunter, 'About the Dialectical Historiography of International Law', 4, 5.

[232] IV Hull, *A Scrap of Paper: Breaking and Making International Law During the Great War* (Ithaca and London: Cornell University Press, 2014); Q Slobodian, *Globalists: The End of Empire and the Birth of Neoliberalism* (Cambridge: Harvard University Press, 2018). See further the discussion of the arguments made by Hull and Slobodian in Chapter 6.

well as the interpretative approaches taken to understanding specific treaty provisions, are embedded within the argumentative institutional practice of international law.[233] The claim that historians can offer an impartial account of the role that treaties play within international law and an evidence-based account of their meaning and purpose is hard to sustain if we turn to consider the place of treaties within the argumentative practice of international lawyers.

As a starting point, the questions of which instruments or statements amount to a treaty, whether and why treaties are a source of international law, and which agreements are legally binding upon states raise foundational issues about the nature of international law.[234] During much of the twentieth century, it was commonplace to see international lawyers express the view that treaties should not be considered as sources of law but rather as sources of obligation for the parties that had entered into them.[235] Treaties were simply a record of the obligations undertaken by states parties who had entered into a transaction on the basis of the customary rule of *pacta sunt servanda*.[236] The consent of states to treaties could be understood to create legal obligations only because that act of consent took place within a juridical system that included the principle that consent shall produce that effect.[237]

Lawyers continued to debate the relative weight that should be placed upon treaties well into the twentieth century. Some international lawyers argued that treaties might prove to be the ephemeral expression of a temporary balance of power and that the enduring weight of custom was what mattered in the long term.[238] For the most extreme proponents of a statist

---

[233] See generally M Bowman and D Kritsiotis (eds), *Conceptual and Contextual Perspectives on the Modern Law of Treaties* (Cambridge: Cambridge University Press, 2018).

[234] J Klabbers, *The Concept of Treaty in International Law* (The Hague: Kluwer, 1996).

[235] Allott, 'Language, Method, and the Nature of International Law', 133 (arguing that treaties should not be regarded as a source of law, but rather as a '*product* of law ... The regrettable consequence of regarding treaties as a source of law is that the consensual character of the treaty thereby appears to be the origin of the obligation. But *ad hoc* consent is a political act').

[236] GG Fitzmaurice, 'The General Principles of International Law Considered from the Standpoint of the Rule of Law' (1957) 92 *Recueil des Cours* 1, at 41.

[237] JL Brierly, 'Le Fondement du Caractère Obligatoire du Droit International' (1928) 23 *Recueil des Cours* 463, at 486 ('Il est vrai que la part de la convention s'accroît de plus en plus aujourd'hui dans le développement du droit international, mais il est également vrai qu'un grand nombre des droits et devoirs des individus sont contractuels à l'origine. Dans les deux cas, le consentement est le créateur immédiat d'un principe de droit, mais seulement parce que l'acte du consentement se produit dans un système juridique dont l'un des principes est que le consentement produira précisément cet effet').

[238] L Oppenheim, 'The Science of International Law: Its Task and Method' (1908) 2 *American Journal of International Law* 313, at 321, 322 ('the law of ... law-making treaties is a grafting-twig on the trunk of the old customary law which might one day have again to be severed from the tree').

approach – perhaps unsurprisingly lawyers from the United States writing during its period as unchallenged global hegemon – treaties could be understood as at best signalling devices that provided information as to what states would interpret as cooperation or coordination in a particular context.[239] According to that view, treaties at best offer a weak guide to predicting what states might do in a given situation, but the parties to treaties have no normative obligation to comply with them. The role played by *pacta sunt servanda* as the foundation of an international legal system was merely a tale that weak-minded 'traditionalist' international lawyers told themselves so they could fall asleep at night. For others, who saw *pacta sunt servanda* as the founding principle of international law or who represented states that sought to challenge inherited conceptions of international law, treaties should not only be honoured but could potentially have the capacity to create or express 'general international law'.[240] In that vein, international lawyers argued that certain treaties may be capable of having a 'law-making' effect,[241] or that some multilateral treaties gave rise to objective regimes that bind third parties.[242]

Some disputes involving treaties have turned on the apparently empirical question of whether particular instruments count as a treaty.[243] The 1969 Vienna Convention on the Law of Treaties (VCLT) presents this as a

---

[239] Goldsmith and Posner, *The Limits of International Law* (arguing that their rational choice model explains 'the logic of treaties without reference to notions of "legality" or *pacta sunt servanda* or related concepts'); Goldsmith and Posner, 'The New International Law Scholarship', 463, at 466, 482–483 (comparing their own rational choice approach, which they describe as exhibiting the 'social science virtues' of 'methodological self-consciousness, empiricism, and theoretical rigor', with the 'traditionalist' approach to international law, which confuses 'normative and positivism claims', is based on 'anecdotes' rather than empirical studies, and has a 'Whiggish rather than scholarly' historical sense).

[240] G Tunkin, 'Is General International Law Customary Law Only?' (1993) 4 *European Journal of International Law* 534.

[241] C Brölmann, 'Law-Making Treaties: Form and Function in International Law' (2005) 74 *Nordic Journal of International Law* 383.

[242] The UN Charter is often considered to give rise to an objective regime, for reasons expressed in the *Reparations for Injuries* opinion, in which the ICJ held that the UN Charter was binding on Israel even though it was not a party because 'fifty States, representing the vast majority of the members of the international community, had the power, in conformity with international law, to bring into being an entity possessing objective international legal personality, and not merely personality recognized by them alone': *Reparations for Injuries Sustained in the Service of the United Nations* [1949] ICJ Rep 179, at 185. Another candidate for a treaty giving rise to an objective regime is the Antarctic Treaty. See the discussion in B Simma, 'The Antarctic Treaty as a Treaty Providing for an "Objective Regime"' (1986) 19 *Cornell International Law Journal* 189; J Crawford and D Rothwell, 'Legal Issues Confronting Australia's Antarctica' (1992) 13 *Australian Yearbook of International Law* 53.

[243] *Case Concerning Maritime Delimitation and Territorial Questions between Qatar and Bahrain (Qatar v. Bahrain)* (Juris & Admissibility) [1994] ICJ Reports 112.

technical, definitional issue.[244] Article 2(1) provides that '"treaty" means an international agreement concluded between States in written form and governed by international law, whether embodied in a single instrument or in two or more related instruments and whatever its particular designation'. Despite the apparently empirical nature of the initial interpretative question, the attempt to distinguish treaties from other political agreements has given rise to disputes in practice and debates in theory.

For example, do treaties have to be made public (as we would expect of domestic legislation) or can they be kept secret (as many legal systems would allow for contracts or trusts)?[245] If treaties are only a subset of international agreements, how is a distinction to be made between treaties and other agreements (such as agreements taking the form of memoranda of understanding, political agreements, joint declarations, side letters, 'gentleman's agreements', or informal agreements) which are not treated as binding under international law?[246] The requirement that an international agreement must be 'governed by international law' to have the status of a treaty is usually taken to distinguish treaties from agreements that were not intended to create rights or obligations under international law, giving rise to a fresh set of issues around how such intention is to be inferred.[247] Within the United States, the heated discussion of those questions has been driven by issues related to the authority

---

[244] Vienna Convention on the Law of Treaties (opened for signature 23 May 1969, entered into force 27 January 1980) 1155 UNTS 331.

[245] The requirement that treaties be registered with the United Nations was one response to the expression of popular resistance to secret treaties during the interwar period. The combined effect of Article 80 of the VCLT and Article 102 of the UN Charter, however, is that failure to register a treaty does not deny it treaty status but (in theory) gives rise to the consequence that no party to the treaty can invoke it before a UN organ. See further M Donaldson, 'The Survival of the Secret Treaty: Publicity, Secrecy, and Legality in the International Order' (2017) 111 *American Journal of International Law* 575.

[246] PM Eisemann, 'Le *Gentleman's agreement* comme source du droit international' (1979) 106 *Journal du Droit International* 326; RR Baxter, 'International Law in "Her Infinite Variety"' (1980) 29 *International and Comparative Law Quarterly* 549; C Chinkin, 'A Mirage in the Sand? Distinguishing Binding and Non-binding Relations between States' (1997) 10 *Leiden Journal of International Law* 223; K Raustiala, 'Form and Substance in International Agreements' (2005) 99 *American Journal of International Law* 581; AT Guzman, 'The Design of International Agreements' (2005) 16 *European Journal of International Law* 579; A Aust, 'Alternatives to Treaty-Making: MOUs as Political Commitments' in DB Hollis (ed), *The Oxford Guide to Treaties* (Oxford: Oxford University Press, 2012), 46.

[247] See DB Hollis, 'Defining Treaties' in DB Hollis (ed), *The Oxford Guide to Treaties* (Oxford: Oxford University Press, 2012), 10, at 25–26; Aust, 'Alternatives to Treaty-Making', 48–53. In addition, agreements not intended to have legal effect might still give rise to rights and obligations through notions of estoppel or legitimate expectations: see A Aust, 'The Theory and Practice of Informal International Instruments' (1986) 35 *International and Comparative Law Quarterly* 787; J Klabbers, 'The Commodification of International Law' in H Ruiz Fabri,

of the President to enter into certain agreements without Congressional approval. US international lawyers thus contrast treaties to a proliferating set of alternative forms, including 'congressional-executive agreements', 'sole executive agreements', 'ex ante congressional executive agreements', 'ex post congressional executive agreements', and 'executive agreements plus'.[248]

Even if states agree that a particular instrument is a treaty, debates over which canons, rules, or methods should be adopted to interpret treaty provisions are a central element of the adversarial legal process. All those involved in proposing, negotiating, or drafting a legal text know that it will be interpreted by other lawyers in the future, and seek to influence that future interpretation or 'to programme it so far as possible'.[249] That involves not only trying to envisage what effect future interpreters will give to the text, but also what interpretative approach they will adopt in doing so.[250]

Thus an awareness of the approaches that are likely to be taken in interpreting legal texts informs the techniques and strategies used in their negotiation and drafting. If the legal field is one in which 'context' (for example, in the form of *travaux préparatoires*) is likely to be given weight as a source for interpreting a particular treaty, then experienced negotiators will 'know how to make "good record" surrounding a text' by providing detailed explanations of votes and public statements.[251] Where the field is one with a stronger focus on

---

E Jouannet, and V Tomkiewicz (eds), *Select Proceedings of the European Society of International Law*, Vol. 1 (Oxford: Hart, 2008), 341, at 344.

[248] For an introduction to those debates, see MS McDougal and A Lans, 'Treaties and Congressional-Executive or Presidential Agreements: Interchangeable Instruments of National Policy' (1945) 54 *Yale Law Journal* 181; S Slonim, 'Congressional-Executive Agreements' (1975) 14 *Columbia Journal of Transnational Law* 434; B Ackerman and D Golove, 'Is NAFTA Constitutional?' (1995) 108 *Harvard Law Review* 799; LH Tribe, 'Taking Text and Structure Seriously: Reflections on Free-Form Method in Constitutional Interpretation' (1995) 108 *Harvard Law Review* 1221; PJ Spiro, 'Treaties, Executive Agreements, and Constitutional Method' (2001) 79 *Texas Law Review* 961; OA Hathaway, 'Treaties' End: The Past, Present, and Future of International Lawmaking in the United States' (2008) 117 *Yale Law Journal* 1236; OA Hathaway, 'Presidential Power over International Law: Restoring the Balance' (2009) 119 *Yale Law Journal* 140; HH Koh, 'Remarks: Twenty-First Century International Lawmaking' (2013) 101 *Georgetown Law Journal* 725; D Bodansky and P Spiro, 'Executive Agreements+' (2016) 49 *Vanderbilt Journal of Transnational Law* 885; HH Koh, 'Triptych's End: A Better Framework to Evaluate 21st Century International Lawmaking' (2017) 126 *Yale Law Journal Forum* 338; CA Bradley and JL Goldsmith, 'Presidential Control over International Law' (2018) 131 *Harvard Law Review* 1201.

[249] P Allott, 'Interpretation: An Exact Art' in A Bianchi, D Peat, and M Windsor (eds), *Interpretation in International Law* (Oxford: Oxford University Press, 2015), 373, at 380.

[250] Allott, 'Interpretation: An Exact Art', 380–381.

[251] Allott, 'Interpretation: An Exact Art', 381.

the text more narrowly conceived, negotiators will spend far more time pinning down each comma and arguing over every phrase.

The interpretation of those texts that set out rules for interpreting treaties is in turn part of that conflictual process. While, in theory, the question of how treaties are to be interpreted is resolved by Articles 31 and 32 of the VCLT, those articles nonetheless leave a great deal of scope to interpreters and include numerous modes of interpretation.[252] Not only did the project of codifying the rules of treaty interpretation in the VCLT fail to prevent interpretative controversies, but the interpretation of the rules set out in the convention is itself regularly central to those controversies.[253] As Philip Allott has noted, 'it is a source of special intellectual pleasure to note that, from the moment they were put on paper, the Vienna Convention provisions on the interpretation of treaties have themselves been subjected to interpretation of an exceptionally intense and contentious kind'.[254]

States faced with the reality of ideological and political conflict have generally been loath to accept that arbitrators are authorised to base their treaty interpretation on the subjective 'intention' of the parties to a treaty rather than its text. In particular, for newly independent states, intentionalism was rejected as a method for treaty interpretation both because it was perceived to involve 'a serious risk of manipulation' of the rights and obligations resulting from treaty commitments, and perhaps more significantly, because intention-alism worked to privilege the supposed common intention of the original

---

[252] The 'general' rule of interpretation set out in Article 31(1) is that '[a] treaty shall be interpreted in good faith in accordance with the ordinary meaning to be given to the terms of the treaty in their context and in the light of its object and purpose'. A focus on the 'text' of a treaty ('ordinary meaning', 'terms of the treaty') thus jostles with approaches that focus on 'context' and on 'object and purpose'. Article 31(2) explains that 'context' here refers to the broader 'text' of the treaty, any agreement made between all parties in connection with the treaty, and any instrument made by one or all parties in connection with the conclusion of the treaty and accepted as an instrument related to the treaty. Article 31(3) notes that any 'subsequent agreement' between the parties regarding the treaty's interpretation shall be taken into account in interpreting the treaty, as shall 'any subsequent practice' in relation to the treaty's application and any relevant rules of international law applicable in relations between the parties. In addition, Article 31(4) provides that a special meaning shall be given to a term if the parties 'so intended'. Article 32 states that recourse may only be had to what the VCLT calls 'supplementary means of interpretation' (and a contextualist historian would call 'context'), including 'the preparatory work of the treaty and the circumstances of its conclusion', in order to confirm the meaning derived from the 'application' of the methods set out in Article 31, or to determine the meaning of the treaty if those methods leave the meaning 'ambiguous or obscure' or lead to a result that is 'manifestly absurd or unreasonable'.

[253] F Zarbiyev, 'A Genealogy of Textualism in Treaty Interpretation' in Bianchi, Peat, and Windsor (eds), *Interpretation in International Law*, 251, at 267.

[254] Allott, 'Interpretation: An Exact Art', 375.

drafters of a treaty over the commitments of states that acceded to treaties later (for example, after independence).[255] Far from being the product or reflection of a common will, state officials have tended to see treaties as 'disagreement reduced to writing'.[256]

States often also disagree over the character of multilateral treaties and whether they should be interpreted as contracts reflecting a series of bilateral bargains, as legislation serving a law-making function, or as constitutions expressing foundational values.[257] To take one example, for decades US administrations expressed concerns about the approach taken by WTO adjudicators to the interpretation of the WTO agreements.[258] Even at the time of the creation of the WTO, shots had already been fired by member states, and particularly the United States, across the bow of a more assertive or activist 'self-understanding' on the part of Appellate Body members.[259] However, the combination of the compulsory nature of the WTO dispute settlement process, the limited institutional capacity for state control over the process in practice, the existence of a standing Secretariat that provided support to Panellists and Appellate Body members, and the constraining effect that a commitment to consensus decision-making had on collective action amongst the Members saw the WTO dispute settlement bodies gain increasing autonomy and independence.[260]

That steady expansion of adjudicative authority and activism was welcomed by those who saw the WTO as a key vehicle for realising a particular vision of global economic integration. The field of international economic law was one of the first areas in which rational choice analysis was applied, with international economic lawyers and trade economists developing a detailed literature on international trade norms and their economic rationale to inform decision-makers.[261] For many in that community, it made sense for the

---

[255] Zarbiyev, 'A Genealogy of Textualism in Treaty Interpretation', 266.

[256] P Allott, 'The Concept of International Law' (1999) 10 *European Journal of International Law* 31, at 43.

[257] For an early statement of such distinctions, see AD McNair, 'The Functions and Differing Legal Character of Treaties' (1930) 11 *British Yearbook of International Law* 100.

[258] R McDougall, *Crisis in the WTO: Restoring the WTO Dispute Settlement Function*, Centre for International Governance Innovation Paper No. 194, October 2018.

[259] See, for example, JH Bello, 'The WTO Dispute Settlement Understanding: Less Is More' (1996) 90 *American Journal of International Law* 416, at 417.

[260] R Howse, 'The World Trade Organization 20 Years On: Global Governance by Judiciary' (2016) 27 *European Journal of International Law* 9; A Lang, 'The Judicial Sensibility of the WTO Appellate Body' (2017) 27 *European Journal of International Law* 1096.

[261] A van Aaken, 'Rational Choice Theory' in Anthony Carty (ed), *Oxford Bibliographies Online: International Law* (Oxford: Oxford University Press, 2012).

Appellate Body to take a teleological approach to interpretation of the WTO agreements, to treat them as incomplete contracts, or more controversially to understand them as having a constitutional character.[262]

Yet for others the result was a form of 'judicial power unleashed'.[263] While many states bridled at the limitations on freedom of action and regulation that broad and evolutive interpretations by the Appellate Body imposed, the United States in particular took dramatic steps to restore the balance of rights and obligations to which it understood itself to have agreed in joining the WTO.[264] The United States insisted that WTO agreements should be strictly interpreted as contracts rather than as multilateral, law-making treaties, that Panel and Appellate Body rulings apply only to specific disputes and had no precedential value, that the Appellate Body was wrong to consider itself as something akin to a court with rulings that carry some level of precedential value, and that the Appellate Body was insufficiently accountable to WTO members. Under the Obama administration, the United States blocked a series of appointments and reappointments to the Appellate Body because the candidates were not considered to share the interpretative approach preferred by the United States.[265] Those simmering disagreements with and challenges to the Appellate Body were intensified after the election of President Trump. While the United States had expressed concerns about the Appellate Body's overreach for decades, those concerns were summarised in the US 2018 Trade Policy Agenda,[266] which criticised specific decisions of the WTO adjudicative bodies, the interpretative approach taken by the Appellate Body, and procedural actions taken by the Appellate Body.

---

[262] H Horn, G Maggi and RW Staiger, 'Trade Agreements as Endogenously Incomplete Contracts' (2010) 100 *American Economic Review* 394; E-U Petersmann, *International Economic Law in the 21st Century: Constitutional Pluralism and Multilevel Governance of Interdependent Public Goods* (Oxford: Hart, 2012); JH Jackson, 'Constitutional Treaties: Institutional Necessity and Challenge to International Law Fundamentals' in M Cremona, P Hilpold, N Lavranos, SS Schneider, and AR Ziegler, *Reflections on the Constitution of International Economic Law* (Leiden and Boston: Martinus Nijhoff, 2014), 193; EU Petersmann, 'The Establishment of a GATT Office of Legal Affairs and the Limits of "Public Reason" in the GATT/WTO Dispute Settlement System' in G Marceau (ed), *A History of Law and Lawyers in the GATT/WTO: The Development of the Rule of Law in the Multilateral Trading System* (Cambridge: Cambridge University Press, 2015), 182.

[263] H Ruiz Fabri, 'The WTO Appellate Body or Judicial Power Unleashed: Sketches from the Procedural Side of the Story' (2017) 27 *European Journal of International Law* 1075.

[264] See further Orford, 'The Crisis of Liberal Internationalism'.

[265] G Shaffer, 'Will the US Undermine the World Trade Organization?', *Huffington Post*, 23 May 2016; J Hillman, 'Independence at the Top of the Triangle: Best Resolution of the Judicial Trilemma?' (2017) 111 *AJIL Unbound* 364, at 367.

[266] Office of the USTR, 2018 *Trade Policy Agenda and 2017 Annual Report of the President of the United States on the Trade Agreements Program*, March 2018.

The Trump administration subsequently blocked the appointment of any new Appellate Body members, leading to the situation in which the Appellate Body ceased to be able to function after December 2019.[267]

As that example makes clear, 'treaty *interpretation* is an especially interesting game' played in an adversarial context and 'as an *act of power*'.[268] A case can turn on whether a particular term should be read as evolutive or static, whether and when the object and purpose of a treaty governs interpretations of particular terms, or how far if at all the interpretation of treaties should be informed by their preambles.[269] International lawyers express widespread scepticism about the capacity of rules concerning treaty interpretation to operate as a science, and very few international lawyers would claim that the adoption of the methods listed in the VCLT could give access to a treaty's true meaning.[270] Nonetheless, international lawyers continue to rely on the VCLT rules for shared protocols of reading and as a guide to framing and channelling communication both between states and, perhaps more importantly, between states and potential future treaty interpreters. The use of those rules can only be understood as part of a 'practice into which the members of the relevant community have been socialized'.[271] It is part of becoming a member of the international law community that 'one does not experience every theoretically imaginable doubt as an actual doubt',[272] unless, that is, the introduction of doubt is useful to your client.

For contextualist historians, the question of what counts as a treaty and whether particular agreements should be considered binding is one that can simply be answered empirically by the adoption of 'evidence-based' approaches to the past and does not require the imposition of a 'hermeneutic template' on past material.[273] Yet claims that the meaning of a treaty can be identified as a matter of fact or that attending to the 'context' in which a treaty

---

[267] G Shaffer, M Elsig, and M Pollack, 'The Slow Killing of the World Trade Organization', *Huffington Post*, 11 November 2017; CP Brown and S Keynes, 'Why Trump Shot the Sheriffs: The End of WTO Dispute Settlement 1.0', *Peterson Institute for International Economics Working Paper 20–4*, March 2020.

[268] Allott, 'Interpretation: An Exact Art', 377 (emphasis in the original).

[269] See J Klabbers, 'Treaties and Their Preambles' in Bowman and Kritsiotis (eds), *Conceptual and Contextual Perspectives on the Modern Law of Treaties*, 172; D Kritsiotis, 'The Object and Purpose of a Treaty's Object and Purpose' in Bowman and Kritsiotis (eds), *Conceptual and Contextual Perspectives on the Modern Law of Treaties*, 237.

[270] F Zarbiyev, 'The "Cash Value" of the Rules of Treaty Interpretation' (2019) 32 *Leiden Journal of International Law* 33.

[271] Zarbiyev, 'The "Cash Value" of the Rules of Treaty Interpretation', 44.

[272] Zarbiyev, 'The "Cash Value" of the Rules of Treaty Interpretation', 44.

[273] Hunter, 'About the Dialectical Historiography of International Law', 6.

is authored will somehow give privileged access to the verifiable intentions of its authors are misguided.[274] Given the process of intergovernmental negotiation through which treaties are drafted, it is 'difficult to say, after the event, how and why and when the language emerged and took on its independent existence'.[275] As the legal realists taught us, determining the 'will' or 'intention' of the parties to an agreement 'is not the object of the interpretative process, but its product'.[276] Any argument by empiricist historians suggesting that their approach to interpretation offers an impartial and undistorted account of what a treaty is, what its authors intended, or the relation of its purpose to its meaning, will simply join forces with other partisans on the legal battlefield.

5.4.4 *Custom and the Interpretation of Past Practice*

International lawyers have been explicitly engaged in arguments about how to interpret the legal meaning of state practice for as long as there have been international lawyers. In addition, historians of international law have regularly placed questions regarding the role of state practice front and centre in their methodological debates.[277] Yet the 'turn to history' moment in the post-Cold War has seen the new generation of professional historians of

---

[274] MH Arsanjani and WM Reisman, 'Interpreting Treaties for the Benefit of Third Parties: The "Salvors' Doctrine" and the Use of Legislative History in Investment Treaties' (2010) 104 *American Journal of International Law* 597, at 602 ('Many proponents of unrestricted resort to *travaux préparatoires* assume, curiously, that while the authoritative text may be ambiguous, hence justifying resort to *travaux*, somewhere in the ocean of delegate statements and proposals that have been recorded and from which the authoritative text emerged, one can find not only clear evidence but also the *real* intention of the parties. This is an odd conceit . . .').

[275] Allott, 'Interpretation: An Exact Art', 377.

[276] M Koskenniemi, 'Law, Teleology and International Relations: An Essay in Counterdisciplinarity' (2011) 26 *International Relations* 3, at 17.

[277] See, for example, WG Grewe, *The Epochs of International Law* (trans M Byers) (Berlin: Walter de Gruyter, 2000 [1984]), 2 (claiming that previous authors 'examining the history of the law of nations adopted a peculiar and methodologically questionable separation of theory and State practice. In doing so they were placing themselves at a disadvantage'); R Lesaffer, 'International Law and Its History: The Story of an Unrequited Love' in M Craven, M Fitzmaurice, and M Vogiatzi (eds), *Time, History, and International Law* (Leiden: Martinus Nijhoff, 2007), 27, at 35–36 (suggesting that historians have 'traditionally' stressed 'the analysis of historical doctrine while state practice largely remains in the shadows', and that in this respect 'little has changed since [Wolfgang] Preiser stated this complaint in 1964'); A Carty, 'Doctrine versus State Practice' in B Fassbender and A Peters (eds), *The Oxford Handbook of the History of International Law* (Oxford: Oxford University Press, 2012), 972 (describing as 'age-old' the 'question of how much attention somebody writing the history of international law should devote to doctrine on the one hand . . . and state practice on the other hand').

international law discover state practice and sternly rebuke international lawyers for not having thought to look at practice before.

Lauren Benton and Lisa Ford, for example, have claimed that 'most contributions' to studying the past of international law, whether undertaken by historians or by 'law school scholars', have failed to notice the world of practice and instead sought to place the emergence of international law 'solely within the framework of intellectual history'.[278] Andrew Fitzmaurice has in turn praised historians for 'turning to state practice which has for so long been neglected for a history of doctrine'.[279] By drawing attention to the 'practice of law', Fitzmaurice claims, historians have 'helped to revolutionize our understanding of legal history'.[280] Not only do contextualist historians claim to have discovered a neglected world of practice, but, as we have seen, they claim to be able to provide 'evidence-based' accounts of legally relevant practice without imposing any 'hermeneutic template' on the past.

The role of past practice in international legal argument is largely an effect of the role that custom plays as a source of modern international law. International law remains a customary law system.[281] The modern conception of custom as a source of international law emerged in the nineteenth century.[282] Before that time the practice of states and their diplomats was studied and treated as a guide to future conduct, but the idea that such practice accompanied by *opinio juris* contributed to the formulation of a broader body of customary law was not a familiar one. While eighteenth-century students of the law of nations had a sense of practice giving rise to a presumption about future intentions, the idea of state practice as we now use it was 'an invention of international legal doctrine in the course of the 19th century'.[283] By the

---

[278] L Benton and L Ford, *Rage for Order: The British Empire and the Origins of International Law, 1800–1850* (Cambridge: Harvard University Press, 2016), 20–21, 210.

[279] Fitzmaurice, 'Context in the History of International Law', 6.

[280] Fitzmaurice, 'Context in the History of International Law', 16, 18.

[281] Allott, 'Language, Method, and the Nature of International Law, 119; J Crawford, *Chance, Order, Change: The Course of International Law* (The Hague: Academy of International Law Pocketbooks, 2014), 57 ('international law is a customary law system, despite all the treaties; even the principle of *pacta sunt servanda*, the obligation to comply with treaties, is a customary law obligation. If we cannot explain custom, we might have to conclude that international law as a whole is built on shaky normative foundations').

[282] See further P Guggenheim, 'Contribution a l'histoire des sources du droit des gens' (1958) 94 *Recueil des Cours* 3; A Carty, *The Decay of International Law: A Reappraisal of the Limits of Legal Imagination in International Affairs* (Manchester: Manchester University Press, 1986), 30–35; Onuma, *A Transcivilizational Perspective on International Law*, 220–221; Carty, 'Doctrine versus State Practice', 972; Crawford, *Chance, Order, Change*, 64–65.

[283] Carty, 'Doctrine versus State Practice', 972.

twentieth century, custom had come to be imagined by at least some international lawyers as the real source of international law.[284]

The idea of state practice as a contribution to the creation of a customary law was in part a product of the influence that the historical school in Germany had on the first generation of professional international lawyers.[285] A number of the 'men of 1873' who participated in the founding of the *Institut de Droit International* understood their role in the establishment of international law as an academic and professional field in the terms made available by Friedrich Carl von Savigny and his colleagues.[286] Savigny was, along with Goethe, 'the most admired German intellectual of his age',[287] and was considered one of the greatest jurists of all time by the end of his career.[288] He succeeded in dominating German legal education throughout his lifetime and beyond, with the only significant counterweight to his influence being that of Hegel.[289] Savigny taught, amongst others, Karl Marx, Rudolf Jhering, Otto von Bismarck, and, importantly for our discussion here, Johann Caspar Bluntschli.[290]

Savigny was one of a number of lawyers who established the historical school of jurisprudence. Of particular relevance to our focus on custom was Savigny's 1814 pamphlet, *Vom Beruf unserer Zeit für Gesetzgebung und Rechtswissenschaft* (Of the Vocation of Our Age for Legislation and

---

[284] Oppenheim, 'The Science of International Law: Its Task and Method'; JL Kunz, 'The Nature of Customary International Law' (1953) 47 *American Journal of International Law* 658, at 663 (custom is 'not only the older, but also the hierarchically higher form of creating norms of international law. Custom-produced general international law is the basis; the customary principle of *"Pacta sunt servanda"* is the reason for validity of all particular international law created by the treaty procedure'; Guggenheim, 'Contribution a l'histoire des sources du droit des gens', 3, at 36 ('en effet, la coutume, au point de vue de la doctrine, est la source originaire et la plus importante. C'est d'elle que la seconde des sources, la convention tire sa validité').

[285] Guggenheim, 'Contribution a l'histoire des sources du droit des gens', 52–53; Carty, *The Decay of International Law*, 30–35.

[286] M Koskenniemi, *The Gentle Civilizer of Nations: The Rise and Fall of International Law 1870–1960* (Cambridge: Cambridge University Press, 2001), 42–45; BB Röben, 'The Method behind Bluntschli's "Modern" International Law' (2002) 4 *Journal of the History of International Law* 249; BB Röben, *Johann Caspar Bluntschli, Francis Lieber und das moderne Völkerrecht 1861–1881* (Baden-Baden: Nomos, 2003).

[287] J Getzler, 'Law, History, and the Social Sciences: Intellectual Traditions of Late Nineteenth- and Early Twentieth-Century Europe' in A Lewis and M Lobban (eds), *Law and History* (Oxford: Oxford University Press, 2003), 215, at 229.

[288] H Kantorowicz, 'Savigny and the Historical School' (1937) 53 *Law Quarterly Review* 326, at 328.

[289] Kantorowicz, 'Savigny and the Historical School', 330.

[290] Kantorowicz, 'Savigny and the Historical School'; Röben, 'The Method behind Bluntschli's "Modern" International Law'; G Stedman Jones, *Karl Marx: Greatness and Illusion* (Cambridge: Belknap Press, 2016), 62–68.

Jurisprudence).[291] The pamphlet was a response to the rationalist liberal jurist Anton Thibaut, head of the philosophical school and chair at the University of Heidelberg, who had proposed that with the defeat of the French and the throwing off of their *Code Napoléon*, Germany should adopt a new unified civil code. Savigny's challenge to Thibaut's proposal contained the broader program of what would become the historical school. While Savigny agreed with Thibaut about the desirability of recovering a properly German law and about the evils of the Napoleonic code, he considered that German law should be established through a historical rather than a rationalist process.

Savigny argued that codes dated from the mid-eighteenth century when 'the whole of Europe was actuated by a blind rage for improvement'.[292] The longing for new codes that could 'insure a mechanically precise adminis-tration of justice' and be 'divested of all historical associations' so as to apply 'to all nations and all times' was driven by a naïve desire for 'absolute perfec-tion'.[293] However, '[a]n historical spirit has been everywhere awakened'.[294] Historical study revealed that law was organically connected with 'the being and character of the people' as 'manifested in the progress of the times'.[295] For law, like language, 'there is no moment of absolute cessation; it is subject to the same movement and development as every other popular tendency'.[296] Savigny argued that 'the common consciousness of the people' was 'the peculiar seat of law'.[297] However, as societies progressed, national tendencies became more distinct and particular classes developed, including a class of jurists. The result was that while law 'formerly existed in the consciousness of the community, it now devolves upon the jurists, who thus, in this depart-ment, represent the community'.[298]

Savigny in this way argued that the teaching and systematisation of Roman law should be understood as the romantic expression of the German *Volk* and could properly be the basis of a unified German law.[299] In his historical account, Roman lawyers were the unlikely conscience of the German nation and thus able to offer an organic law to counter the foreign code imposed by

---

[291] FV von Savigny, *Of the Vocation of Our Age for Legislation and Jurisprudence* (trans A Hayward) (London: Littlewood & Co, 1831).
[292] Savigny, *Of the Vocation of Our Age for Legislation and Jurisprudence*, 20.
[293] Savigny, *Of the Vocation of Our Age for Legislation and Jurisprudence*, 21.
[294] Savigny, *Of the Vocation of Our Age for Legislation and Jurisprudence*, 22.
[295] Savigny, *Of the Vocation of Our Age for Legislation and Jurisprudence*, 27.
[296] Savigny, *Of the Vocation of Our Age for Legislation and Jurisprudence*, 27.
[297] Savigny, *Of the Vocation of Our Age for Legislation and Jurisprudence*, 28.
[298] Savigny, *Of the Vocation of Our Age for Legislation and Jurisprudence*, 28.
[299] Kantorowicz, 'Savigny and the Historical School', 340.

Napoleon. Savigny's theory of the 'twofold life' of the law both gestured towards the people as the foundation of the law and away from them towards the jurists who could represent the people by articulating that law. He concluded that 'all law is originally formed in the manner, in which, in ordinary but not quite correct language, customary law is said to have been formed: ie that it is first developed by custom and popular faith, next by jurisprudence – everywhere, therefore, by internal silently-operating powers, not by the arbitrary will of a law-giver'.[300]

The historical school dreamt of reconciling the ideals of organic community and individual liberty with the modernisation of the economy and the creation of a unified state.[301] They joined their legal project with the 'romantic nationalism of the German intelligentsia, who were intent on redefining their nation and culture in the wake of the Napoleonic wars'.[302] The subsequent popularity of the historical school was in part driven by 'patriotic rejection of French codified law for the German states',[303] and in part by its appeal to both democrats and princes.

> The democrats liked the idea that the people and not the princes were the real law-givers, and the princes and their councillors were delighted to find a formula allowing them to stifle the outcries for legislative reform which now could be rejected as arbitrary, unnatural and un-German.[304]

Bluntschli and his generation of European international lawyers followed in Savigny's conservative footsteps. The men of the *Institut* took from Savigny the idea that the role of the jurist was to act as the representative of the people or, in the case of late nineteenth-century international lawyers, of the civilised world. Out of the mass of state practice, they claimed to discern the doctrines and principles of a customary international law.[305] Customary international law in that account was not the result of a conscious will to create law. Rather, it emerged from a diffuse consciousness that customary laws had developed

---

[300] Savigny, *Of the Vocation of Our Age for Legislation and Jurisprudence*, 30.

[301] Getzler, 'Law, History, and the Social Sciences', 227.

[302] Getzler, 'Law, History, and the Social Sciences', 227.

[303] Getzler, 'Law, History, and the Social Sciences', 229.

[304] Kantorowicz, 'Savigny and the Historical School', 337.

[305] L Nuzzo, 'History, Science and Christianity: International Law and Savigny's Paradigm' in L Nuzzo and M Vec (eds), *Constructing International Law: The Birth of a Discipline* (Frankfurt am Main: Vittorio Klostermann, 2012), 25, at 44 (noting that in order to transform international law into '"a historically oriented science" a simple collection of data and facts was not sufficient' and in addition 'it was necessary to give them an organic form, to reassemble the internal connections' through the approach adopted by the historical school).

spontaneously out of the practices and usages of the international community.[306]

To the contribution of the international lawyers informed by the historical school, we should add the role played by the more empirically focused British and later American lawyers, whose carefully accumulated digests and records of state practice have ever since provided much of the material from which those who understand themselves to be channelling the conscience of the civilised (or free) world continue to rely for their evidence. Just as Savigny's jurists distilled the consciousness of the German people from the digests of Roman law, so too European international lawyers distilled the consciousness of the international community from the digests of Anglo-American practice. That combination of an Anglophone empirical attention to data and facts and the continental work of assembling them into the simulacrum of an 'organic form' through the artifice of the German historical method was the key to the emergence of a doctrine of customary international law.

Other legal systems that still make a place for custom, in particular Anglophone common law systems, do not treat custom as something that is discovered out in the world. While 'community custom' is understood to provide 'the historical foundation of the common law', common lawyers do not consider that contemporary practice can by itself generate binding law.[307] Rather, the development of custom is 'the preserve of judges'.[308] To the extent that the common law is a customary system, the custom to which it refers is better understood as that 'of the English courts, not of the English people', while the materials upon which judges rely to 'explain and elaborate' the common law are 'those which had been incorporated into the system by their own decisions'.[309] For international lawyers, however, customary international law is still understood to emerge out of a world of state practice. In contrast to common law reasoning, international lawyers theoretically refer directly to the social world of states for evidence of custom, rather than to principles or precedents arising out of case law.

---

[306] A Carty, *The Philosophy of International Law* (2nd edition) (Edinburgh: Edinburgh University Press, 2017), 41.

[307] M Lobban, 'Custom, Common Law Reasoning and the Law of Nations in the Nineteenth Century' in A Perreau-Saussine and JB Murphy (eds), *The Nature of Customary Law: Legal, Historical and Philosophical Perspectives* (Cambridge: Cambridge University Press, 2007), 256, at 257.

[308] Lobban, 'Custom, Common Law Reasoning and the Law of Nations', 257.

[309] Lobban, 'Custom, Common Law Reasoning and the Law of Nations', 277.

That relation between the doctrine of customary international law and the empirical world of state practice is relatively straightforward in the abstract. For a new customary law to crystallise or existing law to change, there must be evidence of acts that amount to a settled practice accompanied by *opinio juris* (or evidence that states believe that the practice is accepted or required by law).[310] The claim that international law is developed through state practice and *opinio juris* appears deceptively factual. Yet that claim raises the (non-factual) questions of which practice is normative, why that practice is treated as normative, and who has the authority to interpret the legal meaning of that practice.

Perhaps unsurprisingly, it has proved difficult to identify the practice that has led to the creation of new rules of customary international law in the rapidly changing and contested field of international legal argument. 'Practice' as a source of law possesses force and normative meaning only within a broader conceptual framework and becomes legally intelligible through written records of that practice.[311] Debates within the discipline of international law decisively shape what comes to count as relevant historical material or 'legally significant' practice.[312] One way to think about the normative work that appeals to custom do in international legal argument is by attending to the set of actors that such arguments assemble as authorised to communicate, test, and speak to the existence of international legal obligations and entitlements.[313]

The problems to which a doctrine of customary international law gives rise in both theory and practice are well explored. As generations of international lawyers have shown, it is very easy to poke holes in this doctrine and its foundations. Some of the many critiques of custom have been internal to the logic of the system. For example, when does a shift in practice come to

---

[310] *North Sea Continental Shelf (Federal Republic of Germany/Denmark; Federal Republic of Germany/Netherlands) (Judgment)* [1969] ICJ Reports 3, at 44; *Military and Paramilitary Activities in and against Nicaragua (Nicaragua v. United States of America) (Judgment)* [1986] ICJ Reports 14, at 97–98, 108–109; *Jurisdictional Immunities of the State (Germany v. Italy: Greece intervening) (Judgment)* [2012] ICJ Reports 99, at 122–123.

[311] GJ Postema, 'Custom in International Law: A Normative Practice Account' in A Perreau-Saussine and JB Murphy (eds), *The Nature of Customary Law: Legal, Historical and Philosophical Perspectives* (Cambridge: Cambridge University Press, 2007), 279, at 292–293 ('Customary norms make practical sense in the context of a discursive normative practice ... To understand custom in international law, we need to consider the social environment in which customs typically function and to which they are directly responsive').

[312] Carty, 'Doctrine versus State Practice', 974–975.

[313] DF Vagts, 'International Relations Looks at Customary International Law: A Traditionalist's Defence' (2004) 15 *European Journal of International Law* 1031, at 1036.

signal the crystallisation of a new norm rather than the breach of an old one?[314] How can evidence of a 'subjective' notion of the *opinio juris* of an artificial entity like a state be derived?[315] Some are practical – how can there be a system supposedly premised on the actual practice and *opinio juris* of states when in a world of closed archives there are no contemporary records of that practice or *opinio juris* available?[316] Some are political – why should a system be premised on a form of law that relies on secretive state practice and is not subject to democratic participation in its formation or democratic accountability in its outcomes,[317] particularly when the details of that form of law seem to be dreamed up in the writings of arbitrators or judges with little reference to the world of practice in fact?[318] Some are geopolitical – why, to the degree that there really is a good faith empirical reliance on state practice in determining the existence of customary international law, should the practice of powerful states be treated as more relevant than that of Third World states?[319]

For many international lawyers, the conventional account of customary international law is an embarrassment for a field that imagines itself as professional, rigorous, and scientific.[320] Custom thus appears to be a fragile and easily challenged source of law and might be expected to receive short

[314] Kunz, 'The Nature of Customary International Law', 667–668; Postema, 'Custom in International Law: A Normative Practice Account', 291 ('change typically comes through the same kind of actions that might as easily be seen by some participants as violations').

[315] A Carty, 'The Practice of International Law' in D Armstrong (ed), *The Routledge Handbook of International Law* (London: Routledge, 2009), 81.

[316] Carty, 'The Practice of International Law', 83–85, 98–99; A Carty, 'The Need to be Rid of the Idea of General Customary Law' (2018) 112 *AJIL Unbound* 319, at 321 ('Since the international system is still broadly based upon nation states that are aggressively distrustful of others, there is simply no possibility of any [customary international law] of significance emerging ... There are no reliable records at all, because such "state practice" as is published consists of official declarations, whose meaning is difficult to evaluate in the absence of background materials').

[317] JP Trachtman, 'The Growing Obsolescence of Customary International Law' in CA Bradley (ed), *Custom's Future: International Law in a Changing World* (Cambridge: Cambridge University Press, 2016), 172, at 173.

[318] Trachtman, 'The Growing Obsolescence of Customary International Law', 173; Carty, 'The Need to Be Rid of the Idea of General Customary Law', 319 ('general customary international law is not an intelligible concept and not actually used in practice to demonstrate the existence of any rule of law').

[319] Onuma, *A Transcivilizational Perspective on International Law*, 227; Chimni, 'Customary International Law: A Third World Perspective', 1; KJ Heller, 'Specially-Affected States and the Formation of Custom' (2018) 112 *American Journal of International Law* 191.

[320] JP Kelly, 'The Twilight of Customary International Law' (2000) 40 *Virginia Journal of International Law* 449, at 500; JL Goldsmith and EA Posner, 'A Theory of Customary International Law' (1999) 66 *The University of Chicago Law Review* 1113; Trachtman, 'The Growing Obsolescence of Customary International Law', 186.

shrift in highly contested or politically significant areas of international law. Yet it continues to be invoked frequently before international courts, tribunals, and arbitral bodies,[321] and to play a major part in some of the most highly contested debates in the field, for example concerning the lawfulness of humanitarian intervention or state responsibility for the lost profits of foreign investors.

Any scholarly work that claims to have identified relevant practice out of the mass of archival material available from past eras has had to make normative choices about which practices are relevant to the history of international law and why. My point in this book is not that historians are incapable of making those choices and intervening in debates about the meaning of international law. Rather, my point is that they cannot do so in ways that are impartial or verifiable. Arguments about which practices are relevant to the history of international law are already part of the legal field and cannot operate as neutral interventions offering verifiable explanations of what practice really means. The process of interpreting practice is just as contested and partisan as the process of interpreting texts. The continued relevance of custom to contemporary international law means that any description of past practice in turn becomes a legal argument. To suggest otherwise is to ignore the theoretical and normative debates that underpin the work that practice does in and for international law.

5.4.5 *Transmitting Legal Concepts and Fictions*

In addition to referring to specific precedents, treaties, or state practice when making legal arguments, international lawyers work by invoking a history of meaning that has accrued to legal concepts, principles, doctrines, instruments, or fictions over time. Indeed, one goal of legal education is to teach legal students about the complex set of political debates and logical moves that are condensed into particular legal concepts or fictions, such as the prohibition against the resort to 'force' or the 'right to self-defence' in the UN Charter, 'fair and equitable treatment', 'expropriation', or the 'most-favoured nation principle' in international investment law, and 'like products' or 'subsidies' in international trade law – the list could go on and on. The failure to recognise that legal terms can have a history of meaning attached to them or that interpreters rely on a 'general background understanding' of what

---

[321] M Wood, 'The Present Position within the ILC on the Topic "Identification of Customary International": In Partial Response to Sienho Yee, Report on the ILC Project on "Identification of Customary International Law"' (2016) 15 *Chinese Journal of International Law* 3, at 5–6.

specific clauses mean could have serious implications (for example, if the negotiator of a treaty did not recognise the legal implications conventionally attributed to a particular legal term being proposed by other negotiating parties).[322]

As a result, legal concepts or texts are not simply the product of a single act of creation by a powerful agent at a particular moment. They are also produced through the process of handing on from one legal actor to the next. Riles has invoked this mode of legal production through transmission in her discussion of the 'afterlife' of legal judgements, exploring the way that legal fictions are sustained through being 'passed from legal hand to legal hand' – analysed by scholars in journal articles, invoked in arguments before courts and tribunals, cited by later judges, and taught in classrooms.[323] Through the often arcane rituals of legal life involving transmission and testing of interpretations, lawyers give to legal texts a heightened sense of coherence and purpose. The end result is often that over time, inherited concepts are worn smooth. They cease, at least for lawyers who have grown accustomed to them, to be politically volatile. Legal fictions, terms, and concepts are highly condensed forms of rhetorical material that allow often controversial political or philosophical propositions to be passed on as part of legal routine.

This has implications for how we research and teach international law. Historians insist that we study the 'context' in which a text is authored, whether that is the moment at which a judgement is written, legislation is drafted, or a treaty is negotiated. Yet what is more emblematic of legal knowledge production is the practice of repetition through which legal concepts, principles, and fictions are handed on. While historians are comfortable with the idea that historical time signifies difference, 'they have difficulties with time understood as repetition or identity'.[324]

Many legal scholars (and historians studying the law) tend to direct their attention, whether in celebration or critique, to those they take to be the ideological innovators or inventors of legal concepts or ideas. However, as Riles argues, a focus on individual creators does not offer 'a satisfactory account of the workings of legal knowledge'.[325] In studying international

---

[322] For a discussion of the reliance by treaty negotiators on the 'general background understanding' or 'default meaning' of clauses, see M Waibel, 'Putting the MFN Genie Back in the Bottle' (2018) 112 *AJIL Unbound* 60.

[323] A Riles, 'Is the Law Hopeful?' in H Miyazaki and R Swedberg (eds), *The Economy of Hope* (Philadelphia: University of Pennsylvania Press, 2017), 126, at 141.

[324] KM Parker, 'Repetition in History: Anglo-American Legal Debates and the Writings of Walter Bagehot' (2014) 4 *UC Irvine Law Review* 121, at 123.

[325] Riles, 'Is the Law Hopeful?', 139.

law, it is essential to grasp not only how the concepts, principles, and institutions that shape the field came to be enshrined in particular treaty texts or judgements but also how routine legal techniques of repetition and transmission continue to give such concepts, principles, and institutions authority and meaning. Thinking of history through the idea of repetition as well as innovation gives a better sense of the range of ways that meaning is made in international law.[326]

5.4.6 *Teleology: From Technique to Ideology*

Having considered how international lawyers engage with the past as fact and the past as law, we come to one final way in which lawyers make use of history. International legal arguments construct teleological accounts of what a particular treaty, regime, or international law as a whole is for and where it is headed. Arguments about the end, aim, purpose, or goal of the law are routine aspects of legal interpretation. In addition, for every teleological argument made along those lines, there will be an anti-teleological counterargument that a particular treaty, regime, or field of international law cannot be understood purposively and that we must keep our gaze firmly on the concrete situation in front of us. International lawyers are adept at relating specific technical issues or interpretations to larger abstractions or broad ideological goals such as justice, peace, humanitarianism, prosperity, welfare, liberty, or democracy, to show why one approach should be preferred to alternatives. For David Kennedy, learning to make but also to oppose such connections is a core aspect of legal training:

> To be trained for rulership today means learning the large visions shared among elites and becoming adept at linking broad ideological commitments to technical changes which might generate a favorable result within the frame of those visions ... It means listening to other people asserting things with suspicion, attentive to the context they imagine, alert to the potential that their convictions about how things are and what must occur might be dislodged.[327]

Teleological and anti-teleological arguments are conducted at different scales across international law. For example, lawyers routinely make purposive or

---

[326] See further A Orford, 'Food Security, Free Trade, and the Battle for the State' (2015) 11 *Journal of International Law and International Relations* 1, at 24–28.

[327] D Kennedy, 'The Context for Context: International Legal History in Struggle' in A Brett, M Donaldson, and M Koskenniemi (eds), *History, Politics, Law: Thinking Internationally* (Cambridge: Cambridge University Press, forthcoming 2021).

teleological arguments about the meaning of treaty provisions. The possibility of purposive or teleological interpretation is provided for in Article 31(1) of the VLCT, which provides that '[a] treaty shall be interpreted in good faith in accordance with the ordinary meaning to be given to the terms of the treaty in their context and in the light of its object and purpose'. In addition to Article 31, the VLCT invokes a treaty's 'object and purpose' in discussion of what kinds of reservations are permissible,[328] the obligations that arise for a state after it signs but before it ratifies a treaty,[329] in relation to the modification and suspension of multilateral treaties,[330] and in relation to material breach.[331] Those references direct the interpreter's gaze 'away from the four corners' of the treaty text and 'to something that is altogether more mercurial but which is also, if the Vienna Convention is to be believed, no less real than the written word'.[332] Yet while the direction to adopt a 'teleological approach' might seem straightforward, in practice the meaning of a treaty's 'object and purpose' often proves 'elusive'.[333] The object and purpose of a treaty, like any aspect of law, 'is there to be interpreted, argued, contested and adjudicated'.[334]

Teleological arguments are also made in relation to broader subfields or regimes of international law. For example, the law relating to the use of force is a field in which debates involving teleology feature regularly. During the first decades after the Cold War, government lawyers from the United Kingdom and the United States argued strongly that international law was moving towards acceptance of humanitarian intervention and away from a strong defence of sovereignty.[335] Liberal international lawyers offered broad teleological accounts to support such claims for increased military

---

[328] Article 19 VCLT. In relation to the compatibility of a reservation with the object and purpose of the treaty, Article 19 adopted the formulation developed by the ICJ in *Reservations to the Convention on the Prevention and Punishment of the Crime of Genocide (Advisory Opinion)* [1951] ICJ Rep 15. See further the discussion in JK Koh, 'Reservations to Multilateral Treaties: How International Legal Doctrine Reflects World Vision' (1982) 23 *Harvard International Law Journal* 71.

[329] Article 18 VCLT. See further P Gragl and M Fitzmaurice, 'The Legal Character of Article 18 of the Vienna Convention on the Law of Treaties' (2019) 68 *International and Comparative Law Quarterly* 699.

[330] Article 41(1) and Article 58(1) VCLT.

[331] Article 60(3) VCLT.

[332] Kritsiotis, 'The Object and Purpose of a Treaty's Object and Purpose', 238.

[333] Gragl and Fitzmaurice, 'The Legal Character of Article 18', 709.

[334] Kritsiotis, 'The Object and Purpose of a Treaty's Object and Purpose', 286.

[335] See, for example, D Bethlehem, 'Stepping Back a Moment – The Legal Basis in Favour of a Principle of Humanitarian Intervention', *EJIL: Talk!*, 12 September 2013, available at www.ejiltalk.org/?s=bethlehem; HH Koh, 'Syria and the Law of Humanitarian Intervention (Part II: International Law and the Way Forward)', *Just Security*, 2 October 2013, available at http://justsecurity.org/1506/koh-syria-part2/; A-M Slaughter, 'A Regional Responsibility to Protect' in

interventionism, perhaps best illustrated by Anne Peters' argument that '[h]-umanity is the A and Ω of Sovereignty' and that 'this humanistic principle is also the *telos* of the international legal system'.[336] In a piece that has been widely discussed amongst government advisers, Daniel Bethlehem offered a historical narrative in which the world was witnessing 'the end of geography' as international society became increasingly integrated (under the leadership of liberal states).[337] For Bethlehem, while international law had its historical roots in the Middle Ages, the emergence of the states system, and a world of interacting sovereign entities, the 'geography of statehood' was 'becoming increasingly less important' in a world of global integration, where (the right kind of) 'people, goods, services, and funds flow across borders' and 'individuals and corporations engage directly with one another without the intermediation of states or of their paraphernalia'.[338] In that new world, 'sovereignty and boundaries are like rocks in a river' which may temporarily dam up the water but will not long impede its flow.[339]

Similar narratives feature in other subfields of international law. The natural law world view of human rights, the game theory underpinning new approaches to self-defence, and the liberalising economic thinking underpinning international trade and investment agreements each carry with them specific philosophies of history and specific visions of the purpose of their sub-field.

International lawyers also make teleological arguments in relation to international law imagined as a whole. As is the case with many other academic fields, international law's claim to legitimacy is in part founded upon the broader teleology offered by invented traditions, in which historical figures, texts, and narratives are invoked to situate international lawyers, practices, projects, and institutions within a longer story. The tendency to equate the development of international law with the progress of humanity accompanied the emergence of international law as a profession in the late nineteenth century.[340] The narrative that the history of international law represents

---

D Held and K McNally (eds), *Lessons from Intervention in the 21st Century: Legality, Feasibility and Legitimacy* (London: Global Policy, 2014) 60.

[336] A Peters, 'Humanity as the A and Ω of Sovereignty' (2009) 20 *European Journal of International Law* 513.

[337] D Bethlehem, 'The End of Geography: The Changing Nature of the International System and the Challenge to International Law' (2014) 25 *European Journal of International Law* 9.

[338] Bethlehem, 'The End of Geography', 15.

[339] Bethlehem, 'The End of Geography', 15.

[340] M Koskenniemi, 'A History of International Law Histories' in B Fassbender and A Peters (eds), *The Oxford Handbook of the History of International Law* (Oxford: Oxford University Press, 2012), 943, at 943–944.

progress towards freedom has continued to shape the field, particularly during the eventful period when the United States was the sole superpower. The invocation of historical texts or figures often forms part of such arguments. Lawyers draw on historical references to offer a source of authority for core concepts or new doctrines, situate current innovations as part of longer narratives of human progress, or narrate romantic stories about founding 'fathers' and their visions which have now been realised, all in the context of arguments in which there is a great deal at stake politically, militarily, or economically.

Given the conflictual nature of international law, however, challenges to that liberal teleology have also been a central feature of the field. While many liberal internationalists would still have us believe that the history of the world is determined by the promises and projects of nineteenth-century Europe,[341] powerful challenges to that world view have been offered by TWAIL scholars and critical international lawyers whose thinking about history challenges the uniform teleologies of the enlightenment.[342]

This is the level at which historians are often motivated to engage and join in debates about the history of international law, either to 'correct' legal arguments by showing the 'real origins' of a field of the law or by criticising lawyers for producing progress narratives or morality tales. My point is not that historians should refrain from joining in such arguments about where the field came from or, on a more abstract level, whether teleological arguments are a good thing or a bad thing. My point is simply that such arguments about teleology will operate within the adversarial field of international law and thus will necessarily be partisan. Any account of international law that engages with issues of teleology, including whether or not international lawyers should adopt purposive interpretative methods, whether progress narratives are a good thing or a bad thing, or where the origins or destiny of international law lie, will take their place within that conflictual system. As a result, their effect 'must be intrinsically polemical'.[343]

---

[341] See further H Trüper with D Chakrabarty and S Subrahmanyam, 'Introduction: Teleology and History – Nineteenth-Century Fortunes of an Enlightenment Project' in H Trüper, D Chakrabarty, and S Subrahmanyam (eds), *Historical Teleologies in the Modern World* (London: Bloomsbury, 2015), 4, at 16.

[342] See, for example, Onuma, 'When Was the Law of International Society Born?'; L Eslava, M Fakhri, and V Nesiah (eds), *Bandung, Global History, and International Law: Critical Pasts and Pending Futures* (Cambridge: Cambridge University Press, 2017); R Parfitt, *The Process of International Legal Reproduction: Inequality, Historiography, Resistance* (Cambridge: Cambridge University Press, 2019); N Tzouvala, *Capitalism as Civilisation: A History of International Law* (Cambridge: Cambridge University Press, 2020).

[343] Allott, 'Language, Method, and the Nature of International Law', 93.

5.5 THE REALIST CHALLENGE AND THE MAKING
OF INTERNATIONAL LEGAL ARGUMENT

International lawyers invoke past texts, study past practice, and argue over the histories of meaning attached to legal concepts while working within a field and an institutional context characterised by its adversarial nature. Appealing to past concepts, texts, practices, or cases is central to the legal process of adversarial interpretation, in which something is always at stake in the present. In the post-Cold War era, international law has been the site of an enormous investment of time and energy by politicians and public officials, who are in turn intent on ensuring that this symbolic economy remains within their control, and who know that lawfare or verbal strategy play an increasingly significant role in alliance politics. Controversies over and changes in the meaning of legal concepts are hard fought, as suggested by the time and resources devoted to multilateral negotiations over issues such as the inclusion of a crime of aggression in the Rome Statute to the International Criminal Court, the terms of the Paris Agreement on climate change, or the mega-regional trade agreements that dominated the US agenda in the early decades of the twenty-first century. The increasingly central role played by international adjudication in key areas of trade and investment law has only intensified the struggle over the meaning of the legal texts that result from hard-fought political negotiations.

In making legal arguments, international lawyers draw upon varied resources and materials from the past, including treaties and their negotiating records, diplomatic acts and correspondence, resolutions adopted by international organisations, decisions of international courts and tribunals, arbitral awards, decisions of national courts, legislative and administrative acts of governments, public statements made on behalf of states, government legal opinions, the reports of fact-finding bodies, and the teachings of 'the most qualified publicists'. International lawyers incorporate such material into persuasive legal arguments through processes of abstraction, which may include arguing that particular state practice combined with *opinio juris* gives rise to customary international law, that certain international agreements constitute treaties giving rise to particular rights or obligations, that proposed techniques or interpretations can be linked to grander philosophies, economic models, or other ideological commitments, or that specific events or situations can be understood as part of broader patterns or historical narratives. And those resisting such arguments will seek to disrupt them with whatever tools are at hand.

Debates over what the past means and how to interpret past texts or practices take their place in a politicised field that is fragmented, and in which the forms of law and the means of its change, development, and transform-ation are multiple. International law is a field in which old ideas about custom, the conscience of humanity, and the general principles of civilised nations jostle with detailed treaties and algorithmic targeting protocols as relevant legal materials. International legal arguments move between varying levels of abstraction, between deductive, empirical, and teleological forms of reasoning, and between a bewildering variety of heterogeneous sources with a view to persuading an audience to derive the same patterns from the data as does the speaker.[344]

In that field, methods of interpretation, including those currently advocated by contextualist historians, are deeply contested and vary amongst regimes, with no strong basis for explaining why, for example, bilateral ad hoc invest-ment treaties should be interpreted as if they were part of some shared common law of property, or why 'instant custom' should be able to form in some areas but not others, or why nuclear powers should be given priority as interpreters of the norms governing nuclear weapons, or why reservations to human rights treaties should have a different status to those of less politically volatile or normatively dense agreements, and so on. Being an international lawyer involves trying to persuade people to see the patterns that you see in the material that the community of international lawyers currently treat as legally relevant and intelligible.

Why then does this focus on the academic and professional worlds of international law matter to the debate over method in the turn to history? It matters because the historical debate we have been exploring makes a set of claims about what historicising can do. These claims are premised upon 'assumptions about the historical position and normative commitments' of both the historian and the reader.[345] In order for the work of historicising the law to have the kind of analytical and critical purchase that is claimed for it, lawyers would have to believe that contemporary international law is time-less, natural, universal, and ahistorical. Historical work would then have a revolutionary effect through its ability to invalidate such beliefs. It would be radical to show that international law has a history, that its metaphysics is just a physics, or that its 'tradition' was a recent invention. Contextualist approaches to history are designed to destroy particular forms of orthodoxy that depend upon or are committed to 'metaphysical ideals' or timeless

---

[344] Allott, 'Language, Method, and the Nature of International Law'.
[345] L Carlson, 'Critical for Whom? Genealogy and the Limits of History' (2019) 31 *Method and Theory in the Study of Religion* 185, at 187.

origins.[346] For empirical historiography to have that kind of critical effect, there needs to be a tradition committed to that orthodoxy.

This chapter has argued, however, that there are very few lawyers today for whom the idea that international law is political and a human creation is novel. Such arguments are already an entrenched part of the argumentative field of international law. To put this differently, the reader for whom context-ual history or even genealogy is written is not stable through time.[347] What might have been a radical proposition about Roman law in Italy in the fifteenth century or German law in the nineteenth century is not a radical proposition today. Historians imagine that lawyers speak from the position of scholastic philosophers or metaphysical critics. Rather than assuming that the persona of the lawyer is modelled upon those figures, I have suggested that we need to understand the practice of training law students for practice in public life in terms of a 'tradition of rhetoric, casuistry, emblematics, and philology rather than Roman and German legal science'.[348]

Much historical work about international law wants to keep teaching us that law is not transcendent and that it is historically situated. Historians fail to notice that this approach to law was incorporated within international law's operation by at least the early twentieth century. In order to understand why that matters, it is helpful to remember the place of both metaphysical *and* anti-metaphysical claims about law in the ideology of the academic and profes-sional arms of international law. It is also helpful to think about the place of particular versions of originalism or contextualism in battles over legal mean-ing in specific situations. Once we attend to the situation in which historicis-ing claims about law are made, the idea that placing a text into its context somehow offers us an impartial and verifiable account of legal meaning becomes much less plausible.

For those historians who have engaged in debates over the proper methods to be applied when engaging with the past, international lawyers are under-stood to be writing histories that judge the past. There is little recognition that international legal scholarship might function as advocacy, or legal argument, or rhetoric, in which case the test of its success would not be whether it conformed with empiricist historical standards but rather whether it inter-vened effectively in the present-day operation of international law. Determining the success or failure of legal scholarship in that respect would require some engagement with the mainstream academic or professional

---

[346] Carlson, 'Critical for Whom? Genealogy and the Limits of History', 199.
[347] Carlson, *Contingency and the Limits of History*.
[348] McVeigh, 'Office and the Conduct of the Minor Jurisprudent', 504.

practice in the field of international law with and against which scholarly arguments are working. There has to date been no such engagement undertaken in the turn to history debate.

Perhaps most importantly, the fetishisation of historical context offers a hiding place for neoformalism in international law. In the aftermath of the realist challenge the turn to a 'contextualization of law' offered a 'privileged fetishism of "context"'.[349] The 'context' of the 'law in context' movement involved the project of studying law in relation to an empirically determinable 'society'. Many of the same empiricist moves are repeated in the argument that determinative historical context can offer us a verifiable means of interpreting past legal texts or practice. Believing the claims made by contextualist historians allows lawyers to escape interpretative uncertainty and our own responsibility for legal argument. We act as if historians can discover truths about international law by pointing to the 'origins' of a regime or a field – truths that are lying around waiting to be revealed rather than being actively constructed. For those of us attempting to embrace realist insights and anti-metaphysical commitments within law, this is a cop out. We need 'to engage in normative legal argument without the crutch of formalism'.[350]

The attitude inspired by legal realism asks us to treat law 'as made, not found'.[351] This stress on the language of 'making' rather than 'finding' draws attention to the decisions involved, for example, in choosing a context in which to place a text, or in creating a series, pattern, or analogy to support a particular interpretation of the law. It is this active legal work of making links, choosing analogies, or creating patterns that is explicitly criticised by those who promote empiricist history as a means of finding the history of international law rather than making it. Yet to the extent historians are making arguments about what international law is and where its origins are really to be found, they are engaged in the same law-making project. The choice to focus on particular texts, institutions, figures, or concepts in writing histories of international law has an unavoidably partisan role to play in present political struggles.

In the next chapter, I ask what it might mean to take seriously that writing the history of an object called 'international law' involves participating in the process of making rather than finding that object. As that chapter will show, historians, it turns out, make rather than find international law too.

---

[349] Fraser, 'What a Long, Strange Trip It's Been', 37.
[350] Singer, 'Legal Realism Now', 533.
[351] Singer, 'Legal Realism Now', 474, 533.

6

The History of What?

6.1 HOW HISTORIANS MAKE LAW TOO

International lawyers make legal arguments in part through drawing on the past. For some historians of international law, the way that lawyers use the past in the process of making legal arguments is a problem. As we have seen throughout this book, historians and like-minded lawyers have criticised international legal scholars for misusing the past to tell stories, draw analogies, or bring material from diverse periods into relation. That criticism takes many forms, but the basic idea is that international lawyers improperly impose some kind of organising scheme on past material, often with a view to addressing presentist legal issues. For example, Ian Hunter has criticised international lawyers for imposing 'a hermeneutic template' on the past.[1] Samuel Moyn has dismissed as 'church history' the narratives about human rights offered by the American mainstream of liberal internationalists,[2] and criticised those who 'recast world history as raw material for the progressive ascent of international human rights' or used it to provide 'uplifting backstories' for 'recent enthusiasms'.[3] He characterises such story-telling as a 'misuse of history' that 'distorts the past to suit the present'.[4] Others have criticised international lawyers for '[m]ining the past for analogues',[5] writing history 'from present to past',[6]

---

[1] I Hunter, 'About the Dialectical Historiography of International Law' (2016) 1 *Global Intellectual History* 1, at 6.

[2] S Moyn, *The Last Utopia: Human Rights in History* (Cambridge: Belknap Press, 2010), 8.

[3] Moyn, *The Last Utopia*, 5.

[4] S Moyn, *Human Rights and the Uses of History* (2nd edition) (London: Verso, 2017), 1.

[5] K Purcell, 'On the Uses and Advantages of Genealogy for International Law' (2020) 33 *Leiden Journal of International Law* 13, at 27.

[6] R Lesaffer, 'International Law and Its History: The Story of an Unrequited Love' in M Craven, M Fitzmaurice, and M Vogiatzi (eds), *Time, History, and International Law* (Leiden: Martinus Nijhoff, 2007), 27, at 34–35.

making 'fanciful connections' between texts from different periods,[7] taking 'daring jumps' that destroy the 'complexity and pluralism of the discourses from various (and often very divergent) centuries',[8] or engaging in 'a cherry-picking of historical events'.[9]

In contrast to all that connecting, cherry-picking, story-telling, distorting, analogising, and misusing, a growing number of historians have presented their scholarship as offering value-free, impartial, and verifiable observations about the past of something called 'international law'. Their work, we are told, is about finding rather than making, reality rather than fiction. So Moyn promises to reveal the 'true origins' of human rights and their 'real history'.[10] His methodological essays emphasise the importance of 'distinguishing the abuses from the uses of history', by showing the difference between 'ideologues' who 'through selective evidence or misleading interpretation, betray the dead', and those who are 'anxious about the threat of anachronism' and respect the alterity of the past.[11] Lauren Benton and Lisa Ford have described their work on the 'origins of international law' in the language of finding – they 'observe historical actors', 'uncover projects of reforming the imperial legal order', and 'find' that empire played a complicated role in the history of international law.[12] Benton and Ford compare their own work to that of scholars who impose 'organizing rubrics' that offer 'oversimplified, but ever fashionable, proofs of imperial indifference' or 'the more uplifting but misleading fictions of the origins of human rights law'.[13] Their scholarship, in contrast, is an 'effort to capture the complexity of imperial legal change' and its relation to the history of international law.[14] For Hunter, the 'historical reality' of international law during the seventeenth and eighteenth centuries has been 'retrospectively erased' by twenty-first-century international lawyers.[15] It is contextualist historians who can take a 'properly impartial or historical view'

---

[7] G Cavallar, 'Vitoria, Grotius, Pufendorf, Wolff, and Vattel: Accomplices of European Colonialism and Exploitation or True Cosmopolitans?' (2008) 10 *Journal of the History of International Law* 181, at 207.

[8] Cavallar, 'Accomplices of European Colonialism and Exploitation or True Cosmopolitans?', 207–208.

[9] CR Rossi, *Whiggish International Law: Elihu Root, the Monroe Doctrine, and International Law in the Americas* (Leiden: Brill, 2019), 36.

[10] Moyn, *The Last Utopia*, 5, 7.

[11] Moyn, *Human Rights and the Uses of History*, xii.

[12] L Benton and L Ford, *Rage for Order: The British Empire and the Origins of International Law, 1800–1850* (Cambridge: Harvard University Press, 2016), 21.

[13] Benton and Ford, *Rage for Order*, 25.

[14] Benton and Ford, *Rage for Order*, 25.

[15] Hunter, 'About the Dialectical Historiography of International Law', 5, 19.

of the past,[16] and demonstrate objectively that international law is grounded on 'statist facticity' rather than 'juridical norms'.[17] Isabel Hull introduced her history of 'international law during the Great War' as a corrective to accounts that 'mislead us about what international law is and how it works, and about its relation to power and high politics'.[18] In so doing, she claimed to be taking on 'self-styled "realists", international-legal skeptics, cynics, and pacifists',[19] while being 'careful to avoid the anachronistic practice of reading backward'.[20] For Andrew Fitzmaurice, it is contextualist historians of international law who offer the means to resist 'the political manipulation of the past for present political purposes' and the growing 'indifference to the verifiability of political discourse' in contemporary culture.[21]

Those historians claim to be able to provide impartial and verifiable accounts of international law in a hyper-partisan field in which partisan accounts are all that anybody else has to offer. In this chapter, I argue that their accounts are necessarily as partisan and political as those produced by the most pragmatic of lawyers. That is because any study that is presented as a history of international law, or of a subfield such as human rights law or international economic law, involves an account of what 'international law' or 'human rights' or 'international economic law' is. The question that arises prior to the writing of such a history is: what is the history of international law a history of?[22] International lawyers fiercely debate what 'international law' (or any component of international law) actually 'is'. As the realist Karl Llewellyn

---

[16] I Hunter, 'The Contest over Context in Intellectual History' (2019) 58 *History and Theory* 185, at 192.

[17] Hunter, 'About the Dialectical Historiography of International Law', 5, 6.

[18] IV Hull, *A Scrap of Paper: Breaking and Making International Law during the Great War* (Ithaca and London: Cornell University Press, 2014), 3.

[19] Hull, *A Scrap of Paper*, 322.

[20] Hull, *A Scrap of Paper*, x.

[21] A Fitzmaurice, 'Context in the History of International Law' (2018) 20 *Journal of the History of International Law* 5, at 13, 15, 30.

[22] See Y Onuma, 'When Was the Law of International Society Born? – An Inquiry of the History of International Law from an Intercivilizational Perspective' (2000) 2 *Journal of the History of International Law* 1, at 2 ('International lawyers dealing with the history of international law inevitably faced this critical question of the definition or the concept of international law'); A Carty, 'Doctrine versus State Practice' in B Fassbender and A Peters (eds), *The Oxford Handbook of the History of International Law* (Oxford: Oxford University Press, 2012) 972, at 974 ('the reason international legal history is almost impossible to write is that there is no consensus on what international law is'); A Orford, 'Food Security, Free Trade, and the Battle for the State' (2015) 11 *Journal of International Law and International Relations* 1, at 19–24. For related formulations and questions, see I Hacking, *The Social Construction of What?* (Cambridge: Harvard University Press, 1999); D Ibbetson, 'What Is Legal History a History of?' in A Lewis and M Lobban (eds), *Law and History* (Oxford: Oxford University Press, 2003), 33.

argued, 'if Law and all the relevant vocabulary were not a fighting matter as well as a confused one, it would be possible to make one's own definitions, stick to them, and still hope for understanding. But it is a fighting matter'.[23] In choosing one account or version of the object 'international law' for which to provide a history, the historian becomes a participant in that fight.

Presenting a history of something called 'international law' involves generalising and abstracting. To see an action, event, person, concept, or text as somehow related to 'international law', it is necessary to have in mind a general picture, image, or concept of 'international law'. That work of generalisation and abstraction is creative and political work – '[t]o see a pattern is to make a pattern'.[24] The same is true about writing histories of international law. The author of such a history gives form, shape, direction, scope, content, character, and meaning to something called 'international law' by choosing how to narrate the history of that object.

Writing a history of international law involves writing a history of something for which there is no stable referent or fixed object. As we saw in Chapter 5, there is no neutral story to be told about something called 'international law'. There is no impartial and agreed account of what 'international law' is, the context into which particular legal texts or concepts should be placed, the methods by which texts should be interpreted, whose interpretation of a text or concept is authoritative, who counts as a 'subject' of international law, what counts as a 'source' of international law, the sites in which international law is made, and thus what kinds of archives offer what kinds of 'evidence' about what international law really meant at any given moment or where it really originated. The answer to any of these questions is political rather than technical.

When a historian presents their work as offering a history of something called 'international law', they throw their hat into the presentist ring.[25] And in so doing, they will necessarily take a partisan position. There is no objective, impartial, or 'verifiable' answer to the question 'what is international law a history of?', because there is no objective answer to the question 'what is international law?'. International law is an object whose representation matters to those who exercise power, including professionals who have a great deal at stake in competitive struggles over its meaning and role. As a result, 'all writing

---

[23] KN Llewellyn, 'The Normative, the Legal, and the Law-Jobs: The Problem of Juristic Method' (1940) 49 *Yale Law Journal* 1355, at 1358.

[24] Llewellyn, 'The Normative, the Legal, and the Law-Jobs', 1359.

[25] For a related argument about the principle of choice that informs the framing of any historical project, see further M Rubin, 'Presentism's Useful Anachronisms' (2017) 234 *Past and Present* 236, at 238.

on international law', including histories of international law, 'must be intrinsically polemical'.[26] Any work that settles on 'international law' as an object will accept and indeed consolidate one out of a range of contested presentist accounts of what international law is. To offer a history of 'international law' requires explicitly taking a position on what 'international law' is or implicitly accepting someone else's account of what international law is. Neither is politically neutral. Each historical project that takes international law as an object is part of the contemporary struggle over how international law should be understood and represented.

To show how this works in practice, this chapter explores three empiricist historical accounts that are overtly presented as offering correctives to the distorted, presentist, or incomplete histories of international law produced to date. My focus in each case is on the politics involved in deciding what the history of international law, international human rights law, or international economic law is properly a history of. As we'll see, each of those histories assumes that there is a stable object called 'international law' (or human rights law or international economic law) in the present for which historians can then provide a history of contingency and political struggle.

6.2 BRITISH COLONIAL NETWORKS AS THE ORIGINS OF INTERNATIONAL LAW

In *Rage for Order: The British Empire and the Origins of International Law, 1800–1850*, Lauren Benton and Lisa Ford claimed to have discovered 'the origins of international law' in the practice of early nineteenth-century British imperial officials.[27] According to Benton and Ford, '[m]ost accounts of the history of international law make a mad dash from late eighteenth-century revolutions to late nineteenth-century imaginings of international law', mentioning few international lawyers and 'few major events other than the Congress of Vienna'.[28] In addition, they believe that histories of international law have paid too little attention to the British Empire, and that most histories of international law 'have a tendency to place the history of international law solely within the framework of intellectual history'.[29] Those scholars who have paid attention to colonialism 'too often flattened history by turning it into a

---

[26] P Allott, 'Language, Method and the Nature of International Law', (1970) 45 *British Yearbook of International Law* 93.

[27] Benton and Ford, *Rage for Order*.

[28] Benton and Ford, *Rage for Order*, 18.

[29] Benton and Ford, *Rage for Order*, 21.

morality play', but '[f]ortunately there are other, better ways to take the measure of influence of British imperial formations in world history'.[30] Benton and Ford presented their work as correcting the various 'distortions' of the past produced by international lawyers,[31] by offering a focus on practice rather than doctrine, and on writing the British Empire into the history of international law. According to Benton and Ford, if we want to 'make sense of the early nineteenth century as a phase in the history of international law, we must look away from international law and international lawyers'.[32] The result is that the origins of international law turn out to be the correspondence, reports, commissions, and charters of 'middling officials' of the British Empire.[33] Their account of the British Empire as the origin of international law in the early nineteenth century 'draws attention to the law-producing capacities of imperially organized networks and practices'.[34]

Rage for Order has been cited by Andrew Fitzmaurice, another historian of international law, as an example of the approach to the past that should be adopted by those inside and outside law schools. For Fitzmaurice, the work of Benton and Ford is 'more deeply contextual than any previously seen in the field' and reveals that existing histories of international law have been 'super-ficial'.[35] According to Fitzmaurice, international lawyers and historians of international law had failed to notice the world of legal practice, which had 'for so long been neglected for a history of doctrine'.[36] As a result, *Rage for Order* had 'helped open up a vast domain of international law'.[37] For Fitzmaurice, the book is an example of historical work that is careful not to engage in presentism. Contextualist historians exercise '[v]igilance about imposing present concepts upon the understanding of the past'.[38] One of the main reasons for a contextual approach is 'to contest the political manipulation of the past for present political purposes' and 'the use of the present to produce distorted understandings of the past'.[39]

How then did Benton and Ford make the normative decision about which practices were relevant to the history of international law without engaging in

---

[30] Benton and Ford, *Rage for Order*, 180.
[31] Benton and Ford, *Rage for Order*, 202.
[32] Benton and Ford, *Rage for Order*, 21.
[33] Benton and Ford, *Rage for Order*, 21.
[34] Benton and Ford, *Rage for Order*, 190.
[35] Fitzmaurice, 'Context in the History of International Law', 16.
[36] Fitzmaurice, 'Context in the History of International Law', 6.
[37] Fitzmaurice, 'Context in the History of International Law', 29.
[38] Fitzmaurice, 'Context in the History of International Law', 14.
[39] Fitzmaurice, 'Context in the History of International Law', 13, 15.

presentism? Benton and Ford made clear that in their search for the origins of international law, they were not limited to studying what people who understood themselves to be international lawyers were doing. This raises the question of how they decided that the practices of British 'middling officials' in the nineteenth century were the origins of international law. While, as we saw in Chapter 5, international lawyers have focused on practices for as long as there have been international lawyers, what shifts in the work of Benton and Ford is whose practices count as relevant and why.

According to Benton and Ford, their reason for positing the practice of British imperial officials in the nineteenth century as the origin of international law was because they had used the scholarly work of US-based international lawyers in the twenty-first century as the basis for their understanding of what 'international law' is. According to Benton and Ford:

> Recent studies teach us that international law is not a corpus of doctrines but consists in such diffuse phenomena as nongovernmental networks and administrative procedures.[40]

In an endnote, they explain that those 'recent studies' that 'teach us' what international law is are 'approaches to international law in the twentieth and twenty-first centuries that characterize networks or procedures as the stuff of international law', and specifically the work of Anne-Marie Slaughter, Benedict Kingsbury, Nico Krisch, and Richard Stewart.[41] As those references make clear, Benton and Ford found the origins of that US-based account of international law in the practice of nineteenth-century British imperial officials. Yet the theories of Slaughter and of Kingsbury and his colleagues involved in the Global Administrative Law (GAL) project did not offer neutral or objective accounts that can 'teach us' what the 'stuff of international law' really is. Rather, their theories were overtly normative interventions that attempted to reshape perceptions of the nature and future of international law.

In her influential book *A New World Order*, Anne-Marie Slaughter presented a novel answer to the question of how best to govern the world. Slaughter argued that global governance already existed, but that it was not to be found where most people expected to find it. She focused particularly on the emergence of 'government networks' as a 'key feature of world order in the

---

[40] Benton and Ford, *Rage for Order*, 190.
[41] Benton and Ford, *Rage for Order*, 271, citing A-M Slaughter, *A New World Order* (Princeton: Princeton University Press, 2004); B Kingsbury, N Krisch, and R Stewart, 'The Emergence of Global Administrative Law' (2005) 68 *Law and Contemporary Problems* 15.

twenty-first century'.[42] For Slaughter, the state could best be understood as the sum of its aggregate parts (legislatures, regulators, judiciaries), with those parts increasingly having the capacity (and at times the imperative) to interact with their foreign counterparts in order to address issues of common concern. For Slaughter, rather than continue to imagine ways of creating an international system that could bring unitary states closer together, it made more sense to start thinking about ways in which states had been 'disaggregated', with their now functional parts (legislators, regulators, judiciaries) increasingly operating in functionally specialised 'government networks'.[43]

As Slaughter's book made clear, that claim was both descriptive and normative.[44] For Slaughter, the emergence of a 'world of government networks' was not just an 'underappreciated' fact of international life but also 'a more effective and potentially just world order' than either 'what we have today' or 'a world government in which a set of global institutions perched above nation-states enforced global rules'.[45] Government networks, operating alongside international institutions, could provide a more efficient and just way of ordering a globalised world. In Slaughter's view, a networked world order would be more efficient, because management of transnational problems required flexibility and an ability to harmonise and coordinate responses between counterpart officials free of political interference. And a networked world order would be more just, because the decentralised and dispersed nature of the network offered a means of exercising power without a centralised coercive authority.[46] Slaughter concluded that '(g)lobal governance through government networks is good public policy for the world', as a 'world order self-consciously created out of horizontal and vertical government networks' could 'create a genuine global rule of law without centralized global institutions'.[47]

Slaughter's vision of a new world order was thus not a neutral and impartial account of the true nature of contemporary international law but an argument about which tendencies in contemporary practice should be intensified and consolidated. Giving transnationally networked experts increased authority to make regulatory decisions might seem like a noble dream to some and a nightmare to others. The form of expert rule that Slaughter there championed

---

[42] Slaughter, *A New World Order*, 1.
[43] Slaughter, *A New World Order*, 5–6.
[44] See further A Orford, 'Foreword' in H Cullen, J Harrington, and C Renshaw (eds), *Networks, Experts, and International Law* (Cambridge: Cambridge University Press, 2017), xiii.
[45] Slaughter, *A New World Order*, 1, 7.
[46] Slaughter, *A New World Order*, 30.
[47] Slaughter, *A New World Order*, 261.

has since become the subject of populist challenge within the world of liberal states which she saw as her constituency, and of geopolitical challenge by those arguing that a world of law-making by specific expert guilds means less attention paid to the practices and interests of the global South.[48]

Similarly, Kingsbury and his colleagues presented GAL as an attempt to 'bridge description and prescription'.[49] On the one hand, GAL studies described tendencies that were 'emergent in institutional practice', in particular a 'body of law or law-like principles and mechanisms governing the procedural dimensions' of 'transnational administration'.[50] However while the proponents of GAL renounced 'any a priori normative foundation', their approach was nonetheless 'a normative intervention' to the extent that it sought to 'systematize and disseminate this practice', 'to encourage adoption of certain mechanisms', and 'to name them collectively as GAL'.[51] It was also a normative project to the extent that it involved taking a position in 'perennial debates about the definition and nature of "law"', looking beyond formal sources of international law to treat as relevant other practices that were said to have a 'law-like quality'.[52]

For those who were more sceptical about the GAL project, the ideological aspects of the normative work involved in foregrounding procedural innovations and downplaying questions of consent, status, democracy, and agency were a cause for concern.[53] As Susan Marks cautioned, 'a new noun phrase like global administrative law seems to create a thing. It seems to bring an object into being, with a solidity and even a monumentality that risk putting in

---

[48] See further A Orford, *International Law and the Social Question* (The Hague: Asser Press, 2020); A Orford, 'The Sir Elihu Lauterpacht International Law Lecture 2019: The Crisis of Liberal Internationalism and the Future of International Law' (2021) 28 *Australian Year Book of International Law* 3.

[49] B Kingsbury, M Donaldson, and R Vallejo, 'Global Administrative Law and Deliberative Democracy' in A Orford and F Hoffmann (eds), *The Oxford Handbook of the Theory of International Law* (Oxford: Oxford University Press, 2016), 526, at 528.

[50] Kingsbury, Donaldson, and Vallejo, 'Global Administrative Law and Deliberative Democracy', 527.

[51] Kingsbury, Donaldson, and Vallejo, 'Global Administrative Law and Deliberative Democracy', 528.

[52] Kingsbury, Donaldson, and Vallejo, 'Global Administrative Law and Deliberative Democracy', 529–530; B Kingsbury, 'The Concept of "Law" in Global Administrative Law' (2009) 20 *European Journal of International Law* 23.

[53] See, for example, C Harlow, 'Global Administrative Law: The Quest of Principles and Values' (2006) 17 *European Journal of International Law* 187; BS Chimni, 'Co-option and Resistance: Two Faces of Global Administrative Law' (2005) 37 *New York University Journal of International Law and Politics* 799; A Orford, 'International Territorial Administration and the Management of Decolonization' (2010) 59 *International and Comparative Law Quarterly* 227, at 229, 247–248.

the shade disputes over process, agency, and orientation'.[54] While, as Marks noted, such 'reifying effects are not inevitable', it takes conscious effort to keep in view that such an image of the world is contentious and contingent.[55]

A number of normative choices were therefore involved in the decision by Benton and Ford to equate a search for the precursor of transnational bureaucratic networks with a search for 'the origins of international law'. Why we should treat some actors or practices as more significant or relevant for making international law than others is never made explicit by Benton and Ford. Yet privileging US accounts in the present and British sources in the past as a guide to the nature and meaning of international law is not politically neutral. To do so is to take a position, one that works to reinforce the role of liberal Anglophone lawyers and their vision of networked governance as the truth of international law. Benton and Ford shored up a claim about the nature of international law in the present by looking for something that resembled it in the nineteenth century and calling it 'the origins of international law'. Their book assisted in bringing an object into being through writing its history. It would be more accurate and better clarify the stakes of their project if we think of it as an account of the origins of what some US-based liberal internationalists writing in the early twenty-first century proposed that global law should be and was becoming.

6.3 US INTERNATIONALISM AND THE REAL HISTORY OF HUMAN RIGHTS

A second example of the interrelationship of history-writing and presentist conceptions of international law involves the heated debates about the history of international human rights law. Judging by the explosion of work debating the history of human rights, we seem to agree that human rights has a history, but there is less agreement on where to locate the invention, origins, or breakthrough of human rights. Proposed starting points for human rights histories have included the Enlightenment and the French Revolution,[56] opposition to the slave trade,[57] nineteenth-century

---

[54] S Marks, 'Naming Global Administrative Law' (2005) 37 *New York University Journal of International Law and Politics* 995, at 996.

[55] Marks, 'Naming Global Administrative Law', 996.

[56] L Hunt, *Inventing Human Rights: A History* (New York and London: WW Norton & Company, 2007).

[57] R Blackburn, 'Reclaiming Human Rights' (2011) 69 *New Left Review* 126; JS Martinez, *The Slave Trade and the Origins of International Human Rights Law* (New York: Oxford University Press, 2012).

humanitarian interventions,[58] comparative constitutionalism,[59] Christian movements of the 1930s and 1940s,[60] the Universal Declaration of Human Rights,[61] the complex ideological and geopolitical interests that shaped the European Convention on Human Rights,[62] or the US imperial adventures of the 1970s and since.[63] The debate turns in part on the question of what kind of thing a historian would be looking for in trying to find the origins or write a history of human rights. The risk of focusing on too narrow a definition of human rights is that many influences on the emergence of contemporary human rights may be lost as a result, but the risk of moving beyond a defined focus is, as Lynn Hunt has noted, that 'the history of human rights' becomes 'the history of the entire world'.[64] Perhaps tracing the history of human rights involves tracing the usage of a particular word or concept.[65] If so, what is that word or concept? Perhaps the history of human rights should properly be the history of a form, value, quality, or ideal that is embodied today in the vocabulary of human rights. But if so, to which earlier forms, values, qualities, or ideals do we look to find that history?[66] Or perhaps a historian should search the past for a pattern of argumentation or some kind of language game – perhaps human rights law is what human rights lawyers or activists did in a particular time and place. If so, who is characterisable as a human rights lawyer or activist at any particular point? Perhaps we see rights as inherently a function of particular kinds of institutions or social movements, and if so which institutions or movements?

In the most provocative contribution to that debate, Moyn argued that such disputes turned on questions that were empirical rather than normative.

---

[58] GJ Bass, *Freedom's Battle: The Origins of Humanitarian Intervention* (New York: Random House, 2008).

[59] C McCrudden, 'Human Rights Histories' (2015) 35 *Oxford Journal of Legal Studies* 179.

[60] L Lindkvist, *Shrines and Souls: The Reinvention of Religious Liberty and the Genesis of the Universal Declaration of Human Rights* (Malmö: Bokbox, 2014). See also S Moyn, *Christian Human Rights* (Oxford: Oxford University Press, 2015).

[61] MA Glendon, *A World Made New: Eleanor Roosevelt and the Universal Declaration of Human Rights* (New York: Random House 2002).

[62] AWB Simpson, *Human Rights and the End of Empire: Britain and the Genesis of the European Convention* (Oxford: Oxford University Press, 2001); M Duranti, *The Conservative Human Rights Revolution: European Identity, Transnational Politics, and the Origins of the European Convention* (Oxford: Oxford University Press, 2017).

[63] Moyn, *The Last Utopia*.

[64] Hunt, *Inventing Human Rights*, 20.

[65] See further P de Bolla, *The Architecture of Concepts: The Historical Formation of Human Rights* (New York: Fordham University Press, 2013).

[66] For the influential argument that the candidate should be human dignity, see H Joas, *The Sacredness of the Person: A New Genealogy of Human Rights* (Washington, DC: Georgetown University Press, 2013).

Earlier historians had misunderstood their task because they had failed to understand what the history of human rights was really a history of. According to Moyn, human rights cannot be said to have emerged until a series of key elements were in place – the rights being claimed were minimalist and individualist, secular rather than religious, claimed against the sovereign nation-state 'from above and outside' rather than bound up with the construction of the state, promoted by a transnational movement, and protected through international law rather than state enforcement.

That definition of what human rights meant in the present was then used as the basis to exclude historical precursors that did not include that set of features. As a result, Moyn could claim that human rights 'emerged in the 1970s seemingly from nowhere', when a 'genuine social movement around human rights made its appearance' in the form of US NGOs, US President Jimmy Carter embraced human rights as part of US foreign policy, and 'human rights became central to American international law for the first time'.[67] Moyn's account thus offered up a history of the US approach to enforcing civil and political rights globally as the real history of human rights.[68] Moyn presented his work as scrupulously empirical, aimed at correcting 'the glaring confusions' that had marred other attempts to find 'the "precursors" of human rights'.[69] His 'alternative history' would reveal the 'true origins' of the human rights program and its place in 'real history'.[70] He would counter the 'misuse of history' by the church historians of rights, whose narrative 'distorts the past to suit the present'.[71]

Yet despite his criticism of other scholars for offering backstories that served to make particular presentist accounts of human rights appear more plausible, Moyn's revisionist history had the same effect. His history purported to establish that, after all, international human rights law was simply what the United States at the height of its powers had wanted human rights to be. Other histories of human rights could then be dismissed, not on normative or

---

[67] Moyn, *The Last Utopia*, 8, 155, 201.

[68] For critiques of Moyn's histories for their US-centric focus, see P Alston, 'Does the Past Matter? On the Origins of Human Rights' (2013) 126 *Harvard Law Review* 2043, at 2072; A Anghie, 'Whose Utopia? Human Rights, Development, and the Third World' (2013) 22 *Qui Parle* 63; JR Slaughter, 'Hijacking Human Rights: Neoliberalism, the New Historiography, and the End of the Third World' (2018) 40 *Human Rights Quarterly* 735; J Lemaitre, 'The View from Somewhere: On Samuel Moyn's Not Enough', *Law and Political Economy Blog*, 9 July 2018, available at https://lpeblog.org/2018/07/09/the-view-from-somewhere-on-samuel-moyns-not-enough/.

[69] Moyn, *The Last Utopia*, 12.

[70] Moyn, *The Last Utopia*, 5, 7.

[71] Moyn, *Human Rights and the Uses of History*, 1.

political grounds, but based on the allegedly empirical claim that they did not present the 'real history' of human rights.

6.4 ORDOLIBERALISM AND THE INTELLECTUAL HISTORY OF INTERNATIONAL ECONOMIC LAW

A final example relates to international economic law, which offers the opportunity for a more detailed examination of the shift in orientation and tone that accompanies the move from law to history. As I noted in Chapter 2, for many of us who had been working to understand the relation of international law to the rapidly accelerating project of global economic liberalisation unfolding during the 1990s, the publication (in 2004 in French and in 2008 in English) of Michel Foucault's 1978–1979 lectures at the Collège de France was a turning point.[72] Foucault's lectures offered a detailed analysis and reconstruction of the economic and legal concepts underpinning the thinking of Ludwig Erhard, Wilhelm Röpke, Alexander Rüstow, Ludwig von Mises, Friedrich von Hayek, Walter Eucken, Franz Böhm, and Alfred Müller-Armack. In those lectures, Foucault brought Ordoliberalism into relation with many other trends in liberal and conservative economic thinking since the eighteenth century.

Foucault himself made few direct links between the material he was studying and the question of international law and governance, but there were some intriguing hints of the relation of Ordoliberals to projects of economic ordering on a transnational or global scale in his lectures. For instance, Foucault touched on the relation of Ordoliberals to European reconstruction, the Marshall Plan, and the negotiation of the Rome Treaty.[73] While a handful of legal scholars and economic historians in France, Germany, Italy, and Sweden had been studying the Ordoliberal approach to economic ordering and its relation to the project of European integration since the 1960s,[74] the publication of Foucault's lectures led to an

---

[72] M Foucault, *Naissance de la Biopolitique: Cours au Collège de France, 1978–1979* (Paris: Éditions de Seuil/Gallimard, 2004); M Foucault, *The Birth of Biopolitics: Lectures at the Collège de France, 1978–79* (translated by Graham Burchell) (Hampshire and New York: Palgrave Macmillan, 2008).

[73] Foucault, *The Birth of Biopolitics*, 79, 104, 123.

[74] See, for example, F Bilger, *La pensée economique libérale dans l'Allemagne contemporaine* (Paris: Librairie Générale de Droit et de Jurisprudence, 1964); H Willgerodt and A Peacock, 'German Liberalism and Economic Revival' in A Peacock and H Willgerodt (eds), *Germany's Social Market Economy: Origins and Evolution* (London: Palgrave Macmillan, 1989); C Joerges, 'The Market without the State? The "Economic Constitution" of the European

explosion of interest in that relationship. Legal scholars and economic historians have since developed a significant body of scholarship linking Ordoliberals to contemporary transnational and international economic ordering through law.

Perhaps the most extensive study of the relation of Ordoliberalism to transnational economic integration has been undertaken in relation to the European Union, fuelled in part by two decades of work by Christian Joerges and different constellations of colleagues.[75] A lively debate concerning the

Community and the Rebirth of Regulatory Politics' (1997) European Integration online Papers (EIoP), Vol. 1, No. 19, http://eiop.or.at/eiop/texte/1997-019a.htmJoerges; C Joerges, 'State without a Market? Comments on the German Constitutional Court's Maastricht-judgement and a Plea for Interdisciplinary Discourses', European Integration online Papers (EIoP), Vol. 1, No. 20, http://eiop.or.at/eiop/texte/1997-020a.htm; C Joerges, 'The Science of Private Law and the Nation-State' in F Snyder (ed), *The Europeanisation of Law: The Legal Effects of European Integration* (Oxford: Hart, 2000), 47; M Wegmann, *Früher Neoliberalismus und Europäische Integration* (Baden-Baden: Nomos, 2002); P Commun (ed), *L'ordolibéralisme allemande: Aux sources de l'Économie sociale de marché* (Cergy-Pontoise: CIRAC, 2003); C Joerges, 'Europe a Großraum? Shifting Legal Conceptualisations of the Integration Project' in C Joerges and NS Ghaleigh (eds), *Darker Legacies of Law in Europe: The Shadow of National Socialism and Fascism over Europe and Its Legal Traditions* (Oxford and Portland: Hart, 2003), 167; VJ Vanberg, 'The Freiburg School: Walter Eucken and Ordoliberalism', Freiburg Discussion Papers on Constitutional Economics, No. 04/11 (2004).

75   See, for example, C Joerges and F Rödl, '"Social Market Economy" as Europe's Social Model?', EUI Working Paper Law No. 2004/8; C Joerges, 'What Is Left of the European Economic Constitution? A Melancholic Eulogy' (2005) 30 *European Law Review* 461; H Schulz-Forberg and B Stråth, *The Political History of European Integration: The Hypocrisy of Democracy-Through-Market* (Abingdon: Routledge, 2010); P Dardot and C Laval, *La nouvelle raison du monde. Essai sur la société néolibérale* (Paris: La Découverte, 2010); K Tuori and S Sankari (eds), *The Many Constitutions of Europe* (Surrey: Ashgate, 2010); C Joerges and E-U Petersmann (eds), *Constitutionalism, Multilevel Trade Governance and International Economic Law* (Oxford: Hart, 2011); S Audier, *Néo-libéralisme(s). Une archéologie intellectuelle* (Paris: Grasset, 2012); S Audier, *Le colloque Lippmann: Aux origines du 'néo-libéralisme'* (Paris: BDL editions, 2012); M Maduro, K Tuori, and S Sankari (eds), *Transnational Law: Rethinking European Law and Legal Thinking* (Cambridge: Cambridge University Press, 2014); C Joerges and C Glinski (eds), *The European Crisis and the Transformation of Transnational Governance: Authoritarian Managerialism versus Democratic Governance* (Oxford: Hart, 2014); C Joerges, 'Europe's Economic Constitution in Crisis and the Emergence of a New Constitutional Constellation' (2014) 15 *German Law Journal* 986; JE Fossum and AJ Menéndez (eds), *The European Union in Crises or the European Union as Crises?* (Oslo: Arena Report Series, 2014); J Solchany, 'Wilhelm Röpke as a Key Actor of Transnational Neoliberalism after 1945' in H Schulze-Forberg and N Olsen (eds), *Re-Inventing Western Civilisation: Transnational Reconstructions of Liberalism in Europe in the Twentieth Century* (Cambridge: Cambridge Scholars, 2014), 95; J Solchany, *Wilhelm Röpke, l'autre Hayek. Aux origines du néolibéralisme* (Paris: Publications de la Sorbonne, 2015); D Chalmers, M Jachtenfuchs, and C Joerges (eds), *The End of the Eurocrats' Dream: Adjusting to European Diversity* (Cambridge: Cambridge University Press, 2016); P Commun, *Les Ordolibéraux: Histoire d'un libéralisme à l'allemande* (Paris: Les Belles Lettres, 2016); J Hien and C Joerges (eds),

influence of Ordoliberalism on EU competition law has also developed over the past two decades, inspired in part by the work of David Gerber and fuelled by debates over the principles that should shape the interpretation of EU competition law.[76] In the context of law and development, Kerry Rittich was one of the first critical legal scholars to stress the significance of Hayek and Röpke for understanding the 'theoretical antecedents of neoliberalism' and show their significance for grasping the role of law in economic globalisation.[77] My work brought Ordoliberal thinking on law, planning, and the market into relation with projects of remaking the state through three sites: the United Nations in the early era of decolonisation under the leadership of the economist Dag Hammarskjöld, the project of European integration, and the free trade regimes established under the General Agreement on Tariffs and Trade (GATT) and later the World Trade Organization (WTO).[78]

Ordoliberalism, Law and the Rule of Economics (Oxford and Portland: Hart, 2017); T Biebricher and F Vogelmann (eds), *The Birth of Austerity. German Ordoliberalism and Contemporary Neoliberalism* (London and New York: Rowman & Littlefield, 2017); J Hien and C Joerges, 'Dead Man Walking? Current European Interest in the Ordoliberal Tradition' (2018) 24 *European Law Journal* 14; C Joerges, '"Where the Law Runs Out": The Overburdening of Law and Constitutional Adjudication by the Financial Crisis and Europe's New Modes of Economic Governance' in S Garben, I Govaere, and P Nemitz (eds), *Critical Reflections on Constitutional Democracy in the European Union* (Oxford: Hart, 2019), 168; C Joerges and M Everson, 'The Legal Proprium of the Economic Constitution' in PF Kjaer (ed), *The Law of Political Economy: Transformations of the Function of Law* (Cambridge: Cambridge University Press, 2020), 33.

[76] DJ Gerber, 'Constitutionalizing the Economy: German Neo-liberalism, Competition Law and the "New" Europe' (1994) 42 *American Journal of Comparative Law* 25; DJ Gerber, *Law and Competition in Twentieth Century Europe: Protecting Prometheus* (Oxford: Oxford University Press 2001); R O'Donoghue and AJ Padilla, *The Law and Economics of Article 82 EC* (London: Hart, 2006); I Rose and C Ngwe, 'The Ordoliberal Tradition in the European Union, Its Influence on Article 82 EC and the IBA's Comments on the Article 82 EC Discussion Paper' (2007) 3 *Competition Law International* 8; LL Gormsen, 'The Conflict between Economic Freedom and Consumer Welfare in the Modernisation of Article 82 EC' (2007) 3 *European Competition Journal* 329; P Akman, 'Searching for the Long-Lost Soul of Article 82 EC' (2009) 29 *Oxford Journal of Legal Studies* 267; KK Patel and H Schweitzer, 'EU Competition Law in Historical Context: Continuity and Change' in KK Patel and H Schweitzer (eds), *The Historical Foundation of EU Competition Law* (Oxford: Oxford University Press 2013), 207.

[77] K Rittich, *Recharacterizing Restructuring: Law, Distribution and Gender in Market Reform* (The Hague: Kluwer, 2002).

[78] For the relationship of Ordoliberal and Hayekian thinking to the GATT and WTO, see Orford, 'Food Security, Free Trade, and the Battle for the State', 1; A Orford, 'Law, Economics, and the History of Free Trade: A Response' (2015) 11 *Journal of International Law and International Relations* 155; A Orford, 'Theorizing Free Trade' in A Orford and F Hoffmann (eds), *The Oxford Handbook of the Theory of International Law* (Oxford: Oxford University Press, 2016), 701. For an analysis of the shifting relationship of Hayek's thinking on planning and the rule of law to the project of EU integration through law, see A Orford, 'Europe Reconstructed' (2012) 75 *Modern Law Review* 275. For the relationship of Ordoliberal,

I did so in order to argue that the battle for the state and an attack on planning were central to international economic law, and that the end of empire, decolonisation, and the perceived threats to liberalism posed by communism and socialist planned economies were significant contexts for the initial focus of Ordoliberals on the possibilities offered by the pursuit of economic integration through international law.

In the field of international investment law, David Schneiderman developed the language of 'neoliberal globalism' to describe the emerging regime of international investment law.[79] Inspired by Foucault's lectures, he also analysed 'the place of international investment law in the contemporary neo-liberal project' by linking the constitutionalism of international investment law to German Ordoliberalism and Freiburg school theorising.[80] Ntina Tzouvala also explored the Ordoliberal origins of modern international investment law, tracing a series of episodes beginning with the role of Deutsche Bank head Hermann Abs in drafting a proposal for protecting private property rights in foreign countries, through his collaboration with Sir Hartley Shawcross in drafting the Draft Convention on Investments Abroad in 1959, to the translation of many of the Abs-Shawcross convention provisions into the West Germany/Pakistan BIT in 1959.[81] In addition, a substantial critical legal literature also began to emerge on the topic of the relation of neoliberalism to law and legalism more broadly.[82]

Schmittian, and Hayekian thinking about the state and economic order to the processes of managing decolonisation at the United Nations, see A Orford, 'On International Legal Method' (2014) 1 *London Review of International Law* 166; A Orford, 'Hammarskjöld, Economic Thinking, and the United Nations' in H Melber and C Stahn (eds), *Peace, Diplomacy, Global Justice, and International Agency: Rethinking Human Security and Ethics in the Spirit of Dag Hammarskjöld* (Cambridge: Cambridge University Press, 2014), 156. For the Suez crisis and the economic consequences of decolonisation as a spur to the European integration project and to the remaking of the state through the United Nations, see A Orford, *International Authority and the Responsibility to Protect* (Cambridge: Cambridge University Press, 2010), 67–69. The full argument is forthcoming in A Orford, *The Battle for the State: Democracy, International Law, and Economics*.

[79] D Schneiderman, *Constitutionalizing Economic Globalization: Investment Rules and Democracy's Promise* (Cambridge: Cambridge University Press, 2008), 6.

[80] D Schneiderman, 'Constitutional Property Rights and the Elision of the Transnational: Foucauldian Misgivings' (2015) 24 *Social and Legal Studies* 65.

[81] N Tzouvala, 'The Ordo-Liberal Origins of Modern International Investment Law: Constructing Competition on a Global Scale' in JD Haskell and A Rasulov (eds), *New Voices and New Perspectives in International Economic Law* (Cham: Springer, 2020), 37. That chapter was posted on Academia in 2015.

[82] See, for example, DS Grewal and J Purdy, 'Law and Neoliberalism' (2015) 77 *Law and Contemporary Problems* 1; H Brabazon (ed), *Neoliberal Legality: Understanding the Role of*

For most of us, that historically informed scholarship on economic integration through law was self-consciously undertaken in the spirit of making rather than finding. In my case, reading Foucault's lectures had helped me to articulate and make visible aspects of the European and international economic integration projects about which I had already been writing for a decade.[83] I had argued that WTO agreements were as much about an attempt to mandate a form of regulatory alignment as about quotas or tariffs, and as much about competition within states between groups or classes as about competition between states or between North and South.

It was hard to get much purchase on thinking about international economic law with this critical work. While trade lawyers slowly began to talk about the impact of trade agreements on the right to regulate, they still made constraints on the regulatory state seem like a problem of collateral damage rather than a goal of international economic integration through law. Trade agreements were said to address 'behind the border' rules only when necessary to avoid engaging in discrimination between national and foreign producers in the guise of regulation. The problem I kept coming up against was that trying to talk about the effects on regulation with trade lawyers involved using language that was already coded to mean something else. Trade agreements embed a particular way of thinking about 'discrimination' and 'protectionism' that does different work to the meanings that such language might convey to the lay person.

The flash of recognition I felt when reading the early Ordoliberals was because their work offered a normative account of the vocabulary and assumptions underlying the project of European integration, the GATT, and the WTO agreements. The writings and strategising of the Ordoliberals provided a snapshot of a moment when the connections between a specific economic ideology and the project of transnational economic integration were being made through the language of non-discrimination, economic federation, and

---

Law in the Neoliberal Project (Oxon: Routledge, 2017); B Golder and D McLoughlin (eds), *The Politics of Legality in a Neoliberal Age* (Oxon: Routledge, 2017).

[83] For that earlier work, see A Orford, 'Locating the International: Military and Monetary Interventions after the Cold War' (1997) 38 *Harvard International Law Journal* 443, at 471–476 (predicting what some of the (then newly finalised) WTO agreements meant for democracy); A Orford, 'Globalization and the Right to Development' in P Alston (ed), *Peoples' Rights* (Oxford: Oxford University Press, 2001) 127, at 157–170 (critically analysing the structure and political effect of two WTO Agreements: the Agreement on Sanitary and Phytosanitary Measures (SPS Agreement) and the TRIPS Agreement); A Orford, 'Beyond Harmonization: Trade, Human Rights and the Economy of Sacrifice' (2005) 18 *Leiden Journal of International Law* 179, at 187–194 (exploring the form of law mandated by the SPS Agreement and the General Agreement on Trade in Services (GATS) as interpreted by the Appellate Body).

the rule of law. The conceptual relationship between law, market, state, and sovereignty in Ordoliberal writing appeared strikingly familiar to me because I had for so long been immersed in the arguments made in WTO Appellate Body decisions, the judgments of the European Court of Justice, and the work of the international legal scholars who analysed that jurisprudence. In their lectures, books, meetings, and edited collections, Ordoliberal lawyers and economists offered refreshingly frank explanations of the relation between the language of protection or non-discrimination and the constraints they saw as necessary on democratic decision-making and planning. This helped illuminate how international trade lawyers could talk about ending non-discrimination and mean the dismantling of the regulatory state.

Yet as Foucault himself would have been the first to recognise, it was not possible simply to take 1930s Ordoliberalism as a model or a programme for thinking about the relation of the state and the market in other times and places. Rather, Foucault's lectures offered a way of thinking about the movement between historical problems, ideological framings, and technical practices that I found extremely useful for thinking about international law. In an article reflecting upon the impact of those lectures for legal scholarship, I noted:

> *The Birth of Biopolitics* is not available to be slotted into a predetermined critical programme. Instead, these lectures suggest that if we want to understand the state-law theory that carried the day throughout the latter half of the twentieth century and that remade both Europe and its colonies, we can no longer simply look to the pronouncements of philosophers, legal theorists, or revolutionaries – not even those of Foucault. Instead, these lectures suggest that there is much to be gained from the work of assembling new archives that might make visible the transformations articulated in the doctrines, practices, and rationalizations of the myriad administrators who now shape everyday life for many people on this planet.[84]

In a subsequent series of books, articles, and chapters, I then began that work of 'assembling new archives' through which to understand one influential approach to the projects of remaking the state conducted through development at the UN and through economic integration under the auspices of the EU and the WTO.[85] My work deliberately created a series that linked mid-century European Ordoliberal thinkers to the legal project of economic

---

[84] A Orford, 'In Praise of Description' (2012) 25 *Leiden Journal of International Law* 609 at 621.

[85] On the methodological work involved in making (rather than finding) a new series, see A Orford, 'The Past as Law or History? The Relevance of Imperialism for Modern International Law', *NYU Institute for International Law and Justice Working Paper* 2012/2; D Armitage,

integration undertaken in part through the EU, the GATT, and the WTO. The series I assembled connected, amongst other things, the work of Röpke and Rüstow on how best to confront the perceived "disintegration" of international law and economic order during the 1930s, the centrality of communism, fascism, and the end of empire to that perception of disintegration, the place of law in Ordoliberal proposals for approaching the goals of constraining collectivism and founding a new liberalism on a transnational scale, the relevance of Lionel Robbins' *Economic Planning and International Order* to understanding his later role in the GATT negotiations, Hayek's proposals for neoliberal federation as an articulation of the constraints on domestic regulation made possible by economic integration, the relevance of Röpke's Hague lectures and his conceptualisation of *dominium* and *imperium* for understanding the relation between property and sovereignty imagined in trade agreements, the role of the Suez crisis in shaping the thinking of European neoliberals about the economic consequences of decolonisation, the Ordoliberal thinking underlying the Haberler report as a key to understanding its role in linking trade liberalisation with the dismantling of the social state in Europe and a neoliberal vision of Third World 'development', and the relevance of John Jackson's vision of 'the crumbling institutions of the liberal trade system' for understanding the Tokyo Round of the GATT.[86] The series was designed to focus on attempts at remaking the state through transnational law, and brought Ordoliberal theorising into relation with contemporary legal material including WTO treaty provisions, Appellate Body decisions, rulings of the European Court of Justice, contemporary scholarly debates, and sociological studies of the project of European integration through law.

Importantly for the point I am stressing here, I made clear why I was putting together this assemblage and what it was designed to make visible.[87] In other words, I presented that series or pattern as made not found and explained my reasons for making it. This is a necessary move for those of us committed to the realist position that portraying particular interpretations of law as inevitable is part of the problem. The impetus for my work was to make the Ordoliberal tendencies of present legal arguments visible, while also making clear their contested and contingent status within the EU, the WTO, and other transnational economic ordering projects. In so doing, my aim was to draw

---

'What's the Big Idea? Intellectual History and the *Longue Durée*' (2012) 38 *History of European Ideas* 493, at 497.

[86] See the references in footnote 78.

[87] For reflections on the choices informing that assemblage, see Orford, 'On International Legal Method', 184–196; Orford, 'Free Trade, Food Security, and the Battle for the State', 19–32, 48–49, 64–67; Orford, 'Theorizing Free Trade', 701–710.

attention to those background aspects of the GATT and later of the WTO agreements that kept being passed over or assumed away. Overall, I presented that work as the first step in 'a new history of the free trade project undertaken through international law as one aimed centrally at restructuring the state'.[88] Or to put this more emphatically, I argued that '[w]hat is at stake' in debates over free trade 'is a battle for the state – who or what the state will represent in the twenty-first century, and who will decide'.[89]

The work of Christian Joerges and his colleagues has similarly been clearly positioned as an active and reflexive interpretation of the shifting relevance of Ordoliberalism for the law and politics of European integration. As controversies about German Ordoliberalism and its role in shaping responses to the Eurozone crisis became central to the public debate across Europe, legal scholars and historians cautioned that the impact of the Ordoliberal concept of an economic constitution on the European economic integration project and more broadly had not been stable or straightforward.[90] For example, while German officials nurtured the myth that EU competition rules were inspired by Ordoliberalism, legal scholars cautioned that the claims Ordoliberals made for their own influence 'should not ... be taken at face value'.[91] It was necessary to attend to the 'discrepancy between an ideology and its actual implementation', as ideologies are inevitably 'incomplete and riddled with contradictions'.[92] As Joerges and Michelle Everson noted in relation to their work on the legacies of Ordoliberalism in and for the contemporary economic constitution of Europe, '[w]e are also engaged in this contest and are clearly partisan in our conceptual allegiance'.[93]

Given all the work that had been undertaken by legal scholars and economic historians linking the mid-century Central European Ordoliberals to contemporary projects of international economic ordering through the EU, the WTO, and the international investment regime, it might seem difficult to suggest that a historian might be responsible for 'finding' these connections. Yet this is precisely what happened when an intellectual historian took an

---

[88] Orford, 'Free Trade, Food Security, and the Battle for the State', 67.
[89] Orford, 'Free Trade, Food Security, and the Battle for the State', 67.
[90] J Hien and C Joerges, 'Introduction: Objectives and Contents of the Volume' in J Hien and C Joerges (eds), *Ordoliberalism, Law and the Rule of Economics* (Oxford and Portland: Hart, 2017), 1.
[91] A Wigger, 'Debunking the Ordoliberal Myth in Post-War Europe' in J Hien and C Joerges (eds), *Ordoliberalism, Law and the Rule of Economics* (Oxford and Portland: Hart, 2017), 161, at 177.
[92] Wigger, 'Debunking the Ordoliberal Myth in Post-War Europe', 177.
[93] Joerges and Everson, 'The Legal Proprium of the Economic Constitution', 33.

interest in the history of economic integration through international law. Quinn Slobodian's *Globalists: The End of Empire and the Birth of Neoliberalism* appeared in 2018.[94] It was his first publication to discuss international law or to mention the WTO. Until publishing *Globalists*, Slobodian had been developing a career as a historian of modern German social movements.[95] The links to international law and institutions were central to the promotion and reception of *Globalists*. Slobodian claimed to 'produce an understanding of the European Economic Community (EEC) and later the World Trade Organization (WTO)'[96] and to offer a 'field guide' to international economic institutions and to the 'transnational legal instruments' that regulate the world's resources.[97] According to Slobodian, the creation of the WTO 'was the crowning moment in the twentieth century for the Geneva school'.[98] Indeed, the publisher's website for *Globalists* linked to a video of Slobodian conducting a tour of the WTO building in Geneva.[99]

In the opening chapter of *Globalists*, Slobodian presented himself as introducing a set of forgotten and overlooked thinkers to the history of neoliberalism and international law. According to Slobodian, previous scholars had completely ignored the work of mid-century Central European neoliberals such as Röpke, Robbins, and Haberler on questions of international law and global order. *Globalists* would provide an 'illumination of those aspects of neoliberal thought related to world order that have remained more or less in the shadows',[100] 'introduce a set of thinkers who had not been central to the English language literature and reframe those like Hayek who have been'.[101] According to Slobodian, Hayek's writings on 'neoliberal federation' had been 'largely passed over',[102] as had the fact that they 'came out of incredibly wide-ranging, and now largely forgotten, discussions about which political form might be used to reform, reinvigorate, or replace that of

---

[94] Q Slobodian, *Globalists: The End of Empire and the Birth of Neoliberalism* (Cambridge: Harvard University Press, 2018).

[95] Q Slobodian, *Foreign Front: Third World Politics in Sixties West Germany* (Durham: Duke University Press, 2012); Q Slobodian (ed), *Comrades of Color: East Germany in the Cold War World* (New York: Berghahn Books, 2015).

[96] Slobodian, *Globalists*, 266.

[97] Q Slobodian, 'Making Sense of Neoliberalism', *Harvard University Press Blog*, 15 March 2018.

[98] Slobodian, *Globalists*, 273.

[99] The video is available at www.versobooks.com/blogs/3706-the-walls-of-the-wto-a-film-by-ryan-s-jeffery-and-quinn-slobodian.

[100] Slobodian, *Globalists*, 8.

[101] Slobodian, *Globalists*, 8.

[102] Slobodian, *Globalists*, 105.

empire'.[103] The focus of Röpke, Robbins, Haberler, and Hayek on global order 'has been neglected', and their 'distinct contributions' are 'often neglected in English-language discussions'.[104] Slobodian portrayed himself as '[c]orrecting this elision', which 'is critical because it was the European neoliberals who were most attentive to questions of international order'.[105] 'My narrative', Slobodian declares, will present a 'vision of neoliberal globalism from Central Europe',[106] and put 'the neoliberal project into a broader framework than other scholars have provided to date'.[107]

In addition to unearthing thinkers supposedly ignored by other scholars of international law and neoliberalism, Slobodian claimed to have discovered new themes linking Ordoliberalism with international economic law, international investment law, EU law, and the WTO. The insights that Slobodian claimed to have found through his intellectual history included that early neoliberals were concerned with questions of international law and economic order, that Ordoliberals saw democracy as a problem for capitalism and looked to international law in response, that the end of empire and decolonisation were significant contexts for the initial project of neoliberal ordering pursued through international law, and that the battle for the state and an attack on planning were central to both neoliberalism and international economic law.

In relation to each of those themes, Slobodian claimed to be correcting and completing existing scholarship. According to Slobodian, 'the question of international and global governance has been surprisingly neglected' in accounts of neoliberalism.[108] His historical research had discovered 'a key point of origin of neoliberal globalist thinking within the epochal shift of order that occurred at the end of empire'.[109] The fact that 'questions of empire, decolonization, and the world economy were at the heart of the neoliberal project' had been '[a]ll but ignored',[110] and scholars had 'chronically overlooked the fact that the end of global empires was essential to the emergence of neoliberalism'.[111] The 'extra-European context for the creation of Europe' and in particular the role of the Suez crisis had been 'overlooked'.[112] Other

---

[103] Slobodian, *Globalists*, 100.
[104] Slobodian, *Globalists*, 6–7.
[105] Slobodian, *Globalists*, 8.
[106] Slobodian, *Globalists*, 9.
[107] Slobodian, *Globalists*, 24.
[108] Slobodian, *Globalists*, 4.
[109] Slobodian, *Globalists*, 5.
[110] Slobodian, *Globalists*, 24.
[111] Slobodian, *Globalists*, 14.
[112] Slobodian, *Globalists*, 193.

scholars 'fail to notice that the real focus of neoliberal proposals is not on the market per se but on redesigning states, laws, and other institutions to protect the market'.[113] Slobodian claimed that 'a sense of the animating ideas behind the enterprise itself' had been 'lost in the description of the WTO' but that his intellectual history would 'recover' the 'genealogy of thought that linked the neoliberal world imaginary from the 1920s to the 1990s'.[114] Overall, Slobodian claimed that his book offered 'an alternative account of the modern era',[115] by revealing for the first time that neoliberalism involved 'a project of redesigning the state' through law.[116]

Slobodian insisted on the distance of his account from any existing scholarship. He repeatedly referred to the connections and conceptual themes presented in *Globalists* as 'my narrative',[117] arguing that by discovering this 'neglected' history he had recovered a genealogy of thought that had been 'lost' in accounts of the WTO.[118] 'My narrative', says Slobodian, 'corrects' the existing storyline to reveal that neoliberals 'focused on designing institutions ... to inoculate capitalism against the threat of democracy ... and to reorder the world after empire'.[119] '[M]y narrative' knits together strands of scholarship on the intellectual history of neoliberalism and international law that have remained 'strangely disconnected'.[120] 'My narrative has traced a line that leads from the end of the Hapsburg Empire to the foundation of the World Trade Organization'.[121] 'My narrative', he claims in conclusion, 'has shown that Geneva School neoliberalism is less a theory of the market or of economics than of law and the state'.[122] But in what sense does *Globalists* present a narrative that Slobodian can so relentlessly claim as his own – that is, a narrative produced through the methods of intellectual history?

---

[113] Slobodian, *Globalists*, 6.
[114] Slobodian, *Globalists*, 257.
[115] Slobodian, *Globalists*, 16.
[116] Slobodian, *Globalists*, 18.
[117] Slobodian's ownership of this narrative is one of the messages communicated most insistently and it seems effectively by *Globalists*. Slobodian uses the phrase 'my narrative' numerous times throughout the book, often at moments where he echoes most closely the work of critical legal scholars.
[118] Slobodian, *Globalists*, 257.
[119] Slobodian, *Globalists*, 2.
[120] Slobodian, *Globalists*, 3.
[121] Slobodian, *Globalists*, 264.
[122] Slobodian, *Globalists*, 268.

Slobodian declares that intellectual history was the method that made *Globalists* possible. He describes his study as a 'fairly contained story, presented largely through biography'.[123]

> I use the biographies of Geneva School neoliberals as a way to weave through a discussion of a series of institutions that were designed to encase the global markets from interference by national governments. The following chapters offer a historical field guide to these institutions, for some of which neoliberal intellectuals were the original architects, but for most of which they played the role of advocate, adopter, or adapter.[124]

In Slobodian's telling, he developed that 'field guide' without departing from any of the methodological canons of intellectual history. His approach involved exploring 'political projects populated by discrete individuals occupying specific places and moments in time'.[125] As a result, his history offered a story 'about three generations of thinkers, from the Mises Circle in 1920s Vienna to the international economic lawyers of Geneva who helped theorize the WTO'.[126] The method of contextualist history allowed him 'to tell one story with enough detail to avoid the generalizations that plague the social science literature'.[127]

Slobodian makes it seem that he has simply done what empiricist historians consistently claim they are able to do in relation to international law. Without any attention to presentist concerns, he simply went and found a collection of empirical facts in the archives and brought them to the attention of readers in order to describe the past objectively rather than engage in a process of interpretation. According to this self-presentation, Slobodian did not have to work back from present law in order to decide what facts about the past were relevant. Rather, by engaging in a biographical study of a handful of interwar Ordoliberal theorists along with the writings of three GATT lawyers who had been 'students or followers' of Hayek,[128] Slobodian had been able to generate a new understanding of international economic law. He claimed to have discovered 'the animating ideas' behind the WTO in the writings of the 'Hayekians at the GATT'.[129]

---

[123] Slobodian, *Globalists*, 24.
[124] Slobodian, *Globalists*, 20.
[125] Slobodian, *Globalists*, 25–26.
[126] Slobodian, *Globalists*, 24.
[127] Slobodian, *Globalists*, 24.
[128] Slobodian, *Globalists*, 23.
[129] Slobodian, *Globalists*, 257.

The method that was reinforced through Slobodian's description of his research was thus contextualist intellectual history.

Yet far from 'correcting' existing histories of international law and neoliberalism, 'introducing' a group of thinkers who are 'neglected' or 'chronically overlooked', and providing a new framework in which to understand the neoliberal project, Slobodian's book used the framework that had already been constructed by international legal scholars, and linked the same people and texts that we had already connected to international economic law, international investment law, and EU law. Legal scholarship had already put the neoliberal project into precisely the framework that Slobodian claimed to have discovered, studied the same 'chronically overlooked' thinkers that Slobodian claimed to introduce, and connected the same texts, figures, events, and contexts to help make visible aspects of twentieth-century international law. Despite the misleading and repeated references Slobodian made to his project as one that corrected the received legal and political history of the twentieth century, the story told in *Globalists* came straight out of the work of legal scholars, brought together the same elements that had been assembled in our work, and drew out the themes that we had already made visible, although with some significant differences of tone and analysis to which I will return.

The most generous reading I can give of all that 'introducing' and 'correcting' given the body of existing legal literature making the same arguments is that Slobodian believed that international lawyers simply provide an account of a narrow and pre-given set of texts, authors, and ideas. At best, then, Slobodian did not acknowledge how much his argument leaned upon the work of legal scholars because he did not realise that legal work involves creatively making connections between material and drawing that material into conceptual arguments based on those connections, rather than glossing material that is just to be found lying around.[130] Slobodian made no mention of the decades of legal scholarship that had actively made the connections that he presented as his own and nowhere acknowledged that the elements, structure, and themes of his narrative were laid out in the work of international

---

[130] I am assuming that Slobodian knew about that large body of literature. I do so because it is not possible that a vaguely competent scholar making the kinds of claims Slobodian makes about the originality of his work on international economic law, international investment law, and EU law would not have found the legal literature that had already introduced these Ordoliberal thinkers and made the connections between their work and international law, particularly when much of our work is easily accessible in open access formats through a simple Google search (for example of 'Röpke and international law' or 'Ordoliberalism and European law').

lawyers.[131] His failure to acknowledge, and perhaps even to understand, the work that legal scholarship had done to provide the scaffolding for his argument posed three significant problems for his analysis, for his readers, and for a critical understanding of law.

The first problem created by that failure relates to understanding how law works. Slobodian presented the transmission of ideas from mid-century neoliberals to the WTO as an effect of personal, academic relations of collaboration or mentorship in a specific place, Geneva. Because he was committed to telling a 'fairly contained story, presented largely through biography', he departed from the work of international lawyers when it comes to telling the part of the story that focuses on contemporary international law and institutions. Our work has focused on the negotiation and interpretation of international agreements as a site of struggle and developed conceptual analyses through studies of negotiating records, the decisions of international adjudicators, committee work, state practice, and scholarly argumentation.

Slobodian, however, was committed to telling a story about innovating ideologists. He therefore departed from the work of international legal scholars as he moved closer to the present. Rather than tracking the work of negotiators and later interpreters of the WTO agreements, Slobodian argued that the key architects of the WTO were a small group of Hayek's 'students and followers', namely Jan Tumlir, Director of Economic Research and Analysis at the GATT Secretariat, who died in 1985, Frieder Roessler, who resigned in 1994 as director of the GATT Legal Affairs Division, and Ernst-Ulrich Petersmann, a counsellor in the GATT Legal Affairs Division until 1989. According to Slobodian, those 'devotees of Hayekian thought' were the 'three most important GATT reformers in Geneva' and worked to 'formulate' a 'Hayekian theory of international order'.[132] His account of the creation and role of the WTO focuses on their articles and talks, alongside a passing reference to Jackson's article on the crumbling institutions of the liberal trade system.[133]

---

[131] Slobodian does cite a small number of legal scholars on fairly technical points, but nowhere does he acknowledge that legal scholars had spent decades drawing out the relation of Ordoliberal thinkers to genealogies of international economic law, international investment law, and EU law. Lawyers are in good company in that respect. Slobodian only acknowledges the existence of Foucault's lectures on Ordoliberalism twice, once to correct what Slobodian claims (wrongly in my view) to be Foucault's 'misunderstanding' of Austrian neoliberals and once to say that Foucault 'was correct to see neoliberalism as a project of "legal interventionism"': see Slobodian, *Globalists*, 33, 92.

[132] Slobodian, *Globalists*, 244.

[133] Slobodian, *Globalists*, 242.

Slobodian did not explain what made Tumlir, Roessler, and Petersmann the most important GATT reformers, how those three figures had shaped the Uruguay Round of trade negotiations leading to the creation of the WTO, or how a 'trio of Hayekian GATT experts' subsequently managed to impose their interpretations of what the WTO is for on the rest of us.[134] To do so, Slobodian would have needed to offer a specific analysis of where and how those three lawyers shaped the work of the organisation in their roles at the GATT Secretariat or subsequently as legal academics.[135] Alternatively, he could have offered a more general account of the relation of Secretariat officials to the broader operation of the GATT and WTO or of academic trade lawyers to the interpretation of WTO agreements. His failure to do either was a problem that Slobodian himself recognised. So while Slobodian presented his work as focusing 'on a relatively small number of individuals',[136] he noted that '[t]he story told in these pages cannot substitute for reconstructing the scrum of negotiation and bargaining that led to the creation of the WTO in 1995'.[137] He did not want to 'nominate the writings of Hayek or any other thinker as a Rosetta Stone for descrying an internal logic to a necessarily complex reality'.[138] And yet his narrative did just that.

In particular, Slobodian devoted a great deal of attention to Petersmann, whom he described as 'one of the most internationally visible practitioners and advocates of the field of international economic law' and one of 'the GATT's major intellectual architects'.[139] Slobodian believed Petersmann was important because 'he was one of the leading figures promoting the idea of "constitutionalizing" the world economy in the discipline of international economic

---

[134] Slobodian, *Globalists*, 249.
[135] For their own accounts of their roles at the GATT, see F Roessler, 'The Role of Law in International Trade Relations and the Establishment of the Legal Affairs Division of the GATT' in G Marceau (ed), *A History of Law and Lawyers in the GATT/WTO: The Development of the Rule of Law in the Multilateral Trading System* (Cambridge: Cambridge University Press, 2015), 161; E-U Petersmann, 'The Establishment of a GATT Office of Legal Affairs and the Limits of "Public Reason" in the GATT/WTO Dispute Settlement System' in Marceau (ed), *A History of Law and Lawyers in the GATT/WTO*, 182. For their reviews of *Globalists*, both of which dispute Slobodian's account of their thinking, their ambitions for the WTO, and the extent to which WTO law reflects their vision, see E-U Petersmann, 'Book Review: *Globalists: The End of Empire and the Birth of Neoliberalism*' (2018) 21 *Journal of International Economic Law* 915; F Roessler, 'Democracy, Redistribution and the WTO: A Comment on Quinn Slobodian's Book *Globalists: The End of Empire and the Birth of Neoliberalism*' (2019) 18 *World Trade Review* 353.
[136] Slobodian, *Globalists*, 19.
[137] Slobodian, *Globalists*, 257.
[138] Slobodian, *Globalists*, 20.
[139] Slobodian, *Globalists*, 244–245.

law'.[140] Yet Petersmann has been a visible and controversial figure in the WTO field precisely because the ideological character of his arguments have been clearly apparent, long after ideologues had ceased to be necessary for the field of international economic law to function. In some ways that made a figure like Petersmann less rather than more effective, as Petersmann's frequently expressed frustration about the failure of the WTO to head in the right direction makes clear.

Slobodian's shoring up of historical method comes at the cost of understanding *how* law transmits such ideas. While, as I have argued elsewhere, the Appellate Body has adopted reasoning that embeds aspects of a neoliberal vision of economic relations into decisions about the limits of domestic regulation, to understand that as an effect of the driving role played by Hayek's students is to miss a great deal about the way politics and ideology work most effectively in international law. Neoliberal ideas and values can be transmitted through a process of routinisation that does not require all participants to be card-carrying members of the Mont Pèlerin society.[141] By presenting his narrative as a product of and in the form of intellectual history, Slobodian translated the work of legal scholars into a methodologically conventional story about 'generations' of intellectuals connected by the fact that the later generation are 'students and followers' of the first, and that they all share a location in Geneva.[142] Legal attempts to understand the operation of law in practice is replaced by a conventional story about male tutelage.

This led to a second and broader conceptual and political problem. Slobodian made it seem as if he had been able to produce a conceptual analysis of law by focusing on a small number of European men rather than by studying and trying to make sense of the routine operation and technical detail of legal practice and institutions. Such an approach does not help us to understand how international economic law (or any other form of law) operates, or to train people to engage with international law in practice. As I argued in Chapter 5, law works by making politically volatile material appear smooth. To understand that work, we need to study the ongoing processes of

---

[140] Slobodian, *Globalists*, 257.

[141] See Orford, 'Theorizing Free Trade', 733 (noting the Appellate Body's tendency in interpreting WTO agreements 'to expand the constraints on states to regulate in ways that are seen as trade-distorting and limit the scope for states to take "exceptional" measures ... The end result is a form of "neoliberalism without neoliberals". While few international trade lawyers would see themselves as card-carrying members of the Mont Pèlerin Society, it becomes harder and harder to distinguish much trade law jurisprudence from the core doctrines produced by neoliberals in earlier decades'.)

[142] Slobodian, *Globalists*, 23.

transmission, interpretation, and transformation of the law rather than some imaginary origin.[143] Critical lawyers have long sought to emphasise that 'the distinction between interpreting and making law is unstable'.[144]

Understanding the movement between grand ideological visions and routine techniques of interpretation is central to grasping the work that international lawyers do. In other words, international economic law works as a means of embedding neoliberalism not because it locks in the designs dreamed up by a handful of Hayekians, but because international arguments make it seem self-evident that something called a 'subsidy' exists and is bad,[145] or that it is unfair for a state to put in place restraints on exports of vital products in times of scarcity,[146] or that it is rational to require that governments seeking to regulate the safety of novel food technologies fund and undertake a scientific risk assessment before adopting such regulations rather than requiring the corporations seeking to profit from new technologies to establish their safety.[147]

Legal scholars wrestle with the question of how to convey such tendencies in a particular field of law while at the same time not making it appear as if the law is mechanical and its operations determinate. It is not helpful to make it seem that somehow the WTO was able to lock in the fantasies of Röpke or for that matter of Petersmann.[148] Realist and critical legal scholars have tried to

---

[143] A Orford, 'Law, Economics, and the History of Free Trade: A Response' (2015) 11 *Journal of International Law and International Relations* 155, at 163 ('[I]nternational law is made not only at the point of negotiation of a treaty or handing down of a decision, but also in the process through which legal fictions or concepts or rules or principles are interpreted, transmitted, and handed on between legal professionals and between legal professionals and other people. I [have] noted that international lawyers and political economists ... have consistently worked together on the project of realising liberalism through the creation of an international legal order. So international law is made, expanded, and handed on through a process of transmission that involves legal scholarship, commentary, and teaching as well as legal negotiations, advocacy, and judgment').

[144] NM Perrone and D Schneiderman, 'International Economic Law's Wreckage: Depoliticization, Inequality, Precarity' in E Christodoulidis, R Dukes, and M Goldoni (eds), *Research Handbook on Critical Legal Theory* (Cheltenham: Edward Elgar, 2019), 446, at 465.

[145] Orford, 'Law, Economics, and the History of Free Trade', 172–175; Orford, 'Theorizing Free Trade', 732–733.

[146] Orford, 'Law, Economics, and the History of Free Trade', 158–164.

[147] Orford, 'Globalization and the Right to Development', 158–167; Orford, 'Beyond Harmonization', 188–191.

[148] See A Lang, *World Trade Law after Neoliberalism: Re-imagining the Global Economic Order* (Oxford: Oxford University Press, 2011), 57 (portraying his work on the encounter between international trade law and human rights law as an attempt to 'de-reify' both the trade and the human rights regimes, by arguing that both regimes have 'highly contested ideological foundations', and that in different periods each regime represents 'a contingent compromise between the partisans of each perspective').

show that the law is not a machine that can be programmed by a few sinister Svengalis and then operationalised to 'enforce' their visions upon the world, and that social institutions cannot be successfully designed to realise particular ends. Instead, we explore the ways that the law works to embed and transmit ideas so as to 'generate the experience of necessity'.[149] Slobodian presents his history as a narrative in which the ideas of a few key thinkers were turned into constitutions and in turn then made 'enforceable'. Such arguments work precisely because they largely reproduce, rather than upset, the familiar moves of dogmatic legal argumentation,[150] in this case by making particular contested interpretations of what WTO agreements mean appear necessary and inevitable.

The idealist visions of even the most confident ideologues cannot be translated directly into concrete institutional practice. The sense that they can be is part of the problem, in that it gives these institutional practices greater coherence (this is all mapped out), inevitability (the constitution is determining, it makes things happen), legitimacy (it was all there in the treaty, we had no choice but to apply it), and power (the WTO will enforce its laws). Slobodian claims that neoliberals were able to produce a system of 'rules, enforced through internationally enforceable constitutional laws'.[151] Does it help analytically and politically to imagine that WTO agreements are constitutional laws that can be 'enforced' or that they 'lock in liberal trade rules'?[152] If so, who does it help?

In asking these questions, let me make clear that I too want to change those aspects of our situation that certain officials, lawyers, and economists have sought to present as somehow legally locked in through constitutional measures. However, I would be both dishonest and defeatist if I taught my students that law, even 'constitutional' forms of law, was able to lock in anything or that they should accept that a particular interpretation of a legal provision was locked in. How the routine work of international lawyers makes certain interpretations or arguments appear incontestable is part of what has to be understood rather than reinforced. As David Kennedy has argued:

---

[149] D Kennedy, 'A Semiotics of Legal Argument' in Academy of European Law (ed), *The Protection of Human Rights in Europe* (Dordrecht/Boston/London: Kluwer/Martinus Nijhoff, 1994), 309, at 319.
[150] F Johns, 'Guantánamo Bay and the Annihilation of the Exception' (2005) 16 *European Journal of International Law* 613, at 626.
[151] Slobodian, *Globalists*, 18.
[152] Slobodian, *Globalists*, 281.

The world simply is not constituted in the sense that things fit together in ways articulated in foundational legal documents. Stories about the UN charter, the WTO, the human rights corpus as world 'constitutions' are fairy tales and international law is far too fluid to serve as a judge of the permitted and prohibited.[153]

Third, critical legal scholars also wrestle with the difficulties of making visible the way that law works by linking grand ideological claims and technical legal details. Slobodian instead just focuses on the grand claims. Indeed, Slobodian makes clear that this is his starting methodological premise. 'Labelling neoliberalism helps us to see it as one body of thought and one mode of governance'.[154] That approach simply shores up the coherence of ideologies such as 'neoliberalism' rather than showing that those ideologies, like any other grand ideological claim, are contested and contestable. Attention to the work of embedding and transmitting Ordoliberalism, neoliberalism, or any other 'ism' through law should remind us that neoliberalism, like other isms, is not coherent. The intense conflicts over whether WTO agreements really have the evolutive constitutional character claimed by Ordoliberals like Petersmann has been strongly resisted since the WTO's creation by US officials, some of them representing other variants of what we might call neoliberalism. While the thinkers Slobodian explores had to engage in 'very practical activity' and in 'getting their hands dirty',[155] Slobodian never dirties his own hands or tries to make sense of that 'practical activity'. In such forms of critique, ideology is magically translated into reality, while the 'technical legal instruments that accomplish this magic somehow fade into the background'.[156] The result is to make the power and effect of ideological projects appear far more clear-cut than careful attention to practical influence and institutional embeddedness would reveal.

6.5 HISTORIANS AND THE INTERNATIONAL LEGAL FIELD

Through the kinds of narratives I have explored here, historians of international law try to have their cake and eat it too. They point to the current relevance of their contextualist work while at the same time claiming

---

[153] D Kennedy, 'Law and the Political Economy of the World' (2013) 26 *Leiden Journal of International Law* 7, at 47.
[154] Slobodian, *Globalists*, 3.
[155] Slobodian, *Globalists*, 20.
[156] A Riles, *Collateral Knowledge: Legal Reasoning in the Global Financial Markets* (Chicago and London: University of Chicago Press, 2011), 9.

scrupulously to be ignoring presentist debates when engaging with the past. They shore up particular understandings of international law in the present, while not acknowledging that their sense of what law means in the present is part of a partisan debate in which their histories will play a role. The choice to focus on particular texts, institutions, figures, or concepts in writing histories of international law has an unavoidably partisan effect. Similarly, the methods proposed by contextualist historians are already embedded within the debates about interpretation which structure the legal field. The argument for a focus on the intentions of particular individuals as a guide to the meaning of a text, or the priority of particular ideological understandings of a treaty regime as determinative of its purpose, or the claim that one set of practices are the true origin of international law, turn out to be part of the political struggle for the law rather than above it.

As a result, historians become part of the international law field. The more successful they are at presenting a plausible account of the history of an object that they are able to present as 'international law' (or international human rights law or international economic law), the more they become part of the network of professional knowledge producers who are treated as authoritative sources of information and expertise about international law. Through that process, historians enter the international law game. They become participants in struggles over what international law is and does in the world.

None of that would matter so long as the readers of historical scholarship didn't believe the claim that such scholarship is somehow empirical and objective as opposed to normative and partisan. Increasingly, however, history is treated as a source of authority about international law's past and of empirical methods by which to improve the objectivity of legal scholarship. Historical work is presented and received as offering a non-partisan, objective account of 'meaning', including the meaning of international law. In the final chapter, I will suggest that with those moves, history has become a new foundation for formalism in international law.

7

Why Study the Past of International Law?

History as Politics

This book has explored the turn to history in international law that has taken place since the early 1990s. I have drawn attention to a particular pattern of argument that has shaped the resulting encounter between international lawyers and historians and suggested that we can see in that encounter a hermeneutic of suspicion playing out across and between disciplines. In this chapter, I explore the situation in which that hermeneutic has been adopted and consider the functions it serves for international lawyers. In short, my argument is that the interplay between international law and history serves to offer a new grounding for formalism in an extremely fraught political context. Yet turning to history in search of the real origins of international law or the contextual meaning of international legal texts is a problem both analytically and politically. There are no historical methods that can save us from the political character of international legal interpretation and the suggestion that there are undermines the realist attempt to make the deeply political character of international adjudication apparent.

In Section 7.1, I return to the legal realist insight that lawyers make rather than find the law. As we saw in earlier chapters, international lawyers make legal arguments in part through drawing on the past. We try to assemble past practices and texts into persuasive patterns, construct disparate fragments and sources into a narrative whole, bring different events or cases into relation, and choose specific precedents or analogies as part of the process of legal reasoning. Creative legal work involves creating plausible patterns, analogies, or narratives by assembling past material from disparate sources in ways that are persuasive to legal audiences. Few international lawyers today would present that work as purely technical and mechanical.

Yet while in a sense 'we are all realists now',[1] international lawyers still struggle with the unresolved conflicts between the role played by formalism in justifying the place of international adjudication in global politics and the widespread acceptance of realist premises that challenge the foundations of formalism. As Duncan Kennedy has argued, the adoption of a hermeneutic of suspicion offers one way for lawyers to avoid the contradictions to which legal realism drew our attention.[2] Rather than fully embrace the legal realist scepticism about the possibility of finding rather than making the law, the adoption of a hermeneutic of suspicion allows the projection of that scepticism onto the other side in a legal debate while holding on to the idea that a correct legal interpretation is available. Just such a hermeneutic of suspicion has structured the encounter between international law and history.

Section 7.2 considers the ways in which historical work has been brought into international legal arguments to offer an objective ground for neoformalism. Appeals to contextualist histories allow lawyers to present their arguments as being grounded on evidence and to characterise the other side in a legal debate as ideologically motivated, presentist, or engaged in myth-making rather than proper scholarship. In that way, the fetishisation of historical context can offer a new empiricist ground on which to base neoformalist arguments about what international law really is or means. As we'll see, openly partisan arguments about the nature of international law that were initially developed in international legal scholarship have been taken up by historians and brought back into the legal field as empiricist histories. Appeals to historical scholarship can also work as a form of method laundering, through which partisan legal approaches to interpreting the past are repackaged and presented as empiricist historical methods.

What then is to be done if we accept that international law and its histories are made rather than found? In Section 7.3, I argue that lawyers cannot look to historians (or anyone else for that matter) to save the day with impartial and verifiable evidence-based interpretations of what international law really is, means, or stands for. Nor, I will suggest, is it productive to continue reproducing the hermeneutic of suspicion, accusing others of improperly politicising, instrumentalising, or misusing history while claiming that our side uses history in a properly scientific manner. Yet that is not to say that studying historical material is worthless. I conclude this book by considering why we might still

---

[1]   W Twining, *Karl Llewellyn and the Realist Movement* (London: Weidenfeld and Nicholson, 1973), 382.

[2]   D Kennedy, 'The Hermeneutic of Suspicion in Contemporary American Legal Thought' (2014) 25 *Law and Critique* 91.

want to study the past of international law even if we accept that such study will involve politics all the way down. Rather than shore up a hermeneutic of suspicion in our encounter with histories of international law, I explore other ways that creative lawyers might use the past as part of an overtly political and value-driven engagement with international law in the present.

How we study the past of international law will be determined by why we study the past of international law. Why we study the past of international law in turn depends upon our situation in time and space. And our situation in time and space will also shape what we think this thing called 'international law' is. In my professional life, I talk about international law in many parts of the world with people who call themselves international lawyers and with people who don't. I talk about international law at public events with people who have a financial or strategic interest in how international law works, at closed events with officials from various governments, international organisations, and other non-state actors, at conferences involving both practising and academic international lawyers, at academic events with scholars from a range of disciplines, and with the students I teach or supervise. Very often, I find myself having to translate (for myself and for my audience) between the different objects that the participants at these events take international law to be. In such a context, any history of 'international law' will take as its starting point only one specific, and inevitably contested and partisan, view of what 'international law' is. Such histories will by design or effect be caught up in struggles over the past, present, and future of international law.

7.1 LEGAL ARGUMENT AS MAKING NOT FINDING

The idea that law is a social product rather than a set of rules handed down from time immemorial or from some divine source is now a commonplace feature of legal thought. As we saw in Chapter 5, a version of that idea informed early international lawyers through the influence of the German historical school, while a politically charged version of that argument in the form of Scandinavian and American legal realism would eventually come to shape international legal thought in the twentieth century.

Yet realism took longer to gain ground in international legal thinking than it did in US legal thought. As late as 1940, Hans Morgenthau could argue that unlike other areas of law, positivism remained the determining influence on the study of international law.[3] It had withstood challenges from natural law,

---

[3] HJ Morgenthau, 'Positivism, Functionalism, and International Law' (1940) 34 *American Journal of International Law* 260, at 263.

Kelsen's neo-positivist criticism, and legal sociology. Morgenthau argued that just as internationalist scholarship was still based on positivist assumptions and followed the positivist method, so too the Permanent Court of International Justice (PCIJ) and those who argued before it still followed the 'pseudo-logical method of traditional positivism'.[4] Where advocates before domestic courts and judges of those courts had 'dared to break through the network of positivist formulae', it was striking that there were no instances of such advocacy or decision-making involving international tribunals. Indeed, Morgenthau noted that when Judge Hudson, the US judge on the PCIJ, had sought to find an example of a 'realistic decision' about international law, he was forced to turn to the Court of Appeals of New York.[5]

In order to understand why American legal realism in its strong form came somewhat late to international legal thinking, it is helpful to remember the political intervention that legal realists were staging and the context in which they were staging it. Realists not only challenged any remnants of metaphysical thinking about the grounds or foundations of law but also sought to undermine forms of argument that characterised legal decisions as the effect of mechanically applied decision-making procedures or interpretative techniques.[6] In particular, legal realists stressed that law is 'made, not found' in order to challenge formalist modes of legal reasoning deployed to legitimise the role of judges and adjudicators.[7]

The political sting in the tail of legal realism lay in the second or negative aspect of the argument – that is, that lawyers do not find the law. The 'not finding' part of the argument had – and has – significant implications for the political ideology that we encapsulate in the idea of a 'rule of law'. The argument that judges are restrained by the letter or at the very least the spirit of the law is a core part of the claim that they properly have the authority to make decisions with large-scale implications for the distribution of wealth and privilege or for questions of punishment and sanction.

Indeed, the legal realist challenge to formalism in the first half of the twentieth century was directed at delegitimising the nullifying of progressive social legislation by conservative US judges in the name of protecting property, liberty, and freedom of contract.[8] The move towards a social or welfare

---

[4] Morgenthau, 'Positivism, Functionalism, and International Law', 264.
[5] Morgenthau, 'Positivism, Functionalism, and International Law', 264.
[6] For the characterisation of formalism as 'mechanical jurisprudence', see R Pound, 'Mechanical Jurisprudence' (1908) 8 *Columbia Law Review* 605.
[7] JW Singer, 'Legal Realism Now' (1988) 76 *California Law Review* 465, at 474, 533.
[8] For explorations of the political context and stakes of legal realism, see WJ Samuels, 'The Economy as a System of Power and Its Legal Bases: The Legal Economics of Robert Lee Hale'

state made possible through new forms of regulation and administration was strongly resisted by US judges, and much of the early realist scholarship was a response to the resulting cases. The idea that judges could legitimately exercise the power to overturn legislation passed by democratic parliaments and thus make decisions with major distributional consequences relied in part upon the formalist claim that lawyers had the capacity to engage in a principled and objective process of legal reasoning. The formalist claim that it was possible to differentiate law from politics depended on the idea that judges were engaged in a scientific, apolitical, and rational process of applying clear rules with determinative consequences. Formalist legal reasoning 'was pervaded with a sense of certainty'.[9]

The forensic dissection of such claims by the legal realists reshaped the nature of persuasive legal argument. They argued that legal rules or principles 'are not inherent in some universal, timeless logical system', but 'designed by people in specific historical and social contexts for specific purposes to achieve specific ends'.[10] Rules often contained vague terms like 'reasonableness' that could be interpreted in different ways, meaning that such rules could not be applied mechanically. Broad concepts such as property, rights, or freedom of contract encompassed competing values and choosing between those values when interpreting such concepts meant that law was a site of struggle.[11]

In the common law context, it was not possible to derive a specific rule or holding from a case. A judge could always opt to read a case broadly to establish a general rule or narrowly to limit the holding or *ratio* to specific

(1973) 27 *University of Miami Law Review* 261; G Peller, 'The Metaphysics of American Law' (1985) 73 *California Law Review* 1151; Singer, 'Legal Realism Now', 475–503; MJ Horwitz, *The Transformation of American Law, 1870–1960* (Oxford: Oxford University Press, 1992); N Duxbury, *Patterns of American Jurisprudence* (Oxford: Oxford University Press, 1995), 65–159; BH Fried, *The Progressive Assault on Laissez-Faire: Robert Hale and the First Law and Economics Movement* (Cambridge: Harvard University Press, 1998); SM Teles, *The Rise of the Conservative Legal Movement* (Princeton and Oxford: Princeton University Press, 2008), 24–30.

9   Singer, 'Legal Realism Now', 499.
10 Singer, 'Legal Realism Now', 474.
11 R Hale, 'Coercion and Distribution in a Supposedly Non-Coercive State' (1923) 38 *Political Science Quarterly* 470; M Cohen, 'Property and Sovereignty' (1927) 13 *Cornell Law Quarterly* 8. See also the famous dissent of Justice Holmes in *Lochner* v. *New York* (1905) 198 US 45, at 76 ('General propositions do not decide concrete cases. The decision will depend on a judgment or intuition more subtle than any articulate major premise'). On the meaning of rights as a site of struggle today, see K Rittich, 'The Future of Law and Development: Second-Generation Reforms and the Incorporation of the Social' in DM Trubek and A Santos (eds), *The New Law and Economic Development: A Critical Appraisal* (Cambridge: Cambridge University Press, 2006), 245.

facts.[12] Given the existence of competing and contradictory rules in the legal field, a judge had scope to choose which rules should apply or refer to one line of precedent rather than another. The choice between values was often hidden by the taken-for-granted nature of background rules or facts, so that decisions could be made to seem necessary or inevitable by focusing on how one set of rights or interest holders were affected by a decision and ignoring others, or by foregrounding what the law prohibits rather than what it permits.[13]

Realists called for lawyers to make arguments 'without the crutch of formalism'.[14] That meant abandoning the idea that the only legitimate way to engage in decision-making about normative questions involved adopting an impartial, neutral, or universal point of view. It was not possible to reduce law to a set of rules, general principles, or abstract concepts from which specific legal conclusions could be mechanically derived through an objective process of deduction. Accepting that law is made rather than found required giving up the legal language of discovering right answers, ascertaining meaning, elaborating community values, uncovering principles, or balancing interests.[15]

Legal realism did not begin to have a significant effect upon international law until the latter half of the twentieth century, in part due to the imagined audience for international legal writing and the political context in which legal argument went to work. The European writers of international law treatises in the nineteenth century and well into the twentieth century assumed that their audience shared 'certain moral, political and social values', including values related 'to the conduct of academic discourse'.[16] A legal argument needed to continue only long enough to ensure that a person who basically shared the same values could consider the heterogeneous set of materials assembled by the writer and conclude that the writer's proposal was sensible. An international lawyer could otherwise expect academic discourse to proceed like a polite conversation. The lawyer 'would not expect the audience to interrupt at each sentence with fundamental objections about method, verification procedures or basic assumptions', even though in international law there were 'an endless series of receding challenges which could

---

[12] Singer, 'Legal Realism Now', 470.

[13] See the reflections in D Kennedy, 'The Stakes of Law, or Hale and Foucault!' (1991) XV *Legal Studies Forum* 327; P Schlag, 'An Appreciate Comment on Coase's *The Problem of Social Cost*: A View from the Left' (1986) *Wisconsin Law Review* 919, at 944.

[14] Singer, 'Legal Realism Now', 533.

[15] Singer, 'Legal Realism Now', 532–533.

[16] P Allott, 'Language, Method and the Nature of International Law' (1971) 45 *British Yearbook of International Law* 79, at 95.

be made at every level of reasoning'.[17] The overall goal was to create in the reader 'the same sense of certainty as the writer, based on the same completely uncertain grounds'.[18]

The sense that international lawyers could assume an audience with shared values came under challenge in the early twentieth century with the emergence of communist and fascist states in Europe, a challenge that accelerated with the perceived 'disintegration' of liberal internationalism during the 1930s, the destruction and mass slaughter of the Holocaust and the Second World War, the emergence of new states during decolonisation, and the nuclear standoff of the Cold War. By the 1960s, international lawyers had become increasingly concerned about the difficulties of relating legal categories to 'real-world' facts, aware of the competing interpretations about the justice and injustice of war and intervention that divided the Western, Eastern, and Non-Aligned blocs, and attentive to the demands that the expansion of the international community to include newly independent states had placed upon traditional jurisprudential categories and sensibilities.[19]

Yet even as the sense of a shared community of values came under increasing pressure, an increasingly dominant form of liberal internationalism continued to push for the creation and use of international courts and tribunals to ensure the peaceful settlement of disputes between states. The idea that the existence of courts was fundamental to 'the function of law in the international community' had long been a core tenet of much internationalist thinking.[20] The refusal of states to recognise the compulsory jurisdiction and obligatory competence of courts in disputes between members of international society was seen as a major barrier to the realisation of the rule of international law.[21] That 'legalist project for world order' was forcefully sponsored in the early twentieth century by US international lawyers, who were an essential part of the foreign policy establishment and committed to

[17] Allott, 'Language, Method and the Nature of International Law', 95.
[18] Allott, 'Language, Method and the Nature of International Law', 117.
[19] See for example RP Anand, 'Rôle of the "New" Asian-African States in the Present International Legal Order' (1962) 56 *American Journal of International Law* 383; AA Fatouros, 'International Law and the Third World' (1964) 50 *Virginia Law Review* 783; RP Anand, *New States and International Law* (Delhi: Vikas, 1972); PC Jessup, 'Non-Universal International Law' (1973) 12 *Columbia Journal of Transnational Law* 415; M Bedjaoui, *Towards a New International Economic Order* (Paris and New York: UNESCO/Holmes and Meier, 1979). For an overview of those debates, see A Orford, 'Moral Internationalism and the Responsibility to Protect' (2013) 24 *European Journal of International Law* 83, at 91.
[20] H Lauterpacht, *The Function of Law in the International Community* (Oxford: Clarendon Press, 1933).
[21] Lauterpacht, *The Function of Law in the International Community*, 423–438.

reconciling universal principles with American power and its projection into the region and later the globe.[22]

For much of the twentieth century those who advocated a greater role for international courts and tribunals gained little purchase. However, with the end of the Cold War, Western states and their international lawyers began more successfully to promote certain core principles of human rights, investment protection, and trade liberalisation as foundational or constitutional. During the 1990s, ambitious new multilateral and regional economic agreements with sophisticated dispute settlement mechanisms were established, and increasing resort was made to existing processes of international arbitration in the field of investment disputes. As we saw in Chapter 2, it was during this decade that the twin processes of judicialisation and constitutionalisation began to intensify internationally.

That was the context in which the sceptical approach to formalist legal reasoning developed by legal realists in the early twentieth century began to gain more influence in international law. Much of the initial impetus was through scholars who took up the social science tendency in legal realist thinking, such as those associated with the New Haven school. But there was also an increasing adoption of stronger realist arguments and conclusions, in part through the influence of critical legal studies on international law scholarship. In the United States, most international lawyers, from law and economics scholars to new realists to rational choice theorists to critical legal scholars, accept some aspect of the realist argument. It would be hard to pretend that law is an ideology-free zone after decades of televised US Supreme Court appointment hearings or the central place played by judicial appointments in US Presidential campaigning. The direction of American legal thought (and frankly the drama of current US politics) has in turn had an effect on international lawyers.[23] While many lawyers from other countries still look askance at the more extreme forms of political polarisation evident in US Supreme Court decisions that seem unabashedly to put the 'party' back in 'partisan', it is fair to say that most international legal scholars

---

[22] BA Coates, *Legalist Empire: International Law and American Foreign Relations in the Early Twentieth Century* (Oxford: Oxford University Press, 2016), 3.

[23] While Duncan Kennedy has noted that 'it is easy to exaggerate the extent' to which the globalisation of a particular post-realist form of contemporary legal thought is '"really" Americanization', it is hard to overstate the influence of trends in US legal thought on the broader field of international law, particularly after 1989. For Kennedy's reflection on the 'third globalization' of law and legal thought, see D Kennedy, 'Three Globalizations of Law and Legal Thought: 1850–2000' in DM Trubek and A Santos (eds), *The New Law and Economic Development: A Critical Appraisal* (Cambridge: Cambridge University Press, 2006), 19, at 69.

and practitioners today would barely raise an eyebrow at the claim that international law is political.

However, it is one thing to adopt aspects of the realist arguments about legal reasoning and another to accept the consequences of the most sceptical of those arguments for the legitimacy of law in general and adjudication in particular. Legal realism creates a strong sense of ambivalence about the judicial role and about law more generally.[24] Yet international adjudication has taken on an increasingly significant role, not only in the settlement of disputes between states but also more controversially in investor–state dispute settlement. As a result, international lawyers are engaged in determining the outcome of intense group conflicts over the distribution of the world's wealth and resources. It is here that the adoption of a hermeneutic of suspicion has a significant function. That hermeneutic offers a way of reconciling a sceptical attitude towards formalist legal reasoning and the defense of the role of adjudication in contemporary politics. It does so by projecting the resulting bad faith and role conflict onto one's opponent.

This then helps to make sense of the debate I have been exploring in this book. On the one hand, the 'making' part of the legal realist argument resonates with the use of the past in the practice of international lawyers that I analysed in Chapter 5. As we saw there, international lawyers actively choose the contexts in which to place texts, attempt to persuade an audience to see particular patterns in legal material, rely upon inferences and generalisations to hold together reasoning about past texts or practice and legal conclusions, and draw analogies between the present situation and earlier cases to support a particular interpretation of the law. Law professors teach from casebooks that bring together fragments of legal materials from diverse sources and times, and law students are trained to assemble and reassemble those legal fragments into arguments that can persuade other lawyers familiar with the same material. This is an active process of choosing or selecting from past texts and practices, making patterns or relations, communicating those patterns or relations, and persuading an audience that the patterns or relations we describe offer a plausible and useful account of what the law is.

That work of making legal arguments involves engaging with the past in numerous ways. It requires becoming familiar with the accepted patterns of relating material that appear plausible to legal audiences, studying the historical premises that underpin those accepted patterns, and working out how to unsettle those patterns and their underlying premises. It also requires having a

---

[24] Singer, 'Legal Realism Now', 502.

fine attention to detail, the time and willingness to revisit the historical record, and the ability to observe past practices, cases, events, or texts without having an investment in the particular pattern that has been made of them or is currently acceptable to those in power. Making legal arguments also requires creativity – being able to see concepts or facts in a relation not previously seen and to make new connections, linkages, analogies, relations, or associations between details, events, cases, texts, or concepts. Whether or not a legal audience will be persuaded by the resulting argument depends in part on whether the details appear accurate and the links or relations between different cases or events plausible and perceptible, and in part on the social or institutional aspects of legal practice such as whether the pattern made out of the possible legal material describes what powerful players want to see, or whether the interpreter is perceived as having the authority and credibility to say 'what the law is'.[25]

Yet the intensification of the processes of judicialisation and constitutionalisation in fields such as international trade law and international investment law has placed greater stress on the question of whether or not international adjudicators can apply international law in a way that is free from bias, ideology, or politics. In that context, the idea that international law is made not found risks undermining the legitimacy and authority of international adjudication. The cross-disciplinary version of the hermeneutic of suspicion that I have explored in this book represents one of many current attempts to mediate the tensions produced by the widespread acceptance that international law is political at a time when international adjudication plays an increasingly significant role in distributing the world's resources. In the interdisciplinary version of the hermeneutic of suspicion I have explored in this book, international lawyers are presented as instrumentalising and politicising the past in the process of making partisan legal arguments, while the turn to professional historians offers an escape from the sceptical conclusion that all claims about the past of international law are political. Contextualist historians can offer a new foundation for our legal arguments.

7.2 HISTORY OF INTERNATIONAL LAW AS NEOFORMALISM

7.2.1 *Neoformalism in a Post-Realist Field*

One way of responding to anti-formalist or anti-metaphysical arguments has been to rely on other disciplines to give lawyers something solid on which to

---

[25] F Zarbiyev, 'Saying Credibly What the Law Is: On Marks of Authority in International Law' (2018) 9 *Journal of International Dispute Settlement* 291.

stand. Appeals to history play this role in contemporary international law. Of course we sophisticated twenty-first-century lawyers know that the meaning of WTO agreements is contingent and indeterminate, but look, here's an intellectual historian telling us that after all the regime *does* have a coherent ideology. Of course, we lawyers know that international human rights law is a site of struggle that is as indeterminate as any other form of law, but look, here's an intellectual historian who can prove that the real history of human rights reveals that it is simply an expression of US anti-communism, or European Christianity, or transatlantic neoliberalism.

Historians promise lawyers all the things we lost with the triumph of anti-formalism and anti-metaphysics, such as an escape from partisan struggles over meaning, an empirical account of the true origins and purpose of international law, or an evidence-based understanding of what the authors of legal texts really intended them to mean. The idea that lawyers could escape partisan argument, that fields like human rights or WTO law have a determinable function or purpose, or that we can understand the meaning of a text by reconstructing the context in which it was authored, could not be sustained in the twenty-first century without referring somewhere outside the field of law itself.

History offers lawyers a vision of law in which it is possible to find a determinative source of truth about the law's meaning, and law offers historians a new field of operation in which to employ contested claims about empiricism. For this to work, it requires constant differentiation. Historians insist that they are only studying the past, and that if they happen to provide resources through which to think about international law in the present, this is simply due to their careful archival research that just happens, innocently, magically, to inform arguments about law in the present. And international lawyers accept that differentiation. The work of historians is method laundered back into legal argument, so we can claim to have found support for our side of any legal debate in the facts that historians have established. The fetishisation of historical context thus offers a hiding place for neoformalism in international law.[26] Formalist lawyers are able to look outside what they

---

[26] For the related argument that in the aftermath of the realist challenge, the 'law in context school' in turn offered a 'privileged fetishism of "context"' as an empirically determinable social domain, see D Fraser, 'What a Long, Strange Trip It's Been: Deconstructing Law from Legal Realism to Critical Legal Studies' (1988–1989) 5 *Australian Journal of Law and Society* 35, at 37. For a response to the forms of legal historiography that fetishise context and thick description, see C Tomlins, 'After Critical Legal History: Scope, Scale, Structure' (2012) 8 *Annual Review of Law and Social Science* 31; C Tomlins, 'Foreword: "Law As ..." III – *Glossolalia*: Toward a Minor (Historical) Jurisprudence' (2015) 5 *UC Irvine Law Review* 239.

imagine as the closed world of international law for the possibility of openness to the social environment.

It is hard to let go of all the good things that formalism offered – cognitive certainty, solid foundations, and unarguable meanings. When something is presented as the true origin of international law or when the 'real history' of a subfield such as international human rights law or WTO law is discovered, it is a short step to claiming that those origins or that history in turn determine the law's meaning. The effect, which is paradoxical given the historical insistence on contingency, is to produce a sense that the past did in fact involve a moment in which we chose one meaning (for human rights, or the WTO, or international law) over another. Such debates over the past are proxies for struggles over the nature and meaning of law in the present.[27] We can make it seem as if we are not making a choice or a decision to interpret a treaty or the purpose of a functional regime in a specific way, but merely deferring to the objective findings established by those who can offer authoritative accounts of the past.

The turn to history thus allows lawyers to escape the work of making 'normative legal argument without the crutch of formalism'.[28] International lawyers treat historians both as a source of substantive facts about the past and as the source of methods by which to produce such facts. Yet very often, as we will see, what is laundered back into law through history are substantive or methodological arguments that began as partisan positions in legal struggles.

7.2.2 *Fact Laundering through History: Ordoliberalism as the Truth of the WTO*

The reception of Quinn Slobodian's *Globalists* offers a good example of the tendency for international lawyers to treat historians as empirical authority for factual claims about issues such as the real origins of a field of law, the meaning of treaties, or the ideologies programmed into the design of an institution.[29] International lawyers appeal to historical work both as the

---

[27] P Alston, 'Does the Past Matter? On the Origins of Human Rights' (2013) 126 *Harvard Law Review* 2043, at 2077 (arguing that 'there is a struggle for the soul of the human rights movement, and it is being waged in large part through the proxy of genealogy').

[28] Singer, 'Legal Realism Now', 533.

[29] Q Slobodian, *Globalists: The End of Empire and the Birth of Neoliberalism* (Cambridge: Harvard University Press, 2018). For a detailed discussion of the relationship between Slobodian's intellectual history and the decade of earlier legal scholarship making the same connections but stressing the contingency rather than necessity of dominant interpretations, see Chapter 6.

objective foundation for our side in a legal argument and as revealing the ideological motivations of our opponents. We can see both playing out in current debates over the role and future of the WTO.

Globalists has been cited by international lawyers as an authoritative ground for arguments about the determinative nature of international economic law and the purposes of the WTO, both by those who want to critique international economic law and by those who want to defend it. In the process, a decade of legal scholarship making connections between Ordoliberalism and international law has been transformed into empirical intellectual history. The recognition of contingency in that legal work has been replaced with a tone of certainty, before being brought back into international law as a foundation for neoformalist arguments.

Slobodian, for example, is now a go-to authority for Ernst-Ulrich Petersmann, who cites *Globalists* to shore up his controversial vision of what the WTO is for.[30] Petersmann has repeatedly referred to *Globalists* in support of claims that 'ordo-liberal, multilateral principles' underlie the WTO system, in a context in which the 'systemic challenge' currently posed to 'the WTO legal and dispute settlement system by market-distorting US and Chinese power politics' makes it 'uncertain' whether those ordoliberal principles 'can survive the current WTO governance crisis'.[31] Petersmann has cited *Globalists* as authority for the claim that the 'ordo-liberal "Geneva school of law and economics"' influenced 'the design of the WTO agreement',[32] and for the argument that 'the "Geneva ordo-liberalism" underlying the multilevel WTO dispute settlement system offers coherent constitutional and competition principles' for responding to the current impasse over Appellate Body reform.[33] He has approvingly quoted Slobodian's description of the WTO 'as the paradigmatic product of Geneva school neoliberalism' and the 'creation of the WTO [as] a crowning victory of the neoliberal project of finding an extra-economic enforcer for the world economy in the twentieth century'.[34] In so doing, Petersmann has come to rely on *Globalists* as evidence for his

---

[30] See E-U Petersmann, 'How Should WTO Members React to Their WTO Crises?' (2019) 18 *World Trade Review* 503, at 518–519; E-U Petersmann, 'Between "Member-Driven Governance" and "Judicialization": Constitutional and Judicial Dilemmas in the World Trading System' in C-F Lo, J Nakagawa, and T-F Chen (eds), *The Appellate Body of the WTO and Its Reform* (Singapore: Springer, 2020), 15, at 23.

[31] Petersmann, 'Between "Member-Drive Governance" and "Judicialization"', 38.

[32] Petersmann, 'Between "Member-Drive Governance" and "Judicialization"', 38.

[33] Petersmann, 'How Should WTO Members React to Their WTO Crises', 518–519.

[34] Petersmann, 'Between "Member-Drive Governance" and "Judicialization"', 38, citing Slobodian, *Globalists*, 23, 25. Petersmann quotes those same passages from *Globalists* with approval in Petersmann, 'How Should WTO Members React to Their WTO Crises', 518–519.

ideological reading of what the WTO is for and how WTO agreements should be interpreted.

Lawyers seeking to criticise the WTO have made a similar use of *Globalists*. Harlan Cohen has argued that US 'historians of the modern economy' such as Slobodian and Moyn have revealed how international law has shaped the global economic order, while it is US trade lawyers such as Cohen, Gregory Schaffer, Frank Garcia, and Timothy Meyer who offer solutions to the problems diagnosed by US historians.[35] In that neat division of labour, the earlier work done by lawyers from outside the US disappears from Cohen's account of both history and law. For Cohen, the 'value' of 'historical work' is that it can 'reveal' that 'trade's current status is a reflection of the particular politics and power struggles of the past few decades'.[36] Christine Schwöbel-Patel has argued that international lawyers are not aware of the world we inhabit, in part because 'the myth of international law's apolitical nature has been carried down as a myth at the very core of the discipline'.[37] It is Slobodian, not international lawyers, who unsettled that myth through research that 'places the rise of neoliberalism historically', in so doing '[c]orrecting' widely held assumptions about international economic law through a history that 'casts light on the rise of a set of individuals'.[38] In such accounts, American intellectual historians can be relied on as objective sources of authority about the meaning of international economic law while international lawyers who question the status quo cannot.

Those stories make everything seem too easy. If only international lawyers had noticed before now that international law was being used to remake the state in the interests of the market, or international human rights lawyers had noticed inequality or exploitation in the 1990s, things would have turned out

---

[35] HG Cohen, 'Book Review of *Not Enough: Human Rights in an Unequal World*' (2019) 113 *American Journal of International Law* 415, at 419.

[36] HG Cohen, '... And Trade' (2019) *University of Illinois Law Review Online* 48, at 58.

[37] C Schwöbel-Patel, 'Populism, International Law and the End of *Keep Calm and Carry on Lawyering*' (2018) *Netherlands Yearbook of International Law* 97, at 106.

[38] Schwöbel-Patel, 'Populism, International Law and the End of *Keep Calm and Carry on Lawyering*', 109. For a related appeal to the intellectual histories of Slobodian and Moyn as objective sources of authority about the meaning of international economic law, see M Koskenniemi, *International Law and the Far Right: Reflections on Law and Cynicism* (The Hague: Asser Press, 2019), 21. For the treatment of Slobodian rather than European and international legal scholars as a guide to 'the long arc of ordo-liberal or neoliberal international economics', see B Kingsbury, DM Malone, P Mertenskötter, RB Stewart, T Streinz, and A Sunami, 'Introduction: The Essence, Significance, and Problems of the Trans-Pacific Partnership' in B Kingsbury, DM Malone, P Mertenskötter, RB Stewart, T Streinz, and A Sunami (eds), *Megaregulation Contested: Global Economic Ordering after TPP* (Oxford: Oxford University Press, 2019), 1, at 2

differently! Yet international lawyers were fiercely having the same arguments in the 1990s that historians are trying to reintroduce now. Remembering that international law has always been and remains politics all the way down would change the nature of those stories. Studying the reasons those battles were lost within international law would be more useful than trying to pretend those arguments never happened in order to maintain the fantasy that enlightened critics of international law have suddenly arrived to unsettle our myths and correct our assumptions. What we can learn from those lost battles might help us to figure out where we need to focus our energies now.[39]

7.2.3 Method Laundering through History: From Carl Schmitt to Reinhart Koselleck

In addition to relying on historians as a source of authoritative facts about the legal past, international lawyers also rely on the aura of objectivity offered by historical methods. This represents a related response to the challenge posed by realism. Of course, we know that law is politics and that there are no right answers to legal questions waiting to be found by judges or legal scholars, but maybe other fields could offer us methods that we might deploy to produce better legal science. The role of the scholar then is to find and make use of the best methods from those other, more seriously scientific disciplines.

A claim along these lines has been one of the repeated responses that I have received to the arguments I have made in this book. If I consider that contextualist histories are not capable of producing impartial guides to the meaning of past texts or practices, then my job is to offer another historical method that will provide a better account of the legal past based on a

---

[39] For similar arguments about the effect of erasing socialist feminists, trans and queer people, and feminists of colour from the histories of 1970s feminism, see EL Kennedy, 'Socialist Feminism: What Difference Did It Make to the History of Women's Studies?' (2008) 34 *Feminist Studies* 497, at 511–512 (arguing that 'erasing the women of color and the white women of the 1970s and 1980s who worked against racism allows present-day white participants to believe in a narrative of progress that positions them to solve these issues', while knowing the history of those struggles would give 'a more realistic view of the power of racial formations and the level of struggle required to transform them'); F Enke, 'Collective Memory and the Transfeminist 1970s: Toward a Less Plausible History' (2018) 5 *Transgender Studies Quarterly* 9, at 10 (asking '[h]ow did "1970s feminism" enter collective memory as an exclusionary thing distinct from the experiences, labor, and critiques by feminists of color and trans and queer people of the same era? And why, when existing nuanced narratives might invite us to deeper analysis, are stories of exclusion and abjection so magnetic?').

commitment to scientific 'standards of veracity and verifiability'.[40] The next step should be to undertake a thorough overview of the other historical methods on offer in order to help the legal scholar make an informed choice between those methods. The problem is that legal scholars 'lack awareness of historiographical methods',[41] are 'rarely and often superficially engaged' with historiography,[42] or have offered only a 'narrow sampling of approaches to historical inquiry'.[43] The solution is simple; international lawyers must map and 'clarify the range of available options' from which the legal scholar can then choose the appropriate method for the next job.[44]

As I argued in Chapter 1, however, looking to other historical methods does not resolve issues about the inevitably partisan and political quality of historical argument, but merely pluralises them. Such contributions to the method debate still assume that history really is the master discipline for interpreting the past, and that partisan and distorted legal interpretations of past texts, cases, practices, or concepts can be corrected through the application of historical best practices. The problem is still presented as a modernist one – find the right method and you can produce better interpretations. The one thing on which all of these accounts agree is that the discipline of history can offer 'methods' for providing verifiable accounts of past legal material, broadly conceived to include 'past' texts, events, incidents, judicial reasoning, agreements, treaties, practices, actions, and so on.

Not only do historical methods necessarily become partisan and political when they are brought into relation to international law, but they often seem particularly compelling to international lawyers when they offer method-laundered versions of legal approaches. Conceptual history provides an example of this. The approach to conceptual history associated with Reinhart Koselleck has repeatedly been proposed to international lawyers as one of the alternative methods that we should take up in writing about the past.[45] When we understand ourselves simply to be borrowing methods from

---

[40] L Benton, 'Beyond Anachronism: Histories of International Law and Global Legal Politics' (2019) 21 *Journal of the History of International Law* 1, at 3.

[41] V Vadi, 'International Law and Its Histories: Methodological Risks and Opportunities' (2017) 58 *Harvard International Law Journal* 311, at 320.

[42] M Clark, 'Ambivalence, Anxieties/Adaptation, Advances: Conceptual History and International Law' (2018) 31 *Leiden Journal of International Law* 747, at 757.

[43] Benton, 'Beyond Anachronism', 11.

[44] Vadi, 'International Law and Its Histories', 334.

[45] See, for example, M Koskenniemi, 'A History of International Law Histories' in B Fassbender and A Peters (eds), *The Oxford Handbook of the History of International Law* (Oxford: Oxford University Press, 2012), 943, at 968 (arguing that 'there is (and should be) room for a *Begriffsgeschichte*, or a conceptual history that examines changes in the meaning of legal

another field, it is easier to imagine that the borrowed method is somehow free of the politics that we can more readily spot in our own field. The relation between the conceptual history of Koselleck and the legal method of Carl Schmitt can help to illustrate how that process works.

There is an ongoing and heated debate in international law and international relations about the propriety and utility of engaging with the work of Schmitt.[46] Lawyers are sufficiently familiar with both Schmitt's reputation and the material with which he is working that it is easy to recognise that his interpretations express a particular politics of law. As lawyers, we understand the political stakes of the moves that Schmitt was making in the interwar period, or at least we realise that there were such stakes and that lurking somewhere in the murky background of every one of his motivated legal interpretations there is an imagined client, usually Nazi Germany. Working out how that client's interests inform his legal arguments is a necessary part of engaging with Schmitt.

Those political stakes are less clear when we understand ourselves to be borrowing neutral 'methods' from other disciplines. As an example of this, while critical attention to the relation between Schmitt and Koselleck informed the early German reception of Koselleck's work in reviews by scholars such as Jürgen Habermas and Carl Friedrich,[47] there has been less

concepts' and criticising existing conceptual studies of international law for having rarely followed 'a specific method – not to say anything about adopting a formally "conceptual history" approach in the vein of Reinhardt Koselleck'); Clark, 'Conceptual History and International Law', 759, 770–771 (arguing that 'it is still surprising that one major trend in twentieth century historiography – "conceptual history", treated almost synonymously with one of its major primogenitors, Reinhart Koselleck – has received, at best, fleeting notice as a possible pathway for international legal historiography', that legal scholars 'ought to engage with historiography', and 'Koselleck and conceptual history' offered 'one small but important part of the wider historiographical landscape around which engagement might take place').

[46] See, for example, M Koskenniemi, 'International Law as Political Theology: How to Read *Nomos der Erde*?' (2004) 11 *Constellations* 492; D Chandler, 'The Revival of Carl Schmitt in International Relations: The Last Refuge of Critical Theorists?' (2008) 37 *Millennium: Journal of International Studies* 27; L Odysseos and F Petito, 'Vagaries of Interpretation: A Rejoinder to David Chandler's Reductionist Reading of Carl Schmitt' (2008) 37 *Millennium: Journal of International Studies* 463; B Teschke, 'Decisions and Indecisions: Political and Intellectual Receptions of Carl Schmitt' (2011) 67 *New Left Review* 61; G Balakrishnan, 'The Geopolitics of Separation: A Response to Teschke's "Decisions and Indecisions"' (2011) 68 *New Left Review* 57; R Howse, 'Schmitt, Schmitteanism and Contemporary International Legal Theory' in A Orford and F Hoffmann (eds), *The Oxford Handbook of the Theory of International Law* (Oxford: Oxford University Press, 2016), 212.

[47] See further N Olsen, *History in the Plural: An Introduction to the Work of Reinhart Koselleck* (New York and London: Berghahn, 2012), 83–85 (discussing the review by Habermas); S-L Hoffmann, 'Koselleck in America' (2017) 132 *New German Critique* 167 (discussing the reviews by Habermas and Friedrich).

discussion in the Anglophone literature about the politics of adopting Koselleck's vision of history. Yet Koselleck was influenced by Schmitt both in the themes of his writing about history and in his methodology. After the Second World War, Schmitt had found a new audience in academic circles, particularly in Heidelberg, where Koselleck became fascinated with Schmitt. Schmitt became Koselleck's informal mentor while Koselleck wrote his doctoral dissertation, *Kritik und Krise*.[48]

Schmitt's influence on the substance of Koselleck's research is evident from *Kritik und Krise*. During the 1920s and 1930s, Schmitt had developed a critique of parliamentary democracy and its perceived inability to respond to the crisis of the state.[49] Schmitt had agreed with Thomas Hobbes that 'the factual, current accomplishment of genuine protection is what the state is all about'.[50] For Schmitt the authority of the state was premised upon its capacity to defend the will of an 'indivisibly similar, entire, unified people'.[51] Like Hobbes, Schmitt believed that the existence of competing obligations and multiple allegiances could only lead to conflict and potentially to civil war. Schmitt's argument that the state needed to represent a unified people led him to claim that even Hobbes had not gone far enough. Hobbes retained a (minimal) space for private conscience within his vision of political order. Schmitt saw the preservation of even that minimal differentiation between private conscience and public confession as a threat to state authority.

Schmitt argued that the capacity to guarantee protection in turn depended upon the existence of a sovereign who could distinguish between friends and enemies. An authority that was no longer capable of making distinctions between friend and enemy can have no effect in the world.[52] According to Schmitt, this was the fate that had befallen the *jus publicum Europaeum* at the end of the nineteenth century. European international law had depended for its meaning upon a spatial order premised upon the 'notion that European soil

---

[48] For the English translation, see R Koselleck, *Critique and Crisis: Enlightenment and the Pathogenesis of Modern Society* (Cambridge: The MIT Press, 1988 [1959]). For a detailed analysis of Schmitt's influence on *Kritik und Krise*, see Olsen, *History in the Plural*, 23–86.

[49] C Schmitt, *The Crisis of Parliamentary Democracy* (trans E Kennedy) (Cambridge: MIT Press, 1999 [1934]).

[50] C Schmitt, *The Leviathan in the State Theory of Thomas Hobbes: Meaning and Failure of a Political Symbol* (trans G Schwab and E Hilfstein) (Westport: Greenwood Press, 1996 [1938]), 34.

[51] C Schmitt, *Legality and Legitimacy* (trans J Seitzer) (Durham: Duke University Press, 2004 [1932]), 28.

[52] C Schmitt, *Roman Catholicism and Political Form* (trans GL Ulmen) (Westport: Greenwood Press, 1996 [1923]), 26; C Schmitt, *Political Theology II: The Myth of the Closure of Any Political Theology* (trans M Hoelzl and G Ward) (Cambridge: Polity Press, 2008 [1970]), 114.

or soil equivalent to it had a different status in international law from that of uncivilized or non-European peoples'.[53] Once that was abandoned, European international law 'changed into a universal international law lacking any distinctions'.[54] Because international law could no longer properly distinguish between friend and enemy, it no longer had authority. If international law was to be meaningful, it must retain the sense of European international law as a regional form of law and refrain from judging the conduct of European states.

Writing his dissertation in post-war Heidelberg, Koselleck built on Schmitt's arguments regarding the state crisis and its relation to a dangerous form of utopian moralism. Koselleck argued that the seventeenth-century distinction between an inner realm of morality and an external realm of politics was the 'pathogenesis' that had thrown modern politics into a permanent state of crisis. The European state had been founded on the principle of separating politics from religious morality in order to create civil peace. The 'bourgeois citizen' could feel 'safe and protected' in the 'order of European states' that resulted from the 'subordination of morality to politics'.[55] Yet in the subsequent situation of stability and order, the moral conscience of the European bourgeoisie had grown out of all proportion, and those elites had forgotten that their luxury and freedom only existed as a result of the political order provided by the state. That had given rise to a world of voluntary associations and critical Enlightenment philosophers who saw it as their role to 'look at politics ... from the perspective of an enlightened conscience'.[56] Conscience for Koselleck had become a 'source of evil' and a threat to the peace.[57] A crisis of the European state had arisen because 'a conscience lacking outside support degenerates into the idol of self-righteousness'.[58] Like Schmitt, Koselleck saw the idea that international law could offer a standard against which to judge state conduct as part of the problem. The ideal form of the law of nations in Europe had 'voluntarily relinquished all functions of a mental-moral tribunal' judging the conduct of other states.[59] For Koselleck, international law 'must of necessity be and remain morally imperfect'.[60]

---

[53] C Schmitt, *The Nomos of the Earth in the International Law of the Jus Publicum Europaeum* (trans Ulmen, GL) (New York: Telos Press, 2003 [1950]), 230.
[54] Schmitt, *Nomos of the Earth*, 231.
[55] Koselleck, *Critique and Crisis*, 48.
[56] Koselleck, *Critique and Crisis*, 50.
[57] Koselleck, *Critique and Crisis*, 28.
[58] Koselleck, *Critique and Crisis*, 28.
[59] Koselleck, *Critique and Crisis*, 48.
[60] Koselleck, *Critique and Crisis*, 47.

That way of thinking about protection, the state, critique, and international law will be familiar from Chapter 4, where I explored the arguments about international lawyers made by Ian Hunter. Hunter has made clear that his work is indebted to both Schmitt and Koselleck.[61] For Hunter, in their 'uncompromising rejection' of all attempts to treat anything other than security as the goal of the state, 'Schmitt's and Koselleck's work is an important precondition' of his own.[62] Hunter applauded both Schmitt's defence of the 'European *jus publicum*' for its 'restriction of sovereignty to the purely worldly domination of a territory' rather than any concern with 'the good life', and Koselleck's recognition of the 'cultural and political "crisis"' experienced by the state when its 'focus on worldly security' was undermined by 'the Enlightenment intelligentsia's pursuit of moral perfection'.[63] Hunter shares with Schmitt and Koselleck an allergy to expressions of conscience or critique directed at challenging the European state in the name of justice. For Hunter, the problem posed to the state by postcolonial theorists and international lawyers is that which Schmitt and Koselleck saw as the problem posed by conscience and critique.

The move from Schmitt to Koselleck and on to Hunter illustrates the broader argument about international law and the politics of history that I have made in this book. International lawyers understand that Schmitt's arguments about the state and international law are political and partisan. For those familiar with the milieu in Heidelberg, Koselleck's *Kritik und Krisis* was understood to echo Schmitt's interwar thinking. However, in the intervening decades Koselleck has come to be received simply as a scholar who can offer methodological innovations to the study of history and to international law. In turn, Hunter presents himself and is cited by historians of international law and theorists of international relations as an exemplar of empirical historical method who is able to diagnose the methodological errors and political partisanship of other scholars.[64] I want to stress that my aim is not to discredit

---

[61] I Hunter, *Rival Enlightenments: Civil and Metaphysical Philosophy in Early Modern Germany* (Cambridge: Cambridge University Press, 2001), 11.

[62] Hunter, *Rival Enlightenments*, 12.

[63] Hunter, *Rival Enlightenments*, 11–12.

[64] See, for example, L Benton and L Ford, *Rage for Order: The British Empire and the Origins of International Law, 1800–1850* (Cambridge: Harvard University Press, 2016), 202 (citing Hunter as warning 'of the distortions of method' by international lawyers, and as demonstrating that 'the problems' of international legal scholarship are 'compounded by a reliance on methods of dialectical philosophy history'); R Devetak, *Critical International Theory: An Intellectual History* (Oxford: Oxford University Press, 2018), 8, 9, 11, 156–157 (treating Hunter as an exemplar of contextualist approaches that approach concerns about 'the point or purpose of a text' as 'questions to which empirically based evidence can be mobilized for answers', that 'try

Hunter by showing that he plays a partisan role in battles over the meaning of international law. Rather, my point is that he is as much a partisan as are international lawyers. That gets lost when we lose the familiar bearings of our own field and begin to treat work in other fields as somehow free of worldly politics.

A similar point can be made about the influence of Schmitt on Koselleck's development of conceptual history as a method. Koselleck borrowed from Schmitt a central analytical focus on 'concepts',[65] as well as the focus on a particular formalised conception of intellectual 'conflict' as at the heart of conceptual history.[66] As Timo Pankakoski has argued, Koselleck followed Schmitt in claiming that '[a]rgumentation is a form of struggle, words are weapons in political battles, and the domain of concepts is a battlefield'.[67] I would argue that each of those claims was informed by the fact that Schmitt was a lawyer. In other words, Schmitt passed on to Koselleck a lawyer's sensitivity to the operation of politicised concepts in a field of struggle. It is here that the juridical thinking of Schmitt influences the 'conceptual history' that will subsequently become the trademark of Koselleck.

Schmitt was a master of the art of thinking with juridical concepts and making them do new work. He understood the potent role that concepts play in law and he consciously and overtly sought to change the way lawyers made sense of and used inherited concepts, as well as proposing new concepts when he thought they were needed. The method of doing things with concepts was central for Schmitt, with the focus on a concept often appearing in the titles or subtitles of his publications. The concepts with which Schmitt worked over

---

to resist the urge to study and judge the past by imposing the concepts, concerns, and moral and epistemic standards set in "our" present', and that reject the dubious commitment of critical international relations theorists to 'emancipatory change').

[65] J Müller, 'Carl Schmitt's Method: Between Ideology, Demonology, and Myth' (1999) 4 *Journal of Political Ideologies* 61, at 62 (noting that Schmitt's '"scientific" interest in etymology and a historicist view of concepts ... foreshadowed some of the central concerns of the German school of conceptual history', although in Müller's reading Schmitt contradicted that scientific method through his overriding commitment to 'ideological combat and a strategic politics of concepts'); K Tribe, 'Translator's Introduction' in R Koselleck, *Futures Past: On the Semantics of Historical Time* (trans K Tribe) (New York: Columbia University Press, 2004), vii, at xviii (arguing that overlaying conceptual history and its approach to 'charting the course of the reception of concepts and examining the experience that they both contain and make possible' is 'the continuing influence of Carl Schmitt').

[66] See T Pankakoski, 'Conflict, Context, Concreteness: Koselleck and Schmitt on Concepts' (2010) 38 *Political Theory* 749.

[67] Pankakoski, 'Conflict, Context, Concreteness', 749.

the decades included the concept of 'the political',[68] the concept of 'sovereignty',[69] the concept of 'war' (and the related concepts of 'neutrality' and 'intervention'),[70] the concept of the 'partisan',[71] the concept of piracy,[72] and infamously, the concepts of 'Reich' and of '*Großraum*'.[73]

While Schmitt 'was loath to engage in any systematic discussion of his method',[74] many of the passages in Schmitt's writings offer what in the hands of a historian would be termed conceptual historiography. He famously spelt out his politicised vision of concepts in *The Concept of the Political*, claiming that 'all political concepts' have a 'polemical meaning', 'are focused on a specific conflict and are bound to a concrete situation'.[75] Such concepts 'turn into empty and ghostlike abstractions when this situation disappears'.[76] As a result, political concepts 'are incomprehensible if one does not know exactly who is to be affected, combated, refuted, or negated by such a term'.[77] The examples of 'the essentially polemical nature' of 'politically charged terms and concepts' that Schmitt gave there involved disputes over legal terminology. In particular, in a long footnote he discussed the claim made by the socialist lawyer Karl Renner that payments by tenants to landlords should be designated using the language of tribute rather than rent, and the arguments made by 'many socialists of the Second International' that 'the payments which armed France imposes upon disarmed Germany' are 'not "tribute", but

---

[68] See C Schmitt, *The Concept of the Political* (trans G Schwab) (Chicago and London: University of Chicago Press, 1996 [1932]); C Schmitt, *Theory of the Partisan: Intermediate Commentary on the Concept of the Political* (trans GL Ulmen) (New York: Telos, 2007 [1975]).

[69] C Schmitt, *Political Theology: Four Chapters on the Concept of Sovereignty* (trans G Schwab) (Chicago and London: University of Chicago Press, 2005 [1922]).

[70] See, for example, C Schmitt, 'The Turn to the Discriminating Concept of War' in T Nunan (ed), *Carl Schmitt: Writings on War* (Cambridge: Polity Press, 2011), 30, at 62–74.

[71] Schmitt, *Theory of the Partisan*, 14–22 (engaging in a detailed discussion of the partisan as a 'concept').

[72] C Schmitt, 'The Concept of Piracy (1937)' (2011) 2 *Humanity* 27; Schmitt, 'The Turn to the Discriminating Concept of War', 36. On the legal stakes of Schmitt's arguments about the concept of piracy in the context of the Spanish Civil War, see W Rech, 'Rightless Enemies: Schmitt and Lauterpacht on Political Piracy' (2012) 32 *Oxford Journal of Legal Studies* 235.

[73] C Schmitt, 'The *Großraum* Order of International Law with a Ban on Intervention for Spatially Foreign Powers: A Contribution to the Concept of *Reich* in International Law (1939–1941)' in T Nunan (ed), *Carl Schmitt: Writings on War* (Cambridge: Polity Press, 2011), 75. Schmitt's development and use of the *Großraum* concept was one reason for his arrest and detention at Nuremberg from 1945 to 1947. See C Schmitt, 'Appendix I, Response to the Question: "To What Extent Did You Provide the Theoretical Foundation for Hitler's *Grossraum* Policy?"' (1987) 72 *Telos* 109; JW Bendersky, 'Carl Schmitt at Nuremberg' (1987) 72 *Telos* 97.

[74] Müller, 'Carl Schmitt's Method', 63.

[75] Schmitt, *The Concept of the Political*, 30.

[76] Schmitt, *The Concept of the Political*, 30.

[77] Schmitt, *The Concept of the Political*, 31.

"reparations"'.[78] His argument, in other words, was directed to showing that while some legal concepts can be made to seem 'purely juristic, purely legal, purely scientific', all legal concepts are political.[79] Schmitt insisted that all political concepts, a category in which he included legal concepts, invoke antagonistic friend–enemy relations.[80]

Schmitt stressed that legal concepts were both the outcome of past struggles and pointed to the future. The arguments over concepts such as 'state' or 'sovereignty' indicated 'deep-seated political debates and confrontations, and the victor not only wrote the history but also determined the vocabulary'.[81] The 'fact that a certain question' is addressed conceptually in international law 'already anticipates decisive events'.[82] In addition, legal concepts could only be understood as part of a broader conceptual architecture. The 'trajectory' and 'persuasiveness of a concept in international law, is determined not only through the content of its isolated conception but also fundamentally through the position of the concept in a conceptual system'.[83] As a result, in order to understand or undertake 'conceptual formation in international law', it was necessary to recognise that 'all juridical concepts are determined through the conceptual field and coexist and grow in turn with their conceptual neighbours'.[84]

Schmitt, as a lawyer who had no time for positivism, made no pretence that his or anyone else's uses of concepts was somehow objective or impartial. For example, his studies of the concepts of war and intervention were designed to show that the treatment of Germany after the First World War represented what he saw as a radical and dangerous abandonment of the existing conceptual structure of international law, while his study of the concept of *Großraum* was directed to showing that it was 'the concrete concept of the present that we need'.[85] The point of studying the transformation of legal concepts over time was not to 'engage in endless petty chatter' by exploring all the possible meanings for a concept, but rather to determine whether existing concepts still corresponded to 'truth and reality' or had become 'obsolete' and needed to be replaced.[86] For Schmitt, there were no meaningful arguments about legal and

---

[78] Schmitt, *The Concept of the Political*, 31.
[79] Schmitt, *The Concept of the Political*, 31.
[80] Schmitt, *The Concept of the Political*, 32.
[81] Schmitt, 'The *Großraum* Order', 102–103.
[82] Schmitt, 'The Turn to the Discriminating Concept of War', 36.
[83] Schmitt, 'The Turn to the Discriminating Concept of War', 36.
[84] Schmitt, 'The *Großraum* Order', 119.
[85] Schmitt, The *Großraum* Order, 77–78.
[86] Schmitt, 'The *Großraum* Order', 103–104.

political concepts to be had in the abstract. 'What is argued about is the concrete application' of a concept, with the effect that what matters is 'who decides in a situation of conflict' what the concept means.[87] Because all law is 'situational' and 'juristic concepts' are 'governed by actual interests',[88] studying a legal (and thus political) concept such as sovereignty requires focusing on the interests served by the application of the concept in specific situations.

Schmitt's highly politicised sensibility and account of his scholarly role still has the ability to shock. Critics of Schmitt are often not simply concerned with his fascist political visions for international law but with the fact that he took an overtly politicised approach to international law at all. Benno Teschke, for example, has criticised Schmitt's 'conceptual history of the category of war' as 'more of an ideological construction than a reliable and verifiable grand narrative'.[89] For Teschke, Schmitt's approach is troubling because it not only assumes that concepts have a polemical nature and meaning but deliberately puts that polemical quality of concepts to work. Schmitt's method is 'deliberately designed to fabricate counter-concepts in the political and conceptual battles for intellectual hegemony'.[90] According to Teschke, 'Schmitt's polemical (ie combative) approach to concept formation ... is decisive for understanding his hyperpoliticized mode of knowledge production'.[91] Teschke indicts Schmitt for taking the position that 'no intellectual agreement can be reached by following the liberal protocols of removing "extraneous" political commitments from sober "scientific" debate' or moving to a fantasy world of objectivity and value-neutral impartiality.[92] Teschke concludes that Schmitt's approach is 'empirically defective' and 'ultimately ideological'.[93] Similarly, Jan-Werner Müller has argued that Schmitt's method offers an object lesson in 'the uses and abuses of conceptual history'.[94]

Yet once Schmitt's overtly political legal method is represented as a scientific historical method, it becomes respectable. Koselleck repeatedly acknowledged that his approach to conceptual history borrowed from Schmitt. In a letter he sent in January 1953 a few months before finishing his dissertation,

---

[87] Schmitt, *The Concept of the Political*, 6.
[88] Schmitt, *Political Theology*, 13, 16.
[89] B Teschke, 'Carl Schmitt's Concepts of War: A Categorical Failure' in J Meierhenrich and O Simons (eds), *The Oxford Handbook of Carl Schmitt* (Oxford: Oxford University Press, 2016), 367, at 369.
[90] Teschke, 'Carl Schmitt's Concepts of War', 369–370.
[91] Teschke, 'Carl Schmitt's Concepts of War', 370.
[92] Teschke, 'Carl Schmitt's Concepts of War', 370.
[93] Teschke, 'Carl Schmitt's Concepts of War', 383.
[94] Müller, 'Carl Schmitt's Method', 62–63.

Koselleck thanked Schmitt 'for your strict appeal always to trace the concepts back to their specific situation in order to clarify their meaning. There can be no doubt that this approach offers the only way out of historicism for the science of history'.[95] Koselleck 'often drew attention to Schmitt as one of the intellectual fathers of the *Geschichtliche Grundbegriffe*' and described Schmitt's work 'as "methodologically brilliant" conceptual history'.[96] Koselleck included Schmitt as one of the people who had begun in the 1930s to explore systematically 'the reciprocal interlacing of social and conceptual history'.[97] Koselleck's accounts of conceptual history as shifting between a synchronic analysis of concepts in relation to other concepts in a 'situational context' and a diachronic analysis that considered conceptual transformation historically echoed Schmitt's attention to the place of concepts within a broader architecture as well as their transformation across time.[98] Koselleck reproduced Schmitt's insistence that conflict was at the heart of conceptual history,[99] and he echoed Schmitt in claiming that concepts do not merely 'define given states of affairs, but reach into the future'.[100]

Where Koselleck departed from Schmitt was in presenting conceptual history as a science. He argued that *Begriffsgeschichte* was 'a specialized method for source criticism' that could offer 'great advantages for the historical sciences'.[101] Conceptual history was an 'independent discipline' that offers a 'sociohistorical payoff' by 'pursuing its own methods',[102] and a 'methodologically independent part of sociohistorical research'.[103] Despite being in many ways a method-laundered version of Schmitt's legal argumentation, Koselleck's presentation of his historiography as technical and scientific succeeded. His 'conceptual history' is now treated as just one more method with which international lawyers should dutifully familiarise ourselves and which we might choose to produce better histories. Comparing that nonchalant reception to the keen attention still paid – and properly so – to the politics of Schmitt's legal arguments makes visible the effect of method laundering to which I am trying to draw your attention. Indeed, my intuition is that legal

---

[95] Olsen, *History in the Plural*, 58.
[96] Olsen, *History in the Plural*, 187.
[97] R Koselleck, *The Practice of Conceptual History: Timing History, Spacing Concepts* (trans TS Presner and Others) (Stanford: Stanford University Press, 2002), 22.
[98] Koselleck, *The Practice of Conceptual History*, 82–83, 89.
[99] See further Pankakoski, 'Conflict, Context, Concreteness'.
[100] R Koselleck, *Futures Past: On the Semantics of Historical Time* (trans K Tribe) (New York: Columbia University Press, 2004), 80.
[101] Koselleck, *Futures Past*, 81.
[102] Koselleck, *Futures Past*, 84.
[103] Koselleck, *Futures Past*, 89.

scholars find conceptual history useful precisely because conceptual history borrows a great deal from legal method, or to be more specific, because Koselleck borrowed a great deal from Schmitt.

7.3 METHOD AS POLITICS: HOW WE STUDY THE PAST DEPENDS ON WHY WE STUDY THE PAST

7.3.1 *The Hermeneutic of Suspicion and the Global Rule of Lawyers*

This book has argued that a hermeneutic of suspicion structures encounters between international law and history. In this closing section, I turn to consider why the hermeneutic of suspicion plays such a prominent role in international legal argumentation today. When Duncan Kennedy diagnosed the operation of a hermeneutic of suspicion in US legal debates, he saw it as a response to the increased judicialisation and constitutionalisation of domestic politics and ideological debate over the preceding decades. Kennedy argued that the peculiar feature of US debates was that the 'prosecution and denial of the accusation of ideologically motivated error in legal reasoning' had become an aspect of 'everyday practice over the whole domain of law'.[104] The sceptical approach and critical techniques developed by legal realists were being deployed but the more extreme sceptical conclusion that law is politics all the way down was avoided. Rather, lawyers tended 'to uncover hidden ideological motives behind the "wrong" legal arguments of their opponents, while affirming their own right answers allegedly innocent of ideology'.[105]

In the context of US constitutional debates, the hermeneutic of suspicion makes it possible to hold together two contradictory ideas – that there are liberal and conservative justices and that 'the right answers to ideologically charged questions are "in" the constitution'.[106] The hermeneutic mediates that apparent contradiction by making ideological interpretations appear aberrational or incorrect rather than inevitable. The truth is out there, if only the other side would stop manipulating legal meaning for political purposes. That attitude makes it possible to maintain a commitment to the idea that a correct legal interpretation is still available while charging the other side in any dispute with being ideologically motivated partisans. For Kennedy, the mediating function played by the widespread adoption of the hermeneutic of suspicion in debates about law has been central to maintaining acceptance of

---

[104] Kennedy, 'The Hermeneutic of Suspicion in Contemporary American Legal Thought', 107.
[105] Kennedy, 'The Hermeneutic of Suspicion in Contemporary American Legal Thought', 91.
[106] Kennedy, 'The Hermeneutic of Suspicion in Contemporary American Legal Thought', 135.

the judicialisation and constitutionalisation of politics. As a result of those processes, US lawyers are involved in making legal decisions with political, social, or economic consequences about 'every significant ideological controversy'.[107] It would be much harder to accept the amount of power vested in judges, and the justices of the Supreme Court in particular, if the public fully acknowledged the political nature of good faith legal work.

The function of the hermeneutic of suspicion in contemporary international law is similar to its function in US legal debates. As we have seen, since the ending of the Cold War the international adjudication of disputes over trade and investment has come to play an increasingly significant role in justifying the distribution of wealth and the securing of profits on a global scale. The effect has been to make it increasingly costly in terms of time and resources for governments to introduce regulations that do not comply with a particular neoliberal vision of the limited nature of constraints that can properly be imposed on property holders and their interests. The subject matter of the trade and investment disputes brought before international arbitrators is intensely political.

The role of international arbitrators is legitimised through the claim that judicial reason is exercised in service to apolitical external standards developed by transnational experts rather than through making those adjudicators part of a broader political process.[108] In the fields of international trade and investment law, the process of developing and interpreting those standards has been a 'joint enterprise', carried out 'by economists, international lawyers, and rational-choice political scientists' along with corporate and financial stakeholders.[109] The legitimacy of the standards developed in that jurisprudence has depended less on the role of consent to their formulation and adoption, and more on formalist claims that the outcomes are reached through rational processes of decision-making or by reference to neutral principles of efficiency or economic growth.[110] The resulting decisions concerning fundamental normative questions about the meaning of property and its relation to other

---

[107] Kennedy, 'The Hermeneutic of Suspicion in Contemporary American Legal Thought', 132.
[108] M Renner, 'The Dialectics of Transnational Economic Constitutionalism' in C Joerges and J Falke (eds), *Karl Polanyi, Globalisation, and the Potential of Law in Transnational Markets* (Oxford: Hart, 2011), 419.
[109] A van Aaken, 'Rational Choice Theory' in A Carty (ed), *Oxford Bibliographies Online: International Law* (Oxford: Oxford University Press, 2012). See further Orford, 'Theorizing Free Trade', 708–710.
[110] AT Guzman, 'Against Consent' (2012) 52 *Virginia Journal of International Law* 747; LR Helfer, 'Nonconsensual International Lawmaking' (2008) *University of Illinois Law Review* 71; N Krisch, 'The Decay of Consent: International Law in an Age of Global Public Goods' (2014) 108 *American Journal of International Law* 1.

competing values have been justified as technically correct interpretations of trade and investment agreements.[111]

In addition, the legitimacy of international adjudication has relied upon the 'cosmopolitan symbolic capital' and perceived formalism of international law.[112] International arbitrators and public international lawyers jointly participate in institutions such as The Hague Academy of International Law, international arbitrations take place in internationalist cities such as The Hague, and international law professors and ICJ judges have played a core role as participants in investment arbitration processes.[113] The legitimacy of WTO dispute settlement has also relied upon that symbolic capital, from the location of the WTO overlooking Lake Geneva to the appointment of professors and senior practitioners to Panels and the Appellate Body.

The increasingly high stakes of international adjudication have placed stress on the need to present international law as neutral, impartial, and free of politics.[114] The investment regime has been a particular flashpoint, with widespread criticism of the perceived excesses of ISDS awards. As the awards paid out by governments to foreign investors became ever greater, people began to notice that investment treaties placed an enormous amount of power in the hands of international adjudicators, and more specifically in the hands of the small number of European and North American men (and the occasional woman) who are repeat players in the arbitration scene.[115] Those

---

[111] NM Perrone, 'The Governance of Foreign Investment at a Crossroad: Is an Overlapping Consensus the Way Forward?' (2015) 15 *Global Jurist* 1, at 17.

[112] Y Dezalay and BG Garth, *Dealing in Virtue: International Commercial Arbitration and the Construction of a Transnational Legal Order* (Chicago: University of Chicago Press, 1996), 18–22.

[113] Dezalay and Garth, *Dealing in Virtue*, 18–22; P Eberhardt and C Olivet, *Profiting from Injustice: How Law Firms, Arbitrators and Financiers Are Fuelling an Investment Arbitration Boom* (Amsterdam: Corporate Europe Observatory and the Transnational Institute, 2012); N Bernasconi-Osterwalder and MD Brauch, 'Is "Moonlighting" a Problem? The Role of ICJ Judges in ISDS', *IISD Commentary*, November 2017. For the 2018 announcement that ICJ judges would no longer participate in investor–State arbitration, see Speech by HE Mr. Abdulqawi A Yusuf, President of The International Court of Justice, on the Occasion of the Seventy-Third Session of the United Nations General Assembly, 25 October 2018, 11–12, available at www.icj-cij.org/files/press-releases/0/000-20181025-PRE-02-00-EN.pdf.

[114] For a discussion of the political stakes and increased controversy surrounding international investment arbitration, see A Orford, *International Law and the Social Question* (The Hague: Asser Press, 2020).

[115] J Bonnitcha, LN Skovgaard Poulsen, and M Waibel, *The Political Economy of the Investment Treaty Regime* (Oxford: Oxford University Press, 2017), 29 (listing the twenty-one most frequently appointed investment arbitrators, of whom nineteen are from Europe and North America and two from Latin America); UNCTAD, *World Investment Report 2018* (Geneva: United Nations, 2019), 95 (listing the thirteen most frequently appointed ICSID arbitrators

arbitrators are appointed on a case-by-case basis, so that they do not have the security of tenure that is typically considered necessary to ensure independence and impartiality. Activists have criticised the expansive constraints and costs placed on states seeking to implement environmental or public health measures and the empowerment of corporate actors in their role as foreign investors to challenge government decision-making.[116]

Part of the investment law regime's legitimacy crisis flowed from the asymmetrical nature of the system, in which only investors could trigger the dispute settlement process while the costs of the resulting arbitration were born by both parties. This meant that the ISDS regime was a one-way street, in which the best outcome for a state sued by an investor would be that the government would be held not to have breached its investment protection obligations but still find itself paying millions of dollars to cover the costs of the arbitration.[117] While many states have been willing to gamble on the resulting system, perhaps in the hope that their investors would win against other states often enough to make the overall deal worthwhile, the payoff is less clear for those whose citizens are largely not in the foreign investing class. The net effect of the system is to transfer wealth from states to private actors as the price of regulating in a broad range of areas.

The privileging of international adjudication over domestic political processes for resolving conflicts between the protection of property rights and competing values of public health, environmental protection, or survival has inevitably embroiled judges and arbitrators in ideological controversies and political struggles. To the extent that property is a relational concept, every decision to privilege the property rights of one group has implications for the rights and interests of other groups.[118] Yet rather than being seen as a problem, the removal of those disputes from democratic political processes was

---

between 1987 and 2017, of whom twelve are from Europe and North America and one from Chile).

[116] Eberhardt and Olivet, *Profiting from Injustice*; P Eberhardt, C Olivet, and L Steinfort, *One Treaty to Rule Them All: The Ever-Expanding Energy Charter Treaty and the Power It Gives Corporations to Halt the Energy Transition* (Brussels and Amsterdam: Corporate Europe Observatory and the Transnational Institute, 2018); L Verheecke, P Eberhardt, C Olivet, and S Cossar-Gilbert, *Red Carpet Courts: 10 Stories of How the Rich and Powerful Hijacked Justice* (Brussels and Amsterdam: Friends of the Earth Europe and International, the Transnational Institute and Corporate Europe Observatory, 2019).

[117] On the lack of a 'loser pays' principle in the investment regime, see J Bonnitcha, LN Skovgaard Poulsen, and M Waibel, *The Political Economy of the Investment Treaty Regime* (Oxford: Oxford University Press, 2017), 28.

[118] NM Perrone, 'The International Investment Regime and Local Populations: Are the Weakest Voices Unheard?' (2016) 7 *Transnational Legal Theory* 383; Orford, *International Law and the Social Question*.

characterised as a step forward.[119] Increasingly, 'the appeal of a global rule of law' was seen to lie 'in the promise of protection against the pathologies of internal domestic politics', and the idea of a transnational rule of law equated with 'a kind of internal depoliticization'.[120]

As a result, politics has re-entered that supposedly neutral realm in numerous ways. As I showed in Chapter 2, international investment law was the first field in which commentators began to express concerns about a backlash against liberal internationalism.[121] Similar trends began to emerge in the fields of international trade law, international criminal law, and international human rights law, as evidenced for example by the impasse at the WTO Appellate Body, which some have characterised as representing 'the end of an era' for international law more broadly.[122] Yet the subsequent challenge to the legitimacy of the system has not shaken the conviction that the settlement of disputes through international adjudication is a universally agreed upon ideal that exists independently of ideology, politics, national interest, or substantive visions of the good. The call to continue defending those forms of international adjudication has intensified, despite the signs that they have produced a world order that is not sustainable.[123]

This then is the situation in which the cross-disciplinary hermeneutic of suspicion is being deployed in debates about the uses and misuses of history in international law. As I argued in Chapter 2, appeals to the history of international law have played a significant role in the debates about how to make sense of the perceived crisis of liberal internationalism and in debates over the legitimacy of international adjudication. Those who have sought to muster a defence of existing international institutional arrangements and treaty regimes link their development to progress narratives, while those who have sought to challenge aspects of existing international regimes have linked them to

---

[119] F Kratochwil, 'Has the "Rule of Law" Become a "Rule of Lawyers"?' in G Palombella and N Walker (eds), *Relocating the Rule of Law* (Oxford and Portland: Hart, 2009), 171.

[120] PW Kahn, 'American Exceptionalism, Popular Sovereignty, and the Rule of Law' in M Ignatieff (ed), *American Exceptionalism and Human Rights* (Princeton: Princeton University Press, 2005), 198.

[121] See M Waibel, A Kaushal, K Chung, and C Balchin (eds), *The Backlash against Investment Arbitration: Perceptions and Reality* (Alphen aan den Rijn: Wolters Kluwer, 2010).

[122] G Shaffer, 'A Tragedy in the Making? The Decline of Law and the Return of Power in International Trade Relations' (2019) 44 *The Yale Journal of International Law Online* 1, at 17.

[123] I Hull, 'Anything Can Be Rescinded' (2018) 40(8) *London Review of Books* 25; J Crawford, 'The Current Political Discourse Concerning International Law' (2018) 81 *Modern Law Review* 1; C McLachlan, 'The Assault on International Adjudication and the Limits of Withdrawal' (2019) 68 *International and Comparative Law Quarterly* 499; Shaffer, 'A Tragedy in the Making?, 1.

imperialism, neoliberalism, and rule by globalists. The appeal to history as a new foundation for making arguments about the meaning of international law has developed alongside the deployment of a hermeneutic of suspicion to unveil the ideological errors of the opposing side.

Taken together, the two moves have functioned to mediate the tension between the power increasingly exercised by international judges and arbitrators on the one hand and the public clash of ideologies that undermine the formalist claim that international adjudication is an apolitical process on the other. The resort to a hermeneutic of suspicion in that highly fraught political context works to hold together two ideas: that it is possible to present an objective account of what international law is really for and that law has a politics. Rather than focusing on the political choices involved in any representation of international law, including our own, the hermeneutic of suspicion makes it seem that the politicisation of international law (by our opponents) is the problem. The real history of international law, or the true meaning of a past text, or the ideological origins of an international institution, are there to be found if only the other side would stop dealing in myths rather than empirical facts or misusing the past to support their vision of politics.

7.3.2 *Politics All the Way Down*

What might it look like to study the past of international law without subscribing to the hermeneutics of suspicion, acknowledging that we assemble relations and construct patterns with past material rather than finding them, and that in so doing our work is openly partisan rather than above the battle? What if we started again with the recognition that international law really is politics all the way down, and accepted the conclusions that flow from that? Rather than continue trying to use history as a way of establishing the truth of our own account or accusing our opponents of ideological error, what might be possible if we took responsibility for our own creativity and generativity in the project of making the law and its history? What if we fully acknowledged the work we do, individually and collectively, in assembling and conferring power on the objects of our research and practice?[124]

---

[124] For such an approach, see E Sedgwick, 'Paranoid Reading and Reparative Reading: Or, You're So Paranoid: You Probably Think This Essay Is about You' in E Sedgwick, MA Barale, J Goldberg, and M Moon, *Touching Feeling: Affect, Pedagogy, Performativity* (Durham: Duke University Press, 2002), 123, at 149–150.

Once we accept that 'our concepts are not simply describing the world but are actually "constitutive" of what we see',[125] we are left with the task of constructing an argument and committing to the premises underpinning it without any formalist foundations. When we try to understand and communicate what international law is, what it means, what it does, or who it represents, we are trying to make visible what is already visible, and to understand what is unfolding in front of us in ways that make it amenable to political action.[126] We work to understand the political choices embedded in apparently technical decisions.[127] And we do so knowing that everything is contested, including what counts as a source of international law, for whom and why, what counts as legally relevant practice, what counts as a treaty, how a treaty should be interpreted, how to choose between precedents or analogies, what counts as a rule and what counts as an exception, and whether our situation is radically new or one to which a routine response applies. It is in that field of argument that stories about the past of international law take their place. In such a context, the question is not which method is objective, impartial, or correct but which method is useful. Which (partisan and political) vision of the history of international law best helps us to grasp the current moment and why? A particular historical method may be extremely useful in one context but get in the way of a clear analysis or a persuasive legal argument in another.

If we approach contextualism in that spirit, we can see that the methods developed by the contextualist intellectual history tradition embody a political and normative content that may be useful for international lawyers in certain situations. Contextualist historiography offers us a vision of politics focused on the individual. As we saw in Chapter 4, the philosophy of history embraced by the proponents of contextualist intellectual history is organised around independent, innovating ideologists whose intentions are central to the meaning and understanding of political thought and thus of politics. It is based on a series of assumptions, including that progress is an optical illusion, that every figure or text has its own temporal context and it is anachronistic to consider a concept or text outside that context, that history on a grand scale is not

---

[125] F Kratochwil, 'Looking Back from Somewhere: Reflections on What Remains "Critical" in Critical Theory' (2007) 33 *Review of International Studies* 25, at 28.

[126] A Orford, 'In Praise of Description' (2012) 25 *Leiden Journal of International Law* 609.

[127] For studies that explore the politics of technical decisions, see D Kennedy, 'The Political Stakes in "Merely Technical" Issues of Contract Law' (2001) 19 *European Review of Private Law* 7; A Riles, 'Collateral Expertise: Legal Knowledge in the Global Financial Markets' (2010) 51 *Current Anthropology* 795; Perrone, 'The International Investment Regime and Local Populations'; Orford, *International Law and the Social Question*.

accessible to human understanding or interpretation, that individual innovators are the real agents of history, and that studying the past through the lens of the present distorts an otherwise politically pristine historical record. It reliably produces accounts that reveal the individualist projects behind any visions of politics or history that present as collective, universalist, or idealistic.

There were many affinities between the politics of contextualist historiography and the politics of much critical work in international law during the late twentieth and early twenty-first centuries. For much of the period since the end of the Cold War, it seemed clear to critical scholars of international law and international relations that the object of concern was a militant liberal ideology expressed through the use of force by alliances of Western states. With the break-up of the Soviet Union, liberal states were the remaining revolutionary force in international politics, and the aim was to understand the practices and the legal justifications for the resort to force by those states. Most of the critique in our field was directed to the use of force by the United States and its allies in the name of human rights, humanitarianism, democracy promotion, or civilian protection, and to the excesses or naivety (or both) of liberal internationalism.

Both empiricist historiography and much critical international legal scholarship could join in challenging that hegemonic version of liberal internationalism, which was organised around a tendency to disregard historical context, treat dominant interpretations of legal materials as natural and uncontestable, minimise the role of chance and contingency in the development of current law, ignore conflict and struggle in the history of the field, present a story of progress from past to present, treat ideas or empty abstractions as agents of history, moralise against enemies, and uncritically celebrate tradition. In that context, many critical lawyers and empiricist historians agreed on the utility of approaches that stressed the role of individual people and their projects as agents of change in the law, focused on the politically constituted and invented nature of progress narratives and legal traditions, and advocated recovering alternate historical meanings of texts, concepts, and ideas.

The assumption that international law is basically liberal has informed critical engagement with international law and has meant that critical moves have remained fairly stable for decades. From the left, there has been a powerful challenge to the naivety of Cold War liberalism, combined with an anarchic and egalitarian cynicism about experts and the state; from the right, a challenge to the residual ways in which government constrained the freedom of the innovator or economic entrepreneur. Both assumed that a particular form of international order organised around liberal capitalist states was the problem. The substance of much historical unveiling is still directed at revealing that liberal internationalism is a politics and that its origin stories are myths. Yet it is worth pausing to notice that liberal internationalism is well and truly unveiled already. It felt dangerous to be challenging humanitarian intervention or the tenets of free trade in the 1990s. It doesn't feel that way now.

Critiques of liberal internationalism have far less purchase in the current environment.[128] In the face of looming climate change- and resource-related catastrophes, mass displacement, a new generation of authoritarian leaders, and a decline in US power, attacking liberal histories of progress no longer seems quite the challenge it once was. Powerful states and their leaders, representing the 'fusion' of a transnational capitalist class with patriarchal religion and authoritarian statecraft,[129] are now fully on board with the message that liberalism is flawed, contradictory, hypocritical, and coercive. A certain kind of cynical reason targeting elites and experts now plays a dominant role in fuelling political movements that depend upon that cynicism for their consolidation and expansion.

Reaching automatically for established critiques makes it difficult even to identify the questions that now need to be posed about the role of international law in the current situation. It may turn out that contextualist methods are a useful resource for making legal arguments in such a context. But it may turn out that an effective legal intervention will require abandoning the axioms of contextualist historiography and instead championing teleological accounts,[130] producing universal histories,[131] creating connections or exploring constellations between present and past,[132] arguing that contingency is overrated,[133] reclaiming

---

[128] For the argument that neoliberal states departed from the tenets of classical liberalism some time ago, see W Brown, 'Neo-liberalism and the End of Liberal Democracy' (2003) 7 *Theory & Event* 1; SM Amadae, *Prisoners of Reason: Game Theory and Neoliberal Political Economy* (Cambridge: Cambridge University Press, 2015); C Weber, 'The Trump Presidency, Episode 1: Simulating Sovereignty' (2017) (S1) *Theory & Event* 132.

[129] I Altamirano-Jiménez, 'Trump, NAFTA, and Indigenous Resistance in Turtle Island' (2017) 20 (S1) *Theory & Event* 3, at 4 (arguing that the Trump Presidency 'represents the fusion of the transnational capitalist class with reactionary political power').

[130] M Koskenniemi, 'Law, Teleology and International Relations: An Essay in Counterdisciplinarity' (2011) 26 *International Relations* 3.

[131] B Robbins, 'Subaltern-Speak' in R Warren (ed), *The Debate on Postcolonial Theory and the Specter of Capital* (London and New York: Verso, 2017), 103.

[132] Tomlins, 'After Critical Legal History'; R Parfitt, *The Process of International Legal Reproduction: Inequality, Historiography, Resistance* (Cambridge: Cambridge University Press, 2019).

[133] S Marks, 'False Contingency' (2009) 62 *Current Legal Problems* 1.

the *longue durée* perspective,[134] embracing the use of history as a morality tale,[135] thinking of human beings as collective (political or geological) agents rather than innovating individuals,[136] or abandoning a relentlessly negative form of critique.[137]

As this book has argued, much historical work on international law implicitly takes a position on what international law is and means. In addition, historians who have positioned themselves as authorities on international law (or the law of the European Union, or international human rights, or the WTO) not only implicitly but now often explicitly address the meaning of treaties or institutions that have been negotiated or created in recent decades by people who are still very much alive. Increasingly, intellectual historians are presented as experts about contemporary legal cases, debates, and institutions. It is not clear that this work is substantively 'historical' rather than legal, if by history we mean a body of work addressing that which is 'past' rather than 'present'. What *is* different about the way that intellectual historians discuss contemporary international law is the tone of certainty that these scholars bring to their accounts of what legal regimes or texts really mean.

The turn to history has become a turn to a particular tone or style of writing about law – what I have called a turn to history as method. This turn to history as a method for thinking about law is strongly neoformalist. Historical scholarship, we are told, is impartial, neutral, and free of political manipulation of the past for presentist purposes. Historians are committed to correcting or completing the factional scholarship produced by international lawyers, responding to our misuse of the past for partisan ends with the use of the past to produce objective scholarship, exposing myths and fictions and replacing them with evidence and facts. Historians of international law and the international lawyers who mirror their style of arguing turn to history as a way to tell

---

[134] D Armitage, 'What's the Big Idea? Intellectual History and the *Longue Durée*' (2012) 38 *History of European Ideas* 493.

[135] A Carty and J Nijman (eds), *Morality and Responsibility of Rulers: European and Chinese Origins of a Rule of Law as Justice for World Order* (Oxford: Oxford University Press, 2018).

[136] D Chakrabarty, 'The Climate of History: Four Theses' (2009) 35 *Critical Inquiry* 197; C Malabou, 'The Brain of History, or, The Mentality of the Anthropocene' (2017) 116 *South Atlantic Quarterly* 39; L Eslava, M Fakhri and V Nesiah (eds), *Bandung, Global History, and International Law: Critical Pasts and Pending Futures* (Cambridge: Cambridge University Press, 2017).

[137] B Latour, 'Why Has Critique Run Out of Steam? From Matters of Fact to Matters of Concern' (2004) 30 *Critical Inquiry* 225; R Felski, *The Limits of Critique* (Chicago: Chicago University Press, 2015); I Roele, 'Policing Critique' (2018) 81 *Modern Law Review* 701; A Orford, 'Epilogue: Critical Intimacy and the Performance of International Law' in LJM Boer and S Stolk (eds), *Backstage Practices of Transnational Law* (London: Routledge, 2019), 174.

origin stories about what the world was like for the people we hold responsible
for making international law, to authenticate certain kinds of responses to
international law, or to offer an objective foundation for arguments about
which interpretations of a legal text or legal regime we ought to take seriously.
Appeals to history function as a way of limiting or defending against the
pluralist meanings that we could make of a legal text or a field of international
law or an institution such as the WTO in the present. To speak as a historian
about international law is to speak in a way that has been rendered implausible
and unpersuasive if it were attempted by a lawyer. Yet neoformalist arguments
about what a text really means or what an international institution is really
designed to achieve or what international law is really for can be smuggled
back into legal argument in the guise of objective history.

The encounter between international law and history has shored up the
idea that historiography offers a master set of methods for interpreting the past,
and that history can offer us a new foundation for formalist arguments about
the meaning of the law. This book has argued that we should resist this turn to
history as neoformalism. In the end, no other discipline or method can save
us, analyse us, offer us therapy or sanctuary or sophistication or the moral high
ground or escape from uncertainty or redemption. The language of facts or of
truth is no longer a trump card. There is no authority to which we can appeal
and no method that will establish that our account of facts or our version of
truth is the correct one. All that is available is to construct an argument and
commit to the premises or values underpinning it, knowing and fully
accepting that everything about that is contingent. We need to take responsibility for those choices and their implications, and to realise that doing so is an
ongoing, evolving process. The recognition that international law is politics all
the way down is not the end of the story, but the beginning of a new chapter.
A particular model of international law triumphed in the late twentieth
century. Its displacement poses challenges and opportunities, calling on us
to choose and defend the politics of international law to which we are
committed. The return of history into this story is valuable, but only if it can
allow us to experience that sense of choice and responsibility anew.

Bibliography

Abi-Saab, G, 'The Third World Intellectual in Praxis: Confrontation, Participation or Operation Behind Enemy Lines?' (2016) 37 *Third World Quarterly* 1957.

Ackerman, B and Golove, D, 'Is NAFTA Constitutional?' (1995) 108 *Harvard Law Review* 799.

Adelman, J, 'What Is Global History Now?' *Aeon*, 2 March 2017, https://aeon.co/essays/is-global-history-still-possible-or-has-it-had-its-moment.

Agbakwa, SC, 'Reclaiming Humanity and Economic, Social and Cultural Rights as the Cornerstone of African Human Rights' (2002) 5 *Yale Human Rights and Development Law Journal* 177.

Akman, P, 'Searching for the Long-Lost Soul of Article 82 EC' (2009) 29 *Oxford Journal of Legal Studies* 267.

Alexander, A, 'A Short History of International Humanitarian Law' (2015) 26 *European Journal of International Law* 109.

'International Humanitarian Law, Postcolonialism and the 1977 *Geneva Protocol I*' (2016) 17 *Melbourne Journal of International Law* 15.

Alexandrowicz, CH, 'Treaty and Diplomatic Relations between European and South Asian Powers in the Seventeenth and Eighteenth Centuries' (1960) 100 *Recueil des Cours* 203.

'Kautilyan Principles and the Law of Nations' (1965–1966) 41 *British Yearbook of International Law* 301.

An Introduction to the History of the Law of Nations in the East Indies (16th, 17th and 18th Centuries) (Oxford: Clarendon, 1967).

'The Afro-Asian World and the Law of Nations (Historical Aspects)' (1968) 123 *Recueil des Cours* 117.

Alford, WP, 'Law, Law, What Law? Why Western Scholars of Chinese History and Society Have Not Had More to Say About Its Law' (1997) 23 *Modern China* 398.

Al Ghunaimi, MT, *The Muslim Conception of International Law and the Western Approach* (The Hague: Martinus Nijhoff, 1968).

Allott, P, 'Language, Method, and the Nature of International Law' (1970) 45 *British Yearbook of International Law* 79.

'The Concept of International Law' (1999) 10 *European Journal of International Law* 31.

'The International Lawyer in Government Service: Ontology and Deontology' (2005) 23 *Wisconsin Journal of International Law* 13.

'Interpretation: An Exact Art' in Bianchi, A, Peat, D, and Windsor, M (eds), *Interpretation in International Law* (Oxford: Oxford University Press, 2015), 373.

'Britain and Europe: Managing Revolution' in McCorquodale, R and Gauci, J-P (eds), *British Influences on International Law, 1915–2015* (Leiden and Boston: Brill Nijhoff, 2016), 56.

Alston, P, 'U.S. Ratification of the Covenant on Economic, Social and Cultural Rights: The Need for an Entirely New Strategy' (1990) 84 *American Journal of International Law* 365.

'The Myopia of the Handmaidens: International Lawyers and Globalization' (1997) 8 *European Journal of International Law* 435.

'Resisting the Merger and Acquisition of Human Rights by Trade Law: A Reply to Petersmann' (2002) 13 *European Journal of International Law* 815.

'Does the Past Matter? On the Origins of Human Rights' (2013) 126 *Harvard Law Review* 2043.

Altamirano-Jiménez, I, 'Trump, NAFTA, and Indigenous Resistance in Turtle Island' (2017) 20(S1) *Theory & Event* 3.

Alvarez, JE, 'Hegemonic International Law Revisited' (2003) 97 *American Journal of International Law* 873.

'A BIT on Custom' (2009) 42 *New York University Journal of International Law and Policy* 17.

Amadae, SM, *Rationalizing Capitalist Democracy* (Chicago: University of Chicago Press, 2003).

Prisoners of Reason: Game Theory and Neoliberal Political Economy (Cambridge: Cambridge University Press, 2015).

Amrith, S and Sluga, G, 'New Histories of the United Nations' (2008) 19 *Journal of World History* 251.

Anand, RP, 'Rôle of the "New" Asian-African States in the Present International Legal Order' (1962) 56 *American Journal of International Law* 383.

New States and International Law (Delhi: Vikas, 1972).

Origin and Development of Law of the Sea: History of International Law Revisited (Leiden: Martinus Nijhoff, 1983).

'Sovereign Equality of States in International Law' (1986) 197 *Recueil des Cours* 9.

New States and International Law, 2nd edition (Gurgaon: Hope India Publications, 2008).

Anghie, A, 'Universality and the Concept of Governance in International Law' in Quashigah, EK and Okafor, OC (eds), *Legitimate Governance in Africa: International and Domestic Legal Perspectives* (The Hague: Kluwer, 1999), 21.

'Civilization and Commerce: The Concept of Governance in Historical Perspective' (2000) 45 *Villanova Law Review* 887.

'Time Present and Time Past: Globalization, International Financial Institutions, and the Third World' (2000) 32 *New York University Journal of International Law and Policy* 243.

'Colonialism and the Birth of International Institutions: Sovereignty, Economy, and the Mandate System of the League of Nations' (2002) 34 *New York University Journal of International Law and Politics* 513.

'The Bush Preemption Doctrine and the United Nations' (2004) 98 *Proceedings of the ASIL Annual Meeting* 326.

'The War on Terror and Iraq in Historical Perspective' (2005) 43 *Osgoode Hall Law Journal* 45.

Imperialism, Sovereignty and the Making of International Law (Cambridge: Cambridge University Press, 2008).

'Whose Utopia? Human Rights, Development, and the Third World' (2013) 22 *Qui Parle* 63.

'Imperialism and International Legal Theory' in Orford, A and Hoffmann, F (eds), *The Oxford Handbook of the Theory of International Law* (Oxford: Oxford University Press, 2016), 156.

Armitage, D, 'The Fifty Years' Rift: Intellectual History and International Relations' (2004) 1 *Modern Intellectual History* 97.

'What's the Big Idea? Intellectual History and the *Longue Durée*' (2012) 38 *History of European Ideas* 493.

Foundations of Modern International Thought (Cambridge: Cambridge University Press, 2013).

'The International Turn in Intellectual History' in McMahon, DM and Moyn, S (eds), *Rethinking Modern European Intellectual History* (Oxford: Oxford University Press, 2014), 232.

Arrighi, G, *Adam Smith in Beijing: Lineages of the Twenty-First Century* (London and New York: Verso, 2007).

Arsanjan, MH and Reisman, WM, 'Interpreting Treaties for the Benefit of Third Parties: The "Salvors' Doctrine" and the Use of Legislative History in Investment Treaties' (2010) 104 *American Journal of International Law* 597, at 602.

Askan, C, and Bailes, J (eds), *One Question Gilets Jaunes* (2019), https://stateofnatureblog.com/one-question-gilets-jaunes/.

Audier, S, *Le colloque Lippmann: Aux origines du 'néo-libéralisme'* (Paris: BDL Editions, 2012).

Néo-libéralisme(s). Une archéologie intellectuelle (Paris: Grasset, 2012).

Aust, A, 'The Theory and Practice of Informal International Instruments' (1986) 35 *International and Comparative Law Quarterly* 787.

'Alternatives to Treaty-Making: MOUs as Political Commitments' in Hollis, DB (ed), *The Oxford Guide to Treaties* (Oxford: Oxford University Press, 2012), 46.

Baker, JH, 'Why the History of English Law Has Not Been Finished' (2000) 59 *Cambridge Law Journal* 62.

Balakrishnan, G, 'The Geopolitics of Separation: A Response to Teschke's "Decisions and Indecisions"' (2011) 68 *New Left Review* 57.

Balibar, É, '"Gilets jaunes": The Meaning of the Confrontation', *Open Democracy*, 20 December 2018, www.opendemocracy.net/en/can-europe-make-it/gilets-jaunes-meaning-of-confrontation/.

Bartelson, J, *A Genealogy of Sovereignty* (Cambridge: Cambridge University Press, 1995).

Baskin, J, 'The Disillusionment of Samuel Moyn', *The Chronicle of Higher Education*, 27 October 2017.

Bass, GJ, *Freedom's Battle: The Origins of Humanitarian Intervention* (New York: Random House, 2008).

Bassbender, B and Peters, A, *The Oxford Handbook of the History of International Law* (Oxford: Oxford University Press, 2012).

Baude, W and Sachs, SE, 'Originalism and the Law of the Past' (2019) 37 *Law and History Review* 809.

Baxi, U, 'Market Fundamentalisms: Business Ethics at the Altar of Human Rights' (2005) 5 *Human Rights Law Review* 1.

Baxter, RR, 'International Law in "Her Infinite Variety"' (1980) 29 *International and Comparative Law Quarterly* 549.

Beard, JL, *The Political Economy of Desire: International Law, Development, and the Nation State* (New York: Routledge, 2006).

Beaulac, S, 'The Rule of Law in International Law Today' in Palombella, G and Walker, N (eds), *Relocating the Rule of Law* (Oxford: Hart, 2009), 197.

Becker Lorca, A, 'Eurocentrism in the History of International Law' in Fassbender, B and Peters, A (eds), *The Oxford Handbook of the History of International Law* (Oxford: Oxford University Press, 2012), 1034.

  Mestizo International Law: A Global Intellectual History 1842–1933 (Cambridge: Cambridge University Press, 2014).

Beckert, S and Sachsenmaier, D (eds), *Global History, Globally* (London: Bloomsbury, 2018).

Bederman, DJ, 'Foreign Office International Legal History' in Craven, M, Fitzmaurice, M, and Vogiatzi, M (eds), *Time, History, and International Law* (Leiden: Martinus Nijhoff, 2007), 43.

Bedjaoui, M, *Towards a New International Economic Order* (Paris and New York: UNESCO/Holmes and Meier, 1979).

Bell, DSA, 'The Cambridge School and World Politics: Critical Theory, History and Conceptual Change', *The Global Site*, 2001.

  'International Relations: The Dawn of a Historiographical Turn?' (2001) 3 *British Journal of Politics and International Relations* 115.

Bell, D (ed), *Victorian Visions of Global Order: Empire and International Relations in Nineteenth-Century Political Thought* (Cambridge: Cambridge University Press, 2007).

Bell, DA, 'Questioning the Global Turn: The Case of the French Revolution' (2014) 37 *French Historical Studies* 1.

Bellinger III, JB, 'Legal Issues in the War on Terrorism' (2006) 8 *German Law Journal* 735.

Bello, JH, 'The WTO Dispute Settlement Understanding: Less Is More' (1996) 90 *American Journal of International Law* 416.

Bendersky, JW, 'Carl Schmitt at Nuremberg' (1987) 72 *Telos* 97.

Bennett, JT, 'The Forgotten Genocide in Colonial America: Reexamining the 1622 Jamestown Massacre within the Framework of the UN Genocide Convention' (2017) 19 *Journal of the History of International Law* 1.

Bentley, M, *Modernizing England's Past: English Historiography in the Age of Modernism 1870–1970* (Cambridge: Cambridge University Press, 2005).

  The Life and Thought of Herbert Butterfield: History, Science and God (Cambridge: Cambridge University Press, 2011).

Benton, L, 'Beyond Anachronism: Histories of International Law and Global Legal Politics' (2019) 21 *Journal of the History of International Law* 1.

Benton, L and Ford, L, *Rage for Order: The British Empire and the Origins of International Law, 1800–1850* (Cambridge: Harvard University Press, 2016).

Berman, N, 'Modernism, Nationalism, and the Rhetoric of Reconstruction' (1992) 4 *Yale Journal of Law and the Humanities* 351.

'"But the Alternative Is Despair": European Nationalism and the Modernist Renewal of International Law' (1993) 106 *Harvard Law Review* 1792.

'Between "Alliance" and "Localization": Nationalism and the New Oscillationism' (1994) 26 *New York University Journal of International Law and Politics* 449.

'Beyond Colonialism and Nationalism? Ethiopia, Czechoslovakia, and "Peaceful Change"' (1996) 65 *Nordic Journal of International Law* 421.

'In the Wake of Empire' (1998–1999) 14 *American University International Law Review* 1521.

Bernasconi-Osterwalder, N and Brauch, MD, 'Is "Moonlighting" a Problem? The Role of ICJ Judges in ISDS', *IISD Commentary*, November 2017.

Besson, S, 'International Legal Theory *qua* Practice of International Law' in d'Aspremont, J, Gazzini, T, Nollkaemper, A, and Werner, W (eds), *International Law as a Profession* (Cambridge: Cambridge University Press, 2017), 268.

Bethlehem, D, 'A Transatlantic View of International Law and Lawyers: Cooperation and Conflict in Hard Times' (2009) 103 *Proceedings of the ASIL Annual Meeting* 455.

'The Secret Life of International Law' (2012) 1 *Cambridge Journal of International and Comparative Law* 23.

'Self-Defense against an Imminent or Actual Armed Attack by Nonstate Actors' (2012) 106 *American Journal of International Law* 770.

'Stepping Back a Moment – The Legal Basis in Favour of a Principle of Humanitarian Intervention', *EJIL: Talk!*, 12 September 2013, .www.ejiltalk.org/?s=bethlehem.

'The End of Geography: The Changing Nature of the International System and the Challenge to International Law' (2014) 25 *European Journal of International Law* 9.

Bevir, M, 'The Role of Contexts in Understanding and Explanation' (2000) 23 *Human Studies* 395.

'Contextualism: From Modernist Method to Post-analytic Historicism' (2009) 3 *Journal of the Philosophy of History* 211.

Biebricher, T and Vogelmann, F (eds), *The Birth of Austerity. German Ordoliberalism and Contemporary Neoliberalism* (London and New York: Rowman & Littlefield, 2017).

Bilder, RB, 'The Office of the Legal Adviser: The State Department Lawyer and Foreign Affairs' (1962) 56 *American Journal of International Law* 633.

Bilger, F, *La pensée economique libérale dans l'Allemagne contemporaine* (Paris: Librairie Générale de Droit et de Jurisprudence, 1964).

Blaas, PBM, *Continuity and Anachronism: Parliamentary and Constitutional Development in Whig Historiography and in the Anti-Whig Reaction between 1890 and 1930* (The Hague: Springer, 1978).

Blackburn, R, 'Reclaiming Human Rights' (2011) 69 *New Left Review* 126.

Blackmore, J, Itagaki, R, and Tanaka, S (eds), *Ernst Mach's Vienna 1895–1930* (Dordrecht: Kluwer, 2001).

Blair, J, 'Taking Aim at the New International Economic Order' in Mirowski, P and Plehwe, D (eds), *The Road from Mont Pèlerin: The Making of the Neoliberal Thought Collective* (Cambridge and London: Harvard University Press, 2009), 347.

Blair, T, 'Doctrine of the International Community', Speech given to the Economic Club of Chicago, Chicago, 22 April 1999.

Blum, G, 'Prizeless Wars, Invisible Victories: The Modern Goals of Armed Conflict' (2017) 49 *Arizona State Law Journal* 633.

'The Paradox of Power: The Changing Norms of the Modern Battlefield' (2019) 56 *Houston Law Review* 745.

Bodansky, D, 'What's So Bad about Unilateral Actions to Protect the Environment?' (2000) 11 *European Journal of International Law* 339.

Bodansky, D and Spiro, P, 'Executive Agreements+' (2016) 49 *Vanderbilt Journal of Transnational Law* 885.

Bolton, JR, 'Is There Really "Law" in International Affairs?' (2000) 10 *Transnational Law and Contemporary Problems* 1.

Bonnitcha, J, Skovgaard Poulsen, LN, and Waibel, M, *The Political Economy of the Investment Treaty Regime* (Oxford: Oxford University Press, 2017).

Bork, RH, *The Tempting of America: The Political Seduction of the Law* (New York: Macmillan, 1990).

Borschberg, P, *Hugo Grotius, the Portuguese, and Free Trade in the East Indies* (Singapore: National University of Singapore Press, 2011).

Bothe, M, 'Terrorism and the Legality of Pre-emptive Force' (2003) 14 *European Journal of International Law* 227.

Bourke, R, 'Pocock and the Presuppositions of the New British History' (2010) 53 *The Historical Journal* 747.

'Revising the Cambridge School: Republicanism Revisited' (2018) 46 *Political Theory* 467.

Bowman, M and Kritsiotis, D (eds), *Conceptual and Contextual Perspectives on the Modern Law of Treaties* (Cambridge: Cambridge University Press, 2018).

Brabazon, H (ed), *Neoliberal Legality: Understanding the Role of Law in the Neoliberal Project* (Oxon: Routledge, 2017).

Bradley, C, 'Rhetoric and the Regulation of the Global Financial Market in a Time of Crisis: The Regulation of Credit Ratings' (2009) 3 *Transnational Law and Contemporary Problems* 24.

Bradley, CA and Goldsmith, JL, 'Presidential Control over International Law' (2018) 131 *Harvard Law Review* 1201.

Brandis, G, 'The Right of Self-Defence against Imminent Armed Attack in International Law', speech presented at the TC Beirne School of Law, University of Queensland (11 April 2017), *EJIL:Talk!*, www.ejiltalk.org/the-right-of-self-defence-against-imminent-armed-attack-in-international-law/.

Bray, HL, 'Understanding Change: Evolution from International Claims Commissions to Investment Treaty Arbitration' in Schill, SW, Tams, CJ, and Hofmann, R (eds), *International Investment Law and History* (Cheltenham: Edward Elgar, 2018), 102.

Breckman, W, 'Intellectual History and the Interdisciplinary Ideal' in McMahon, DM and Moyn, S (eds), *Rethinking Modern European Intellectual History* (Oxford: Oxford University Press, 2014), 275.

Brett, A, 'Scholastic Political Thought and the Modern Concept of the State' in Brett, A and Tully, J with Hamilton-Bleakley, H (eds), *Rethinking the Foundations of Modern Political Thought* (Cambridge: Cambridge University Press, 2006), 130.

Brett, A and Tully, J, 'Preface' in Brett, A and Tully, J with Hamilton-Bleakley, H (eds), *Rethinking the Foundations of Modern Political Thought* (Cambridge: Cambridge University Press, 2006).

Brierly, JL, 'Le Fondement du Caractère Obligatoire du Droit International' (1928) 23 *Recueil des Cours* 463.

Brölmann, C, 'Law-Making Treaties: Form and Function in International Law' (2005) 74 *Nordic Journal of International Law* 383.

Brown, CP and Keynes, S, 'Why Trump Shot the Sheriffs: The End of WTO Dispute Settlement 1.0', Peterson Institute for International Economics Working Paper 20-4, March 2020.

Brown, W, 'Neo-liberalism and the End of Liberal Democracy' (2003) 7 *Theory & Event* 1.

Brownlie, I, 'Friedmann Award Address: The Work of an International Lawyer' (2006) 45 *Columbia Journal of Transnational Law* 1.

Brummer, C, 'Territoriality as a Regulatory Technique: Notes from the Financial Crisis' (2010) 79 *University of Cincinnati Law Review* 499.

Burgis-Kasthala, M, 'How Should International Lawyers Study Islamic Law and Its Contribution to International Law?' in de la Rasilla del Moral, I and Shahid, A (eds), *International Law and Islam: Historical Explorations* (Leiden and Boston: Brill Nijhoff, 2019), 39.

Burke, P, 'Context in Context' (2002) 8 *Common Knowledge* 152.

Butler, J, 'Genius or Suicide' (2019) 41(2) *London Review of Books* 10.

Butterfield, H, *Christianity and History* (London: G Bell and Sons, 1950).
'The Scientific versus the Moralistic Approach in International Affairs' (1951) 27 *International Affairs* 411.
Christianity, Diplomacy and War (London: Epworth Press, 1953).
The Whig Interpretation of History (New York: WW Norton, 1965 [1931]).

Buzan, B and Lawson, G, *The Global Transformation: History, Modernity and the Making of Modern International Relations* (Cambridge: Cambridge University Press, 2015).

Cai, C, 'New Great Powers and International Law in the 21st Century' (2013) 24 *European Journal of International Law* 755.

Cantegreil, J, 'The Audacity of the Texaco/Calasiatic Award: René-Jean Dupuy and the Internationalization of Foreign Investment Law' (2011) 22 *European Journal of International Law* 441.

Carlson, L, *Contingency and the Limits of History* (New York: Columbia University Press, 2019).
'Critical for Whom? Genealogy and the Limits of History' (2019) 31 *Method and Theory in the Study of Religion* 185.

Carter, BE, Weiner, AS, and Hollis, DB, *International Law*, 7th edition (New York: Wolters Kluwer, 2018).

Carty, A, *The Decay of International Law: A Reappraisal of the Limits of Legal Imagination in International Affairs* (Manchester: Manchester University Press, 1986).

'Scandinavian Realism and Phenomenological Approaches to Statehood and General Custom in International Law' (2003) 14 *European Journal of International Law* 817.

'The Iraq Invasion as a Recent United Kingdom "Contribution to International Law"' (2005) 16 *European Journal of International Law* 143.

'Visions of the Past of International Society: Law, History or Politics?' (2006) 69 *Modern Law Review* 644.

Philosophy of International Law (Edinburgh: Edinburgh University Press, 2007).

'The Practice of International Law' in Armstrong, D (ed), *The Routledge Handbook of International Law* (London: Routledge, 2009), 81.

'Did International Law Really Become a Science at the End of the 19th Century' in Nuzzo, L and Vec, M (eds), *Constructing International Law: The Birth of a Discipline* (Frankfurt am Main: Vittorio Klostermann, 2012), 229.

'Doctrine versus State Practice' in Fassbender, B and Peters, A (eds), *The Oxford Handbook of the History of International Law* (Oxford: Oxford University Press, 2012), 973.

The Philosophy of International Law, 2nd edition (Edinburgh: Edinburgh University Press, 2017).

'The Need to be Rid of the Idea of General Customary Law' (2018) 112 *AJIL Unbound* 319.

Carty, A and Lone, FZ, 'Some New Haven International Law Reflections on China, India and Their Various Territorial Disputes' (2011) 19 *Asia Pacific Law Review* 95.

Carty, A and Nijman, J (eds), *Morality and Responsibility of Rulers: European and Chinese Origins of a Rule of Law as Justice for World Order* (Oxford: Oxford University Press, 2018).

Carty, A and Smith, R, *Sir Gerald Fitzmaurice and the World Crisis: A Legal Advisor in the Foreign Office 1932–1945* (The Hague: Kluwer, 2000).

Cassese, A, 'On the Current Trends towards Criminal Prosecution and Punishment of Breaches of International Humanitarian Law' (1998) 9 *European Journal of International Law* 2.

Cassese A, 'Ex iniuria ius oritur: Are We Moving towards Forcible Humanitarian Countermeasures in the World Community?' (1999) 10 *European Journal of International Law* 23.

Cavallar, G, 'Vitoria, Grotius, Pufendorf, Wolff and Vattel: Accomplices of European Colonialism and Exploitation or True Cosmopolitans?' (2008) 10 *Journal of the History of International Law* 181.

Cavanagh, E, 'Legal Thought and Empires: Analogies, Principles, and Authorities from the Ancients to the Moderns' (2019) 10 *Jurisprudence* 463.

Chacko, CJ, 'India's Contribution to the Field of International Law Concepts' (1958) 93 *Recueil des Cours* 117.

Chakrabarty, D, *Provincializing Europe: Postcolonial Thought and Historical Difference* (Princeton: Princeton University Press, 2000).

'The Climate of History: Four Theses' (2009) 35 *Critical Inquiry* 197.

'Planetary Crises and the Difficulty of Being Modern' (2018) 46 *Millennium* 259.

Chalmers, D, Jachtenfuchs, M, and Joerges, C (eds), *The End of the Eurocrats' Dream: Adjusting to European Diversity* (Cambridge: Cambridge University Press, 2016).

Chandler, D, 'The Revival of Carl Schmitt in International Relations: The Last Refuge of Critical Theorists?' (2008) 37 *Millennium: Journal of International Studies* 27.

Charlesworth, H, 'International Law: A Discipline of Crisis' (2002) 65 *Modern Law Review* 377.

'Law-Making and Sources' in Crawford, J and Koskenniemi, M (eds), *The Cambridge Companion to International Law* (Cambridge: Cambridge University Press, 2012), 187.

Charney, JI, 'Universal International Law' (1993) 87 *American Journal of International Law* 529.

Chatterjee, H, *International Law and Inter-State Relations in Ancient India* (Calcutta: KL Mukhopadhyay, 1958).

Chayes, A and Chayes, AH, *The New Sovereignty: Compliance with International Regulatory Agreements* (Cambridge: Harvard University Press, 1995).

Chayes, A, Ehrlich, T, and Lowenfeld, A, *International Legal Process* (Boston: Little Brown & Co, 1968).

Chen, Y, 'Bandung, China, and the Making of World Order in East Asia' in Eslava, L, Fakhri, M, and Nesiah, V (eds), *Bandung, Global History, and International Law: Critical Pasts and Pending Futures* (Cambridge: Cambridge University Press, 2017), 177.

Chimni, BS, 'Third World Approaches to International Law: A Manifesto' in Anghie, A, Chimni, B, Mickelson, K, and Okafor, O (eds), *The Third World and International Order: Law, Politics, and Globalization* (Leiden and Boston: Martinus Nijhoff, 2003), 47.

'International Institutions Today: An Imperial Global State in the Making' (2004) 15 *European Journal of International Law* 1.

'Co-option and Resistance: Two Faces of Global Administrative Law' (2005) 37 *New York University Journal of International Law and Politics* 799.

'The Birth of a "Discipline": From Refugee to Forced Migration Studies' (2009) 22 *Journal of Refugee Studies* 11.

'International Law Scholarship in Post-colonial India: Coping with Dualism' (2010) 23 *Leiden Journal of International Law* 23.

'Customary International Law: A Third World Perspective' (2018) 112 *American Journal of International Law* 1.

Chinese Society of International Law, 'The South China Sea Arbitration Awards: A Critical Study' (2018) 17 *Chinese Journal of International Law* 207.

Chinkin, C, 'A Mirage in the Sand? Distinguishing Binding and Non-binding Relations between States' (1997) 10 *Leiden Journal of International Law* 223.

Clark, M, 'Ambivalence, Anxieties/ Adaptation, Advances: Conceptual History and International Law' (2018) 31 *Leiden Journal of International Law* 747.

Clinton, WJ, 'A Just and Necessary War', *New York Times*, May 23, 1999, www.nytimes.com/1999/05/23/opinion/a-just-and-necessary-war.html.

Coates, BA, *Legalist Empire: International Law and American Foreign Relations in the Early Twentieth Century* (Oxford: Oxford University Press, 2016).

Cohen, F, 'Transcendental Nonsense and the Functional Approach' (1935) 35 *Columbia Law Review* 809.

Cohen, HG, '. . . And Trade' (2019) *University of Illinois Law Review Online* 48.
  'Book Review of *Not Enough: Human Rights in an Unequal World*' (2019) 113 *American Journal of International Law* 415.
Cohen, M, 'Property and Sovereignty' (1927) 13 *Cornell Law Quarterly* 8.
Collins, R and Bohm, A, 'International Law as Professional Practice' in d'Aspremont, J, Gazzini, T, Nollkaemper, A, and Werner, W (eds), *International Law as a Profession* (Cambridge: Cambridge University Press, 2017), 67.
Comment, 'Legal Theory and Legal Education' (1970) 79 *Yale Law Journal* 1153.
Commun, P (ed), *L'ordolibéralisme allemande: Aux sources de l'Économie sociale de marché* (Cergy-Pontoise: CIRAC, 2003).
Commun, P, *Les Ordolibéraux: Histoire d'un libéralisme à l'allemande* (Paris: Les Belles Lettres, 2016).
Connelly, M, 'The Next Thirty Years of International Relations Research: New Topics, New Methods, and the Challenge of Big Data' (2015/2) 14 *Les cahiers Irice* 85.
Constable, M, 'Genealogy and Jurisprudence: Nietzsche, Nihilism, and the Social Scientification of Law' (1994) 19 *Law and Social Inquiry* 551.
Cornell, S, 'Meaning and Understanding in the History of Constitutional Ideas: The Intellectual History Alternative to Originalism' (2013) 82 *Fordham Law Review* 721.
Corten, O, 'The Controversies Over the Customary Prohibition on the Use of Force: A Methodological Debate' (2006) 16 *European Journal of International Law* 803.
  Le droit contre la guerre: l'interdiction du recours à la force en droit international contemporain (Paris: Pedone, 2008).
  'The "Unwilling or Unable" Test: Has It Been, and Could It Be, Accepted?' (2016) 29 *Leiden Journal of International Law* 777.
Craig, C, *Glimmer of a New Leviathan: Total War in the Realism of Niebuhr, Morgenthau, and Waltz* (New York: Columbia University Press, 2003).
Craven, M, 'Introduction: International Law and Its Histories' in Craven, M, Fitzmaurice, M, and Vogiatzi, M (eds), *Time, History, and International Law* (Leiden: Martinus Nijhoff, 2007), 1.
  The Decolonization of International Law (Oxford: Oxford University Press, 2007).
  'Theorizing the Turn to History in International Law' in Orford, A and Hoffmann, F (eds), *The Oxford Handbook of the Theory of International Law* (Oxford: Oxford University Press, 2016), 21.
Crawford, J, *Chance, Order, Change: The Course of International Law* (The Hague: Academy of International Law Pocketbooks, 2014).
  'The Current Political Discourse Concerning International Law' (2018) 81 *Modern Law Review* 1.
Crawford, J and Rothwell, D, 'Legal Issues Confronting Australia's Antarctica' (1992) 13 *Australian Yearbook of International Law* 53.
Creamer, Cosette D, 'From the WTO's Crown Jewel to Its Crown of Thorns' (2019) 113 *AJIL Unbound* 51.
Curthoys, A, Genovese, A, and Reilly, A, *Rights and Redemption: History, Law and Indigenous People* (Sydney: University of New South Wales Press, 2008).
Damrosch, Lori Fisler, 'Human Rights, Terrorism and Trade' (2002) 96 *Proceedings of the ASIL Annual Meeting* 128.
Dardot, P and Laval, C, *La nouvelle raison du monde. Essai sur la société néolibérale* (Paris: La Découverte, 2010).

d'Aspremont, J, Gazzini, T, Nollkaemper, A, and Werner, W (eds), *International Law as a Profession* (Cambridge: Cambridge University Press, 2017).

d'Aspremont, J Gazzini, T, Nollkaemper, A, and Werner, W, 'Introduction' in d'Aspremont, J, Gazzini, T, Nollkaemper, A, and Werner, W (eds), *International Law as a Profession* (Cambridge: Cambridge University Press, 2017), 2.

Daston, L, 'The Sciences of the Archive' (2012) 27 *Osiris* 156.

Davis, DM, 'Adjudication and Transformation: Out of the Heart of Darkness' (2001) 22 *Cardozo Law Review* 817.

Davis, JW, 'The Argument of an Appeal' (1940) 26 *American Bar Association Journal* 895.

de Bolla, P, *The Architecture of Concepts: The Historical Formation of Human Rights* (New York: Fordham University Press, 2013).

Deeks, AS, '"Unwilling or Unable": Toward a Normative Framework for Extraterritorial Self-Defense' (2012) 52 *Virginia Journal of International Law* 483.

de Grazia, M, 'Anachronism' in Cummings, B and Simpson, J (eds), *Cultural Reformations: Medieval and Renaissance in Literary History* (Oxford: Oxford University Press, 2010), 13.

Dehm, J, 'International Law, Temporalities and Narratives of the Climate Crisis' (2016) 4 *London Review of International Law* 167.

'One Tonne of Carbon Dioxide Equivalent (1tCO2e)' in Hohmann, J and Joyce, D (eds), *International Law's Objects* (Oxford: Oxford University Press, 2018), 305.

Dehm, S, 'Framing International Migration' (2015) 3 *London Review of International Law* 133.

Delahunty, RJ and Yoo, J, 'The "Bush Doctrine": Can Preventive War Be Justified?' (2009) 32 *Harvard Journal of Law and Public Policy* 851.

de la Rasilla del Moral, I, *In the Shadow of Vitoria: A History of International Law in Spain (1770–1953)* (Leiden and Boston: Brill, 2017).

Del Mar, M and Twining, W (eds), *Legal Fictions in Theory and Practice* (Heidelberg: Springer, 2015).

Der Derian, J, *On Diplomacy: A Genealogy of Western Estrangement* (Oxford: Basil Blackwell, 1987).

Derrida, J, *Negotiations* (trans Rottenberg, E) (Stanford: Stanford University Press, 2002).

Devetak, R, '"The Battle Is All There Is": Philosophy and History in International Relations Theory' (2017) 31 *International Relations* 261.

Critical International Theory: An Intellectual History (Oxford: Oxford University Press, 2018).

Devetak, R and Walter, R, 'The Critical Theorist's Labour: Empirical or Philosophical Historiography for International Relations?' (2016) 13 *Globalizations* 520.

Dezalay, Y and Garth, BG, *Dealing in Virtue: International Commercial Arbitration and the Construction of a Transnational Legal Order* (Chicago: University of Chicago Press, 1996).

'"Legal Theory", Strategies of Learned Production, and the Relatively Weak Autonomy of the Subfield of Learned Law' in Desautels-Stein, J and Tomlins, C (eds), *Searching for Contemporary Legal Thought* (Cambridge: Cambridge University Press, 2017), 137.

Didi-Huberman, G, *Devant le temps: histoire de l'art et anachronism des images* (Paris: Les Éditions de Minuit, 2000).

Confronting Images: Questioning the Ends of a Certain History of Art (trans Goodman, J) (University Park: The Pennsylvania State University Press, 2005 [1990]).

Donaldson, M, 'The Survival of the Secret Treaty: Publicity, Secrecy, and Legality in the International Order' (2017) 111 *American Journal of International Law* 575.

Doty, RL, *The Politics of Representation in North-South Relations* (Minneapolis: University of Minnesota Press, 1996).

Drayton, R and Motadel, D, 'Discussion: The Futures of Global History' (2018) 13 *Journal of Global History* 1.

Dunn, J, 'The Identity of the History of Ideas' (1968) XLIII *Philosophy* 85.

The History of Political Theory and Other Essays (Cambridge: Cambridge University Press, 1996).

Dunne, T, *Inventing International Society: A History of the English School* (Hampshire: Palgrave, 1998).

Dunne, T and Reus-Smit, C (eds), *The Globalization of International Society* (Oxford: Oxford University Press, 2017).

Duranti, M, *The Conservative Human Rights Revolution: European Identity, Transnational Politics, and the Origins of the European Convention* (Oxford: Oxford University Press, 2017).

Dutton, M, *Policing Chinese Politics: A History* (Durham and London: Duke University Press, 2005).

Duxbury, N, *Patterns of American Jurisprudence* (Oxford: Clarendon Press, 1995).

Dyzenhaus, D, 'The Grudge Informer Case Revisited' (2008) 83 *New York University Law Review* 1000.

Eberhardt, P and Olivet, C, *Profiting from Injustice: How Law Firms, Arbitrators and Financiers Are Fuelling an Investment Arbitration Boom* (Brussels and Amsterdam: Corporate Europe Observatory and the Transnational Institute, 2012).

Eberhardt, P, Olivet, C, and Steinfort, L, *One Treaty to Rule Them All: The Ever-Expanding Energy Charter Treaty and the Power It Gives Corporations to Halt the Energy Transition* (Brussels and Amsterdam: Corporate Europe Observatory and the Transnational Institute, 2018).

Egan, B, 'International Law, Legal Diplomacy, and the Counter-ISIL Campaign: Some Observations' (2016) 92 *International Studies* 235.

Eich, S and Tooze, A, 'The Allure of Dark Times: Max Weber, Politics, and the Crisis of Historicism' (2017) 56 *History and Theory* 197.

Eisemann, PM, 'Le *Gentleman's agreement* comme source du droit international' (1979) 106 *Journal du Droit International* 326.

Elias, TO, *Africa and the Development of International Law* (Leiden: AW Sijthoff, 1972).

'The Doctrine of Intertemporal Law' (1980) 74 *American Journal of International Law* 285.

Enke, F, 'Collective Memory and the Transfeminist 1970s: Toward a Less Plausible History' (2018) 5 *Transgender Studies Quarterly* 9.

Eslava, L, *Local Space, Global Life: The Everyday Operation of International Law and Development* (Cambridge: Cambridge University Press, 2015).

Eslava, L, Fakhri, M, and Nesiah, V (eds), *Bandung, Global History, and International Law: Critical Pasts and Pending Futures* (Cambridge: Cambridge University Press, 2017).

Everson, M and Joerges, C, 'The Legal Proprium of the Economic Constitution' in Kjaer, PF (ed), *The Law of Political Economy: Transformations of the Function of Law* (Cambridge: Cambridge University Press, 2020), 33.

Fakhri, M, *Sugar and the Making of International Trade Law* (Cambridge: Cambridge University Press, 2014).

Falk, R, 'Casting the Spell: The New Haven School of International Law' (1995) 104 *Yale Law Journal* 1991.

Fallon Jr, RH, 'The Meaning of Legal "Meaning" and Its Implications for Theories of Legal Interpretation' (2015) 82 *The University of Chicago Law Review* 1235.

Farer, TJ, 'Intervention in Unnatural Humanitarian Emergencies: Lessons of the First Phase' (1996) 18 *Human Rights Quarterly* 1.

Fasolt, C, *The Limits of History* (Chicago: University of Chicago Press, 2004).

Fassbender, B and Peters, A, 'Introduction: Towards a Global History of International Law' in Fassbender, B and Peters, A (eds), *The Oxford Handbook of the History of International Law* (Oxford: Oxford University Press, 2012), 2.

Fassin, D, *Michel Foucault* (trans B Wing) (London: Faber and Faber, 1992).

Fatouros, AA, 'International Law and the Third World' (1964) 50 *Virginia Law Review* 783.

Felski, R, '"Context Stinks!"' (2011) 42 *New Literary History* 573.
  The Limits of Critique (Chicago: Chicago University Press, 2015).

Fidler, DP, 'A Kinder, Gentler System of Capitulations? International Law, Structural Adjustment, and the Standards of Liberal, Globalized Civilization' (2000) 35 *Texas International Law Journal* 387.

Field, F, *The Last Days of Mankind: Karl Kraus and His Vienna* (London: Macmillan, 1967).

Filmer, R, *Patriarcha and Other Political Works*, ed Laslett, P (Oxford: Basil Blackwell, 1949).

Fisher III, WW, 'Texts and Contexts: The Application to American Legal History of the Methodologies of Intellectual History' (1997) 49 *Stanford Law Review* 1065.

Fitzmaurice, A, 'The Genealogy of *Terra Nullius*' (2007) 129 *Australian Historical Studies* 1.
  'Liberalism and Empire in Nineteenth-Century International Law' (2012) 117 *American Historical Review* 92.
  'Context in the History of International Law' (2018) 20 *Journal of the History of International Law* 5.

Fitzmaurice, G, 'The Law and Procedure of the International Court of Justice 1951–54: Treaty Interpretation and Certain Other Treaty Points' (1951) 28 *British Yearbook of International Law* 1.
  'The General Principles of International Law Considered from the Standpoint of the Rule of Law' (1957) 92 *Recueil des Cours* 1.

Fitzmaurice, M, 'Consent to Be Bound – Anything New Under the Sun?' (2005) 74 *Nordic Journal of International Law* 483.

Foks, F, 'The Sociological Imagination of the British New Left: "Culture" and the "Managerial Society", C. 1956–1962' (2018) 15 *Modern Intellectual History* 801.

Fossum, JE and Menéndez, AJ (eds), *The European Union in Crises or the European Union as Crises?* (Oslo: Arena Report Series, 2014).

Foucault, M, *Naissance de la Biopolitique: Cours au Collège de France, 1978–1979* (Paris: Éditions de Seuil/Gallimard, 2004).

The Birth of Biopolitics: Lectures at the Collège de France, 1978–79 (translated by Graham Burchell) (Hampshire and New York: Palgrave Macmillan, 2008).

Franck, TM, 'Editorial Comments: Terrorism and the Right of Self-Defense' (2001) 95 *American Journal of International Law* 839.

Recourse to Force: State Action against Threats and Armed Attack (Oxford: Oxford University Press, 2002).

'Criminals, Combatants, or What? An Examination of the Role of Law in Responding to the Threat of Terror' (2004) 98 *American Journal of International Law* 686.

Frank, JN, *Law and the Modern Mind* (New York: Coward-McCann, 1930).

Fraser, D, 'What a Long, Strange Trip It's Been: Deconstructing Law from Legal Realism to Critical Legal Studies' (1988–1989) 5 *Australian Journal of Legal Sociology* 35.

'"This Is Not Like Any Other Legal Question": A Brief History of Nazi Law before UK and US Courts' (2003) 19 *Connecticut Journal of International Law* 59.

Fried, BH, *The Progressive Assault on Laissez-Faire: Robert Hale and the First Law and Economics Movement* (Cambridge: Harvard University Press, 1998).

Fukuyama, F, *The End of History and the Last Man* (New York: Free Press, 2006).

Fuller, L, 'Positivism and Fidelity to Law – A Reply to Professor Hart' (1958) 71 *Harvard Law Review* 630.

Legal Fictions (Stanford: Stanford University Press, 1967).

Galindo, GRB, 'Martti Koskenniemi and the Historiographical Turn in International Law' (2005) 16 *European Journal of International Law* 539.

García-Salmones, M, 'Early Twentieth-Century Positivism Revisited' in Orford, A and Hoffmann, F (eds), *The Oxford Handbook of the Theory of International Law* (Oxford: Oxford University Press, 2016), 173.

Gathii, JT, 'Good Governance as a Counter Insurgency Agenda to Oppositional and Transformative Social Projects in International Law' (1999) 5 *Buffalo Human Rights Law Review* 107.

'Neoliberalism, Colonialism and International Governance: Decentering the International Law of Governmental Legitimacy' (2000) 98 *Michigan Law Review* 1996.

'A Critical Appraisal of the International Legal Tradition of Taslim Olawale Elias' (2008) 21 *Leiden Journal of International Law* 317.

Gerber, DJ, 'Constitutionalizing the Economy: German Neo-liberalism, Competition Law and the "New" Europe' (1994) 42 *American Journal of Comparative Law* 25.

Law and Competition in Twentieth Century Europe: Protecting Prometheus (Oxford: Oxford University Press 2001).

Getzler, J, 'Law, History, and the Social Sciences: Intellectual Traditions of Late Nineteenth- and Early Twentieth-Century Europe' in Lewis, A and Lobban, M (eds), *Law and History* (Oxford: Oxford University Press, 2004), 215.

Gienapp, J, 'Historicism and Holism: Failures of Originalist Translation' (2015) 84 *Fordham Law Review* 935.

Gill, S (ed), *Gramsci, Historical Materialism and International Relations* (Cambridge: Cambridge University Press, 1993).

Ginzburg, C, *History, Rhetoric, and Proof* (Hanover and London: University Press of New England, 1999).

    The Judge and the Historian: Marginal Notes on a Late-Twentieth-Century Miscarriage of Justice (London and New York: Verso, 1999).

    'The Bond of Shame' (2019) 120 *New Left Review* 35.

Glendon, MA, *A World Made New: Eleanor Roosevelt and the Universal Declaration of Human Rights* (New York: Random House 2002).

Glennon, MJ, 'The New Interventionism: The Search for a Just International Law' (1999) 78 *Foreign Affairs* 2.

Godden, L, 'Wik: Legal Memory and History' (1997) 6 *Griffith Law Review* 122.

Golder, B, 'Contemporary Legal Genealogies' in Desautels-Stein, J and Tomlins, C (eds), *Searching for Contemporary Legal Thought* (Cambridge: Cambridge University Press, 2017), 80.

Golder, B and McLoughlin, D (eds), *The Politics of Legality in a Neoliberal Age* (Oxon: Routledge, 2017).

Goldie, M, 'The Context of *The Foundations*' in Brett, A and Tully, J, with Hamilton-Bleakley, H (eds), *Rethinking the Foundations of Modern Political Thought* (Cambridge: Cambridge University Press, 2006), 3.

Goldsmith, JL, *The Terror Presidency: Law and Judgment Inside the Bush Administration* (New York and London: WW Norton & Co, 2007).

Goldsmith, J, 'The Contribution of the Obama Administration to the Practice and Theory of International Law' (2016) 57 *Harvard International Law Journal* 455.

Goldsmith, JL and Posner, EA, 'A Theory of Customary International Law' (1999) 66 *The University of Chicago Law Review* 1113.

    The Limits of International Law (Oxford: Oxford University Press, 2005).

    'The New International Law Scholarship' (2006) 34 *Georgia Journal of International and Comparative Law* 463.

Goodrich, P, 'The Critic's Love of the Law: Intimate Observations on an Insular Jurisdiction' (1999) 10 *Law and Critique* 343.

    '"Who Are We?": Persona, Office, Suspicion, and Critique' in Desautels-Stein, J and Tomlins, C (eds), *Searching for Contemporary Legal Thought* (Cambridge: Cambridge University Press, 2017), 43.

Gordon, G, 'Natural Law in International Legal Theory: Linear and Dialectical Presentations' in Orford, A and Hoffmann, F (eds), *The Oxford Handbook of the Theory of International Law* (Oxford: Oxford University Press, 2016), 279.

Gordon, PE, 'Contextualism and Criticism in the History of Ideas' in McMahon, DM and Moyn, S (eds), *Rethinking Modern European Intellectual History* (Oxford: Oxford University Press, 2014), 32.

Gordon, R, 'Saving Failed States: Sometimes a Neocolonialist Notion' (1997) 12 *American University Journal of International Law and Policy* 903.

Gordon, RW, 'J Willard Hurst and the Common Law Tradition in American Legal Historiography' (1975) 10 *Law and Society Review* 9.

    'Critical Legal Studies as a Teaching Method, against the Background of the Intellectual Politics of Modern Legal Education in the United States' (1989) 1 *Legal Education Review* 6.

'Foreword: The Arrival of Critical Historicism' (1997) 49 *Stanford Law Review* 10.

Taming the Past: Essays on Law in History and History in Law (Stanford: Stanford University Press, 2017).

Gormsen, LL, 'The Conflict between Economic Freedom and Consumer Welfare in the Modernisation of Article 82 EC' (2007) 3 *European Competition Journal* 329.

Gragl, P and Fitzmaurice, M, 'The Legal Character of Article 18 of the Vienna Convention on the Law of Treaties' (2019) 68 *International and Comparative Law Quarterly* 699.

Gray, C, *International Law and the Use of Force*, 4th edition (Oxford: Oxford University Press, 2018).

Greenman, K, 'Aliens in Latin America: Intervention, Arbitration, and State Responsibility for Rebels' (2018) 31 *Leiden Journal of International Law* 617.

Greenwood, C, 'Humanitarian Intervention: The Case of Kosovo' (1999) 10 *Finnish Yearbook of International Law* 168.

'International Law and the Pre-emptive Use of Force: Afghanistan, Al-Qaida, and Iraq' (2003) 4 *San Diego International Law Review* 7.

Grewal, DS and Purdy, J, 'Law and Neoliberalism' (2015) 77 *Law and Contemporary Problems* 1.

Grewe, WG, *The Epochs of International Law* (trans Byers, M) (Berlin: Walter de Gruyter, 2000 [1984]).

Grey, T, 'Holmes and Legal Pragmatism' (1989) 42 *Stanford Law Review* 787.

Guest, KJ, 'Exploitation under Erasure: Economic, Social and Cultural Rights Engage Economic Globalisation' (1997) 19 *Adelaide Law Review* 74.

Guggenheim, P, 'Contribution a l'histoire des sources du droit des gens' (1958) 94 *Recueil des Cours* 3.

Guilhot, N, 'Introduction: One Discipline, Many Histories' in N Guilhot (ed), *The Invention of International Relations Theory* (New York: Columbia University Press, 2011), 1.

'Portrait of the Realist as a Historian: On Anti-whiggism in the History of International Relations' (2015) 21 *European Journal of International Relations* 3.

After the Enlightenment: Political Realism and International Relations in the Mid-Twentieth Century (Cambridge: Cambridge University Press, 2017).

Guillaume, G, 'Droit international et action diplomatique: Le cas de la France' (1991) 2 *European Journal of International Law* 136.

Guldi, J and Armitage, D, *The History Manifesto* (Cambridge: Cambridge University Press, 2014).

Gunneflo, M, *Targeted Killing: A Legal and Political History* (Cambridge: Cambridge University Press, 2016).

Guzman, AT, 'The Design of International Agreements' (2005) 16 *European Journal of International Law* 579.

'Against Consent' (2012) 52 *Virginia Journal of International Law* 747.

Hacking, I, *The Social Construction of What?* (Cambridge: Harvard University Press, 1999).

Hägerström, A, *Inquiries into the Nature of Law and Morals* (Uppsala: Almquist & Wiksell, 1953).

Philosophy and Religion (Oxon: Routledge, 1964), 33, 74.

Hale, R, 'Coercion and Distribution in a Supposedly Non-Coercive State' (1923) 38 *Political Science Quarterly* 470.

Hall, I, 'History, Christianity, and Diplomacy: Sir Herbert Butterfield and International Relations' (2002) 28 *Review of International Studies* 719.

Hall, S, 'Introducing NLR' (1960) I/1 *New Left Review* 1.

'Life and Times of the First New Left' (2010) 61 *New Left Review* 177.

Halley, J, Kotiswaran, P, Rebouché, R, and Shamir, H (eds), *Governance Feminism: Notes from the Field* (Minneapolis and London: University of Minnesota Press, 2019).

Halperin, DM, *Saint Foucault: Towards a Gay Hagiography* (Oxford: Oxford University Press, 1995).

Hamilton, S, 'Foucault's End of History: The Temporality of Governmentality and Its End in the Anthropocene' (2018) 46 *Millennium* 371.

Harlow, C, 'Global Administrative Law: The Quest of Principles and Values' (2006) 17 *European Journal of International Law* 187.

Harootunian, H, *Marx after Marx: History and Time in the Expansion of Capitalism* (New York: Columbia University Press, 2015).

Hart, HLA, 'Positivism and the Separation of Law and Morals' (1958) 71 *Harvard Law Review* 593.

Hartog, F, 'The Present of the Historian' (2014) 4 *History of the Present: A Journal of Critical History* 203.

Regimes of Historicity: Presentism and Experiences of Time (New York: Columbia University Press, 2015).

Haslam, J, *No Virtue Like Necessity: Realist Thought in International Relations since Machiavelli* (New Haven: Yale University Press, 2002).

Hathaway, OA, 'Treaties' End: The Past, Present, and Future of International Lawmaking in the United States' (2008) 117 *Yale Law Journal* 1236.

'Presidential Power over International Law: Restoring the Balance' (2009) 119 *Yale Law Journal* 140.

Hay, D, Linebaugh, P, Rule, JG, Thompson, EP, and Winslow, C, *Albion's Fatal Tree: Crime and Society in Eighteenth-Century England* (London and New York: Verso, 2011 [1975]).

Head, JW, 'The Global Financial Crisis of 2008–2009 in Context – Reflections on International Legal and Institutional Failings, "Fixes", and Fundamentals' (2010) 23 *Global Business and Development Law Journal* 43.

Helfer, LR, 'Nonconsensual International Lawmaking' (2008) *University of Illinois Law Review* 71.

Heller, KJ, 'Specially-Affected States and the Formation of Custom' (2018) 112 *American Journal of International Law* 191.

Henkin, L, 'Kosovo and the Law of "Humanitarian Intervention"' (1999) 93 *American Journal of International Law* 826.

Hernández-Uriz, G, 'To Lend or Not to Lend: Oil, Human Rights and the World Bank's Internal Contradictions' (2001) 14 *Harvard Human Rights Journal* 197.

Hien, J and Joerges, C, 'Dead Man Walking? Current European Interest in the Ordoliberal Tradition' (2018) 24 *European Law Journal* 14.

'Introduction: Objectives and Contents of the Volume' in Hien, J and Joerges, C (eds), *Ordoliberalism, Law and the Rule of Economics* (Oxford and Portland: Hart, 2017), 1.

Hien, J and Joerges, C (eds), *Ordoliberalism, Law and the Rule of Economics* (Oxford and Portland: Hart, 2017).

Higgins, R, 'Diverging Anglo-American Attitudes to International Law' (1972) 2 *Georgia Journal of International and Comparative Law* 1.

'Time and the Law: International Perspectives on an Old Problem' (1997) 46 *International and Comparative Law Quarterly* 502.

'The Judicial Determination of Relevant Facts, Speech to the Sixth Committee of the General Assembly, 2 November 2007' in Higgins, R, *Themes and Theories* (Oxford: Oxford University Press, 2009), 1369.

'Introduction to the Symposium' (2018) 87 *British Yearbook of International Law* 101.

Hill, C, *Puritanism and Revolution* (London: Sicker & Warburg, 1958).

The Intellectual Origins of the English Revolution (New York: Oxford University Press, 1965).

The World Turned Upside Down (New York: Viking, 1972).

Hillman, J, 'Independence at the Top of the Triangle: Best Resolution of the Judicial Trilemma?' (2017) 111 *AJIL Unbound* 364.

Hilton, B, *A Mad, Bad, and Dangerous People? England 1783–1846* (Oxford: Clarendon Press Oxford, 2006).

Hirsch, E and Stewart, C, 'Introduction: Ethnographies of Historicity' (2005) 16 *History and Anthropology* 261.

Hobsbawm, E, *The Age of Revolution: Europe 1789–1848* (New York: Vintage, 1962).

Industry and Empire (New York: Pantheon, 1968).

Interesting Times: A Twentieth-Century Life (London: Allen Lane, 2002).

Hobsbawm, E and Ranger, T (eds), *The Invention of Tradition* (Cambridge: Cambridge University Press, 1983).

Hobsbawm, E and Rudé, G, *Captain Swing* (London: Phoenix Press, 1969).

Hodges, M, 'History's Impasse: Radical Historiography, Leftist Elites, and the Anthropology of Historicism in Southern France' (2019) 60 *Current Anthropology* 391.

Hoffmann, S-L, 'Koselleck in America' (2017) 132 *New German Critique* 167.

Holden, G, 'Who Contextualizes the Contextualizers? Disciplinary History and the Discourse about IR Discourse' (2002) 28 *Review of International Studies* 253.

Hollis, DB, 'Defining Treaties' in Hollis, DB (ed), *The Oxford Guide to Treaties* (Oxford: Oxford University Press, 2012), 10.

Holmes, DR, 'Communicative Imperatives in Central Banks' (2014) 47 *Cornell International Law Journal* 15.

Holmes, OW, 'The Path of the Law' (1897) 10 *Harvard Law Review* 457.

Hont, I, *Jealousy of Trade: International Competition and the Nation-State in Historical Perspective* (Cambridge, MA: Harvard University Press, 2005).

Höpfl, HM, 'Scholasticism in Quentin Skinner's *Foundations*' in Brett, A and Tully, J with Hamilton-Bleakley, H (eds), *Rethinking the Foundations of Modern Political Thought* (Cambridge: Cambridge University Press, 2006), 113.

Horn, H, Maggi, G, and Staiger, RW, 'Trade Agreements as Endogenously Incomplete Contracts' (2010) 100 *American Economic Review* 394.

Horwitz, MJ, *The Transformation of American Law, 1870–1960* (Oxford: Oxford University Press, 1992).

Howse, R, 'Adjudicative Legitimacy and Treaty Interpretation in International Trade Law: The Early Years of WTO Jurisprudence' in Weiler, JHH (ed) *The EU, the WTO, and the NAFTA: Towards a Common Law of International Trade* 35 (Oxford: Oxford University Press, 2000).

'Schmitt, Schmitteanism and Contemporary International Legal Theory' in Orford, A and Hoffmann, F (eds), *The Oxford Handbook of the Theory of International Law* (Oxford: Oxford University Press, 2016), 212.

'The World Trade Organization 20 Years On: Global Governance by Judiciary' (2016) 27 *European Journal of International Law* 9.

Hu, J, 'Build towards a Harmonious World of Lasting Peace and Common Prosperity', New York, September 15, 2005, https://www.un.org/webcast/summit2005/state ments15/china050915eng.pdf.

Hueck, IJ, 'The Discipline of the History of International Law – New Trends and Methods on the History of International Law' (2001) 3 *Journal of the History of International Law* 194.

Hull, I, 'Anything Can Be Rescinded' (2018) 40(8) *London Review of Books* 25.

Hull, IV, *A Scrap of Paper: Breaking and Making International Law during the Great War* (Ithaca and London: Cornell University Press, 2014).

Humphreys, S and Otomo, Y, 'Theorizing International Environmental Law' in Orford, A and Hoffmann, F (eds), *The Oxford Handbook of the Theory of International Law* (Oxford: Oxford University Press, 2016), 797.

Hunt, L, 'Against Presentism', *Perspectives on History* (May 2002).

Inventing Human Rights: A History (New York and London: WW Norton & Company, 2007).

Writing History in the Global Era (New York and London: WW Norton and Company, 2014).

Hunter, I, 'Metaphysics as a Way of Life' (1994) 23 *Economy and Society* 93.

Rival Enlightenments: Civil and Metaphysical Philosophy in Early Modern Germany (Cambridge: Cambridge University Press, 2001), 12.

'The State of History and the Empire of Metaphysics' (2005) 44 *History and Theory* 289.

'The History of Theory' (2006) 33 *Critical Inquiry* 78, at 98.

'The History of Philosophy and the Persona of the Philosopher' (2007) 4 *Modern Intellectual History* 571.

'Natural Law, Historiography, and Aboriginal Sovereignty' (2007) 11 *Legal History* 137.

'Talking about My Generation' (2008) 34 *Critical Inquiry* 583.

'Postmodernist Histories' (2009) 19 *Intellectual History Review* 265.

'Vattel's Law of Nations: Diplomatic Casuistry for the Protestant Nation' (2010) 31 *Grotiana* 108.

'Global Justice and Regional Metaphysics: On the Critical History of the Law of Nature and Nations' in Dorsett, S and Hunter, I (eds), *Law and Politics in British Colonial Thought: Transpositions of Empire* (New York: Palgrave Macmillan, 2010), 11.

'The Figure of Man and the Territorialisation of Justice in "Enlightenment" Natural Law: Pufendorf and Vattel' (2013) 23 *Intellectual History Review* 289.

'The Mythos, Ethos, and Pathos of the Humanities' (2014) 40 *History of European Ideas* 11.

'About the Dialectical Historiography of International Law' (2016) 1 *Global Intellectual History* 1.

'The Contest over Context in Intellectual History' (2019) 58 *History and Theory* 185.

Huntington, SP, *The Clash of Civilizations and the Remaking of World Order* (New York: Touchstone, 1996).

Hurrell, A, 'Hegemony, Liberalism and Global Order: What Space for Would-Be Great Powers?' (2016) 82 *International Affairs* 1.

Ibbetson, D, 'What Is Legal History a History of?' in Lewis, A and Lobban, M (eds), *Law and History* (Oxford: Oxford University Press, 2004), 33.

Ikenberry, GJ, 'The Rise of China and the Future of the West: Can the Liberal System Survive?' (2008) 87 *Foreign Affairs* 23.

Irving, H, 'Outsourcing the Law: History and the Disciplinary Limits of Constitutional Reasoning' (2015) 84 *Fordham Law Review* 957.

Isaac, J, 'Progress, Innovation and the Problem of Conceptual Change', Paper presented at the *History, Politics, Law: Thinking through the International Conference*, May 2016.

Jackson, JH, 'Constitutional Treaties: Institutional Necessity and Challenge to International Law Fundamentals' in Cremona, M, Hilpold, P, Lavranos, N, Schneider, SS, and Ziegler, AR (eds), *Reflections on the Constitution of International Economic Law* (Leiden and Boston: Martinus Nijhoff, 2014), 193.

James, S, 'JGA Pocock and the Idea of the "Cambridge School" in the History of Political Thought' (2019) 45 *History of European Ideas* 83.

Janik, A and Toulmin, S, *Wittgenstein's Vienna* (Chicago: Ivan R Dee, 1996).

Jay, M, 'Historical Explanation and the Event: Reflections on the Limits of Contextualization' (2011) 42 *New Literary History* 557.

Jessup, 'Non-Universal International Law' (1973) 12 *Columbia Journal of Transnational Law* 415.

Jiang, S, 'Philosophy and History: Interpreting the "Xi Jinping Era" through Xi's Report to the Nineteenth National Congress of the CCP', *The China Story*, May 11, 2018, www.thechinastory.org/cot/jiang-shigong-on-philosophy-and-history-interpreting-the-xi-jinping-era-through-xis-report-to-the-nineteenth-national-congress-of-the-ccp/.

Jiang, S, 'The Internal Logic of Super-Sized Political Entities: "Empire" and World Order' (trans D Ownby), www.readingthechinadream.com/jiang-shigong-empire-and-world-order.html.

Joas, H, *The Sacredness of the Person: A New Genealogy of Human Rights* (Washington, DC: Georgetown University Press, 2013).

Joerges, C, 'State without a Market? Comments on the German Constitutional Court's Maastricht-Judgement and a Plea for Interdisciplinary Discourses' (1997) European Integration online Papers (EIoP), Vol. 1, No. 20, http://eiop.or.at/eiop/texte/1997-020a.htm.

'The Market without the State? The "Economic Constitution" of the European Community and the Rebirth of Regulatory Politics' (1997) European Integration online Papers (EIoP), Vol. 1, No. 19, http://eiop.or.at/eiop/texte/1997-019a.htmJoerges.

'The Science of Private Law and the Nation-State' in Snyder, F (ed), *The Europeanisation of Law: The Legal Effects of European Integration* (Oxford: Hart, 2000), 47.

'Continuities and Discontinuities in German Legal Thought' (2003) 14 *Law and Critique* 297.

'Europe a Großraum? Shifting Legal Conceptualisations of the Integration Project' in Joerges, C and Ghaleigh, NS (eds), *Darker Legacies of Law in Europe: The Shadow of National Socialism and Fascism over Europe and Its Legal Traditions* (Oxford: Hart, 2003), 167.

'What Is Left of the European Economic Constitution? A Melancholic Eulogy' (2005) 30 *European Law Review* 461.

'German Perspectives and Fantasies' (2011) 12 *German Law Journal* 10.

'Europe's Economic Constitution in Crisis and the Emergence of a New Constitutional Constellation' (2014) 15 *German Law Journal* 986.

'The Overburdening of Law by Ordoliberalism and the Integration Project' in Hien, J and Joerges, C (eds), *Ordoliberalism, Law and the Rule of Economics* (Oxford and Portland: Hart, 2017), 179.

'"Where the Law Runs Out": The Overburdening of Law and Constitutional Adjudication by the Financial Crisis and Europe's New Modes of Economic Governance' in Garben, S, Govaere, I, and Nemitz, P (eds), *Critical Reflections on Constitutional Democracy in the European Union* (Oxford: Hart, 2019), 168.

Joerges, C and Everson, M, 'The Legal Proprium of the Economic Constitution' in Kjaer, PF (ed), *The Law of Political Economy: Transformations of the Function of Law* (Cambridge: Cambridge University Press, 2020), 33.

Joerges, C and Ghaleigh, NS, *Darker Legacies of Law in Europe: The Shadow of National Socialism and Fascism over Europe and Its Legal Traditions* (Oxford and Portland: Hart, 2003).

Joerges, C and Glinski, C (eds), *The European Crisis and the Transformation of Transnational Governance: Authoritarian Managerialism versus Democratic Governance* (Oxford: Hart, 2014).

Joerges, C and Petersmann, E-U (eds), *Constitutionalism, Multilevel Trade Governance and International Economic Law* (Oxford: Hart, 2011).

Joerges, C and Rödl, F, '"Social Market Economy" as Europe's Social Model?', EUI Working Paper Law No. 2004/8 (2004).

Johns, F, 'Guantánamo Bay and the Annihilation of the Exception' (2005) 16 *European Journal of International Law* 613.

'Financing as Governance' (2011) 31 *Oxford Journal of Legal Studies* 391.

Johns, F, Skouteris, T, and Werner, W, 'The League of Nations and the Construction of the Periphery Introduction' (2011) 24 *Leiden Journal of International Law* 797.

Jones, O, 'Introduction' in Williams, R (ed), *May Day Manifesto 1968* (London: Verso, 2018), 1.

Jouannet, E and Ruiz Fabri, H (eds), *Le droit international et l'impérialisme en Europe et aux Amériques* (Paris: Société de droit et de legislation comparée, 2007).

Jütersonke, O, 'Realist Approaches to International Law' in Orford, A and Hoffmann, F (eds), *The Oxford Handbook of the Theory of International Law* (Oxford: Oxford University Press, 2016), 327.

Kagan, R, *Paradise and Power: America and Europe in the New World Order* (London: Atlantic, 2003).

Kahn, PW, 'American Exceptionalism, Popular Sovereignty, and the Rule of Law' in Ignatieff, M (ed), *American Exceptionalism and Human Rights* (Princeton: Princeton University Press, 2005), 198.

Kahn-Freund, O, 'Hugo Sinzheimer 1875–1945' in Kahn-Freund, O (ed), *Labour Law and Politics in the Weimar Republic* (Oxford: Basil Blackwell, 1981), 73.

Kammerhofer, J, 'The Future of Restrictive Scholarship on the Use of Force' (2016) 29 *Leiden Journal of International Law* 13.

 'The Challenges of History in International Investment Law: A View from Legal Theory' in Schill, SW, Tams, CJ, and Hofmann, R (eds), *International Investment Law and History* (Cheltenham: Edward Elgar, 2018), 164.

Kantorowicz, H, 'Savigny and the Historical School' (1937) 53 *Law Quarterly Review* 326.

Kaplan, RD, 'How We Would Fight China' (June 2005) *The Atlantic* 49.

Karl, R, 'Foreword to the English Edition' in Wang, H, *The End of the Revolution: China and the Limits of Modernity* (London and New York: Verso, 2009), vii.

Kattan, V, 'Furthering the "War on Terrorism" through International Law: How the United States and the United Kingdom Resurrected the Bush Doctrine on Using Preventing Military Force to Combat Terrorism' (2018) 5 *Journal on the Use of Force and International Law* 97.

Kaye, H, *The Education of Desire: Marxists and the Writing of History* (New York and London: Routledge, 1992).

Keene, E, *Beyond the Anarchical Society: Grotius, Colonialism and Order in World Politics* (Cambridge: Cambridge University Press, 2002).

 'The English School and British Historians' (2008) 37 *Millennium* 381.

 'International Intellectual History and International Relations: Contexts, Canons and Mediocrities' (2017) 31 *International Relations* 341.

Keishiro, I, 'The Principles of International Law in the Light of Confucian Doctrine' (1967) 120 *Recueil des Cours* 1.

Kelley, DR, 'Legal Humanism and the Sense of History' (1966) 13 *Studies in the Renaissance* 184.

 Foundations of Modern Historical Scholarship: Language, Law, and History in the French Renaissance (New York: Columbia University Press, 1970).

 'History, English Law, and the Renaissance' (1974) 65 *Past and Present* 24.

Kelly, AH, 'Clio and the Court: An Illicit Love Affair' (1965) 119 *Supreme Court Review* 121.

Kelly, JP, 'The Twilight of Customary International Law' (2000) 40 *Virginia Journal of International Law* 449.

Kelly, P, 'Rescuing Political Theory from the Tyranny of History' in Floyd, J and Stears, M (eds), *Political Philosophy versus History? Contextualism and Real Politics in Contemporary Political Thought* (Cambridge: Cambridge University Press, 2011).

Kelsen, H, *General Theory of Law and State* (Cambridge: Harvard University Press, 1945).

 Pure Theory of Law (trans Knight, M.) (Berkeley: University of California Press, 1967).

 General Theory of Norms (trans Hartney, M) (Oxford: Clarendon Press, 1991 [1979]).

Kennedy, D(avid), 'The Sources of International Law' (1987) 2 *American University Journal of International Law and Policy* 1.

'The Move to Institutions' (1986–1987) 8 *Cardozo Law Review* 841.

'Autumn Weekends: An Essay on Law and Everyday Life' in A Sarat and TR Kearns (eds), *Law in Everyday Life* (Ann Arbor: University of Michigan Press, 1993), 191.

'The International Style in Postwar Law and Policy: John Jackson and the Field of International Economic Law' (1995) 10 *American University Law Review* 671.

'International Law and the Nineteenth Century: History of an Illusion' (1997) 17 *Quinnipiac Law Review* 99.

'What Is New Thinking in International Law?' (2000) 94 *Proceedings of the ASIL Annual Meeting* 104.

'When Renewal Repeats: Thinking against the Box' (2000) 32 *New York University Journal of International Law and Politics* 335.

'The International Human Rights Movement: Part of the Problem?' (2002) 15 *Harvard Human Rights Journal* 101.

The Dark Sides of Virtue: Reassessing International Humanitarianism (Princeton: Princeton University Press, 2005).

Of War and Law (Princeton: Princeton University Press, 2006).

'Law and the Political Economy of the World' (2013) 26 *Leiden Journal of International Law* 7.

A World of Struggle: How Power, Law, and Expertise Shape Global Political Economy (Princeton and Oxford: Princeton University Press, 2016).

'The Context for Context: International Legal History in Struggle' in Brett, A, Donaldson, M, and Koskenniemi, M (eds), *History, Politics, Law: Thinking Internationally* (Cambridge: Cambridge University Press, forthcoming 2021).

Kennedy, D(uncan), 'Distributive and Paternalistic Motives in Contract and Tort Law, with Special Reference to Compulsory Terms and Unequal Bargaining Power' (1982) 41 *Maryland Law Review* 563.

'Legal Education as Training for Hierarchy' in D Kairys (ed), *The Politics of Law* (New York: Pantheon Books, 1982), 54.

'The Stakes of Law, or Hale and Foucault!' (1991) XV *Legal Studies Forum* 327.

'A Semiotics of Legal Argument' in Academy of European Law (ed), *The Protection of Human Rights in Europe* (Dordrecht/Boston/London: Kluwer/Martinus Nijhoff, 1994), 309.

A Critique of Adjudication: Fin de Siècle (1997).

'The Political Stakes in "Merely Technical" Issues of Contract Law' (2001) 19 *European Review of Private Law* 7.

'The Disenchantment of Logically Formal Legal Rationality, or Max Weber's Sociology in the Genealogy of the Contemporary Mode of Western Legal Thought' (2004) 55 *Hastings Law Journal* 1031.

'Three Globalizations of Law and Legal Thought: 1850–2000' in Trubek, DM and Santos, A (eds), *The New Law and Economic Development: A Critical Appraisal* (Cambridge: Cambridge University Press, 2006), 19.

'The Hermeneutic of Suspicion in Contemporary American Legal Thought' (2014) 25 *Law and Critique* 91.

Kennedy, D and Stiglitz, J (eds), *Law and Economics with Chinese Characteristics* (Oxford: Oxford University Press, 2013).

Kennedy, D and Tennant, C, 'New Approaches to International Law: A Bibliography' (1994) 35 *Harvard International Law Journal* 417.

Kennedy, EL, 'Socialist Feminism: What Difference Did It Make to the History of Women's Studies?' (2008) 34 *Feminist Studies* 497.

Khadduri, M, 'Islam and the Modern Law of Nations' (1956) 50 *American Journal of International Law* 358.

    The Islamic Law of Nations: Shaybānī's Siyar (Baltimore: John Hopkins Press, 1966).

Kingsbury, B, 'International Courts: Uneven Judicialisation in Global Order' in Crawford, J and Koskenniemi, M (eds), *The Cambridge Companion to International Law* (Cambridge: Cambridge University Press, 2012), 203.

    'The Concept of "Law" in Global Administrative Law' (2009) 20 *European Journal of International Law* 23.

Kingsbury, B, Donaldson, M, and Vallejo, R, 'Global Administrative Law and Deliberative Democracy' in Orford, A and Hoffmann, F (eds), *The Oxford Handbook of the Theory of International Law* (Oxford: Oxford University Press, 2016), 526.

Kingsbury, B, Krisch, N, and Stewart, R, 'The Emergence of Global Administrative Law' (2005) 68 *Law and Contemporary Problems* 15.

Kinnear, M, Fischer, GR, Almedia, JM, Torres, LF, and Bidegain, MU (eds), *Building International Investment Law: The First 50 Years of ICSID* (Alphen aan den Rijn: Wolters Kluwer, 2016).

Kirby, J, 'History, Law and Freedom: FW Maitland in Context' (2019) 16 *Modern Intellectual History* 127.

Kissinger, H, *On China* (New York: Penguin, 2011).

Klabbers, J, 'The Commodification of International Law' in Ruiz Fabri, H, Jouannet, E, and Tomkiewicz, V (eds), *Select Proceedings of the European Society of International Law, Volume 1* (Oxford: Hart, 2008), 341.

    The Concept of Treaty in International Law (The Hague: Kluwer, 1996).

    'Treaties and Their Preambles' in Bowman, M and Kritsiotis, D (eds), *Conceptual and Contextual Perspectives on the Modern Law of Treaties* (Cambridge: Cambridge University Press, 2018), 172.

Klein, N, *Dispute Settlement in the UN Convention on the Law of the Sea* (Cambridge: Cambridge University Press, 2009).

Kleinberg, E, Scott, JW, and Wilder, G, *Theses on Theory and History* (Wild on Collective, May 2018).

Kleinberg, E, Wallach Scott, J, and Wilder, G, 'From the Authors of the "Theses on Theory and History"', *In the Moment Blog*, July 10, 2018, available at https://critinq.wordpress.com/2018/07/10/from-the-authors-of-the-theses-on-theory-and-history/.

Knop, K, 'The Hart-Fuller Debate's Silence on Human Rights' in Cane, P (ed), *The Hart-Fuller Debate in the Twenty-First Century* (London: Hart, 2010), 61.

Knox, R and Tzouvala, N, 'Looking Eastwards: The Bolshevik Theory of Imperialism and International Law' in Greenman, K, Orford, A, Saunders, A, and Tzouvala, N (eds), *Revolutions in International Law: The Legacies of 1917* (Cambridge: Cambridge University Press, 2020), 27.

Koh, HH, 'Is There a "New" New Haven School of International Law?' (2007) 32 *Yale Journal of International Law* 559.

'Remarks: Twenty-First Century International Lawmaking' (2013) 101 *Georgetown Law Journal* 725.

'The State Department Legal Adviser's Office: Eight Decades in Peace and War' (2012) 100 *Georgetown Law Journal* 1747.

'Syria and the Law of Humanitarian Intervention (Part II: International Law and the Way Forward)', *Just Security*, 2 October 2013, http://justsecurity.org/1506/koh-syria-part2/.

'Transnational Legal Process' (1996) 75 *Nebraska Law Review* 181.

'Triptych's End: A Better Framework to Evaluate 21st Century International Lawmaking' (2017) 126 *Yale Law Journal Forum* 338.

Koh, JK, 'Reservations to Multilateral Treaties: How International Legal Doctrine Reflects World Vision' (1982) 23 *Harvard International Law Journal* 71.

Koikkalainen, P, 'Peter Laslett and the Contested Concept of Political Philosophy' (2009) 30 *History of Political Thought* 336.

'The Politics of Contextualism: Normativity and the New Historians of Political Thought' (2015) 9 *Journal of the Philosophy of History* 347.

Korhonen, O, *International Law Situated: An Analysis of the Lawyer's Stance Towards Culture, History and Community* (The Hague: Kluwer, 2000).

'New International Law: Silence, Defence or Deliverance?' (1996) 7 *European Journal of International Law* 1.

Koselleck, R, *Critique and Crisis: Enlightenment and the Pathogenesis of Modern Society* (Cambridge: The MIT Press, 1988 [1959]).

Futures Past: On the Semantics of Historical Time (trans K Tribe) (New York: Columbia University Press, 2004).

The Practice of Conceptual History: Timing History, Spacing Concepts (trans Presner, TS and Others) (Stanford: Stanford University Press, 2002).

Koskenniemi, M, 'Between Commitment and Cynicism: Outline for a Theory of International Law as Practice' in *Collection of Essays by Legal Advisors of States, Legal Advisers of International Organizations and Practitioners in the Field of International Law* (New York: United Nations, 1999), 495.

'Letter to the Editors of the Symposium' (1999) 93 *American Journal of International Law* 351.

The Gentle Civilizer of Nations: The Rise and Fall of International Law 1870–1960 (Cambridge: Cambridge University Press, 2001).

'"The Lady Doth Protest Too Much" Kosovo, and the Turn to Ethics in International Law' (2002) 65 *Modern Law Review* 159.

'Introduction: Alf Ross and Life Beyond Realism' (2003) 14 *European Journal of International Law* 653.

'Why History of International Law Today?' (2004) 4 *Rechtsgeschichte* 61.

'International Law as Political Theology: How to Read *Nomos der Erde*?' (2004) 11 *Constellations* 492.

'International Law and Hegemony: A Reconfiguration' (2004) 17 *Cambridge Review of International Affairs* 197.

From Apology to Utopia: The Structure of International Legal Argument, Reissue with New Epilogue (Cambridge: Cambridge University Press, 2005).

'International Legislation Today: Limits and Possibilities' (2005) 23 *Wisconsin Journal of International Law* 61.

'Law, Teleology and International Relations: An Essay in Counterdisciplinarity' (2011) 26 *International Relations* 3.

'Histories of International Law: Dealing with Eurocentricity' (2011) 19 *Rechtsgeschichte* 152.

'A History of International Law Histories' in Fassbender, B and Peters, A (eds), *The Oxford Handbook of the History of International Law* (Oxford: Oxford University Press, 2012), 943.

'Epilogue: To Enable and Enchant – On the Power of Law' in Werner, W, de Hoon, M and Galan, A (eds), *The Law of International Lawyers: Reading Martti Koskenniemi* (Cambridge: Cambridge University Press, 2017), 393.

International Law and the Far Right: Reflections on Law and Cynicism (The Hague: Asser Press, 2019).

Koskenniemi, M, Rech, W, and Jiménez Fonseca, M (eds), *International Law and Empire: Historical Explorations* (Oxford: Oxford University Press, 2017).

Kratochwil, F, 'Looking Back from Somewhere: Reflections on What Remains "Critical" in Critical Theory' (2007) 33 *Review of International Studies* 25.

'Has the "Rule of Law" Become a "Rule of Lawyers"?' in Palombella, G and Walker, N (eds), *Relocating the Rule of Law* (Oxford and Portland: Hart, 2009), 171.

Kreitner, R, 'The Jurisprudence of Global Money' (2010) 11 *Theoretical Inquiries in Law* 177.

Krieger, Heike, *The Kosovo Conflict and International Law: An Analytical Documentation 1974–1999* (Cambridge: Cambridge University Press, 2001).

Krisch, N, 'International Law in Times of Hegemony: Unequal Power and the Shaping of the International Legal Order' (2005) 16 *European Journal of International Law* 369.

'The Decay of Consent: International Law in an Age of Global Public Goods' (2014) 108 *American Journal of International Law* 1.

Kritsiotis, D, 'Theorizing International Law on Force and Intervention' in Orford, A and Hoffmann, F (eds), *The Oxford Handbook of the Theory of International Law* (Oxford: Oxford University Press, 2016), 655.

'The Object and Purpose of a Treaty's Object and Purpose' in Bowman M and Kritsiotis, D (eds), *Conceptual and Contextual Perspectives on the Modern Law of Treaties* (Cambridge: Cambridge University Press, 2018), 237.

Kunz, J, 'The Nature of Customary International Law' (1953) 47 *American Journal of International Law* 658.

LaCapra, D, *Rethinking Intellectual History: Texts, Contexts, Language* (Ithaca and London: Cornell University Press, 1983).

Lacey, N, 'Reinterpreting the Context and Reassessing the Significance of the Hart-Fuller Debate' in Cane, P (ed), *The Hart-Fuller Debate in the Twenty-First Century* (London: Hart, 2010), 1.

Laghmani, S, *Histoire du droit des gens: du jus gentium impérial au jus publicum europaeum* (Paris: Pedone, 2004).

'L'ambivalence du renouveau du *jus gentium*' in Ruiz Fabri, H, Jouannet, E, and Tomkiewicz, V (eds), *Select Proceedings of the European Society of International Law, Volume 1 2006* (Oxford and Portland: Hart, 2008).

Landauer, C, 'Antinomies of the United Nations: Hans Kelsen and Alf Ross on the Charter' (2003) 14 *European Journal of International Law* 767.

'Erwin Panofsky and the Renascence of the Renaissance' (1994) 47 *Renaissance Quarterly* 255.

Lang, A, *World Trade Law after Neoliberalism: Re-Imagining the Global Economic Order* (Oxford: Oxford University Press, 2011).

'The Judicial Sensibility of the WTO Appellate Body' (2017) 27 *European Journal of International Law* 1096.

Laslett, P, 'Introduction' in Laslett, P (ed), *Philosophy, Politics and Society* (Oxford: Basil Blackwell, 1956), vii.

'Sir Robert Filmer: The Man versus the Whig Myth' (1948) 5 *The William and Mary Quarterly* 523.

'The English Revolution and Locke's "Two Treatises of Government"' (1956) 12 *Cambridge Historical Journal* 40.

'The Face to Face Society' in Laslett, P (ed), *Philosophy, Politics and Society* (Oxford: Basil Blackwell, 1956), 157.

Latour, B, 'Why Has Critique Run Out of Steam? From Matters of Fact to Matters of Concern' (2004) 30 *Critical Inquiry* 225.

Lauterpacht, H, *The Development of International Law by the International Court* (London: Stevens and Sons, 1958).

The Function of Law in the International Community (Oxford: Oxford University Press, 2011 [1933]).

Lechevalier, A, 'Why and How Has German Ordoliberalism Become a French Issue? Some Aspects about Ordoliberal Thoughts We Can Learn from the French Reception' in Hien, J and Joerges, C (eds), *Ordoliberalism, Law and the Rule of Economics* (Oxford and Portland: Hart, 2017), 23.

Lehto, M, 'The Fight against ISIL in Syria. Comments on the Recent Discussion of the Right of Self-defence against Non-state Actors' (2018) 87 *Nordic Journal of International Law* 1.

Lemaitre, J, 'The View from Somewhere: On Samuel Moyn's Not Enough', *Law and Political Economy Blog*, July 9, 2018, available at https://lpeblog.org/2018/07/09/the-view-from-somewhere-on-samuel-moyns-not-enough/.

Lepsius, O, 'The Problem of Perceptions of National Socialist Law Or: Was There a Constitutional Theory of National Socialism?' in Joerges, C and Ghaleigh, NS (eds), *Darker Legacies of Law in Europe: The Shadow of National Socialism and Fascism over Europe and Its Legal Traditions* (Oxford: Hart, 2003), 19.

Lesaffer, R, 'International Law and Its History: The Story of an Unrequited Love' in Craven, M, Fitzmaurice, M, and Vogiatzi, M (eds), *Time, History, and International Law* (Leiden: Martinus Nijhoff, 2007), 27.

'Law and History. Law between Past and Present' in van Klink, B and Taekema, S (eds), *Law and Method: Interdisciplinary Research into Law* (Tübingen: Mohr Siebeck, 2011), 133.

Levine, JM, *Humanism and History: Origins of Modern Historiography* (Ithaca: Cornell University Press, 1987).

Li, M, *Five Principles of Peaceful Coexistence: Continuity and Challenges*, A Series of Lectures at the Xiamen Academy of International Law, 2017.

Lim, CL (ed), *Alternative Visions of the International Law on Foreign Investment: Essays in Honour of Muthucumaraswamy Sornarajah* (Cambridge: Cambridge University Press, 2016).

Lim, CL, 'The Strange Vitality of Custom in the International Protection of Property, Contracts, and Commerce' in Bradley, CA (ed), *Custom's*

Future: International Law in a Changing World (Cambridge: Cambridge University Press, 2016), 205.

'The Worm's View of History and the Twailing Machine' in Lim, CL (ed), *Alternative Visions of the International Law on Foreign Investment: Essays in Honour of Muthucumaraswamy Sornarajah* (Cambridge: Cambridge University Press, 2016), 3.

Lindkvist, L, *Shrines and Souls: The Reinvention of Religious Liberty and the Genesis of the Universal Declaration of Human Rights* (Malmö: Bokbox, 2014).

Linklater, A, *The Transformation of Political Community: Ethical Foundations of the Post-Westphalian Era* (Cambridge: Polity Press, 1998).

Liu, X, 'New China and the End of American "International Law"' (2019) III(3) *American Affairs* 155.

Llewellyn, K, 'On the Problem of Teaching "Private" Law' (1941) 54 *Harvard Law Review* 775.

'On What Is Wrong with So-Called Legal Education' (1935) 35 *Columbia Law Review* 651.

Llewellyn, KN, 'The Normative, the Legal, and the Law-Jobs: The Problem of Juristic Method' (1940) 49 *Yale Law Journal* 1355.

Jurisprudence: Realism in Theory and Practice (Chicago: University of Chicago Press, 1962).

Lo, VI and Hiscock, M (eds), *The Rise of the BRICS in the Global Political Economy* (Cheltenham: Edward Elgar, 2014).

Lobban, M, 'Custom, Common Law Reasoning and the Law of Nations in the Nineteenth Century' in Perreau-Saussine, A and Murphy, JB (eds), *The Nature of Customary Law: Legal, Historical and Philosophical Perspectives* (Cambridge: Cambridge University Press, 2007), 256.

Locke, J, *Two Treatises of Government*, ed Laslett, P (Cambridge: Cambridge University Press, 1988 [1960]).

Long, D, and Schmidt, BC (eds), *Imperialism and Internationalism in the Discipline of International Relations* (Albany: State University New York Press, 2005).

Loraux, N, 'Éloge d'anachronisme en histoire' (1993) 27 *Le Genre Humain* 23.

Lovejoy, A, *The Great Chain of Being* (New York: Torchbook, 1960).

Mach, E, *Contributions to the Analysis of the Sensations* (trans CM Williams) (Chicago: Open Court, 1897).

Maduro, M, Tuori, K, and Sankari, S (eds), *Transnational Law: Rethinking European Law and Legal Thinking* (Cambridge: Cambridge University Press, 2014).

MARHO: The Radical Historians Organization, *Visions of History: Interviews with EP Thompson, Eric Hobsbawm, Sheila Rowbotham, Linda Gordon, Natalie Zemon Davis, William Appleman Williams, Staughton Lynd, David Montgomery, Herbert Gutman, Vincent Harding, John Womack, CLR James, and Moshe Lewin* (New York: Pantheon, 1983).

Maitland, FW, *Domesday Book and Beyond: Three Essays in the Early History of England* (Cambridge: Cambridge University Press, 1897).

'A Prologue to a History of English Law' (1898) 14 *Law Quarterly Review* 13.

English Law and the Renaissance (Cambridge: Cambridge University Press, 1901).

Constitutional History of England – A Course of Lectures Delivered (Cambridge: Cambridge University Press, 1908).

'The Law of Real Property' in HAL Fisher (ed), *The Collected Papers of Frederic William Maitland* (Cambridge: Cambridge University Press, 1911 [1879]), 162.

'The Making of the German Civil Code' in Fisher, HAL (ed), *The Collected Papers of Frederic William Maitland Volume 3* (Cambridge: Cambridge University Press, 1911 [1879]), 474.

'The Mystery of Seisin' in Fisher, HAL (ed), *The Collected Papers of Frederic William Maitland* (Cambridge: Cambridge University Press, 1911 [1879]), 358.

'Why the History of English Law Is Not Written' in Fisher, HAL (ed), *The Collected Papers of Frederic William Maitland* (Cambridge: Cambridge University Press, 1911 [1888]), 480.

The Forms of Action at Common Law (Cambridge: Cambridge University Press, 1965 [1909]).

State, Trust and Corporation, eds Runciman, D and Ryan, M (Cambridge: Cambridge University Press, 2003).

Maitland, FW and Montague, FC, *A Sketch of English Legal History* (New York and London: GP Putman's Sons, 1915).

Mäki, U, Walsh, A, and Pinto, MF (eds), *Scientific Imperialism: Exploring the Boundaries of Interdisciplinarity* (London and New York: Routledge, 2018).

Malabou, C, 'The Brain of History, or, the Mentality of the Anthropocene' (2017) 116 *South Atlantic Quarterly* 39.

Mälksoo, L, 'Russia and China Challenge the Western Hegemony in the Interpretation of International Law', *EJIL: Talk!*, 15 July, 2016, www.ejiltalk.org/russia-and-china-challenge-the-western-hegemony-in-the-interpretation-of-international-law/.

Mallard, G and Sgard, J (eds), *Contractual Knowledge: One Hundred Years of Legal Experimentation in Global Markets* (Cambridge: Cambridge University Press, 2016).

Mann, H, 'International Investment Agreements: Building the New Colonialism?' (2003) 97 *Proceedings of the ASIL Annual Meeting* 247.

Maogoto, JN, *Battling Terrorism: Legal Perspectives on the Use of Force and the War on Terror* (London and New York: Routledge, 2005).

Marks, S, 'Empire's Law' (2003) 10 *Indiana Journal of Global Legal Studies* 449.

'Naming Global Administrative Law' (2005) 37 *New York University Journal of International Law and Politics* 995.

'False Contingency' (2009) 62 *Current Legal Problems* 1.

'Human Rights and Root Causes' (2011) 74 *Modern Law Review* 57.

Martinez, JS, *The Slave Trade and the Origins of International Human Rights Law* (New York: Oxford University Press, 2012).

Matheson, M, 'Justification for the NATO Air Campaign in Kosovo' (2000) 94 *Proceedings of the ASIL Annual Meeting* 301.

Mattei, U, 'A Theory of Imperial Law: A Study on US Hegemony and the Latin Resistance' (2003) 10 *Indiana Journal of Global Legal Studies* 383.

Maurer, B, 'Regulation as Retrospective Ethnography: Mobile Money and the Arts of Cash' (2011) 21 *Banking and Finance Law Review* 299.

Mavroidis, PC and Sapir, A, 'China and the world trade organisation: Towards a better fit', Working Paper, Issue 06, 11 June 2019, Bruegel, available at www.bruegel.org/2019/06/china-and-the-world-trade-organisation-towards-a-better-fit/.

Mazower, M, *No Enchanted Palace: The End of Empire and the Ideological Origins of the United Nations* (Princeton: Princeton University Press, 2013).

McAdam, J, 'An Intellectual History of Freedom of Movement in International Law: The Right to Leave as a Personal Liberty' (2011) 12 *Melbourne Journal of International Law* 27.

McCrudden, C, 'Human Rights Histories' (2015) 35 *Oxford Journal of Legal Studies* 179.

McDougal, MS, 'The Law School of the Future: From Legal Realism to Policy Science in the World Community' (1946–1947) 56 *Yale Law Journal* 1345.

McDougal, MS and Lans, A, 'Treaties and Congressional-Executive or Presidential Agreements: Interchangeable Instruments of National Policy' (1945) 54 *Yale Law Journal* 181.

McDougal, MS and Lasswell, HD, 'The Identification and Appraisal of Diverse Systems of Public Order' (1959) 53 *American Journal of International Law* 1.

McDougall, R, Crisis in the WTO: Restoring the WTO Dispute Settlement Function, Centre for International Governance Innovation Paper No. 194, October 2018.

McIntyre, KB, *Herbert Butterfield: History, Providence, and Skeptical Politics* (Wilmington: ISI Books, 2011).

McLachlan, C, 'The Assault on International Adjudication and the Limits of Withdrawal' (2019) 68 *International and Comparative Law Quarterly* 499.

McNair, AD, 'The Functions and Differing Legal Character of Treaties' (1930) 11 *British Yearbook of International Law* 100.

McVeigh, S, 'Afterword: Office and the Conduct of the Minor Jurisprudent' (2015) 5 *UC Irvine Law Review* 499.

Meese III, E, 'Toward a Jurisprudence of Original Intent' (1988) 11 *Harvard Journal of Law and Public Policy* 5.

Mégret, F, 'From "Savages" to "Unlawful combatants": A Postcolonial Look at International Humanitarian Law's "Other"' in Orford, A (ed), *International Law and Its Others* (Cambridge: Cambridge University Press, 2006), 265.

Melber, H and Stahn, C (eds), *Peace, Diplomacy, Global Justice, and International Agency: Rethinking Human Security and Ethics in the Spirit of Dag Hammarskjöld* (Cambridge: Cambridge University Press, 2014).

Merali, I and Oosterveld, V (eds), *Giving Meaning to Economic, Social and Cultural Rights* (Philadelphia: University of Pennsylvania Press, 2001).

Mertens, T, 'Radbruch and Hart on the Grudge Informer: A Reconsideration' (2002) 15 *Ratio Juris* 186.

    'Nazism, Legal Positivism, and Radbruch's Thesis on Statutory Injustice' (2003) 14 *Law and Critique* 277.

Meyler, B, 'Accepting Contested Meanings' (2013) 82 *Fordham Law Review* 803.

    'Law, Literature, and History: The Love Triangle' (2015) 5 *UC Irvine Law Review* 365.

Michael, J, *Elements of Legal Controversy* (Brooklyn: The Foundation Press, 1948).

Mickelson, K, 'Rhetoric and Rage: Third World Voices in International Legal Discourse' (1998) 16 *Wisconsin International Law Journal* 353.

    'Leading towards a Level Playing Field, Repaying Ecological Debt, or Making Environmental Space: Three Stories about International Environmental Cooperation' (2005) 43 *Osgoode Hall Law Journal* 135.

    'International Law as a War against Nature? Reflections on the Ambivalence of International Environmental Law' in Stark, B (ed), *International Law and Its*

Discontents: Confronting Crises (Cambridge: Cambridge University Press, 2015), 84.

Miles, K, *The Origins of International Investment Law: Empire, Environment and the Safeguarding of Capital* (Cambridge: Cambridge University Press, 2013).

Milsom, SFC, 'Maitland' (2001) 60 *Cambridge Law Journal* 265.

Mitchell, R, 'Chinese Receptions of Carl Schmitt Since 1929' (2020) 8 *Penn State Journal of Law and International Affairs* 181.

Mitchell, J, 'Women: The Longest Revolution' (1966) I/40 *New Left Review* 11.

Morgenthau, HJ, 'Positivism, Functionalism, and International Law' (1940) 34 *American Journal of International Law* 260.

Morosini, FC and Badin, MS, 'Petrobras in Bolivia: Is There a Rule of Law in the "Primitive" World?' in Muir Watt, H, Bíziková, L, Brandão de Oliveira, A, and Arroyo, DPF (eds), *Global Private International Law: Adjudication without Frontiers* (Cheltenham: Edward Elgar, 2019), 381.

Motha, S, 'As If – Law, History, Ontology' (2015) 5 *UC Irvine Law Review* 327.

Moyn, S, *The Last Utopia: Human Rights in History* (Cambridge and London: Belknap Press, 2010).

The Last Utopia: Human Rights in History (Cambridge: Belknap Press, 2010).

'Imaginary Intellectual History' in McMahon, DM and Moyn, S (eds), *Rethinking Modern European Intellectual History* (Oxford: Oxford University Press, 2014), 112.

Christian Human Rights (Oxford: Oxford University Press, 2015).

'Martti Koskenniemi and the Historiography of International Law in the Age of the War on Terror' in Werner, W, de Hoon, M, and Galán, A (eds), *The Law of International Lawyers: Reading Martti Koskenniemi* (Cambridge: Cambridge University Press, 2016), 340.

Human Rights and the Uses of History, 2nd edition (London: Verso, 2017).

Not Enough: Human Rights in an Unequal World (Cambridge and London: Belknap Press, 2018).

Moyn, S and Sartori, A (eds), *Global Intellectual History* (New York: Columbia University Press, 2013).

Mullen, ML, 'Anachronism' (2018) 46 *Victorian Literature and Culture* 567.

Müller, J, 'Carl Schmitt's Method: Between Ideology, Demonology, and Myth' (1999) 4 *Journal of Political Ideologies* 61.

Murphy, S, 'The Intervention in Kosovo: A Law-Shaping Incident' (2000) 94 *Proceedings of the ASIL Annual Meeting* 303.

'Terrorism and the Concept of "Armed Attack" in Article 51 of the UN Charter' (2002) 43 *Harvard International Law Journal* 41.

Murphy, SD, 'The Doctrine of Preemptive Self-Defense' (2005) 50 *Villanova Law Review* 699.

Musson, A, 'Myth, Mistake, Invention? Excavating the Foundations of the English Legal Tradition' in Lewis, A and Lobban, M (eds), *Law and History* (Oxford: Oxford University Press, 2003), 63.

Myrdal, G, 'Postscript' in Streeten, P (ed), *Value in Social Theory* (Oxon: Routledge, 1958), 237.

Nagel, A and Wood, CS, *Anachronic Renaissance* (New York: Zone Books, 2012).

Namier, LB, *The Structure of Politics at the Accession of George III* (London: Macmillan and Co, 1929).

Navarro, P, *Death by China: Confronting the Dragon – A Global Call to Action* (New Jersey: Pearson FT Press, 2011).

Natarajan, U, 'Creating and Recreating Iraq: Legacies of the Mandate System in Contemporary Understandings of Third World Sovereignty' (2011) 24 *Leiden Journal of International Law* 799.

'TWAIL and the Environment: The State of Nature, the Nature of the State, and the Arab Spring' (2012) 14 *Oregon Review of International Law* 177.

Natarajan, U and Khoday, K, 'Fairness and International Environmental Law from Below: Social Movements and Legal Transformation in India' (2012) 25 *Leiden Journal of International Law* 415.

'Locating Nature: Making and Unmaking International Law' (2014) 27 *Leiden Journal of International Law* 573.

Nawaz, MK, 'The Law of Nations in Ancient India' (1957) 6 *Indian Yearbook of International Affairs* 172.

Neff, SC, *War and the Law of Nations: A General History* (Cambridge: Cambridge University Press, 2005).

Neuwithr, RJ, Svetlicinii, A, and Halis, DDC (eds), *The BRICS-Lawyers' Guide to Global Cooperation* (Cambridge: Cambridge University Press, 2017).

Nijman, JE, *The Concept of International Legal Personality: An Inquiry into the History and Theory of International Law* (Asser: The Hague, 2004).

Nilakanta Sastri, KA, 'International Law and Relations in Ancient India' (1952) 1 *Indian Yearbook of International Affairs* 97.

Nolte, G, 'Preventive Use of Force and Preventive Killings: Moves into a Different Legal Order' (2004) 5 *Theoretical Inquiries in Law* 111.

Nuzzo, L, 'History, Science and Christianity: International Law and Savigny's Paradigm' in Nuzzo, L and Vec, M (eds), *Constructing International Law: The Birth of a Discipline* (Frankfurt am Main: Vittorio Klostermann, 2012), 25.

Nuzzo, L and Vec, M (eds), *Constructing International Law: The Birth of a Discipline* (Frankfurt am Main: Vittorio Klostermann, 2012).

Nuzzo, L and Vec, M, 'The Birth of International Law as a Legal Discipline in the 19th Century' in Nuzzo, L and Vec, M (eds), *Constructing International Law: The Birth of a Discipline* (Frankfurt am Main: Vittorio Klostermann, 2012), ix.

Oakley, F, *Politics and Eternity: Studies in the History of Medieval and Early-Modern Political Thought* (Leiden: Brill, 1999).

Obregón, L, *Completing Civilization: Nineteenth Century Criollo Interventions in International Law*, PhD Thesis, Harvard Law School, 2002.

'The Colluding Worlds of the Lawyer, the Scholar and the Policymaker: A View of International Law from Latin America' (2005) 23 *Wisconsin International Law Journal* 145.

'Completing Civilization: Creole Consciousness and International Law in Nineteenth-Century Latin America' in Orford, A (ed), *International Law and Its Others* (Cambridge: Cambridge University Press, 2006), 247.

O'Connell, ME, 'New International Legal Process' (1999) 93 *American Journal of International Law* 334.

Odinkalu, C, 'Analysis of Paralysis or Paralysis of Analysis: Implementing Economic, Social and Cultural Rights under the African Charter on Human and Peoples' Rights' (2001) 23 *Human Rights Quarterly* 328.

O'Donoghue, R and Padilla, AJ, *The Law and Economics of Article 82 EC* (London: Hart, 2006).

Odysseos, L and Petito, F, 'Vagaries of Interpretation: A Rejoinder to David Chandler's Reductionist Reading of Carl Schmitt' (2008) 37 *Millennium: Journal of International Studies* 463.

Office of Legal Affairs (ed), *Collection of Essays by Legal Advisers of State, Legal Advisers of International Organizations and Practitioners in the Field of International Law* (New York: United Nations, 1999).

Office of the USTR, *2018 Trade Policy Agenda and 2017 Annual Report of the President of the United States on the Trade Agreements Program*, March 2018.

Okafor, OC, 'The Global Process of Legitimation and the Legitimacy of Global Governance' (1997) 14 *Arizona Journal of International and Comparative Law* 117.

'Newness, Imperialism, and International Legal Reform in Our Time: A TWAIL Perspective' (2005) 43 *Osgoode Hall Law Journal* 171.

'Poverty, Agency and Resistance in the Future of International Law: An African Perspective' (2006) 27 *Third World Quarterly* 799.

Okoye, FC, *International Law and the New African States* (London: Sweet and Maxwell, 1972).

Oloka-Onyango, J, 'Beyond the Rhetoric: Reinvigorating the Struggle for Economic and Social Rights in Africa' (1995) 26 *California Western International Law Journal* 1.

Olaka-Onyango, J, 'Reinforcing Marginalised Rights in an Age of Globalization' (2003) 18 *American University International Law Review* 851.

Olaka-Onyango, J and Udagama, D, Economic, Social and Cultural Rights: Globalization and Its Impact on the Full Enjoyment of Human Rights, Final Report (E/CN.4/Sub.2/2003/14).

Globalization and Its Impact on the Full Enjoyment of Human Rights, Progress Report to the UN Sub-Commission on the Promotion and Protection of Human Rights (E/CN.4/Sub.2/2001/10).

The Realization of Economic, Social and Cultural Rights: Globalization and Its Impact on the Full Enjoyment of Human Rights, Preliminary Report to the UN Sub-Commission on the Promotion and Protection of Human Rights (E/CN.4/Sub.2/2000/13).

Olsen, N, *History in the Plural: An Introduction to the Work of Reinhart Koselleck* (New York and London: Berghahn, 2012).

Onuma Y, 'When Was the Law of International Society Born? – An Inquiry of the History of International Law from an Intercivilizational Perspective' (2000) 2 *Journal of the History of International Law* 1.

Onuma, Y, *A Transcivilizational Perspective on International Law* (Leiden and Boston: Martinus Nijhoff, 2010).

Oppenheim, L, 'The Science of International Law: Its Task and Method' (1908) 2 *American Journal of International Law* 313.

Orford, A, 'Locating the International: Military and Monetary Interventions after the Cold War' (1997) 38 *Harvard International Law Journal* 443.

'Contesting Globalization: A Feminist Perspective on the Future of Human Rights' (1998) 8 *Transnational Law and Contemporary Problems* 171.

'Embodying Internationalism: The Making of International Lawyers' (1998) 19 *Australian Year Book of International Law* 1.

'Muscular Humanitarianism: Reading the Narratives of the New Interventionism' (1999) 10 *European Journal of International Law* 679.

'The Subject of Globalization: Economics, Identity, and Human Rights' (2000) 94 *American Society of International Law Proceedings* 146.

'Globalization and the Right to Development' in Alston, P (ed), *Peoples' Rights* (Oxford: Oxford University Press, 2001), 127.

Reading Humanitarian Intervention: Human Rights and the Use of Force in International Law (Cambridge: Cambridge University Press, 2003).

'The Destiny of International Law' (2004) 17 *Leiden Journal of International Law* 441.

'Beyond Harmonization: Trade, Human Rights and the Economy of Sacrifice' (2005) 18 *Leiden Journal of International Law* 179.

'Biopolitics and the Tragic Subject of Human Rights' in Dauphinee, E and Masters, C (eds), *The Logics of Biopower and the War on Terror: Living, Dying, Surviving* (Hampshire and New York: Palgrave Macmillan, 2007), 205.

'Jurisdiction without Territory: From the Holy Roman Empire to the Responsibility to Protect' (2009) 30 *Michigan Journal of International Law* 981.

'International Territorial Administration and the Management of Decolonization' (2010) 59 *International and Comparative Law Quarterly* 227.

International Authority and the Responsibility to Protect (Cambridge: Cambridge University Press, 2011).

'Europe Reconstructed' (2012) 75 *Modern Law Review* 275.

'In Praise of Description' (2012) 25 *Leiden Journal of International Law* 609.

'Moral Internationalism and the Responsibility to Protect' (2013) 24 *European Journal of International Law* 83.

'The Past as Law or History? The Relevance of Imperialism for Modern International Law' in Toufayan, M, Tourme-Jouannet, E and Ruiz Fabri, H (eds) *Droit international et nouvelles approches sur le tiers-monde: entre repetition et renouveau* (Paris: Société de Législation Comparée, 2013), 97.

'On International Legal Method' (2014) 1 *London Review of International Law* 166.

'Scientific Reason and the Discipline of International Law' (2014) 25 *European Journal of International Law* 369.

'Hammarskjöld, Economic Thinking, and the United Nations' in Melber, H and Stahn, C (eds), *Peace, Diplomacy, Global Justice, and International Agency: Rethinking Human Security and Ethics in the Spirit of Dag Hammarskjöld* (Cambridge: Cambridge University Press, 2014), 156.

'Food Security, Free Trade, and the Battle for the State' (2015) 11 *Journal of International Law and International Relations* 1.

'Law, Economics, and the History of Free Trade: A Response' (2015) 11 *Journal of International Law and International Relations* 155.

'Theorizing Free Trade' in Orford, A and Hoffmann, F (eds), *The Oxford Handbook of the Theory of International Law* (Oxford: Oxford University Press, 2016), 701.

'International Law and the Limits of History' in Werner, W, de Hoon, M, and Galán, A (eds), *The Law of International Lawyers: Reading Martti Koskenniemi* (Cambridge: Cambridge University Press, 2016), 297.

'Foreword' in Cullen, H, Harrington, J, and Renshaw, C (eds), *Networks, Experts, and International Law* (Cambridge: Cambridge University Press, 2017), xiii.

'NATO, Regionalism, and the Responsibility to Protect' in Shapiro, I and Tooze, A (eds), *Charter of the North Atlantic Treaty Organisation together with Scholarly Commentaries and Essential Historical Documents* (New Haven: Yale University Press, 2018), 302.

'Epilogue: Critical Intimacy and the Performance of International Law' in Boer, LJM and Stolk, S (eds), *Backstage Practices of Transnational Law* (London: Routledge, 2019), 174.

'International Law and the Populist Moment' (2020) 35 *American University International Law Review* 427.

International Law and the Social Question (The Hague: Asser Press, 2020).

'The Sir Elihu Lauterpacht International Law Lecture 2019: The Crisis of Liberal Internationalism and the Future of International Law' (2021) 28 *Australian Year Book of International Law* 3.

'A Global Rule of Law' in Loughlin, M and Meierhenrich, J (eds), *The Cambridge Companion to the Rule of Law* (Cambridge: Cambridge University Press, 2021), 538.

'Regional Orders and the Future of International Law: The End of Geography or a New Geopolitics?' (2021) 73 *Current Legal Problems* (forthcoming).

Orford, A and Beard, J, 'Making the State Safe for the Market: The World Bank's *World Development Report 1997*' (1998) 22 *Melbourne University Law Review* 196.

Ortino, M, 'The Governance of Global Banking in the Face of Complexity' (2019) 22 *Journal of International Economic Law* 177.

Owens, P, *Economy of Force: Counterinsurgency and the Historical Rise of the Social* (Cambridge: Cambridge University Press, 2015).

'International Historical What?' (2016) 8 *International Theory* 448.

Ownby, D and Cheek, T, 'An Introduction to Jiang Shigong on "Philosophy and History: Interpreting the 'Xi Jinping Era' through Xi's Report to the Nineteenth National Congress of the CCP"', *The China Story*, May 11, 2018, www.thechinastory.org/cot/jiang-shigong-on-philosophy-and-history-interpreting-the-xi-jinping-era-through-xis-report-to-the-nineteenth-national-congress-of-the-ccp/.

Pahuja, S, *Decolonizing International Law* (Cambridge: Cambridge University Press, 2011).

Palfrey, S, 'The Truth of Anachronism' in *Shakespeare's Possible Worlds* (Cambridge: Cambridge University Press, 2014).

Palonen, K, *Quentin Skinner: History, Politics, Rhetoric* (Cambridge: Polity Press, 2003).

Panofsky, E, *Renaissance and Renascences in Western Art* (Stockholm: Almqvist & Wiksells, 1960).

Pankakoski, T, 'Conflict, Context, Concreteness: Koselleck and Schmitt on Concepts' (2010) 38 *Political Theory* 749.

Pappe, HO, 'On the Validity of Judicial Decisions in the Nazi Era' (1960) 23 *Modern Law Review* 260.

Parfitt, R, 'The Spectre of Sources' (2014) 25 *European Journal of International Law* 297.

'Fascism, Imperialism and International Law: An Arch Met a Motorway and the Rest Is History . . .' (2018) 31 *Leiden Journal of International Law* 509.

The Process of International Legal Reproduction: Inequality, Historiography, Resistance (Cambridge: Cambridge University Press, 2019).

'Series Introduction – Fascism and the International: The Global South, the Far-Right and the International Legal Order', TWAILR: Reflections #5/2019.

'Is This (Brazilian) Fascism? The Far-Right, the Third World and the Wrong Question', TWAILR: Reflections #6/2019.

Parker, KM, 'Law "In" and "As" History: The Common Law in the American Polity, 1790–1900' (2011) 1 *UC Irvine Law Review* 587.

'Repetition in History: Anglo-American Legal Debates and the Writings of Walter Bagehot' (2014) 4 *UC Irvine Law Review* 121.

'Writing Legal History Then and Now: A Brief Reflection' (2016) 56 *American Journal of Legal History* 168.

Parra, AR, *The History of ICSID* (Oxford: Oxford University Press, 2012).

Patel, KK and Schweitzer, H, 'EU Competition Law in Historical Context: Continuity and Change' in Patel, KK and Schweitzer, H (eds), *The Historical Foundation of EU Competition Law* (Oxford: Oxford University Press, 2013), 207.

Paulus, AL, 'International Law after Postmodernism: Towards Renewal or Decline of International Law?' (2001) 14 *Leiden Journal of International Law* 727.

Pauwelyn, J, 'At the Edge of Chaos? Foreign Investment Law as a Complex Adaptive System, How It Emerged and How It Can Be Reformed' (2014) 29 *ICSID Review* 372.

'Rational Design or Accidental Evolution? The Emergence of International Investment Law' in Douglas, Z, Pauwelyn, J, and Viñuales, JE (eds), *The Foundations of International Investment Law: Bringing Theory into Practice* (Oxford: Oxford University Press, 2014), 11.

Peden, K, 'The Burden of Intelligibility' (2014) 40 *History of European Ideas* 70.

Pedersen, S, 'Review Essay: Back to the League of Nations' (2007) 112 *The American Historical Review* 1091.

The Guardians: The League of Nations and the Crisis of Empire (Oxford: Oxford University Press, 2015).

Peller, G, 'The Metaphysics of American Law' (1985) 73 *California Law Review* 1151.

Pellet, A, 'Brief Remarks on the Unilateral Use of Force' (2000) 11 *European Journal of International Law* 385.

Perreau-Saussine, E, 'Quentin Skinner in Context' (2007) 69 *The Review of Politics* 106.

Perrone, NM, 'The Governance of Foreign Investment at a Crossroad: Is an Overlapping Consensus the Way Forward?' (2015) 15 *Global Jurist* 1.

'The International Investment Regime and Local Populations: Are the Weakest Voices Unheard?' (2016) 7 *Transnational Legal Theory* 383.

Perrone, NM and Schneiderman, D, 'International Economic Law's Wreckage: Depoliticization, Inequality, Precarity' in Christodoulidis, E, Dukes, R, and Goldoni, M (eds), *Research Handbook on Critical Legal Theory* (Cheltenham: Edward Elgar, 2019), 446.

Peters, A, 'Humanity as the A and Ω of Sovereignty' (2009) 20 *European Journal of International Law* 513.

Petersmann, E-U, *International Economic Law in the 21st Century: Constitutional Pluralism and Multilevel Governance of Interdependent Public Goods* (Oxford: Hart, 2012).

'The Establishment of a GATT Office of Legal Affairs and the Limits of "Public Reason" in the GATT/WTO Dispute Settlement System' in Marceau, G (ed), *A History of Law and Lawyers in the GATT/WTO: The Development of the Rule of Law in the Multilateral Trading System* (Cambridge: Cambridge University Press, 2015), 182.

'Book Review: *Globalists: The End of Empire and the Birth of Neoliberalism*' (2018) 21 *Journal of International Economic Law* 915.

'How Should WTO Members React to Their WTO Crises?' (2019) 18 *World Trade Review* 503.

'Between "Member-Driven Governance" and "Judicialization": Constitutional and Judicial Dilemmas in the World Trading System' in Lo, C-F, Nakagawa, J, and Chen, T-F (eds), *The Appellate Body of the WTO and Its Reform* (Singapore: Springer, 2020), 15.

Philadelphoff-Puren, N and Rush, P, 'Fatal (F)laws: Law, Literature and Writing' (2003) 14 *Law and Critique* 191.

Phillipson, N and Skinner, Q, 'Preface' in Phillipson, N and Skinner, Q (eds), *Political Discourse in Early Modern Britain* (Cambridge: Cambridge University Press, 1993), xii.

Pihlajamäki, H, 'Against Metaphysics in Law: The Historical Background of American and Scandinavian Legal Realism Compared' (2004) 52 *American Journal of Comparative Law* 469.

Pistor, K, 'A Legal Theory of Finance' (2013) 41 *Journal of Comparative Economics* 315.

'From Territorial to Monetary Sovereignty' (2017) 18 *Theoretical Inquiries in Law* 491.

Pitts, J, *A Turn to Empire: The Rise of Imperial Liberalism in Britain and France* (Princeton: Princeton University Press, 2005).

'Empire and Legal Universalisms in the Eighteenth Century' (2012) 117 *American Historical Review* 92.

'The Critical History of International Law' (2015) 43 *Political Theory* 541.

'International Relations and the Critical History of International Law' (2017) 31 *International Relations* 282.

Boundaries of the International: Law and Empire (Cambridge: Harvard University Press, 2018).

Plehwe, D, 'The Origins of the Neoliberal Economic Development Discourse' in Mirowski, P and Plehwe, D (eds), *The Road from Mont Pèlerin: The Making of the Neoliberal Thought Collective* (Cambridge and London: Harvard University Press, 2009), 238.

Pocock, JGA, 'The History of Political Thought: A Methodological Inquiry' in Laslett, P and Runciman, WG (eds), *Philosophy, Politics, and Society*, Second Series (Oxford: Oxford University Press, 1962), 183.

Politics, Language and Time: Essays on Political Thought and History (Chicago: University of Chicago Press, 1971).

'Languages and Their Implications: The Transformation of the Study of Political Thought' in Pocock, JGA, *Politics, Language and Time: Essays on Political Thought and History* (Chicago: University of Chicago Press, 1971).

Virtue, Commerce, and History: Essays on Political Thought and History, Chiefly in the Eighteenth Century (Cambridge: Cambridge University Press, 1985).

The Ancient Constitution and the Feudal Law: A Reissue with a Retrospect (Cambridge: Cambridge University Press, 1987 [1957]).

'Foundations and Moments' in Brett, A and Tully, J with Hamilton-Bleakley, H (eds), *Rethinking the Foundations of Modern Political Thought* (Cambridge: Cambridge University Press, 2006), 37.

Political Thought and History: Essays on Theory and Method (Cambridge: Cambridge University Press, 2008).

'Time, Institutions and Action: An Essay on Traditions and their Understanding' in Pocock, JGA (ed), *Political Thought and History: Essays on Theory and Method* (Cambridge: Cambridge University Press, 2009), 187.

'A Response to Samuel James's "JGA Pocock and the Idea of the 'Cambridge School' in the History of Political Thought"' (2019) 45 *History of European Ideas* 99.

Pollock, F, 'Frederic William Maitland, 1850–1906' (1905–1906) 2 *Proceedings of the British Academy* 1.

Pollock, F and Maitland, FW, *The History of English Law*, 2nd edition (Cambridge: Cambridge University Press, 1968 [1898]).

Porras, I, 'Appropriating Nature: Commerce, Property, and the Commodification of Nature in the Law of Nations' (2014) 27 *Leiden Journal of International Law* 641.

'Binge Development in the Age of Fear: Scarcity, Consumption, Inequality, and the Environmental Crisis' in Stark, B (ed), *International Law and Its Discontents: Confronting Crises* (Cambridge: Cambridge University Press, 2015), 25.

Postema, GJ, 'Custom in International Law: A Normative Practice Account' in Perreau-Saussine, A and Murphy, JB (eds), *The Nature of Customary Law: Legal, Historical and Philosophical Perspectives* (Cambridge: Cambridge University Press, 2007), 279.

Pound, R, 'Mechanical Jurisprudence' (1908) 8 *Columbia Law Review* 605.

Pue, WW, 'In Pursuit of Better Myth: Lawyers' Histories and Histories of Lawyers' (1995) 33 *Alberta Law Review* 732.

Purcell, K, 'On the Uses and Advantages of Genealogy for International Law' (2020) 33 *Leiden Journal of International Law* 13.

Purdy, J, 'The Politics of Nature: Climate Change, Environmental Law, and Democracy' (2010) 119 *Yale Law Journal* 1122.

Quirk, J and Vigneswaran, D, 'The Construction of an Edifice: The Story of a First Great Debate' (2005) 31 *Review of International Studies* 89.

Rabban, DM, *Law's History: American Legal Thought and the Transatlantic Turn to History* (Cambridge: Cambridge University Press, 2013).

Radbruch, G, 'Gesetzliches Unrecht und übergesetzliches Recht' (1946) 1 *Süddeutsche Juristenzeitung* 105.

'Statutory Lawlessness and Supra-Statutory Law (1946)' (2006) 26 *Oxford Journal of Legal Studies* 1 (trans B Litschewski Paulson and SL Paulson).

Rancière, J, 'Le concept d'anachronisme et la vérité de l'historien' (1996) 6 *L'Inactuel: Psychoanalyse & Culture* 53.

Rasulov, A, 'What Is Critique?' in d'Aspremont, J, Gazzini, T, Nollkaemper, A, and Werner, W (eds), *International Law as a Profession* (Cambridge: Cambridge University Press, 2017), 189.

Raustiala, K, 'Form and Substance in International Agreements' (2005) 99 *American Journal of International Law* 581.

Rech, W, 'Rightless Enemies: Schmitt and Lauterpacht on Political Piracy' (2012) 32 *Oxford Journal of Legal Studies* 235.

Reid, JP, 'Law and History' (1993) 27 *Loyola of Los Angeles Law Review* 193.

Reimann, MW, 'Holmes's *Common Law* and German Legal Science' in Gordon, RW (ed), *The Legacy of Oliver Wendell Holmes, Jr* (Stanford: Stanford University Press, 1992), 72.

Reisman, WM, 'Kosovo's Antinomies' (1999) 93 *American Journal of International Law* 860.

'Theory about Law: Jurisprudence for a Free Society' (1999) 108 *Yale Law Journal* 935.

'Assessing Claims to Revise the Laws of War' (2003) 97 *American Journal of International Law* 82.

Reisman, WM and Armstrong, A, 'The Past and the Future of the Claim of Preemptive Self-Defense' (2006) 100 *American Journal of International Law* 525.

Reisman, WM, Wiessner, S, and Willard, AR, 'The New Haven School: A Brief Introduction' (2007) 32 *Yale Journal of International Law* 575.

Renner, K, *The Institutions of Private Law and Their Social Functions* (trans A Schwarzschild) (London: Routledge and Kegan Paul, 1949).

Renner, M, 'The Dialectics of Transnational Economic Constitutionalism' in Joerges, C and Falke, J (eds), *Karl Polanyi, Globalisation and the Potential of Law in Transnational Markets* (Oxford: Hart, 2011), 419.

Richardson III, HJ, 'US Hegemony, Race, and Oil in Deciding United Nations Security Council Resolution 1441 on Iraq' (2003) 17 *Temple International and Comparative Law Journal* 27.

Ricœur, P, *Freud and Philosophy: An Essay on Interpretation* (New Haven: Yale University Press, 1970).

Riles, A, 'Aspiration and Control: International Legal Rhetoric and the Essentialization of Culture' (1993) 106 *Harvard Law Review* 723.

'The View from the International Plane: Perspective and Scale in the Architecture of Colonial International Law' (1995) 6 *Law and Critique* 39.

'Collateral Expertise: Legal Knowledge in the Global Financial Markets' (2010) 51 *Current Anthropology* 795.

Collateral Knowledge: Legal Reasoning in the Global Financial Markets (Chicago and London: University of Chicago Press, 2011), 9.

'Managing Regulatory Arbitrage: A Conflict of Laws Approach' (2014) 47 *Cornell International Law Journal* 63.

'New Approaches to International Financial Regulation', Cornell Law School Research Paper No 15-03, Cornell Law School, 2014.

'Legal Amateurism' in Desautels-Stein, J and Tomlins, C (eds), *Searching for Contemporary Legal Thought* (Cambridge: Cambridge University Press, 2017), 499.

'Is the Law Hopeful?' in Miyazaki, H and Swedberg, R (eds), *The Economy of Hope* (Philadelphia: University of Pennsylvania Press, 2017), 126.

Rittich, K, 'Transformed Pursuits: The Quest for Equality in Globalized Markets' (2000) 13 *Harvard Human Rights Journal* 231.

'Who's Afraid of the *Critique of Adjudication?*: Tracing the Discourse of Law in Development' (2001) 22 *Cardozo Law Review* 929.

Recharacterizing Restructuring: Law, Distribution, and Gender in Market Reform (The Hague: Kluwer, 2002).

'The Future of Law and Development: Second-Generation Reforms and the Incorporation of the Social' in Trubek, DM and Santos, A (eds), *The New Law and Economic Development: A Critical Appraisal* (Cambridge: Cambridge University Press, 2006), 245.

Röben, BB, 'The Method behind Bluntschli's "Modern" International Law' (2002) 4 *Journal of the History of International Law* 249.

· *Johann Caspar Bluntschli, Francis Lieber und das moderne Völkerrecht 1861–1881* (Baden-Baden: Nomos, 2003).

Robbins, B, 'Subaltern-Speak' in Warren, R (ed), *The Debate on Postcolonial Theory and the Specter of Capital* (London and New York: Verso, 2017), 103.

Roberts, Adam, 'NATO's "Humanitarian War" over Kosovo' (1999) 41 *Survival* 102, at 106.

Roele, I, 'Policing Critique' (2018) 81 *Modern Law Review* 701.

Roessler, F, 'The Role of Law in International Trade Relations and the Establishment of the Legal Affairs Division of the GATT' in Marceau, G (ed), *A History of Law and Lawyers in the GATT/WTO: The Development of the Rule of Law in the Multilateral Trading System* (Cambridge: Cambridge University Press, 2015), 161.

'Democracy, Redistribution and the WTO: A Comment on Quinn Slobodian's Book *Globalists: The End of Empire and the Birth of Neoliberalism*' (2019) 18 *World Trade Review* 353.

Rose, I and Ngwe, C, 'The Ordoliberal Tradition in the European Union, Its Influence on Article 82 EC and the IBA's Comments on the Article 82 EC Discussion Paper' (2007) 3 *Competition Law International* 8.

Rosenberg, J, *The Empire of Civil Society: A Critique of the Realist Theory of International Relations* (London and New York: Verso, 1994).

Ross, A, 'Tû-Tû' (1957) 70 *Harvard Law Review* 812.

Rossi, CR, *Whiggish International Law: Elihu Root, the Monroe Doctrine, and International Law in the Americas* (Leiden: Brill, 2019).

Roth, BR, 'Governmental Illegitimacy and Neocolonialism: Response to Review by James Thuo Gathii' (2000) 98 *Michigan Law Review* 2065.

Rothschild, E, 'The Archives of Universal History' (2008) 19 *Journal of World History* 37.

Rowbotham, S, *Women, Resistance and Revolution* (New York: Pantheon, 1972).
Hidden from History (London: Pluto, 1973).

Rubin, M, 'Presentism's Useful Anachronisms' (2017) 234 *Past and Present* 236.

Ruiz Fabri, H, 'The WTO Appellate Body or Judicial Power Unleashed: Sketches from the Procedural Side of the Story' (2017) 27 *European Journal of International Law* 1075.

Runciman, D, 'History of Political Thought: The State of the Discipline' (2001) 3 *British Journal of Politics and International Relations* 84.

Rupert, M and Smith, H *Historical Materialism and Globalization* (London and New York: Routledge, 2002).

Ruskola, T, 'China in the Age of the World Picture' in Orford, A and Hoffmann, F (eds), *The Oxford Handbook of the Theory of International Law* (Oxford: Oxford University Press, 2016), 138.

Ruys, T, 'Armed Attack' and Article 51 of the UN Charter: Evolutions in Customary Law and Practice (Cambridge: Cambridge University Press, 2010).

Ruys, T and Corten, O with Hofer, A (eds), The Use of Force in International Law (Oxford: Oxford University Press, 2018).

Saberi, H, 'Yale's Policy Science and International Law: Between Legal Formalism and Policy Conceptualism' in Orford, A and Hoffmann, F (eds), The Oxford Handbook of the Theory of International Law (Oxford: Oxford University Press, 2016), 427.

Sacerdoti, G, 'From Law Professor to International Adjudicator: The WTO Appellate Body and ISCID Arbitration Compared, a Personal Account' in Caron, DD, Schill, SW, Smutny, AC, and Triantafilou, EE (eds), Practising Virtue: Inside International Arbitration (Oxford: Oxford University Press, 2015), 204.

Samuels, WJ, 'The Economy as a System of Power and Its Legal Bases: The Legal Economics of Robert Lee Hale' (1973) 27 University of Miami Law Review 261.

Sands, P, 'Conflict and Conflicts in Investment Treaty Arbitration: Ethical Standards for Counsel,' in A Rovine (ed), Contemporary Issues in International Arbitration and Mediation: The Fordham Papers (New York: Brill, 2012), 28.

Sands, P and Sarvarian, A, 'The Contributions of the UK Bar to International Law' in McCorquodale, R and Gauci, J-P (eds), British Influences on International Law, 1915–2015 (London and Boston: Brill Nijhoff, 2016), 497.

Sayed, H, 'The Humanization of the Third World' in Eslava, L, Fakhri, M, and Nesiah, V (eds), Bandung, Global History, and International Law: Critical Pasts and Pending Futures (Cambridge: Cambridge University Press, 2017), 431.

Scalia, A, 'Originalism – The Lesser Evil' (1989) 57 University of Cincinnati Law Review 849.

Schachter, O, 'The Invisible College of International Lawyers' (1977–1978) 22 Northwestern University Law Review 217.

Scharf, MP, Customary International Law in Times of Fundamental Change: Recognizing Grotian Moments (Cambridge: Cambridge University Press, 2013).

Scharf, MP and Williams, PR, Shaping Foreign Policy in Times of Crisis: The Role of International Law and the State Department Legal Adviser (Cambridge: Cambridge University Press, 2010).

Schill, SW, 'W(h)ither Fragmentation? On the Literature and Sociology of International Investment Law' (2011) 22 European Journal of International Law 875.

'Private Enforcement of International Investment Law: Why We Need Investor Standing in BIT Dispute Settlement' in Waibel, M, Kaushal, A, Chung, K-HL, and Balchin, C (eds), The Backlash against Investment Arbitration: Perceptions and Reality (Alphen aan den Rijn: Wolters Kluwer, 2010), 29.

Schlag, P, 'An Appreciate Comment on Coase's The Problem of Social Cost: A View from the Left' (1986) Wisconsin Law Review 919.

Schmidt, BC, The Political Discourse of Anarchy (New York: State University New York Press, 1998).

Schmitt, A, 'Appendix I, Response to the Question: "To What Extent Did You Provide the Theoretical Foundation for Hitler's Grossraum Policy?"' (1987) 72 Telos 109.

Schmitt, C, Roman Catholicism and Political Form (trans Ulmen, GL) (Westport: Greenwood Press, 1996 [1923]).

The Concept of the Political (trans Schwab, G) (Chicago and London: University of Chicago Press, 1996 [1932]).

The Leviathan in the State Theory of Thomas Hobbes: Meaning and Failure of a Political Symbol (trans Schwab, G and Hilfstein, E) (Westport: Greenwood Press, 1996 [1938]), 34.

The Crisis of Parliamentary Democracy (trans Kennedy, E) (Cambridge: MIT Press, 1999 [1934]).

The Nomos of the Earth in the International Law of the Jus Publicum Europaeum (trans Ulmen, GL) (New York: Telos Press, 2003 [1950]), 220.

Legality and Legitimacy (trans Seitzer, J) (Durham: Duke University Press, 2004 [1932]).

Political Theology: Four Chapters on the Concept of Sovereignty (trans Schwab, G) (Chicago: University of Chicago Press, 2005 [1922]).

Theory of the Partisan: Intermediate Commentary on the Concept of the Political (trans GL Ulmen) (New York: Telos, 2007 [1975]).

Political Theology II: The Myth of the Closure of Any Political Theology (trans Hoelzl, M and Ward, G) (Cambridge: Polity Press, 2008 [1970]).

'The Concept of Piracy (1937)' (2011) 2 *Humanity* 27.

'The *Großraum* Order of International Law with a Ban on Intervention for Spatially Foreign Powers: A Contribution to the Concept of *Reich* in International Law (1939–1941)' in Nunan, T (ed), *Carl Schmitt: Writings on War* (Cambridge: Polity Press, 2011), 75.

'The Turn to the Discriminating Concept of War (1937)' in Nunan, T (ed), *Carl Schmitt: Writings on War* (Cambridge: Polity, 2011).

Schmitt, MN, 'Preemptive Strategies in International Law' (2002–2003) 24 *Michigan Journal of International Law* 534.

Schneiderman, D, *Constitutionalizing Economic Globalization: Investment Rules and Democracy's Promise* (Cambridge: Cambridge University Press, 2008).

Resisting Economic Globalization: Critical Theory and International Investment Law (Hampshire and New York: Palgrave Macmillan, 2013).

'Constitutional Property Rights and the Elision of the Transnational: Foucauldian Misgivings' (2015) 24 *Social and Legal Studies* 65.

Schulz-Forberg, H and Stråth, B, *The Political History of European Integration: The Hypocrisy of Democracy-Through-Market* (Abingdon: Routledge, 2010).

Schuyler, RL, 'The Historical Spirit Incarnate: Frederic William Maitland' (1952) LVII *American Historical Review* 303.

Schwebel, SM, 'Remarks on the Role of the Legal Advisor of the US State Department' (1991) 2 *European Journal of International Law* 131.

Schwebel, S, 'The Influence of Bilateral Investment Treaties on Customary International Law' (2004) 98 *Proceedings of the ASIL Annual Meeting* 27.

'In Defense of Bilateral Investment Treaties' (2015) 31 *Arbitration International* 181.

Schwöbel-Patel, C, 'Populism, International Law and the End of Keep Calm and Carry on Lawyering' (2018) *Netherlands Yearbook of International Law* 97.

Scott-Smith, G and Rofe, JS, *Global Perspectives on the Bretton Woods Conference and the Post-War World Order* (London: Palgrave Macmillan, 2017).

Sedgwick, E, 'Paranoid Reading and Reparative Reading: Or, You're So Paranoid: You Probably Think This Essay Is about You' in Sedgwick, E, Barale, MA, Goldberg, J, and Moon, M, *Touching Feeling: Affect, Pedagogy, Performativity* (Durham: Duke University Press, 2002), 123.

Sedgwick, EK, *Epistemology of the Closet* (Berkeley: University of California Press, 1990).

Seppänen, S, *Ideological Conflict and the Rule of Law in Contemporary China: Useful Paradoxes* (Cambridge: Cambridge University Press, 2016).

'Anti-formalism and the Preordained Birth of Chinese Jurisprudence' (2018) 14 *China Perspectives* 31.

'Performative Uses of Sovereignty in the Belt and Road Initiative' in Zhao, Y (ed), *International Governance and the Rule of Law in China under the Belt and Road Initiative* (Cambridge: Cambridge University Press, 2018), 32.

Shaffer, G, 'The New Legal Realist Approach to International Law' (2015) 28 *Leiden Journal of International Law* 189.

'Will the US Undermine the World Trade Organization?', *Huffington Post*, 23 May 2016.

'A Tragedy in the Making? The Decline of Law and the Return of Power in International Trade Relations' (2019) 44 *The Yale Journal of International Law Online* 1.

Shaffer, G, Elsig, M, and Pollack, M, 'The Slow Killing of the World Trade Organization', *Huffington Post*, 11 November 2017.

Shaffer, G and Ginsburg, T, 'The Empirical Turn in International Law Scholarship' (2012) 106 *American Journal of International Law* 1.

Shalakany, AA, 'Arbitration and the Third World: A Plea for Reassessing Bias under the Specter of Neoliberalism' (2000) 41 *Harvard International Law Journal* 419.

Sharp, P, 'Herbert Butterfield, the English School and the Civilizing Virtues of Diplomacy' (2003) 79 *International Affairs* 855.

Shilliam, R, *German Thought and International Relations: The Rise and Fall of a Liberal Project* (Hampshire and New York: Palgrave Macmillan, 2009).

Simma, B, 'The Antarctic Treaty as a Treaty Providing for an "Objective Regime"' (1986) 19 *Cornell International Law Journal* 189.

'NATO, the UN and the Use of Force' (1999) 10 *European Journal of International Law* 1.

Simpson, AWB, *A History of the Land Law*, 2nd edition (Oxford: Clarendon Press, 1986).

Human Rights and the End of Empire: Britain and the Genesis of the European Convention (Oxford: Oxford University Press, 2001).

Simpson, G, *Great Powers and Outlaw States: Unequal Sovereigns in the International Legal Order* (Cambridge: Cambridge University Press, 2004).

Singer, JW, 'Legal Realism Now' (1988) 76 *California Law Review* 465.

Singh, N, *India and International Law* (Delhi: S. Chand and Co, 1969).

Skinner, Q, 'Hobbes's "Leviathan"' (1964) VII *The Historical Journal* 321.

'History and Ideology in the English Revolution' (1965) VIII *The Historical Journal* 178.

'The Limits of Historical Explanations' (1966) 41 *Philosophy* 199.

'Meaning and Understanding in the History of Ideas' (1969) 8 *History and Theory* 3.

'Motives, Intentions and the Interpretation of Texts' (1972) 3 *New Literary History* 393.

The Foundations of Modern Political Thought, 2 volumes (Cambridge: Cambridge University Press, 1978).

'A Reply to My Critics' in Tully, J (ed), *Meaning and Context: Quentin Skinner and His Critics* (Princeton: Princeton University Press, 1988), 231.

'The Idea of a Cultural Lexicon' in Skinner, Q, *Visions of Politics: Volume I, Regarding Method* (Cambridge: Cambridge University Press, 2002), 158.

Visions of Politics: Volume I, Regarding Method (Cambridge: Cambridge University Press, 2002).

'General Preface' in *Visions of Politics: Volume I, Regarding Method* (Cambridge: Cambridge University Press, 2002), vi.

'Interpretation and the Understanding of Speech Acts' in *Visions of Politics: Volume I, Regarding Method* (Cambridge: Cambridge University Press, 2002), 103.

'Moral Principles and Social Change' in *Visions of Politics: Volume I, Regarding Method* (Cambridge: Cambridge University Press, 2002), 145.

'Retrospect: Studying Rhetoric and Conceptual Change' in *Visions of Politics: Volume I, Regarding Method* (Cambridge: Cambridge University Press, 2002), 175.

'On Encountering the Past: Interview by Petri Koikkalainen and Sami Syrämäki' (2002) 6 *Finnish Yearbook of Political Thought* 34.

'Surveying the *Foundations*: A Retrospect and Reassessment' in Brett, A and Tully, J with Hamilton-Bleakley, H (eds), *Rethinking the Foundations of Modern Political Thought* (Cambridge: Cambridge University Press, 2006), 236.

Skouteris, T, 'The Force of a Doctrine: Art 38 of the PCIJ Statute and the Sources of International Law' in Johns, F, Joyce, R, and Pahuja, S (eds), *Events: The Force of International Law* (Oxon: Routledge, 2011), 69.

'The Idea of Progress' in Orford, A and Hoffmann, F (eds), *The Oxford Handbook of the Theory of International Law* (Oxford: Oxford University Press, 2016), 939.

'The Turn to History in International Law' in Carty, A (ed), *Oxford Bibliographies Online* (Oxford: Oxford University Press, 2016).

Slaughter, A-M, 'International Law in a World of Liberal States' (1995) 6 *European Journal of International Law* 503.

A New World Order (Princeton: Princeton University Press, 2005).

'A Regional Responsibility to Protect' in Held, D and McNally, K (eds), *Lessons from Intervention in the 21st Century: Legality, Feasibility and Legitimacy* (London: Global Policy, 2014) 60.

Slaughter, A-M and Burke-White, W, 'An International Constitutional Moment' (2002) 43 *Harvard International Law Journal* 1.

Slaughter, JR, 'Hijacking Human Rights: Neoliberalism, the New Historiography, and the End of the Third World' (2018) 40 *Human Rights Quarterly* 735.

Slobodian, Q, *Foreign Front: Third World Politics in Sixties West Germany* (Durham: Duke University Press, 2012).

Globalists: The End of Empire and the Birth of Neoliberalism (Cambridge: Harvard University Press, 2018).

'Making Sense of Neoliberalism', *Harvard University Press Blog*, 15 March 2018.

Slobodian, Q (ed), *Comrades of Color: East Germany in the Cold War World* (New York: Berghahn Books, 2015).

Slonim, S, 'Congressional-Executive Agreements' (1975) 14 *Columbia Journal of Transnational Law* 434.

Sluga, G, 'Turning International: *Foundations of Modern International Thought* and New Paradigms for Intellectual History' (2015) 41 *History of European Ideas* 103.

Sluga, G and Clavin, P (eds), *Internationalism: A Twentieth-Century History* (Cambridge: Cambridge University Press, 2017).

Snyder, FE and Sathirathai, S (eds), *Third World Attitudes toward International Law* (Dordrecht: Nijhoff, 1987).

Sofaer, A, 'International Law and Kosovo' (2000) 36 *Stanford Journal of International Law* 13.

  'On the Necessity of Pre-Emption' (2003) 14 *European Journal of International Law* 209.

Soffer, R, *History, Historians, and Conservatism in Britain and America: From the Great War to Thatcher and Reagan* (Oxford: Oxford University Press, 2008).

Solchany, J, 'Wilhelm Röpke as a Key Actor of Transnational Neoliberalism after 1945' in Schulze-Forberg, H and Olsen, N (eds), *Re-Inventing Western Civilisation: Transnational Reconstructions of Liberalism in Europe in the Twentieth Century* (Cambridge: Cambridge Scholars, 2014), 95.

  Wilhelm Röpke, l'autre Hayek. Aux origines du néolibéralisme (Paris: Publications de la Sorbonne, 2015).

Solum, LB, 'Intellectual History as Constitutional Theory' (2015) 101 *Virginia Law Review* 1111.

Sornarajah, M, 'Power and Justice in Foreign Investment Arbitration' (1997) 14 *Journal of International Arbitration* 103.

  'Power and Justice in International Law' (1997) 1 *Singapore Journal of International and Comparative Law* 28.

  'Power and Justice: Third World Resistance in International Law' (2006) 10 *Singapore Year Book of International Law* 19.

  Resistance and Change in the International Law on Foreign Investment (Cambridge: Cambridge University Press, 2015).

  'On Fighting for Global Justice: The Role of a Third World International Lawyer' (2016) 37 *Third World Quarterly* 1972.

  The International Law on Foreign Investment, 4th edition (Cambridge: Cambridge University Press, 2017).

Sornarajah, M and Wang, J, 'China, India, and International Law: A Justice Based Vision between the Romantic and Realist Perceptions' (2019) 9 *Asian Journal of International Law* 217.

Spaulding, NW, 'Independence and Experimentalism in the Department of Justice' (2011) 63 *Stanford Law Review* 409.

  'The Historical Consciousness of the Resistant Subject' (2011) 1 *UC Irvine Law Review* 677.

Spiro, PJ, 'Treaties, Executive Agreements, and Constitutional Method' (2001) 79 *Texas Law Review* 961.

Stahn, C, *The Law and Practice of International Territorial Administration: Versailles to Iraq and Beyond* (Cambridge: Cambridge University Press, 2008).

Staples, ALS, *The Birth of Development: How the World Bank, Food and Agriculture Organization, and World Health Organization Changed the World, 1945–1965* (Kent: The Kent State University Press, 2006).

Stark, B, 'Postmodern Rhetoric, Economic Rights and an International Text: "A Miracle for Breakfast"' (1993) 33 *Virginia Journal of International Law* 433.

Stedman Jones, G, *Karl Marx: Greatness and Illusion* (Cambridge: Belknap Press, 2016).

Stephens, T, 'Reimagining International Environmental Law in the Anthropocene' in Kotzé, L (ed), *Environmental Law and Governance for the Anthropocene* (Oxford: Hart, 2017), 31.

Stewart, C, 'History and Anthropology' (2016) 45 *Annual Review of Anthropology* 79.

Stolleis, M, 'Prologue: Reluctance to Glance in the Mirror. The Changing Face of German Jurisprudence after 1933 and Post-1945' in Joerges, C and Ghaleigh, NS (eds), *Darker Legacies of Law in Europe: The Shadow of National Socialism and Fascism over Europe and Its Legal Traditions* (Oxford: Hart, 2003), 1.

Strang, J, 'Two Generations of Scandinavian Legal Realists' (2009) 32 *Retfærd Årgang* 62.

Sugarman, D and Pue, WW, 'Introduction: Towards a Cultural History of Lawyers' in Pue, WW and Sugarman, D (eds), *Lawyers and Vampires: Cultural Histories of Legal Professions* (Oxford: Hart, 2003).

Suk Gersen, J, 'The Socratic Method in the Age of Trauma' (2017) 130 *Harvard Law Review* 2320.

Sur, S, 'Le recours à la force dans l'affaire du Kosovo et le droit international', *Les notes de l'Ifri – no 22* (Paris: Institut français des relations internationales, 2000).

    'Peut-on parler d'une hégémonie américaine?' in *Travaux et Recherches de l'IFRI, Observation et théorie des relations internationales* (Paris: Institut français des relations internationales, 2001), 83.

Suri, J, *Power and Protest: The Global Revolution and the Rise of Détente* (Cambridge: Harvard University Press, 2005).

Szasz, PC, 'The Security Council Starts Legislating' (2002) 96 *American Journal of International Law* 901.

Talmon, S, 'The Security Council as World Legislature' (2005) 99 *American Journal of International Law* 175.

Teles, SM, *The Rise of the Conservative Legal Movement* (Princeton and Oxford: Princeton University Press, 2008).

Teschke, B, 'Carl Schmitt's Concepts of War: A Categorical Failure' in Meierhenrich, J and Simons, O (eds), *The Oxford Handbook of Carl Schmitt* (Oxford: Oxford University Press, 2016), 367.

    The Myth of 1648: Class, Geopolitics and the Making of Modern International Relations (London: Verso, 2003).

    'Decisions and Indecisions: Political and Intellectual Receptions of Carl Schmitt' (2011) 67 *New Left Review* 61.

Tesón, FR, 'Collective Humanitarian Intervention' (1996) 17 *Michigan Journal of International Law* 232.

Thomas, C, 'Causes of Inequality in the International Economic Order: Critical Race Theory and Postcolonial Development' (1999) 9 *Transnational Law and Contemporary Problems* 1.

    'Transnational Migration, Globalization, and Governance: Theorizing a Crisis' in Orford, A and Hoffmann, F (eds), *The Oxford Handbook of the Theory of International Law* (Oxford: Oxford University Press, 2016), 882.

Thompson, EP, *The Making of the English Working Class* (London: Victor Gollancz, 1963).

    Whigs and Hunters: The Origins of the Black Act (New York: Pantheon, 1975).

'The New Left' in Winslow, C (ed), *EP Thompson and the Making of the New Left* (New York: Monthly Review Press, 2014), 119.

Tomlins, C, 'After Critical Legal History: Scope, Scale, Structure' (2012) 8 *Annual Review of Law and Social Science* 31.

'Foreword: "Law As ..." III – *Glossolalia*: Toward a Minor (Historical) Jurisprudence' (2015) 5 *UC Irvine Law Review* 239.

Toufayan, M, Tourme-Jouannet, E, and Ruiz Fabri, H (eds) *Droit international et nouvelles approches sur le tiers-monde: entre repetition et renouveau* (Paris: Société de Législation Comparée, 2013).

Trachtman, JP, 'The Growing Obsolescence of Customary International Law' in Bradley, CA (ed), *Custom's Future: International Law in a Changing World* (Cambridge: Cambridge University Press, 2016), 172.

Trexler, RC, 'Florentine Religious Experience: The Sacred Image' (1972) 19 *Studies in the Renaissance* 7.

Triantafilou, EE, 'Contemporaneity and Its Limits in Treaty Interpretation' in Caron, DD, Schill, SW, Smutny, AC, and Triantafilou, EE (eds), *Practising Virtue: Inside International Arbitration* (Oxford: Oxford University Press, 2015), 449.

Tribe, K, *Strategies of Economic Order: German Economic Discourse 1750–1950* (Cambridge: Cambridge University Press, 1995).

'Translator's Introduction' in Koselleck, R, *Futures Past: On the Semantics of Historical Time* (trans Tribe, K) (New York: Columbia University Press, 2004), vii.

Tribe, LH, 'Taking Text and Structure Seriously: Reflections on Free-Form Method in Constitutional Interpretation' (1995) 108 *Harvard Law Review* 1221.

Trubek, D, 'Where the Action Is: Critical Legal Studies and Empiricism' (1984) 36 *Stanford Law Review* 575.

Trüper, H with Chakrabarty, D, and Subrahmanyam, S, 'Introduction: Teleology and History – Nineteenth-Century Fortunes of an Enlightenment Project' in Trüper, H, Chakrabarty, D, and Subrahmanyam, S (eds), *Historical Teleologies in the Modern World* (London: Bloomsbury, 2015), 3.

Tuck, R, *The Rights of War and Peace: Political Thought and the International Order from Grotius to Kant* (Oxford: Oxford University Press, 1999).

Tully, J (ed), *Meaning and Context: Quentin Skinner and his Critics* (Princeton: Princeton University Press, 1988).

Tully, J, *An Approach to Political Philosophy: Locke in Contexts* (Cambridge: Cambridge University Press, 1993).

Tunkin, G, 'Is General International Law Customary Law Only?' (1993) 4 *European Journal of International Law* 534.

Tuori, K and Sankari, S (eds), *The Many Constitutions of Europe* (Surrey: Ashgate, 2010).

Twining, W, *Karl Llewellyn and the Realist Movement* (London: Weidenfeld and Nicholson, 1973).

'The Bad Man Revisited' (1973) 58 *Cornell Law Review* 275.

'Other People's Power: The Bad Man and English Positivism 1897–1997' (1997) 63 *Brooklyn Law Review* 189.

'RG Collingwood's Autobiography: One Reader's Response' (1998) 25 *Journal of Law and Society* 603.

Rethinking Evidence: Exploratory Essays, 2nd edition (Cambridge: Cambridge University Press, 2006).

'Lawyers' Stories' in *Rethinking Evidence: Exploratory Essays*, 2nd edition (Cambridge: Cambridge University Press, 2006), 286.

'Narrative and Generalizations in Argumentation about Questions of Fact' in *Rethinking Evidence: Exploratory Essays*, 2nd edition (Cambridge: Cambridge University Press, 2006), 332.

'Taking Facts Seriously' in *Rethinking Evidence: Exploratory Essays*, 2nd edition (Cambridge: Cambridge University Press, 2006), 14.

Tzouvala, N, 'TWAIL and the "Unwilling or Unable" Doctrine: Continuities and Ruptures' (2016) 109 *AJIL Unbound* 266.

Capitalism as Civilisation: A History of International Law (Cambridge: Cambridge University Press, 2020).

'The Ordo-Liberal Origins of Modern International Investment Law: Constructing Competition on a Global Scale' in Haskell, JD and Rasulov, A (eds), *New Voices and New Perspectives in International Economic Law* (Cham: Springer, 2020), 37.

Umozurike, UO, *International Law and Colonialism in Africa* (Enugu: Nwamife, 1979).

UNCTAD, *World Investment Report 2018* (Geneva: United Nations, 2019).

Vadi, V, 'International Law and Its Histories: Methodological Risks and Opportunities' (2017) 58 *Harvard International Law Journal* 311.

Vagts, DF, 'Hegemonic International Law' (2001) 95 *American Journal of International Law* 843.

'International Relations Looks at Customary International Law: A Traditionalist's Defence' (2004) 15 *European Journal of International Law* 1031.

Vaihinger, H, *The Philosophy of 'As-If'. A System of the Theoretical, Practical and Religious Fictions of Mankind* (trans CK Ogden) (London: Routledge and Kegan Paul, 1924).

van Aaken, A, 'Rational Choice Theory' in Carty, Anthony (ed), *Oxford Bibliographies Online: International Law* (Oxford: Oxford University Press, 2012).

Vanberg, VJ, 'The Freiburg School: Walter Eucken and Ordoliberalism', Freiburg Discussion Papers on Constitutional Economics, No. 04/11 (2004).

Van Harten, G, 'Perceived Bias in Investment Treaty Arbitration' in Waibel, M, Kaushal, A, Chung, K-HL, and Balchin, C (eds), *The Backlash against Investment Arbitration: Perceptions and Reality* (Alphen aan den Rijn: Wolters Kluwer, 2010), 43.

van Ittersum, MJ, *Profit and Principle: Hugo Grotius, Natural Rights Theories and the Rise of Dutch Power in the East Indies (1595–1615)* (Leiden: Brill, 2006).

van Ittersum, M and Jacobs, J, 'Are We All Global Historians Now? An Interview with David Armitage' (2012) 36 *Itinerario* 7.

Vergerio, C, 'Context, Reception, and the Study of Great Thinkers in International Relations' (2019) 11 *International Theory* 110.

Verheecke, L, Eberhardt, P, Olivet, C, and Cossar-Gilbert, S, *Red Carpet Courts: 10 Stories of How the Rich and Powerful Hijacked Justice* (Brussels and Amsterdam: Friends of the Earth Europe and International, the Transnational Institute and Corporate Europe Observatory, 2019).

Vicuña, FO, 'Time in International Law and Arbitration' in Caron, DD, Schill, SW, Smutny, AC, and Triantafilou, EE (eds), *Practising Virtue: Inside International Arbitration* (Oxford: Oxford University Press, 2015), 584.

Vigneswaran, D and Quirk, J, 'Past Masters and Modern Inventions: Intellectual History as Critical Theory' (2010) 24 *International Relations* 107.

Vinen, R, *The Long '68: Radical Protest and Its Enemies* (Milton Keynes: Allen Lane, 2018).

Vitalis, R, *White World Order, Black Power Politics: The Birth of American International Relations* (Ithaca: Cornell University Press, 2015).

von Bernstorff, J, *Der Glaube an das universale Recht: Zur Völkerrechtstheorie Hans Kelsens und seiner Schüler* (Baden-Baden: Nomos, 2001).

   The Public International Law Theory of Hans Kelsen: Believing in Universal Law (Cambridge: Cambridge University Press, 2011).

   'Hans Kelsen and the Return of Universalism' in Orford, A and Hoffmann, F (eds), *The Oxford Handbook of the Theory of International Law* (Oxford: Oxford University Press, 2016), 192.

   'The Relationship between Theory and Practice in International Law' in d'Aspremont, J, Gazzini, T, Nollkaemper, A, and Werner, W (eds), *International Law as a Profession* (Cambridge: Cambridge University Press, 2017), 222.

von Bernstorff, J and Dann, P (eds), *The Battle for International Law: South-North Perspectives on the Decolonization Era* (Oxford: Oxford University Press, 2019).

von Savigny, FV, *Of the Vocation of Our Age for Legislation and Jurisprudence* (trans A Hayward) (London: Littlewood & Co, 1831).

Waibel, M, 'Putting the MFN Genie Back in the Bottle' (2018) 112 *AJIL Unbound* 60.

Waibel, M, Kaushal, A, Chung, K-HL, and Balchin, C (eds), *The Backlash against Investment Arbitration: Perceptions and Reality* (Alphen aan den Rijn: Wolters Kluwer, 2010).

Walker, EC, 'The Long Revolution of Raymond Williams' (2006) 37 *The Wordsworth Circle* 60.

Walker, RBJ, *Inside/Outside: International Relations as Political Theory* (Cambridge: Cambridge University Press, 1993).

Wang, H, *China's New Order: Society, Politics and Economy in Transition* (Cambridge: Harvard University Press, 2003).

   The End of the Revolution: China and the Limits of Modernity (London and New York: Verso, 2009).

   China's Twentieth Century: China's Twentieth Century: Revolution, Retreat and the Road to Equality (London and New York: Verso, 2016).

Wang, T, 'International Law in China: Historical and Contemporary Perspectives' (1990) 221 *Recueil des Cours* 195.

Wæver, O, 'The Speech Act of Realism: The Move That Made IR' in Guilhot, N (ed), *The Invention of International Relations Theory* (New York: Columbia, 2011), 97.

Weber, C, 'The Trump Presidency, Episode 1: Simulating Sovereignty' (2017) 20 *Theory & Event* 132.

Wedgwood, R, "NATO's Campaign in Yugoslavia' (1999) 93 *American Journal of International Law* 828.

Weeramantry, CG, *Islamic Jurisprudence* (New York: St Martin Press, 1988).

Wegmann, M, *Früher Neoliberalismus und Europäische Integration* (Baden-Baden: Nomos, 2002).

Weiler, JHH, 'The Rule of Lawyers and the Ethos of Diplomats: Reflections on the Internal and External Legitimacy of WTO Dispute Settlement' (2001) 35 *Journal of World Trade* 191.

Weiler, T, *The Interpretation of International Investment Law: Equality, Discrimination and Minimum Standards of Treatment in Historical Context* (Leiden and Boston: Martinus Nijhoff, 2013).

Weinstein, B, 'History without a Cause? Grand Narratives, World History, and the Postcolonial Dilemma' (2005) 50 *International Review of Social History* 71.

Weis, R and Twining, W, 'Reconstructing the Truth about Edith Thompson: The Shakespearean and the Jurist' in Twining, W (ed), *Rethinking Evidence: Exploratory Essays*, 2nd edition (Cambridge: Cambridge University Press, 2006), 344.

Weiss, TG, 'On the Brink of a New Era? Humanitarian Interventions, 1991–94' in Daniel, DCF and Hayes, BC (eds), *Beyond Traditional Peacekeeping* (Hampshire and New York: Palgrave Macmillan, 1995).

White, JB, *Heracles' Bow: Essays on the Rhetoric and Poetics of the Law* (Madison: University of Wisconsin Press, 1985).

White, H, *The Content of the Form: Narrative Discourse and Historical Representation* (Baltimore and London: The John Hopkins University Press, 1987).

Whitman, JQ, *The Verdict of Battle: The Law of Victory and the Making of Modern War* (Cambridge: Harvard University Press, 2014).

Wigger, A, 'Debunking the Ordoliberal Myth in Post-War Europe' in Hien, J and Joerges, C (eds), *Ordoliberalism, Law and the Rule of Economics* (Oxford and Portland: Hart, 2017), 161.

Wilde, R, *International Territorial Administration: How Trusteeship and the Civilizing Mission Never Went Away* (Oxford: Oxford University Press, 2008).

Wilf, S, 'Law/Text/Past' (2011) 1 *UC Irvine Law Review* 543.

Willgerodt, H and Peacock, A, 'German Liberalism and Economic Revival' in Peacock, A and Willgerodt, H (eds), *Germany's Social Market Economy: Origins and Evolution* (London: Palgrave Macmillan, 1989).

Williams, R, *Culture and Society 1780–1950* (London: Chatto & Windus, 1958).

The Long Revolution (London: Chatto & Windus, 1961).

The Country and the City (New York: Oxford University Press, 1973).

Keywords: A Vocabulary of Culture and Society (Oxford: Oxford University Press, 2015 [1976]).

Williams, R (ed), *May Day Manifesto 1968* (London: Verso, 2018).

Wilson, P, 'The Myth of the "First Great Debate"' (1998) 24 *Review of International Studies* 1.

Winslow, C (ed), *EP Thompson and the Making of the New Left* (New York: Monthly Review Press, 2014).

Winslow, C, Hay, D, and Linebaugh, P, 'Introduction to the Second Edition' in Hay, D, Linebaugh, P, Rule, JG, Thompson, EP, and Winslow, C (eds), *Albion's Fatal*

Tree: Crime and Society in Eighteenth-Century England (London and New York: Verso, 2011), xix.

Woldemarian, SB, Maguire, A, and von Meding, J, 'Forced Human Displacement, the Third World and International Law: A TWAIL Perspective' (2019) 20 *Melbourne Journal of International Law* 1.

Wood, CS, *Forgery Replica Fiction: Temporalities of German Renaissance Art* (Chicago and London: University of Chicago, 2008).

Wood, M, 'The Present Position within the ILC on the Topic "Identification of Customary international": In Partial Response to Sienho Yee, Report on the ILC Project on "Identification of Customary International Law' (2016) 15 *Chinese Journal of International Law* 3.

'The Iraq Inquiry: Some Personal Reflections' (2018) 87 *British Yearbook of International Law* 149.

Wright, J, 'The Modern Law of Self-Defence', speech presented at the International Institute for Strategic Studies, London (11 January 2017), *EJIL:Talk!*, www.ejiltalk.org/the-modern-law-of-self-defence/.

Wu, M, 'The WTO and China's Unique Economic Structure' in Liebman, BL and Milhaupt, CJ (eds), *Regulating the Visible Hand? The Institutional Implications of Chinese State Capitalism* (Oxford: Oxford University Press, 2015), 313.

'The "China, Inc" Challenge to Global Trade Governance' (2016) 57 *Harvard International Law Journal* 261.

Xue, H, *Chinese Contemporary Perspectives on International Law: History, Culture, and International Law (Pocketbooks of The Hague Academy of International Law)* (Leiden/Boston: Brill/Nijhoff, 2012).

'Meaningful Dialogue through a Common Discourse: Law and Values in a Multi-Polar World' (2011) 1 *Asian Journal of International Law* 13.

Yackee, JW, 'The First Investor-State Arbitration: The Suez Canal Company v Egypt (1864)' (2016) 17 *The Journal of World Investment and Trade* 401.

Yee, S, 'Towards a Harmonious World: The Roles of the International Law of Co-progressiveness and Leader States' (2008) 7 *Chinese Journal of International Law* 99.

'Dispute Settlement on the Belt and Road: Ideas on System, Spirit and Style' (2018) 17 *Chinese Journal of International Law* 907, at 911.

Young, JP, *Yesterday's Hero*, 1975, www.youtube.com/watch?v=KVSEiveFY7g.

Young, B, 'The Tyranny of the Definite Article: Some Thoughts on the Art of Intellectual History' (2002) 28 *History of European Ideas* 101.

Zapatero, P, 'Legal Imagination in Vitoria: The Power of Ideas' (2009) 11 *Journal of the History of International Law* 221.

Zarbiyev, F, 'A Genealogy of Textualism in Treaty Interpretation' in Bianchi, A, Peat, D, and Windsor, M (eds), *Interpretation in International Law* (Oxford: Oxford University Press, 2015), 251.

'Saying Credibly What the Law Is: On Marks of Authority in International Law' (2018) 9 *Journal of International Dispute Settlement* 291.

'The "Cash Value" of the Rules of Treaty Interpretation' (2019) 32 *Leiden Journal of International Law* 33.

Zeng, K and Liang, W, *China and Global Trade Governance: China's First Decade in the World Trade Organization* (London and New York: Routledge, 2013).

Zeng, L, 'Conceptual Analysis of China's Belt and Road Initiative: A Road towards a Regional Community of Common Destiny' (2016) 15 *Chinese Journal of International Law* 517.

Zhao, T, 'A Political World Philosophy in Terms of All-Under Heaven (*Tian-xia*)' (2009) 56 *Diogenes* 1.

Index

abridgment, Whig history and, 84, 120–122
Abs, Hermann, 268
Alberti, Valentin, 166
Alciato, Andrea, 148
Alexander, Sally, 137
Althusser, Louis, 166
Ames, James Barr, 118
anachronisms
  art and, 154–155
  Butterfield's critique of, 107, 119–120, 125,
    138–139
  Cambridge School on, 109
  concept of, 81, 86
  defense of, 86–87, 154–155, 154–155
  Fitzmaurice on, 82
  heterotemporality, 87–89
  international lawyers and, 82, 84–85, 91–92,
    171, 172–173
  Maitland on, 116, 119
  Moyn on, 79, 254
  prohibition of, 13, 82, 85
  Skinner on, 140–141
Anaya, S. James, 166
The Ancient Constitution and the Feudal Law
  (Pocock), 128
Anghie, Antony, 166, 195, 198
Annales School, 138
anti-formalism, 208–212
anti-metaphysical approaches, to international
  law, 212–217
Aristotelian university metaphysics, 165
Armitage, David, 89–90, 93–94, 270–271
art history, 92, 149–152, 149–152, 154–155, 154–155

Badiou, Alain, 166
Bandung Conference, 59–60

Barthes, Roland, 166
Bartolus of Saxoferrato, 146–147
Baudouin, François, 148
Bederman, David, 76
Bell, Duncan, 93–94
Bellinger, John, III, 38
Belt and Road Initiative, 62–64
Benton, Lauren, 81, 100, 236, 254, 257–259
Berger, Sandy, 27–28
Bethlehem, Daniel, 39, 65, 247
Bethlehem principles, 39
bilateral investment treaties (BITs), 24–25, 46,
  268
The Birth of Biopolitics (Foucault), 50–53, 265,
  270, 270
Bismarck, Otto von, 237
BITs. *See* bilateral investment treaties
Blair, Tony, 27
Bluntschli, Johann Caspar, 237, 239–240
Böhm, Franz, 265
Braudel, Fernand, 136
Brazil, international law in, 57
Brett, Annabel, 93–94
BRICS, 12, 18–19, 57
Budé, Guillaume, 148
Burke-White, William, 37
Burrow, John, 93–94
Butterfield, Herbert, 84–85, 93–94, 93–94, 107
  on abridgment, 121–122
  on anachronism, 119–120, 125
  Cambridge School of Political Thought
    influenced by, 112–115
  challenge to constitutional history, 112–115
  Christian realism and, 122–127
  critical reactions to, 125
  in Nazi Germany, 123, 125–126

Butterfield, Herbert (cont.)
  on presentism, 119–120, 125
  Whig Constitutionalism and, 112–127
  on Whig history, 119–122, 125, 126–127,
    127–128, 194–195
  The Whig Interpretation of History, 107–109,
    113, 113, 119–120

Cambridge School of Political Thought, 83.
    See also Butterfield, Herbert; Hunter,
    Ian; Pocock, J. G. A.; Skinner, Quentin
  Butterfield as influence on, 112–115
  contextualist approach and, 94–95, 98
  Hunter on, 168–172
  interpretation and, 93–99
  methodological arguments of, 94, 108–109,
    108–109, 135–138, 135–138, 156–157,
    156–157
  Pocock and, 127–130, 168–169, 168–169, 183, 183
    *The Ancient Constitution and the Feudal
      Law*, 128
    emergence of, 128–129
    empiricist methods as influence on,
      129–130
    Laslett and, 128–130
  proponents of, 93–94, 108–109, 108–109
  Skinner and, 135–144, 168–169, 168–169
Canada
  EU-Canada Comprehensive Economic and
    Trade Agreement, 46
  North American Free Trade Agreement,
    24–25, 46
capitalism, 22–23, 30–31, 50, 58, 60, 143–144,
    274, 275, 318, 318
Carter, Jimmy, 264
Cassirer, Ernst, 166
causality. *See* model of historic causality
Chayes, Abram, 211
Chayes, Antonia, 211
China
  aggression, opposition to, 28–29, 59–60,
    64–65
  Bandung Conference and, 59–60
  Belt and Road Initiative of, 62–64
  break-up of Soviet Union and, 57–58
  Five Principles of Peaceful Coexistence and,
    59–60
  histories of international law and, 57–58
  imperialism and, 59, 64–65
  international law approach to, 58–60, 64–65,
    64–65

Korean War and, 59–60
  model of historic causality, 67
  neoliberalism and, 57–58, 61–62
  New Left in, 60, 62–63
  People's Republic of China, 58–59
    founding of, 59
    international recognition of, 60–61
    reform and opening-up policy, 57–58
    reformist economic policy in, 61–63
    revolutionary politics and, 58
    rise of, 3–4, 12, 18–19, 56–68, 57, 56–68
    Russia and, 64–65
    Third World Approaches to International
      Law movement and, 65
    in World Trade Organization, accession to,
      62
Chomsky, Noam, 166
Christian movements, human rights and,
    262–263
Christian realism, Butterfield and, 122–127
civilizational cultures, 159
climate change, 3–4, 44–56, 47–56, 88, 249
Clinton, Bill, 28
CLS movement. *See* Critical Legal Scholars
    movement
Cohen, Felix, 210–211
Cohen, Harlan, 298
Coke, Edward, 133–134
Cold War, 2–3, 19–20, 22, 28, 28, 32–33, 291
colonialism. *See also* postcolonial scholarship
  China and, 59
  histories of, 71–75, 77–78, 77–78, 159,
    257–259, 257–259
  international lawyers on legacy of, 195, 198,
    201, 201–206
Commentaries on American Law (Kent), 209
common law
  Maitland on, 116, 118, 134
  Pocock on, 131–135
common lawyers, 13–14, 110, 127–128, 134, 176,
    240
'common-law mind,' 133–134
completion, history as, 75–81
The Concept of the Political (Schmitt),
    306–307
conceptual history, 72–73, 142–143, 300–301,
    305, 306–307, 309
Connan, François, 148
Constitution, US, originalist approach to,
    96–98
constitutional historians, 170

constitutionalization, international law and, 3, 22, 53, 55, 268, 268, 279–280, 282–283, 282–283, 291–292, 294, 294, 310–311

contextualist history, 72, 105–112, 165, 169–172, 197, 206–208, 206–208, 316–317

contextualist method, 172–177. *See also* Butterfield, Herbert; Hunter, Ian; Pocock, J. G. A.; Skinner, Quentin

Critical Legal Scholars (CLS) movement, 6

Cujas, Jacques, 148

custom, 29, 98–99, 133, 134, 155, 182, 182, 207–208, 216, 226, 227, 235–238, 242–243, 249–250, 249–250

customary international law, 24–25, 37, 49, 98–99, 98–99, 189, 189, 235–243, 239–243, 249

Davis, Natalie Zemon, 136

decolonization, international law and, 23–24, 34, 53, 101, 215, 215–217, 268

Deng Xiaoping, 57–58

Derrida, Jacques, 166

Devetak, Richard, 171–172

dialectical historiography, 165

disciplinary history, 78–79

dispute settlement mechanisms
    International Convention on the Settlement of Investment Disputes between States and Nationals of Other States, 23–24
    under UN Convention on the Law of the Sea, 22
    for World Trade Organization, 232–233

dominium, 271, 276

Douaren, François Le, 148

Dunn, John, 93–94, 108

Dyzenhaus, David, 203

Eagleton, Terry, 166

Economic Planning and International Order (Robbins), 271

EEC. *See* European Economic Community

Ehrlich, Thomas, 211

empire
    British Empire, 113–114, 136, 254, 257–259, 257–262
    Hapsburg Empire, 275
    historians of, 74
    Holy Roman Empire, 144–147, 175–176, 175–176
    informal empire, 33

international law and, 5, 34–35, 34–35, 254, 257–259, 257–259, 271
    of metaphysics, Hunter on, 166–167
    Ordoliberalism and end of, 101, 266–268, 271, 274–276, 274–276, 283, 283

empiricism
    challenges to, 10, 60, 67–68, 67–68, 73–74, 73–74, 86–92, 86–92, 98–99, 98–99, 180–181, 226–235, 226–235
    historical methods as, 5–7, 8–9, 8–9, 12, 13, 77–78, 77–78, 81–92, 81–92, 94–95, 107, 107, 109–110, 109–110, 119–120, 129–130, 173, 173, 225–226, 295–296, 295–296

Horkheimer on, 90–91

Hunter on, 169

international law and, 5–6, 8–9, 15, 16–17, 29–30, 29–30, 70, 74–75, 76, 77–78, 80, 84–85, 85, 91–92, 92, 100, 103, 105–106, 105–106, 110–111, 110–111, 175–176, 176, 180–181, 208, 226–235, 226–235, 252, 252, 286, 317, 317

Energy Charter Treaty, 24–25, 46

English common lawyers. *See* common lawyers

Enlightenment, 113, 172, 175–176, 248, 262–263, 303, 304

Erhard, Ludwig, 265

EU. *See* European Union

EU-Canada Comprehensive Economic and Trade Agreement, 46

Eucken, Walter, 265

Eurocentric law of nations, 215–216

European Convention on Human Rights, 262–263

European Economic Community (EEC), 273

European Union (EU)
    economic crisis in, 52
    EU-Canada Comprehensive Economic and Trade Agreement, 46
    international economic law in, 266–268
    international law in, 182, 212–217, 212–217

expansionism, by US, 30–36

fact-finding, for past
    historian's role in, 222–223
    in international law practice, 218–223
    juridical facts in, 221

fascism, 124–125, 201–206, 271, 291, 308. *See also* National Socialism

Febvre, Lucien, 136

feminist movements, 299

Filmer, Robert, 128
Fitzmaurice, Andrew, 93–94, 195, 206, 236, 255, 255, 258
Five Principles of Peaceful Coexistence, 59–60
Forbes, Duncan, 93–94
Ford, Lisa, 81, 236, 254, 257–259
Foucault, Michel, 50–53, 72–73, 136, 265, 268, 268. *See also* Ordoliberalism
The Foundations of Modern Political Thought (Skinner), 144–146
Frank, Jerome, 211
French Revolution, human rights and, 262–263
Freud, Sigmund, 6
Friedrich, Carl, 301–302
Fuller, Lon, 203

GAL project. *See* Global Administrative Law project
game theory, 7, 14–15, 192, 247
Garcia, Frank, 298
General Agreements on Tariffs and Trade (GATT), 22–23, 279–280
    decolonization and, 101, 267–275
    Ordoliberalism and, 53, 101, 266–275
    Tokyo Round, 271
    Uruguay Round, 21
Gentili, Alberico, 161–162
The Gentle Civilizer of Nations (Koskenniemi), 160–161
Gerber, David, 267
German historical school, 237–238, 240, 287. *See also* Savigny, Friedrich Carl von
Ginsburg, Tom, 211–212
Ginzburg, Carlo, 103, 195–196
Global Administrative Law (GAL) project, 259, 261–262
global history, 5, 66, 70–71, 70–71
Globalists (Slobodian), 273–281, 296–298, 297–298
Goldsmith, Jack, 211–212
Goodrich, Peter, 191, 209
Gordon, Linda, 136
gradualism, 113–114
Großraum, concept of, 65–66, 305–307
Grotius, Hugo, 161–162
'grudge-informer' case, 203–204
Guevara, Che, 136
Guldi, Jo, 89–90

Habermas, Jürgen, 166, 301–302
Hägerström, Axel, 214–215

Hall, Stuart, 137, 166
Hammarskjöld, Dag, 53, 214, 267–275
Hart, H. L. A., 203–204
Hartog, François, 196
Hayek, Friedrich von, 53, 101, 265, 271, 273–274, 273–274, 276–277, 278, 280
Hegel, Georg Wilhelm Friedrich, 166
hegemony, 18–19, 30–34, 42, 57, 57, 65–66
hermeneutic of suspicion
    Critical Legal Scholars movement as response to, 6
    cross-disciplinary version of, 6–9, 285, 294, 314–315
    dangers of, 286–287
    deployment of, 314–315
    function of, 310–312
    international adjudication and, 312–314
    international investment law and, 314
    international law and, 5–9, 310–315, 310–315
    Kennedy, Duncan, and, 5–6, 286, 310
    legal formalism and, 7
    meaning of, 6–7
    Ricoeur and, 6
Hill, Christopher, 136–138
historic causality. *See* model of historic causality
historical consciousness, 132, 144–149
    classical antiquity and, 147–148
    Roman law and, 145–147
historical materialism, 72–74
The History Manifesto (Armitage and Guldi), 89–90
Hobsbawm, Eric, 136–138
Holmes, Oliver Wendell, 118, 200–201, 210
Hont, Istvan, 93–94
Hu Jintao, 61
Huber, Max, 221
Hull, Isabel, 81, 226, 255, 255
human rights
    definitions of, 263
    European Convention on Human Rights, 262–263
    historical starting points for, 262–263
    Moyn on, 79, 81, 253–254, 254, 263–265, 264
    narratives of, 253–254
    Universal Declaration of Human Rights, 262–263
    US expansionism and, 31–32
human rights lawyers, 31–32, 102, 103, 263, 263, 296–299, 296–299

humanism, 1–5, 111–112, 131, 144–149, 149, 174–175, 174–175
   mos gallicus, 132, 134–135
   Renaissance and, 145, 149–156, 156–157, 169, 172
   scholasticism and, 148–149
   study of classical antiquity and, 147–148
humanitarian interventions, 25–26, 28–29, 32, 246–247, 246–247, 262–263, 317–318
Hunt, Lynn, 263
Hunter, Ian, 78, 107–111, 157–164, 157–164, 206–207, 304, 304–305
   on Cambridge School, 168–172
   on civilizational cultures, 158
   on contextualist historians, 165, 169–172
   on German constitutional historians, 161–162, 170
   on indigenous lawyers, 158
   on international lawyers, 157–172, 195, 195
   on Third World Approaches to International Law scholars, 158, 198
Hurst, J. Willard, 118

ICC. *See* International Criminal Court
ICJ. *See* International Court of Justice
ICSID Convention. *See* International Convention on the Settlement of Investment Disputes between States and Nationals of Other States
imperialism
   China and, 58, 60, 65–66
   humanitarian intervention and, 32
   international law and, 19, 34–35, 42, 42, 47, 47, 50, 50, 201, 201–206
   on Third World Approaches to International Law and, critique of, 34–35, 77–78, 77–78
imperium, 271, 276
India
   Five Principles of Peaceful Coexistence and, 59–60
   use of force against Pakistan, 33
indigenous lawyers, 158, 166
indigenous rights, in Australia, 205
inequality, 3–4, 31–32, 31–32, 34, 35–36, 55–56, 102, 298–299
intellectual history, 5, 71, 72, 89–90, 94–95, 101, 108, 109–110, 138, 139–141, 157–164, 157–164, 171, 273–281, 273–281, 295–296, 295–296, 298, 298, 316–317

international adjudication
   China and, 61
   conflictual style of, 198
   consolidation of investment protection through, 24–25, 249, 292–293, 311–312
   constitutionalization and, 22
   expansion of, 3, 21–24
   judicialization and, 3, 22
   neoformalism and, 7, 314–315
   political stakes of, 25, 249, 286, 286, 294, 311–312, 314
International Convention on the Settlement of Investment Disputes between States and Nationals of Other States (ICSID Convention), 23–24, 45–46
International Court of Justice (ICJ), 21, 25, 25, 185–189, 187–189, 192, 221–222, 221–222, 312–314, 312–314
International Criminal Court (ICC), 22, 46, 249
international crises, historicization of, 44–56
   climate change crisis, 44–56
   in European Union, 50–53
   financial crisis, 44–56
   food crisis, 44–56
   international investment law and, 45–46, 49–50, 49–50
international economic law
   decolonization and, 101, 267–275
   European Economic Community and, 273
   European Union and, 266–268
   General Agreement on Tariffs and Trade and, 22–23, 53, 101, 267–275, 279–280, 279–280
   intellectual history of, 265–283
   Ordoliberalism as influence on, 101, 266–275
   Slobodian on, 277
   World Trade Organization and, 21, 46, 53, 62, 62–63, 232, 233–234, 267–275, 276–277, 279–280, 279–280, 282, 297–298, 297
international investment law, 45–46, 49–50, 49–50, 268, 268, 314, 314
international relations scholars
   Butterfield and, 112, 123, 124, 126–127
   contextual history and, 71, 73–74, 94, 94–95, 109, 109, 171, 171–172, 304
international trade law. *See* international economic law
International Tribunal for the Law of the Sea (ITLOS), 22

international tribunals. *See* tribunals
interpretation
    Cambridge School of Political Thought
        and, 13, 72, 93–99, 168–169, 170
        Skinner on, 96, 136–140, 144–146, 147
    of Chinese history, 67–68
    customary international law and, 235–243
    empiricist methods, 5–7, 8–9, 8–9, 75–81,
        75–81, 90–91
    in international law practice, 93–99, 182, 182,
        218–223, 223–226, 235–243, 235–243,
        245–248, 249–250, 256, 273–281, 273–281
    neoformalism and, 6, 8–9, 252, 252, 282, 282,
        320, 320
    originalist approach to, 96–98
    of treaties, 4, 24, 29–30, 49–50, 98–99,
        98–99, 170, 170, 226–235, 226–235,
        249–250, 249–250, 296–298, 296–298,
        311–312, 320, 320
    Whig approach to. *See The Whig
        Interpretation of History*
investment protection regimes
    bilateral investment treaties and, 24–25
    under Energy Charter Treaty, 24–25
    in international courts and tribunals, 24–25
    under North American Free Trade
        Agreement, 24–25
investor-state dispute settlement (ISDS), 45–46
Italian Renaissance, 149–156
    historicist approach to, 154–155
    interpretation of images and texts, 152–153
    myth of, 149–156
    narratives on, 153–154
    Panofsky lectures on, 149–151
ITLOS. *See* International Tribunal for the Law
    of the Sea

Jackson, John, 271
Jameson, Frederic, 166
Jay, Martin, 166
Jhering, Rudolf, 237
Jiang Shigong, 65–66
Joerges, Christian, 202, 266–268, 266–268, 272
Jouannet, Emmanuelle, 166
judges
    'grudge-informer' case, 203–204
    historians and, 84–85, 119–122, 120, 124–125,
        125–126, 174–175, 174–175, 180–181, 195,
        197, 206
    legal realist view of, 287–289, 310–311
    in postcolonial context, 198, 201–206

role of, in common law, 133, 240
role of, in international law, 25, 188–189,
    188–189, 194–197, 198, 287–288,
    287–288, 310–315, 310–315
standpoint of, 116–117, 181, 190, 190, 197–198,
    200–201, 227–229, 227–229
judicialization
    consolidation of investment protection and,
        24–25
    international courts and tribunals and, 22
    of international law, 3, 294
Justinian's Code, 146, 148, 153

Kagan, Robert, 38–39
Kahn-Freund, Otto, 118
Kant, Immanuel, 166
Kelley, Donald, 132, 134–135
Kelsen, Hans, 155–156, 212, 212–214
Kennedy, David, 163, 211–212, 211–212, 245, 282–283
Kennedy, Duncan, 6
    on globalization of legal realism, 292
    on hermeneutic of suspicion, 5–6, 286, 310
Kent, James, 209
Keywords (Williams, Raymond), 137–138
King, Martin Luther, 136
Kingsbury, Benedict, 259
Kleinberg, Ethan, 90–91
Klüber, Johan Ludvig, 161–162
Koh, Harold, 188, 211–212
Korean War, 59–60
Koselleck, Reinhart, 300–310
    conceptual history, 309
    conscience, 303
    early reception of work, 301–302
    Schmitt influence on, 299–310
Koskenniemi, Martti, 95, 160–164, 166, 298,
    298
Kosovo, NATO intervention in, 26–29
Krisch, Nico, 259
Kristeva, Julia, 166
Kritik und Krise (Koselleck), 302, 304

Laslett, Peter, 93–94, 128–129, 130
The Last Utopia (Moyn), 74, 79
lawyers. *See* common lawyers; human rights
    lawyers
legal education. *See* legal training
legal formalism. *See also* anti-formalism;
    neoformalism
    hermeneutic of suspicion and, in
        international law, 7

US legal realism as challenge to, 118,
    210–211, 210–211, 252, 252, 288–289, 290
legal humanism, 132, 134–135
legal realism
    American legal realism, 287–294
    early international influences on, 287
    formalism challenged by, 118, 210–211,
        210–211, 252, 252, 288–289, 290
    globalization of, 292
    international law influenced by, 287–288,
        290–294, 291
    positivism and, 287–288
    rule of law and, 288–289
    socio-historical context for, 289
    Scandinavian legal realism, 214–215
legal training, 100, 115–118, 176–177, 180,
    185–186, 185–186, 189–194, 189–194,
    245
Leibniz, Gottfried Wilhelm, 166
Leo, Heinrich, 166
Lesaffer, Randall, 76–77
liberal internationalism
    crisis of, 44, 57, 314, 314–315
    critiques of, 30–36, 55, 55, 316–317, 318–319
    inter-war 'disintegration' of, 291
    legal realism and, 291–292
    Ordoliberalism and, 53, 101, 265–283,
        265–283, 297–298, 297–298
    post-Cold War era of, 18–19, 21
    US war on terror and, 36–39
Liu Xiaofeng, 65–66
Llewellyn, Karl, 255–256
Locke, John, 128
longue durée history, 79–80, 88, 119–120, 169,
    318–319
Lowenfeld, Andreas, 211

Mach, Ernst, 212–213
Mackinder, Halford, 65–66
Macpherson, C. B., 138
Maitland, F. W., 115–119
    on changing social function of legal
        concepts, 116–117
    on common law doctrines, 116, 118, 134
    as legal historian, 115–116
    on real property, 116
    on scope of modern law, 117–118
Marks, Susan, 261–262
Martens, Georg Friedrich von, 161–162
Marx, Karl, 6, 237
Marxism, 66, 135

'Meaning and Understanding in the History of
    Ideas' (Skinner), 139–142
metaphysical approach, to international law,
    157–172, 206–208, 206–217
metaphysical hermeneutics of history, 165
Meyer, Timothy, 298
Mises, Ludwig von, 265
Mitchell, Juliet, 137
mixed commissions, 23
model of historic causality, 67
Mont Pèlerin society, 280
Morgenthau, Hans, 287–288
mos gallicus, 132, 134–135
Moser, Johann Jakob, 161–162, 168
Moyn, Samuel, 27–28, 43, 43, 79, 79–80
    on human rights, 263–265
    on human rights lawyers, 102
    on international lawyers, 99–100, 207, 207
    on narratives of human rights, 253–254
Müller-Armack, Alfred, 265
Myrdal, Gunnar, 214

NAFTA. *See* North American Free Trade
    Agreement
narratives. *See also* progress narratives
    of contextualist historians, 197
    empiricist rules for, 84
    evidentia in narration, 196
    of human rights, 253–254
    in myth of Italian Renaissance, 153–154
    past as, 100–102
National Socialism, 202
NATO. *See* North Atlantic Treaty
    Organization
Nazi Germany, 202
    Butterfield on, 123, 125–126
    'grudge-informer' case, 203–204
    interpretation of German law after fall of,
        201–206
neoformalism, history of international law as,
    294–310, 320, 320
neoliberalism, 283
    within Chinese characteristics, 57–58, 62–63
    human rights and, 27–28, 31–32, 31–32, 102
    international law and, 45–46, 53, 53, 268,
        268, 277, 277, 283, 283, 297–298,
        297–298, 311–312
    Ordoliberals and, 52–53, 101, 267, 267, 271,
        273, 273–281, 297–298, 297–298
A New World Order (Slaughter), 259–261
Nietzsche, Friedrich, 6

North American Free Trade Agreement (NAFTA), 24–25, 46
North Atlantic Treaty Organization (NATO), intervention in Kosovo by, 26–29
Nussbaum, Martha, 166

Onuma, Yasuaki, 215–216
Operation Allied Force, 26–29. *See also* Kosovo
Ordoliberalism
  in European Union, 101, 266–268
  General Agreements on Tariffs and Trade, 101
  Geneva school of law and economics and, 297
  international economic crises and, 50–53
  international economic law and, 265–283
  international law and, 265–283
  neoformalism and, 296–299
  World Trade Organization and, 101, 296–299
originalism, 96–98

Pakistan, India's use of force, 33
Pankakoski, Timo, 305
Panofsky, Erwin, 149–151
Paris Agreement, on climate change, 249
PCIJ. *See* Permanent Court of International Justice
People's Republic of China (PRC), 58–59. *See also* China
  founding of, 59
  international recognition of, 60–61
Permanent Court of International Justice (PCIJ), 287–288
Perrot, Jean-Claude, 136
Peters, Anne, 246–247
Petersmann, Ernst-Ulrich, 278, 297–298
philosophical history, 165
Pitts, Jennifer, 93–94
Pocock, J. G. A.
  Cambridge School of Political Thought and, 93–94, 107, 108, 127–130, 128–129, 168–169, 168–169, 183, 183
  The Ancient Constitution and the Feudal Law, 128
  on common lawyers, 127–135
  'common-law mind,' 131–135
  on historiography, 108–111, 131–135, 131–135, 183
  Laslett and, 128, 130
  Maitland as influence, 115–119, 128, 133–134, 133–134

on Roman law, 131–133
on traditions, 183
The Political Theory of Possessive Individualism (Macpherson), 138
positivism, 90–91, 129–130, 155–156, 287–288, 287–288
Posner, Eric, 211–212
postcolonial scholarship, 34, 77–78, 84–85, 86, 162–163, 165–166, 198, 201, 216–217, 304
Pound, Roscoe, 118
PRC. *See* People's Republic of China
presentism, 83, 85
  Butterfield on, 107–108, 119–120, 120, 125
  concept of, 83
  Fitzmaurice on, 258
  Hunter on, 78, 109–110, 158, 158
  international lawyers and, 11, 29–30, 85, 86, 105–106, 105–106, 172–173
progress narratives
  Butterfield and Whig history as, 107, 113, 119–121, 125, 126–127, 194–195
  contextualist methodological accounts as, 110–111, 127, 144–145, 144–145, 148–149, 153–154, 153–154, 170, 170, 172–173, 173
  critique of, 13, 30–34, 30–34, 36, 106, 110, 125, 248, 318–319
  history of international law as, 4, 19–20, 25, 25, 29–30, 30–34, 44, 44, 55–56, 247–248, 247–248
  human rights history as, 79, 254
property, 23–24, 30, 33, 36, 114–115, 115–118, 122, 141, 250, 268, 271, 288, 311, 313–314
Pufendorf, Samuel, 161–162, 168
Purcell, Kate, 207
Pütter, Johann Stephan, 161–162

Radbruch, Gustav, 203
Rage for Order (Benton and Ford), 257–259
Ranke, Leopold von, 168
rational choice theory, 211–212, 232–233, 292
realism. *See also* Christian realism; legal realism
  American anti-formalism and, 209–210
  in international law, 208–212, 217, 249–252, 249–252
reform and opening-up policy, in China, 57–58
Regarding Method (Skinner), 139–142
Renaissance humanism, 145, 149–156, 156–157, 169, 172
Renner, Karl, 118, 306–307
Reynolds, Henry, 166

Ricoeur, Paul, 6
Riles, Annelise, 18, 184
Rittich, Kerry, 53, 267, 267
Robbins, Lionel, 271
Roessler, Frieder, 278
Roman law, 131–133, 145–146, 147–148,
    207–208, 214–215, 214–215, 239, 251, 251
Rome Statute, 249
Röpke, Wilhelm, 53, 101, 265, 271, 273–274,
    273–274, 281
Ross, Alf, 215
Rossi, Christopher, 195
Rowbotham, Sheila, 137
rule of law, 22–23, 25, 30–34, 30–34, 40–41,
    40–41, 64–65, 64–65, 171–172,
    171–172, 202, 202, 259–261, 259–261,
    269–270, 288–289, 288–289, 312–314,
    312–314
Runciman, David, 156–157
Russia
    China and, relationship after end of Cold
        War, 64–65
    withdrawal from Energy Charter Treaty, 46
Rüstow, Alexander, 265, 271

Saussure, Ferdinand de, 166
Savigny, Friedrich Carl von, 237–239
Schachter, Oscar, 186
Schaffer, Gregory, 298
Schmitt, Carl, 55, 65–66, 168, 301–310
    juridical concepts for, 305–308
    Koselleck influence on, 299–310
Schneiderman, David, 268
scholasticism, 135–157, 165, 174, 175–176,
    206–207, 209–210, 211
Schwöbel-Patel, Christine, 298
Scott, Joan Wallach, 90–91, 136
September 11 attacks. *See* war on terror
settler colonial courts, in Australia, 205
Shaffer, Gregory, 211–212
Shawcross, Hartley, 268
Sinzheimer, Hugo, 118
Skinner, Quentin, 93–94, 107, 108–111, 134–135,
    134–135
    on Annales School, 138
    Cambridge School of Political Thought
        and, 135–144, 168–169, 168–169
    conceptualization of historical method,
        135–138, 144–145, 224
    *The Foundations of Modern Political
        Thought*, 144–146

on historical consciousness, 144–149
    classical antiquity and, 147–148
    Roman law and, 145–147
on history of political thought, 142–143
on humanists, 144–149
on individual agency, 143–144
on Italian Renaissance, myth of, 144–146,
    149–156, 149–156
    Panofsky lectures as influence on, 149–151
    'Meaning and Understanding in the History
        of Ideas,' 139–142
    Regarding Method, 139–142
on scholastic lawyers, 135–157
Slaughter, Anne-Marie, 37, 211–212, 259,
    259–261
Slobodian, Quinn, 101–102, 226, 273–281,
    273–281, 283, 283, 296–298, 296–298
Soffer, Reba, 112–113
South Africa, international law in, 57
Soviet Union. *See* Russia
Stewart, Richard, 259

teleology, 245–248
Teschke, Benno, 308
Thayer, James Bradley, 118
Theses on Theory and History (Kleinberg and
    Scott and Wilder), 90–91
Thibaut, Anton, 237–238
Third World Approaches to International Law
    (TWAIL) scholars, 34, 56, 77–78,
    77–78, 192, 195
    China and, 65
    Hunter on, 158, 198
    international lawyers and, 195
Thomasius, Christian, 168
Thompson, E. P., 136–138
Trans-Pacific Partnership (TPP), 46
treaties
    interpretation of, 4, 24, 29–30, 49–50, 98–99,
        98–99, 170, 170, 226–235, 226–235,
        249–250, 249–250, 296–298, 296–298,
        311–312, 320, 320
    obligation of, 227
    pacta sunt servanda and, 227–229
    publicity and, 229
    as source of law, 163, 227–229
    unequal, China and, 58–59
    Vienna Convention on the Law of Treaties,
        229, 231, 246, 246
    withdrawal from, 36–39, 46, 46–47
tribunals, international, creation of, 23

Trump, Donald, 45
Tuck, Richard, 93–94
Tully, James, 93–94
Tumlir, Jan, 278
TWAIL scholars. *See* Third World Approaches
    to International Law scholars
Twining, William, 181, 206, 219–220
Tzouvala, Ntina, 268

UK. *See* United Kingdom
UN Charter. *See* United Nations
UNCLOS. *See* United Nations
United Kingdom (UK)
    Brexit and, 45
    Chagos Archipelago and, 221–222
    humanitarian intervention and, 26–27,
        246–247
    Kosovo intervention and, 26–27
    Minquiers and Ecrehos case, 221–222
    origins of international law and, 257–262
    radical historians in, 136
    U.S. war on terror and, 39
United Nations (UN)
    Convention on the Law of the Sea, dispute
        settlement mechanisms under, 22
    Security Council, 25–26
    treaty registration with, 229
    UN Charter, 228
        U.S. war on terror and, 38, 40–41, 40–41
United States (U.S.)
    anti-formalism as legal tradition,
        international law and, 208–212
    expansionism of, critical response to, 30–36
        by human rights lawyers, 31–32
        by international legal scholars, 30–34
        postcolonialism and, 34
        Third World Approaches to International
            Law scholars and, 34
    international law and, transformation of,
        19–36, 262–263, 262–265
    legal realism in. *See* legal realism
    North American Free Trade Agreement,
        24–25, 46
    war on terror. *See* war on terror
    withdrawal from Trans-Pacific Partnership,
        46
    World Trade Organization and, 21, 233–234,
        233–234
Universal Declaration of Human Rights,
    262–263

Uruguay Round, GATT, 21
U.S. *See* United States

Valla, Lorenzo, 148
Vattel, Emer de, 161–162
Vienna Convention on the Law of Treaties
    (VCLT), 229, 231, 246, 246
*Vom Beruf unserer Zeit für Gesetzgebung und
    Rechtswissenschaft* (Of the Vocation of
    our Age for Legislation and
    Jurisprudence) (Savigny), 237–238

Wang Hui, 57–58, 60, 65–66
war on terror, 36–43
Whig Constitutionalism, 112–127
Whig history, 113–115, 119–122, 119–122, 125,
    127–128, 194–195
    abridgement and, 85, 107–108, 107–108,
        120–121, 121–122
    anachronism and, 120
    Butterfield on, 107–108, 113, 113, 119–122,
        119–122, 194–195
    international law and, 77–78, 84–85, 85, 195, 195
    judgment of the past and, 119–122, 195, 195
    Pocock on, 133–135
    progress narratives and, 115–119, 121–122, 125,
        126–127
The Whig Interpretation of History
    (Butterfield), 107–109, 113, 113, 119–120
White, Hayden, 136, 196–197
Wilder, Gary, 90–91
Williams, Raymond, 136–138
Williams, Robert A., Jr., 166
Wolff, Christian, 166
World Trade Organization (WTO)
    China and, 62–63, 297, 297
    creation of, 21
    dispute settlement process, 21–23, 232,
        232–233, 297, 297
    international economic law and, intellectual
        history of, 271–273, 276–277, 279–280,
        279–280, 296–298, 296–298
    Ordoliberalism and, 53, 101, 267–275,
        296–299, 297–298
    U.S. and, 21, 46, 232, 233–234, 297, 297
    WTO agreements, 269, 282
Wright, Martin, 125
WTO. *See* World Trade Organization

Xi Jinping, 62

CPSIA information can be obtained
at www.ICGtesting.com
Printed in the USA
BVHW092146270721
613020BV00013B/142